AMERICAN DREAMS & REALITY:
A Retelling of the American Story
Volume II, Fifth Edition

AMERICAN DREAMS & REALITY:
A Retelling of the American Story
Volume II, Fifth Edition

Louise A. Mayo
County College of Morris
Randolph, New Jersey

Anne Kearney
Jefferson Community & Technical College
Louisville, Kentucky

John Moretta
Houston Community College System
Houston, Texas

Abigail Press   Wheaton, IL 60187

Design and Production: Abigail Press
Typesetting: Abigail Press
Typeface: AGaramond
Cover Art: Sam Tolia

AMERICAN DREAMS & REALITY:
A Retelling of the American Story, Volume II

Fifth Edition, 2005
Printed in the United States of America
Translation rights reserved by the authors
ISBN 1-890919-36-5

ABOUT THE AUTHORS

Louise Mayo is the Chairperson of the Department of History/ Political Science at County College of Morris, Randolph, NJ, where she has been a professor for the past twenty-three years. She is the author of *The Ambivalent Image* (1988), *A House Divided: America in the Era of Civil War and Reconstruction*, and numerous articles and papers in the fields of women and minority history. She has an M.A. from Cornell University in Modern European and Russian History and a Ph.D. from City University of New York in American History, specializing in immigration and minority history. She teaches courses in Twentieth Century America, History of American Women, History of Minorities, History of American Cities and Suburbs, and Civil War and Reconstruction. She wishes to thank members of her department who read her chapters and offered helpful suggestions, particularly Dr. Rita Heller.

Anne has a B.A. from Saint Mary's College (Notre Dame, IN), an M.A. and a Ph.D. from the University of Notre Dame in American History, and an M.L.S. in academic librarianship from Indiana University at Bloomington. She presently teaches American History and the History of American Women at Jefferson Community and Technical College - Kentucky Community and Technical College System in Louisville while pursuing a law degree at Brandeis School of Law, University of Louisville. She is listed in *Who's Who in America* and *Who's Who in the World*. She has written articles for the Oxford Biographical Dictionary and Salem Press and presented scholarly papers at the annual meetings of the Catholic Historical Association, Popular Cultural Association, and Community College Humanities Association.

John A. Moretta earned a B.A. in History from Santa Clara University in CA., an M.A. in History from Portland State University in Oregon, and a Ph.D. in History from Rice University in Houston, Texas. He is currently Professor of History and Chair of the Social Sciences Dept. of Central College, Houston Community College System in Houston, Texas. Dr. Moretta is also an adjunct professor at the University of Houston. Dr. Moretta's first book, *William Pitt Ballinger, Texas Lawyer, Southern Statesman*, won the 2003 San Antonio Conservation Society's award for one of the best books in Texas history. In addition to his book, Dr. Moretta has also written several articles on Texas history, published in both local and national historical journals, such as *Civil War History*. He is a co-author of *The Western Dream of Civilization* and *American Dreams, American Reality*. He is currently completing a biography of William Penn for Addison Wesley Longman's Library of American Biography Series. Expected publication date is fall, 2005.

Contents in Brief

Contents

Chapter Twelve

RECONSTRUCTION:
The Turning Point That Never Turned

April 14, 1865, was Good Friday. It was the fourth anniversary of the surrender of Fort Sumter. At a ceremony in the remains of the old fortress, Major Robert Anderson, its former commander, hoisted the weather-beaten, ragged old flag he had been forced to pull down in 1861. That evening, a weary President Lincoln and his wife relaxed at Ford's Theater, which was showing a popular comedy, "Our American Cousin," in a benefit performance for disabled Union veterans. The theater was packed, and the cast ad-libbed "many pleasant allusions" to the president, to the delight of Lincoln and the audience.

The nation had come through the greatest threat ever to its existence and now faced further overwhelming challenges. But the leader whose burdens and trials had made him appear to be much older than his fifty-six years seemed to be equal to the task. "I am a tired man," Lincoln said at the end of the war. "Sometimes I think I am the tiredest man on earth." He had overcome his frequent bouts of depression and his personal grief over the death of his lively, inquisitive, and much-loved eleven-year-old son, Willie. (Mary, his wife, never completely regained her stability after a nervous break-

down brought on by her child's death.) Lincoln had also managed to surmount the despair he felt at the death of thousands of Americans in the war. His success in meeting national and personal crises underscored both his greatness and his compassion.

The president was haunted by his dreams. Some, like those about the dead Willie, gave him comfort. Others were alarming, particularly recurring images of assassination. In one such dream, Lincoln was awakened by the loud weeping of mourners surrounding a body lying in state. When he asked a soldier who the corpse was, he was told, "The President. He was killed by an assassin." His friend, Ward Lamon, his self-appointed bodyguard, and Secretary of War Stanton were both alarmed enough about possible dangers to the president's safety to provide cavalry escorts for his carriage and a District of Columbia policeman to accompany him to the theater.

Amidst the joy of surrender celebrations and the merriment of the theater, however, the security precautions had disintegrated. The policeman, who had been charged with guarding the president, carelessly left his post at the door of the president's box to see the play.

Right about the time of the Fort Sumter ceremony, John Wilkes Booth, a young actor, had gone to the theater to pick up his mail. There, he learned about the special performance that the president would attend. As the laughter rose in the theater, Booth made his way to the president's box, derringer pistol and dagger in hand. At the outer door, he was briefly stopped but showed his card and confidently claimed that the president, who was known to enjoy actors, had asked him to come.

Booth was a member of one of America's great acting families. Although overshadowed by his father and his brother, Edwin (who was believed by many to be America's finest actor), John was a fairly successful actor in his own right, earning an impressive $20,000 a year. He was, however, unstable, egotistical, and a fanatical Confederate sympathizer. He obsessed about Lincoln whom he saw as a tyrant responsible for all the nation's problems. Booth had recruited a strange group of malcontents from Washington's underworld, including a Confederate deserter, a Rebel spy, and a mentally handicapped druggist's clerk. Lee's surrender thwarted his original plan to kidnap the president and bring him to Richmond. So, he resolved instead to kill Lincoln, Vice President Johnson, and Secretary of State Seward. The conspirator assigned to kill Johnson lost his nerve. The other accomplice did stab and seriously wound Seward, who eventually recovered.

Meanwhile, Booth, after downing two brandies for courage, stepped into the president's box and fired his pistol into Lincoln's head. After slashing the arm of a major who tried to detain him, Booth vaulted over the box and landed on stage, breaking a leg. He shouted something to the dazed audience. Some said it was "sic temper tyrannis" ("thus be it ever to tyrants"), Virginia's state motto. Then he hobbled off stage out into the alley where he mounted his waiting horse and clattered off into Washington's dark streets. Booth's bullet tore into the president's brain. An army surgeon, who had been sitting in the audience, pronounced the wound to be mortal.

Soldiers carried the unconscious president across the street to a room in a boarding house. There he lingered for the night, surrounded by stricken members of his cabinet, with his wife sobbing uncontrollably in the next room. He died the next morning at 7:22. Tears cascading down his face, Edmund Stanton declared, "Now he belongs to the ages."

John Wilkes Booth assassinated
President Abraham Lincoln.

Within minutes, the telegraph carried the tragic news to a stunned nation. No American president had ever been killed before. People openly wept in the streets. Navy Secretary Gideon Welles noted that blacks were especially overwhelmed by Lincoln's death just as victory over slavery occurred: "the hopeless grief (of those poor colored people) affected me more than almost anything else." For fourteen days, millions of Americans stood along the tracks and watched silently as a nine-car train carried Lincoln's body, and the small coffin of his son, Willie, the 1,662 miles from Washington back home to Springfield, Illinois. The president's murder on Good Friday had made him into a Christ-like figure. It gave new meaning to the final verse of the "Battle Hymn of the Republic": "As He died to make men holy, Let us die to make men free."

By April 26, Union troops had trapped John Wilkes Booth in a burning Virginia barn and shot him in the head. As he lay dying, he whispered, "Tell my mother I died for my country...I did what I thought was best." Four of his accomplices were hanged and four others were sentenced to hard labor, including the hapless Dr. Samuel Mudd, whose sole crime seemed to be setting Booth's broken leg. The mood of the Northern public after the assassination caused anger, bitterness, and cries for vengeance against Confederate leaders. Yet Lincoln, in his moving second inaugural address, had declared, "With malice toward none; with charity for all; with firmness in the right...let us strive...to bind up the nation's wounds." With the death of this great man, would it be possible to balance "charity" and "firmness" and create "a just and a lasting peace"?

WARTIME RECONSTRUCTION

The questions that formed the core of Reconstruction surfaced during the war. After the Emancipation Proclamation, Northerners of every political stripe assumed that the South would emerge from the war as a society without slavery. But what system of labor would replace the institution of slavery? Would four million newly freed slaves become citizens? If they did, what rights would they enjoy, and what role would they play in the social and political life of the South? Could the states of the Confederacy rejoin the union? If so, under what terms? Should the president or Congress set these terms?

Military officers, during the war, often had to make decisions about what to do with thousands of ragged freed slaves who flocked to Union armies when they learned about emancipation. Despite his openly expressed contempt for both radical ideas and freedmen, General Sherman issued a special order reserving confiscated land for the resettlement of freed people on plots of forty acres per family. He also sanctioned lending army mules to the new farmers (leading, perhaps, to the later poignant demand for "forty acres and a mule"). By the end of the war, more than forty thousand people had been resettled in that area of coastal South Carolina and Georgia. By 1865, 20 percent of the farmland under Union control was being worked by independent black farmers. In 1863 General Grant declared that Davis Bend, the estate of Jefferson Davis and his brother, should become a "negro paradise." Davis' former

slaves and other black farmers leased its thousands of acres. By 1865 they were raising successful cotton and food crops and earning a profit of nearly $160,000. They formed their own government, including elected judges and sheriffs. Black people desired, above all, to become independent farmers, and some radical Republicans hoped that the future would see a South of black yeoman farmers working their own land.

Events in Louisiana, however, were more indicative of the labor system that would develop in the South. There, the military commander believed that the army's burden of caring for black refugees could be ended by restoring the plantation system. Former slaves would be coerced into signing yearly contracts with loyal planters and forbidden to leave without permission of the owners. Despite the program's limited success in reviving the state's agricultural system, most army officials operated under the assumption that freed slaves should continue to be plantation laborers.

Northern freedmen's aid societies, founded by abolitionists, attempted to accomplish another radical vision of the future, that of an educated black population able to fulfill the demands of citizenship. During the war, they sent more than a thousand teachers to the occupied South, precursors of two thousand more who arrived in the early postwar period. Most came from New England, and three-quarters were women. Most were white (although 20 percent were blacks, many of whom were themselves only minimally educated). They strove to instill the Protestant work ethic and the values of self-discipline in the 200,000 or so students they reached. After the war, the freedmen's education program was greatly expanded in a concentrated effort to erase illiteracy. The black scholar and leader, W. E. B. Du Bois, later commented that these missionary teachers were the unsung heroes of the Civil War who "came not to keep the Negroes in their place, but to raise them out of the defilement of the places where slavery had wallowed them....This was the gift of New England to the freed Negro."

Lincoln attempted to deal with the issue of restoration of the Southern states to the Union in December 1863, a year after the Emancipation Proclamation. He issued the Proclamation of Amnesty and Reconstruction, his first extensive program for reconstruction. In it, Lincoln offered the re-establishment of all rights "except as to slaves" to those in conquered areas who took a loyalty oath to the federal constitution. Only high-ranking confederate military and civil officials would be excluded. When 10 percent of the 1860 voting population had taken the oath, a new state government would be established, abolishing slavery. Lincoln based his policy on the theory of the "indissoluble Union." Since states could not legally secede, they were still a part of the Union. The purpose of reconstruction was to enable loyal citizens to regain control of their governments. Lincoln never saw this policy, issued in the midst of war, as an unchangeable blueprint for postwar reconstruction. He hoped to use his "Ten Percent Plan" to weaken the Confederacy by gaining the support of former Southern Whigs, at best hesitant secessionists. He also wanted to get emancipation into as many Southern state constitutions as possible.

Radical Republicans, led by Charles Sumner and Benjamin Wade in the Senate and Thaddeus Stevens in the House, objected to allowing former rebels back into the Union so easily. They wanted to ensure that committed Unionists controlled Southern governments and that the freedom and civil rights of blacks would be protected. They argued that, by seceding, Southern states had committed "state suicide," reverting to territories that had to apply to Congress for readmission to the Union. When representatives of a Louisiana government that followed Lincoln's plan showed up in 1864, Congress refused to seat them. That same year, Republicans in Congress produced their own view of reconstruction in the Wade-Davis Bill. This law would have required an oath of allegiance from a majority of the voters, rather than 10 percent. Then elections would be held for delegates to a state constitutional convention, with the vote restricted to those who could take an "iron clad oath" that they had never voluntarily aided the Confederacy. This measure would have postponed Reconstruction for a very long period. Lincoln, fearing its consequences for the war effort, pocket-vetoed it.

Congressman Thaddeus Stevens of Pennsylvania advocated seizing land from Southern planters and distributing it among the freed blacks.

Although some historians later saw this as evidence of the irreconcilable differences between the moderate, charitable views of the president and the harsh unyielding attitudes of Radicals in Congress, Lincoln himself insisted that he was not "inflexibly committed to any single plan of restoration." Lincoln tended to be flexible and pragmatic, adjusting his ideas to the political circumstances. He worked with his radical opponents in January 1865 to gain passage of the Thirteenth Amendment, abolishing slavery throughout the nation and ensuring that wartime emancipation measures could never be overturned. He also signed a bill creating the Freedmen's Bureau as a relief agency in the South for refugees of both races. It was empowered to draft and enforce labor contracts, to aid blacks to become independent farmers, and to assist in the operation of freedmen's schools.

Lincoln moved closer to compromise with Congress. He confided to a friend that he "had no plan for reorganization, but must be guided by events." He tried to meet partially the demands of radical critics and free blacks for black suffrage in the South. He suggested, in his last public speech (April 11, 1865), that the vote be extended to literate blacks and the larger group of those who had served in the Union armies. The *New York Times* noted that Lincoln did not seem to feel the time had yet come for "the statement of a settled reconstruction policy." At a cabinet meeting on the morning of his assassination, Lincoln endorsed a plan to substitute military occupation for civilian government in the Confederate states to ensure the enforcement of black civil rights. The bullets from Booth's gun prevent us from ever knowing whether this gifted and practical politician could have successfully negotiated the contradictions between the competing goals of "charity," "firmness" and "justice."

PRESIDENTIAL RECONSTRUCTION

Andrew Johnson, the man who succeeded Lincoln, seemed to many to have a remarkably similar background to his predecessor. Both rose from rural poverty with little or no formal education to realize their ambitions and achieve success in the public arena. Johnson had been an illiterate tailor whose school teacher wife taught him to write. He acquired a farm and slaves and climbed the political ladder in Tennessee, eventually becoming governor and senator. Johnson resented the snobbery he felt from the old-time plantation Southern leadership. "Some day I will show the stuck-up aristocrats who is running the country," he once vowed. When the Civil War broke out, Johnson was an ardent Unionist, the only senator from a Confederate state who spoke out against secession. As wartime governor of occupied Tennessee, he sternly declared, "Treason must be made odious, and traitors must be punished and impoverished." He promised anxious blacks that he would "be your Moses, and lead you through the Red Sea of war and bondage to a fairer future of liberty and peace." Such comments, coupled with the need to build bisectional support, particularly in the border states, led Lincoln to pick Johnson for vice president in 1864. His thunderous speeches against the "slaveocracy" also led many Radical Republicans to believe that the new president would be more sympathetic to their point of view than Lincoln had been.

Lincoln and the radicals had misread Johnson, however. The struggle to overcome poverty seemed to have given Lincoln an empathy for others, wit, and the political skills of tact and flexibility. The same struggle embittered Johnson and made him into a suspicious man who, despite personal courage, was intolerant of other views, stubborn, and unable to compromise. Unlike Lincoln, Johnson never viewed slavery as a great moral evil. "Damn the Negroes," he once declared, "I am fighting these traitorous aristocrats, their masters." He believed that nonslaveholding whites were the main victims of slavery, oppressed by the combination of slaves and their masters. He saw no role for the freedmen in a reconstructed South and hoped that they would leave the country. "White men alone must manage the South," he announced. He insisted to Congress that blacks had "less capacity for government than any other race of people....Wherever they have been left to their own devices they have shown a constant tendency to relapse into barbarism." He was a committed Jacksonian in that he favored states' rights and was as suspicious of the "bloated, corrupt aristocracy" of the banks and corporations emerging in the North as he had been of the Southern patricians.

With Congress not due to meet again until December 1865, Johnson was free to implement his own reconstruction policy. Lincoln's tentative reconstruction initiatives based on the wartime theory of indestructible states had become set in stone in Johnson's limited imagination. This was coupled with a rigid view of states' rights that would not allow any real role for the federal government in Reconstruction. Johnson's restoration policy (as he insisted on calling it) became clear in two proclamations he issued in May 1865. One offered amnesty and return of all property, except slaves, to every white man who swore to an oath of future loyalty. Political and military leaders of the Confederacy and those with property valued at more than $20,000 were excluded but given the opportunity to apply to the president for individual pardons. Under the second proclamation, the newly loyal electorate would choose members to a constitutional convention in each state. Despite his stated support for states' rights, Johnson made it clear that he expected each convention to nullify secession, accept the abolition of slavery, and repudiate all Confederate debts. After that, elections would

The Freedmen's Bureau established schools attended by ex-slaves. Many of the teachers were white women from the North.

be held for state and federal officials, and Reconstruction would be complete. Under these terms, presidential Reconstruction moved along rapidly. Southern congressmen arrived to claim their seats by the time Congress reconvened in December. But Johnson had misinterpreted Northern and congressional opinion as completely as the radicals had misunderstood Johnson's true nature earlier. As a result of the actions of these reconstructed governments, Congress refused to seat the Southern congressmen.

The same president who had spoken sternly about "treason" in April was speaking eloquently of the need to be "forbearing and forgiving" about the past sins of the South by the fall. Despite his often expressed hatred of the old aristocrats, the ego of the former illiterate tailor's apprentice was gratified when members of the proud Southern ruling class came to him to beg humbly for pardons. "I remember the taunts, the jeers, the scowls with which I was treated," the president noted. He was gratified by their confessions of error and their expressions of "sincere respect" for his "desire and intention to sustain Southern rights in the Union." He quickly granted 13,500 pardons to ex-Confederates who were now free to return to power in their states.

Southern Defiance and the Black Codes

When the Confederate armies surrendered, Southerners, as an observer remarked at the time, were "so despondent that if readmission at some future time under whatever conditions had been promised, it would have been looked upon as a favor." But presidential generosity and support led to obstinate overconfidence by Southern leaders. Johnson, now the captive of Southern interests, could not respond to their open defiance. As a result, several states repealed secession instead of repudiating it. Mississippi refused to ratify the Thirteenth Amendment, and Arkansas even appropriated funds for Confederate veterans' pensions. Northerners, who expected some acknowledgment of defeat by the South, were astounded when some states elected the newly pardoned ex-Confederates to local, state, and even national office. In the most publicized example, Georgia chose Alexander Stephens, the former vice president of the Confederacy, as one of its senators.

The inability of Southern whites to accept the free labor ideology of the North was even more disturbing to many Northerners. Southern state legislatures in 1865 and 1866 passed a series of Black Codes, ostensibly to define the legal rights of the newly freed blacks. Most Southern whites were unable or unwilling to accept even minimal notions of legal equality between the races. The codes did concede blacks the rights to have legal marriages, sign contracts, sue and be sued, and obtain property. Southerners claimed that these were substantial advances. However, the codes denied the freed people such basic rights as that of free assembly, bearing arms, serving on juries, testifying against whites in court, voting, or holding office. Although many of these prohibitions existed in the still white supremacist North as well, these open attempts to restrict the Union's most loyal followers in the South irritated many Northerners.

The provisions of the codes that related to labor and vagrancy angered Northerners the most, as they seemed to foreshadow an attempt to bring back plantation slavery. The laws defined vagrancy so broadly that any black who did not have an annual contract to work on a plantation could be arrested, fined, and hired out as an unpaid laborer to any planter who paid the fine. Blacks, who wanted to enter any other occupation but agriculture, needed special licenses from the state. Children, in homes not deemed to be "adequate," could be sent as "apprentices" to white "guardians," their former owners. Although the army and Freedmen's Bureau suspended enforcement of the worst provisions of the Black Codes, their implications had a deep impact on Northern public opinion. Stories in Northern newspapers bolstered the image of unrepentant, arrogant Confederates. One influential Republican commentator reported, "It is a stubborn fact that our truest friends are threatened and persecuted and that the negro is denied his freedom whenever the population has a chance to act upon its own impulses without immediately being checked."

The Split Between President and Congress

When the representatives of the Johnson governments arrived to take their seats in December 1865, the stage was set for a direct conflict between the president and Congress. Johnson had hoped to cre-

ate a new centrist Union coalition of Democrats, Southern whites, and moderate Republicans. To do so, however, he would have to compromise on the issue of freedmen's rights. Johnson's friends knew that he would never compromise, preferring a messy struggle. "A fight between the Radicals and the Executive is inevitable," said one. "Let it come. The sooner the better for the whole country."

Many Republicans believed that the future of their party was at stake. An ironic result of the Thirteenth Amendment came out of the elimination of the three-fifths clause in the Constitution. The South would increase its political power by adding 15 to 20 seats, as the entire black population would now count in allotting seats in the House. This hardly seemed fair to Republicans, since these Johnsonian governments were denying the most basic rights to blacks. In addition, rebels whose treason had been ignored by presidential pardons were running those governments. (Ten Confederate generals and nine former Confederate congressmen were in the group of Southern representatives asking to be seated.) It was not surprising that Congress refused to seat the eighty Southern representatives. Congressional Republicans also rejected Johnson's "restoration" plans. Instead, Congress appointed a Joint Committee of Fifteen on Reconstruction.

Moderates, however, dominated the Joint Committee. Compromise still seemed possible. These moderate Republicans conferred with Johnson and believed they had his support for two bills to protect the rights of freed people. The first extended the life of the Freedmen's Bureau, enlarged its legal powers in civil rights cases, and authorized it to build and maintain schools. Johnson dismayed the moderates in February 1866 by vetoing the bill. Democrats organized a mass rally to support the veto. Johnson delivered an extraordinarily unrestrained speech attacking the radicals as traitors and Judases. He portrayed himself as Christ who would willingly shed his blood to "vindicate the Union and the preservation of this government in its original purity and character." The speech was so intemperate that many Americans wondered if the president was drunk.

Despite their disillusionment over the president's behavior, most moderate Republicans still hoped to

Many African-American families received little help during Reconstruction.

avert a complete break. They modified the Freedmen's Bureau bill to meet some of the presidential objections and passed a relatively modest Civil Rights bill. The bill sought to overturn the Dred Scott decision and the Black Codes. It defined blacks as citizens entitled to protection, property, contracts, and equality under the law. To appease Johnson, the bill did not give blacks the vote or the right to desegregated public facilities. Despite this attempt at compromise, the president shocked the moderates again by vetoing the Civil Rights bill and the second Freedmen's Bureau bill. He made any future reconciliation with Congress virtually impossible by arguing that Reconstruction was already complete under his policies, and only the individual states could deal with the freedmen. Democrats applauded his stand. If Congress had its way, one Democratic paper declared, "how long will it be...before it will say the negro shall vote, sit in a jury box, and intermarry with your families? Such are the questions put by the President." But the veto turned potential allies among moderate Republicans into unyielding enemies. "He has broken the faith, betrayed his trust, and must sink from detestation to contempt," declared one disillusioned senator who had tried to work with Johnson. Rather than isolating the radicals, Johnson's actions pushed the moderates closer to the radical position. Congress was able to override both presidential vetoes.

The Fourteenth Amendment

The Joint Committee on Reconstruction faced with the break with the president sought to develop a constitutional amendment that would unify Republicans. It would do so by placing the rights of freedmen under national protection where they could not be touched by presidential actions or shifting political currents. Republicans also hoped that the Fourteenth Amendment would provide the terms under which the defeated South could return to the Union. This amendment, which quickly gained the necessary two-thirds vote in Congress, may well be the most important single amendment in the United States Constitution. Much of its significance came from later interpretations. But even at the time, it provided a national guarantee of equality before the law.

The first section of the amendment defined citizenship in the nation as belonging to "all persons born or naturalized in the United States." Thus, any blacks born in America were now automatically citizens, nullifying the Dred Scott decision. No state could abridge "the privileges and immunities" of a citizen of the United States, "deprive any person of life, liberty, or property without due process of law," or deny "equal protection of the laws." In later years this section, the heart of the amendment, was subject to a variety of interpretations. Conservative courts at the end of the century ruled that corporations were "legal persons," and state attempts to regulate them were unconstitutional. In the mid-twentieth century, the "equal protection" provision became the foundation for overturning state mandated segregation of the races.

The second section was a compromise on the issue of black suffrage. It did not grant blacks the right to vote, but it did provide for a reduction in a state's representation, proportional to the number of male citizens denied the vote. If Southern states declined to extend the votes to blacks, at least they would not benefit from the increased representation that derived from the end of the three-fifths clause. The third section was the most controversial at the time, since it barred from national or state office all men who had aided the rebellion after swearing allegiance to the Constitution. This was designed to exclude the pre-war ruling class from power. The fourth section guaranteed the Union debt and repudiated the Confederate debt.

As a whole, the Fourteenth Amendment presented the minimum terms Northern public opinion expected from the defeated South. After all, it did not confiscate land from Confederate supporters or leaders, did not deny them the vote, or even force them to accept black suffrage. It seems likely that Reconstruction would have been over if the South accepted the amendment. Tennessee, controlled by political enemies of Johnson, quickly ratified the amendment in 1866 and was promptly admitted back into the Union. Johnson, however, still totally misunderstanding Northern public opinion, urged the excluded states to reject the amendment. He argued that the amendment was illegal because it kept the Southern states out of the Congress that passed it. The ex-confederate states unwisely followed his advice.

Johnson convinced his Southern admirers that he could rally popular support in the North for his Reconstruction plans and administer a well-deserved whipping to the Radicals in the congressional elections of 1866. The president attempted to launch a National Union movement to support his objectives. This movement, however, failed to get off the ground as a result of basic problems that undermined it in the eyes of the Northern public. Growing violence in the South alarmed Northerners. In May 1866, a quarrel in Memphis between recently discharged black veterans and local whites, led by Irish policemen, erupted into a three-day riot. The white mobs killed forty-six blacks, raped five black women, and burnt or looted hundreds of black homes, schools, and churches. The Memphis riot proved, the *New York Tribune* observed cynically, "that the Freedmen's Bureau ought to be abolished forthwith, and the blacks remitted to the paternal care of their old masters, who 'understand the nigger...a great deal better than the Yankees can.'" Three months later, a similar riot rocked New Orleans when a mob attacked delegates to a black suffrage convention, killing thirty-four blacks and three of their white allies, and injuring over one hundred more. Many Northerners agreed with the assessment of one observer that Johnson's lenient policies had caused this "barbarism of the rebellion in its renaissance." The president certainly did not ease these concerns when he delivered a speech in which he blamed the Republicans for inciting the mob and offered no sympathy for the victims.

In fact, the greatest problem faced by the National Union movement may well have been the president himself. Johnson had been an effective speaker in Tennessee, so he decided to take his case to the Northern public. He launched his August-September 1866 "swing around the circle," a campaign tour to influence Northern voters in the upcoming congressional elections. (He was the first president ever to do this.) The trip was an unmitigated disaster. His rough country style, which played so well in Tennessee, turned off Northern voters. He allowed hecklers, planted by radicals, to draw him into shouted exchanges of insults. "Why not hang Thad Stevens and Wendell Phillips," he exclaimed at one stop. The president had lost all control of himself, and, in doing so, he lost command of the country.

Finally, the Republicans were able to brush the Democrats, by now Johnson's main supporters, with the tar of treason against the Union. This was a tactic later known as "waving the bloody shirt." One Republican speaker declared, "Every unregenerate rebel calls himself a Democrat....Every man who labored for rebellion in the field, who murdered Union prisoners...who conspired to bring about civil war in the loyal states...calls himself a Democrat." The election had also become a referendum on the Fourteenth Amendment, overwhelmingly favored by Northern public opinion.

All these factors help explain a victory so lopsided that it surprised even the most committed Radical Republican. The Radicals now had a veto-proof majority of more than two-thirds in both Houses of Congress. The Northern electorate had clearly decided that the victory in the war must lead to a fundamental transformation of the South. Republicans even swept Johnson's own state of Tennessee. Its new Republican governor gleefully said, "Give my respects to the dead dog in the White House."

Reconstruction Acts

Led by Thaddeus Stevens, Speaker of the House, and Benjamin Wade, President Pro Tem of the Senate,

Radicals believed that they had won a mandate from the public to substitute a congressional reconstruction plan for the president's failing program. Egged on by the president, the Southern states continued to reject the Fourteenth Amendment, the easiest terms they could have reasonably expected. Exasperated moderates then reached a compromise with Radicals on a Reconstruction Act.

The Reconstruction Act of 1867 rejected Johnson's views that the Southern states should be immediately admitted to the Union without qualifications. It also rebuffed Radical demands for an indefinite military occupation, coupled with confiscation and redistribution of plantation lands to provide a foundation for the economic independence of the freedmen. Instead, the act temporarily divided the old Confederacy (except Tennessee) into five military districts. Each would be supervised by an army general who could use the army and the Freedmen's Bureau to register voters and protect lives and property. The act then laid out the steps to create new state governments and admit them to the Union. First, each state would hold a constitutional convention with delegates chosen by all adult males regardless of "race, color, or previous condition." (But not ex-Confederates barred by the Fourteenth Amendment.) The new governments had to allow the same "impartial" suffrage and ratify the Fourteenth Amendment. When these conditions were met, states could send representatives to Congress. The president vetoed the act, protesting that "the people of the South...were to be trodden under foot to protect niggers."

Congress rapidly and overwhelmingly overrode the veto. All but three states—Mississippi, Texas, and Virginia—agreed to these requirements by June 1868. The Fourteenth Amendment became part of the Constitution in July. (Those last three states were readmitted in 1870.) The Reconstruction Act, in insisting on black suffrage in the South, combined the idealism of the Radicals with political realism. The black vote might make it possible to establish the Republican Party in the South. Some people felt that it would allow blacks to defend themselves and free the nation of the need for continued federal occupation and intervention.

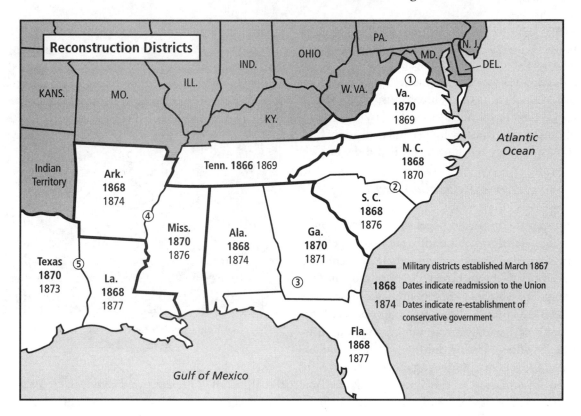

President Johnson, firm in his belief that Reconstruction was a dangerous revolution, sought to thwart the will of Congress with his appointment powers. Congress, in turn, tried to limit Johnson's ability to do mischief by passing the Tenure of Office Act. This act prevented the president from dismissing any federal official whose appointment had required Senate confirmation until the Senate approved his successor. This was designed to prevent Johnson from removing Republican officials who supported congressional reconstruction, particularly Secretary of War Edwin Stanton. Stanton not only supported Radical Reconstruction but he was in a key position to aid in its enforcement and act as an internal cabinet spy for his friends in Congress.

Radical Republicans turned their attentions to reforms at the state level in the North, designed to eliminate obstacles to individual advancement. This was in accord with the party's free-labor ideology that had been at the heart of its opposition to slavery. Michigan expanded state institutions for orphans and the disabled, outlawed racial segregation, and instituted free compulsory public education. Massachu-

setts' Republicans succeeded in banning racial discrimination in public accommodations and limiting child labor. An ambitious program of reform in New York included a Tenement House Act, Free School Law, Metropolitan Health Act, a Normal School Act that set up eight state teachers' colleges, and the establishment of a State Board of Charities. Despite these undoubted advances, however, most Northern blacks remained in unskilled, low-wage jobs and substandard housing. The arrival of increasing numbers of European immigrants caused many to lose such jobs as barbers and construction workers where they had long predominated. Nevertheless, public life and political rights were now open to them in ways unheard of before the war. The overwhelming majority of blacks, however, continued to live in the South.

The most important effort for radical reform in the North was the push to extend the vote to blacks. But Northern voters, frightened by the vicious, racist rhetoric of the Democrats and their conservative allies, rejected black suffrage amendments. A French newspaperman noted wryly, "Any Democrat who did not manage to hint in his speech that the negro is a degenerate gorilla, would be considered lacking in enthusiasm." As a result, the Democrats made major gains in the local and state elections of 1867. This emboldened Johnson and his allies. The president treated serenaders at the White House to a "victory speech." One of his aides crowed, "Any party with an abolition head and a nigger tail will soon find itself with nothing left but the head and the tail."

Presidential Impeachment

Johnson, in the mistaken belief that Northern public opinion was now behind him, renewed his efforts to obstruct congressional reconstruction. Ignoring the advice of General Grant, he removed military commanders who seemed too enthusiastic in their enforcement of Radical reconstruction policies and replaced them with officers more sympathetic to Southern whites. Finally, Johnson decided to challenge Congress by removing Secretary of War Stanton, in violation of the Tenure of Office Act. (Congress had refused to confirm Stanton's suspension.) At the advice of Republican senators, Stanton barricaded himself in his office and refused to turn over the keys to his supposed replacement. The latter arrived complete with a major hangover from a premature celebration of his new position.

After this debacle, the House voted to impeach (indict) Johnson by a strictly party-line vote of 126 to 47 even before the actual charges had been listed. Nine of the eventual charges referred to violations of the Tenure of Office Act. The tenth accusation was that Johnson had been "unmindful of the high duties of his office" and had tried to bring Congress into "disgrace, ridicule, hatred, contempt, and reproach."

As the Constitution provides, the Senate acts as jury in cases of impeachment, with the Chief Justice of the Supreme Court serving as presiding judge. A two-thirds vote is required to remove a president. Despite the elaborate legal language, it was clear that the president was really being tried for his unyielding opposition and attempts to sabotage Republican reconstruction, as well as his general incompetence. An influential group of moderate Senate Republicans worried about establishing a precedent by which

Andrew Johnson escaped conviction by a single vote.

two-thirds of Congress could remove any president who disagreed with them. This might destroy the constitutional system of checks and balances by creating an all-powerful legislative branch like that of Great Britain. In addition, these moderates distrusted the Radical views and temperament of Benjamin Wade, the president pro tem of the Senate, who would succeed Johnson. (The vice presidency was vacant.) The president's lawyers quietly let these moderates know that, in the future, he would stop denouncing Congress and would enforce the Reconstruction Acts. As a result, thirty-five senators voted for conviction, one short of the necessary two-thirds. Seven Republicans voted with the twelve Democrats to provide the margin of Johnson's "victory." Several others were ready to support the president if their votes were needed. Contrary to later myths, the seven were not "martyrs" who were read out of the party. The crisis that had the potential to shake up the entire constitutional system ended without changing it in any fundamental way.

The Election of 1868

Although Johnson had been humbled by his narrow escape, the acquittal also weakened the position of the Radicals within the Republican Party. General Ulysses S. Grant had emerged from the Civil War as the Union's leading military hero. Although he had supported congressional actions in a bitter split with Johnson, Grant was not known to have any particular ideological convictions. Conservative Northern businessmen, although unenthusiastic about Radical Reconstruction, felt that any attempt to reopen the now settled issue would cause political and economic chaos. They believed a Grant presidency would bring stability and conditions conducive to investment in the South. Grant easily won the Republican nomination on a platform that bragged about "the assured success of the reconstruction policy of Congress."

The Democrats rejected Johnson and his many liabilities and drafted the colorless Governor of New York, Horatio Seymour. Since Seymour had denounced Lincoln during the war as a military despot and had referred to the draft rioters as "my friends," he handed the issue of loyalty and patriotism to the Republicans. As a result, Democrats ran on a platform denouncing Reconstruction as "unconstitutional, revolutionary, and void." Frank Blair of Missouri, the party's vice presidential candidate, had an outstanding record as a Union general during the War. But he frightened many Northern voters by suggesting that the army should be used to break up the unconstitutional Republican governments in the South. He also condemned Republicans for putting the South under the heels of "a semi-barbarous race of blacks who are worshippers of fetishes and polygamists" and want only to "subject white women to their unbridled lust." Racist comments like these made this the last presidential campaign to openly bring up the issue of white supremacy.

Republicans replied by "waving the bloody shirt" even more vigorously. The same Democrats who had betrayed their country during the war, Republicans charged, were now proposing "government by assassination and violence, instead of government by law." Events in the South seemed to confirm Republican warnings. Extra-legal terrorist groups began to wreak havoc on law and order in the South. The Ku Klux Klan was founded as a social club in 1866 in Tennessee. Its members came from all classes

The Ku Klux Klan was dedicated to preserving white supremacy.

within Southern white society. Its leaders included Confederate generals and other officers, headed by the renowned cavalry leader, General Nathan Bedford Forrest. By 1868, it had become an organization of hooded vigilantes, dedicated to preserving white supremacy. In the 1868 election the Klan engaged in an organized reign of terror directed at blacks and white Republican leaders. Assassins murdered a Republican congressman from Arkansas and three members of the South Carolina legislature. In Georgia, threats and beatings kept blacks from the polls. Eleven Georgia counties with black majorities did not tabulate a single Republican vote. In Louisiana more than a thousand people, mostly blacks, were killed by rampaging Klansmen. In one parish (county) alone, the estimated death toll was 200 blacks, leading a local Democratic leader to declare that this taught blacks a "wholesome lesson." On election day, there wasn't even one Republican vote in an area that had cast over 4,700 Republican votes seven months earlier.

These methods enabled the Democrats to carry Georgia and Louisiana and reduce Republican margins elsewhere in the South. By lending credence to Republican charges that the Rebels were trying to regain power through terror, however, the lawlessness in the South probably helped Republicans in the North. Grant won just about the same percentage of the Northern vote (55 percent) as Lincoln had in 1864 and carried all but three of the Northern states. Grant won an overwhelming electoral majority of 214 to 80. The Republicans retained a substantial margin in the House and Senate. Nevertheless, the great Civil War hero had actually received only about 53 percent of the popular vote against a weak and discredited opponent.

The Fifteenth Amendment

Grant's election assured the continuation of Reconstruction, but it also meant that a new Republican leadership would direct it. House Speaker Thaddeus Stevens, the leading exponent of protecting the rights of freed people and guaranteeing their economic independence, died in August 1868. The mass of mourners that filed past his body as it lay in state in the Capital was eclipsed only by Lincoln. True to his principles, he was buried in a black cemetery so that "I might illustrate in death the principles which I advocated through a long life, Equality of Man before his Creator." His death, followed the next year by that of Edwin Stanton and the loss of his Senate seat by Benjamin Wade, signaled the passing of the old generation of Radicals. The new leadership was more practical than idealistic and driven more by economic concerns.

These Republican leaders worried that a resurgent Democratic Party, bolstered by "rebel" votes, might evict them from power. It seemed to many that it was now crucial to ensure their electoral base by extending black suffrage throughout the country. Blacks still could not vote in eleven of the twenty-one Northern states or the five border states. In addition, the vote in the ten former Confederate states depended on the Reconstruction Acts that could easily be repealed once reconstruction was over. Many Republicans felt a moral obligation to secure the vote for blacks. Naturally, blacks who could vote overwhelmingly favored the party of emancipation, the Republicans. Thus, as one Republican congressman noted, "Party expediency and exact justice coincide for once."

When Congress assembled in December 1868, it moved quickly to pass the Fifteenth Amendment to secure black suffrage. It rejected a Radical proposal to guarantee the right to vote to all male citizens over 21. Such an amendment might be rejected by Northern and Western states who imposed their own limits on voting directed against the foreign born and the Chinese in the Far West. As approved, the amendment prohibited the states from denying the right to vote only "on account of race, color or previous condition of servitude." The warnings of one Radical congressman: "Let it remain possible to still disfranchise the body of the colored race in the late Rebel states and I tell you it will be done," proved to be prophetic. Southern whites were ultimately able to use loopholes that seemed to permit denial of the right to vote on supposedly nonracial grounds. These included literacy and property qualifications. Within thirty years, few Southern blacks were able to vote.

The Fifteenth Amendment was ratified by March 1870. Many relieved Republicans agreed that the passage of the amendment was "the last great point that remained to be settled of the issues of the war." Blacks were already playing a significant role in the newly established Southern governments.

RADICAL RECONSTRUCTION: MYTH AND REALITY

A remarkable period began in Southern history after the passage of the Reconstruction Acts. For the first time ever, governments rested on universal manhood suffrage, without regard to race. All citizens were entitled to "equal protection of the laws." Blacks could now vote, serve on juries, and even hold office. For whites, this was a profoundly disquieting experience, a world "suddenly turned bottom-side up."

The confusion and agitation of the whites led them to characterize Reconstruction as the "tragic era" of an occupied South. Bolstered by later books and films, like *Birth of a Nation* and *Gone With the Wind*, they painted a picture of a society gone mad. In this legend ignorant blacks dominated the governments and ran wild: "It is barbarism overwhelming civilization by physical force. It is the slave rioting in the halls of his master," said one observer. These power mad slaves were aided by villainous Northern "carpetbaggers" who came South "like buzzards" to strip the helpless South of its few pitiful possessions. They, in turn, were abetted by the even more treacherous "scalawags," Southerners who sold out their own people for profit.

This myth, which remained embedded in the American psyche for over a century, bore little resemblance to reality. Blacks did not dominate any of the new governments. (Only South Carolina had a black majority in its legislature.) Military occupation was never widespread and lasted as long as eight years in only three states (South Carolina, Florida, and Louisiana). A small minority of carpetbaggers were the unscrupulous adventurers of the legend. The majority were middle class Union veterans who decided to make their homes in the South. Some of these were entrepreneurs who came for business opportunities. Many were teachers, missionaries, and Freedmen's Bureau agents. Some were idealists like Adelbert Ames, the future Governor of Mississippi, convinced that he "had a Mission with a large M" to help the freed people. Southern supporters of Reconstruction, the so-called "scalawags," also had varied motives. Most had been wartime Unionists in upland counties or pre-war Whigs who had been reluctant secessionists. Some were formerly ardent secessionists who concluded that accommodation would bring economic development to the South. These included General Longstreet, Lee's old lieutenant, who accepted a federal post and campaigned for Grant.

Blacks and Reconstruction

Blacks saw Reconstruction as an opportunity to gain independence and equality. They long remembered the time when "de freedom sun shine out" as the great turning point of their lives. One man recalled, "I felt like a bird out of a cage. Amen. Amen. Amen. I could hardly ask to feel any better...." Now they sought to achieve personal independence and a black community apart from white authority.

Right at the beginning of Reconstruction, blacks tested their new freedom by holding meetings and unsupervised religious services, previously forbidden under slavery. They purchased prohibited items like guns and liquor, flaunted outrageous finery, and even refused to move aside for whites on the sidewalks. Anxious whites complained bitterly about this "insolence" and "insubordination." Many, now free from slavery's restrictions on travel, took to the roads. Between 1865 and 1870 the black population of the ten largest cities in the South doubled. Unfortunately, jobs were scarce, and new segregated neighborhoods arose, consisting largely of broken-down shanties.

The most poignant reason for movement was the attempt to reunite family, the central institution of the black community. One freedman, for example, requested the assistance of the Freedman's Bureau in locating "my own dearest relatives," whom he had not seen in twenty-four years. Slave marriages had not been recognized under Southern law, so couples rushed to make their relationships legal. By 1870, the overwhelming majority of African Americans lived in two-parent households.

Relationships within the family also changed. Under slavery, black men and women had experienced "the rough equality of powerlessness." Now, many hoped to create the type of patriarchal family that was typical in white American households. In the early years of Reconstruction many black women withdrew from field labor, hoping to devote themselves to more domestic responsibilities. Black men were able to play a role in political and public life, while black women, like white women, were not. The Freedman's Bureau reinforced these separate roles by appointing men as heads of household who could sign labor contracts for their families. Black ministers preached that the woman's role was to make the house "a place of peace and comfort" for her husband. The shift from field to home, however, was

The schools built by the Freedman's Bureau were segregated but allowed the children in the South to get a formal education.

only temporary. The rise of sharecropping made families responsible for their plots of land. All members had to work this land. In addition, the extreme poverty of most black families, which worsened in the depression of the 1870s, made women's labor a necessity. Thus, a much higher percentage of married black women than white women had to work outside the home. Still, both black men and women struggled to maintain family stability as the cornerstone of the African-American community.

The other key community institution was the black church. Freedmen quickly withdrew from bi-racial congregations in which they had been required to sit in the back or in the gallery. They pooled their limited resources and built separate black churches. The church was "the first social institution fully controlled by black men in America." Churches became

the centers of community life. Ministers were the most respected members of the community, active in political as well as religious life. They fostered a spirit of community self-help that led to the formation of fraternal, charitable, mutual aid, and burial societies.

The freed people's thirst for self-improvement was evident in the push to establish schools, another key institution. In 1860, over 90 percent of the black population in the South was illiterate. Observers have noted, "the almost sacred nature to the Negroes' attitude towards education." Despite all obstacles put in their way, most agreed with Frederick Douglass that, "the pathway from slavery to freedom was literacy." The freed people, themselves, took the initiative to raise money for schools and teachers' salaries. Many of the schools were supported, at least in part, by tuition, generally $1 to $1.50 a month per child. This was a substantial burden to a man who may have earned $10 a month for his labors. The Freedman's Bureau generally came into the picture after schools had been started, offering some modest financial support and supplies of books. This drive for education continued long after the Freedmen's Bureau ended.

The records of the Bureau contained poignant requests for aid: "You must kno that our people are very poor and if we are not helpt we will remain in ignorants a long time." Many of the schools faced active, even violent, hostility from local whites. Particularly in the smaller towns, most of the teachers were freed people, often only semiliterate themselves. One apologized, "I never had the chance of goen to school for I was a slave until freedom....I am the only teacher because we cannot doe better now." Most of these black teachers earned a modest living, often hardly more than that of a field hand. Some became leaders of the community, even gaining political office.

Surprisingly, many Southern whites taught in the small town and rural schools for blacks. Most were people of limited means who hoped to earn a modest livelihood. One wrote, "I consider myself a pioneer in this laudable cause and being a widow with three children to support, I have undertaken this at the sacrifice of my friends." Northern philanthropic and religious groups also played a part by opening schools in the cities and sending New England "schoolmarms" to inculcate accepted middle class standards of behavior. Eventually, reconstructed state governments began using tax dollars to support separate public schools for children of both races. By 1900, the black illiteracy rate had been cut in half. Even more might have been accomplished had the early valiant efforts been sustained by later white governments. Despite the limitations, W. E. B. Du Bois (a noted African-American scholar and writer) believed that the establishment of a public school system enabled blacks to avoid re-enslavement. It helped them to build an inner culture that withstood the shocks of the outer world.

Blacks, rebuilding their lives and creating their own institutions, realized that true freedom would be achieved solely through economic independence. That, they believed, could only be attained by ownership of land. "What's de use of being free if you don't own land enough to be buried in?" one freedman asked. African Americans also believed that they were entitled to land that had been developed

Most blacks worked as sharecroppers on land owned by whites. In this photograph, black sharecroppers pick cotton. Because the price remained low, sharecroppers often fell into debt and were tied to the land.

through the sweat of their own and their ancestors' labor over many generations. Some Radicals, like Thaddeus Stevens, favored confiscation of Confederate plantations and their redistribution in 40 acre plots to freedmen. Radicals warned that "to give the slaves only freedom without the land, is to give them only the mockery of freedom which the English or Irish peasant had." But the idea was too extreme for most Republicans. As a result, only a few freedmen gained the economic autonomy for which they had dreamed. Most had to work for white landowners.

Nevertheless, blacks did manage to force basic changes in plantation agriculture. While many worked for wages, more settled for an arrangement under which they would get a share of the crop. Planters divided their estates into small plots that they rented to the freedmen. The sharecropper generally could keep one-third of the year's crop after paying for use of the land and necessary supplies, seed, and work animals. Blacks preferred a system that freed them from gang labor and daily white supervision. Poor whites, as well as blacks, became sharecroppers. Planters gained greater stability, as all members of the sharecropping family worked to produce a crop. Eventually, many families were caught up in a web of debt. Even had they been given the small plots of land that they expected, black families, lacking credit or power, would undoubtedly still have suffered economically. But land redistribution would certainly have shaken the foundations of Southern society by creating a group of middle class black farmers.

Despite setbacks, Southern blacks had taken important steps in organizing their own lives. They sponsored newspapers that became a powerful resistance force. They sought to protect these gains by mobilizing and voting in large numbers. At the beginning of Reconstruction, about half of the men qualified to vote were black. Freedmen were the majority of voters in Alabama, Florida, Louisiana, Mississippi, and South Carolina. Despite this, they held only 15 to 20 percent of the government positions. Blacks served as lieutenant governors, secretaries of states, treasurers, and superintendents of education. Sixteen blacks sat in Congress during Reconstruction, including two senators (Hiram Revels

Senator Blanche Bruce

and Blanche Bruce of Mississippi). Over 600 were state legislators, and countless more held local positions like sheriff, justice of the peace, and even mayor. Most of these black politicians were young men. Those at the upper levels tended to come from the free black community, largely from the North, and were often college-educated. Many of those at the state and local levels were far less-educated ex-slaves who had held positions of trust within the slave community, particularly drivers and artisans.

Freedmen eagerly joined Union Leagues that mobilized their votes for the Republicans. Black voters were not the ignorant, easily led dupes described by disgruntled whites. The political agenda of freed people included protection of their wages or shares of crops, a tax-supported public school system, assurance of equality before the law, and defense against the violence of white vigilantes. They were, perhaps surprisingly, uninterested in vengeance against their former masters or in any real push for genuine social integration. The Reconstruction governments, established with their support, now faced the substantial challenge of fulfilling the aspirations of these constituents for a better, more just South. At the same time, they confronted the daunting task of rebuilding a war-torn land in which the average wealth of whites had fallen by one-half.

Republican Rule in the South

Under the rule of the Radical Republicans, both races were able to make considerable social and political progress. The new constitutions ended property qualifications for voting for whites, as well as blacks. They abolished imprisonment for debt and, for the first time, recognized the property rights of married women. Above all, these constitutions established the rights of blacks and whites to public schools.

Still, many white Southerners were deeply disturbed by the support of black schools at public expense. They believed that education would "spoil" blacks, making them discontented and difficult to handle. Despite this, Reconstruction governments increased support for schools, including night schools for adults. Poor white children also, for the first time, were able to take advantage of the new educational system. The Freedman's Bureau and northern philanthropic agencies helped establish black colleges such as Fisk, Hampton, and Tougaloo, initially to train black teachers. Republican governments, for the first time ever in the South, accepted the principle that the state should be responsible for public education.

Also for the first time, Republican state governments built hospitals, orphan asylums, and institutions for the blind, deaf, and mentally ill. Some local governments even provided food, firewood, and free medical care for the poor. State governments attempted to rebuild bridges, public buildings, roads, and other facilities demolished by the war. They provided state aid to railroads destroyed by the war. Most of the investment and construction had to go to rebuilding the railroads. This was accomplished by 1872, and 3300 additional miles were added. Southern Republicans also set up industrial commissions to attract investors to the South, with rather limited success.

Though the achievements of these Reconstruction governments were substantial, they were costly. An entire public school system had to be built. Railroads and rebuilding a war-torn land required substantial funds. As a result, taxes and debts ballooned during Republican rule. Economic problems brought many of the railroads to the verge of bankruptcy. Although no higher than the taxes in the rural Midwest at the time, Southern taxes in 1870 were four times as high as they had been in 1860. Small white landowners had to pay a larger share of taxes than ever before. Their anger at their increased financial burden turned many of these early supporters against the Republicans. In addition, many refused or were unable to pay their taxes. This diminished the services Republican state governments tried to provide, led to economic turmoil, and discredited those governments in northern, as well as southern, eyes.

Corruption in the Reconstruction South further tarnished the image of these governments. One contemporary observer exclaimed, "Such a Saturnalia of robbery and jobbery has seldom been seen in a civilized country...greed was unchecked and roguery unabashed." This view became accepted as the key historical truth about Reconstruction. Certainly, profiteering was widespread. The unprecedented sums of money that these new governments were handling led to bribery, kickbacks, and skimming of public funds. Many officials, in fact, saw nothing wrong with helping themselves to a share of the expanding state budgets. This was, however, only a reflection of what was happening throughout the nation. The Tweed Ring (a Democratic machine in New York) probably stole more from the people than all the Southern governments combined. Southern railroad "rings" were only pale imitations of Wall Street "robber barons." Although it may have been unfair, the dishonesty in the Southern governments further damaged Reconstruction in the view of Northern public opinion.

Despite its achievements, Republican Reconstruction government never met its original exalted goals of remaking Southern society in a more egalitarian mold. For example, it was one thing to build schools and quite another to integrate them. White parents did not want their children to share classrooms with blacks. Although New Orleans successfully integrated several thousand students, this bold experiment was not repeated elsewhere. Even black legislators did not seem to believe that interracial schooling was practical and preferred to stress fair division of school funds. Although the system of legalized segregation in public accommodations did not yet exist, discrimination was widespread. Black demands led to laws establishing the right to equal access to public places and transportation. These laws, however, were rarely enforced.

Land ownership presented another fundamental issue that Republican governments failed to confront. Only South Carolina set up a land commission to purchase acreage and resell it to freed people on easy credit terms. After a shaky start, the commission did succeed in establishing 14,000 black families on homesteads. One such community, Promised Land, is still in existence. Outside South Carolina, the hopes of the freed people were disappointed. Most white Republicans, although committed to equality of citizenship, opposed any state attempts to redistribute property. As one paper pointed out at the time, the lack of any land of their own, coupled with the antagonism of the white elite, meant that freedmen "cannot rise....They must be servants to others, with no hope of bettering their condition." In the long run, this proved to be only too true and was, perhaps, the greatest failure of Reconstruction.

THE GRANT ADMINISTRATION AND NORTHERN POLITICS

When they elected Grant president in 1868, most Americans assumed that he would bring the same superb leadership skills to the job that he had demonstrated as a victorious general. But Grant's experiences on the battlefield did not adequately prepare him for the complexities of the presidential office. His lack of any deep ideological convictions, as demonstrated by his slogan, "Let Us Have Peace," further limited his forcefulness in office. Although he had shrewder political instincts than he is generally given credit for, Grant was often naive in choosing his associates. As someone who had consistently failed in business, he particularly admired successful businessmen and turned to them for advice.

Government Corruption

During the Grant years, it seemed as though corruption infected officials in every region and at every level of government. As the economy soared in the North (by 1873 industrial production was 75 percent greater than its 1865 level), opportunities for profiteering also grew. Influence-peddlers crowded state legislatures, seeking advantages for their railroad, mining, or lumber companies. Even relatively honest officials saw nothing wrong in accepting money or favors from businessmen in return for preferential laws or contracts. Local, state, and even federal governments were not well equipped to deal with the demands created by economic growth and increased government services and benefits. This led to alliances between businessmen and politicians that produced the ever expanding corruption of the era.

Although he himself was honest, Grant surrounded himself with people who saw public office as a road to personal profit. During his two terms, his secretary of war, his vice president, many treasury and naval officials, and even his private secretary were involved in public scandals. Government promotion of railroad development offered one prime opportunity. By 1872, the federal government had distributed well over 100 million acres of public land and millions of dollars for railroad construction, particularly to the new transcontinental lines, the Central Pacific and the Union Pacific. This led to the era's most famous scandal, that of the Credit Mobilier. This was a "dummy" corporation created to receive construction contracts from the Union Pacific. It was formed by an inner circle of Union Pacific stockholders. These men made exorbitant profits by awarding themselves contracts at greatly inflated costs. To forestall congressional inquiry, the company distributed stock to important members of Congress and federal government officials. The resulting scandal that broke in 1872 implicated several important Republican leaders, including the vice president.

Other scandals hit the Grant administration even harder. The Secretary of War had to resign or face impeachment when it was revealed that he had taken kickbacks from government-appointed traders in Indian Territory. Another investigation uncovered the widespread Whiskey Ring that looted millions of dollars from federal excise taxes. Investigations revealed that the president's secretary was at the center of the ring. Only Grant's intervention saved him from prison. One observer has noted, "It was the age of the audacious confidence man, and Grant was the incurable sucker. He easily fell victim to their trickery...because he could not believe that such people existed."

Foreign Policy in the Grant Years

Grant's best cabinet appointment was, undoubtedly, his Secretary of State, Hamilton Fish, an aristocratic New Yorker. His greatest success resulted from quiet and persistent diplomacy to settle damage claims against the British. These were based on the wartime destruction caused by the *Alabama* and other British-built vessels that had preyed on Union shipping. Eager to maintain American friendship, the British agreed to the 1871 Treaty of Washington, which set up an international arbitration tribunal to settle claims. The tribunal awarded the United States $15.5 million for damages done by the British-made ships. This was not only a victory for American diplomacy, it also established an important precedent for settling international disputes and helped improve relations with Britain.

The biggest foreign policy disaster during the Grant years was the attempt to take over Santo Domingo (the Dominican Republic today). After the victory of nationalism in the Civil War, many Americans again embraced the ideas of Manifest Destiny. In 1867, Secretary of State Seward had negotiated a treaty with Russia to purchase Alaska for $7.2 million. Despite derisive comments about "Seward's Folly," this set a precedent for annexing territory not connected to the continental United States. Various promoters and speculators used their influence with Grant's private secretary to lobby for annexation of Santo Domingo. Although they succeeded in getting Grant to agree to a treaty, the Senate refused to ratify it, leading to further splits within the Republican Party.

Elizabeth Cady Stanton and Susan B. Anthony were a strong team in the suffrage and abolition movements.

Women and Reconstruction

When blacks achieved political rights, women continued to be "the only class of citizens wholly unrepresented in the government." Abolitionists and feminists had long been allied in the American reform movement. When the issues of black male citizenship and suffrage arose in the debates over the Fourteenth and Fifteenth Amendments, women's rights advocates hoped that woman suffrage would be next. They were disappointed when many of their old abolitionist allies deserted them, declaring, "It is the Negro's hour, not the woman's."

The Fourteenth Amendment added the word "male" to the Constitution for the first time (in its description of inhabitants entitled to vote). Militant feminists, led by Elizabeth Cady Stanton and Susan B. Anthony, opposed the Fifteenth Amendment for prohibiting racial, but not sexual, discrimi-

Susan B. Anthony (left) and Lucy Stone (right), feminist leaders whose followers split over support for the Fifteenth Amendment. Anthony headed the more radical wing while the moderate group accepted the Reconstruction Amendments.

nation in voting. Stanton believed that an extension of the vote that led to universal manhood suffrage only underscored the powerlessness of women and their declining status. Educated and informed women like the reformers, Stanton argued, were far more qualified to make political decisions than immigrants and freedmen "who do not know the difference between the monarchy and the republic." The already small feminist movement split into a radical wing, headed by Stanton and Anthony, and a more moderate group that accepted the reconstruction amendments. Susan B. Anthony actually faced trial for voting in the election of 1872. Both groups continued to fight for women's suffrage, although they were unable to achieve their goals in this era. They were more successful in obtaining property rights for married women. The abolitionist-feminist alliance had totally disintegrated, further weakening supporters of reconstruction.

The Election of 1872

As Grant's renomination became a certainty by 1872, a group of members of his own party, who disagreed with his appointments and policies, launched the Liberal Republican movement. They stressed civil service reform to end the abuses of political corruption and urged amnesty in the South. They hoped to attract candidates of "superior intelligence and superior virtue." As a compromise candidate for the presidency, they nominated Horace Greeley, editor of the *New York Tribune*, the most prominent newspaperman in the country. In his 40 years as a journalist Greeley had supported a wide variety of contradictory positions. Before the Civil War, he had been a staunch abolitionist. After, he moved from advocating tough postwar reconstruction to becoming the leading spokesman for self-government and amnesty in the South. Despite his years of attacks directed at Democrats, the Democratic Party decided to endorse Greeley under the slogan, "Anything to beat Grant."

Greeley's eccentricities, however, made him vulnerable to ridicule. In addition, Greeley's stress on Southern self-government proved to be counter-productive, as many Northern voters still distrusted the white South. Thomas Nast, the *Harper's Weekly* cartoonist who had helped destroy the Tweed Ring, had a similar field day with Greeley. His best known campaign cartoon showed pirate captain Greeley bringing his boat next to the ship of state while armed Confederates waited below to board and demolish it. Another portrayed Greeley stretching a hand over Lincoln's grave to clasp the hand of John Wilkes Booth!

Despite vigorous campaigning, Greeley's candidacy began to lose steam. Grant won 56 percent of the popular vote, the largest margin of any candidate from 1828 to 1904. He carried every Northern state and ten of the sixteen Southern or border states. The Republicans were also able to regain their two-thirds margin in both Houses of Congress. Weary from campaigning, depressed by the results, and mourning the death of his wife, Greeley died three weeks later. The Liberal Republican movement also collapsed. But, when the nation's prosperity dissolved into depression in 1873, Republicans grew more vulnerable to the issues of reform and reconciliation that had been raised unsuccessfully in the election.

RETREAT FROM RECONSTRUCTION

Grant's landslide re-election victory seemed, at least on the surface, to reaffirm the nation's support for continued reconstruction. Many Northerners, however, were becoming increasingly disillusioned with Southern Republicans. Except for the Radical Republicans, few Northerners had ever been deeply committed to racial equality. New issues arising from depression and unemployment led Northern voters, who had never had much real sympathy for the difficulties of Southern blacks, to lose any remaining interest in their plight.

Increase in Terrorism

The waves of terror instituted by the Klan and Klan-like organizations in the South directed against blacks and Republicans continued to grow during the 1870s. The death toll was in the hundreds. Northerners expressed their amazement at the inability of Southern Republicans to maintain order. Attempts by Republican officials to use militia to contain the violence proved to be ineffective. White troops were unreliable because the Klan often infiltrated their ranks. Black militia units increased white anger and led to fears of race warfare. Even when Klansmen were arrested, it was difficult to protect witnesses and find a jury that would convict. One case in Mississippi was dismissed when five key witnesses were murdered. When the governor of North Carolina sought to crush the Klan by declaring marital law, the Democratic-controlled legislature impeached him and discharged him from office in 1871. (He was the first American governor ever to be so removed.)

Congress finally responded to the increasing violence by passing a series of Enforcement Acts, the most extensive of which was the Ku Klux Klan Act of 1871. For the first time, conspiracies to deny citizens equal protection of the law could be prosecuted in federal courts. The president could declare martial law in any community victimized by terror and could even suspend habeas corpus. Led by a new, crusading attorney general, the federal government did intervene in South Carolina and successfully prosecuted several hundred Klansmen elsewhere in the South. By 1872, federal power had broken the back of the Klan and appeared to have returned the rule of law to the South.

Unfortunately, the return to some semblance of order was short-lived. Congressional Republicans began to retreat from their commitment to "carpetbag governments" in the South. One politician bluntly announced, "The truth is our people are tired out with this worn out cry of 'Southern outrages'!!!" By 1872, Congress had extended amnesty to all but a handful of Confederate leaders and the Freedman's Bureau was allowed to expire. "White Leaguers" in Louisiana killed over one hundred blacks in the town of Colfax. But the entrance of federal troops into the state to end the increasingly bitter conflict provoked cynical complaints in Congress about "federal despotism."

In 1873, the great postwar economic growth suddenly collapsed in a financial panic. Disastrous unemployment and wage cuts led to bitter strikes and protests. Class divisions threatened social harmony. Frightened Republican businessmen became more sympathetic to Southern whites who seemed to be facing the same problems of disorder with lower class blacks. Conservative doctrines, stressing business interests, replaced equal rights for blacks as the Republican Party's central ideology.

As always in hard economic times, the voters turned against the party in power. In the greatest turnaround in the nineteenth century, the huge Republican majority in the House of Representatives became a 60 seat Democratic majority. In New York, where Democrat Samuel Tilden piled up an amazing 50,000 vote majority for governor, a paper declared, "The election is not merely a victory but a revolution." For the first time in a generation, even Massachusetts elected a Democratic governor. Although the depression was the main reason for the Republican defeat, many leaders blamed the party's Southern reconstruction policies for the debacle. *The Prostrate State*, an influential and widely read book by James Pike, a Northern journalist, indicted supposed "Negro rule" in South Carolina. It reinforced the idea that governmental corruption and extravagance were the results of power given to "a mass of black barbarism...the most ignorant democracy that mankind ever saw." Some Republican leaders openly spoke of "unloading" the weight of Southern Reconstruction governments.

The Civil Rights Act of 1875

The second Grant administration witnessed a general retreat from Reconstruction. The Supreme Court issued a series of decisions in the 1870s that seriously undercut the protections for blacks, seemingly guaranteed by the Fourteenth Amendment. In one particularly devastating decision, the Court overturned convictions obtained against violent terrorists under the Enforcement Act. The Court ruled that the amendment allowed the federal government to act only against violations of rights by *states*, rather than individuals. Only local or state authorities could punish individual crimes. This made it almost impossible to prosecute criminals whose violence against blacks was ignored by local officials.

The last of the old radical "lions," Charles Sumner, senator from Massachusetts, tirelessly labored to secure the passage of the Civil Rights Act to safeguard the fast-fading dream of equality. This measure prohibited racial discrimination in public accommodations, jury selection, cemeteries, and transportation. On his death bed Sumner entreated a visitor, "You must take care of the civil-rights bill,...don't let it fail." Its passage was the final tribute of his colleagues to a man whose entire public life had been devoted to ending slavery and achieving civil rights for African Americans. Although the law seemed to call for an unparalleled demonstration of federal powers, in practice it was rarely enforced. It remained a statement of principles, rather than action, until it was declared unconstitutional by the Supreme Court in 1883.

The "Redeemers" Regain Power

The nationwide depression had hit rural white Southerners with particular force. High taxes and a precipitous drop in crop prices combined to undermine the economic position of independent white small farmers. Many joined black farmers in the ranks of the landless. Democrats were able to use racism to rally back country whites whose economic frustrations turned them against Southern Republican governments.

The "Mississippi Plan," which enabled Democrats to regain power in that state in 1875, became the model for "redeemers" throughout the South. The Democrats were trying to "redeem" their states from Republican and carpetbagger control. The first step of the plan was to force the 15 percent of the state's whites who considered themselves Republicans to switch sides through threats and ostracism. The next step was to use violence to intimidate black voters and break up Republican rallies. In broad daylight "Rifle Clubs" marched undisguised and shot down blacks "just the same as birds." In one such incident, mobs murdered thirty-five blacks and two whites in Vicksburg. Democratic newspapers in the state proclaimed the slogan, "Carry the election peacefully if we can, forcibly if we must." The governor of Mississippi, a Civil War Medal of Honor winner and one of the best carpetbag governors, appealed to President Grant for federal troops to control the violence. Northern party leaders, worried that military intervention would cost the Republicans a closely fought contest in Ohio, persuaded the president not to act. In a sentence that summarized the Northern retreat from reconstruction, the attorney general informed the governor, "The whole public are tired out with these annual autumnal outbreaks in the South, and the great majority are now ready to condemn any interference on the part of the Government." As a result, armed men threatened to kill freedmen who voted and openly destroyed ballot boxes with Republican votes. They shot one black state senator in the back. This contempt for federal law and the Constitution of the United States resulted in an overwhelming Democratic victory in Mississippi. It seemed apparent that whatever the results of the presidential election of 1876, Reconstruction itself would not survive.

The Disputed Centennial Election

Millions of Americans flocked to Philadelphia in 1876 to celebrate America's centennial at an enormous Exposition dedicated to the "Progress of the Age." Despite the continuing economic depression and rampant labor conflict, the exhibits extolled new inventions and the possibilities of technological progress. Many groups were left out of the displays. Native Americans were seen only as quaint contrasts to an advanced civilization. A Woman's Pavilion featured women weavers but failed to mention the struggle for women's rights. Susan B. Anthony disrupted the July 4th program at the exposition to read a "Woman's Declaration of Independence." Blacks were not only invisible in the exhibits, they had even been barred from the construction crews that built the display halls.

American politics were nothing to celebrate about either in 1876. Successful intimidation of black voters and the declining courage of white Republicans resulted in Democratic "Redemption" of all Southern states except South Carolina, Louisiana, and Florida. On the national level, the scandals that had overwhelmed the Grant administration burst into public view. This forced the Republicans to find a candidate of unquestioned honesty. They chose a former Civil War general, Governor Rutherford B. Hayes of Ohio, a drab "third-rate nonentity." The Democrats tried to seize the issue of reform by nominating Governor Samuel Tilden of New York, a millionaire corporate lawyer. Tilden had won a national reputation as a reformer when he broke up the infamous Tweed Ring in New York City. Both candidates were conservative men who favored sound money, reform, and limited government. The Democrats hoped to gain Northern swing states by downplaying the "bloody shirt" issues of Civil War and Reconstruction.

Reports of a massacre in Hamburg, South Carolina hampered this Democratic strategy. There, whites murdered five captured black militiamen in cold blood and looted and demolished black shops and homes. This atrocity enabled Republicans to revive Northern fears of Democrats as unreconstructed rebels. Although Hayes did not do as well as Grant had in 1872, he was able to win all but four of the Northern states, giving him 165 electoral votes. Tilden won a 250,000 popular vote plurality. (Although it has been estimated that at least 250,000 Southern Republicans had been terrorized to prevent them from voting, neutralizing that margin of victory.) He carried New York, New Jersey, Connecticut, Indiana, and all the Southern states under Democratic control, a total of 184 electoral votes. With only 185 electoral votes needed for victory, Tilden's triumph seemed evident. Two sets of conflicting returns, however, had arrived from South Carolina, Louisiana, and Florida. On the face of the returns, it appeared that Tilden had carried at least two of the states, but the Republican-controlled election boards certified Hayes as the winner in each state. While this might seem to have been a subversion of honest returns, it was actually impossible to tell what the results of an accurate count of the votes would have been. The Democrats had used fraud and force to keep blacks and Republicans from voting in the first place. For example, one Louisiana parish that had 1688 Republican voters in 1874, recorded only one in 1876.

Congress, lacking any clear guidance in the Constitution, faced an extraordinary predicament in determining who had really won. With a Republican Senate and a Democratic House, Congress decided to turn the problem over to an Electoral Commission consisting of five senators, five representatives, and five Supreme Court justices. The commission was balanced with seven Republicans and seven Democrats. The fifteenth member was to be an impartial Supreme Court justice. But, after some political maneuvering, this final member turned out to be Justice Joseph Bradley, a Republican, who cast the swing vote with the Republicans. By an eight to seven margin, the commission voted to award all 20 disputed electoral votes to Hayes, giving him the 185 electoral votes needed for victory. Many infuriated Democrats felt that they had been robbed and threatened action in the House.

While these proceedings were going on in public, negotiations continued behind the scenes between Republican leaders and "moderate" Southern Democrats. Under this "Compromise of 1877," Southerners agreed to withdraw their opposition to Hayes' inauguration in return for Hayes' assurance that he would remove the remaining federal troops from the South. This was merely the final step in the abandonment of Reconstruction. A month after his inauguration, in April 1877, Hayes ordered the withdrawal of federal troops from Louisiana and South Carolina, causing the collapse of the last two Re-

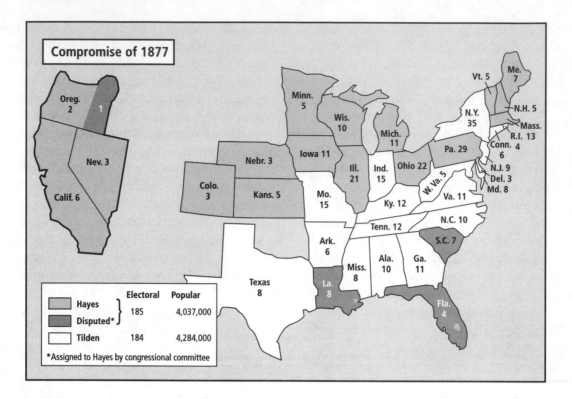

Compromise of 1877

	Electoral	Popular
■ Hayes	185	4,037,000
■ Disputed*		
□ Tilden	184	4,284,000

*Assigned to Hayes by congressional committee

publican governments in the South. The Republican governor of South Carolina sorrowfully informed his distressed black supporters, "Today, by order of the President whom your votes alone rescued from overwhelming defeat, the Government of the United States abandons you...." Thus, the real losers of the 1876 election were not the Democrats but Southern blacks whose last hopes for equality were crushed.

THE NEW SOUTH

The nation recovered from the depression after 1878. In the 1880s the American economy leaped forward at an astonishing pace. The South shared the buoyant mood that swept the country in the 1880s. The collapse of the last few Radical governments led to the domination of Southern politics by a new class of men. These included merchants, bankers, railroad promoters, and even some industrialists. They allied with the old planter class that, despite a decline of its prewar power, retained considerable influence in rural areas. They called themselves Redeemers, claiming that they had "redeemed" the

South from corrupt and extravagant carpetbag rule. They proclaimed the beginning of a "New South" devoted to economic modernization and frugal government. They promised to relieve the North of a burden most Northerners did not want: the burden of Reconstruction and the establishment of equal rights for blacks.

Henry Grady, editor of the *Atlanta Constitution*, was the foremost exponent of the expansive New South ideology. He announced that there would be a new stress on the "gospel of work as the South's great need." He assured Northerners that the South had learned its lesson in its defeat and was now willing to embrace Northern economic and social standards. In his famous 1886 speech, he promised that the New South understood "that her emancipation came because through the inscrutable wisdom of God her honest purpose was crossed, and her brave armies beaten." Southerners, he declared, were now glad that "the American Union was saved from the wreck of war."

Booker T. Washington emerged as an African-American exponent of the New South. Washington, who had been born a slave, had worked his way

Booker T. Washington believed that vocational education was the answer for African Americans.

erate cause had been wrong, most Southerners believed it had always been right. They were defenders of the "Lost Cause," including even slavery. Every Confederate Memorial Day, they paraded the red Confederate battle flag down the streets of small and large towns. (Even today, that flag remains a source of confrontation between white and black Southerners.)

A more important difficulty with the New South conception was the continuing backwardness of the Southern economic and social system. The new state governments set out to reduce government spending and property taxes. In doing so, they retreated from reconstruction commitments to a state that had responsibilities for the welfare of its citizens. Florida abandoned a nearly completed college, leaving the state without any institution of higher learning. Alabama closed public hospitals. Public schools were the principal victims of the cutbacks. Louisiana spent so little on its system that the percentage of literate whites actually declined between 1880 and 1900. Above all, black schools, so laboriously built and maintained, were hit the hardest as the gap between spending for black and white schools invariably widened.

Agriculture in the New South

up from poverty after being educated at Virginia's Hampton Institute. He hoped that other blacks would follow in his footsteps in seeking self-improvement. In a famous 1895 speech at the Cotton States Exposition, Washington outlined his "Atlanta Compromise." Blacks would give up agitation for their rights and would concentrate on hard work to make them economically indispensable to whites. This economic importance would eventually lead to white acceptance. His New South institution, Tuskegee in Alabama, emphasized industrial education and improved agricultural methods as the path for black students. George Washington Carver did his pioneer research on the uses of the peanut at Tuskegee.

Despite the widespread publicity given to the ideas of New Southerners, the problem with the image they sought to build was that much of it was not accurate. Far from admitting that the Confed-

This backwardness was nowhere more apparent than in agriculture. Broad new vagrancy laws reinforced planters' control over their labor force. These permitted the arrest of any unemployed person and made it a crime to leave a job before the expiration of a contract. Criminal laws increased the penalty for even the most petty offense. The convict lease system expanded to permit the hiring out of most prisoners. Mines, railroads, lumber companies, and planters vied for these new forced laborers, most of whom were blacks convicted of minor transgressions.

Other laws gave planters control of property and credit, including precedence to their claims for their share of the crops. Even during Reconstruction, sharecropping had perpetuated black economic dependence upon whites. As the system evolved, the sharecropper had to borrow against future crops to pay his debts to the landowner and supply merchant. Inevitably, he became enmeshed in a web of debt from which escape was virtually impossible. The continued reliance on cotton led inescapably to overproduction and declining prices, compounding the misery. The sharecropping system and its labor control worked against any efforts to mechanize Southern agriculture. Most small white farmers succumbed to the same economic forces. In the Deep South, per capita income remained unchanged even in the great era of economic growth in America, 1880 to 1900.

Industry in the New South

Many New South crusaders concentrated on a campaign to develop industry. They achieved some success in the expansion of Southern textile mills. The new fad of cigarette smoking led to the growth of the tobacco industry. Railroad construction continued at a rapid pace. Southern lines were integrated into the national railroad network under the control of Northern capitalists. Despite these advances in industrialization, fueled by promises of low taxes, special concessions, and a docile labor force, the South remained overwhelmingly agricultural. In fact, even by 1900, the New South accounted for a smaller percentage of the nation's industry than the Old South had in 1860. (Industrialization had proceeded at a far more rapid pace in the North.)

While the new upper class continued to prosper, most Southerners, white and black, fell into even deeper poverty. Publicists touted the cotton mills as the salvation of poor whites. But when the poor white farmers gave up their struggle with the land and went to work in the mills, they replaced one life of destitution with another. Men earned wages of about 50 cents a day, and women and children supplemented family income at even lower wages. Companies controlled all aspects of life in company towns and the poor white worker found that, "I owe my soul to the company store." These mill villages did remain all-white and consciousness of racial superiority grew in importance as the century ended.

The Rise of Jim Crow

Illiteracy, lack of adequate nutrition and housing, and a system of social, economic, and political injustice trapped blacks in the "brave" New South. The disillusionment with the end of Reconstruction led more than 50,000 blacks to seek opportunities in Kansas. These "Exodusters" represented only a small percentage of those who would have migrated if opportunities in the North were not still closed to them. Over 90 percent of black Americans in 1900 continued to live in the South.

Despite the end of Reconstruction in 1877 and the continuing intimidation and violence, black voting had not been entirely eliminated in the South. With their economic clout, the conservative upper classes felt that they could effectively manage the black vote. In the late 1880s and early 1890s, however, the growing agricultural unrest led to the formation of the Populist movement. For a while, it seemed that oppressed white and black farmers might get together and challenge conservative rule in the South. The Democratic leadership responded by reviving racist propaganda and returning to warnings about "Negro domination" and "revival of black Reconstruction" to discredit the Populists. The Democrats were successful in maintaining their power and reinforcing a one-party South. A major component of their efforts was the disfranchisement of black voters. Between 1890 and 1910 every Southern state imposed poll taxes, literacy requirements, and property qualifications for voting. Four states even instituted a "grandfather" clause that allowed men to vote only if their ancestors had voted before 1867 (before blacks had been granted the vote). The Supreme Court eventually overturned this obvious violation of the Fifteenth Amendment but not until 1915. These measures succeeded in an almost total elimination of black voting in the South. As late as 1896, 130,000 blacks continued to vote in Louisiana. By 1904, only 1,342 were still able to do so. Although there were loopholes to permit whites to vote, poll taxes and property qualifications did reduce the number of poor illiterate white voters as well.

Southern customs had long separated the races, but in the 1890s a series of Jim Crow laws made segregation into a rigid system. The term *Jim Crow* came from old blackface minstrel shows. It had come to mean a code for racial segregation in schools, industry, transportation, and all areas of public accommodation. In 1896, the Supreme Court in *Plessy v. Ferguson* ruled that state-mandated separate railroad cars for blacks did not violate equal protection guaranteed by the Fourteenth Amendment if the separate facilities were equal. In an impassioned dissent, Justice John Harlan, a Southerner himself, declared, "The Constitution is colorblind." Later decisions, however, extended this "separate but equal" doctrine to other public facilities, particularly schools. Of course, accommodations were never really equal, and Jim Crow became central to the Southern way of life.

Ida B. Wells is perhaps best remembered for her antilynching crusade.

There was also a dramatic increase in white violence in the 1890s, designed to keep blacks more firmly "in their place." The decade averaged 187 lynchings each year. The overwhelming majority of the victims were black. Some were well-planned public events, attracting large audiences and family outings. Some victims were accused of crimes, but the "crime" of many of the victims was "uppityness." Others supposedly made sexual advances to white women. The fear that white women might be attracted to black sexuality, encouraged as a strategy to terrify whites, was one of the underpinnings of rigid segregation. The lack of protection for African Americans in the South made Booker T. Washington's ideas of racial cooperation more popular. Other blacks, however, favored a more militant approach. In 1892, Ida B. Wells, a crusading black journalist in Memphis, launched an international anti-lynching movement. When she investigated the charges of "rape," she found virtually all of them untrue.

Segregation, combined with sharecropping and debt tenancy, stifled the ingenuity and economic potential of a large percentage of the Southern population. The South succeeded in marginalizing itself in the name of white domination. The New South, thus, had very little meaning for most Southerners— white or black. For African Americans, it meant the end of the dream that Reconstruction had encouraged. A black politician, ending his nine-year congressional career, conceded the extravagance of the earlier Reconstruction governments. But, he asked, "can the saving of a few thousand or a few hundred thousands of dollars compensate for the loss of the political heritage of American citizens?"

CONCLUSION

As the Civil War and Reconstruction faded from view, a romantic haze suffused the era. Organizations staged grand reunions of the "Blue and the Gray." Popular books and plays were devoted to reconciliation (particularly through romances between Southern women and Northern men). Black abolitionist Frederick Douglass struggled unsuccessfully to oppose remembering "with equal admiration...those who fought for slavery and those who fought for liberty and justice." Racism even reached the Grand Army of the Republic, which segregated its posts and forced black veterans to march behind whites in Memorial Day parades.

In the early twentieth century, historians, led by William Dunning of Columbia University, rewrote the history of Reconstruction. They believed that blacks were "children," incapable of understanding the freedom that Northerners unwisely thrust upon them. One bestseller even argued that under Reconstruction, Southern whites "literally were put to the torture" by "emissaries of hate" who inspired "lustful assaults" by blacks against white women. The black community understood a different version of Reconstruction. As one 88-year-old former slave told an interviewer in the 1930s, "I know folks think books tell the truth, but they shore don't."

Reconstruction certainly succeeded in bringing the nation along a relatively peaceful path after the ending of the worst war in American history. The victorious and outraged North did not turn on the helpless South in an orgy of revenge through executions or confiscation of property. Except in songs and books, the defeated South did not inaugurate a period of guerrilla warfare. Perhaps most surprisingly, newly freed blacks did not seek revenge against their former masters. They never even attempted to seize the plantations.

In view of the pervasive racism of America of this era, it is less surprising that the constitutional amendments, the Freedmen's Bureau, and the civil rights laws did not bring about permanent change than that they were passed in the first place. In view of deeply held ideas about property rights, limited government, and black inferiority the failure of Reconstruction seems almost inevitable. W. E. B. Du Bois commented, "The slave went free; stood a brief moment in the sun; then moved back again toward slavery." The failure of the experiment in equal rights was a tragedy for blacks and for the whole nation. The issue of race remained a sore on the nation's body for years to come. Nevertheless, the amendments and civil rights laws passed during Reconstruction became the basis of a renewed and more effective struggle for equal rights almost a hundred years later, a struggle that continues to this day.

Chronology

1863	Lincoln issues Proclamation of Amnesty and Reconstruction
1864	Congress passes stringent Wade-Davis Bill
1865	Freedmen's Bureau established Civil War ends Lincoln assassinated (April 14) Black Codes enacted by Southern legislatures Thirteenth Amendment abolishing slavery added to the Constitution
1866	Congress approves 14th Amendment Congress passes Civil Rights Act and Freedmen's Bureau Act over Johnson's veto Ku Klux Klan founded in Tennessee Republicans triumph in congressional elections despite Johnson's efforts
1867	Congressional Reconstruction Act passed U. S. purchases Alaska
1868	President Johnson is impeached but acquitted Fourteenth Amendment ratified Ulysses S. Grant elected president
1869	Ratification of the Fifteenth Amendment
1870	Last four Southern states admitted to the union
1871	Ku Klux Klan Act passes to end terrorism in the South
1872	Grant re-elected president
1873	Financial panic leads to five-year depression
1875	Whiskey Ring scandal further discredits Grant administration
1876	Disputed presidential election of Hayes vs. Tilden
1877	Electoral commission awards presidency to Rutherford B. Hayes
1890s	"Jim Crow" laws passed in the South
1896	*Plessy v. Ferguson* upholds segregation "separate but equal"

SUGGESTED READINGS

Edward L. Ayers, *The Promise of the New South: Life After Reconstruction* (1992).

LaWanda Cox, *Lincoln and Black Freedom* (1981).

Richard Nelson Current, *Those Terrible Carpetbaggers* (1988).

W.E.B. Dubois, *Black Reconstruction* (1935).

Eric Foner, *Reconstruction: America's Unfinished Revolution* (1988).

___ ,*A Short History of Reconstruction* (1990).

George Frederickson, *The Black Image in the White Mind* (1971).

William Gillette, *Retreat From Reconstruction, 1869-1879* (1980).

Herbert Gutman, *The Black Family in Slavery and Freedom, 1750-1925* (1976).

William Hesseltine, *Lincoln's Plan of Reconstruction* (1960).

Jacqueline Jones, *Labor of Love, Labor of Sorrow: Black Women, Work, and the Family from Slavery to the Present* (1985).

Leon Litwack, *Been in the Storm So Long: The Aftermath of Slavery* (1979).

William S. McFeely, *Grant: A Biography* (1981).

___ ,*Frederick Douglass* (1990).

Eric McKitrick, *Andrew Johnson and Reconstruction* (1960).

James McPherson, *Ordeal by Fire* (1992).

Michael Perman, *Emancipation and Reconstruction, 1862-1879* (1987).

Willie Lee Rose, *Rehearsal for Reconstruction* (1964).

Theodore Rosengarten, *All God's Dangers: The Life of Nate Shaw* (1974).

Hans L. Trefousse, *Andrew Johnson* (1989).

Joel Williamson, *The Crucible of Race* (1984).

C. Vann Woodward, *Origins of the New South, 1877-1913* (1951).

___ ,*The Strange Career of Jim Crow* (1974).

Chapter Thirteen

THE RISE OF INDUSTRIAL AMERICA & THE POLITICS OF THE NEW ORDER

It was a cool, clear crisp October morning in the Italian Alpine town of Piantedo—population 650—when fourteen-year-old Aurelia Rossotti awoke at 6 a.m. to catch the train to Milano, which left at 7 a.m. The year was 1903. Aurelia was the third oldest child in a family of ten children—six girls and four boys. Her older brother Pietro and older sister Lena had left for "America" two years earlier. Now it was her turn to leave for the "Promise Land" of the United States. Her siblings had sent her the money for her trip over on a steamer—the same way they had come—that left once a month out of the port city of Genoa. It had taken "Pep"—that is now what Pietro called himself because it was easier for Anglo-Americans to pronounce and sounded "less foreign"—and Lena six months each of work to save enough money to send to their sister, Aurelia. Pep had gotten a job in a lumber mill in northern California, earning about a dollar a day for 12 hours of work. Lena worked as a "domestic" for the mill's owner, a man named Pierce, whose Anglo-American family had been in California since the Gold Rush days of the early 1850s. Indeed, the Pierce family was not only the richest in the area, owning several businesses, including the Eureka Hotel, and thousands of acres of prime land, but also controlled the city government—a Pierce was mayor and another relative was Chief-of-Police. At the time, the most lucrative enterprise was timber, and the Pierce family owned several mills worth millions of dollars. At first, the Pierces used cheap Chinese labor in their mills, but white California nativism raised its ugly head and drove the Chinese out of the area decades earlier. Filling that labor void would be the "new" immigrants, who, beginning in the 1880s on, were primarily from southern and eastern Europe, like "Pep" Rossotti. Pep was just one of several of these new immigrants working in the mill. Working alongside him as he fed raw timber into the cutting saws were other immigrants—a "Bohunk" (the generic WASP pejorative for a Slav or Hungarian) and a Russian, whom the WASP bosses simply called "Ivan," even though that was not his real name. Since these three men did not speak a word of each other's languages, if they wished to communicate with each other, they all had to learn English. None of the Rossotti children had much formal education—the equivalent of the sixth or seventh grade in the United States—so learning a language as difficult as English was not easy. But they all did and were quite proud of that accomplishment until the day they died.

A the time of Aurelia's emigration, a one-way ticket to America cost around $200 (which would be well over

$1,000 in present U.S. value) and that was for space in "steerage"—the bottom of the ship. This was not a luxury liner or cruise ship—no sun decks, no swimming pools, no all-you-can-eat buffets, no exotic shore-leaves, and no shuffle board. This was a ship built for simply packing into its cargo hold as many human beings as possible and transporting them across the Atlantic to the New World, that strange and distant land discovered some five hundred years earlier by another Italian hoping to find fame and fortune. Living conditions on these immigrant steamers were at best barely tolerable and most of the time deplorable. Quarters were cramped with no privacy, rats roamed freely, and the food was usually not worth eating, and so many of the immigrants brought their own familiar fare with them in their packs—salami, cheese, bread, and fruit from the homeland. Despite the rather wretched conditions on board, hundreds of immigrants believed it was worth enduring for the opportunity to have a new and better life in America. This was what Aurelia hoped for. Aurelia was also somewhat of a "rarity"; she was one of only a relative handful of northern Italians on board. The steamer, after picking up Aurelia and some others at Genoa, then steamed south to Naples and then to the island of Sicily, where the majority of the "cargo" got on board. Why were the majority of Italian immigrants who came to America from southern Italy? The answer was simple: southern Italy was by far the poorest region in the country, especially so for the inhabitants of the island of Sicily. Southern Italy was (and still is) overwhelmingly agricultural and rural, its farmers dependent on the cultivation of olives, some wheat, livestock, and that's about it. Land is not that fertile, especially that of Sicily, which is essentially an island of rocks, whose soil and terrain is only conducive to the growing of olives and the making of olive oil. Today, such commodities, especially in the United States, are considered to be "healthy" foods; a hundred years ago, few, if any, WASP Americans even knew what olive oil was. Sicily was also a very violent place, run by very powerful warlord-type of families who were constantly feuding with each other for control of the island. Violence was endemic, part of daily life, which saw murder and assassination become commonplace as gun-battles between the families raged in broad daylight, fought with "luparas"—shotguns used for the killing of

wolves, which once roamed the island. All too frequently, innocent bystanders were killed for just being in the wrong place at the wrong time. Thus, one can easily understand why someone would want to leave such a place.

After about two weeks of travel, Aurelia's steamer entered New York City's harbor, where it unloaded its passengers at the newly built "processing" facility at Ellis Island. There, Aurelia and hundreds, if not thousands, of immigrants were put through a battery of different questions, physical examinations, baggage checks, in short, as thorough of a "screening" as was possible to determine whether the individual was physically and mentally healthy enough to enter the United States. Aurelia was. However, her only problem was her first name—none of the Irish or Welsh "processors" could pronounce it correctly. Finally, as her "papers" were approved and had stamped on them "WOP"—which meant "without passport" but has since come to be one of the pejoratives for Italians—a Welsh immigration official looked at Aurelia, noticed her red hair and rosey-red cheeks, and decided that henceforth her "new" American name would be "Rosie." From that moment on, Aurelia Rossotti became "Rosie" Rossotti.

After spending a few days in New York City in an Italian-owned boarding house, "Rosie" boarded the train at Penn Station in NYC and headed west for California to join her brother and sister. It only took about seven days for the train to reach San Francisco, as it stopped only twice along the way to take on more passengers. To travel 3,000 miles in that short of time was remarkable testimony to the speed and facility of the American railway system, which had only finished its transcontinental lines a decade and a half earlier. When Aurelia arrived at the station in San Francisco, her brother and sister were there to meet her. She was so excited and relieved to see them, especially since she could "speak" again. Ever since she left Italy, Aurelia had spoken hardly at all for there were very few people with whom she could converse! Even on board the steamer with fellow Italians, Aurelia had difficulty speaking with them because of their different "dialects." Aurelia spoke "Lombardia," a northern Italian dialect very different from the "Italian" spoken by a "Siciliano," "Napolitano," or "Calabrese." There was no "official" Italian language yet; the Italian government was still trying to create one when Aurelia left Italy. She spoke not a word of English but did speak surprisingly a little German, which she had been taught in school. The region of Italy, Lombardia, where Aurelia was from had once been part of the Austro-Hungarian empire and while under Habsburg rule, all Italians were forced to learn German. Along the way to California, Aurelia met some "tdeschi"—the Italian word for Germans—and had brief but pleasant conversations with them. She was amazed by how quickly they were able to switch from German to English and English to German. She someday wanted to be able to do that as well.

After spending the day in San Francisco with her siblings and other Italians (many of whom were also from Lombardia and other areas of northern Italy, with whom she very much enjoyed the company of, especially their cooking!) in the North Beach area of that city, the Rossottis boarded a train for Eureka, arriving there late the next day. No sooner was "Rosie" in her "new home," a flat that Lena and Pep rented near the town's hospital, than Aurelia got a job at the hospital as a "cleaning woman" for about 80 cents a day. It obviously was very little money for such hard work, but it helped Lena and Pep pay the rent. Aurelia stayed with her brother and sister for two years, all the while working in the hospital. One day a local "lumberjack" came in with a badly cut hand. His name was Amadeo Acquistapace, was also from Piantedo, and whom Aurelia knew by name only. The Acquistapaces were legendary in the area for their passionate support of socialism. They were outspoken critics of the constitutional monarchy that ruled Italy at the time and vociferously urged its overthrow by revolutionary means, if necessary. Such public advocacy got young Amadeo into trouble with the law, and thus to escape possible imprisonment, he fled to the United States in 1900. By the time Aurelia met him, he was known as "Andy" and spoke "perfect English," at least according to Aurelia. He was twenty-six when they met; Aurelia was sixteen. They married in 1906 and went to San Francisco for their honeymoon, which turned into the most frightful event of their lives. The young couple experienced one of the worst natural disasters in United States history: the 1906 San Francisco earthquake. The quake itself did not destroy the city; it was the ensuing fires that did the most damage to life and property. The newlyweds escaped the calamity, returning to Eureka as

soon as they could get out of the city. Andy and Rosie remained in Eureka until 1931. In those years, they worked hard, saved their money, and in 1920, they bought the Eureka Hotel from the Pierce family. They prospered as hotel owners. During the 1920s Californians discovered the "north Coast" of the state—coming there to vacation. Also, beginning in that decade, Italians began buying land in the area to start vineyards, and today, as a result of Italian entrepreneurship, many California wines are recognized as some of the best in the world.

Andy and Rosie had six children—four girls and two boys. In 1931, as a result of the Great Depression, Andy and Rosie were forced to sell their hotel. The tourists weren't coming anymore—they had no money to spend on vacations and other amenities—and so for many small business owners like Andy and Rosie, dependent on tourism for survival, the depression meant the end of their dream. They swept up their children and moved to Auburn, California, a small town of about 2,000 people, nestled in the foothills of the Sierra Nevada Mountains. Andy and Rosie moved there because it reminded them of Piantedo. They briefly thought about going back to Italy but quickly dismissed that idea for Andy was still a hardcore socialist. The fascist Mussolini had been in power since 1922, and since that time, had declared "open season" on all opposition, especially targeting socialists and communists for his reign of terror. Moreover, they were Americans now; proud of their citizenship, which they both attained in 1914. Rosie was proud of her English, though spoken with a noticeable accent. Rosie got a job in the post office, "the lady who gave you your stamps," while Andy opened a hardware store. They made it even through the darkest days of the Great Depression. All six of their children became "one hundred percent American"—that is, they refused to speak Italian, especially in public, refused to eat or cook Italian food, went to public schools, and some even married non-Italians!! However, I am proud of my "one hundred percent Italian heritage," for I am one of Andy's and Rosie's ten grandchildren. My mother is Anna Acquistapace, who married an "Italian boy," John Anthony Moretta, from Brooklyn, New York in 1946. John and Anna named one of their five sons, John Anthony Moretta, Jr., co-author of **American Dreams and Reality.**

In the decades following the Civil War, the United States underwent one of the most rapid and profound economic transformations of any nation in world history. Perhaps only Japan's equally rapid rise at the same time, from a feudal, agrarian society to a modern, industrial one, rivaled that of the United States in historical importance. Slavery and sectionalism, the two dominant forces of antebellum America, gave way to industry and the various social and political issues that were associated with it. Although industrial development began in the Northeast before the Civil War, it speeded to a fever pitch from 1865-1890. By the end of the nineteenth century the United States led the world in manufacturing, far surpassing Great Britain, the undisputed leader in production throughout most of the nineteenth century. In the years between 1865 and the 1890s, the country was transformed from an overwhelming agrarian and rural society to a nation of factories and cities. Industrial progress, however, caused unprecedented socioeconomic and political upheaval, as cycles of boom and bust dominated the economic landscape. Panics, sharp economic downturns usu-

ally precipitated by stock market crashes and accompanied by bank failures and unemployment, occurred more often than not and caused two major depressions, one following the Panic of 1873 and a deeper depression after the Panic of 1893. Industrialization was an exclusively Northeastern phenomenon, while the South and the West remained predominantly rural and agricultural. Outside of the Northeast, only the cities/states bordering the Great Lakes, such as Chicago, Illinois, or Cleveland, Ohio, experienced industrial expansion. In those places busy ports witnessed an influx of cheap labor and a correspondingly impressive outflow of American industrial, finished, or processed goods.

Post-Civil War industrialization created a new class in the United States, men whose wealth and concomitant political power were derived from the new industrial order. These "plutocrats" as they came to be called, represented only a handful of individuals, but their dominance of the economy and politics of the Gilded Age was so complete that they have had few rivals since. Their names are legendary still: Andrew Carnegie, Jay Gould, John D. Rockefeller,

Immigrants from Antwerp, Belgium, sit on the deck while bound for Ellis Island. The wave of immigration had a major impact on the way America developed. New customs, manners, languages, food, religious practices, and cultures flooded the country.

and J. P. Morgan, to name but a few, were larger-than-life figures who controlled not only the economy and politics but the popular imagination as the heroes and villains in the high drama of industrialization.

Bound closer by a network of railroads and telegraphs, with the fate of small towns linked as never before to the fortunes of big cities, the United States was finally becoming the vision of Alexander Hamilton and Henry Clay: an integrated, national, self-sufficient economy, a nation united in fact as well as in name. Perhaps ideologically as important as the realization of the Hamiltonian vision or of Henry Clay's American system was the fact that industrialization meant the end of Jeffersonian agrarianism as the nation's ethos. By the 1890s, the businessman had replaced the yeoman farmer as the new symbol of America; upon his shoulders now rested the future of the democratic republican experiment begun one hundred years earlier. Not until the 1930s, with the Great Depression and the New Deal, would Americans reject the values of big business. During that decade they would find a new value system based on justice, compassion, and cooperation—values totally antithetical to the principles of the amoral market place of laissez faire capitalism, of which the plutocrats of the Gilded Age were the progenitors.

OLD INDUSTRIES TRANSFORMED, NEW INDUSTRIES BORN

In the aftermath of the Civil War the magnitude of American industrial development was unprecedented and dramatic. Old industries evolved into the nation's first corporations or "big businesses," while discovery and invention stimulated a whole host of new industries, such as oil and electricity. However, without question the most important and dominant postwar industry was the railroad, without which virtually none of the others would have existed. The rise of the railroad played the key role in the transformation of the American economy, helping to create a more consolidated, unified economy and network that enabled a variety of businesses to become truly national in scope and scale.

THE RAILROADS: THE UNITED STATES' FIRST BIG BUSINESS

From the end of the Civil War to 1900, the United States embarked on one of the most ambitious infrastructure undertakings in world history: the building of one of the largest railroad networks. In the process, the railroad builders also created the nation's first big business. The Republic's first transcontinental rail system was completed in 1869 when the Union Pacific and Central Pacific lines met at Promontory Point, Utah and drove the famous golden spike into the ground commemorating the occasion. Over the course of the next thirty years, the amount of track laid quadrupled, totaling over 193,000 miles by 1900. That total was greater than all of the track laid in all of Europe and Russia combined. The impressive amount of track belied the fact that most of the nation's system was haphazard at best with poor organization and very few integrated networks. Most of the early lines, except for the first transcontinental, did not connect with one another and trains ran on tracks of varying gauges. During the 1870s, more than one thousand roads appeared, often built for financial speculation rather than for viable transportation. Speculation in railroad stock became notorious and an easy way to make fortunes (or lose them as the case was more often than not) by "watering stock"—that is stock issued in excess of the actual assets of the railroads. Unfortunately, this practice carried over into the twenty-first century—witness the rise and fall of the Enron Corporation in Houston, Texas, which resurrected this practice first "developed" by railroad speculators. As with Enron, as long as investors remained optimistic about the future, a boom mentality prevailed. Buyers could be found for the overvalued stock, and a handful of individuals turned huge profits.

Perhaps the most interesting and personal way to gain an understanding of the rise of the railroad industry is to look at the career of Jay Gould, one of the nation's most legendary plutocrats and railroad developers par excellence. Gould bought his first rail line before he was twenty-five. It was only sixty-two miles long, in bad repair, and on the brink of failure. Within two years, however, Gould refurbished it and sold it at a profit of $130,000. Thus began the ascendancy of the individual who would pioneer the development of the nation's railway system and become the era's most notorious and ruthless speculator.

Gould admitted he knew little about railroads and cared less about their operation. Nevertheless he came "to write the book" on the concept of corporate expansion, the architect of the vast railroad system that developed in the 1870s. In short, Gould bought and sold, or controlled, railroads only as a means to make money: immediate profit. He had no intention of owning any lines forever, or of even controlling the network for an indefinite period of time. He was simply a stock market "player" who looked for vulnerable lines to buy, purchasing enough of its stock to give him controlling interest and then threatened to undercut his competitors until they bought him out at a high profit. The railroads that fell into his hands fared badly and often went bankrupt. Gould's genius and wealth was the result of his shrewd buying and selling of railroad stock, not in providing transportation.

The ease with which Gould was able to manipulate railroad stock and control lines illustrates the haphazard nature of the early rail industry. Partly responsible for this was the federal government, which was so anxious to develop the West in the post-war years that it gave vast amounts of the public domain to the railroad builders for free. The railroads not only received land for rights-of-way but were granted liberal sections on alternating sides of the track (sometimes up to twenty square miles on both sides of the track!) to do with as they pleased, most often to sell to settlers who followed the lines west. Between 1870 and 1900, the federal government granted the lines a total of 180 million acres, an area larger than the state of Texas. But the lion's share of the capital for the roads came from private investors, a good portion of whom were foreigners, mostly Englishmen.

Lack of planning led to over-expansion of lines. Already by the 1870s, the railroads competed fiercely for business on the eastern seaboard. A manufacturer who needed to ship goods to market and who was fortunate enough to be in an area inundated by competing lines could get a greatly reduced shipping rate in return for promising to use that particular road

exclusively. This type of cutthroat competition between the lines caused many to lose money and go under. Those that survived realized that such competition was ruinous to all and thus set up agreements or "pools" to divide up territory more equitably and set uniform rates. But these informal combinations invariable failed because they were never legally formalized and because "corsairs" like Gould were determined to destroy all competitors by undercutting whatever rates they offered their customers.

In the 1880s, Gould attempted to put together from existing lines, and from the construction of new ones, a second transcontinental system to compete with the Union and Central Pacific. His decision meant that other railroads had no choice but to defend their interests by adopting his strategy of expansion and consolidation. Beginning in that decade and stretching into the next, the other railroad titans went to war with Gould, resulting ultimately in his defeat, but in the process, by the 1890s, the lines west of the Mississippi had been consolidated into three major roads that controlled all rail travel—the Southern Pacific, the Northern Pacific, and the Atchison, Topeka, and Santa Fe.

One of the most important by-products of the emerging railroad industry was the introduction of new, more efficient business practices such as new cost accounting methods and new business structures that enabled the railroads to run at a profit and give new meaning to the term "big business." In the antebellum period, even the largest Northern textile mill employed only 800 workers, most often working in one town or even one factory. By 1874, the Pennsylvania Railroad, the largest line in the East, and for awhile in the country, employed more than 55,000 workers and managers and controlled more than 6,000 miles of track spanning half of the nation. Capitalized at over $400 million, the Pennsylvania could boast that it was the largest private enterprise in the world. The Pennsylvania could rightly be called one of the nation's first corporations, and its organization, size, and profitability pointed the way toward the future for all other businesses wanting to become as powerful and profitable. Consolidation became the key to such status, and thus the transformation began from small partnerships to huge "incorporated" entities.

An equally important revolution in communications coincided with the growth of the railroads. In the 1840s Samuel F. B. Morse developed a code to send messages across electrical wire. Morse's intricate series of dots and dashes, tapped out on a single key, allowed telegraphers to send messages virtually instantaneously over the wires, thus giving the country its first national communication system. The telegraph marched across the continent with the railroads, on rights-of-way furnished by the lines themselves. The telegraph system became the nerve center for the railroads, providing the companies with the instantaneous communication they needed to control their far-flung rail empires. Here again, Gould played a crucial role. In 1878, through his mastery of stock manipulation, the robber baron gained control of Western Union, the company that monopolized the telegraph industry. With control of Western Union, Gould could thus dictate to the other roads the price they had to pay for such services. Needless to say, Gould's acquisition of Western Union only made him that much more powerful and that much more hated by his competitors, such as they were.

Not all of the early railroad magnates were as ruthless as Gould. James J. Hill, owner of the Great Northern (Minneapolis, Minnesota to Seattle, Washington), built his line well and without the benefit of federal largesse. Hill had to plan carefully and calculate which areas would best be served by the line to maximize returns to his investors. As a result, the Great Northern was one of the few major roads able to remain solvent and running during the 1890s, when depression hit the country in 1893. In contrast, speculators like Daniel Drew and Jim Fisk, Gould's partners at the Erie Railroad, could more accurately be described as wreckers than as builders. They ruined the Erie, one of the East's most important early lines, by gambling with its stock to line their own pockets. In the West, the Big Four railroad moguls—Collis P. Huntington, Richard Crocker, Leland Stanford, and Mark Hopkins—became so powerful that critics claimed the Southern Pacific held California in the grip of an "octopus."

The public's increasing alarm at the railroad tycoons' control of the economy provided a barometer of attitudes toward big business itself. When Jay Gould died in 1892, the press described him as "the world's richest man," estimating his fortune at over $100 million. His competitor for that title, the "Commodore," Cornelius Vanderbilt, who built the New York Central Railroad, judged Gould "the smartest man in America." But to the public who found in Gould a symbol of all that most troubled them about the rise of big business, he was, as he himself admitted shortly before his death, "the most hated man in America." Why? Many, no doubt, remembered Gould's attempt to corner the gold market in 1869. Anti-Semitism also was a factor since many mistakenly believed Gould to be Jewish. Finally, many Americans had long hated men who earned great wealth by "shuffling paper" and speculation with other people's money rather than by their own physical exertions or producing goods. Since Gould did neither, his image was further tarnished. However, by the time of his death, more than 150,000 miles of track stretched across the country, and no one could claim to have had a greater hand in its building than Jay Gould.

The Panic of 1873

The nefarious, speculative activities of railroad barons such as Gould, Fisk, Drew, and others helped to precipitate one of the worst and most prolonged economic contractions in United States history: the Panic of 1873. As noted above, the exhilarating yet frenzied railroad expansion of the immediate postwar years came to a wrenching halt in the fall of 1873. In September, Jay Cooke and Company, the cornerstone of the nation's banking system, went under after being unable to market millions of dollars of bonds of the Northern Pacific Railroad, a line that was to provide the country's second transcontinental system. The failure of Cooke's company precipitated a national financial panic as hundreds of banks and brokerage houses failed as well. So intertwined was the stock market with railroad speculation that it temporarily suspended operation while investors attempted to recoup losses and rally the market back to health. Factories throughout the land laid off thousands of workers as a result of the railroad industry's collapse. Of the nation's 364 railroads, 89 went into bankruptcy by the end of the panic's first year. Eighteen thousand related businesses failed in two years. Unemployment rose to 14 percent by 1876, as hard times settled across the land like a pall. The downturn lasted for over ten years; not until the mid-1880s did the economy recover and stabilize, and then, as will be seen, "good times" lasted for only a few years as yet another depression hit the nation in 1893.

ANDREW CARNEGIE AND THE RISE OF THE STEEL INDUSTRY

Railroad construction stimulated the development of a second major industry—steel. The first railroads ran on iron rails, which cracked and broke with alarming regularity. Steel, stronger and more flexible than iron, remained too expensive for use in rail until an Englishman named Henry Bessemer developed a way to make steel from pig iron, which the United States had vast quantities of near the Great Lakes. With such an abundance of iron ore, the Bessemer process found its most enthusiastic employers among American steel manufacturers. Andrew Carnegie was one of the first steel producers to use the Bessemer process and the first champion of the new "King Steel." Within a decade, Carnegie monopolized the steel industry.

Unlike Jay Gould, who by the time of his death was despised, almost from the beginning of his rise to industrial preeminence, Andrew Carnegie became an American icon. The hatred toward Gould and the affection for Carnegie testified to the country's divided reaction to industrialism. Carnegie, a barely literate Scots immigrant, came to personify the American dream (or myth!) of rags-to-riches. He rose from a job in a textile factory cleaning bobbins at age twelve for a $1.20 a week to become one of the richest men in America. Before he died, he gave away more than $300 million of his fortune, most notably to public libraries. His alleged generosity or philanthropy, combined with his own rise from poverty, went far to promote a popular image with the

Andrew Carnegie

public. In reality, Carnegie was a shrewd, often ruthless, manipulative businessman, in many respects no different than Gould. He simply atoned for his callousness and greed in his twilight years by becoming a philanthropist.

Carnegie's swift rise to plutocrat coincided with the propagation of the popular myth promoted by the writer Horatio Alger, whose novels, such as *Ragged Dick, Mark the Matchboy, and Pluck and Luck*, filled Americans' heads with the notion that if one just worked hard, led a clean, sober life, like Carnegie allegedly did, they too could become millionaires. To a certain degree, such was possible in the immediate aftermath of the Civil War, which allowed a few men, such as Carnegie, to take advantage of such a wide-open economic system in a state of constant flux and change. In many ways, Carnegie did embody an Algeresque quality: pluck and luck to be in the right place at the right time. After he left the textile factory, while still a teenager, he got a job as a telegraph operator for the Pennsylvania Railroad. Under the auspices of Tom Scott, the line's superintendent, Carnegie rose through the ranks, all the while maintaining Scott's friendship. It was Scott who loaned Carnegie the money for his first investments in the stock market that netted him enough money to plunge into the steel business. Carnegie's twelve years with the railroad also provided him with a great education in business management that he put to good use when he struck out on his own to reshape the iron and steel industries.

In 1872 Carnegie began his rise in the steel industry. By applying the lessons of cost accounting and efficiency he had learned at the Pennsylvania Railroad, Carnegie turned steel into the nation's first manufacturing big business. In the town of Braddock, on the outskirts of Pittsburgh, Pa., he built the most modern Bessemer steel plant in the world and began turning out steel at an unprecedented rate. By the 1890s, Carnegie's blast furnaces poured out an incredible ten thousand tons of steel a week. Using railroad accounting methods, he cut the cost of making rails in half, from $58 to $25 a ton. Carnegie's formula for success was simple: "Cut the prices, scoop the market, run the mills full; watch the costs and profits will take care of themselves." Indeed, by 1900, Carnegie Steel earned more than $40 million in a single year. But at what human costs? "Cut the prices" meant, like for Gould, you simply destroy all competitors by having lower prices than anyone else. Lower prices meant lowering the costs of production, which meant cutting potentially the most expensive production cost—labor. Carnegie's workers were grossly overworked and underpaid—exploited callously by a man who had become a hero known for his supposed humanity and compassion, for he himself had "once been there." Workers toiled at least twelve hours a day in most of his plants, and when the shift changed every other week, they worked twenty-four hours at a stretch in the hazardous steel mills. Carnegie held an absolute majority of stock in his company and rarely paid dividends to his shareholders. Instead, he poured the profits back into new plants and new machinery—not into higher wages, safer working conditions, nor shorter hours

for his workers. Obviously, the richer Carnegie became the more he forgot "where he came from."

Carnegie's steel monopoly was the result of a system of business organization or incorporation called vertical integration. Vertical integration simply means that all facets of a given manufacturing enterprise, from the procuring of essential raw materials to the finished product, including transportation, are under the control of one business or ownership. In Carnegie's case, as one contemporary observer noted, "from the moment these crude stuffs were dug out of the earth until they flowed in a stream of liquid steel in the ladles, there was never a price, profit, or royalty paid to any outsider." Between 1875 and 1900, Carnegie sought to control every aspect of the steel making process, from the mining of iron ore on the Great Lakes to its transport to his mills, to the production of crude steel and rails.

Carnegie dominated the steel industry for three decades, building Carnegie Steel into an industrial giant, the largest steel producer in the world. Carnegie's steel built the nation's first skyscraper, formed the skeleton of the Washington Monument, supported the elevated trains in Chicago and New York, and provided the superstructure for the Brooklyn Bridge. By 1900, Andrew Carnegie was world famous, and steel had replaced iron as the most important heavy construction material.

JOHN D. ROCKEFELLER, STANDARD OIL AND THE TRUST

Edwin Drake's oil discovery in Pennsylvania in 1859 sent thousands rushing to that state's oil fields searching for "black gold." In the days before electricity, the automobile, and gasoline, crude oil was refined for lubrication oil for machinery and kerosene for lamps to light homes and streets. Observing the difference between the price of crude oil gushing from wells at fifty cents a barrel (forty-two gallons) and the kerosene sold in the East at fifty cents a gallon, smart entrepreneurs turned to oil refining as the key to making a potential fortune from this particular resource. The amount of capital required to buy or build an oil refinery in the 1860s and 1870s was rela-

John D. Rockefeller

He borrowed constantly to build up his profits, making other people's money work for him. A taciturn young man with an all-consuming passion for business, Rockefeller, like his cohorts, Gould and Carnegie, hired a substitute to fight for him during the Civil War, so he could remain on the homefront, profiting from the war while others fought and died to keep him safe and making money. Like many other shirkers, Rockefeller became wealthy during the war years. In 1865, he bought out his partner with borrowed money and took over the largest oil refinery in Cleveland. Like a growing number of his fellow plutocrats, Rockefeller realized that a partnership was no way to maximize profit and minimize personal liability; a corporation was. Thus, in 1870, he incorporated his oil business, founding the Standard Oil Company, the precursor of today's Exxon Corporation.

As the largest refiner in Cleveland, Rockefeller demanded rebates or "kickbacks" from the railroads, which they gave. Indeed, his volume of shipping was so great that the railroads not only gave him the rebates on his fares but also slipped him "under the table" a portion of the fares paid by his competitors. Such wheeling and dealing allowed Rockefeller to undercut his competitors. He not only could ship his oil at a dollar a barrel cheaper but he also received a dollar a barrel "rake-off" on every barrel his competitors shipped. Using this kind of leverage, Rockefeller soon pressured competing refiners to sell out to him or face ruin. By 1871 Standard Oil had "cornered" the petroleum business in Cleveland, and now John D. set his sights on the national market.

The cities of Cleveland, Pittsburgh, Philadelphia, and New York City competed to become the center of the nation's petroleum business. By combining railroad rebates with efficient production, Standard Oil strengthened its position. Major refiners began to sell out. In a series of secret mergers, or combinations, they received stock in Rockefeller's company and continued to run their refineries as before under their own names. Stubborn independents who refused to capitulate to Rockefeller's often menacing demands to sell, either unwittingly sold to companies that were secretly controlled by Standard Oil or somehow mysteriously blew up!! Rockefeller was in-

tively low, about $25,000, the cost of laying one mile of railroad track. Since investment cost was low, the story of the new petroleum industry was one of riotous, cutthroat competition among the plethora of small refineries. Inspired by both Gould's and Carnegie's ruthlessness and single-mindedness, one man, John D. Rockefeller, came to dominate oil refining through the use of yet another new business organizational strategy called the trust. By the 1890s, Rockefeller controlled nine-tenths of the oil refining business through his Standard Oil Company.

John D. Rockefeller grew up the son of a shrewd Yankee doctor who peddled quack cures for cancer. Under his father's tutelage, he learned early some of the more invidious skills that would help him establish his oil empire. "I cheat my boys every time I get a chance," Bill Rockefeller boasted. "I want to make 'em sharp." John D. started out rather humbly, a bookkeeper in Cleveland, but owned his own business by the time he was twenty-one. One of the secrets of his success lay in his ability to obtain loans.

famous for doing whatever it took to eliminate his competition; in that sense he may have been more shameless and ruthless than either Gould or Carnegie. Not until 1879, when a New York legislative committee investigated railroad practices did the American people learn the extent of Standard Oil's hidden empire.

Rockefeller's clandestine activities were necessary because such combinations were illegal. Laws forbade one corporation from controlling another. Rockefeller, however, circumvented the laws by shrewdly developing yet another new organizational structure that came to be called a trust. Such an entity was a form of horizontal integration, which differed from Carnegie's vertical approach in steel. In a trust, several "trustees" hold stock in the various companies doing the same business in "trust" for the parent company's stockholders. In the case of Standard Oil, trustees held stock in the various refineries "in trust" for Standard's stockholders. Initially, Rockefeller did not attempt to control every facet of the oil business from crude oil at the well to the final product. Rather, he opted to move horizontally to control only the refining process by taking over all the refineries he could. He used the trust to increase profits by controlling output, thus raising prices consumers had to pay. Because Standard Oil monopolized the market and controlled the output of an essential commodity, "heating oil," and in effect "lighting" for homes, schools, hospitals, businesses, and street lights, the public soon cried out against the company, accusing it of conspiring against the public for private profit. When the federal government threatened to outlaw the trust as a violation of free trade, Rockefeller simply changed his tactics and organized Standard Oil into a holding company, which operated in much the same way as a trust but was legal. Instead of competing companies agreeing to set prices and determine territories, such as the railroads did for awhile, the holding company simply combined competing companies under one central administration. The state of New Jersey helped to promote this new form of consolidation and monopoly by passing laws that allowed state-chartered corporations to hold stock in out-of-state enterprises. Suffice it to say, very quickly conglomerates such as Standard Oil company and a host of other large combinations transferred their company "headquarters" to New Jersey, which by the end of the century was "home" to some of the nation's largest corporations.

As Rockefeller's empire grew, central control became essential. Interestingly, Rockefeller personally did not move to New Jersey but to neighboring New York City, where from his office at 26 Broadway, he began to vertically integrate á la Carnegie steel, Standard Oil. In reality, Standard Oil became unique: it was both horizontally and vertically integrated, allowing it to ultimately control the entire petroleum industry from crude oil sources in the ground (which at this time were exclusively located east of the Mississippi in the states of Pennsylvania, Ohio, and parts of West Virginia) to home and business delivery of the final product.

Rockefeller enjoyed unprecedented business success. Before he died in 1937 at the age of ninety-eight, he had become the nation's first billionaire. For most of his adult life, he was undeniably the richest man in the Republic. Despite his modest habits, his pious Baptist habits, and his many philanthropic acts, the American people never embraced him the way they had Carnegie. The individual most responsible for Rockefeller's negative public image was journalist/muckraker Ida M. Tarbell, whose classic magazine expose, *History of the Standard Oil Company*, published in *McClure's Magazine* beginning in 1902, revealed to the American people that Rockefeller was perhaps the most ruthless and callous of all the plutocrats. Tarbell's devastatingly thorough history showed an individual so determined in his business pursuit that he willingly and unashamedly used whatever tactics—threats, assassination, sabotage—that would bring the desired result: complete control of the petroleum industry of the United States. By the time Tarbell finished her story, Rockefeller had become such a demon in the public's eye that he literally slept with a loaded revolver by his bed to defend himself against possible assassins.

Even though Andrew Carnegie was at times as cold and ruthless, it was Rockefeller who aroused the people's fear of industrial concentration. Americans vilified him because they feared the vast power of one company to so completely control the pro-

Alexander Graham Bell, inventor of the telephone, made the first successful call on March 10, 1876.

duction and supply of so vital a resource such as oil. At any time, Standard Oil could shut the nation down if its unscrupulous, greedy owner thought he could make more money by doing so! However, plutocrats such as Rockefeller, despite having their own personal fears for their safety, were secure for years to come from any laws being passed by the federal government that curtailed their power or ability to do as they pleased, regardless of the harm done to the public welfare.

Although Americans may have feared and despised the plutocrats such as Rockefeller, they warmly embraced the inventors, even though many of them were closely tied to the plutocracy. At the turn of the century, Alexander Graham Bell and Thomas Alva Edison had become folk heroes. However, regardless of how profound or revolutionary the invention, the inventor and his "creation" ultimately came under

the plutocrats' control. Such was the case for two of the most important innovations in technological history—the telephone and electricity—both of which were the brain child of American genius.

Alexander Graham Bell, like Carnegie, a Scots immigrant, developed a way to transmit voice over wires—the telephone. The emperor of Brazil, Dom Pedro II, who attended the 1876 Philadelphia Centennial Exposition was dumfounded by a telephone on display and cried out, "My God, it talks!" Bell's demonstration of his new device immediately caught the attention of Western Union, which wanted to buy Bell's patent but was distracted from doing so because it was involved in its own battle for survival against Jay Gould. Bell, seeing the possibility of losing control of his own invention, wisely formed his own company, American Bell, with himself as owner. But Bell was an inventor, not a business man, and thus wisely deferred such matters to his brilliant professional manager, Theodore N. Vail, who over the course of two decades built Bell America and its subsidiary, American Telephone and Telegraph (AT&T) into one of the nation's largest communications corporations. In 1900, AT&T became the parent company of the entire "Bell system." Taking a page from Rockefeller's book, Vail organized first Bell America and then AT&T both vertically and horizontally, which meant that AT&T had a complete monopoly of the new telephone industry and would remain in control of it until the late twentieth century. Via Western Electric, which AT&T also owned, the company manufactured and installed its own equipment as well as controlling long-distance telephone service. In practical terms, AT&T meant that Americans could communicate not only locally in their towns and cities but across the country. Unlike a telegraph message, which had to be written out and taken to a telegraph office, sent over the wire, and then delivered by hand to the recipient, the telephone connected both parties immediately and privately. Bell's invention proved a boon to business, contributing greatly to speed and efficiency.

However, since AT&T monopolized this new communication industry, it, like any of the other big businesses discussed so far, dictated supply, service, and prices. If one wanted "phone service," then it

Edison not only invented the light bulb but designed power plants and generators to make the entire system work. Before the electric light bulb, homes were lit by candles, kerosene lanterns, and gaslights.

would be provided but at AT&T's convenience and price. Many rural folk, for example, would not have a telephone in their homes for decades after it became a household item for most urban dwellers. Why? It simply was not "profitable" for AT&T to supply service to people living in the country. It would cost the company too much money to build lines for such limited use. However, if one lived in the country and wanted to be "connected," then rates would be exorbitant compared to those paid by city folk. Thus, ironically, the telephone, which could have brought Americans closer together (which it did for urban residents), only served to further separate country folk from city folk, creating over time a serious socioeconomic and cultural chasm that grew ever wider in the twentieth century.

In the eyes of Americans, Thomas Edison came to personify the virtues of rugged individualism and Yankee ingenuity, working twenty hours a day in his laboratory in Menlo Park, New Jersey, vowing to turn out "a minor invention every ten days and a big thing every six months or so." Edison almost fulfilled his pledge. At the height of his career, he averaged a patent every eleven days and invented such "big things" as the phonograph, the motion picture camera, and the electric light bulb. No industry that developed in the post-Civil War period faced more

obstacles than electric light and power. Edison's invention of a filament for the electric light bulb in 1879 ushered in the age of electricity. But perplexing Edison was the way to sell this most important product. Before he could begin marketing electric light and power, he had to develop an integrated system of conductors, power stations, generators, lamps, and electrical machines. Because electricity was so technically complex and so potentially dangerous, it

Edison's incandescent light bulb.

demanded an entirely new system of marketing, one that relied on skilled engineers. Initially, the new industry depended on private generators. Financier J.P. Morgan had electricity installed in his New York City mansion on Madison Avenue in 1882, making it the first private home in the country with electric lighting. An engineer visited the house daily to start the generator. When the lamp in Morgan's library short-circuited and set fire to his desk, the engineer promptly fixed the problem and restored Morgan's faith in electricity, so much so that he invested heavily in the Edison General Electric Company.

Edison worked diligently to build power stations and provide electric current. But his system had one serious drawback: it relied on direct current, which meant that he could only supply electricity for up to two miles from a power station. George Westinghouse, a contemporary of Edison's and inventor of the air brake for trains, solved the problem by "inventing" alternating current, which could travel much greater distances. Westinghouse saw great—profitable—potential in supplying people with this new product and created his own company to compete with Edison General Electric. Both companies created large, complex, vertically integrated enterprises to meet their unique marketing and distribution needs. They staffed sales offices with technicians trained to advise consumers, safely install and operate equipment, and provide repair services. Despite Edison's protests, Westinghouse's superior alternating current became the accepted standard for electric power.

By 1900 electricity had become, like the telephone, part of American urban life. It powered trolley cars, subways, and factory machinery. It lighted homes, apartments, factories, and office buildings. Indeed, electricity became so exclusively associated with urban life that it became one of the most visibly symbolic manifestations of the increasing gap between city and country. As will be seen in a later chapter, as late as the 1930s, only 10 percent of rural America enjoyed or had access to this most important product. As was the case with the telephone, those who controlled the electrical power business, like Westinghouse and others, hoped to personally profit and thus only provided to markets where

money could be made—the cities. Poor farmers and other rural folk could not afford the rates charged because to provide such a desultory population with electricity would have "cost" too much for the electric companies to profit. Thus, rural Americans would have to wait until the New Deal to have what had become a necessity of life for urban Americans some forty years earlier.

While Americans thrilled to the new electric cities, the day of the inventor quietly yielded to the heyday of the corporation. In 1892, J.P. Morgan consolidated the electric industry, selling Edison General Electric, of which he had become its major investor and shareholder, out from under its inventor and dropping Edison's name from the corporate title. The new General Electric Company, which was four times the size of its closest competitor, Westinghouse, soon dominated the market.

The Emergence of Mass Marketing

By the 1880s, thanks largely to the railroads, a national mass market emerged for producers of consumer goods. Indeed, the United States was one of the first industrial nations to produce simultaneously capital and consumer goods, the latter often in greater quantities than the former. Manufacturers of consumer goods integrated methods of mass production with those of mass distribution via the railroads to establish some of the first major consumer-oriented enterprises in America. Some of the first and most important of the new consumer industries to emerge were in the meatpacking and food processing industries, where innovative ownership allowed producers to reap huge profits from hot dogs and ketchup.

What Carnegie did for steel, Gustavus Swift did for meatpacking. Until well after the Civil War, cattle were transported out of the West (mainly Texas until the 1880s) on the hoof (actual live steers) to be slaughtered by local butchers. To feed an expanding Northern and Eastern population, Texas cowboys would drive large herds to the closest railheads, and then from there the live steers would be shipped to the meatpacking plants where they would be slaughtered. The problem was that much of the cattle had

Cattle are forced up the chute into a railroad boxcar. Scenes like this were common before the 1870s.

already lost weight from long drives out of south Texas and thus would not be of very good quality once they reached the packing house and were slaughtered. Swift believed it would be more efficient and produce a better quality of beef if the cattle were slaughtered in the Midwest, such as in cities like Kansas City, Missouri, and then transported North or East in refrigerated railcars while still fresh. To accomplish this, Swift created a vertically integrated meatpacking business headquartered in Chicago that controlled the entire process—from the purchase of cattle for slaughter to the mass distribution of initially fresh then processed meat to retailers and consumers. Swift was the first to use the refrigerated railcars, and through high quality, low prices, and effective advertising, he won over consumers who worried about buying meat not butchered locally. Swift's success led the older meatpackers, such as Philip Armour, to build similarly integrated businesses to compete with Swift. Armour, for example, was able to initially "corner the market" on processed meat in the form of bologna and hot dogs. By the 1890s, the city of Chicago had become, thanks to Swift and

Armour, the center of the nation's meatpacking industry. From the Windy City, all manner of fresh and processed meat found its way into homes all across the nation. Though the quality of processed and even fresh meat was often questionable, the innovative ideas of Swift and Armour provided American consumers with a quantity and variety of food that was envied by the rest of the world.

Just as Swift combined mass production with mass distribution to revolutionize meatpacking, Henry John Heinz transformed the processed food industry. In 1880 Heinz was a local producer of pickles, sauces, and condiments. Operating on the outskirts of Pittsburgh, Heinz was still recovering from the Panic of 1873, which caused him to go bankrupt, when he adopted new, more efficient methods of canning and bottling and built a network of sales offices to advertise his fifty-seven varieties of condiments and sell them across the nation. To ensure the necessary and continuous flow of vegetables and other foodstuffs into his factories, he created a large buying and storing organization to contract with local farmers. By 1888 Heinz had become one of

Pittsburgh's wealthiest citizens, and ketchup had become a household staple. Using similar methods, the owners of other processed food companies, such as Quaker Oats, Campbell Soup, and Borden Condensed Milk, coordinated mass production with mass distribution to produce inexpensive, canned, and easily prepared foods for a national market. Companies producing other commodities such as tobacco, grain, matches, and soap integrated manufacturing and distribution to dominate their respective markets. American Tobacco, Procter & Gamble, Quaker Oats, and Pillsbury Flour all started during the Gilded Age, becoming giants in that time and are still flourishing today.

To boost and sustain sales in a nationally expanding market of consumers, businesses realized the importance of promoting their goods by advertising. Just as the railroads made possible a national market, newspapers made possible advertising on a national scale. Gilded Age advertising bore little resemblance to the slick, sophisticated industry of today. Nineteenth-century advertising agents neither wrote the copy nor selected the illustrative materials. All of that was done by the advertiser, "the client" or business wishing to display its products, primarily in newspapers and later in magazines. What the agent did do was buy and sell space in the newspapers and magazines. With more than 8,000 papers printed in the United States by 1876, few business owners could afford the time away from their companies to learn the names and locations of the papers, let alone check the circulation figures and bargain for advertising space. That became the agent's job, taking the client's prepared copy and placing it in specified papers. The ad agent earned his livelihood by being paid a commission, not by the advertiser but the newspaper publishers.

Gilded Age advertising was tainted by its frequent association with all manner of questionable products, ranging from quack medicine cure-alls to rotten canned or processed meats. Products like Lydia Pinkham's Vegetable Compound, a "sure cure for female complaints," pioneered early advertising and made Lydia Pinkham a household name. Reputable firms eschewed advertising because of its dubious, unethical practices. Organizations like the American Medical Association, which emerged in the late Gilded Age to try to purge the medical profession of quacks and phony medicines, prohibited its members from plying their trade in print. By the turn of the century, however, advertising and attitudes toward it began to change. As companies pursued a larger share of the national market, they turned to advertising to boost sales by extolling the virtues of their products. Ivory Soap—"99.44% pure—so pure it floats;" Quaker Oats—"the easy food;" and Coca Cola—"The ideal brain tonic"—cashed in on the growing trend toward national advertising. As companies competed for the national market, advertising became more professionalized, as ad agents began increasingly to not just place ads but actually write them as well. By the end of the century full-service advertising agencies started appearing in the larger urban areas such as New York City, soon to become the home to the burgeoning advertising industry. In short, advertising became an integral part of the product package.

FROM COMPETITION TO CONSOLIDATION: THE RISE OF THE CORPORATION

Even as plutocrats like Rockefeller and Carnegie built their empires, their days of independent ownership and autonomy were numbered. Once privately-owned and operated companies were selling out to impersonal, anonymous entities called corporations, which by the beginning of twentieth century were becoming the dominant form of business organization. Soon corporations, managed by faceless boards of directors—supposedly educated, professional business "experts"—replaced the great business titans of the previous decades. Already by the end of the nineteenth century, the corporation had begun to eclipse the partnership and sole proprietorship as the major business enterprise. Corporations had the advantage of limited liability, which protected investors from losing their own assets should the company go under. A corporation could "outlive" its owners and was not susceptible to the vagaries that frequently destroyed family businesses, as one generation could ruin a company painstakingly created by its predecessors. Corporations also separated ownership and management, placing the company's daily operations in the hands of professional managers. Since the corporation could raise money by issuing stocks and bonds, the owners in most instances were individual investors, a consortium of the majority stockholders, who were more than glad to leave management to elected or chosen boards of directors and the daily operations to trained experts. Also, because the law—the Fourteenth Amendment—recognized the corporation as a "person" and granted it protection under that legislation's due process clause, it was difficult to regulate or redress corporate abuse through legislation. Finally, corporations could buy out and control other corporate entities, and it was this power that came to dominate in the early twentieth century as businesses consolidated into ever larger corporate giants.

The merger trend that resulted in the formation of Standard Oil and General Electric intensified in the years between 1890 and 1903. When trusts came under scrutiny, businesses consolidated into holding companies, as Standard Oil had done, to avoid prosecution. As many companies went under as a result of the depression of the 1890s, many went into bankruptcy courts where they were restructured, reorganized, and consolidated by court-appointed receivers. Banks and financiers played a key role in this consolidation, so much so that the era of the individual entrepreneur gave way to the dominance of the financial capitalist. No one better defined this role than J.P. Morgan, the great New York banker, who single-handedly reshaped American business at the turn of the century, consolidating several major industries, including the railroads and steel, into large corporate entities. During these years, a new social philosophy, based on Darwinian theory, helped to justify consolidation and to prevent state or federal intervention to regulate or control the excesses or corporate capitalism. The Supreme Court, a bastion of conservatism during this time, further promoted consolidation by "strictly" interpreting the Constitution and thus declaring unconstitutional legislation designed to regulate railroad rates and to outlaw trusts and monopolies.

J.P. MORGAN AND FINANCE CAPITALISM

The new consolidationists loathed competition and whenever possible pursued a policy of incorporation and central control. No one was a more zealous promoter of consolidation than J. Pierpont Morgan, whose life seemed circumscribed by three things: the pursuit of order, predictability, and profit. Morgan was one of the most dominant Wall Street financiers and "players" of all time. A large man (over six feet tall, which was several inches more than Carnegie or Gould, both of whom were under five feet five, the average height for an adult male) with a prominent acne-scarred nose and a cold, aloof demeanor, with eyes that seemed to pierce right through you, Morgan disdained the climbers and speculators with a haughtiness that led his enemies to call him "Jupiter" after the Roman god. The son of a successful banker, J.P. Morgan inherited along with his wealth the stern business code of the old-fashioned merchant bankers, men who valued character and reputation. From his own age, Morgan embraced the new business ethos and believed that investment banking could play a decisive role in reorganizing business and transforming the stock market.

Morgan acted as a power broker in the reorganization of the railroads and in the creation of corporations like General Electric and United States Steel. When depression engulfed the nation in the early 1890s, once again the railroad industry was hit hard. Morgan, with his passion for order and his access to capital, decided it was time to restructure the entire industry, consolidating as many of the lines as possible to prevent the industry's future collapse when hard times hit. He had already restructured the Baltimore and Ohio, the Reading, and the Chesapeake and Ohio Railroads in the 1880s. After the panic of 1893, he added the Santa Fe, the Erie, and the Northern Pacific and Southern Railroads to his list. In 1901, Morgan's railroad empire reached its zenith when he created the Northern Securities Company, a supersystem designed to bring peace between the feuding Great Northern and Northern Pacific Railroads. Other investment bankers did the same as Morgan for other lines but none did it on the scale of J.P. Morgan.

Morgan's purpose for creating the Northern Securities Company was to establish a "community of interest" among the new entities managers, men he handpicked. Often, Morgan partners sat on the boards of competing firms, forming interlocking directorates. By the time Morgan was finished reorganizing the railroad industry, seven major groups, all under his auspices, controlled two-thirds of the nation's rail lines.

Banker-control of the railroads rationalized or coordinated the industry. But such cooperation and harmony among the lines belied the fact that Morgan heavily watered the stock of the railroads, issuing new stock lavishly to keep old investors happy and to guarantee large profits. Morgan's firm made millions from commissions and from blocks of stock acquired in the reorganization process. The blatant overcapitalization caused by the watered stock negatively affected the railroads, saddling them with enormous debts. Equally detrimental was the management style of the Morgan directors, who were not railroad men but essentially "cost analysts" whose background was banking and accounting, and thus their conservative policies discouraged the continued technological and organizational innovation necessary to run the line effectively.

In 1898 Morgan believed it was time to consolidate the steel industry. The story of his acquisition of Carnegie Steel is not only legendary but symbolic of the passing of an old era and the coming of a new one. The heyday of the individual entrepreneur was ending by the late nineteenth century, and in its wake came the rise of the corporation. Carnegie represented the old order—Morgan the new. As he began to challenge Carnegie's empire, Morgan wisely first merged all the smaller steel companies, thus eliminating the last remnant of competition in the steel industry. In the merger process, Morgan also vertically integrated his new cartel by having his companies move from the manufacture of finished steel products into actual steel production. Carnegie, who for decades had monopolized crude steel production, countered this obvious move by creating a new plant for the manufacturing of finished steel products such as tubing, nails, wire, and hoops.

The press covered the impending war between the feisty Scot and the arrogant Wall Street broker as if it were a major sporting event, but the battle of the titans proved in the end to be little more than the wily maneuvering of two shrewd businessmen so adept that even today it is hard to discern who won. The sixty-six-year-old Carnegie, for all his obstinacy, longed to retire to his castle in Scotland and may well have invited Morgan's bid for power. Surely Carnegie knew that Morgan was probably the only individual who had enough money to buy him out. When an intermediary sought Carnegie out on the golf course and asked him to name his price, Carnegie scrawled a number on his score card, and the go-between scurried back to Morgan's office and handed him the card. Morgan, who disdained haggling, accepted the price; he agreed to pay $480 million for Carnegie Steel. Carnegie's personal "take" was more than $250 million. According to legend, when Carnegie later teased Morgan that he should have asked for a $100 million more, Morgan had the last laugh, telling the Scotsman, "You would have got it if you had."

Morgan quickly merged Carnegie Steel with his other steel companies, forming one of the largest conglomerates in United States history and in the world at the time: United States Steel, known today as USX. Created in March 1901, U.S. Steel became the country's first billion dollar corporation. Yet despite its monolithic size and despite Morgan's attempt to gain a monopoly on steel production, he could not. There remained enough smaller, independent producers, such as Bethlehem Steel, to create a competitive system know as oligopoly, in which several large combinations, not one alone, controlled production. Other industries, such as meatpacking and electricity, were also oligopolies. Businesses in this new arrangement did not compete with each other by cutting prices; rather they simply followed the lead of giants like U.S. Steel in setting prices and dividing the market so that each business held a comfortable, profitable share. Although oligopoly did not eliminate competition all together, it definitely limited the competitors to a handful of companies.

When J.P. Morgan died in 1913, he estate was worth $68 million, not counting an additional $50 million in art treasures. Andrew Carnegie, who gave away more than $300 million before he died six years later, is said to have quipped, "And to think he was not a rich man!" But Carnegie's remark missed the point. Morgan was driven by the pursuit of personal power and order, which he believed consolidation of businesses into corporations would achieve. Morgan's imprint on the Gilded Age, and even down to today, was far greater than that of either Carnegie or Rockefeller. When the country faced bankruptcy in 1895, it was Morgan to whom the president turned. And as the reorganizer of American's railroads and the creator of U.S. Steel, General Electric, and other large combinations, Morgan ushered in the era of oligopoly that has continued to be an integral feature of the nation's business scene to the present.

SOCIAL DARWINISM AND THE GOSPEL OF WEALTH

As the plutocrats made their fortunes, many worried how they would be publicly perceived. Would the people embrace them as the epitome of rugged individualism, the realization of the American dream that hard work and a clean, sober life brings material success and rewards? Or, would they be viewed as ruthless, self-serving scoundrels who made their money by callously exploiting others? Even those who cared less about their public image, nonetheless, believed it essential to find justification or rationalization for how and why they "made it" while the majority of people suffered in miserable poverty, despair, and hopelessness. As already noted, the plutocrats often engaged in cutthroat competition from which fewer and fewer winners emerged. The road to wealth and power taken by these "robber barons" was strewn with ruined competitors and brutally exploited labor. Such ruthlessness not only seemed to become increasingly necessary for personal aggrandizement, it was also transformed into a "virtue" by the twin ideologies of Social Darwinism and the "gospel of wealth."

For men like Andrew Carnegie, the writings of Social Darwinists Herbert Spencer and William Graham Sumner helped expiate feelings of personal guilt. "I remember that light came as in a flood and all was

clear," Carnegie remarked after reading Spencer's work. Spencer and his disciples believed that the same natural forces or laws that determined evolution and survival in the animal world were applicable to the human condition as well. As in the animal world, Darwin's concept of natural selection meant that in human society, the "fittest" individuals survived and flourished in the marketplace while those less "endowed" were destined or predetermined to be swept away by obviously superior individuals. Survival of the fittest supposedly enriched not only the winners but also society as a whole. Human evolution would produce what Spencer called "the ultimate and inevitable development of the ideal man" through a culling process of eliminating supposedly weaker, inferior human beings.

According to the Social Darwinists, poverty and slums were as inevitable as the concentration of wealth. Spencer argued that "there should not be a forcible burdening of the superior for the support of the inferior." His protégé, Sumner, asserted "If we do not like the survival of the fittest, we have only one possible alternative, and that is the survival of the unfittest." Both men believed that government or charitable intervention to improve the conditions of the poor interfered with the functioning of supposed "natural law" and prolonged the life of "defective gene pools" to the detriment of society as a whole. In short, Social Darwinists propagated a perverted Darwinism designed to bolster or justify not just the plutocrats' ruthless rise to power and wealth but to denigrate and keep oppressed as well the masses, whom they regarded as the "unfit." The Social Darwinist theory was imbued with overt racism and ethnocentrism, for the "fit" or superior individuals were clearly Anglo-Saxon or white Northern Europeans (excluding the "degenerate" Irish, of course!), while the unfit or inferior were the rest of humanity who were not of that "stock" and were thus to be either subordinate at all times to the superior race or ultimately "extinguished." As will be seen shortly, Social Darwinism became very popular among the nation's WASP (White, Anglo-Saxon Protestants) elite, especially from the 1890s on because of the massive influx of Southern and Eastern European immigrants whom they regarded as the "unfit."

Suffice it to say, plutocrats like Carnegie and Rockefeller enthusiastically embraced this theory. Rockefeller told his Baptist Sunday school class, "The growth of large business is merely the survival of the fittest. This is not an evil tendency in Business. It is merely the working out of nature and a law of God." Some who found the callousness of Social Darwinism unpalatable sought religious justification instead. Since colonial times, the Protestant work ethic had informed the American creed, denouncing idleness and viewing material success as evidence of being among the "elect"—God's chosen people for whom salvation was a certainty. Expanding on this assumption, the more religiously affected plutocrats constructed the "gospel of wealth."

In this context, some were simple and direct in their certainty, like Rockefeller, that their rise to industrial preeminence and wealth was ordained by God: "God gave my riches," Rockefeller sanctimoniously declared as a "reward" for having led a most clean, sober, diligent and righteous life. Carnegie produced a written, logically argued rationale for his success: "Not evil but good, has come to the race," he wrote, "from the accumulation of wealth by those who have the ability and energy that produces it." To justify his exploitation of labor, Carnegie was certain that the masses would waste any extra income "on the indulgence of appetite." "Wealth, passing through the hands of the few," Carnegie wrote, "can be a much more potent force for the elevation of our race than if it had been distributed in small sums to the people themselves," whom the steel magnate was convinced would only spend it on the pleasures derived from vice and dissipation. In short, Carnegie believed that individuals like himself who have clearly demonstrated their "fitness," or superiority, should decide what other people needed. In Carnegie's case, he took that responsibility seriously, distributing over $300 million to such philanthropic causes as the founding of libraries and the Carnegie Foundation.

Among the most effective apologists for the wealthy were religious leaders such as the Episcopal Bishop William Lawrence, who proclaimed that "Godliness is in league with riches." Not only did the elite deserve their wealth, but the poor were responsible for their low status because of their obvi-ous personal flaws and defectiveness. God was punishing them for their alleged "sins" of depravity and laziness. The eminent preacher Henry Ward Beecher reaffirmed this belief when he announced that "no man suffers from poverty unless it be more than his fault—unless it be his sin."

Thus, according to supposed scientific and religious thought, the maldistribution of wealth was not only inevitable but desirable, for it ultimately would "cleanse" society of all the "unfit" and leave only those "worthy" of continued existence. Probably more important was the support and propagation of such perversion by popular culture. *McGuffey Readers* stressed the virtue of hard work and its inevitable rewards. Popular literature reinforced the idea that success always came to those who deserved it in America, the land of opportunity.

INTERNAL MIGRATION AND EUROPEAN IMMIGRATION

The appeal of Social Darwinism among WASP America intensified during the last decade of the nineteenth century and into the early twentieth century because of unprecedented European immigration. Never before or since had so many human beings come to the United States seeking a new and better life. Indeed, between 1880 and 1920, some 23 million people arrived in the United States, mainly from Europe but from Canada, Mexico and Latin America, and Japan as well. Europe, however, provided over 80 percent of the total, and in that context, after 1880 and until 1914, the majority of immigrants came from southern and eastern Europe. Among them were 4 million Italians, 2 million Russian and Polish Jews, 2 million Hungarians, 4 million Slavs, and 1 million from Lithuania, Greece, and Portugal. Hundreds of thousands came as well from Turkey, Armenia, Lebanon, Syria, and other Near Eastern lands abutting the European continent. It was this particular phase of immigration that resurrected the nativism, prejudice, and discrimination WASP America had previously displayed in the antebellum period toward the Irish and Germans. The same fears WASP America had about the Irish and

This is a scene in one of New York's immigrant ghettos. People were forced to live in small apartments with little or no sanitation facilities.

Germans they now simply transferred to the Italians, Hungarians, eastern European Jews, Turks, Armenians, Poles, Russians, and other Slavic peoples. Not only did WASP America fear the Catholicism and supposed ethnic/racial inferiority of the new arrivals (the same "anxieties" they felt about the Irish in the 1840s), but compounding those trepidations was the fact that many of the new people weren't even Christian—they were Jewish or Muslim, two faiths the majority of white Americans had no understanding or knowledge of in any capacity and had always viewed with suspicion, contempt, and hostility. Up to this time, except for the momentary "fear" the influx of Irish and Germans created in the 1840s, WASP America's supremacy was unchallenged. Now, that was about to potentially change with the massive "invasion" of Europe's unwanted and "unfittest." Indeed, as the popular journal *Public Opinion* edito-

rialized, "they are the very scum and offal of Europe." Though a very high percentage of these immigrant groups were indeed illiterate peasants from some of the most impoverished areas of southern and eastern Europe who were "coming to America" to escape such despair, they were nonetheless all castigated for being uneducated, backward, and outlandish in appearance. Terence Powderly, head of the labor organization the Knights of Labor, complained—with a degree of accuracy because they were discriminated against and segregated into the city's most wretched areas—that the newcomers "herded together like animals and lived like beasts."

Old-stock WASP elites like Henry Cabot Lodge of Massachusetts, formed an unlikely alliance with organized labor (which was also at this time WASP-dominated and feared that the influx of unskilled labor, which the immigrants represented, would adversely affect their jobs and status) to press for immigration restriction. A precedent for keeping out "undesirables" had been established in 1882, when labor agitation and racism in California led to passage of the Chinese Exclusion Act, which stopped the legal immigration of Chinese nationals. On the east coast Lodge and his nativist followers championed a literacy test, a device designed to limit immigration from Italy and eastern Europe by requiring immigrants to demonstrate the ability to read and write in their own language. As mentioned above, since the vast majority of Italian and Slavic peasants had little to no formal education, it was assumed few would be able to pass the test. In 1896, Congress approved a literacy test for immigrants, but President Grover Cleveland promptly vetoed it. "It is said," the president reminded Congress, "that the quality of recent immigration is undesirable. The time is quite within recent memory when the same thing was said of immigrants, who, with their descendants, are now numbered among our best citizens." Cleveland's veto forestalled immigration restriction but did not stop the forces seeking to build such a "moat" around the United States. Hard-core nativist like Lodge would continue to press for restriction until they achieved their goal in the 1920s.

Why They Came

The new wave of immigration that brought southern and eastern Europeans to the United States beginning in the 1880s resulted from a number of factors. Improved economic conditions in northwestern Europe, as well as immigration to Australia, Canada, and Argentina, curtailed the flow of "old" immigrants to the United States. Prior to the 1880s, the overwhelming majority of new arrivals—the "old" immigrants— came from Germany, Ireland, Great Britain, Scandinavia, the Low Countries, and France. At the same time, a protracted economic depression in southern Italy, the religious persecution of Jews in eastern Europe, especially in Russia, with the infamous "pogroms," and a general desire to avoid conscription into the Russian army (which affected both Slavs and Poles) led many in southern and eastern Europe to come to the United States.

Economic factors in the United States also played a role, the most important of which was American industries' insatiable demand for cheap, unskilled labor, especially during good times. So important was immigrant labor in the rise of American industrial preeminence that without it the United States would not have become the leading industrial power in the world, at least not as rapidly. Had the millions of Europeans remained in their respective homelands or migrated instead to Germany, England, or France, then it was possible that one of those nations, not the United States, would have been the greatest industrial power by 1900. Nor would the plutocrats' profits and wealth been as great or as legendary had it not been for such cheap labor costs. Although the U.S. government did not offer direct inducements to immigrate (despite some pressure to do so by big business), the steamship companies solicited immigrants who provided a highly profitable self-loading cargo. Agents from large lines traveled throughout Europe drumming up business. Colorful pamphlets and posters mingled fact with fantasy to promote America as the land of promise and opportunity.

Though socioeconomic factors played a key role in European migration, in the final analysis, the decision whether to leave the Old Country and come to the United States, remained an individual or family choice. Immigrants were neither the "huddled masses" nor the bold adventurers determined at any cost to enter the "golden door." Nevertheless, immigration fever affected whole villages, as the entire population of a rural hamlet in southern Italy or in the Balkans would collectively decide to come to America or at least pool resources and send its most able-bodied. Would-be immigrants eager for information about America relied on letters, advertisements, and word of mouth—sources not always reliable or truthful. Promotional pamphlets all too frequently exaggerated the United States' economic opportunities, especially those that advertised "free land" or other such wild notions. Such falsehoods helped to create an image in the peasant/immigrant mind of an America whose "streets were paved with gold." Glowing letters from immigrants to friends and relatives back home boasted of how wonderful and better life was in America. In most cases, it was all fabrication, for those who left certainly did not want to appear failures when so many were counting on them to succeed and either be able to bring more over or return with the promised riches. As one Italian immigrant recalled, "Everything emanating from America reached [Italy] as a distortion. News was colored, success magnified, comforts and advantages exaggerated beyond all proportions." No wonder immigrants left for America believing "that if they were ever fortunate enough to reach America, they would fall into a pile of manure and get up brushing the diamonds out of their hair."

In at least one respect, life in the New World differed markedly from that in the old. In their home countries the majority of immigrants were farmer/peasants living in often very isolated rural villages. In America they became reluctant urbanites and industrial/manufacturing workers. Once they arrived and reality set in—there was no free land for them to have, even in the West—they were forced to stay and work in the urban, industrial centers where their wages were so low that their dream of ever moving out of such an environment and owning land was an illusion. The concentration of immigrants in the nation's industrial cities became symbiotic with urbanization. By 1900, almost two-thirds of the country's immigrants resided in cities. Although nowhere yet did the foreign-born population outnumber old-stock Anglo-Saxon inhabitants, the immigrants and their American-born children did makeup a majority in many of the nation's cities. By 1900, 50 percent of Philadelphia's population was foreign-born or the progeny of such parents, and the percentages were even higher in other cities: 66 percent in Boston, 75 percent in Chicago, and an amazing 80 percent in New York City.

Not all newcomers came to stay. Over the time period 1880-1910, perhaps eight million, mostly young men, came to the U.S., worked for a year or a season, trying to earn as much money as they could, and then went home. American immigration officers referred to such individuals as "birds of passage" because they followed a regular pattern of migration to and from the United States. By 1900, almost 75 percent of the new immigrants were single young men. Intent on making money as quickly as pos-

Pushcart peddlers on Hester Street on New York's Lower East Side. Hester Street was the place to live for newly arrived Jewish immigrants.

sible, they were willing to accept jobs and conditions others, especially native white workers, would not. They showed little interest in labor unions, which initially did not welcome them anyway because of the early union's often virulent nativism. Only later, when they realized that they were not going to return home, that America was now their permanent home, did they join unions.

Jews from eastern Europe most often came as family units and came to stay. In the 1880s, a wave of violent persecutions, or pogroms, in the Russian empire led to the departure of more than a million Jews in the next two decades. They settled mostly in the port cities of the East coast. New York City's Lower East Side replicated the Jewish ghettoes of eastern Europe, teeming with street peddlers and push carts. Hester Street, at the heart of New York's Jewish section, rang with the calls of vendors hawking their wares from pickles to feather beds. Jews were not the only immigrants to have their own "neighborhoods" in American cities. Soon after their arrival, virtually all the immigrant groups were segregated into their

Working in the underground mine shafts was extremely dangerous. Poor working conditions also caused illnesses, such as black lung disease. Explosions and cave-ins were a constant danger.

own enclaves by a WASP America fearful of their possible "mixing" or integration. Thus, springing up in New York City or Boston were the "Little Italys," or "Little Polands," and a whole host of other such communities in the inner city of the nation's major urban centers. In such enclaves the immigrants would remain (some forever) for several generations. As will be seen in subsequent chapters, as their numbers swelled and their affect on the city landscape became more pronounced, WASP America realized that no matter how deplorable their existence, the "new" Americans were here to stay. Once old-stock Americans accepted this reality, they then stopped running and wisely realized that if the immigrants intended to make the United States their permanent home, then the best policy to pursue was the newcomers' acculturation and assimilation. As will be seen, such a new attitude proved successful in transforming the once "unwanted" into "acceptable" citizens.

Immigrant Labor

How important were the immigrants to the industrial work force? In the first decade of the twentieth century, immigrant men and their sons constituted 70 percent of the workforce in 15 of the 19 leading U.S. industries. Their concentration was highest in industries where the work was most exploitive and dangerous: railroad construction and tunnels; in the coal, iron ore, and other mineral mines; in the steel mills, and in the putrid, disease-infested meatpacking houses. Within this context, certain ethnic groups predominated. For example, after 1900, Slovaks and Poles overwhelmingly worked the coal mines and steel mills of western Pennsylvania, Buffalo, and Cleveland, while Poles, Lithuanians, and Italians were the rank and file in the meatpacking and food processing industries. Italians also exceeded all other groups in the heavy construction business, such as the building of New York City's subway system. In

Women and children earned additional income in the home by doing "piece work." Employers paid for each finished item.

the "lighter" but no less arduous work of garment manufacturing, Jews and Italians predominated. Most egregious, however, was the preponderance of immigrant children in the garment industry "sweat shops." Here, hunched over sewing machines, twelve to fourteen hours a day, with tiny, nimble fingers often getting torn to shreds by the rapidly-moving needles, could be found young immigrant women and boys and girls as young as ten-years old, earning pennies per piece of clothing. Not only did these sweat shops callously exploit immigrant youth, they also were physically some of the most deplorable, hazardous, and sometimes fatal workplaces.

Immigrant labor workweeks averaged 60 hours—10 hours per day except Sunday. Workers who were granted Saturday afternoons off—thus reducing their workweek to 55 hours—considered themselves fortunate. Steel workers were not so lucky. They labored from 72 to 89 hours a week and were required to work one 24-hour shift every two weeks. Immigrants were forced to work long hours just to

barely make ends meet. In 1900 the annual earnings of American industrial workers averaged between $400 and $500 a year, although there were substantial variations from region to region and level of skill. Southern workers only earned on average $300 annually, while Northern counterparts earned $460. The better paying jobs by the late nineteenth century went to the "older immigrants"—Yankees, Germans, Irish, and Welsh. Through their unions, workers of Northern European extraction also controlled access to new jobs that opened up and usually managed to fill them with a son, a relative, or fellow countrymen. Consequently, relatively few of the new immigrants rose into the prosperous ranks of skilled labor. Ironically, though old immigrant skilled workers earned more than the recent arrivals, as the nineteenth century progressed, the old immigrants found themselves increasingly unemployed as the captains of industry replaced them with machines, easily operated by the unskilled new immigrants.

From the Farm to the City

Certainly not all of urban America's newcomers were foreign-born immigrants. Indeed, until the 1880s, the majority of a city's new inhabitants came from within the country, the result of an internal migration that brought hundreds of thousands of farm boys and girls looking for jobs in the burgeoning urban industrial centers and hoping to make their fortunes. The lure of the bright lights and the promise of wages, coupled with the theaters, the dance halls, the great amusement parks like Coney Island in New York City, and the cultural and educational advantages offered by the city, the likes of which they never dreamed existed, all served as a powerful magnet for many young folk.

For at least one group of Americans, the city promised something more. African Americans came north, not just looking for jobs, but to escape as well violence and oppression. Beginning in the 1880s, ex-Confederate states one by one put in place a series of laws called Jim Crow, that completely segregated black folk and white folk in the South. Further, by the 1890s, black voters were completely disfranchised in the South and with such laws, apartheid became complete. Worse, the 1890s marked the high point of a vicious racism against black folk, which saw the lynching of African Americans living in the south reach an all-time high. Southern white supremacy and segregation were further buttressed by the Supreme Court of the United States, which ruled in its 1896 landmark decision in *Plessy v. Ferguson,* that segregated facilities were legal under the doctrine of "separate but equal." With such an endorsement by the highest court in the land, white Southerners felt free to use whatever intimidation and violence necessary to "keep the Negro in his place." These indignities combined with the lack of economic choices to impel many southern blacks to leave their homes and seek a safer and materially better life in the North. "To die from the bite of frost is far more glorious than at the hands of a mob," proclaimed the *Defender,* Chicago's largest African-American newspaper. By the 1890s, many southern black folk agreed. Black migrants, nearly all of them from the rural South, headed to northern cities, either in the Mid-

west or the Northeast. There they found jobs, usually at the bottom of the occupational ladder, as janitors, cooks, common unskilled laborers, or domestic servants. Unfortunately, racism in the North was as commonplace as it was in the South, though often not as overt. In the North, Jim Crow's slick cousin, James Crow, was alive and well, covertly, insidiously, oppressing black folk, keeping them a segregated, subordinate class. Despite the existence of James Crow, the urban North continued to attract African Americans. By 1900, New York, Philadelphia, and Chicago contained the largest black communities in the nation. Although the greatest black exodus out of the South would occur during and after World War I, 185,000 African Americans had already moved north by 1890. The great migration was underway.

LAISSEZ FAIRE IN THEORY AND PRACTICE

Prevailing economic theory also bolstered greed, exploitation, and opposition to any government or private intervention to alter the "natural" laws of the free marketplace and the forces of unbridled capitalism. Since the nation's founding, Adam Smith's theory had informed the nation's economic system. Smith asserted that the market was directed and controlled by an "invisible hand" composed of a multitude of individual choices. If government did not meddle, competition would naturally lead to production of desired goods and services at reasonable prices—the natural laws of supply and demand. In short, Smith believed that since all humanity was motivated by self-interest, no individual or group of individuals would willingly succumb to greed or avarice, for to do so would only hurt their realization of personal—material— happiness. Thus, individuals must be left alone to act according to self-interest and in the process, the resulting economy would be best suited to meet society's demands.

Acceptance of Smith's theory led to a policy called laissez-faire. Government was to leave the economy alone and not disrupt the operation of these natural forces. Business leaders naturally endorsed the theory's rejection of governmental intervention and regulation, yet they saw no contradiction in asking government for aid and subsidies to further promote industrialization and modernization. To a large extent, Gilded Age capitalists got what they wanted: a laissez-faire policy that left them alone to pursue their objectives, free from all government interference, and government assistance whenever they asked to further expand and protect their enterprises, regardless of the harm their pursuit of "self-interest" had on people and the environment. Ironically, this distortion of Smith's theory helped produce an economy where business consolidation wreaked havoc on the very competition needed for natural regulation of the economy.

Unfettered industrial capitalism boggles the modern mind. Yet, as will be seen in a later chapter, such a possibility did not occur until the Progressive period, and really not until the 1930s and the New Deal. Until then, no laws protected the consumer from adulterated foods, spurious claims for ineffective or even dangerous patent medicines, the sale of stock in non-existent companies, any sort of regulation of the stock market, no laws abolishing child labor or establishing a forty-hour work week, or unsafe and overpriced transportation services. No national regulating agency of any kind existed before the establishment of the Interstate Commerce Commission in 1887. The proclamation, "Let the buyer beware," asked people to make decisions and choices without enough information to protect their interests.

While denying support and protection to consumers and workers, government at all levels willingly aided the plutocrats. Alexander Hamilton's vision of an industrializing nation promoted and protected by government participation had never entirely died. Indeed, it was resurrected by the Republican Party by 1860. In that year, the party pledged to enact higher tariffs to protect domestic northern industry, to subsidize the completion of a transcontinental railroad, and to establish a stable national banking system—all Hamiltonian ideas first introduced in the 1790s. As will be seen shortly, the Republican victory in that year and for the next several decades undoubtedly boded well for the emerging business and industrial elite, as the party evolved into the strongest supporter and promoter of big business and their interests.

Big business not only found a strong ally in the Republican Party but in the U.S. Supreme Court as well. During the 1880s and 1890s, the Court increasingly reinterpreted the Constitution to protect business from taxation, regulation, labor organization, and antitrust legislation. In a series of landmark decisions, the Court used the Fourteenth Amendment, originally intended to protect freed slaves from state laws violating their rights, to protect corporations. The Fourteenth Amendment declares that no state can "deprive any person of life, liberty, or property, without due process of law." By defining corporations as "persons" under the law, the Court determined that legislation designed to regulate corporations deprived them of "due process." Using this rationale, the Court struck down state laws regulating railroad rates, declared income tax unconstitutional, and judged labor unions as a "conspiracy in restraint of trade." As the plutocrats and their enterprises destroyed the environment, exploited labor, and generally ran roughshod over anyone or anything they felt not worth their time or energy, the Court insisted on elevating the "rights of property"—the capitalist interests—over the rights of people. According to Justice Stephen J. Field, the Constitution "allows no impediments to the acquisition of property." Field, born to a wealthy family and educated at the best schools of his day, spoke with the bias of the privileged class to whom property rights were sacrosanct. Imbued with this ideology, the Court refused to restrain corporate consolidation and did nothing to curb the excesses of industrial capitalism.

Labor Strife

With such attitudes shared by the government and plutocrats toward the working class, it was inevitable that sooner than later, the nation's working classes would rise up in protest against the plutocracy's exploitation and oppression. Perhaps the violent confrontations between labor and the industrial capitalists could have been avoided had the government been more concerned with the workers' plight. Since it was not, workers, finding no redress of their grievances through either the established political or legal system, decided to take matters into their own hands and through their own efforts, try to win the rights and respect they were entitled to as citizens.

Several factors drove workers toward protest and organizing and joining unions. Workplace safety, for example was one such cause. The drive for greater speed and productivity on railroads and in factories gave the United States the unfortunate distinction of having the world's highest rate of industrial accidents. Another factor was the erosion of worker autonomy in factories, as increasingly machinery replaced skilled workers and managers made operational decisions about pace and procedure rather than the workers. In short, as the Gilded Age progressed, once proud, skilled craftsmen became commodities to be bought for wages rather than a mastery whereby the worker sold the product of his labor rather than the labor itself. For skilled artisans this was an alarming trend. Their efforts to preserve or recapture independence from "bosses" and robber barons fired much of the era's labor unrest, which often escalated into violent, bloody confrontations between workers and owners.

The Great Railroad Strike of 1877

Because railroads were the nation's first, most important, industrial corporations it would only be natural that they would become the focal points of early labor strife. Citing declining revenues during the depression of the 1870s, several railroads cut wages by as much as 35 percent between 1874 and 1877. When the Baltimore and Ohio Railroad announced its third 10 percent cut on July 16, 1877, workers struck and prevented the line's trains from running. The strike spread rapidly to other roads and within weeks all rail traffic from St. Louis to the East coast was brought to a standstill. Ten states called out their militias to try to force strikers back to work but workers would not succumb to such intimidation and fought back, not only firing on the troops but setting fire to rolling stock and roundhouses as well. By the time federal troops restored order in the first week of August, at least one hundred railroad workers, militia, and bystanders had been killed and

hundreds more injured, as well as millions of dollars of railroad property razed. It was the worst episode of labor violence in U.S. history to that time; the specter of class conflict frightened many upper and middle class Americans who believed that the nation was headed for social revolution.

As a result of the Great Railroad Strike, many workers hoped that through better organization they could win a redress of grievances without having to resort to striking, which they just witnessed would be brutally suppressed by the plutocrats and the government. Thus emerged the Knights of Labor, initially a secret fraternal society founded in 1869 in Philadelphia. However, in 1879, under the leadership of Terence Powderly, a skilled machinist by trade, the Knights "came out" and declared themselves a federation of unions, or "assemblies," as they were officially known. Powderly organized the Knights' assemblies by industry rather than by craft, giving many unskilled and semiskilled workers union representation for the first time. Some assemblies admitted women and black workers as well but despite this inclusiveness, tendencies toward exclusivity of craft, gender, and race divided and weakened many assemblies.

Terence Powderly was president of the Knights of Labor for more than ten years. Powderly detested strikes.

Women delegates at a national meeting of the Knights of Labor. Women belonged to separate associations affiliated with local all-male unions.

A paradox of purpose also handicapped the Knights. The goal of most the union's members was to improve their situation within the system through higher wages, shorter hours, better working conditions, and job security—the nuts and bolts objectives of working class Americans from this time forward. This meant collective bargaining with employers; it also meant striking if such concessions were not granted. The assemblies won some strikes and lost some. Powderly and Knights' leadership, however, discouraged the calls for strikes for they believed that in the end, strikes only weakened assemblies because workers, more often than not, lost to management who replaced the striking workers with strikebreakers or scabs, if not breaking the strike all together with the use of force. Powderly also opposed strikes for ideological reasons. Powderly was a "closet" socialist, who believed that strikes constituted a tacit recognition of the legitimacy of the wage system, which siphoned off to capital a part of the wealth created by labor. Like a good but visionary socialist, Powderly believed capitalism would ultimately give way to worker's cooperatives, which would own the means of production. But if workers continued to strike and alienate especially the middle class, which he believed would become sympathetic to the workers' plight and support them, then there was no hope for workers to someday through cooperatives to own and operate mines, factories, and railroads to the benefit of all Americans. Despite Powderly's pleas for workers to avoid strikes, the Knights gained their greatest triumphs by striking. In 1884 and 1885 successful Knight-led strikes against the Union Pacific and Missouri Pacific railroads won enormous prestige and a rush of new members, which by 1886 totaled 700,000. But defeat in a second strike against the lines in 1886 was a serious blow. Then came the Haymarket bombing in Chicago.

The Haymarket meeting in Chicago in 1886 breaks into violence.

Haymarket Square

Since the late 1870s, Chicago had become the center of labor radicalism, home to not only the Socialist Labor Party but to anarchism as well. The majority of anarchists were foreign-born, mostly Germans, and by 1886 they had gained significant influence within the Windy City's Socialist Party. The anarchists called for the violent destruction of the capitalist system so that a new socialist order could be built on its ashes. Anarchist had also infiltrated some of the city's unions, and from such bases of operation they led the call for a general strike on May 1, 1886, to achieve the eight-hour workday. Compounding an already nervous environment was the fact that Chicago police were notoriously hostile to labor organizers and strikers, so the scene was ripe for an inevitable violent confrontation between workers and police.

The object of the strike was the McCormick farm machinery plant in Chicago. A fight broke out between striking workers and "scabs," which resulted in a police attack on the strikers in which four people were killed. Anarchist used the incident to call for a massive protest rally at Haymarket Square on May 4.

Toward the end of the meeting, as the rain-soaked crowd dispersed, the police suddenly arrived in force. When someone threw a bomb into their midst, the police opened fire indiscriminately. When the melee was over, 50 people lay wounded and 10 dead, 6 of them policemen.

The alleged "riot" unleashed a wave of anti-labor hysteria throughout the city and even the nation. Chicago police rounded up hundreds of labor leaders, including eight German-born anarchists they believed responsible for the bombing incident. They were tried for conspiracy to commit murder, though not a shred of evidence ever surfaced to prove that any of them had thrown the bomb. Nonetheless, all eight were convicted, and seven were sentenced to be hanged, of which only four ended up swinging from the gallows. One committed suicide and two others' sentences were commuted to life imprisonment. The affair became a cause celebre that bitterly divided the country; some Americans believed it a blatant act of repression of civil rights and judicial murder; others, the majority of citizens, applauded the court's actions and hoped it would send a warning signal to labor radicals that their ideas and actions faced "zero tolerance."

In the aftermath of the Haymarket affair, the Knights of Labor soon dissolved. However, a new national labor organization emerged to take its place: the American Federation of Labor founded in 1886 by immigrant cigar-maker Samuel Gompers. Gompers organized the new union not by industry as Powderly had done but by trade or craft, which in effect made the new union for skilled workers only. Under Gompers' leadership the AFL shunned radical crusades, accepted capitalism and the wage system, and worked for better conditions, higher wages, shorter hours, and job security—"pure and simple unionism" as Gompers called his organization's agenda. The AFL's endorsing of the capitalist order, his condemning of militancy and radicalism, and its not too outlandish demands for workers' rights allowed the AFL to not only survive but to prosper in a difficult climate. In short, Gomper's call for "working within the system" did not alienate or arouse the hostility of the capitalist plutocrats. As a result, the union's membership grew from 140,000 in 1886 to nearly one million by 1900. Though Gompers was able to calm the fears of capitalists and the anxieties of Americans in general that labor was not going to plunge the nation into social revolution if its demands were not met, labor militancy did not die. Two bestselling books helped to keep it alive, especially the call for a more egalitarian social order. Although neither of the two works had the impact of an *Uncle Tom's Cabin,* they nevertheless affected the millions who read them.

Henry George

Progress and Poverty, written by the self-educated author, Henry George, in 1879, seemed an unlikely candidate for best-seller status. Prior to becoming a newspaper editor in California, George had spent fifteen years traveling and working in various occupations. In his travels across the nation, he was appalled by the contrast between wealth and poverty. He came to believe that "land monopoly" was the cause: the control of land and resources by the few at the expense of the majority of citizens. His solution was 100 percent taxation on the "unearned increment" in the value of land—that is, on the differ-

ence between the initial purchase price and the eventual market value (minus improvements), or what today we would call capital gains. Such gains were created by society, he insisted, and thus should be confiscated by taxation for the benefit of society. This would eliminate the need for all other taxes, George argued, and help narrow the gap between rich and poor by either giving all the unused land to the landless or using the money to provide work for all.

Though not an easy book to read, by 1905, *Progress and Poverty* had sold over 2 million copies and had been translated into several languages. A single-tax movement emerged to propagate George's ideas, but they mostly fell on deaf ears. The book's real impact came from George's descriptions of grinding, abject poverty and despair in the midst of plenty. George became a hero to labor. He joined the Knights, moved to New York City, and ran for mayor in 1886 and narrowly lost. His campaign dramatized labors' grievances and alerted the major parties to the power of that constituency. George's legacy lasted well into the next century. As will be seen in a later chapter, many Progressive reformers were first sensitized to social issues by their reading of *Progress and Poverty.*

Edward Bellamy

The other Gilded Age work that had mass appeal was Edward Bellamy's *Looking Backward.* A devout Christian reformer, Bellamy wrote a utopian romance that took place in the year 2000 and contrasted the America of that year with the America of his time, 1887. In 2000, all industry is controlled by the government; everyone works for equal pay; there are no rich and no poor, no strikes, and no class conflict. *Looking Backward* had obviously a socialist "leaning," even though Bellamy preferred to call his collectivist order "nationalism," not socialism. He definitely was not a Marxist socialist for he condemned the idea of class conflict as the only means to achieve the cooperative state. His vision of a world without social strife appealed to many middle class Americans, who bought 500,000 copies of his book every year for several years in the early 1890s. So inspired by Bellamy's work, that Nationalist clubs sprang up throughout the nation, advocating government or public ownership if not of all industries at least public utilities—"gas and water socialism."

An offshoot of Bellamy's Nationalist movement and inspired by his work was the Social Gospel movement that emerged in the 1890s in American cities, and significantly affected mainstream Protestantism and many Catholic leaders as well. Appalled by the poverty and overcrowding in the sprawling tenement districts of urban America, clergymen and laypeople associated with the movement embraced a new theology of social activism: helping to ameliorate the plight of the poor was just as important, or should be, to religious leaders as saving souls. They were willing to go into the bowels of the immigrant tenement slums and not only help "save" the inhabitants from engaging in "sinful" activities but help to deliver them as well from poverty. Social Gospelites pressed for legislation to curb the immigrant worker exploitation and provide them with opportunities for betterment.

The Homestead Steel Strike

By the 1890s, there was plenty of evidence to feed the fears of many middle class Americans that the nation was unraveling. Strikes occurred with a frequency and fierceness that made 1877 and 1886 look like mere preludes to Armageddon. The most dramatic confrontation took place in 1892 at the Homestead plant of the Carnegie Steel Company. Carnegie and his plant manager, Henry Clay Frick, were determined to break the power of the country's strongest union, the Amalgamated Association of Iron, Steel, and Tin Workers. Frick used a dispute over wages and work rules as his opening salvo in his war with the union. He staged a "lockout" to reopen the plant with nonunion workers. Union workers, however, called for a strike and refused to leave the plant. Frick then called in 300 Pinkerton guards to oust them. The Pinkerton detective agency had evolved since the Civil War era into a "big business" private security force that specialized in "union busting." A full-scale gun battle erupted between workers and Pinkertons on July 6, leaving nine workers and seven detectives dead and scores wounded. Frick persuaded

the Pennsylvania governor to send in 8,000 militia to protect the strikebreakers or "scabs, and the plant reopened. Public sympathy, much of it pro-union at first, shifted when an anarchist tried to murder Frick in his office. Frick was severely wounded but lived. The result, however, was the turning of the public against the union, which allowed the militia to brutally crush the union and the strike with popular support.

The Pullman Strike

Even more alarming than the Homestead strike, which remained local from start to finish, was the Pullman Strike of 1894, which had national repercussions. In 1880 George Pullman, manufacturer of elegant dining, parlor, and sleeping cars for the nation's railroads, had constructed a factory town, called Pullman, ten miles south of Chicago. The "planned" community provided solid brick homes for workers, beautiful parks and playgrounds, and even its own sewage-treatment plant. Pullman also closely watched his workers' activities, outlawing saloons, and insisting that his properties turn a profit. When the 1893 depression hit, Pullman slashed his workers' wages without reducing rents. In response, thousands of workers joined the newly formed American Railway Union, led by the fiery young organizer Eugene V. Debs. The union called for a strike, which Pullman's workers willingly joined. Union members working for the nation's largest railroads refused to switch Pullman cars, paralyzing rail traffic in and out of Chicago, one of the nation's most important rail hubs. In response, the General Manager's Association, an organization of top railroad executives, set out to break the union. The managers imported jobless "scabs" from the East coast and asked U.S. Attorney General Richard Olney, a former railroad attorney, for a federal injunction (court order) against the strikers for allegedly refusing to move railroad cars carrying U.S. mail. In truth, the strikers volunteered to switch mail cars onto any trains not pulling Pullman cars, and it was the railroad's managers who were delaying the mail by refusing to send their trains without the full complement of cars. Nevertheless, Olney, bolstered by Presi-

On July 3, 1894, President Cleveland ordered federal troops to Chicago to end the Pullman strike. By July 20, the federal troops had been withdrawn, and military guards were operating the trains. The union had been defeated.

dent Cleveland and citing the Sherman Antitrust Act, secured an injunction against the union's leaders for restraint of commerce. Despite the government's crackdown, union leaders refused to back down and return to work. But the government was determined to break the union. Debs was arrested and federal troops were sent to Pullman to crush the strike, which they eventually did but not after the loss of thirteen lives, fifty-three wounded and the burning of seven hundred freight cars. By exploiting and fabricating middle class fears that strikers and unions in general were hotbeds of labor radicalism, crafty corporate leaders persuaded state and federal officials to help them squash organized labor's desire to negotiate with business for basic worker rights. When the Supreme Court in the 1895 case, *In re Debs,* upheld Deb's prison sentence and legalized the use of injunctions against labor unions, the judicial system made its blatant support of big business clear and that in the future, the plutocrats could count on that body to help preserve the status quo and their hegemony over it. By the beginning of the new century, it was painfully clear that the United States and its middle class citizenry had no intention of embracing unions or even the idea that its industrial workers were entitled to basic rights. Working class America was viewed with suspicion and hostility, and even its slightest attempt at a redress of grievances was regarded as "radical." The Pullman strike made it clear that from this point on, federal and state officials would side with the plutocrats against its working class citizenry. Ineffective in the political arena, blocked by state officials, and frustrated by court decisions, American unions failed to expand their base of support. Post-Civil War labor turmoil had drained the vitality of organized labor and given it a negative public image that it would not shed until the 1930s, when a change in middle class values and attitudes would find common cause with that of the working classes.

GILDED AGE POLITICS

As can be easily discerned from reading this chapter so far, the most dominant and interesting, if not dramatic individuals of the era, were not politicians but the businessmen-entrepreneurs and financiers who so dominated the time period. Indeed, political leadership, especially at the national level, is marked by some of the most uninspiring, complacent, and outright lackluster men ever to sit in the Oval Office. While men like Carnegie, Rockefeller, and Morgan jump vividly from the pages of the past, the presidents lie pallid on those same pages. Though many Americans today complain about the lack of strong, vibrant, and purposeful presidential leadership, if they had lived in the Gilded Age with those same expectations and hopes, they would feel even more depressed and disassociated. The weakness of the presidency and the federal government in general in the years between Abraham Lincoln (1861-65) and Theodore Roosevelt (1901-1909) was one of the most pronounced and prolonged periods in the nation's history. Beginning with Reconstruction and the pathetic, tumultuous presidency of Andrew Johnson, presidential leadership seemed to plummet to an all-time low. Concomitantly, the lack of quality men in the White House allowed Congress to gain ascendancy, and it was that body the plutocrats manipulated and controlled to ensure that there would be no governmental interference in their affairs. During the Gilded Age, a good portion of both the House and Senate membership were on the plutocrat's "payroll." This waning of federal power, especially in the executive branch, became a persistent pattern in American government, interrupted only by the activism of the progressive movement under the leadership of Theodore Roosevelt, and later, during the Great Depression of the 1930s, when Franklin Roosevelt assumed the Oval Office.

The presidents from Rutherford B. Hayes (1877-1881) to Grover Cleveland (1885-1889, 1893-97), are indeed forgotten men. All too frequently when Americans are asked "who were these men?" rarely does anyone say, "Oh, wasn't he a president?" More often than not, the responses range from, "Oh, wasn't he a major league pitcher?" or "Didn't he invent something?" Or, most revealing, when someone is told he was a president of the United States, a look of complete surprise crosses his or her face and out comes "I didn't know that—I never heard of the guy!" Sad but understandable because so little was expected of these presidents and the federal government in general. Until the 1890s, when the excesses of industrial capitalism became apparent, few Americans believed that the president or the national government should have any role in addressing the problems accompanying the industrial transformation. The dominant creed of laissez-faire coupled with the tenets of Social Darwinism warned government to leave business alone; intervention to ameliorate even the most vile effects of industrialization would only retard the natural "evolutionary" progress allegedly taking place in the United States, led by those best "fit" to do so—the plutocrats. This belief in nongovernment intervention in the economy and society reduced the role of the federal government to something of a sideshow. The real energy and action took place elsewhere—in party politics on the local and state levels and in the centers of business and industry. Nevertheless, important changes transformed American political life in the decades following the Civil War, as industrialism replaced sectionalism as the driving force in national politics. The corruption and abuses associated with party politics produced civil service reform. By the 1880s, important economic issues such as the protective tariff, the currency, and federal regulation of the trusts and railroads moved to the forefront.

The Political Culture of the Gilded Age

Looking back on Gilded Age politics, there is some irony in the fact that voters of that time turned out in record numbers to elect those lackluster presidents. Voter turnout in the Gilded Age averaged a hefty 80 percent, compared with a turnout of only 51 percent in 2000. Why were voters in a supposed politically apathetic and complacent period so eager to cast their ballots?

The answer lies in the "political culture" of the late nineteenth century. Since the Jacksonian Period, political parties had used patronage or the "spoils system" to reward voters for their support. Many voters owed their livelihood to party bosses—the local party leader or "hack" responsible for sustaining the spoils system. Often these local politicos were involved in all manner of graft and corruption in order to maintain party loyalty and control of local politics. During the Gilded Age, "machine politics," particularly at the municipal level, became the order of the day. In essence, machine politics meant the control of every level of city government by either of the dominant parties, Republic or Democrat, depending upon the city involved. Under the guiding hand and sharp eye of the boss, political power was organized vertically within the machine in a hierarchical system of patrons and clients. The style of the Gilded Age boss was new and coarse, more personalized and direct than that of his eighteenth-century gentleman predecessor. The urban political machine's stock and trade was jobs and appointments, transit franchises, paving contracts, public construction bids, licenses, permits, and hundreds of other saleable items needed to conduct city business.

The impulse motivating the city boss was essentially conservative: the need to bring a semblance of order to his district. From at least mid-century, bosses like New York City's William Marcy Tweed and Philadelphia's James McManes had watched the aimless spreading of their cities and understood the problem of managing them. Tweed frankly admitted that New York's population was "too hopelessly split into races and factions to govern under universal suffrage, except by bribery of patronage and corruption." Their domains, the bosses realized, were fragmented like giant jigsaw puzzles. Only a professional could provide the liberal application of patronage to glue them together, even though his workmanship might be both slipshod and expensive. In New York City immediately after the Civil War, Boss Tweed secured a grip on the city government, built a mammoth new county courthouse, completed plans for Central Park, and began work on a city-wide transit system. All these achievements came at the cost of widespread corruption and an astronomical increase in the city's debt.

Bosses seldom achieved the efficiency they sought. At best they surrounded themselves with oligarchies that presided over loose federations of wards and precincts. In the 1890s the bosses' failings in efficiency and accountability would give progressive reformers much ammunition in attacking the urban machines. But in the absence of a genuine science of public administration and of a corps of professional managers to apply it, the bosses at least provided a

William Marcy Tweed

minimum of order and services—however lavishly and corruptly they improvised with the materials at hand. It also must be remembered that the bosses and their machines provided one of the chief forms of entertainment for voters and nonvoters alike in an age before mass recreation and amusement. The local machine sponsored parades, rallies, speeches, picnics, torchlight processions, and Fourth of July fireworks, attracting thousands of city dwellers, all for the purpose of ensuring machine support and keeping machine candidates elected.

Patronage Politics in the States

In the 1870s such state bosses as Roscoe Conkling in New York and James G. Blaine, the "Plumed Knight" from Maine, were highly visible, colorful characters who were masters of the art of demagoguery and personal leadership. By the 1880s, however, a new generation was taking over, achieving political control in many states and building loyal machines. The new bosses of the 1880s were quieter, behind-the-scenes operators who were much cleverer and more cautious than their more raucous predecessors. They were determined to avoid the constant feuding among placemen, which helped to contribute to their forerunner's demise. Matt Quay in Pennsylvania, Tom Platt in New York, Nelson Aldrich in Maine, William Vilas in Wisconsin, and George Hearst in California were typical of a new breed of party chieftains who conducted national business in Washington while keeping a vigilant eye on their cronies back home, solving patronage quarrels, settling factional disputes, and smoothing discontent.

The key device for harmonizing party interests at the state level was the caucus, where local bosses, county chairmen, and state legislators gathered to approve the state's boss choice of candidates for various offices. Here was the real power-base of the men mentioned above, and their ability to more or less force subordinates to accept their "men" was what kept them in power. Naturally, the process involved bribery, even extortion if necessary, to ensure the "system's" survival. Democratic Party bosses won control over their states more slowly than Republicans and, particularly in the one-party South, kept a looser grip on the party reins. Yet, southern Democratic, or "Bourbon," conservatism soon became the model for long-time Democrats who continued to invoke the name of Jefferson in deploring the "spirit of centralization" while quietly employing just that concept in staffing and strengthening their organizations. In both parties, as in the business world after 1880, consolidation was the order of the day.

Increasingly in the 1890s, politics became limited to white males only. Although black men voted during Reconstruction, the abandonment by the Republican Party of southern black folk after the Compromise of 1877, greatly affected black voting thereafter. One of the main goals of the Redeemers was to wrest political power from the freedmen and that was accomplished by the 1890s. Through the use of terror and intimidation, white Southerners denied black men their right to vote, and those who attempted or asserted their right usually ended up swinging from a tree at the end of a rope! White supremacy and rule was entrenched by the 1890s

and so was one-party rule, that of the Democracy. From the end of Reconstruction and for the next seventy years, the old Confederate South voted Democratic in every election. Labeling the Republican Party the agent of "Negro rule," white southern Democrats engaged in all manner of race-bating and white-line bombast to keep southern voters (white, of course) voting straight Democrat—the party of white supremacy.

Opposing the "Solid South" was the Republican Northeast, with nearly enough electoral votes to guarantee its control of the White House. To preserve Republican ascendancy at the national level, the party had to carry key states such as Ohio, Indiana, and New York and had to prevent an alliance from developing between the agricultural South and the West. Northern Republican politicians, like their southern Democratic counterparts, continued to fan the flames of sectionalism with emotional appeals to the Civil War, a tactic known as "waving the bloody shirt," which was used effectively by the party in the 1868 election to get U.S. Grant into the Oval Office. Strong Unionist states in the Midwest responded by voting consistently Republican. "Iowa will go Democratic," one observer joked, "when Hell goes Methodist." Veterans of the Grand Army of the Republic formed an important base of Republican Party support, which rewarded their loyalty with generous pensions. By 1886, an astounding one-quarter of the federal budget went to pensions, not a penny of that to ex-Confederates.

Despite being left out of pension benefits and being labeled as "traitors," ex-Confederates and southern whites, in general, were fine with Republican hegemony at the national level. This was true because as long as the Republicans did not interfere with their "Negro problem" and allowed southern whites to oppress black folk, then the "trade-off" was more than acceptable. Southern white priority was not seeing one of their "own" in the White House but control of the region's black majority. As long as the Republicans turned a blind eye toward Jim Crow and other forms of southern apartheid, then southern whites willingly accepted Republican hegemony at the national level, including the White House.

Religion and ethnicity also played a significant role in politics. In the North, Protestants, from the old-line denominations, particularly Presbyterians and Methodists, were drawn to the Republican Party, which championed a series of moral reforms such as temperance. The Democratic Party courted immigrants and attracted Catholic and Jewish voters by consistently opposing laws to close taverns and other businesses on Sunday and by charging that crusades against liquor only masked the real intention of temperance crusaders: a blatant, ethnocentric attack on immigrant culture.

The power of the two major parties remained about equally divided throughout the 1870s and 1880s and into the 1890s. Although the Republicans dominated the White House, they rarely controlled Congress. The Democrats, noted more for their local control and appeal than for their national unity, for the most part, dominated the House of Representatives. Not until the Seventeenth Amendment was passed were senators directly elected by voters. Until then, (1912), the state legislatures selected senators. In an era legendary for its tolerance of all but the most flagrant bribery and corruption, state legislatures rather easily and all too frequently came under the control of the powerful capitalist-industrialist interests. In *Wealth Against Commonwealth* (1894), his book on the Standard Oil Company, journalist Henry Demarest Lloyd wrote, "The Standard has done everything with the Pennsylvania legislature except to refine it." Senators were often closely allied with business interests, as in the case of Nelson Aldrich, the powerful Republican from Rhode Island, whose daughter married John D. Rockefeller, Jr. and who didn't mind being called "the senator from Standard Oil."

The Shadow Presidents

Since real political power at the national level resided in Congress during the Gilded Age, the principal task given by party managers to the era's presidents was to get themselves elected without compromising their reputations by saying anything provocative and then to dispense patronage to party worthies. Winning the presidency was not easy, especially when neither

party's platforms differed to any noticeable degree. James Bryce, the British minister in Washington who observed the 1884 presidential election, between Republican James G. Blaine and the Democratic nominee, Grover Cleveland, was amazed that neither party had a distinctive agenda. "Neither party has any principles, any distinctive tenets. Both have traditions. Both claim to have tendencies. . . .All has been lost, except office or the hope of it."

President Rutherford B. Hayes, whose disputed 1876 election marked the end of Reconstruction, proved to be a hard-working, well-informed executive who wanted peace, prosperity, and an end to party strife. Although ridiculed by the Democratic press as "Rutherfraud," and "His Fraudulency," Hayes was a man of integrity and honesty, who seemed well-suited for his role as a national leader. But Hayes faced a formidable task in attempting to end party strife, which greatly handicapped his implementation of any national agenda or vision he might have had. Unfortunately for Hayes and his Republican successors, his party remained wracked by internal factionalism and was controlled by party bosses who boasted that they could make or break a president.

The three Republican factions bore the colorful names Stalwarts, Half-Breeds, and Mugwumps. The Stalwarts, led by New Yorker Roscoe Conkling, were Grant supporters and thus were associated with the scandals of his administration and consequently were perceived to be willing to continue that legacy. Opposing them were the Half-Breeds, led by Senator James G. Blaine of Maine, a group that was only slightly less corrupt than Conkling's bunch in its pursuit of party dominance and spoils. Against both factions was a small but noteworthy group of liberal Republican reformers, mostly from Massachusetts and New York, whose critics dubbed them the Mugwumps, the name of an Algonquian Indian chief, but was used derisively by the faction's opponents who asserted that the Mugwumps were fence-straddlers when it came to the most important issue of party loyalty. The Mugwumps were determined to purge the Republican Party of all those who had so tarnished its image as the party of the Union and the Grand Army of the Republic. They were determined to drive the other factions out of the party and institute badly needed governmental reforms to ensure that competent, honest men like themselves were in control. In their pursuit of reform, they evaded the complex and divisive economics issues, such as tariff reform and monopolies, and instead focused on government reform through civil service reforms designed to set standards for office holders and put an end to the spoils system.

Hayes, despite his virtues, soon managed to alienate powerful party members. A realist, he used federal patronage to build Republican strength by selecting for government jobs if not the best men, the best—most qualified and honest—Republicans he could find. To the Stalwarts, he was a traitor; to the Mugwumps, his appointments still smacked of the spoils system. Hayes soon found himself without a party and thus, come election time, announced that he would not pursue his party's nomination in 1880.

Party bosses like Blaine and Conkling easily overpowered and destroyed Hayes' modest though sincere attempts at party reform. Fiery, dynamic, shrewd, manipulative, petty, and vindictive, as well as tied to corporate interests, Blaine and Conklin dominated national politics at this time. The imperious Conkling had nothing but contempt for the Mugwumps. He lambasted "snivel service" reform. "Parties," he declared, "are not built up by deportment, or by ladies' magazines, or gush." His archrival, the "plumed Knight," James G. Blaine, was a charismatic Irish-American, with a devoted following so fanatical in their support that they were dubbed "Blaniacs." Blaine condemned blatant Stalwart corruption but was himself tarnished by questionable dealings in railroad bonds. More careless than criminal in his business relations, Blaine, typical of so many of his cohorts, drew no fine distinction between public service and private gain; indeed they were symbiotic to men of Blaine and Conkling's ilk. Yet, Blaine's shady dealings caused enough public disaffection to cost him the Republican nomination in 1880 and the presidency four years later.

In 1880, the Mugwumps had just enough influence to block a Stalwart attempt to bring U.S. Grant out of retirement and run again for the presidency. Blaine, too, was passed over, and instead a dark-horse candidate, Representative James A. Garfield of Ohio, a virtual "nobody," was nominated. Conkling, however, insisted that one of his "boys," Chester Alan Arthur, a fellow Stalwart from New York, be put on the ticket as vice-president. The Democrats, still trying to unite a sectionalized party, nominated ex-Union general (the Republicans had had great success with such nominees—Grant, Hayes, and now Garfield), Winfield S. Hancock. But such a choice was not going to endear southern Democrats even though the "Solid South" voted for Hancock over Garfield. As one observer noted, "It is a peculiarly constituted party which sends rebel brigadiers to Congress because of their rebellion, and which nominated a Union General as its candidate for president because of his loyalty." Although the popular vote was close, Garfield won 214 electoral votes to Hancock's 155.

"My God," Garfield cried out after only a few months in the Oval Office, "what is there in this place that a man should ever want to get into?" Garfield, like Hayes, confronted the difficult task of remaining independent while attempting to placate the screaming bosses for "jobs" and the howling reformers for a massive overhaul of the federal bureaucracy. To an indecisive and easily overwhelmed man like Garfield, the presidency was a nightmare. He found the job of dispensing federal patronage grueling and distasteful, especially as he was forced to award positions to individuals whom he knew were not only completely unqualified for the job but venal and corrupt as well. More than 140,000 federal civil service jobs needed filling. Thousands of office seekers swarmed into Washington, each clamoring for a place. In an era before constant Secret Service protection for the president was established, the White House door was literally wide open. Garfield took a fatalistic view: "Assassination," he told a friend, "can no more be guarded against than death by lightning, and it is best not to worry about either."

On July 2, 1881, less than four months after taking office, Garfield was indeed assassinated, waiting for a train at a Washington, D.C. railroad station. His assassin, Charles Guiteau, though clearly insane, was a disgruntled office seeker who claimed to be motivated by political partisanship. He told the police officer who arrested him, "I did it; I will go to jail for it; Arthur is president, and I am a Stalwart. Garfield did not die instantly or in a few days; he lingered on through the summer, finally succumbing in September 1881. The press was outraged, holding the Stalwarts responsible for the president's tragic, violent death. Even though the Stalwarts were not responsible for Guiteau's actions, they nonetheless helped to create the hostile political environment that produced such individuals and violence. Stalwart leader Roscoe Conkling, who came under heavy attack for his partisanship in the wake of the assassination, had to give up his presidential ambitions and retire from politics and assumed a career as a corporate lawyer. Assaults on the spoils system increased, as did public demand for civil service reform. Though Garfield's death galvanized support for civil service reform, the ensuing congressional, as well as public, debate was long and hard. Those opposing reform cried out that it was class and ethnically biased. When Mugwumps spoke of government run by the "best men," they meant men of their own class and ethnic stock—WASPs. Reform would be particularly detri-

mental to Irish-Americans, who by this time were attaining increasing numbers of positions of political power in Northeastern cities. They would not want to see government once again in the hands of an educated Yankee elite. At a time when few men had more than an elementary school level of education, office seekers would not want to take a written civil service examination. One opponent argued, "George Washington would not have passed examination for a clerkship," noting that "in his will written by his own hand, he spells clothes, cloathes."

Despite acrimonious debate, civil service reform at the national level was instituted with the passage of the Pendleton Act in 1883. Both parties claimed credit for the act, which established a permanent Civil Service Commission of three members, appointed by the president. Some 14,000 jobs were placed under a merit system that required examinations for office and made it impossible to remove individuals for political reasons. Half of the postal jobs and most of the customhouse jobs—long two of the most "rewarded" jobs under the spoils system—passed to the control of the Civil Service Commission. The new

This cartoon pictures Winfield Scott Hancock as the biblical Samson against the "Republican Philistines."
Hancock lost to the favored James A. Garfield by less than 10,000 popular votes but Garfield won the electoral votes.

law prohibited federal officeholders from contributing to political campaigns, thus helping to dissolve a major portion of the party bosses' revenue. Soon business interests replaced officeholders as the nation's chief political "fund-raisers." Ironically, civil service reform thus gave the plutocracy an even greater influence in political life than it already had.

"Chet Arthur, president of the United States! Good God!" exclaimed many Americans upon hearing of Garfield's death. Such foreboding was not unwarranted, for there was little in Arthur's background that qualified him for the highest office in the land. Only four years earlier he had been dismissed from his customhouse position in New York on charges of corruption. But a sort of metamorphosis took place as Arthur, now free of Conkling's grasp, quickly dispelled the nation's fears and acted independently, signing the Pendleton Act that his fellow Stalwarts had so long opposed. Arthur himself had little "faith in reform" but was politically savvy enough not to stand in the path of public sentiment. Beyond signing the Pendleton Act, Arthur's presidency was one of the most lackluster in history, doing nothing else of consequence except to refurbish the White House with his own money and in keeping with his bachelor taste. He put a billiard table in the basement. As long-time Mugwump Carl Schurz observed, "whenever Arthur did a creditable thing, people would say, 'He is after all a better man than we thought he was.'" Arthur surprised his critics by turning out to be a competent president, but his was a boring, mundane administration. As election year 1884 approached, Republicans were excited that their most charismatic standard bearer, James G. Blaine, would breathe new, more exciting life into the party and carry them to victory once again.

1884: THE DEMOCRATS FINALLY WIN THE BIG ONE

Grover Cleveland in the White House

At their tumultuous Chicago convention, the Republicans, as predicted, turned to their "Plumed Knight," James G. Blaine, to lead them to victory in 1884. Blaine represented the younger, more dynamic wing of the Republican Party that was now eager to shed the taint of Grantism with Conkling out of the way. Blaine and his supporters also promoted continued economic development and a more assertive foreign policy. Unfortunately for Blaine, however, his charisma could not overcome the stigma of being involved in the tawdry politics of the Gilded Age. It was "leaked" that in 1876, while serving as Speaker of the House, Blaine had offered political favors to a railroad company in exchange for stock. Blaine also supported the spoils system, though not as rabidly as Conkling. Nonetheless, in the eyes of staunch Mugwumps like E. L. Godkin, editor of the respected magazine, *The Nation,* Blaine "wallowed in spoils like a rhinoceros in an African pool."

Sensing Blaine's vulnerability, the Democrats chose an individual who politically represented a sharp contrast to Blaine: Grover Cleveland of New York. Cleveland's rather meteoric rise from reform mayor of Buffalo to governor was noteworthy because along the way he fought the bosses and spoilsmen and won. He was short, rotund, and resembled a bull dog, but he was his own man. The savvy of the Democrats' choice became readily apparent when reform stalwarts such as Godkin and Carl Schurz bolted the Republican Party and supported Cleveland. But Cleveland was not without liabilities, the most notorious of which was his admission that he had fathered an illegitimate child as a young man. The Republicans naturally exploited this, jeering at rallies, "Ma, Ma, where's my pa?" Cleveland also had to overcome the powerful influence of New York City's Tammany Hall who hated Cleveland for his attempts while governor to destroy their machine. Tammany still controlled the immigrant vote of the city, which was increasingly more important as that population grew. If immigrant voters "stayed home" come election day, Cleveland could lose his own state. But in October a rabid Protestant Republican clergyman denounced the Democrats as the party of "Rum, Romanism, and Rebellion." Blaine failed to immediately repudiate the remark, which allowed Cleveland's supporters to claim that such a statement only showed that the Republicans were anti-Catholic, anti-drink, and were insulting patriotic Democrats tired of the "bloody shirt." This blunder and the Mugwumps' defection allowed Cleveland to carry New York state by 1200 votes and with it the election. Cleveland won the popular vote by only 25,685 votes and in the electoral college the margin of victory was 37 votes.

Tariffs and Pensions

Though he had established himself as his own man when it came to dealing with machine politicians, Cleveland showed no such boldness or courage when it came to challenging the business elite. Indeed, in most respects Cleveland demonstrated that he was the plutocrats' friend, embracing the belief that government must not meddle in the economy. In the Jacksonian period, laissez faire had been a radical "liberal" idea endorsed by ambitious small entrepreneurs who wanted business conditions favorable to competition; by the 1880s it had become the plutocrat's rallying cry against any form of government intervention in their affairs. Approving of this ethos, Cleveland asserted presidential power mostly through his vetoes and displayed a limited understanding of industrialization's impact. For example, he vetoed a bill that would have provided seeds to drought-stricken Texas farmers, admonishing that people should not expect the government to solve their problems.

One public issue did arouse Cleveland from his legislative slumber: the tariff, a matter involving a tangle of conflicting economic and political interests. Tariff duties were a major source of federal revenue in the era before an income tax, so the tariff was really a form of taxation. But which imported goods should be subject to duties, and how much? Opinions differed radically. The producers of such commodities as coal, hides, timber, and wool demanded tariff protection against foreign competition, and industries that prospered behind tariff walls— iron and steel, textiles, machine tools—wanted protection to continue. Workers in these industries agreed, convinced that protection meant higher wages and secure jobs. Other manufacturers, however, while seeking protection for their finished goods, wanted low tariffs on the raw materials they required

but had to import. Massachusetts shoe makers, for example, urged high duties on imported shoes but low duties on imported hides. Most farmers, by contrast, hated the protective tariff, charging that it inflated farm-equipment prices (because large farm machinery companies such as John Deere and International Harvester had monopolies because tariffs had locked out foreign farm equipment makers), and by impeding trade, made it hard to sell American farm products abroad.

Cleveland's call for the lowering of tariffs arose initially from the fact that in the 1880s the high tariff, generating millions of dollars in federal revenue, was feeding a growing budget surplus. Since government expenditures were negligible during this time, a huge surplus of money had accrued in the treasury, largely from tariff and land sales revenue. This surplus tempted many legislators, especially those from the low-income and undeveloped South and West, to demand that the money be distributed in the form of veterans' pensions or expensive public works projects in their home districts. Believing paternalistic government an anathema, Cleveland viewed the budget surplus as a corrupting influence. In his annual congressional message in 1887, Cleveland argued that lower tariffs would not only cut the federal surplus but would also reduce prices and slow down mergers and consolidations by introducing a degree of competition (foreign) in many markets. Although the 1888 Democratic campaign gave little attention to the issue, Cleveland's talk of lowering the tariff alienated many once-supportive plutocrats.

Cleveland stirred up another hornet's nest when he took on the Grand Army of the Republic. Veterans' disability pensions cost the government millions of dollars annually. No one opposed pensions for the deserving, but by the 1880s fraudulent claims had become a public scandal. Unlike his predecessors— who were all Republicans and who did not want to lose this most important voting bloc—Cleveland investigated these claims and rejected many of them. In 1887 he vetoed a bill that would have pensioned the disabled veterans (even if their disability had nothing to do with military service) and their dependents. The pension list should be an honor roll, he declared, not a boondoggle.

THE 1888 ELECTION

The Plutocrats and the GAR Strike Back

By 1888, many disaffected Democrats, and even Republicans who had defected, concluded that Cleveland was not the man they had hoped for and thus must go. "The Plumed Knight," Blaine, decided he was through seeking the big prize and bowed out of seeking the Republican nomination. Party chieftains, especially those tied to the plutocracy, believed it necessary to find someone who could win but whom they could control as well. They turned to Benjamin Harrison of Indiana, the grandson of old "Tip," former president William Henry Harrison. A corporation lawyer and former senator, Harrison was so void of personality and aloof that some ridiculed him as the human iceberg. His campaign managers learned to scurry him away after speeches before anyone could engage him in conversation or experience his effete handshake.

Soon after the hustings began, the issues quickly distilled down to two: the tariff and veterans' pensions, which Harrison hit hard. Cleveland was falsely accused of "free trade"—the elimination of all tariffs. Harrison asserted that the high protective tariff ensured prosperity, decent wages for industrial workers, and a healthy home market for farmers. Thanks to donations from big business, the Republicans amassed a campaign chest of $4 million. Such a war chest went far, not only for posters and buttons but also votes. Despite Republican chicanery, Cleveland beat Harrison in the popular vote by over 100,000 but unfortunately for the Democrat, the popular vote doesn't matter in the end; the electoral vote does and Harrison carried the key states of Indiana and New York and triumphed in the electoral college by winning 233 votes to Cleveland's 167. The Republicans held the Senate and regained the House. When Harrison righteously stated that Providence aided the Republican cause, his campaign chairman retorted that "Providence hadn't a damn thing to do with it. . . . A number of men approached the gates of the penitentiary to make him president."

Harrison quickly rewarded his supporters via the spoils system, handing out hundreds of jobs to individuals whom the plutocrats and other Republican power brokers "recommended." He appointed as commissioner of pensions a GAR official, who on taking office declared, "God help the surplus!" The pensions soon ballooned from 676,000 to nearly a million. This massive pension system, coupled with medical care in a network of veterans' hospitals, became the nation's first large-scale public welfare program. In 1890 the triumphant Republicans also enacted the McKinley Tariff, which raised the rates on many imported manufactured goods to an all-time high of over 40 percent ad valorem. This new tariff stirred a hornet's nest of protest. The people had elected Harrison to preserve protection not to enact a higher tariff. The McKinley Tariff helped deplete that "vexing" surplus by raising duties so high that many foreign producers simply stopped selling their goods in the United States. Democrats naturally seized on the unpopularity of the tariff, labeling the Republican Congress that passed it as "The Billion Dollar Congress," as it unleashed an unprecedented spending frenzy of the entire surplus. Most of the money was spent on "pork-barrel" programs, that is, legislation passed for no real benefit other than to bring federal largesse to a congressman's or senator's "favorite" constituents. So upset were voters with such programs and spending that in the off-year election of 1890, they swept the hapless Republicans, including McKinley, out of office. Two years later, in a rather remarkable come back, Cleveland defeated Harrison for the presidency, promising to lower the tariff.

THE RAILROADS, THE TRUSTS, AND THE FEDERAL GOVERNMENT

American voters may have disagreed on the tariff, but increasingly they concurred on the need for federal regulation of the railroads and federal legislation against the trusts. As early as the 1870s, farmers had organized to combat the railroads and their exploitive, discriminatory policies toward especially small farmers. One of the first such organizations was the Grange, founded in 1867, initially as a social and educational association for farmers. However, by the 1870s, the Grange became politicized

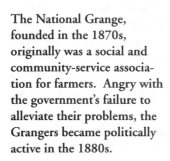

The National Grange, founded in the 1870s, originally was a social and community-service association for farmers. Angry with the government's failure to alleviate their problems, the Grangers became politically active in the 1880s.

because of railroad abuse and launched an independent political party for a redress of their grievances against the railroads. Surprisingly, at the local and state level, the Grangers elected a number of officials that made it possible for several Midwestern states to pass laws regulating the railroads. At first, the Supreme Court upheld their right to do so. In *Munn v. Illinois* (1877), the Court ruled in favor of regulation. But in 1886, the Supreme Court reversed itself in the *Wabash* case (*Wabash, St. Louis, and Pacific Railway Co. v. Illinois*) and ruled that because railroads crossed state lines, they fell outside state jurisdiction. With more than three-fourths of railroads crossing state lines, the Supreme Court's decision effectively stopped regulation.

Public outcry was so great over the Court's ruling that the first Cleveland administration passed the first federal law to regulate the railroads, the Interstate Commerce Act of 1887. The act established the nation's first federal regulatory agency, the Interstate Commerce Commission, which was charged with the power to investigate and oversee railroad activities. In its early years, the ICC was never strong

enough or sure enough of its role to pose a serious threat to the railroads' continued monopolistic practices. In the end, the act and the commission proved more important as a precedent than as an effective watchdog.

Concern over the growing power of the trusts led the federal government during the Harrison administration to pass the Sherman Antitrust Act in 1890. By then enough Democrats and disaffected reform Republicans coalesced in Congress to pass such a law if it could be accomplished without hurting the economy, which whether one liked it or not, was inextricably tied to the vagaries of consolidated enterprises, whether they were trusts, holding companies, or whatever "bigness" implied. The Sherman Act allowed for corporations but struck at the trusts. Businesses could no longer enter into agreements to restrict competition. The law outlawed pools and trusts but did nothing to prohibit huge holding companies like Standard Oil, since a holding company, no matter how big, was one entity and not an agreement among separate businesses to set prices or restrict trade.

The Sherman Act proved to be a weaker, more feeble attempt at government regulation than the Interstate Commerce Act. In the decade after its passage, the government successfully mandated the break up of only six trusts. However, the law was used four times against labor by outlawing unions as a "conspiracy in restraint of trade." In 1895, the Supreme Court dealt the law a crippling blow in the *E.C. Knight* case. The Court drastically narrowed the law by allowing the American Sugar Refining Company, which controlled 98 percent of the nation's sugar production, to continue its monopoly on the grounds that manufacture did not constitute trade. Both the Sherman Act and the Interstate Commerce Act testified to the nation's growing concern about the excesses of corporate capitalism and an increasing willingness to turn to the federal government as a source of redress for such abuses. Not until the twentieth century would more reform-minded activist presidents be willing to engage the corporations and use the full power of the federal government to protect the public welfare.

The Fight for Free Silver

Though many Americans wanted the government to curtail the power of the trusts, the most important issue of the 1880s and 1890s had to do with the currency. During the Civil War, the Union printed greenbacks (paper money), which provided funds for the war effort and simultaneously created inflation because the dollars were not backed by gold or silver. Debtors, who could pay back their loans with the devalued dollars, liked inflation; creditors, of course, opposed it. Because most debtors were Southern and Western farmers and most creditors and investors were Northeastern bankers, the controversy assumed intense sectional partisanship and overtones, as the issues of inflation versus deflation, of greenbacks versus hard money, and later gold versus silver, pitted the Northeast against an allied South and West.

In the 1870s, supporters of cheap money (paper) organized a third-party movement, the Greenback Labor Party, whose platform argued that the nation needed an expanding monetary system to keep up with population growth and commercial expansion. Greenbackers insisted the paper money was "the people's currency, elastic, cheap, and exportable, based on the entire wealth of the country." But in 1879, Congress voted to resume the gold standard, thus siding with creditors as opposed to debtors by tying the nation's currency to its gold reserves. Greenbackers responded by running General James B. Weaver for president in 1880. Despite the appeal of inflation among Southerners and Westerners, especially the farmers of those regions, voters below the Mason-Dixon line could not bring themselves to cast their ballot for a former Union general, and the party soon dissolved after the election. Despite Congresses' resolve with the gold standard, the currency issue would not go away. As a result of the return to the gold standard, money became even tighter. By the 1890s, the call for easier money and credit reappeared, with debtors calling not for the reissuing of greenbacks but for backing the dollar with silver.

The silver controversy stirred passions like no other issue of the day. On one side stood the "gold bugs"—mainly Northeastern creditors who believed that gold constituted the only honest money and who did not want to be paid in devalued dollars, which they asserted silver would do. On the opposite side, stood the "silverites"—led by the Western silver mining interests, whose stake in the battle was obvious. In the 1860s and 1870s, the West exploded in a silver bonanza, producing far more silver than gold. However, there was so much silver on the market that the price of silver plummeted. Mining states like Colorado and Nevada wanted the government to buy silver and mint silver dollars to help raise the price. Allied with the silver mining companies for very different reasons were Southern and Western farmers who had fallen on hard times during the 1870s and 1880s and who saw in silver a panacea for their problems. A grinding cycle of debt and deflation had left farmers in those regions in need of relief. Farmers hoped that increasing the money supply—inflation—with silver dollars would give them some relief.

Silverites pointed out that until 1873, the country had enjoyed a system of bimetallism, with both silver and gold coins minted. In that year, Congress demonetized (stopped buying and minting) silver, an act bimetallist denounced as the "crime of '73." They accused the domenetizers of a conspiracy to limit the money in circulation and place the West and the South at the mercy of Northeastern financiers. In 1878 Congress took steps to appease the silverites by passing the Bland-Allison Act over Hayes' veto. The measure required the government to buy silver and issue silver certificates. The act also helped mine owners, who now had a buyer for their ore, but it had little inflationary impact. Pressure for inflation continued, but the silverites were unable to make any progress until 1890, when in return for their support of the McKinley Tariff, Congress passed the Sherman Silver Purchase Act, increasing the amount of silver the government bought. Once again, the measure fell far short of generating inflation, and advocates began to call for "the free and unlimited coinage of silver," a plan whereby virtually all the silver that was mined would be minted into silver coins and circulated at the rate of sixteen ounces of silver to one ounce of gold.

The silver issue crossed party lines, but the Democrats hoped to use it to achieve an alliance between Western and Southern voters. Though the Democrats recaptured the White House in 1892 with Grover Cleveland's second administration, the president was still as economically conservative as he was during his first term. Cleveland supported the gold standard unequivocally; so much so that in 1893 he called a special session of Congress and brow-beat that body into repealing the Sherman Silver Purchase Act. Repeal only further divided the country, making the Mississippi River for a time as potent a political boundary as the Mason-Dixon line. Angry farmers warned Cleveland not to travel west of the river if he valued his life.

Compounding the silver controversy was the Panic of 1893, which the silver-gold issue helped to cause. As was the case in the Panic of 1873, the railroad industry once again was responsible for initiating this most recent downturn. As was true with industry in the 1870s, investment in the railroad boom of the 1880s triggered speculation among investors. Typical of the previous decade, railroad companies fed the speculative mania by issuing more stock (and enticing investors with higher dividends) than the soundness of the line warranted. Weakened by agricultural stagnation, railroad expansion halted in the early 1890s, affecting many related industries, including iron and steel. The first hint that this most vital industry was faltering came with the failure of one of the East's most important roads, the Philadelphia and Reading Railroad.

The line's failure occurred at the same time as the silver-gold controversy was intensifying, especially as the public's confidence in the gold standard waned. This diminished faith had several sources. First, when a leading London investment bank collapsed in 1890, hard-pressed British investors sold millions of dollars worth of stock in American railroads and other corporations and converted their dollars to gold, draining U.S. gold reserves. Second, as noted earlier, was the Harrison administration's lavish pork-barreling and veteran payouts, which drained government resources at a time when tariff revenue was declining because of the high McKinley Tariff. Third, the 1890 Sherman Silver Purchase Act further strained the gold reserve by requiring the government to pay for its monthly silver purchases with treasury certificates redeemable in either gold or silver; naturally certificate holders chose gold over silver. Between January 1892 and March 1893, when Cleveland took office, the gold reserve had plummeted to around $100 million, the minimum considered necessary to support the dollar. This decline alarmed those who viewed the gold standard as the only sure evidence of the government's solvency.

As typical in financial panics, fear fed on itself as fearful investors converted their stock holdings to gold. Stock prices plunged in May and June 1893; gold reserves sank; by the end of the year, seventy-four railroads had gone under as well as more than 15,000 commercial institutions, including 600 banks. After the Panic of 1893 came four years of depression.

The Depression of 1893–1897

By 1897, about a third of the nation's railroads were in bankruptcy. Just as the railroad boom had stimulated the industrial prosperity of the 1880s, so had its collapse caused the entire economy to be adversely affected. The Depression of 1893 took a heavy human toll, more so than that of 1873. Industrial unemployment soared to almost 25 percent, leaving millions of factory workers with no money to feed their families and heat their homes. Recent immigrants faced disaster. Jobless men tramped the streets and rode freight trains from city to city, region to region, looking for work. The unusually harsh winters of 1893 and 1894 only made things worse. In New York City, where the crisis quickly overwhelmed local relief agencies, a minister reported actual starvation. Amid the suffering, a rich New Yorker named Bradley Martin threw a lavish costume ball costing several hundred thousand dollars. When news of such foppish frivolity and insensitivity reached the city's masses, the outrage was so great that Martin, fearing for his life (and rightly so!), wisely moved his family abroad.

Rural America, already hard-hit by declining agricultural prices, faced ruin. Farm prices dropped by more than 20 percent between 1890 and 1896. Corn plummeted from fifty cents to twenty-one cents a bushel and wheat from eighty-four cents to fifty-one cents. Cotton sold for five cents a pound in 1894. Some desperate Americans turned to protest. In Massillon, Ohio, a self-taught monetary expert, Jacob Coxey, proposed as a solution to unemployment a $500 million public-works program funded with paper money not backed by gold or silver, simply designated "legal tender" (just as it is today). A man of action as well as ideas, Coxey organized the first serious "march on Washington," to lobby for his scheme. Thousands joined him en route, and several hundred actually reached the Capital in late April 1894. Police arrested Coxey and other leaders when they attempted to enter the Capitol grounds, and his "army" disbanded. Although some considered Coxey an eccentric, his proposal closely resembled programs the New Deal implemented during the 1930s to help relieve the unemployed.

In the harsh winter of 1894-95, Cleveland aggravated an already highly charged political climate by his deal with J.P. Morgan to save the country's gold reserves by having the financier lend the gov-

ernment $62 million in exchange for U.S. bonds at a special discount. With this loan from "the House of Morgan," the government purchased enough gold to replenish its reserve, which had dwindled to $41 million by 1895. Naturally, Morgan and his partner, August Belmont, resold the bonds for a substantial profit. Cleveland saved the gold standard but at a high price. His dealings with Morgan and Belmont and the bankers' handsome profits on the deal only underscored many people's suspicions of an unholy alliance between Washington and Wall Street. Cleveland's policies split the Democratic Party. Farm leaders and silver Democrats condemned his repeal of the Sherman Silver Purchase Act. South Carolina's Ben Tilman, running for the Senate in 1894, announced that Cleveland was a "scoundrel" and an "old bag of beef and I am going to Washington with a pitch-fork and prod him in his fat old ribs." This split in Democratic ranks affected the 1894 and 1896 elections and reshaped politics as the century ended.

The 1893 depression also helped change social thought. Middle-class charitable workers and reformers, long convinced that individual character flaws caused poverty, now realized—as socialists had long argued and as the poor well knew—that even sober, hardworking people could succumb to economic forces beyond their control. As the social work profession developed in the early twentieth century, its disciples spent less time preaching to the poor and more time investigating the social and environmental sources of poverty. Many Americans also began to question the sanctity and validity of the laissez-faire ethos as many depression-worn citizens began embracing the idea of government intervention on behalf of the public welfare to ameliorate the more egregious social consequences of industrialization. In the early twentieth century, this new view would energize powerful political forces. The depression, in short, not only brought suffering; it also taught lessons.

CONCLUSION

Mark Twain, one of America's greatest writers, humorists, and one of its shrewdest social critics, called the period following Reconstruction the "Gilded

A picture of the Brooklyn Bridge under construction. The separation of the Brooklyn residents from Manhattan by the East River demanded the building of the Brooklyn Bridge between the boroughs. It had the longest span of any bridge previously built and was the first to use suspension cables. Construction began in 1869 and was not completed until May 24, 1883.

Age." He chose that term to ridicule the ugliness, crass materialism, and sham of a time when glitter on the outside masked what lay beneath. Twain's label has stood for more than a century as a fair representation of an era when political corruption strutted with the haughty arrogance of a Conkling and industrialists like William Vanderbilt cried, "The public be damned!" But if the age spawned greed, corruption, and vulgarity on a grand scale, it was not without its share of solid achievements. In the three decades after the Civil War, America made the leap into the industrial age. Indeed, by 1900 it was the leading industrial/manufacturing nation in the world, whose standard of living was fast becoming the envy of other nations. Where dusty roads and cattle once sprawled across the continent, steel rails now bound together a nation. Cities grew from the ground into the sky. In New York City, the Brooklyn Bridge spanned the East River with steel and stone, more strikingly beautiful than all the showy mansions on Fifth Avenue. In the offices and business boardrooms, men like Rockefeller, Carnegie, and Morgan consolidated American industry. By the end of the century, the country had achieved industrial maturity. No other era in the nation's history witnessed such a rapid transformation. However, it remained to be seen whether the nation could curb the plutocrats' vast and overwhelming power and work to solve the social and economic problems accompanying industrialization.

Chronology

1869 Completion of first transcontinental railroad
Knights of Labor founded.

1870 John D. Rockefeller incorporates Standard
Oil Company in Cleveland, Ohio.

1873 "Crime of 1873" demonetizes silver
Panic on Wall Street leads to major economic
depression.

1874 Pennsylvania Railroad capitalized at $400
million and employing 55,000; largest
private enterprise in the world.

1876 Alexander Graham Bell demonstrates telephone
at Philadelphia Centennial Exposition.

1877 Rutherford B. Hayes sworn in as president
after disputed election
Great Railroad Strike cost 100 lives and
millions of dollars in damage
U.S. Supreme Court upholds right of states
to regulate railroads in *Munn v. Illinois.*

1878 Bland-Allison Act to remonetize silver passed
over Hayes' veto.

1879 Henry George publishes *Progress and Poverty*
Congress votes to resume gold standard
Thomas Alva Edison perfects filament for
incandescent lightbulb.

1880s Jay Gould attempts to build a second
transcontinental railway system
Gustavus Swift revolutionizes meatpacking
with refrigerated rail cars to transport fresh
meat to the east
H.J. Heinz pioneers mass production and
distribution of his fifty-seven varieties of
condiments.

1880 Greenback Labor Party runs General James
B. Weaver for president
Dark horse Republican candidate James A.
Garfield elected president.

1881 Garfield assassinated by Charles Guiteau
Vice-President Chester A. Arthur becomes
president.

1882 Standard Oil develops the trust

1883 Railroads establish four standard time zones
Congress passes Pendleton Act establishing
civil service reform

1884 Grover Cleveland elected president; first
Democrat to serve since before the Civil War
Mark Twain's *Huckleberry Finn* published
and subsequently banned in Boston

1886 Knights of Labor membership peaks at 700,000
Haymarket riot causes antilabor backlash
American Federation of Labor founded
In *Wabash* case, U.S. Supreme Court reverses
itself and disallows state regulation of
railroads that cross state lines

1887 Edward Bellamy publishes *Looking Backward*
Interstate Commerce Act creates first federal
regulatory agency.

1888 Benjamin Harrison elected president of the
United States.

1889 Standard Oil reorganizes into a holding company

1890 Congress passes the McKinley Tariff, Sherman
Antitrust Act and Sherman Silver Purchase Act

1892 Grover Cleveland elected to second term as
president
J.P. Morgan consolidates electric industry,
creating the General Electric Company
Homestead steel strike erupts into violence
and bloodshed and eventually suppressed

1893 Financial panic begins economic depression
Congress repeals Sherman Silver Purchase Act

1894 Coxey's Army of the unemployed marches
on Washington
Pullman strike paralyzes the railroads and
provokes federal intervention

1895 J.P. Morgan bails out U.S. Treasury and saves
nation's gold reserves

1901 J.P. Morgan buys out Carnegie Steel and creates
U.S. Steel, first billion dollar corporation in
the United States.

SUGGESTED READINGS

Paul Avrich, *The Haymarket Tragedy* (1984).

David H. Bain, *Empire Express: Building the First Transcontinental Railroad* (1999).

Robert V. Bruce, *Alexander Graham Bell and the Conquest of Solitude* (1973).

Sean Dennis Cashman, *America in the Gilded Age* (1984).

Alfred D. Chandler, *The Visible Hand: The Managerial Revolution in American Business* (1977).

Alfred D. Chandler Jr., *The Railroads: The Nation's First Big Business* (1965).

——*Scale and Scope: The Dynamics Of Industrial Capitalism* (1990).

Dino Cinel, *From Italy to San Francisco: The Immigrant Experience* (1982).

Peter Collier and David Horowitz, *The Rockefellers: An American Dynasty* (1976).

Vincent P. DeSantis, *The Shaping of Modern America, 1877-1920* (2nd. Ed., 1989).

Melvyn Dubofsky, *Industrialism and the American Worker, 1865-1920* (1975).

Richard Ellis, *American Political Cultures* (1993).

Saul Engelbourg, *Power and Morality: American Business Ethics, 1840-1914* (1980).

Philip S. Foner, *The Great Labor Uprising of 1877* (1977).

Donna Gabaccia, *From the Other Side: Women, Gender, and Immigrant Life in the U.S., 1820-1990* (1994).

John A. Garraty, *The New Commonwealth, 1877-1890* (1968).

Ray Ginger, *Age of Excess* (1963).

Julius Grodinsky, *Jay Gould, 1867-1892* (1957).

Herbert C. Gutman, *Work, Culture, and Society in Industrializing America: Essays in American Working-Class and History* (1976).

Robert Higgs, *The Transformation of the American Economy, 1865-1914* (1971).

John Higham, *Strangers in the Land* (1955).

Richard Hofstadter, *The Age of Reform* (1955).

Ari Hoogenboom, *Outlawing the Spoils: The Civil Service Reform Movement, 1865-1883* (1961).

___,*The Presidency of Rutherford B. Hayes* (1988).

Irving Howe, *World of Our Fathers* (1976).

Jacqueline Jones, *The Dispossessed: America's Underclass from the Civil War to the Present* (1992).

Mathew Josephson, *The Robber Barons: The Great American Capitalists, 1861-1901* (1934).

Thomas Kessner, *The Golden Door: Italian and Jewish Mobility in New York City, 1880-1915* (1977).

Maury Klein, *The Life & Legend of Jay Gould* (1987).

Sidney Lens, *The Labor War: From the Molly Maguires to the Sitdowns* (1974).

Andre Millard, *Edison and the Business of Innovation* (1990).

Gwendolyn Mink, *Old Labor and New Immigrants in American Political Development* (1986).

David Montgomery, *The Fall of the House of Labor: The Workplace, the State, and American Labor Activism, 1865-1925* (1987).

Humbert Nelli, *Italians of Chicago, 1880-1920* (1970).

James D. Norris, *Advertising and the Transformation of American Society, 1865-1920* (1990).

Nell Irvin Painter, *Standing at Armageddon: the United States, 1877-1919* (1987).

Glen Porter, *The Rise of Big Business, 1860-1910* (1973).

Andrew Sinclair, *Corsair: The Life of J. Pierpont Morgan* (1980).

John Sproat, *The Best Men: Liberal Reformers in the Gilded Age* (1968).

David J. Rothman, *Politics and Power: The United States Senate, 1869-1901* (1966).

Ronald Takaki, *Stringers From A Different Shore: A History of Asian Americans* (1989).

George R. Taylor and Irene D. Neu, *The American Railroad Network, 1861-1890* (1956).

Peter Temin, *Iron and Steel in Nineteenth-Century America* (1964).

Irwin Unger, *The Greenback Era: A Social and Political History of American Finance* (1964).

James A. Ward, *Railroads and the Character of America, 1820-1887* (1986).

Allen Weinstein, *Prelude to Populism: Origins of the Silver Issue, 1867-1878* (1970).

Robert H. Wiebe, *The Search for Order, 1877-1920* (1967).

Virginia Yans-McLaughlin, *Family and Community: Italian Immigrants in Buffalo, 1880-1930* (1977).

Chapter Fourteen

THE TRANS-MISSOURI WEST: The Last Frontier

The Nez Percé Indians were a small tribe living peacefully in the beautiful Wallowa Valley of Oregon, a fertile area of mountain forests, meadows, winding rivers, and a pure blue lake. Earlier in their history, when the half-starved and illness-weakened Lewis and Clark expedition entered their territory, they had welcomed the whites, supplied them with food, and looked after their horses. In seventy years of contact, they had never killed a white settler. In the 1850s, the Christian, "progressive" branch of the tribe agreed to turn over large tracts of mineral-rich land to the federal government. They accepted the white man's offer to live on a large reservation set aside for them in Idaho. In 1863, the discovery of gold greatly diminished this reservation. But the larger group under its leader, the dignified and statesman-like Chief Joseph, refused to sign any treaty giving up more land. Joseph reflected the views of most Native Americans when he declared: "The earth was created by the assistance of the sun, and it should be left as it was....The country was made without lines of demarcation, and it is no man's business to divide it." While most whites saw the land and its resources as there to be exploited, Native Americans believed that people were

a part of nature, not its master. Chief Joseph affirmed, "The earth and myself are of one mind. The measure of the land and the measure of our bodies are the same." Like other Indians, he felt that land could be used but could no more be owned than the air all people breathed.

An advocate of peaceful coexistence with whites, Joseph and his tribe were able to survive on their little piece of paradise until the 1870s. White settlers began to covet this prime area. They pressured the government into forcing the rest of the Nez Percés onto the Idaho reservation in 1877. With a heavy heart, Joseph convinced his people that resistance was futile, and they began their long journey from the land they loved to the reservation. On the way, however, some of the younger hot-heads in the tribe, fortified by alcohol and angry at their plight, killed four white settlers.

Joseph understood that retribution would be swift and terrible. He persuaded his people to flee with him, hoping to gain sanctuary in Canada where many Sioux Indians had received refuge. At the battle of White Bird Canyon, he was able to drive off the pursuing American troops. Then the Nez Percés scattered in many directions. Joseph led the largest group of 200 men and

491

350 women, children, and old people. A remarkable chase followed through Idaho and Montana. The Nez Percés traveled east through Yellowstone Park where they frightened some of the astonished tourists and almost encountered General Sherman fishing in the area. Then they headed north. The weary band of Indians covered 1,321 miles in 75 days, hunted by some 5,000 embarrassed government troops. Fascinated readers of Eastern newspapers, uniformly sympathetic to the underdog Indians, eagerly followed each day's story. (Native Americans had long since been eliminated there, so Easterners could far more easily feel tolerance toward the Indian.) The embarrassed generals explained their ineptitude by dubbing Joseph, "the red Napoleon."

The army regiments finally caught up with the Nez Percés within sight of the Canadian border. Some bands of resolute warriors were able to slip across the border where Sitting Bull in his Sioux Canadian village welcomed them. But Joseph and most of his tribe surrendered, exhausted, freezing, and broken hearted. Of the four hundred Nez Percés left, only eighty-seven were fighting men. General Nelson Miles, who greatly admired Joseph's efforts for his people, agreed to allow the band to return to the Idaho reservation. After meeting with the general, Joseph declared, "Hear me, my chiefs. I am tired; my heart is sick and sad. From where the sun now stands, I will fight no more forever." Then, the chief swept his blanket across his face as a symbol of mourning and surrendered. It had cost almost $2 million to vanquish Joseph and his followers.

The American government reneged on the promise General Miles had made to the Nez Percés. Rather than sending them to the Idaho reservation, it moved them from one desolate place to another, finally settling them in a flatlands reservation in Oklahoma. Many died from malnutrition and disease, including Joseph's six children. In 1885, the government transferred the survivors to a reservation near Spokane, Washington, where their descendants remain to this day. Chief Joseph puzzled Buffalo Bill Cody when he joined the "Wild West" shows. The chief was willing to repeat his famous speeches, but he always refused to don war paint and re-enact the end of his people's quest. He died in 1904. The Indian agency physician listed the cause of death as "a broken heart."

THE STRUGGLE OF NATIVE AMERICANS

On the eve of the Civil War, there were approximately 250,000 Indians who shared the Great Plains and mountains of the West with wild animals such as the wolf, coyote, wild horse, jack rabbit, and, above all, the buffalo. These constituted about two-thirds of the Native Americans remaining in the United States (compared to approximately 2.5 million who lived here at the time of Columbus). There were many different languages, customs, and tribes among these Indians. Some, such as the Zuni, Navaho, and Hopi, were fairly well settled farmers, sheep herders, and gardeners. Most, like the Sioux, Apache, and Cheyenne, were nomads and hunters who followed the vast buffalo herds (numbering anywhere from 13 to 25 million) over immense distances.

The buffalo was central to the existence of most of the Plains tribes. Bands (smaller groups of about 500 within the tribe) would pursue the herds through the grasslands, riding powerful small horses descended from those introduced to the New World by the Spaniards. When they stopped, they constructed temporary dwellings (teepees). When they left, the land was virtually undisturbed as a result of the deep respect for nature that was characteristic of Indian religion and culture. The buffalo provided virtually all the basic necessities for these Native Americans. The meat was their main food source. Buffalo hides could be turned into clothing, blankets, robes, shoes, and teepees. The bones became arrow tips, knives, hoes, and even children's sleds. The tendons were used as thread or strings for bows. Fats became cosmetics, and bladders turned into water bags. Even the buffalo droppings—"buffalo chips"—were burned for fuel!

Native Societies

Despite the tribal differences, there were some basic similarities among these Native Americans. Their societies rested upon extended family networks. Unlike the individualism emphasized by white American capitalist competition, Indians stressed cooperation and the welfare of the group. Their reli-

Joseph, Chief of Nez Percé

6

gion focused on the intimate interrelationship between human beings and nature. Most agreed with Chief Joseph that land could never be owned by man. To some, this reverence for the land meant that farming was a sacrilege. One chief explained, "You ask me to plow the ground! Shall I take a knife and tear my mother's bosom?...You ask me to cut the grass and make hay....But how dare I cut my mother's hair?" Many tribes had special pieces of land or water that they considered particularly sacred. Often, these were burial grounds where ancestral spirits lived. Whites tended to ignore or even desecrate these holy lands, leading to bitter conflicts.

Most tribes had loose governmental structures in which authority was shared. Although the chiefs were ceremonial leaders, they had relatively limited power. This led to misunderstandings with whites who thought treaties and agreements with an individual chief would automatically be accepted by the whole tribe. Many bands followed a method of decision-making in which most members took part. As in white society, gender tended to determine responsibilities. Women's work consisted of cooking, raising children, gathering food, sewing, and tanning hides. If a band remained settled for any length of time, women tended the farms. They also created most of the beautiful works of art produced by Native American culture. Women had rights respected by their husbands and often participated in ceremonial dances and tribal councils. Men were the hunters, traders, warriors, and religious leaders.

To whites, the most important attribute of Plains Indian tribes like the Sioux and Cheyenne was their prowess as mounted warriors resisting white advances. Their nomadic lifestyle clashed with the interests of the oncoming railroads, miners, ranchers, and farmers. Their herds of buffalo interfered with westward expansion by knocking over telegraph poles, overturning construction, and even derailing trains when they stampeded. Worst of all, the military skills of the Plains Indians made them the fiercest enemies the whites had ever met. As early as the 1850s, a "scientific" discourse explained, "The *Barbarous* races of America...although nearly as low in intelligence as the Negro races, are essentially untamable....Our Indian tribes submit to extermination, rather than wear the yoke under which our negro slaves fatten and multiply." Thus, while black labor could be valuable under suitable controls, the only solution to the Indian problem was elimination. Most settlers agreed with Theodore Roosevelt that the West was not destined to be "kept as nothing but a game reserve for squalid savages."

When Americans believed that much of the trans-Missouri West was the "Great American Desert," of little value and virtually uninhabitable, the tribes had been largely free to roam its vast spaces. In fact, the federal government considered the area west of the Missouri River "one big reservation." It had even relocated the Five Civilized Tribes of the Old Southwest to the "permanent Indian territory" in the area. By the 1850s, traders, explorers, and settlers advanced into Indian lands and demanded protection. The government began to adopt a new policy of "concentration" under which each tribe would be dealt with separately and confined to smaller reservations. Treaties, often obtained through dishonest means, divided land between Indians and settlers and limited the rights of each on the lands of the other. Whites lived up to these treaties only when the lands in question were undesirable for farming or mining.

As threats to their way of life grew, Indians began to mount a formidable resistance. Warriors, traveling in raiding parties of twenty or thirty, attacked isolated farms and ranches, wagon trains, and stagecoaches. The United States Army intervened, and battles with the tribes broke out. Despite their considerable military abilities, the Plains Indian fighters had many limitations that, in the long run, would make their defeat inevitable. They were unable to centralize, either politically or militarily, to resist white aggression. In fact, they frequently became involved in battles with each other. Many Native Americans were particularly vulnerable to the white man's contagious diseases, such as smallpox that killed thousands. Of course, the most obvious difficulty was that they faced a numerically and technologically superior force.

Destruction of the Buffalo

The destruction of the buffalo herds may well have been the most significant factor in the ultimate defeat of the Plains tribes. After the Civil War, a nationwide craze developed for buffalo robes from the fabled West. This was followed by a brief period in which buffalo tongue became a highly sought delicacy in posh restaurants in the East. In 1871 a tannery in Pennsylvania discovered that buffalo hides could be turned into valuable leather. Groups of professional hunters armed with repeating rifles flooded the area, shooting vast numbers of the huge beasts. Amateurs, sometimes firing from the windows of passing railroad trains, often joined in the "sport" of shooting down the slow-moving animals. Sometimes hundreds of carcasses were left to rot on the open plains (either with only their tongues removed or for no apparent reason at all). Railroad companies hired hunters like Buffalo Bill Cody to mount shooting junkets to remove impediments to railroad traffic. Cody claimed that he killed four thousand buffalo in eighteen months. Even a few Indian tribes, such as the Blackfeet, joined in the kill to make profits from the new demand. Much of the slaughter was not very profitable as the supply of buffalo robes glutted the market, driving down prices. One hunter reported, "I saw buffaloes lying dead on the prairie so thick that one could hardly see the ground. A man could have walked for twenty miles upon their carcasses." Eventually, scavengers created a minor occupation gathering the tons of buffalo bones strewn over the plains for five dollars a ton.

The army and Bureau of Indian Affairs agents encouraged the destruction of the buffalo herds to lessen Indian resistance. "Kill every buffalo you can" one army officer suggested. "Every buffalo dead is an Indian gone." In 1872, the Indian commissioner accurately predicted that before long the "most powerful and hostile bands of today" would be "reduced to the condition of supplicants for charity." By 1883, there were few of the huge beasts left on the plains. The designer of the famous "buffalo nickel" had to go to the Bronx Zoo in New York to find a model. Just as modern Americans are totally dependent upon the oil supply, Native American society on the plains could not survive this decimation of the buffalo.

Indian Wars

Despite this inevitable result, however, small scale skirmishes began to escalate into full scale battles. The first of these conflicts took place during the Civil War when regular army units went to fight the Confederacy and raw recruits replaced them. Led by Little Crow, the eastern Sioux in Minnesota rebelled against conditions in a cramped reservation where corruption by white Indian agents ran rampant. Before being defeated, they killed seven hundred whites. A court martial condemned three hundred to death, but President Lincoln commuted all but thirty-nine of the sentences. Thirty-eight of the Sioux were hanged in a public ceremony, and the rest of the tribe was shipped to the Dakotas. Little Crow, who had managed to escape the noose, left his hiding place to pick raspberries. Deer-hunting settlers spotted him and, motivated by the $25 bounty Minnesota had placed on Sioux scalps, shot him. The state awarded them a $500 bonus and displayed Little Crow's preserved skull and scalp at an exhibition in St. Paul.

Meanwhile, warfare raged in Colorado when miners grabbed lands that the government had guaranteed to the Cheyenne and Arapaho only ten years earlier. In 1864, in response to attacks on settlements and stagecoaches, the army threatened to launch a campaign of retribution. The territorial governor promised that friendly Indians who exhibited the American flag and camped at army posts would be under official protection. In response, one band gathered near an army post in Sand Creek. Colonel Chivington, the "Fighting Parson," declaring, "I believe it is right and honorable to use any means under God's heaven to kill Indians," led a volunteer militia against the unsuspecting, unguarded camp. Despite attempts by the Indians to show peaceful intentions by hoisting a white flag, the militia butchered hundreds of innocent men, women, and children. The bodies were mutilated. The "heroes" of Sand Creek brought over 100 scalps, some of them women's pubic hair, back to Denver. There, they were stretched across the stage of a local theater

MAJOR INDIAN BATTLES

Bear Paw Mountain 1877
WASH. Blackfeet
MONT.
Chief Joseph's Route
Sioux N. DAKOTA
Nez Percé Crow
ORE. Little Big Horn 1876
Klamath Rosebud 1876
Modoc War 1872-1873 Sioux Sioux
Yurok Sioux IDAHO Fetterman Massacre 1866 S. DAKOTA
Shasta WYO.
Wounded Knee 1890
NEV. NEBR.
CALIF. Arapaho Pawnee
UTAH
TERRITORY COLO.
Ute Cheyenne
Sand Creek KANSAS
Navajo Massacre 1864
Hopi Jicarilla
Apache Kiowa
Zuñi
ARIZ. TERRITORY Comanche Red River War
N. MEXICO 1874-1875
Apache TERRITORY
Skeleton Canyon
(Geronimo surrenders) 1886 TEXAS

✹ Major Indian Battles

for public approval. "Colorado soldiers have again covered themselves with glory," a local paper exulted. The massacre destroyed the lives or influence of every Cheyenne and Arapaho chief who favored peace with the whites, and Indian hostility greatly intensified as a result.

A congressional committee investigated the causes of strife in the West. It recommended an Indian Peace Commission to negotiate agreements. In 1867 and 1868, there were conferences to persuade tribes to relocate to reservations in the Black Hills of the Dakotas and to undesirable land in "Indian Territory"—Oklahoma. In return, the government promised supplies and assistance. While some tribes acquiesced in the inevitable, many resisted. Between 1869 and 1875, over two hundred battles erupted between the army and the Indians. The army commander in the West, General S. R. Curtis, was clear about his intentions: "I want no peace until the Indians suffer more."

In 1868 a band of Cheyenne was caught at the Washita River in Oklahoma by an army unit led by the "fair-haired boy" of the military, Colonel George Armstrong Custer. Custer was undoubtedly the most picturesque and charismatic army officer of the era. He was over six feet tall, slim, and broad shouldered. He swaggered when he walked and wore his golden hair past his shoulders. His entire life was a reckless pursuit of glory. With his long blond hair flying behind him as he rode, Custer supervised the slaughter of the chief and his tribe at the Washita. His fame for this encounter came from a widely publicized exaggerated report he wrote that failed to mention that, of the 103 Cheyenne killed, only eleven were warriors. The rest were women and children. Many whites justified such actions by dehumanizing Native Americans. Oregon whites who hanged a seven-year-old Indian child echoed a widely held view that, "nits breed lice."

A new Board of Indian Commissioners, created in 1869, attempted to undermine the collective nature of Indian life, weaken tribal structure, and force the people to assimilate into white culture by becoming farmers. President Grant favored a policy of

Custer first distinguished himself during the Civil War. At the Battle of Washita, Custer defeated Black Kettle's Cheyennes. The battle marked the culmination of the campaign against the Indians of the southern Great Plains.

pacifying the natives through peace overtures rather than battles. This was known as "Quaker Policy," because of the number of Quakers (and other church people) involved in its implementation. The poor quality of the land on reservations and the Indians' view of farming as "women's work" undercut their efforts. Another problem lay in the management of Indian concerns by the Bureau of Indian Affairs. The agents, who gained their jobs through political patronage, were often corrupt and incompetent. Even the best of them had little understanding of tribal culture. The Indians, in effect on welfare and totally dependent on the government, received rotten meat, spoiled flour, and threadbare blankets. It became harder and harder to keep them on the reservations.

The Northern plains were the domain of the Sioux, the one tribe that had never suffered a major defeat at the hands of whites. Poor conditions on their Dakota reservation became even more intolerable when miners invaded sacred lands in the Black Hills. The miners were drawn by rumors that there was "gold in the grass roots." One Indian lamented, "The white man is in the Black Hills just like maggots." As the Sioux resisted the trespassers, the whites

demanded government protection. The government, following its customary policy of resorting to force, ordered all hostile Sioux back to their reservation or face punishment. Bands of warriors, under the leadership of Crazy Horse and Sitting Bull, gathered in Montana. Numbering between 2,500 and 4,000, it was one of the largest Indian armies ever formed in North America. Three army columns arrived to round them up. The glory-seeking Custer led the Seventh Cavalry. He firmly believed that his men could beat any Plains Indians and that this might be his "lucky turn" to achieve renown. Custer's attitude towards Native Americans was apparent in his *My Life on the Plains*. He described the Indian as "a savage in every sense of the word...one whose cruel and ferocious nature far exceeds any wild beast of the desert."

Although his scouts reported large numbers of hostile Indians in the area, Custer believed that he could strike a quick and decisive blow as he had at Washita. Perhaps fearful that he might have to share some of the accolades, Custer did not wait for the other parts of the expected three-prong attack. His grandiosity led him to deny his troops any reasonable rest and to fail to order the most basic recon-naissance. On June 25, 1876, Custer ordered a charge at the Little Big Horn River against an Indian force that outnumbered his by more than eight to one. The Sioux benefitted from the superior generalship of Crazy Horse, rallying to the cry, "It's a good day to die!" Taking no prisoners, all 260 soldiers were annihilated. Word of "Custer's Last Stand," burst into headlines to an astounded public on July 5, 1876, the day after the nation's great centennial celebration. The defeat, described as a "massacre," led to a general cry for revenge against the Indians. The *New York Times* reported, "It is agreed on all hands that there must now be an Indian war till the hostile Indians of the Northwest have been chastised and subjugated." Despite the sensation, this famous Indian victory was short-lived. The Indians discovered, as one historian has commented, that "the slaying of a big white chief could spell the doom of a people." Within a few months, lacking food, supplies, and unity, the hostile bands of Sioux and Cheyenne were broken up, surrounded, and defeated. Most moved into reservations where disease, starvation, and alcohol succeeded in diminishing their numbers and destroying their spirit. Sitting Bull and a handful of his followers escaped into Canada. But, in 1881, he chose to return to his people on the reservation.

In the Southwest, tribesmen known as hunters and warriors resisted the narrow confinements of windswept desert reservations. For seventeen years there was almost continuous warfare with the Apaches whom Westerners saw as particularly tricky, fierce, and slippery. In 1871, a group of angry ranchers slaughtered over a hundred sleeping Apaches and captured twenty-nine children who they sold as slaves to rival tribes. These murders horrified Easterners. President Grant threatened to place Arizona under martial law if the murderers were not brought to trial. Local authorities arrested the leaders of the group and quickly acquitted them.

Meanwhile, leading generals attempted to persuade the Apaches to surrender peacefully. One tough-minded old warrior, Cochise, agreed to peace in exchange for a reservation that included some traditional tribal land. After his death, however, his

tribe found themselves increasingly frustrated by pressures to assimilate and by the famine that resulted from inadequate rations. One leader of the Chiricahua Apaches, Geronimo, established mountain bases in Arizona and Mexico and led raids against white outposts for more than a decade. By 1886, Geronimo's tiny band numbered no more than thirty-six, even though they had kept more than five thousand soldiers occupied with their lightening-fast tactics. The government spent about $1 million for every Apache killed. Finally, Apache scouts talked Geronimo into surrendering. He and his followers were sent to a Florida reservation. Later, he was transferred to Fort Sill, Oklahoma, where he became quite a celebrity. Described by one observer as "half clown and half monster," he enjoyed riding in Wild West shows and parades, wearing a high silk hat. He made a living selling souvenir bows and arrows to impressionable tourists. He died in 1909. A legend arose that his bones were secretly removed and taken to the mountains he loved. His fame was revived in World War II when American parachuters shouted his name as they jumped from their planes. Geronimo's surrender marked the end of formal warfare between whites and Native Americans.

Wounded Knee: The Final "Battle"

The success of the government in forcing Indians onto reservations meant that the old economic system and, with it, the traditional culture were in danger of extinction. Civilizations facing such crises often turn in hope to a messiah. The prophet many turned to was a Paiute Indian named Wovoka. While living with the family of a white rancher, Wovoka had studied the Bible and learned of the miraculous powers of the white medicine man, Jesus. During an eclipse of the sun in 1889, he experienced a vision in which God told him that he was the Indian messiah. When pilgrims from Western reservations journeyed to his lodge for inspiration, Wovoka showed them scars on his hand where whites had nailed him to a cross many centuries ago. He preached a spiritual reawakening in which the mystical "Ghost Dance," performed by ecstatic masses of Indians, would hasten the return of dead relatives.

Wovoka, the Paiute prophet

ans. When one hidden gun was fired by an Indian (It is not clear whether accidentally or on purpose.), the nervous soldiers turned their new Hotchkiss machine guns at point-blank range on the Indians. They mowed the Indians down in the snow, where an approaching blizzard froze the bodies. The next day they were thrown into a mass grave. The wounded, four men and forty-seven women and children, were carried to a local missionary church where they lay beneath a banner declaring, "Peace on Earth; Good Will to Men." Three days later, the cleanup troops found a baby beneath the snow, wrapped in a blanket and wearing a buckskin cap with a beadwork embroidery of the American flag. Incredibly, she was still alive. General L. W. Colby, commander of the troops at Wounded Knee, adopted her and named her Marguerite. The Indians dubbed her Lost Bird.

The cavalry believed that Custer was finally avenged. Congress gave special medals to the soldiers for their roles in this last "military engagement." Frank Baum, who ten years later wrote *The Wizard*

These ghosts would drive out the whites, bring back the buffalo, and restore the old way of life. Participants also wore "ghost shirts," decorated with mystical designs and conferring invulnerability to the white man's bullets. The proud Sioux, their glories fading and close to starvation, were particularly committed followers of Wovoka. Dancing was so widespread on Sioux reservations that virtually all other activities were halted.

Alarmed settlers and Indian agents, believing that the rapturous dancing might lead to renewed conflict, sought to suppress it by calling in troops. In the melees that followed, an Indian policeman killed the old chief, Sitting Bull. Worried that this might result in Indian resistance, the Seventh Cavalry (Custer's old regiment) tried to round up more than three hundred cold and hungry Sioux. The group had left the reservation and camped at Wounded Knee, South Dakota, December 29, 1890. The troops surrounded the band, two-thirds of whom were women and children, and disarmed the Indi-

**Brigadier General L. W. Colby,
commander of the troops at Wounded Knee, holds his
adopted Indian daughter, Marguerite, whose parents
had been killed in the massacre.**

of Oz, noted approvingly that whites were now "masters of the American continent." He proposed that the few "miserable wretches" who remained among the Indians would be better off with "total annihilation." Forty years later, Black Elk, a Sioux holy man, recalled Wounded Knee: "I can still see the butchered women and children lying heaped and scattered....And I can see that something else died there in the bloody mud, and was buried in the blizzard. A people's dream died there." On December 29, 1890, one historian commented, "the Indian frontier of the American West vanished in the smoke of Hotchkiss shells bursting over the valley of Wounded Knee Creek."

The Reformers and Their Vision

Some Americans were appalled by the consequences of the army's "victories" over the Indians. Public sympathy had been aroused by such events as Chief Joseph's dramatic plea to be allowed to return to his homeland in the Northwest and the tragic attempt by Dull Knife's Cheyennes to escape from Indian Territory and return to their old home in Montana, only to be gunned down by soldiers. Native Americans appeared to be on the brink of extinction, their population declining rapidly, their game gone, their land taken. Arapaho dancers mournfully sang:

My Father have pity on me!
I have nothing to eat,
I am dying of thirst—
Everything is gone.

The destruction of independence, traditional authority, and culture led many Indians to turn to alcohol to escape bleak reality. Others followed peyotism in using the powerful drug to experience sensational dreams and a heightened feeling of personal worth. Some turned to a revival of the Sun Dance, which involved days of fasting, dancing, and self-mutilation through skewers in the skin of the chest to achieve oneness with the Great Spirit.

The end of any real danger from the Indians allowed some people to demonstrate greater tolerance and sympathy. Prominent whites were alarmed by the catastrophe they believed stemmed from humiliating dependency and pagan practices. They formed reform organizations like the Indian Rights Association. Helen Hunt Jackson was a particularly pas-

Slaughtered frozen bodies of the Sioux at Wounded Knee were piled like cordwood.

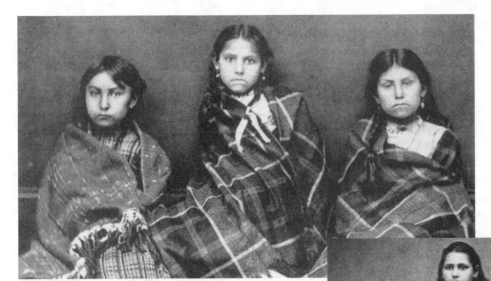

The Hampton Institute in Virginia took these before and after photographs of three young Crow Indian girls who had been sent East from their reservation. They had been "civilized" with a book, new dresses, a doll, and checkers.

sionate crusader for Indian rights. She hoped that her 1881 book, *A Century of Dishonor*, would awaken the public to the hardships of Indians in the same way that *Uncle Tom's Cabin* had done thirty years earlier to the plight of slaves. Her book, while not as huge a best seller as that earlier novel, was widely read and did arouse the public conscience. Three years later, her romanticized novel, *Ramona*, about the tragic annihilation of the California Indians, also was enormously popular. Despite being dismissed by Theodore Roosevelt as "foolish sentimentalists," the reformers were gaining influence.

The paternalistic vision of these white liberals rested on the desire to Americanize the Indians by stripping them of their cultural heritage, converting them to Christianity, educating them in English, and preparing them to function in a white capitalist economy. Then, these reformers were confident, white hostility would disappear. The first step would be to "individualize" or "detribalize" Native Americans. They would be taught individual responsibility and labor, according to the Protestant work ethic. Then, they could break free of the tribe that held them back and jump into the mainstream of American life.

The first step in this process would be to hasten the breakup of the reservations and of tribal lands by allotting small farms to individual Indians. Sensing the possibilities of great profit, land speculators supported the reformers. After all, as one Indian Commissioner observed, it seemed a shame that public lands, rich in resources and waiting to be farmed "in obedience to the divine command, can long be kept simply as a park, in which wild beasts are hunted by wilder men." Jubilant reformers hailed the passage of the Dawes Act in 1887 that envisioned the creation of Indian yeoman farmers. One reformer compared the act to the Magna Charta, the Declaration of Independence, and the Emancipation Proclamation, all in one! Under this law, the president could divide tribal lands, giving 160 acres to each head of family and smaller allotments to single Indians. To protect the Indians from being fleeced, the Bureau of Indian Affairs would hold the land in trust for twenty-five years. After allotments, "surplus" reservation lands could be sold to whites.

What reformers failed to understand was that even though reservation policy had been a failure, its original purpose, at least, had been to set up boundaries that not only limited Indians but also restricted white access. They did not foresee the consequences of the Dawes Act. The disastrous result was the loss of more than 60 million "surplus" acres by Indian tribes. The 2,000 Sisseton Sioux of South Dakota, for instance, lived on a reservation of 918,000 acres of rich farmland. After allotment, more than 600,000 surplus acres remained and were opened to white farmers. The settlers rapidly moved in among these Sioux and destroyed any remaining tribal culture. Later laws enabled greedy speculators to buy allotted land, often at ridiculously low prices. Some forty years after the passage of the Dawes Act, Indians retained only one-third of the land they had held in 1887, much of it of poor quality.

Education went side by side with individual land ownership as a key element of reformers' ideology. They believed it would provide the transition from savagery to civilization. Schools provided instruction in English, manual and agricultural skills, American patriotism, and Christianity. An Indian pupil in one of the schools clearly described its goals. "I believe in education," he said, "because I believe it will kill the Indian that is in me and leave the man and the citizen." As a result of reformist pressures, the federal government appropriated more than a million dollars for Indian education by 1887. When schools on reservations did not seem to be effective in assimilating Indians, nonreservation boarding schools were set up to remove Indian children, sometimes forcibly, from the tribal environment. Navaho children were chained to rusty pipes to discourage them from using their native language. These schools were patterned on the Carlisle Indian School in Penn-

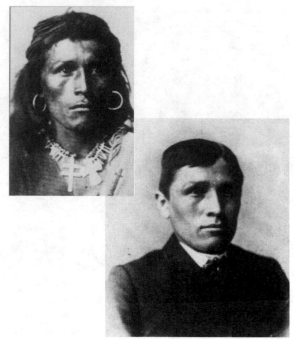

A Navajo Indian before and after his "assimilation" into the Carlisle Indian School in Pennsylvania

sylvania. This school followed a policy of "total immersion" in white civilization and ruthless assimilation. While the Carlisle school displayed its most successful graduates at world's fairs and exhibitions, most found themselves misfits in dress and attitudes when they returned to their old reservations. Some left the reservation, but most returned to their old way of life. (During World War II, the American military was grateful that Navahos had clung to their native language. The Japanese were never able to break the "code" broadcast by Navaho radiomen.) Reformers, who had naively expected the rapid obliteration of Native American culture, were astonished at its tenacity. Despite the poverty, disease, and unemployment endemic on the reservations, Indians remained stubbornly loyal to old tribal ways.

One historian commented, "Except for the internment of the...Japanese during World War II, Indian removal is the only example of large-scale government-enforced migration in American history. For the Japanese, the move was temporary; for the Indians it was not." Even as their lives became increasingly difficult, Indians became part of the romantic folklore of the West. Dime novels recounted tales of Indian fighting on the Plains. Wild West shows, started by Buffalo Bill Cody in 1883, featured Plains Indians attacking innocent whites and their inevitable and well-deserved defeats. The shows began with Wild Bill Hickok galloping on stage, shooting Indians who menaced beautiful heroines while declaiming, "Fear not, fair maid; by heavens you are safe at last with Wild Bill, who is ever ready to risk his life...in defense of weak and helpless womanhood." Thus, the story of the Indian wars was rewritten to make the whites blameless victims of Indian aggression. In 1885, Cody prevailed on Sitting Bull to join his show. The chief drew tremendous crowds, many of whom gave him money for copies of his signed photograph. He returned to his reservation with two gifts from Buffalo Bill—an enormous white sombrero and a performing horse. It is said that when Sitting Bull was killed the old show horse went through his tricks, seeming to onlookers to be performing the Ghost Dance, and then galloped off into the hills, never to be seen again.

MIGRATION TO THE WEST

Waves of new settlers poured into the West from other parts of the United States and from overseas. They came on the heels of earlier migration that had brought California and Oregon into the Union as states before 1860. While these settlers had arrived by the thousands before the Civil War, after the war they numbered in the millions. They spread rapidly over the immense western territories. With the same kind of thoroughness they had demonstrated in the annihilation of both buffalo and Indians, they systematically exploited the natural resources of the West. The mountains and plains, they discovered, were rich in minerals such as gold, silver, lead, zinc, iron, coal, and copper. There were pasture lands suitable for grazing cattle and sheep and some of the world's most productive farm lands. Most of these migrants were white Anglo-Americans who left established communities in the older sections of the country, but other people came as well. Between 1870 and 1900 over two million foreign-born im-

migrants also made their way to the West. Many of these were German, British, or Scandinavian farmers. Others came from Ireland, China, and Eastern Europe to find work. African Americans also sought a better life in the land of seemingly boundless opportunities.

Chinese Immigrants

At the same period in which millions of Europeans crossed the Atlantic in search of new opportunities in the East, thousands of Chinese left their impoverished homeland to cross the Pacific for a better life on the "Golden Mountain" in the West. The first group had come in the 1840s and 1850s to look for gold after the California gold discovery. Discriminatory laws and the hostility of white miners drove most of them away from prospecting. Some worked sites abandoned by white miners. The shift to hydraulic extraction, financed by large eastern corporations, led many Chinese to accept jobs as hired laborers in the mines. Others became servants, laundry workers, and restaurant owners.

After the Civil War, as jobs in mining declined, railroad work became the largest source of employment. Over twelve thousand found jobs building the first transcontinental railroad. These Chinese laborers made up 90 percent of the workforce on the Central Pacific Railroad, building the line from San Francisco to Utah. The railroad company, like many businesses, preferred Chinese laborers because they worked for very modest wages and made few demands. One employer testified before a California Senate committee: "I find this difference: the Chinaman will stay and work, but the white man, as soon as he gets a few dollars, will leave and go elsewhere." Many had been recruited for railroad work in China. When they arrived, they were organized into work gangs under Chinese supervisors. The greatest challenge was the climb up the Pacific slope of the Sierras where tunnels had to be cut through granite cliffs and 40 miles of snowsheds were constructed. The Central Pacific did little to protect its workers from dangerous conditions or from the elements. In the winter, many workers dug shelters in snow banks to find some warmth. These makeshift refuges often collapsed and smothered those trapped inside, but the work continued.

When the first transcontinental railroad was finished in 1869, Chinese workers found jobs on the Southern Pacific Railroad, building dams and irrigation systems, and as the first migratory workers on the large wheat and fruit farms of California. Others established modest farms or set up fishing villages along the Pacific coast. Even more migrated to "Chinatowns" in Western cities, the largest of which was in San Francisco. By 1880, there were 200,000 Chinese in America. Almost all of them lived in the Far West, three-quarters in California.

The specter of "hordes" of Chinese entering the United States rapidly became a heated issue. The New York *World* announced that, "Asiatics are cunning, treacherous and vicious, possessing no conception of American civilization." The paper worried that the western states were "degenerating into Chinese colonies," making any further Chinese immigration "disastrous" to the American way of life.

These fears were increased by the life style of these "exotic" immigrants. Most saw their move to America as a temporary step to secure some wealth and return to their villages in China where they would gain respect and wives. As a result, they brought few women with them (Only 1 in 20 Chinese immigrants was female.), and some of those were prostitutes. Their "bachelor" communities were self-contained. Lives revolved around clan organizations led by wealthy merchants. These groups, like the "Six Companies" of San Francisco, helped meet the social and welfare needs of the poorer immigrants. The *tongs* were independent secret societies that were sometimes involved in criminal activities, particularly prostitution and the opium trade.

Many Americans were frightened by the presence of these nonwhite, nonChristian males. They believed that Chinese men had sexual designs on white women. Chinese "opium dens" seemed far more sinister than the bars popular with white American workingmen. The depression of the 1870s added

The joining of the Union Pacific and Central Pacific Railroads on May 10, 1869 at Promontory, Utah changed life in America. Coast-to-coast travel was possible for the first time.

to the hostility. California was hit particularly hard as land values slumped, gold output from the mines continued to decline, and a lull in railroad construction brought thousands of unemployed Chinese workers back to the state. "Anti-coolie" clubs attacked Chinese workers in the streets. Mobs in Los Angeles lynched fifteen Chinese men and burned homes. Vigilantes in Chico, California murdered Chinese, and a San Francisco riot burned down many Chinese laundries. The worst incident occurred in Rock Springs, Wyoming when frenzied white miners massacred fifty-one Chinese and expelled hundreds more. The Workingmen's Party was formed in San Francisco in 1878 by Denis Kearney, an Irish immigrant. The party charged that the Chinese were stealing all the available jobs. Its manifesto proclaimed, "Treason is better than to labor beside a Chinese slave." Other groups, arguing that the Chinese were "unassimilable," demanded that they be excluded from the country.

Congress responded to this western pressure by passing the Chinese Exclusion Act in 1882, banning future Chinese immigration. In the next forty years, Chinese population in America declined by 40 percent. Western corporations were forced to look elsewhere for cheap labor.

Hispanics in the West

For three centuries most of the Far West had been a part of the Spanish Empire in the New World and then of the Mexican Republic. As a result of the Mexican War, the United States in 1848 had acquired not only a vast additional territory but also almost eighty thousand new citizens. These Mexican Americans were now seen as a "colored," Spanish-speaking, Catholic minority group in a society overwhelmingly white, Protestant, and English-speaking. Spanish-speaking communities, scattered throughout the Southwest, were rapidly altered by the migration of Anglo-Americans and the expansion of the capitalist economy into their areas.

The old Spanish elite quickly lost both their influence and their land. Mexican residents of California once owned 15 million acres of land. Vast numbers of English-speaking immigrants poured into the region, occupying their lands. The completion of the Southern Pacific Railroad in 1876 brought thousands more. The outnumbered Mexican Americans were unable to counter endless litigation and fraud that stripped them of their property. By the 1880s few still owned their own land. In New Mexico, the Santa Fe Ring, a clique of white bankers and merchants, used heavy property taxes to force Mexican-American landowners to sell their land at bargain prices. The ring quickly gained control of several million acres of land. In Texas, increasing white claims on grazing and farming land to meet world demand for beef, sheep, and cotton led to a similar pattern of fraud and intimidation. The southern Protestants who settled Texas were particularly prejudiced against the "colored" *tejanos* (Mexicans). The famed Texas Rangers helped enforce white control and land claims. Historians have estimated that the Rangers killed almost five thousand Mexican Americans in the 1800s. Some of these may have been criminals, others revolutionary *banditos*, but many were simply tejanos whom whites wanted to "dislodge" from the land.

Mexican Americans increasingly became part of the working class in city *barrios* (ghettos) or as migrant farm workers. By 1900, the growth of large commercial farms with heavy investments in sophisticated equipment and irrigation systems priced most of the remaining small Mexican-American farmers out of the business. The use of irrigation and fertilizers caused a threefold increase in farm acreage in the Southwest between 1870 and 1900. At the same time, the dynamic economy, bolstered by the railroads, attracted new waves of Mexican immigrants. They poured across the unregulated border by the thousands in search of new opportunities. The passage of the Chinese Exclusion Act led many growers and businessmen to recruit Mexican laborers.

The new migrants, like the old Hispanic residents, came to a society in which they were subordinate to whites and restricted to the lowest paying jobs. In some places, particularly in Texas, they faced the literacy tests and poll taxes that had already denied voting rights to blacks in the South. They often attended segregated schools. The paternalistic, extended family that had once been part of Hispanic culture faced serious challenges in the new society. The weakened Mexican-American community was not well prepared to confront a western society dominated by the push for progress and modernization.

Other Minorities in the West

The perception of greater opportunities and a more open society in the West attracted many migrants from other groups. Irish workmen came to lay railroad track. Most of the laborers on the Union Pacific, running West from Omaha, Nebraska to Utah, were Irish. Many, more adventurous Irishmen headed west to seek their fortunes as miners or ranchers. Richard King, the son of poor Irish immigrants, founded the King Ranch in south Texas. He bought his original holding of 15,000 acres for two cents an acre. With the help of obliging Texas Rangers, who enforced his often fraudulent land claims, he was able to increase his holding to 600,000 acres. Marcus Daly, a formerly penniless Irish immigrant, established the Anaconda copper mines in Montana and filled his work force with Irish miners. He socialized with his workmen and was popular as a fair employer. Most Irish who came west, however, remained in working class jobs and concentrated in cities.

Just as German Jews had done before them, some Eastern European Jews came west, ready to take risks for better opportunities. A few attempted to found agricultural colonies in North Dakota or in the cooperative community of New Odessa, Oregon, with minimal success. Others took up peddling or ran small businesses. Jews experienced greater social mobility in the West than in the older sections of America. One example was the Madanic family that came from Russia in 1889. After toiling in the sweatshops, they saved enough money to open a reasonably successful clothing store in Illinois. By 1908, they moved to the boomtown of Tulsa, Oklahoma. Their business was so successful there that they were able to open branches in nearby towns. Eventually, they changed their name to the May Brothers, and their stores spread throughout the country. The record of most European pioneer immigrant groups demonstrated that economic success was attainable

and social integration possible, particularly in their children's generation.

African Americans, disillusioned by the failure of Reconstruction, hoped to find the opportunities to farm their own land that they had been denied in the South. Some three hundred of these "Exodusters" were attracted to Nicodemus in northwest Kansas by handbills that read, "All Colored People that want to GO TO KANSAS, on September 5th, 1877, Can do so for $5.00." By 1879, "Kansas Fever" had even spread to desperately poor black families in the lower South. These black settlers had fewer resources than whites and got little or no support from the institutions of local society in the West. Even when their communities survived, they rarely prospered. In the 1880s, a substantial minority of the cowboys working in Texas and Oklahoma, perhaps as many as 25 percent, were African Americans. Some of the famous gunfighters of Western legend were black, including "Deadeye Dick" and "Isom Dart." The peacetime American army, much of it stationed in the West, attracted a large number of black Civil War veterans. Many of these became part of the regiments known as "Buffalo Soldiers," which played a significant role in the Indian wars. San Francisco was the home of the black leaders of the Pacific Coast area. They led an eventually successful 20-year struggle to open the schools to their children and held equal rights conventions. Most of the substantial number of African Americans in the West, however, were laborers seeking work. A household in Tombstone, Arizona, in 1880 was typical. It consisted of a 30-year-old South Carolinian laborer and his younger wife, and eight black men in their 30s and 40s who were blacksmiths, cooks, waiters, and laborers.

Western workers tended to be single, highly mobile, men. Single women often worked in dance halls or as prostitutes. Although Americans perceived of the West as the section of boundless opportunity, real social mobility was no greater than that of the older sections of the country. Those who most rapidly succeeded generally were people who were well off before they arrived. The Western labor force was amazingly multiracial. Even more than in the East, white Anglo-Saxon Americans worked alongside blacks, Chinese, Mexicans, Indians, and immigrants from eastern and southern Europe. But this work force was also racially stratified. Those who did the unskilled and most strenuous jobs in the mines, farms, and on the railroads usually were nonwhites. The limited mobility into more skilled or supervisory jobs was reserved for white workers. An Irish unskilled laborer might expect, over the years, to move up to slightly better work. A Mexican, African-American, or Chinese worker could not look forward to the same opportunity.

THE MINING FRONTIER

The first great economic boom in the Far West occurred in mining, and miners were generally among the advance guard in the frontier. The mining boom had a relatively brief life-span, but its impact was enormous. It encouraged settlement, caused the creation of governments and laws, stimulated transportation, and enticed both capital and labor to the West.

The mining rushes followed the pattern of the 1849 California Gold Rush. A prospector would discover nuggets or dust that had been washed into streams or rivers by the forces of erosion. The news spread quickly to other miners who stampeded into the area searching for a bonanza. The early arrivals found easy pickings, using large metal pans. A handful of prospectors might find as much as $8,000 in gold a day, but most were lucky to end up with an ounce of gold ($16). The initial discoveries played out quickly. Within a few years, as surface yields dwindled, corporations entered the picture to find the veins of gold hidden in rocks and hills. They could pay for the costly heavy machinery and hydraulic mining that brought up the ore hidden beneath the surface. Some disillusioned prospectors took jobs as miners for the big companies, but thousands of others surged to the next strike and the continuing dream of instant wealth.

The first great mineral rush after the California Gold Rush occurred in Colorado just before the Civil War (1859). Thousands poured into the region with the slogan, "Pike's Peak or Bust," painted on the canvas of their wagons. The boom helped make cities out of mining camps, particularly Denver. The placer (surface) boom rapidly fell on hard times. Soon disappointed miners trekked back home with a new slogan, "Busted by Gosh!" Others stayed on and took

African-American cavalrymen were not treated as well as white soldiers.

jobs in shaft mining or tried their hands at farming or grazing. Later, gold was found at Cripple Creek, and a rich bed of silver was discovered at Leadville. The "Mile High City" of Denver became the prosperous center for smelting ore from throughout the Rockies and for the production of mining equipment. By 1876, Colorado gained admission to the union as the Centennial State.

Even before the first Colorado boom ended, news of another strike in Nevada sent miners swarming into the treeless and waterless Washoe Mountains. Two Irishmen found the Ophir silver vein, the richest in history. (The find was called the Comstock Lode after the lackadaisical Henry Comstock who claimed a share of the profits based on his supposed ownership of the stream where the silver was found.) The boomtown of Virginia City quickly emerged at this forlorn site. Although there were no railroads and no means to produce supplies, entrepreneurs rapidly organized to ship everything from equipment and food to prostitutes and liquor from California. The silver in this fabulous strike was embedded in quartz, so crushing machinery was required to reach the treasure.

The big mines needed blasting, drilling, and timbering (building huge wooden bunkers to prevent the mountain from caving in). After twelve substantial strikes, the greatest of all, the "Big Bonanza," took place in 1873. One company, excavating 1,167 feet, found a 54-feet wide vein filled with gold and silver. The $200 million this vein produced created the "Kings of the Comstock." George Hearst from California, father of the newspaper mogul, William Randolph Hearst, was one of these. He and his partners took their huge profits with them back to San Francisco where they built spectacular mansions.

The merchants, bankers, and mine owners erected lavish homes that looked down on the flashy town of Virginia City, which had grown to twenty thousand. They sat on their porches sipping champagne, as Irish, Welsh, Cornish, German, and Mexican miners toiled in the tunnels far below. In the depth of these mines, the working conditions were horrible. The intense heat of over 100 degrees made it difficult to work for more than a few minutes at a time. Cooling stations had tubs of ice and towels that were dipped in ice water and thrown on the miners' bodies. The tunnels filled with the stench of unwashed bodies, blasting powder, rotting timber, and human waste. (There were no toilets.) Tunnel floods, cave-ins, explosions, and accidents were commonplace. In view of the great risk involved, the miners earned $4 a day, decent pay for a workingman. Eventually, even this fabulous source of ore played out, and the price of silver suffered sharp declines. The great mines of the Comstock Lode closed. By the 1890s, Virginia City was a ghost town.

This pattern was repeated in every subsequent strike. Gold was discovered in 1874 in the Black Hills on the Sioux reservation. By 1876, the army gave up any effort to keep the prospectors out. Before long, there were 25,000 people in Deadwood, South Dakota, a town that rivaled Tombstone, Arizona as the toughest in the West. As in other booms, the surface resources quickly disappeared, and a big corporation took over. After ore worth $287 million had been extracted in a remarkably short time, the population rapidly declined, and Deadwood passed into the realm of legend. The Dakotas eventually developed into an agricultural economy.

Other, less exciting, resources ultimately proved to be even more important in the development of the West. Marcus Daly was disappointed when he found out that his Anaconda silver mine contained copper and only small amounts of silver. But his mood turned to joy when he realized that it was one of the largest and purest copper deposits ever discovered. "The Richest Hill on Earth" made millionaires out of Daly and several other investors. Access to railroads enabled Anaconda to market its vast deposits. Copper from Montana played an important role in the miles of electric wiring that were powering factories and lighting cities in both America and Europe. The "Copper Kings" of Montana were involved in continuous conflicts to win control of the state's economy and government, along with its copper output. Eventually, as greater and greater investments were needed to build huge electric generating plants and smelting facilities, Eastern investors with ties to Standard Oil took control. In other places, lead, tin, quartz, and zinc mining proved to be profitable. In 1901, just before the advent of the automobile, Black Gold gushed from the Spindletop fields in Texas, creating the most lucrative industry of all, the oil industry.

The constant danger, lack of safety devices, and terrible discomfort in the mines created a sense of beleaguered brotherhood among many of the miners. They began to form unions to aid the injured and demand better working conditions. In an 1892 Idaho miners' strike, state and federal troops were called in to break up the strike. Seven miners were killed in the resulting melee. The Western Federation of Miners (WFM) had its headquarters in the copper town of Butte, Montana, the "Gibraltar of Unionism." Within a decade, the WFM had over 50,000 members in the region. It became the base for the far more militant Industrial Workers of the World (IWW). The unwillingness of the mining corporations to even discuss issues with their workers and their tendency to call for troops to end strikes led to escalating violence. Despite these labor problems, however, mining created the wealth that laid the grounds for an expanding economy.

THE CATTLE KINGDOM

As prospectors rushed westward to seek their fortunes, cattlemen began moving into the Great Plains. They were attracted by the open range, the expansive grasslands in the public domain where herds could graze without charge, unfettered by the boundaries of private property. The rapid growth of population in northern markets increased the prices offered for steers. Even before the Civil War, there were five million head of wild Texas longhorn roaming the Texas range. These were descendants of stock imported by Spanish colonists. Steers valued at $4 a head in Texas, where they attracted few buyers, sold for $30 to $50 in Chicago. Fortunes, equal to those attainable by miners, could be made by those who could bring the cattle to market. The only issue was how to get them there.

Long before America annexed Texas, the Mexican *vaquero*, the predecessor of the American cowboy, had developed techniques and equipment to capture and herd cattle. These included roundups

and ropings and much of the distinctive cowboy gear, including lariats, saddles, spurs, chaps, and even the five-gallon hat. The coming of the railroad inspired cattlemen to risk a cross-country drive of their stock to the railroad town of Sedalia, Missouri in 1866. In this first "long drive," 260,000 steers were driven north. They were beset by cattle rustlers, Indians, gun-totting farmers trying to protect their crops, and stampedes. Only a fraction of the herd ever arrived in Sedalia, but those that did sold for $35 a head. This inspired other ranchers to try their luck.

A shrewd young Illinois meat dealer, Joseph McCoy, realized that he could make his fortune by providing a place where buyers and breeders could do business. He picked the insignificant little town of Abilene, Kansas. Its main advantage was that it lay on the Kansas Pacific railroad line that ultimately connected to Chicago. There, he built stock pens, stables, railroad loading facilities, and a hotel. By 1868, 75,000 head of cattle arrived in Abilene, and, within a few years, the numbers increased enormously. The arrival of cowboys soon led to the construction of saloons, gambling parlors, and houses of prostitution. Wild Bill Hickok became famous as a fast shooting marshal in this cow town.

As railroads expanded, other cattle towns developed. The most famous was Dodge City on the Santa Fe Railroad. It was called the "Cowboy Capital," particularly in the decade from 1875-85. At its height, 250,000 cattle arrived each year. It also supported the usual assortment of drunks and reckless adventurers, many of whom ended up in the celebrated Boot Hill Cemetery.

The long drive was an amazing sight, so it is understandable that it became the most romanticized sector of western life. In the spring, cattlemen rounded up their herds from the open range. Calves were branded and turned loose with their mothers to pasture. Year-old steers were combined with those of other herds. Then, accompanied by a dozen or so cowboys, the herd of three thousand was moved north at a rate of 300 to 500 miles a month. The cattle wore furrows on the trail so deep that they continued to be visible for years. Despite the myths that grew up about picturesque cowboys, the work, in the words of a veteran of the drive, was a "tire-

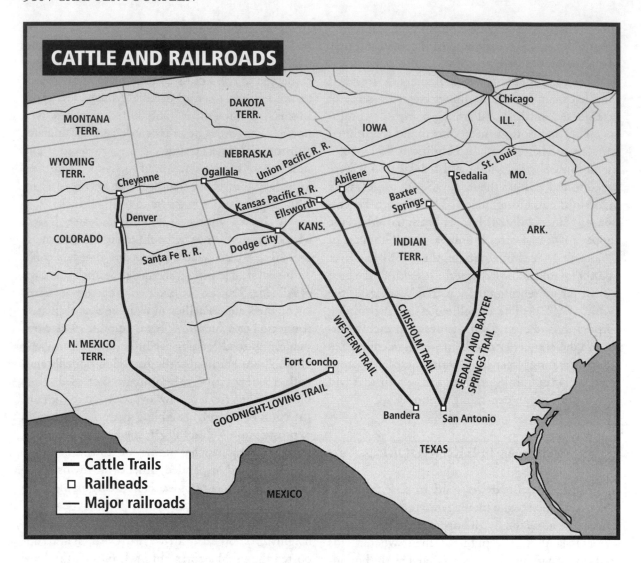

CATTLE AND RAILROADS

some, grimy business for the attendant punchers, who traveled ever in a cloud of dust," with the "constant chorus...from the bellows, lows and bleats of the trudging animals." Despite his romantic image that captured the imagination of Easterners, the cowboy was, in reality, a poorly paid ($25 to $40 a month) worker whose life was hard and monotonous. Few were good shots. Many (at least a third) were Mexicans or blacks, even though they were invariably portrayed in popular legend as white. When Texas cowboys struck for higher wages, the cattlemen crushed their strike. The cattle companies began replacing Anglo cowboys with Mexicans who were given only one-half to two-thirds of the pay.

A successful drive could produce very substantial profits of 40 percent or more. Despite the risks of "Texas fever," a deadly cattle disease, rustlers, Indians, and natural disasters, Eastern and European investors were tempted by dreams of amazing profits. (British investors alone poured some $45 million into the cattle industry in the 1870s and 80s, owning some 20 million acres of grazing land.) The old free-wheeling stockman was rapidly being replaced by large corporations. Businessmen realized that the tough, scrawny longhorns, derided as "8 pounds of hamburger on 800 pounds of bone and horn," were perfect for enduring the long drive but not as suitable to producing tender, juicy steaks. And the long trip did not improve the quality of the meat.

Ranchers began to breed longhorns with better quality imported stock in permanent and fenced ranches.

The long drive was also doomed by the same railroads that had made the drive possible in the first place. They brought thousands of farmers to the plains. These permanent settlers objected to cattle breaking down their fences and trampling their crops. They retaliated by enclosing their homesteads with barbed wire that was deadly to onrushing cattle and by persuading state legislatures to pass laws designed to limit the entrance of the herds. Sheepherders also came to the range in large numbers. Contemptuous cattlemen wrongly argued that sheep spoiled the water and destroyed the grass by eating its roots as well. The sheep owners were often immigrants or nonwhites. Cattlemen believed sheep were "inferior animals herded by inferior men." Eventually, the sheep outnumbered the cattle. Bloody, armed conflicts erupted between sheepmen and cattlemen, between farmers and ranchers, and among arrogant cattle barons for control of an area. In one such episode, the 1892 Johnson County War, the Wyoming Stock Growers Association hired gunmen to eliminate small ranchers they accused of rustling.

Other forces were even more devastating. The feverish, speculative expansion led to overcrowding on ranges reduced by actions of farmers and government. President Cleveland, for example, evicted herds of cattle trespassing on land in the Indian Territory. By 1884, 20 million cattle grazed the American West. Supply was greatly outpacing demand, and the price of beef began a precipitous decline. Nature then delivered the final crushing blow. Two terrible winters of blizzards in 1885-6 and 1886-7, with a blistering, scorching summer between them, devastated the plains. Thousands of cattle piled up and died. Grass and streams dried up. Cattle raisers rushed their weakened and often emaciated steers into the declining market to salvage what they could from the disaster. In Chicago, the price of beef plummeted from $9.35 per hundred pounds in 1882 to $1 in 1887. The old Cattle Kingdom died. But the better run companies that had centralized and modernized survived the bad times. They had fenced in grazing land, raised hay for winter feed, and upgraded their stock. Their cowboys increasingly became workers who were just as liable to build fences, dig irrigation ditches, and cut hay as to ride herd. Eventually, the ranchers produced more beef than ever, although they continued to depend on public lands for grazing and federal projects to bring them irrigation.

Boom Towns, Cities and Lawlessness

Both the mining and cattle booms, as well as the railroads, produced towns that followed similar patterns of overnight development. Virginia City, for example, began its existence as a shantytown, but the mining bonanza turned it into a metropolis containing mansions, an opera house, a six-story hotel, 131 saloons, four banks, and numerous houses of prostitution. Men outnumbered women by more than three to one. The same was true of the cow town of Abilene. There, amidst the streets ankle-deep in mud, the crude wooden sidewalks, and the dilapidated store fronts, a cowboy could find many ways to spend the several months' pay burning a hole in his pocket. Bright lights beckoned from saloons like the Bull's Head and from gambling parlors featuring roulette or poker games. The Novelty Theater presented sleazy entertainment, and the "Devil's Half Acre" featured world-weary prostitutes. Other boom towns exhibited a similar flashy, tawdry picture.

Many Western men were adherents of the "Code of the West," which stressed that a real man never retreated from confrontation; people must redress their own grievances. This popular attitude could be seen in an old folk song:

> Wake up, wake up darlin' Corrie
> And go and get my gun
> I ain't no hand for trouble
> But I'll die before I run.

The code placed great value on personal courage, often leading, in the words of one historian, to "reckless bravado." In a televised address to the nation in 1953, President Dwight Eisenhower admiringly described the old code of Abilene (his hometown) and of its marshal, "Wild Bill" Hickok: "Meet anyone face to face with whom you disagree" and "if you met him face to face and took the same risk as he did, you could get away with almost anything (killing included), as long as the bullet was in front." Westerners were, at the same time, the most heavily armed group of civilians in the world.

Cattle and mining towns presented particular opportunities for men whose guns were their means of livelihood. Some of the gun wielders were outlaws, recast by myth into Robin Hood-like figures. One historian has called them "social bandits," expressing the grievances of many others who would never have dared to commit criminal acts. There were approximately three hundred "glorified gunfighters" whose exploits became Western legend. Some, like Jesse James, whose daring was admired as that of "strong men who could protect and avenge themselves," robbed the banks and railroads that were resented by peaceful ordinary citizens for their unfair charges. When the Southern Pacific Railroad successfully used hired gunslingers to clear out dissident farmers with conflicting land claims, its actions aroused resentment. One result was popular admiration for two holdup men—Chris Evans and John Sontag—who specialized in Southern Pacific Railroad trains and dramatic shoot-outs with railroad detectives.

The famous Lincoln County War, which struck New Mexico in 1878, involved two factions struggling to dominate local commerce. The "War" provided the training ground for at least nineteen gunfighters, including the legendary Billy the Kid. In reality, the "Kid" was neither the mythical hero portrayed at the time nor the "mentally inferior" psychopath depicted by later revisionists. Instead, he was a typical young gunfighter involved in the conflicts of the era and unsuccessful in his attempts to turn to a more peaceful civilian life. In his "short and violent life" of only 21 years, he was probably responsible for ten deaths. Many of the outlaws, like the James and Younger brothers and the terrifying John Wesley Hardin (responsible for at least twenty deaths), learned outlaw tactics of raiding and shooting as Confederate guerrillas during the Civil War.

Some of these gun fighters became law enforcement officers like Wyatt Earp and his brother Virgil.

Cowboy outlaws, who frequently rode into Tombstone, Arizona, to have a rambunctious good time, angered the elite Republican mine owners who ran the booming town. The town leaders turned to Wyatt and his brothers to use their gunfighting skills to end the killings in Tombstone and restore some order. In addition to coming from a strong unionist Republican family, the Earps were ardent speculators in area mines and real estate. In the famous showdown at the O.K. Corral in 1881 the Earps and their ally, Doc Holiday, were able to defeat the cowboy-rustler-outlaw faction headed by the Clantons and McLaurys.

Sometimes the line between lawful and unlawful killer was rather blurred. Wild Bill Hickok, a professional gambler, often found himself on the wrong side of the law. Yet, he also served as an effective law officer at various times. McCoy, the businessman who built Abilene, hired Hickok, a Union veteran from an abolitionist Illinois family, to subdue the violence-prone Texas cowboys who swept into town. His face-to-face shooting of a well-known Texas gunfighter and gambler helped Hickok fulfill his goal of bringing order to Abilene. (Contrary to legend, Hickok killed only one more person in his tenure in Abilene and that one by mistake.) Hickok eventually moved to Deadwood where he was shot in the back while playing poker, assuring his place in Western myth.

Many historians feel that later romantic legends greatly exaggerated accounts of Western gun fighting. Despite their unruly character, homicide rates in the boom towns were not particularly high. The five main Kansas cattle towns, for example, had a total of forty-five homicides over a 15 year period. Western violence, however, was more complex than official homicides. The lack of effective law enforcement institutions to protect life and property resulted in the creation of vigilante bands, usually led by the wealthy elite in the Western towns. Men like California railroad magnate and senator Leland Stanford, engaged in vigilante violence. There were over two hundred vigilante movements west of the Mississippi. In one year, in California alone, mobs executed forty-seven people. They justified their challenge to legal authority by emphasizing the right of self-preservation of the community. Since the Virginia City police force was too small and dishonest to keep order, vigilantes took over the town in 1871 and hanged two infamous outlaws. A Denver newspaper approved of a nearby vigilante hanging in 1879, noting that it was not only "well merited but a positive gain to the county, saving at least five or six thousand dollars."

Other aspects of Western violence involved racial and ethnic tensions that culminated in brutality directed against Indians, Mexicans, Chinese, or blacks. Within the majority white community, tensions exploded when the new forces of industrialization clashed with the old combative Code of the West. Miners, loggers, and mill workers struggled against the new corporate elite. Sometimes the state militia crushed strikes, leading to bitter conflicts. In one shocking incident in Ludlow, Colorado, in 1914, a "Thirty Years War" between miners and a Rockefeller-owned company culminated in the suffocation death of thirteen women and children and the shooting of many other people.

The pattern of violence gradually changed, for the most part, as the boom towns faded. Either they disintegrated into "ghost towns," or they were reformed by the efforts of stable and permanent settlers. As the West urbanized as a result of the advances of technology, the criminal justice system responded to public demands for a more tranquil society. The production and exchange of goods and services requiring an urban setting increased in the West. Theodore Roosevelt, in his *Winning of the West* (1896), noted that when Kentucky became a state in the 1790s, only 1 percent of its population resided in Lexington, its largest city. But when Colorado entered the union in 1876, one-third of its people lived in Denver. "Nowadays," the future president proudly noted, "when new states are formed the urban population in them tends to grow as rapidly as in the old."

Denver, the "Queen City of the Rockies," vividly demonstrated these changes in Western life. Until 1870, the city existed to fulfill the needs and desires of miners, and to outfit and equip them. Visiting observers noted, "Drunkenness and rioting...existed everywhere." Saloons, brothels, and gaming houses were omnipresent and, "in these horrible dens a man's life is worth no more than a dog's." The completion of railroad connections in 1870, however, enabled the city to diversify its economy. The 1870 population of 4,759 grew to 10,500 by 1890. By then, visitors could travel on cable cars. (The electric trolley was introduced the following year.) Observers marveled at the spread out character of the handsome new city and noted, "a general absence of frontier ruggedness." The houses and shops remarked one, "would do credit to Broadway."

San Francisco was, undoubtedly, the paramount city of the nineteenth-century West. By 1890, it had close to 300,000 inhabitants and ranked eighth in population among the nation's cities. The city collected raw materials and produced foodstuffs, shoes, clothing, and equipment distributed throughout the Far West. A British observer compared it to "a New York that has no Boston on one side of it and no shrewd and orderly rural population on the other to keep it in order."

THE WESTERN FARMER

Farmers had begun moving west of the Mississippi and even the Missouri before the Civil War. After the war, however, what had been a trickle became a flood. Between 1870 and 1900, farmers doubled the land under cultivation from 407 to 841 million acres. This newly farmed acreage was greater than the amount of land that had been cultivated in the entire country from its beginning. Many of these new farms were on the Great Plains.

Farmers Settle the Plains

For many years, farmers feared moving into the Great Plains. Besides coarse grass, the area had little vegetation. There were few animals suitable for hunting. The lack of water and wood was even more important. No wonder Americans had dubbed this area the "Great American Desert."

Before the Civil War, the forbidding Great Plains had been reachable only after an obstacle-filled journey by wagon. The building of the transcontinental railroads created an immense railroad network that made access to the Great Plains much easier. To gain customers and to increase the value of their enormous land holdings granted by generous governments, the railroad companies energetically promoted land settlement. Their land bureaus and agents in the East and Europe offered long term loans and low cost transportation to prospective buyers. One promoter assured young men that "this vast region...with its boundless, undeveloped resources," was beckoning. "They will be nobodies where they are—they can be somebodies in building up a new society."

These campaigns were amazingly successful. Along with millions of Americans, mostly from nearby states, over two million foreigners settled in the West. More than two-thirds of the people in the Dakotas in 1880 were of foreign parentage. By 1905, the Santa Fe Railroad alone had moved sixty thousand Mennonites from the Ukraine to Kansas.

Federal government land policy was another key factor in pulling settlers to the West. The Homestead Act of 1862 attempted to make the long-cherished ideal of a nation of independent farmers into a reality. Under the act, public lands in the West were opened to free settlement by citizens and those who declared that they would become citizens. Settlers, who paid a modest $10 fee, could get plots of 160 acres if they occupied the land for five years and improved it. Although 400,000 families gained title to homesteads under the act, the law hardly functioned as Congress had presumably envisioned.

One problem was the 160-acre limit. While 160 acres was more than enough in the fertile soil of older sections, it was not adequate for the drier land of the plains. A second problem was the prevalence of fraud. Dishonest speculators and cattle and mining interests were able to file false claims and grab the choicest locations. Undermanned government land offices were unable to provide the kind of supervision that would have assured that land went to legitimate settlers. Later acts that attempted to rectify the shortcomings of the Homestead Act, by increasing the size of land grants and shortening the period of residence, only seemed to encourage even more extensive fraud. Many more settlers bought their land at prices from $2 to $10 an acre from railroads, land

companies, and state governments that had been given federal land for educational purposes. It has been estimated that less than 15 percent of Great Plains' farmers actually got their land from the Homestead Act. Nevertheless, the idea of ample free land available from the government helped keep the dream alive of the West as a land of opportunity.

A temporary climate change was another factor that contributed to the surge of settlement. For several years, particularly after 1877, rainfall in the plains far exceeded the normal totals. Watching their abundant crops grow, many settlers wondered why the area had ever been called the "Great American Desert." Some went as far as to argue that the cultivation of the plains had caused permanent climate change, particularly increased rainfall!

Farming on the Plains: Overcoming Problems

Those who came to farm on the plains had to confront and overcome daunting obstacles. The lack of trees in the area presented the first challenge. This made it prohibitively expensive to build even rough log cabin homes and to put up fencing to enclose property and protect crops from range cattle. The development of inexpensive barbed wire in 1874, and its rapid availability to farmers, solved the latter problem. The first dwelling the pioneer set up might be a cave, a lean-to, or even a canvas-topped cart. Eventually, settlers hit on the idea of using the tough matted sod, like oversized bricks, to build houses. These homes were invariably dark, dirty, and subject to mud falling down on the furniture when it rained. While these dwellings seemed picturesque to visitors, homes of imported wood or local stone replaced them as soon as improved circumstances permitted. The shortage of wood made it difficult to heat houses in some of the coldest sections of America. Early settlers used dried buffalo "chips" or hay in special slow-burning stoves. But the predicament persisted until the railroads began to bring in coal.

Nature presented a variety of other problems. Prairie fires were a menace to homes and crops. On the northern plains, blizzards were particularly dangerous. Among the pests that plagued the settlers, the grasshoppers were the worst. At times, they were as thick as a heavy snowstorm, and they ate everything in sight, including clothes hanging out to dry. Masses of grasshoppers, making the tracks dangerously slippery, even held up the railroads. The prairie sod was so tough that it required a special steel plow pulled by several oxen to break up one to two acres a day.

The lack of an adequate water supply was the most serious difficulty of all. Some farmers turned to digging wells to reach water as far down as 500 feet. Well-digging crews with expertise and expensive equipment toured the region, charging a dollar a foot. Windmills, harnessing the powerful winds of the area, raised the water from the deep wells. These windmills, however, were limited to supplying household needs and, perhaps, a vegetable garden. Experts developed special varieties of wheat, barley, and other crops requiring less water. Many farmers turned to "dry farming" cultivation techniques. After each rainfall, farmers plowed the field, enabling the turned over mud to serve as a mulch to store water. Irrigation might have been the most effective solution in some areas, but it required capital investment on a scale that only the federal government could provide. In the 1870s and 80s, it was unable or unwilling to fund such projects.

After 1887, climate conditions returned to normal. The dry seasons turned the once fertile lands into a semi-desert. In the earlier booming years farmers were able to obtain easy credit to expand. Crop failures and conflicts in Europe had greatly increased the demand for American grain. As one Kansas farmer noted, "Haste to get rich has made us borrowers, and the borrowing has made booms, and the booms made men wild, and Kansas became a vast insane asylum...." When the droughts came, many farmers found themselves unable to repay their debts. In the drought year of 1888, thousands of wagons of the "defeated legion" rolled eastward, some bearing despondent signs, "In God We Trusted; In Kansas We Busted."

At the same time, farmers, both the successful and the unsuccessful, were deeply affected by the commercialization of farming, especially after the mid 1890s. The open plains country lent itself to large scale farms that specialized in one crop and mechanized almost as much as contemporary factories. Such inventions as cord binders, rotary plows, seeders, mowers, and combines brought economies of scale. By the end of the 1880s, two men and a team of horses could harvest 20 acres of wheat a day. (Earlier farmers had been happy if they managed eight acres of wheat a **season**.) The hours required to farm one acre of wheat dropped from sixty-one to an astonishing three. Farmers learned about "scientific agriculture" from the land-grant colleges established by the 1862 Morrill Act. The result was soaring production. At first, the growing cities and foreign countries bought up these crops. Eventually, Russian wheat production recovered, Australia entered the world market, and a worldwide overproduction caused a precipitous drop in prices. Farmers began steadily to lose ground. In 1860 they received 30 percent of the national income; by 1910 their share fell to 18 percent. The new economic order did not seem nearly as attractive to them as it once had.

The Role of Women

Frontier farms were family enterprises. As in earlier eras, the responsibilities of the farmer's wife could be overwhelming. She carried out the then common household tasks of cleaning, cooking, washing dishes and clothes, mending, and ironing. These were far more difficult on the plains where they might involve washing clothes in the hardest water, keeping a dirt house clean, and giving birth to a succession of children with little or no help. She probably also fed extra men at harvesting time, preserved food, worked in the garden, took care of the barnyard poultry, milked and churned the butter, and sewed the family's clothing on her new, indispensable treadle sewing machine. Accidents, often resulting in tetanus, and diseases like malaria were commonplace. Doctors were a rarity. Generally, women provided the rudimentary medical treatment. "Out here," wrote one, "we have to dope ourselves." Few of these women had the luxury of running water or an indoor toilet.

A wagonload of sod bricks stands ready for roof repairs on this sod house.

The worst problem for many women (as it was for many men) was the loneliness and isolation of life on the prairie. This remained true despite community and church building and such social events as quilting bees. Even the wife of a successful farmer later wrote of her Kansas homestead, "In all the years we spent there we never could see a neighbor's light in the evening. I did wish so much we could, to relieve the loneliness." An empty cabin in the Texas panhandle displayed a more bitter view, "250 miles to the nearest post office; 100 miles to wood; 20 miles to water; 6 inches to hell...Gone to live with the wife's folks."

The fatiguing labor, the hard water, winter blizzards, burning summer heat, and continual winds made many of these pioneer women look old by thirty. Hamlin Garland, a fine American writer, returned to visit his Iowa hometown in 1887. He was taken by the "sordid struggle and half-hidden despair" he found in every house. The sight of a woman he remembered "in the days of her radiant girlhood," particularly moved him. The burdens of wifehood and motherhood had led to "lovely girlhood wasting away into thin and hopeless age."

While women's lives remained difficult and women's roles largely traditional, Western states were more supportive of women's rights. Perhaps as a result of the important part women played in Western settlement or in hopes of attracting the stabilizing influence of more women, Western states were the first to grant women the vote. In the 1890s, Wyoming, Utah, Colorado, and Idaho were the only states to approve of women's suffrage. By 1914, Washington, California, Oregon, Arizona, Kansas, Nevada, and Montana had enfranchised women. All of these states were in the trans-Missouri West.

Farmers' Grievances and Politics

Western farmers were keenly aware that something was seriously wrong in their world. The main cause of farmers' problems was, probably, declining prices for their crops, a result of overproduction. But overproduction and dependence on world markets seemed distant and abstract to most farmers. They sought more comprehensible and tangible explanations for their woes. One writer summed up the views of many when he declared that something was radically wrong with the system: "The railroads have never been so prosperous, and yet agriculture languishes. The banks have never done a better...business and yet agriculture languishes. Manufacturing enterprises never made more money,...and yet agriculture languishes."

The farmers' greatest grievance was against the railroads. They were totally dependent on noncompetitive railroads to ship their products. It seemed to them that the railroads were charging higher rates for farm products than other products and for goods in the West and South than for those in the Northeast. (Railroad officials argued that the sparser population made this differential necessary.) Railroads also ran elevator and warehouse facilities that charged high storage rates. In many western states, railroads controlled the government. As one Oregon senator said about the owner of the Oregon Central Railroad, "Ben Holladay's politics are my politics and what Ben Holladay wants I want."

Farmers also blamed their plight on banks and loan companies that controlled credit. Farmers had taken out loans to expand or buy machinery when farm prices were high. Interest rates ranged from 10 to 25 percent. Many had to pay these loans back at a time when farm prices were declining and currency was scarce. Many agrarian leaders favored increasing the monetary supply to make repayments easier.

Another vital issue involved prices. Farmers had no control over the prices for their crops, which often rose or declined as a result of unpredictable external forces. Usually, they harvested all the crops in one region at the same time. All the farmers had to sell immediately to pay their loans. "Middlemen"— speculators and local or regional agents—seized the opportunity to get the crops at artificially low prices. Then, they sold when the prices rose. Often, their profit margins exceeded that of the farmer who had labored long and hard hours to produce the product. In addition, while farm prices fluctuated, the prices of manufactured goods the farmer bought remained high as a result of tariffs and eastern monopolies.

Many farmers saw the railroad owners, the bankers, and the monopolists as the villains who had conspired to oppress them. "It is," one declared, "a struggle between the robbers and the robbed."

Some farmers realized that, in an era of economic consolidation, they needed to organize. The first effort to create a national farm organization was the Grange or "Patrons of Husbandry" founded in 1867 to provide education, fellowship, and social interaction. By the 1870s, membership had grown to more than a million. Grangers began to address the economic grievances of the farmers by emphasizing railroad regulation and cooperatives. Grangers successfully lobbied several state legislatures to establish railroad commissions to regulate railroad operations and even fix maximum rates for freight shipments. Cooperative stores purchased directly from manufacturers to eliminate the middleman. Some granges even set up cooperative banks and grain storage elevators.

Granger successes, unfortunately, were not permanent. Lacking adequate capital and management skills, the cooperatives began to fail. Some members supported the Greenback movement, which favored inflation and easier credit by increasing the amount of paper money in circulation. When farm prices experienced a temporary revival after 1878, thousands of farmers deserted the Grange and lost interest in government reform. (The Grange did continue as a social and educational institution that helped to ease the burden of social isolation.)

In an early case, the Supreme Court had upheld "Granger laws," regulating grain elevators and their rates. But in the *Wabash* case of 1886, the Court weakened those laws by prohibiting states from regulating interstate railroad rates. Although Congress responded to this by creating the Interstate Commerce Commission in 1887 to provide federal regulation of railroads, the commission did little to limit the monopolistic practices of railroads. Despite these limitations, the Grange movement laid the groundwork for the more militant agrarian protest movement of the 1890s.

The Populist Movement

In the 1880s farmers' Alliances arose to replace the Grange. At first, these organizations existed largely on paper and devoted their energies to educational and social programs. As the decade wore on, the repeating cycles of declining prices, indebtedness, and limited money supply severely rocketed the chronically poor South and the Great Plains. In the South regional groups joined in the Southern Alliance with a membership variously estimated at 1.5 to 3 million. An affiliated Colored Alliance claimed another million members. The blizzards and droughts that hit the Great Plains in the late 1880s spurred the growth of the Northwestern Alliance.

Years of resentment brought forth impassioned leaders who articulated agrarian grievances. In the South, Alliance leaders like Tom Watson of Georgia urged cooperation between black and white farmers to achieve common goals. In the West, fiery orators advocated radical solutions. These included women like Mary E. Lease, a Kansas lawyer and homesteader. "Wall Street owns the country," she declared. "The West and South are bound and prostrate before the manufacturing East." She implored farmers to "raise less corn and more hell."

In the elections of 1890 the Alliances endorsed candidates who supported their objectives, whether Democrats in the South or independents in the West. They were remarkably successful. In the South, Alliance-endorsed candidates captured four governorships, eight state legislatures, forty-four congressmen, and several senators. On the Great Plains, Alliancemen were able to gain control of four legislatures and elect a governor in Kansas and two senators. In 1892, flushed with their new-found respectability, Alliance leaders from the South and West joined hands in a convention in St. Louis to form the People's or Populist Party. As the party's presidential nominee, they chose James B. Weaver, a former Union general and Greenback nominee for president. As a balance, they picked a former Confederate officer for vice president. The Populists conducted a lively and colorful campaign, described by one observer as a blend of "the French Revolution and a western religious revival."

The party's platform reflected a radical agrarian agenda, derided by some as "hayseed socialism." Populist farmers, as landowners, did not consider themselves socialists. They did believe that "natural

Mary E. Lease advised farmers to "raise less corn and more hell."

monopolies," like the railroads, telegraph, and telephone, should be government-owned and operated to benefit all the people. They favored a more activist federal government that would pay for its programs by instituting a graduated income tax under which the rich would pay a larger percentage of their income. They wanted a flexible currency based on free coinage of silver that would increase the money supply. This would enable farmers to repay their debts, while aiding silver miners. The platform also advocated the "subtreasury plan" to help maintain farm prices. Under this proposal, farmers could borrow government funds at modest interest secured by crops stored in government warehouses. The platform proposed that "excess" land in the hands of railroads be reclaimed to benefit legitimate settlers. Government would be restored "to the hands of the people" by direct election of senators (still elected by state legislatures), the secret ballot, and the initiative and referendum. (These enabled the people directly to propose and enact laws.) To broaden support to the urban worker, the party also favored an eight-hour day and immigration restriction. The preamble to the platform announced: "We seek to restore the government of the Republic to the hands of the 'plain people' with which class it originated."

In the 1892 presidential election, Weaver became the first third-party candidate to garner over a million votes. He carried Kansas, Colorado, Idaho, and Nevada and gained respectable totals in most of the Great Plains. He did not do nearly as well in the older agricultural states or in the East. In the South, Democratic Party leaders successfully appealed to racism and intimidated black voters to lessen Populist support. In the future, Southern politicians, like Tom Watson, who hoped to appeal to poor whites, stayed within the Democratic Party and combined their populism with extreme racism. The following year, however, brought the Panic of 1893, followed by a major depression. The resulting disruptions and discontent made the Populists seem far more dangerous to conservative leaders and gave the party serious expectations for the election of 1896.

As the impact of the depression deepened in both urban and rural areas, public anger at Grover Cleveland and his government reached the boiling point. In the midterm elections of 1894, most voters turned to the Republicans, but Populist votes also increased by more than 40 percent. A book backed by Western silver-mine owners, *Coin's Financial School*, aided their cause. This best-seller argued that "the conspiracy of Goldbugs" caused the misery of the depression. The complicated issue of money was reduced to the simplest of terms: the farmers and the nation could be saved only by the free coinage of silver. Then, property values would increase, the debtor could repay his debts, and the country would revive. Unfortunately, this obsession with silver overshadowed the genuine issues once stressed by the Populists.

The Election of 1896

In 1896, the Republicans nominated William McKinley for president. He was a supporter of big business, high tariffs, and continuation of the gold standard. The silverites won control of the Democratic Party and nominated a dynamic, young (36-year old), congressman from Nebraska, William Jennings Bryan. Bryan, a fiery orator whose booming voice could be easily heard in the back of the gallery of the huge hall in Chicago, electrified the delegates. In his famous "Cross of Gold" speech, Bryan declared that American prosperity rested upon "our broad and fertile prairies." He scornfully rejected the gold standard, concluding to wildly enthusiastic applause, "You shall not press down upon the brow of labor this crown of thorns, you shall not crucify mankind upon a cross of gold."

Bryan's nomination presented the Populists with a painful dilemma. If they endorsed him, they would lose their identity as a third party. Free silver was only one plank in their extensive platform of reform. But if they ran their own candidate, the reformist vote would split and a conservative Republican would inevitably be elected president. With obvious reluctance, the Populists endorsed Bryan and attempted to show some independence by picking their own candidate for vice president.

The campaign of 1896 was one of the most important and dramatic in American history, offering the voters a clear choice of vastly different platforms. Bryan crisscrossed the nation, traveling over 18,000 miles, and delivering more than 600 free-silver speeches. The dignified McKinley stayed on his front porch in Canton, Ohio. He issued carefully crafted statements while his campaign operated like a well-oiled machine. Republicans successfully pictured Bryan as a dangerous radical whose ideas would bring inflation, raise food prices, and destroy jobs and industry. Employers went as far as to threaten their workers with pink slips if they didn't vote for the Republicans. McKinley won the popular vote by a margin of over 600,000 and the electoral vote by 271 to 176. Bryan carried the South and most of the Great Plains but lost the settled family farmers of the Midwest, as well as the urban centers of the Northeast.

"God's in his heaven, all's right with the world," the Republican campaign manager wired McKinley when he learned of the victory. Bryan's crushing defeat led to a Republican domination of national politics for all but eight of the next thirty-six years. New discoveries of gold ironically caused the very inflation that farmers had expected from silver. Farm prices rose again. In the election of 1900, McKinley, boasting of prosperity and "The Full Dinner Pail," defeated Bryan again, even more decisively.

The election of 1896 destroyed the Populist movement. The more inclusive progressive movement, however, adopted many of its ideas. Some of its "radical" proposals eventually became law, including direct election of senators, a graduated income tax, and farm price supports.

THE WEST IN CULTURE, MYTH AND IMAGINATION

The image of an unsettled and boundless West had long held a special place in the imaginations of both Americans and Europeans. As early as the seventeenth century, the vast interior areas seemed to many to represent both opportunity and refuge. The trans-Missouri West, with its Great Plains, magnificent mountains, incredible deserts, and other wonders, seemed even more spectacular than anything Americans had seen before. Artists of the new "Rocky Mountain School" painted enormous landscapes that were often sent on tours of the country. The new landscape photographers, some of whom accompanied government geological surveys, matched the grandiose visions of the artists. Viewing these magnificent landscapes helped produce a torrent of public support for the creation of national parks. In 1872 Congress responded by creating Yellowstone National Park to preserve for all time, "wonders within said park...in their natural condition."

The romance of the West's natural beauty led to the development of an organized conservation movement to counter the greedy exploitation and destruction of the environment. The most effective publicist for wilderness protection was John Muir, a Scottish immigrant who fell in love with the redwood forests of the Yosemite Valley. He lyrically advised city people to climb mountains: "Nature's peace will flow into you as the sunshine into the trees...cares will drop off like autumn leaves." His efforts brought about the creation of Yosemite National Park in 1890 and the formation in 1892 of the Sierra Club. That organization committed itself to wilderness protection in the Pacific mountain region.

In many ways, the romanticized, individualistic lifestyle they associated with the West enthralled more Americans than its unequaled landscape. The cowboy, ignoring his reality as a low-paid worker, was transformed into a mythical hero, "the knight of the plains." Cheap paperbacks, known as "dime nov-

els," flooded the country from the 1860s to the 1880s. The most popular were "westerns" that emphasized noble, self-reliant heroes who inevitably defeated the forces of evil, whether "savage" Indians or no-good cattle rustlers. They were often written by men who had never left the East. *Buffalo Bill: King of the Border Men* (1869), very loosely based on the experiences of "Buffalo Bill" Cody, was one of the most successful of the dime novels. Over 121 "Buffalo Bill" books followed.

The success of his fictional counterpart led the real Cody to launch his Wild West show in 1883. The show was an enormous popular hit, seen by millions of Americans. Cody promised his enthralled audiences that he was presenting "actual scenes, genuine characters" from the West. He depicted history as a modern morality pageant in which the Western hero repelled Indian attacks. Whites became victims of Indian aggression in the show. Cody's claim that his myth was reality was reinforced by the presence of real Indians, including the most famous of all, Sitting Bull. The shows also presented such glamorous western skills as bronco riding, roping and shooting. (The most admired shooter was Annie Oakley, an Eastern woman, billed as a perfect frontierswoman.) Cody became an international superstar. One bronco rider, who stayed with the cast for seven years, traveled around the world three and a half times on tours. There were two command performances for Queen Victoria of England. Prince Albert of Monaco journeyed all the way to Wyoming for a chance to "kill a grizzly bear or two" with the help of the great Buffalo Bill. Eventually, the demand for the Wild West Show faded. The rodeo developed as replacement entertainment for Americans who still longed for evidence of the courage and pioneer spirit of the West.

The works of three young men, who left their eastern upper class homes to find fulfillment in the part of the country where life was as simple and heroic as the dime novels, supported the legend of the West. Theodore Roosevelt, Frederick Remington, and Owen Wister found what they were looking for in the West. Roosevelt extolled the glories of the frontier in his four volume, *The Winning of the West* (1889-96). Remington, in his paintings and sculp-

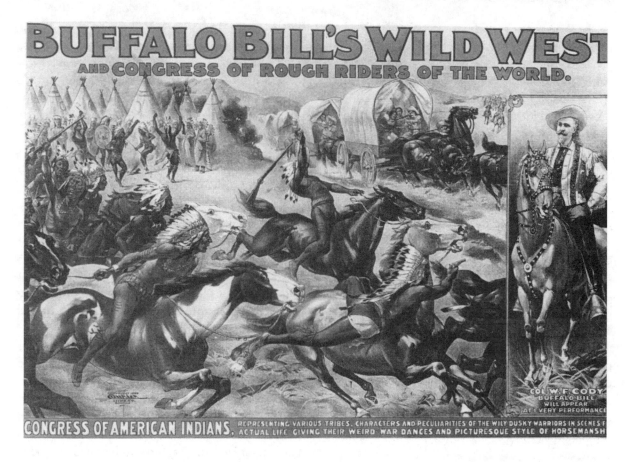

tures, depicted heroic white cowboys and Indian fighters. Wister, a Harvard-educated lawyer, refined the dime novel image of the romantic, manly cowboy in numerous short stories and books. The most famous was *The Virginian*, a gigantic best-seller that sold 50,000 copies in its first two months. The hero, an honest, brave cowboy (who never does any hard physical cowboy work), easily defeats the forces of evil, wins the beautiful school teacher, and becomes a successful businessman.

Even Mark Twain, one of America's greatest authors, reinforced the romantic image of the West as the last escape from the bonds of modern civilization. His 1872 memoir, *Roughing It*, describes his entertaining experiences as a reporter during the Nevada mining boom. His great novel, *The Adventures of Huckleberry Finn* (1882), deals with boyhood on an earlier frontier, a Missouri River town. But the characters' attempts to break away from the repressive forces of order, represent the vision of the West as the last possibility for real freedom.

Probably the clearest statement of this romantic view of the West and the first interpretation of the frontier's importance came in 1893 from Frederick Jackson Turner, a Wisconsin scholar who would become the most eminent historian of his generation. Four years after the Oklahoma land rush had overrun the Indian Territory, the last major tract of Indian land, Turner delivered a paper entitled, "The Significance of the Frontier in American History." In it, he declared that, "the advance of American settlement westward," by white men was the central event of American history. This expansion had brought about opportunities, individualism, and democracy. It had created the distinctive American character. He cited the 1890 census that declared that a continuous frontier line no longer existed. "Now," Turner concluded sadly, "the frontier has gone and with its going has closed the first period of American history."

Later historians argued that Turner's "frontier thesis" was inaccurate. It ignores the civilizations of

Native Americans and Hispanics that already existed in the supposedly empty spaces of the West. Its emphasis on the feats of brave white men neglects the contributions of women, African Americans, Asians, and others. One historian, who studied the lives of prostitutes in Helena, Montana, found that they were their own bosses, saving and investing their earnings, in the early years. Then, men came in and took control of them and their money. This extremely non-Turnerian view of the marker of the closing of the frontier suggests that, "the frontier ends when the pimps come to town." Triumph and individualism in the real West coexisted with failure, greed, exploitation of resources, and, above all, modern industrial capitalism. There were vast areas of unoccupied land in the West still to be settled Nevertheless, the myth endured. Americans felt a real sense of loss at "the passing of the frontier." Where would opportunities arise in the future? What would happen to America's "Manifest Destiny" now that it had completed the conquest of the continent? Would the eyes of American expansionists now be focused overseas?

CONCLUSION

The myth of the individualistic Westerner continued well past the "closing of the frontier." Later popular writers, such as Zane Grey, continued in the tradition of Owen Wister. With the arrival of motion pictures, the "western" gained renewed popularity. One of the first films was a 1903 western, *The Great Train Robbery*. Movie serials and successful films, as well as radio shows, featured such Western heroes as the Lone Ranger, Tom Mix, Hopalong Cassidy, and Roy Rogers. "The Virginian" was later made into a popular Gary Cooper movie and a 1960s television series. The great director, John Ford, relied on the works of Frederick Remington for his lighting, costumes, and color. The brave, self-reliant hero who single handedly destroys the forces of evil was reborn in such excellent movies as *Shane* and *High Noon*. Some of the most popular programs in early television were such westerns as "Gunsmoke," "Wyatt Earp," and "Bonanza." The remarkably successful Marlboro Man advertising campaign depicted a rugged cowboy who rode free and was "not about to take advice from Washington bureaucrats like the surgeon general." More recently, the image has shifted from the old West to the new frontier of space where heroes perform feats of equal daring in such epics as *Star Wars*.

Modern historians have painted a more realistic picture of the West. This includes a variety of peoples of both genders and many nationalities and races. Great mining booms often ended as ghost towns. The farmer faced real problems of weather, water, indebtedness, and uncontrollable market forces. They organized in very non-individualistic movements of protest. Native Americans were more often the victims of aggression than the wild savage aggressors of the Wild West show.

Perhaps the children who for generations dressed as cowboys and Indians were the closest to the real West. They were Catholics, Jews and Protestants, black and white, male and female, and from every conceivable ethnic group. Their imaginary West was an amazingly diverse place. But so was the real West of the nineteenth century.

Chronology

1862	Homestead Act Sioux War erupts in Minnesota
1864	Sand Creek massacre of Cheyennes
1867	The Grangers founded—first national farmers' organization Joseph McCoy organizes cattle drives to Abilene, Kansas
1869	First transcontinental railroad completed
1872	Yellowstone National Park established
1873	Giant silver strike discovered at Nevada's Comstock Lode
1874	Gold found in Black Hills of South Dakota Barbed wire invented
1876	Custer and his troops annihilated at Little Big Horn Colorado, the "Centennial State," admitted to the Union
1881	Helen Hunt Jackson writes *A Century of Dishonor*
1880s	Buffalo herds decimated
1883	Buffalo Bill Cody introduces his Wild West show
1886	Droughts and blizzards on the Plains devastate cattle ranching and wheat farming
1887	Dawes Act passed
1889	Indian territory in Oklahoma opened to settlement Ghost Dance religion rises among western Indians
1890	Massacre of Sioux at Wounded Knee, South Dakota
1892	Populist Party formed and receives over a million votes in presidential election
1893	Frederick Jackson Turner, "The Significance of the Frontier in American History" Major economic depression begins
1896	McKinley defeats Bryan

SUGGESTED READINGS

Stephen Ambrose, *Nothing Like it in the World: The Men Who Built the Transcontinental Railroad* (2000).

Susan Armitage and Elizabeth Jameson, eds., *The Woman's West* (1987).

Dee Brown, *Bury My Heart At Wounded Knee* (1970).

William Cronon, et. al., eds, *Under the Open Sky: Rethinking America's Western Past* (1992).

William F. Holmes, *American Populism* (1994).

Julie Jeffrey, *Frontier Women* (1979).

Patricia Nelson Limerick, *The Legacy of Conquest: The Unbroken Past of the American West* (1987).

Robert D. McGrath, *Gunfighters, Highwaymen, and Vigilantes* (1984).

Robert C. McMath, *American Populism: A Social History* (1993).

Clyde Milner, et. al., eds., *The Oxford History of the American West* (1994).

Nell Irvin Painter, *The Exodusters* (1977).

Rodman W. Paul, *The Far West and the Great Plains in Transition, 1859-1900* (1988).

Robert E. Riegel and Robert G. Athearn, *America Moves West* (1971).

David Roberts, *Once They Moved Like the Wind: Cochise, Geronimo, and the Apache Wars* (1993).

William R. Savage, *The Cowboy Hero* (1986).

Fred A. Shannon, *The Farmer's Last Frontier, 1860-1897* (1945).

Henry Nash Smith, *Virgin Land: The West as Symbol and Myth* (1978).

T.J. Stiles, *Jesse James: Last Rebel of the Civil War* (2002).

Robert Utley, *The Indian Frontier of the American West, 1846-1890* (1984).

——, *The Lance and the Shield: The Life and Times of Sitting Bull* (1993).

Richard White and Patricia N. Limerick, *The Frontier in American Culture (1994).*

Teddy Roosevelt, San Juan Hill in Cuba

Chapter Fifteen

THE IMPERIAL REPUBLIC

In January 1899, the United States Senate was locked in an intense, often acrimonious debate, over whether to ratify the Treaty of Paris, officially ending the recent war with Spain, allegedly fought for the liberation of Cuba. While the politicians argued, thousands of United States soldiers, half-way around the world, were engaged in a vicious, brutal guerrilla war against Filipino rebels, wanting the same thing their Cuban counterparts had longed for—independence. Unfortunately for both groups, neither would receive their independence for decades to come. Both countries became the victims of eventual U.S. colonialism. Ironically, only a few weeks before, Americans and Filipinos had been allies, together defeating the Spanish to liberate the Philippines. The American fleet under Admiral George Dewey had destroyed the Spanish naval squadron in Manila Bay on May 1, 1898. Three weeks later, a U.S. warship brought from exile the Filipino insurrectionary Emilio Aguinaldo to lead rebel forces on land while the United States' gunboats patrolled the seas.

At first, the Filipinos believed the Americans to be their liberators. Although U.S. intentions were never clear, Aguinaldo believed, like his Cuban counterparts, that the Americans had no imperial ambitions; their purpose was pure and altruistic—to help liberate an oppressed people. They would simply drive the Spanish out and then leave the Philippines to the self-determination of the Filipino people. In June, Aguinaldo declared Philippine independence and began setting up a constitutional government. U.S. officials completely discounted the independence ceremonies. When an armistice ended the war in August, American troops denied Aguinaldo's Filipino soldiers an opportunity to liberate their own capital city and shunted them off to the suburbs. The armistice agreement recognized American rights to the "harbor, city, and bay of manila," while the proposed Treaty of Paris gave the United States the entire Philippine Islands archipelago.

When news of the U.S. "acquisition" of the islands reached Filipinos, they protested in the streets of Manila and elsewhere. This was not what they believed would happen. They now viewed Americans, especially the troops stationed there, as an army of occupation, which, in effect, it was. Tensions between American and Filipino soldiers escalated to the point that the streets of Manila became a war zone as both sides dug into trenches *spanning 14 miles through the city. Taunts, obscenities, and racial epithets were shouted across the neutral zone. Barroom skirmishes and knife fights between the soldiers became "normal" occurrences and "pastimes." American soldiers wantonly searched houses without warrants and looted stores. Their behavior was completely unjustified and deplorable.*

On the night of February 4, 1899, Privates William Grayson and William Miller of Company B, 1ˢᵗ Nebraska Volunteers, were on patrol in Santa Mesa, a Manila suburb surrounded on three sides by insurgent trenches. The Americans had orders to shoot any Filipino soldiers who were in the neutral area. As the two Americans cautiously worked their way to a bridge over the San Juan River, they heard a Filipino signal whistle, answered by another. Then a red lantern flashed from a nearby blockhouse. The two froze as four Filipinos emerged from the darkness on the road ahead. "Halt!" Grayson shouted. The native lieutenant in charge answered "Halto!"— either mockingly or because he had similar orders. Standing less than fifteen feet apart, the two men repeated their commands. After a moment's hesitation, Grayson fired, killing his Filipino "ally" with one bullet. As the other Filipinos jumped out at them, Grayson and Miller "opened up" and shot two more. As they fired at the Filipinos, Grayson exulted that he shot "my first nigger." While three Filipino soldiers laid dying in the streets of their own city, killed by men supposedly their friends and comrades-in-arms, Grayson and Miller ran back to their own lines shouting warnings of attack. Within minutes of Grayson's and Miller's return, the Filipinos retaliated, launching a full-scale attack in revenge for the murder of their cohorts.

The next day, Commodore Dewey cabled Washington that the "insurgents have inaugurated general engagement" and promised a quick and decisive suppression of the insurrection. The outbreak of hostilities ended the Senate debates, which had up to this point favored the rejection of the treaty for its obvious imperialist ramifications. But now, with the beginning of a full-fledged revolt against U.S. subjugations, those senators who were wavering voted to support the treaty for they could not vote against it while American soldiers were so engaged. On February 6, 1899, the Senate ratified the Treaty of Paris, thus formally annexing the Philippines and sparking a war between the United States and Aguinaldo's

Filipino revolutionaries who represented a small percentage of the population.

In a guerrilla war similar to those fought in the twentieth century in Eastern Asia, Filipino nationalists tried to undermine the American will by hit-and-run attacks. American soldiers, meanwhile, remained in heavily garrisoned cities and undertook search-and-destroy missions to root out rebels and pacify the countryside. The Filipino-American War lasted until 1902, three years longer than the Spanish-American War that caused it and involving far more troops, casualties, and monetary and moral costs. The United States won its first encounter with a nationalist uprising fought by guerrillas. However, the nation would not be as lucky in its next foray, some sixty years later. In that conflict, against a similarly motivated adversary, the United States would ultimately be defeated. In the aftermath of that "shock," Americans confronted a new reality that forced them to accept the fact that American might and righteousness no longer automatically guaranteed victory, even against an alleged "inferior" foe. In the end, the Vietnam conflict proved that a people's desire for the right of self-determination regardless of the power arrayed against them, if they persevered, they would triumph. Ironically, both the Filipinos and the Vietnamese borrowed a page from the history of the United States, a nation born in a war of national liberation but a nation that forgot its own history somewhere along the way.

AMERICA'S QUEST FOR EMPIRE 1880-1900

The United States had been an expansionist nation since its inception. Throughout the first half of the nineteenth-century, as the nation's population grew and pressed westward, the national government accommodated the movement by continually acquiring, either by purchase or by force, new territory: the trans-Appalachian West, the Louisiana Purchase, Florida, Texas, Oregon, the former Mexican Borderlands of California, Nevada, New Mexico, Arizona, and Colorado, and after the Civil War, Alaska. After the Louisiana Purchase, the second largest territory acquired was that taken from Mexico in the nation's first imperialist war justified by the rhetoric of "Manifest Destiny," which has since become a label for the whole complex of attitudes, concepts, and actions that swept American dominion to the shores of the Pacific Ocean. At the heart of this impulse was an exuberant faith in the democratic creed: Anglo-Americans were a chosen race, and their appointed mission was to extend the area of "freedom." As will be seen later in this chapter, late nineteenth-century imperialists resurrected Manifest Destiny and applied its basic tenets to justify the United States' need to expand beyond the confines of the North American continent in pursuit of an empire. By the end of the century, American hegemony was established in the Western Hemisphere as well as in the Pacific rim. Motivating many Americans to engage in an aggressive, acquisitive foreign policy was the desire to see the United States take its rightful place among the world's great powers, many of whom were themselves intensely involved in drives for empire (most notably England, France, Germany, and Japan) to either expand their existing dominions or, as in the case of Germany and the United States, to "join the imperialist club." By the end of the century, the drive for empire among the great powers, which will include the United States, will bring much of the underdeveloped world under the control of the Western industrial nations.

Voices for Expansion

Several different groups helped to promote American imperialism. One of the earliest and most vociferous were Protestant missionaries. Integration of the world economy made evangelical Protestants, like most Americans, more conscious of the diversity of the world's peoples. Overseas missionary activity intensified between 1870 and 1900, most of it directed toward China, which saw increasing numbers of Western, including American missionaries, penetrate that nation in an attempt to convert the Chinese to Christianity. Convinced of their superiority, Anglo-Saxon Americans and Englishmen considered it their Christian duty to teach the Gospel to the "ignorant" Asian masses and save their souls. Missionaries also believed that their proselytizing would help to "civilize" and "uplift" an inferior people, who resembled

the immigrant masses at home whom they were also trying to "redeem." Thus, American imperialism—as well England's—will be imbued with a sense of righteous duty incumbent upon civilized Christian nations to bring "enlightenment" and "freedom" to the "heathen" and supposedly save them from themselves.

American industrial capitalists and investors also played key roles in promoting overseas expansion, hoping to increase business profits and their personal fortunes in foreign lands. The Asian market was especially alluring to such men, who believed that China, with its 400 million people, was a potential "gold mine" of opportunity. By the late 1880s, James B. Duke, head of American Tobacco, was selling one billion cigarettes a year in East Asian markets. Looking for ways to fill boxcars for his Northern Pacific Railroad, heading west from Minnesota to Tacoma, Washington, J. J. Hill wanted to load them with wheat and steel destined for China and Japan. He actually published and distributed wheat cookbooks throughout East Asia, trying to convince the people there to change their diets and eat less rice and more bread, which he believed would make them "healthier!" Although export trade with East Asia during this period never fulfilled Hill's or others' expectations, their promotion of Asia as a source of great potential markets for the United States convinced many politicians and imperialists that this part of the world was important to the national well-being.

The economic crises of the 1890s also intensified the clamor for foreign markets. The capitalists' agitation for material expansion was reinforced ideologically by one of the most original and important historical theories ever promulgated within the confines of American academic and intellectual circles: Frederick Jackson Turner's "frontier thesis." By 1890, which that year's census revealed, the United States had completed the task of internal westward movement. In 1893, Turner, an assistant professor of history at the University of Wisconsin, published his seminal essay, "The Significance of the Frontier in American History," that articulated what many of Turner's fellow citizens feared: that the frontier had been essential to the nation's economic growth and to the cultivation of democracy. It had provided (white) Americans, filled with wanderlust, an opportunity to own land, which was once in abundance. The fact that land was in such plentiful supply helped to relieve the nation of potential social unrest born of class tensions created by economic inequities. Simply put, as long as there was the frontier, Americans could escape the congested cities and wretched factories and start anew somewhere in the West on their own land. It was in the wilderness, Turner argued, that the American identity was born because that environment forced Europeans coming to the New World to transform themselves into different human beings if they hoped to survive and "make it." As they adapted to the wilderness, the Europeans slowly but steadily shed all their Old World customs, habits, and beliefs and over the decades acquired uniquely "American" characteristics—rugged individualism, egalitarianism, and a democratic faith. Now that the frontier was allegedly "closed," Turner and others wondered could the United States continue to prosper and provide its citizens with the stability and security that had long been the hallmarks of its historical development?

In recent years, historians of the American West have disavowed Turner's thesis, arguing that the very idea of the frontier as uninhabited wilderness negates the fact that already living in the West for thousands of years were tens of thousands of Native Americans. They also assert, and rightly so, that today and even in Turner's time, much of what Americans believed about the West had been highly romanticized and distorted: more myth than reality. Contrary to what Turner claimed, the West was still a very undeveloped region by the 1890s and thus provided Americans with ample opportunity to exploit for their own aggrandizement. Indeed, as will be seen in a later chapter, it was not until the 1930s and after World War II that Western resources were fully exploited and the region developed.

Even though modern historians' assessments of Western development are accurate, they would have meant very little to Turner's contemporaries. For them, as for Turner, concern about the disappearing frontier expressed a fear that the increasingly urbanized and industrialized nation had lost its way.

Turner's essay appeared just as the country was entering the deepest, longest, and most conflict-ridden depression and decade in its history. What could the republic do to regain its economic prosperity and political stability? Where would it find its new "safety valve" frontiers that would save the nation from upheaval and renew the people's faith in the great democratic republican experiment? One answer to these questions came from the proponents of overseas expansion. As Senator Albert J. Beveridge of Indiana declared in 1899: "We are raising more than we can consume. . . .We are making more than we can use. Therefore, we must find new markets for our produce, we must find new occupation for our capital, new work for our labor."

Whatever the effect of such physical phenomena as the expansion of the American frontier to the Pacific Ocean and the enrichment of the nation's economy, much of the impetus for overseas expansion in the last third of the nineteenth century was mental. Old political ideas like the Monroe Doctrine were imbued with more expansionist overtones, and newer ones like manifest destiny offered spiritual sustenance for aggressive behavior. Proliferating theories of racial superiority, buttressed by science or pseudoscience, became accepted "wisdom." Regardless of class or education, the majority of WASP Americans believed their country had a special mission, sanctified by geography and race, to lead and dominate the "unfit" and the "uncivilized" peoples of the world.

The Imperialists

Eager to assist the expansionist capitalists who believed that the acquisition of overseas markets would be the panacea for the nation's economic woes were a group of politicians, intellectuals, and military strategists who viewed such expansion (the acquisition of territory) as essential for great power status. They wanted the nation to take its place alongside Britain, France, Germany, and Russia as a great imperial nation. They believed that the United States should join the intensifying competition among the major European powers for colonies; it should build a strong navy, solidify a sphere of influence in the Caribbean, and extend markets into Asia, just as the Europeans were doing, not only in that region of the world but in Africa and the Middle East as well. Indeed, by the late nineteenth century only one independent nation existed in Africa—Ethiopia. The rest of the continent had been carved up by the European powers. Even tiny Belgium had a "piece of the action," controlling the resource-rich present-day nation, the Congo, while France possessed geographically the largest empire in Africa, even though most of it was desert. Watching the European superpowers carve up the world were the envious American imperialists who began agitating for the United States to get into the race for empire while "the gittin' was still good."

The imperialists, to justify their new outlook, resurrected the pre-Civil War rhetoric of manifest destiny that now became consonant with imperialism; indeed, they were now one-in-the-same. John Fiske, noted American anthropologist and imperialist, as well as a popular lecturer, toured the country giving a set-piece presentation entitled "Manifest Destiny." Fiske asserted that "The work the English race began when it colonized North America is destined to go on until every land on the earth's surface that is not already the seat of an old civilization shall become English in its language, in its religion, in its political habits and traditions, and to a predominant extent in the blood of its people."

As noted in the previous chapter, Darwinian theory was distorted to reinforce the cult of capitalism, allowing plutocrats like Rockefeller and Carnegie a way to justify their ruthless acquisitiveness and their brutal exploitation of their workers. The imperialists also found ideological succor from Social Darwinism to bolster their expansionist assertions. Implicit in Social Darwinism was the claim of Anglo-Saxon racial superiority. The imperialists were overwhelming of such ethnic/racial stock and thus held that America's democratic institutions—i.e., the New England town meeting—came not from ancient Greece but from early German tribes via England. They quickly incorporated Darwinism into their new approach to imperialism. The peripatetic Fiske argued that Anglo-Saxon expansion, based on Teutonic theories of democracy, justified any conquest.

The most popular propagator of Anglo-Saxonism/imperialism was the Protestant evangelical, Josiah Strong, whose paean to Anglo-Saxonism, *Our Country,* was a national bestseller in the late 1880s. In his book, Strong asserted that "the wonderful progress of the United States as well as the character of its people, are the results of natural selection." For Strong and his disciples, the Anglo-Saxon race represented civil liberty and "pure spiritual Christianity." North America was to be "the great home of the Anglo-Saxon, the principal seat of his power, the center of his life and influence." With its obvious genetic and biological superiority, the Anglo-Saxon race "will spread itself over the earth" to Mexico, to Central and South America, and "out upon the islands of the sea" to Africa and beyond. Feeling no remorse for the "inferior races" doomed by the Anglo-Saxon advance, Strong asked rhetorically, "Is there room for reasonable doubt that his race, unless devitalized by alcohol and tobacco, is destined to dispossess many weaker races, assimilate others, and mold the remainder, until, in a very true and important sense, it has Anglo-Saxonized mankind?"

Strong's sanctimonious boosterism and racism would be easy to dismiss as rubbish if it had not been so popular with the nation's increasingly anxious (because of immigration) Anglo-Saxon masses or if his rantings had not been embraced and articulated in the classrooms and lecture halls of some of the nation's best universities. Unfortunately, late nineteenth century American academic institutions lacked today's student diversity, and thus those sitting in the classrooms were overwhelming young WASP males, who wholeheartedly concurred with their professors who preached white, Anglo-Saxon supremacy and the need for their race to dominate all others to prevent the "mongrelization" of humanity. Darwin, to his chagrin, set scholars scrambling to determine racial superiority by measuring facial angles, skull size, brain weight, and even human hair. There was hardly a major university in the United States that did not include racially based courses in its core curriculum. To the imperialists/Social Darwinists, success in international competition and conquest reflected laws of nature. America's destiny required th itself the military equal of the strongest European nations and the master of the "lesser" peoples of the world.

Thus, as the nineteenth century came to a close, the United States was a restless and racist society. Those who believed the myth of Anglo-Saxonism could ascribe inferiority to masses of people at home and abroad: African Americans, Native Americans, workers, immigrants, and most foreigners. Such a cultural atmosphere was extremely conducive to imperialist initiatives, because imperialism—like Anglo-Saxonism, Social Darwinism, and manifest destiny—was also based on the principle of racial inequality.

ADMIRAL ALFRED THAYER MAHAN AND THE RISE OF AMERICAN MILITARISM

Perhaps the most influential imperialist was Admiral Alfred Thayer Mahan, whose seminal work, *The Influence of Sea Power on History, 1660-1783* (1890), laid out the blue-print for the nation's first, most significant peacetime military buildup. In his book, Mahan argued that all the world's great empires, beginning with Rome, sustained their hegemony by controlling the seas. If the United States hoped to attain great power status, it was imperative that it embark immediately on an aggressive expansion and modernization of its navy, with enough ships and fire-power to make its presence felt everywhere in the world. Ironically, during the Civil War, the United States possessed one of the world's largest navies; by the 1880s the United States ranked twelfth behind sleeping China, decrepit Turkey, and tiny Chile. To be effective, that global fleet would require a canal across Central America through which U.S. warships could pass swiftly from the Atlantic to the Pacific Oceans. It would also demand a string of far-flung service bases from the Caribbean to the southwestern Pacific. Mahan thus urged the United States government to take possession of Hawaii and other strategically located Pacific islands with superior harbor

seen, Presidents William McKinley sevelt would eventually make al-

most all of Mahan's vision a reality. In the early 1890s, however, Mahan believed his ideas and exhortations were falling on deaf ears, for he was certain that few Americans were willing to bear the costs and responsibilities of empire. Although the imperialists counted in their ranks prominent individuals like Theodore Roosevelt and Senator Henry Cabot Lodge of Massachusetts, there were still too many Americans who insisted that the United States should not aspire to world power by emulating the Europeans by using military might and force to acquire bases and colonies. Such an approach, they believed, would not only "degrade" the United States, putting the nation on the same "level" as the Europeans, but tarnish, as well, the revered image of a country whose people were known for their sense of justice, decency, and humanity.

Mahan's skepticism quickly dissipated as the government's alarm over the Europeans' expansionist policies moved both Congress and the presidents to action. Every administration from the 1880s on committed itself to a "big navy" policy. By 1898 the U.S. navy had moved from twelfth to fifth in the world; by 1900 it ranked third, behind only England and Germany. Already in 1878, under the farsighted auspices of the "Plumed Knight," James G. Blaine, who was serving as Secretary of State for Rutherford B. Hayes, the United States secured rights to Pago Pago, a superb deepwater harbor in Samoa (a collection of islands in the southwest Pacific inhabited by Polynesians).

These attempts to project U.S. power overseas had already deepened the government's involvement in the affairs of foreign lands. For example, four years after securing harbor rights to Pago Pago, in 1889, the United States established a protectorate (the "uniquely" American term for "colony") over part of Samoa, a move intended to block German and British attempts to weaken American presence and influence on the islands.

In the early 1890s, Grover Cleveland was increasingly drawn into Hawaiian affairs, as tensions between American sugar planters and native Hawaiians upset the islands' economic and political stability. In other words, by that decade, a small but powerful coterie of American sugar planters had pretty much gained economic and thus political control of the islands, relegating the native population to an underclass of subservient lackeys. Tensions between native Hawaiians and whites began as early as the 1820s when American missionaries arrived to try to convert the islanders to Christianity. In the process they began buying up huge parcels of land and to subvert the existing feudal system of landholding. They simultaneously encouraged American businesses to buy into sugar plantations, and by 1875 U.S. corporations dominated the sugar trade. American capitalists, in effect, turned the islands into one vast sugar-producing economy, which they completely controlled. By this time Hawaii appeared in James G. Blaine's opinion to be "an outlying district of the state of California," and he began to push for annexation. In 1887 a new treaty allowed the United States to build a naval base at Pearl Harbor on the island of Oahu. Now, together with Pago Pago, the United States had two Pacific fueling stations for its growing naval fleet.

Emboldened by the Pearl Harbor treaty, American sugar planters took a step further toward hopeful annexation by overthrowing a weak king, Kalakaua, and replacing him with the more pliant Queen Liliuokalani, whom they believed would be their puppet. Queen "Lili," however, chose not to become their lackey and tried to assert her independence. The planters were determined to control the islands, and under the leadership of pineapple magnate, Sanford B. Dole, and with the help of U.S. sailors, the planters overthrew the queen in 1893. The planters then put pressure on Cleveland to make Hawaii a protectorate, which he did in that same year. Congressional imperialists wanted the president to outright annex the islands, but Cleveland refused to acquiesce to their demands. In 1900, however, during the presidency of William McKinley, Hawaii was officially annexed as a territory of the United States. The native Hawaiians were not consulted about this momentous change in their national identity.

Hawaii was often viewed as a stepping-stone to the vast Asian markets, especially those of China. For that purpose, in 1896, a consortium of New York bankers created the American China Development

President William McKinley

Company. They feared, however, that the weak Manchu dynasty would fall to European, Russian, and Japanese imperialism. Once they gained control of China, they would then carve it up into "spheres of influence" (which they already had done to large portions of that beleaguered country) and close off their respective areas of occupation to outside trade, which they already were in the process of doing with the territory they already possessed. Such action would obviously lock the United States out of this most lucrative market. Secretary of State John Hay responded in 1899 by announcing the Open Door Policy. According to this doctrine, outlined in notes to six major powers, the U.S. enjoyed the right to advance its commercial interests anywhere in the world, at least on terms equal to those of other imperialist nations. The Chinese marketplace was too important to lose. Nationalist rebellion, however, threatened to prevent all outsiders' plans to end Chinese sovereignty. An antiforeign secret society known as the Harmonious Righteous Firsts (dubbed "Boxers" by the Western media) rioted repeatedly in 1898 and 1899 in protest against the foreign occupation of their country. In 1899 they actually succeeded in controlling the capital city of Beijing and surrounding all the foreign embassies. Appalled by the deaths of thousands, including many Chinese converts to Christianity, and determined to maintain American economic interests, President McKinley, without requesting congressional approval, sent 5,000 U.S troops to join an international coalition forces, which ultimately put down the uprising. The Boxer Rebellion dramatized the Manchu regime's weaknesses as well as the surging wave of nationalism affecting increasing numbers of Chinese resentful of the foreign occupation and exploitation of their country and people and destruction of their culture. As will be seen in a later chapter, the United States will secretly help the Chinese win their independence from primarily European domination and in return for such assistance, China will "open its doors" to American trade, granting the United States "most favored" nation status.

By this time, imperialist sentiment in Congress and throughout the nation was being energized by "jingoism." Jingoists—the word was originally coined in Great Britain in the 1870s and quickly entered American foreign policy parlance—were supernationalists (hardcore Social Darwinists as well) who believed that an aggressive, arrogant foreign policy with a willingness to go to war would enhance the nation's glory. They were constantly on the alert for insults to their country's honor and prestige and swift to call for military retaliation if so affronted. This predatory brand of nationalism emerged not only in Britain and in the United States, but in France, Germany, and Japan as well. The anti-imperialist editor, E.L. Godkin, of *The Nation* exclaimed in 1894, "The number of men and officials in this country who are now mad to fight somebody is appalling." Spain's behavior in Cuba in the 1890s gave the imperialists the war they sought. The imperialists had grown up in a period of weak presidents, an exploding economy, escalating military power, rising expectations, and disappointing performance. Now the time for action was fast approaching, and they would seize it. In helping make the United States a great power, they were more than simple agents of history. Conditioned by years of frustration in foreign policy, they could now lead it into a new realm and become the movers and shakers of American expansion.

THE SPANISH-AMERICAN WAR

By the 1890s the islands of Cuba and Puerto Rico were virtually all that remained of Spain's once vast New World empire. Ever since the late 1860s the Cubans had been in a constant state of revolt against Spanish rule. Though ultimately suppressing the early uprisings, by the late 1890s, the Spanish were finding it increasingly more difficult to subdue the Cuban rebels, whose numbers were growing each year. Interestingly, helping to ignite the 1895 insurrection was a tariff passed by the United States a year earlier that made sugar, Cuba's main export, too expensive for the U.S. market. The tariff caused economic contraction, which in turn only intensified Cubans' resentment toward their Spanish rulers, even though they had not caused the depression. The fighting between Spanish soldiers and Cuban rebels was brutal, as both sides often committed unspeakable atrocities. The rebels razed large areas of the island, not only destroying tobacco and sugar crops but making it uninhabitable as well. The Spanish army retaliated, responding in kind on the orders of General Valeriano Weyler, who rounded up thousands of Cubans and "relocated" them into concentration camps where they were horribly mistreated, causing thousands to die. Indeed, an estimated 200,000 Cubans—one-eighth of the island's population—died of starvation and disease.

Such reprisals, especially those attributed to "Butcher" Weyler (as he was now being labeled in the U.S. press), inflamed American public opinion. Many Americans sympathized with the Cubans, whom they believed were fighting the same anticolonial war they themselves had waged against another "effete" European power over 100 years earlier. The American public was kept well-apprised of events in Cuba, especially in the newspapers published by either William Randolph Hearst or Joseph Pulitzer, who together owned the majority of the nation's largest dailies. Pulitzer and Hearst were revolutionizing American journalism in the late nineteenth century by creating a new kind of newspaper, which catered openly to a readership of lower socioeconomic status than those citizens who read the more traditional press. In short, they created the first tabloids, which today can be seen in every supermarket check-out stand around the nation. Like today's *National Enquirer*, and other such publications, Hearst's and Pulitzer's papers specialized in lurid, sensational news; when such news did not exist, editors were not above making it up. All such presentation was designed to boost circulation, which meant more money for Hearst and Pulitzer. By the 1890s, both men were engaged in a ruthless circulation war, and they saw the struggle in Cuba as a great opportunity. Both sent hordes of reporters and illustrators to the island with orders to provide accounts of Spanish atrocities committed on innocent Cubans. All too frequently Hearst and Pulitzer reporters greatly exaggerated or distorted what was actually taking place in Cuba, if not blatantly fabricating stories to please their greedy publishers. They were accused by the legitimate press of engaging in "yellow journalism"—embellishing stories with titillating details when the true reports did not seem dramatic enough. "You furnish the pictures," Hearst supposedly told an overly scrupulous artist, "and I'll furnish the war."

Helping the jingoists and interventionists agitate the American public were the thousands of Cuban émigrés in the United States living primarily in the cities of Miami, Philadelphia, New York, and Trenton, New Jersey. These folk gave extensive support to the Cuban Revolutionary Party, headquartered in New York, and helped to make its slain leader, Jose Marti, a "freedom-fighting" hero and martyr in the eyes of many sympathetic but duped Americans. With the financial backing of prominent American capitalists, Cuban Americans formed other clubs and associations to support the cause of *Cuba Libre*. In some areas of the country, the émigrés' activities and solicitations were more important in garnering popular support for U.S. intervention in Cuba than the falsehoods circulated by the yellow journalists.

The increasing public outcry against alleged Spanish brutality and imperialist agitation for U.S. intervention in Cuba failed to move President Grover Cleveland to action. He proclaimed American neutrality and urged New York City officials to muzzle Cuban émigrés there who were trying to rally New Yorkers to the cause of Cuban independence. Cleveland's Republican successor, William McKinley, elected in 1896, appeared more amenable to the jingoists' and imperialists' cries for intervention in Cuba. Soon after taking office, McKinley formally protested Spain's "uncivilized and inhuman" behavior, causing the Spanish government (which was growing more fearful of American intervention) to recall Weyler, significantly modify its "relocation" policy, and grant Cubans limited autonomy. At the end of 1897, because of the concessions granted by the Spanish, the insurrection abated and for the moment it seemed that U.S. intervention might be averted. The jingoists and imperialists naturally believed that it was their "saber-rattling" that had caused Spain to capitulate and modify their Cuban policy. To a degree they were correct; the Spanish government, as will be seen shortly, wanted to avoid a war with the United States at all costs—a war Spain knew it could not win.

Unfortunately, the events of February 1898 mitigated the chances for a peaceful settlement. The first crisis occurred with the publication in U.S. papers of the de Lome letter, a communiqué written by the Spanish minister in Washington, Dupuy de Lome, that had been stolen by a Cuban agent in Havana and "somehow" found its way into American dailies. In this private correspondence, de Lome described McKinley as a weak man and "a bidder for the admiration of the crowd." Interestingly, many Americans felt the same way about McKinley, including fellow Republican Theodore Roosevelt, who declared the president as having "no more backbone than a chocolate éclair." Americans accepted as part of partisan politics the right of citizens to openly criticize their president. But no "foreigner" was allowed such freedom, and if one had the audacity to do so, they would quickly incur the wrath of the American public. Such was the situation for Dupuy de Lome, who promptly resigned after reading his comments in American newspapers.

While anger over the de Lome letter was still high, the U.S. battleship *Maine* blew up in Havana harbor, causing the death of 260 sailors. McKinley had sent the *Maine* into Havana harbor in late 1897 to protect U.S. citizens and property from supposed

The U. S. battleship, *Maine*, exploded in Havana harbor. The ship was destroyed and all of the crew still aboard were killed. "Remember the Maine" became the battle cry.

Spanish loyalists' attacks. No sooner did the ship explode, than the jingoists and imperialists screamed "retribution" and agitated for war. They were certain that the Spanish had sunk the ship, particularly after a hastily assembled naval court of inquiry declared (inaccurately) that an external explosion by a submarine mine had caused the disaster. Later evidence established that the incident occurred as a result of an accidental explosion in the engine rooms. Regardless of the true cause, at the time, sufficient numbers of Americans were convinced it was the dastardly act of the evil Spanish, and thus war hysteria swept the land and Congress, responding to the public clamor for retaliation, unanimously appropriated $50 million for military preparations. Echoing the rallying cry used in Texas by Anglo-Americans some sixty years earlier—"Remember the Alamo"— to defeat an equally perfidious "Latin" people, the Mexicans, "Remember the *Maine*" became the new Anglo-American mantra for revenge against the Spanish.

McKinley still hoped to avoid a conflict; others in his administration, including Assistant Secretary of the Navy, Theodore Roosevelt, clamored for war. In March 1898, the president notified the Spanish government of his conditions for avoiding war: Spain would pay an indemnity for the *Maine,* abandon its concentration camp policy, end the fighting with the rebels, and commit itself to Cuban independence. On April 9, Spain agreed to all the demands but one—Cuban independence. Though McKinley was inclined to accept Spain's bid for peace, the jingoist/imperialist pressure from within his administration and from the public was too great for him to withstand. Jingoist and imperialist propaganda had been successful in whipping the American public into a war frenzy; nothing short of a violent display of new American power would satisfy the American people. Moreover, the nation's new war machines, especially the navy, had been modernized at great expense and now the opportunity presented itself to see whether it was sufficient enough to earn the United States the respect it deserved as a great power. In short, the imperialists believed it was essential for the U.S. to go to war; if Spain simply acquiesced to American

Newspapers printed sensational headline stories, stirring up the public to go to war with Spain as pictured in here in Joseph Pulitzer's *New York World*.

demands then the nation would not have the opportunity to demonstrate its awesome military power nor the "virility," "masculinity," and martial spirit of its people. There was no better way to show the other great powers that the United States had "arrived" militarily and economically than to unleash upon another country its new war machines and in a brief, decisive war earn an empire. Thus, on April 11, 1898, McKinley asked Congress for authority to go to war. Three days later Congress approved a war resolution, which included a declaration (spelled out in the Teller Amendment) that the United States would not use the war as an opportunity to acquire Cuba. On April 24, Spain responded with a formal declaration of war against the United States.

"A Splendid Little War"

Secretary of State John Hay called the Spanish-American conflict "a splendid little war," a view most Americans—with the exception of the actual combatants—seemed to share. Declared in April 1898,

it was over by August of that year. The war was so brief largely because the Cuban rebels, after years of fighting, had significantly weakened Spanish forces on the island, thus making U.S. intervention in many respects nothing more than a "mopping up" operation. Out of the one million men who volunteered to fight, only 460 were killed in battle or died from wounds. However, 5,200 others perished from diseases such as malaria, dysentery, and typhoid, to name just a few. Casualties among the Cuban rebel forces who continued to bear the brunt of the fighting were much higher.

Another factor contributing to the relatively easy American victory was U.S. naval superiority. In the war's first major battle, a naval engagement in Manila harbor on May 1, 1898, in the Philippines, Spain's strategic Pacific possession, a U. S. fleet commanded by Commodore George Dewey, destroyed an entire Spanish fleet while losing only a sailor (to heat stroke). In mid-August, U.S. troops occupied the capital, Manilla. On land the story was different as the nation went to war with a standing U.S. Army of only 26,000 troops, which were scattered throughout the western United States, whose only combat experience had been skirmishing with Indians and

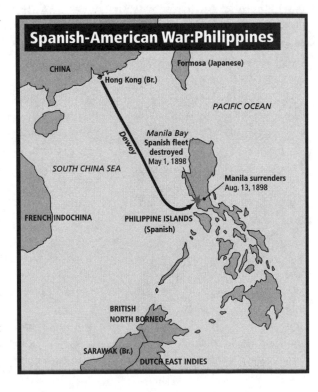

chasing down bandits and other desperadoes. In short, the army was ill-equipped and ill-prepared to fight an all-out war. Even though Spain was not a great power, nor even remotely close to even pretending to be one, it nonetheless was going to fight to try to keep the last vestiges of its once vast empire, and thus greeting American forces on Cuba was a Spanish army of 80,000 regulars. Congress immediately increased the Army to 62,000 and called for an additional 125,000 volunteers. The response to this call was astounding but outfitting, training, and transporting the new recruits overwhelmed the Army's capacities. United States soldiers endured serious supply problems: a shortage of modern rifles and ammunition, having to wear blue flannel uniforms, totally inappropriate attire for the hot, humid Caribbean weather, inadequate medical services, and food rations so bad that many soldiers died from food poisoning! It took more than five days in June to ship an invasion force of 16,000 men the short distance from Tampa, Florida to Daiquiri, Cuba.

There were also racial conflicts. A significant number of the combatants, whether they were volunteers or regular army, were African Americans. In the regular army there were black regiments who had been stationed in the West to defend white settlements from Indian raids and were now transferred east to fight in Cuba. As the "Buffalo Soldiers" traveled through the South toward the training camps, they resented the rigid segregation and name-calling they were subjected to and occasionally fought back. Black soldiers in Georgia deliberately camped out in a "whites-only" park; in Florida, they beat a white soda-fountain worker who refused to serve them; in Tampa, attempted white intimidations provoked a black retaliation that resulted in a nightlong black-white confrontation that left thirty white civilians wounded.

Another interesting and ironic racist taint to the war was the fact that the majority of the Cuban guerrilla fighters were black. This shocked U.S. forces because they believed the Cuban "freedom-fighters, fully nine-tenths of them," were white because U.S. newspaper reports had described them as "intelligent, civilized, and democratic, possessing an Anglo-Saxon tenacity of purpose." The Spanish oppressors, by contrast, were portrayed as dark complexioned—"dark, cruel eyes, dark swaggering men," is how the writer Sherwood Anderson depicted them—and possessing the characteristics of their "dark race": barbarism, cruelty, and indolence. The U.S. troops' first encounters with Cuban and Spanish forces dispelled these myths. Their Cuban allies appeared poorly outfitted, rough in their manners, and primarily dark-skinned. By contrast, the Spanish soldiers were light-complexioned, appeared well-disciplined, and tougher in battle than was expected. The Cuban rebels were actually skilled guerrilla fighters but racial prejudice prevented U.S. soldiers and reporters from crediting their contributions to eventual victory. Instead, they judged the Cubans harshly, asserting that they were primitive, savage, and incapable of self-control or self-government. As will be seen, such ascriptions went far in helping the imperialists persuade the American people that Cuba must become an American protectorate, if for no other reason than to "save" the Cubans from themselves! During the actual fighting, U.S. troops (the majority of the white troops) refused to associate with their black Cuban allies. They refused to fight alongside the Cubans, and increasingly they denied their "allies" information about Spanish movements and other strategy.

Despite the U.S. Army's ineptitude and racial prejudice, its soldiers were filled with the appropriate martial spirit, as all of them—both black and white—were eager for combat. No one was more excited about that prospect than Theodore Roosevelt, who, along with Colonel Leonard Wood, led a volunteer cavalry unit comprised of an interesting and somewhat motley crew of Ivy League gentlemen (Roosevelt's Harvard cronies), western cowboys, sheriffs, prospectors, Indians, and small numbers of Hispanics and ethnic European Americans. Roosevelt's "Rough Riders," as the battalion came to be known, landed with the invasion force and played an active role in the three battles fought in the hills surrounding Santiago de Cuba, the main theater of action on the island's southeastern coast. Their most famous action, the one on which TR would build his lifelong reputation as a warrior/hero, was a furious charge on foot, not on horse, up Kettle Hill into the

Major Battles In Cuba

El Caney
July 1, 1898

Santiago

Santiago Bay

San Juan Hill
July 1, 1898

Kettle Hill
July 1, 1898

Las Guasimas
June 24, 1898

Spanish fleet
destroyed
July 3, 1898

Daiquiri

heart of Spanish defenses. Roosevelt's bravery was remarkable though his judgment was faulty. Nearly 100 men were killed or wounded in the charge. Accounts of TR's bravery overshadowed the equally, if not more courageous, performance of other troops, most notably the 9th and 10th Negro Cavalries, which played a key role in clearing away Spanish fortifications on Kettle Hill and allowing Roosevelt's Rough Riders to make the charge. One of TR's men commented: "If it had not been for the Negro cavalry, the Rough Riders would have been exterminated." Another added, "I am a Southerner by birth, and I never thought much of the colored man. But I never saw such fighting as those Tenth Cavalry men did. They didn't seem to know what fear was, and their battle hymn was 'There'll be a hot time in the old town tonight.'" The 24th and 25th Negro Infantry Regiments performed equally important tasks in the U.S. Army's taking of the adjacent San Juan Hill.

Despite prejudice, discrimination, and segregation, African-American soldiers risked their lives in

Colonel Roosevelt and his Rough Riders at the top of San Juan Hill

proving their patriotism and courage. At the time, Roosevelt and others publicly lauded their contributions to ultimate victory. He praised his black comrades-in-arms as "an excellent breed of Yankee," and declared that no "Rough Rider will ever forget the tie that binds us to the Ninth and Tenth Cavalry." But soon after returning home, he began diminishing their role, even to the point of calling their behavior cowardly. Like most white American officers and enlisted men of the time, TR had difficulty believing blacks could fight well. By the time of U.S. entry into the Great War in 1917, the U.S. military had adopted a policy of excluding black troops from combat roles altogether. Moreover, it must be remembered that if African-American soldiers' bravery and contributions to victory were too exalted by white America, such acclaim could go far toward helping African Americans achieve equality at home—something few white Americans were ready to embrace.

Though victorious on the battlefield, by mid-July 1898, American troops were short of food, ammunition, and medical facilities. Their ranks were so decimated by malaria, typhoid, and dysentery that Roosevelt despaired, "We are within measurable distance of a terrible military disaster." Fortunately, the Spanish had lost the will to fight, realizing that to do so would cause even greater humiliation and death. As Spain's Atlantic fleet tried to retreat from Santiago harbor, the U.S. navy raked and sank their archaic fleet, killing 474 Spanish sailors. The Spanish army in Santiago surrendered on July 16; and on July 18 the Spanish government asked for peace. While Spanish and U.S. officials negotiated an armistice, American forces took Puerto Rico. On August 12 the U.S. and Spanish government agreed to an armistice, but before the news reached the Philippines, the U.S. captured Manila and took prisoner 13,000 Spanish soldiers. In the ensuing formal peace settlement, finalized in the Treaty of Paris in December 1898, Spain recognized Cuban independence, ceded Puerto Rico and the Pacific island of Guam to the United States, and after receiving a payment of $20 million, the Spanish agreed to give the Philippines, as well, to the victorious United States. Americans now possessed an island empire stretching from the Caribbean to the Pacific.

THE UNITED STATES BECOMES A WORLD POWER

The United States' acquisition of the Philippines, Guam, and Puerto Rico had little, if not nothing, to do with the reasons the nation had gone to war. Initially, the U.S. proclaimed to the world and to its own citizens that the Republic was going to war to help liberate the Cuban people from their brutal Spanish oppressors, and in that context, the country would be upholding its democratic creed of self-determination. For the imperialists such rhetoric was simply a ruse to disguise their real intention, which was to incorporate Cuba into a new American empire. Naïve anti-imperialists, who supported the war, believed it was to liberate the Cubans from the last decadent "remnant" of the Old World, Spain. Naturally the imperialists delighted in the Treaty of Paris, which ceded to the U.S. Guam, Puerto Rico, and the Philippines, the last viewed as essential for the projection of U.S. power in the Pacific and Asia. In the end, President McKinley was just as much an imperialist as the men who surrounded him and who were the architects of the expansionist policy and the war. As noted earlier, McKinley annexed Hawaii, giving the U.S. permanent control of its first-rate deep-water port at Pearl Harbor. Then, he set his sights on setting up a naval base at Manila. Never before had the United States pursued such a large military presence outside the Western Hemisphere.

In a departure of even greater significance and future ramifications, the McKinley administration announced that the newly acquired territories would be regarded as colonies and governed as such. Virtually all the territory previously acquired by the United States had been settled by Americans, who eventually petitioned for statehood and were admitted to the Union with the same rights as existing states. In the case of the new possessions, only Hawaii would be allowed to follow the traditional path toward statehood. That occurred largely because of the influence of the powerful American sugar planters, who controlled the island and believed it best for their economic interests if Hawaii was made a "territory" in the traditional sense so that it could someday become a state. In 1900, Congress obliged the sugar planters by passing an act extending U.S. citizenship to all Hawaiian residents and putting the islands on the road to statehood in 1959. The story of the Philippines, as will be seen shortly, was quite different. There, no powerful American clique resided who desired eventual statehood status. The U.S. had little interest in the Philippines beyond controlling Manila harbor. The decision to make the whole country an American colony was proclaimed to prevent other powers, such as Japan and Germany, from gaining a foothold somewhere in the 400-island archipelago and launching attacks on the American naval base at Manila.

The McKinley administration might have taken a different approach toward the Philippines had it not been for the racism that informed much of American imperialist policy and attitudes at this time. Helping U.S. forces to defeat the Spanish in the Philippines was a broad-based indigenous rebel movement led by Emilio Aguinaldo, who, like his Cuban counterparts, looked to the United States as the liberator of his country. However, much to Aguinaldo's eventual disappointment and betrayal, the U.S. never had any intention of granting the islands their independence, which they could have done by simply brokering a deal with Aguinaldo, giving the Philippines independence in exchange for a naval base at Manila. An American fleet stationed there would have protected the islands from other aggressive imperialists, such as Japan or Germany, serving the larger interests of both the U.S. and Filipinos. Outright annexation was also an alternative, granting the Filipinos the same status as the Hawaiians and putting them on the road toward statehood. However, McKinley chose none of these possibilities. He believed, like most other imperialists, that the Filipinos were an "inferior" people incapable of self-government and the right of self-determination. In short, McKinley believed that American rule would enormously benefit the Filipinos, whom he called "our little brown brothers." A devout Methodist, he explained that America's mission was "to educate the Filipinos and to uplift and civilize and Christianize them, and by God's grace do the very best we could by them." In reality, the majority of Filipinos were already Christianized, Catholic in fact, a legacy of

centuries of Spanish rule. Indeed, a substantial percentage of the islanders not only had assumed Spanish names but were bilingual as well, able to speak both Spanish and their native tongue. They were hardly a people bereft of "civilization." Nonetheless, the U.S. would undertake a solemn mission to "civilize" the Filipinos and help to prepare them for independence. Until the U.S. deemed they were sufficiently "civilized," the island would be ruled by American governors appointed by the president. As will be seen shortly, the Filipinos believed they were "civilized" enough and ready for their independence and if it was not given freely, then they would take it from the United States by fighting a second war of national liberation.

Critics of Empire: The Anti-Imperialists

Even before the ink was dry on the Treaty of Paris, strong voices of opposition to empire had emerged, led by the recently organized Anti-Imperialist League. The association's membership was an impressive list of noted Americans, ranging from former president Grover Cleveland to the plutocrat Andrew Carnegie, to the labor leader Samuel Gompers, and to some of the nation's foremost men of letters and intellectuals such as Mark Twain, William James, and William Dean Howells. Disturbing them most was the acquisition of the Philippines, which they believed was a blatant contradiction and violation of the nation's most precious principle: the right of all people to independence and self-government. Moreover, they feared that the large military and diplomatic establishment that would be required to administer the colony would threaten political liberties at home. Though capitalists like Carnegie could be found among the more righteous and altruistic anti-imperialists, the majority of Carnegie's plutocratic cohorts joined the cause out of self-interest. U.S. sugar producers feared competition from Filipino producers. Trade unionists, like Gompers, worried that cheap Filipino labor would stream across the Pacific and flood the U.S. labor market and reduce wage rates. Some businessmen warned that the cost of maintaining an "imperial" outpost in the Philippines would far exceed any economic benefits the colony would provide to the nation. Many Democratic anti-imperialists typically used the acquisition of the islands for partisan purposes, as an entrée to criticize Republican foreign policy in general. Finally, many anti-imperialists were hardcore social Darwinists, who already were anxious about the massive influx of southern and eastern Europeans and their "breeding" potential for mongrelization. They now feared the contaminating effects of contact with "inferior" Asian races.

In February 1899, the anti-imperialist coalition in the Senate failed by one vote to prevent that body's ratification of the expansionist Treaty of Paris. Helping to deliver the imperialist victory was the news on the eve of the vote that the Filipinos had risen in revolt against the U.S. army of occupation. With another war looming and the lives of American soldiers imperiled, a few senators who had been reluctant to vote for the treaty may have felt obligated to support the president. McKinley's overwhelming re-election victory in 1900 and the defeat of the expansionist critic William Jennings Bryan eroded the anti-imperialist cause. Nevertheless, at a time of jingoistic rhetoric and militaristic posturing, many of them had upheld an older and finer vision of the United States.

GUERRILLA WAR IN THE PHILIPPINES, 1898-1902

A Prelude to Vietnam

Unfortunately for both Americans and Filipinos, "uplifting" the latter embroiled the United States in a bloody struggle that lasted for nearly five years and cost the lives of over 4,000 American soldiers and as many as 20,000 Filipino resistance fighters. By the time the fighting ended in the summer of 1902, more than 120,000 U.S. soldiers had served in the Philippines. The conflict cost $160 million, or eight times what the U.S. paid Spain for the archipelago. The war brought Americans face-to-face with a disturbing reality: American actions on the islands were all too often no different than those of the Spanish on Cuba. Like Spain, the United States was refusing to

recognize a people's desire for self-rule. Like "Butcher" Weyler, American generals turned a blind eye as their soldiers used savage tactics to "search and destroy" rebel encampments, units, and any civilian hamlets believed to be harboring rebels or their supplies. In the process, whole communities suspected of supporting the rebels were "relocated" into concentration camps, while their entire village was razed. American soldiers executed so many insurrectionists (whom they called "goo-goos") that the ratio of Filipino dead to wounded reached 15 to 1, a statistic that made the U.S. Civil War, in which one soldier had died for every five wounded, seem relatively humane. One New Yorker wrote home that his unit had killed 1,000 Filipinos—men, women, and children—in retaliation for the killing of a single American soldier. Reflecting the racist attitude of most Americans, whether civilian or military, toward the Filipinos, the infantryman wrote home that "I am in my glory when I can sight my gun on some dark skin and pull the trigger." Estimates of total Filipino deaths from American bullets, starvation, and disease range from 50,000 to 200,000.

The United States finally gained the upper hand after General Arthur MacArthur (father of Douglas) was appointed commander of the islands in 1900. MacArthur did not seek an immediate peace settlement; indeed, the fighting's ferocity continued unabated. He realized, however, that peace could not be won by guns alone and thus initiated an amnesty program for all Filipino rebels who laid down their arms. He also cultivated close relations with the island's wealthy elites. McKinley supported this effort to build a Filipino constituency accepting of U.S. presence. To that end, he sent William Howard Taft to the islands in 1900 to establish a civilian government. A year later, Taft became the colony's first "governor-general" and declared that he intended to prepare the Filipinos for independence. Taking a page from British imperialism, Taft and subsequent American governor-generals, to create the façade that the "colonists" were governing themselves, ruled through puppet local elites. Everyone knew, however, that the United States still controlled the islands and that whatever autonomy had been granted was the result of American "munificent" self-interest. Nonetheless, many governmental functions were transferred to Filipino control, and Taft initiated a vigorous program of public works (roads, bridges, schools) that would give the Philippines the infrastructure necessary for economic development and political independence. Naturally, few such projects were undertaken without an eye toward usefulness to the United States as well. After all, it was an American colony from which benefits were expected. By 1902, the combination of ruthless suppression and concessions ended the revolt. Though sporadic fighting continued until 1913, American control of the Philippines was secure. In 1946, nearly half a century after Admiral Dewey's guns had boomed in Manila Bay, independence finally came to the Philippines.

Controlling Cuba and Puerto Rico

Helping the Cubans free themselves from Spanish oppression and then allowing for their independence had allegedly been the main purpose for war against Spain. However, as in the case of the Philippines, American altruism quickly changed as the McKinley administration made it clear that the United States was not about to relinquish control of the island. At the president's urging, Congress attached the Platt Amendment to a 1901 army appropriations bill that abrogated the earlier Teller Amendment, that in effect had disavowed any American intention of acquiring Cuba. Despite its obfuscating verbiage, the Platt Amendment made Cuba another American colony by stipulating that Cuba would not be permitted to make treaties with foreign powers; that the United States would have broad authority to intervene in Cuban political and economic affairs; and that Cuba would sell or lease land to the United States for naval stations. Suffice it to say, Cuban nationalists felt betrayed and outraged by such American duplicity but, unlike the Filipinos, did not rise in revolt. The dependence of Cuba's vital sugar industry on the U.S. market and the presence of a substantial U.S. army of occupation rendered resistance futile. In short, the Cubans had no choice but to write the Platt Amendment into their constitution if they hoped to have even a modicum of self-rule. Unfortunately for the Cubans, their economic dependence on the United States allowed for their constant political subjugation. Between 1989 and 1914, American trade with Cuba increased more than tenfold—from $27 million to $300 million—while investments more than quadrupled—from $50 million to $220 million. The United States intervened in Cuban political affairs a total of five times between 1906 and 1921 to protect its capitalist interests. As in the Philippines, the United States ruled through a pro-U.S. business indigenous elite that remained in power until 1959, when Cuban rebels, led by Fidel Castro, overthrew the last of such puppet regimes. Until then, the Cubans endured a half century of internal suppression and external exploitation of their country. Needless to say, the economic, military, and political control the United States imposed on Cuba would fuel anti-American sentiment there for years to come and help prepare the way for Castro's victory in 1959.

Puerto Rico received somewhat different treatment. The United States was not going to grant the Puerto Ricans independence, even though ironically under Spanish rule the islanders enjoyed a large measure of political autonomy. Nor did the United States impose Puerto Rico any sort of Platt Amendment that made the island a "colony" like its Caribbean neighbor, Cuba. Instead, the U.S. annexed the island outright via the Foraker Act (1900). This act was unprecedented in U.S. history for unlike all previous annexations, this measure made no provision for making the inhabitants citizens of the United States. Puerto Rico was designated an "unincorporated" territory, which meant that Congress would dictate the island's government and specify its inhabitants' rights. In short, with the Foraker Act, Congress had invented a new imperial mechanism for ensuring sovereignty over lands deemed vital to U.S. economic and military security. Though in effect another U.S. colony, Puerto Rico fared better than allegedly "independent" Cuba. Puerto Ricans were granted U.S. citizenship in 1917 and won the right to elect their own governor in 1947. Still Puerto Ricans did not have the same rights as other Americans in the 48 states. Moreover, as "citizens," Puerto Ricans' standard of living was still far below that of the mainlanders. Indeed, as late as 1998, one-fourth of Puerto Rican households subsisted on $1,000 or

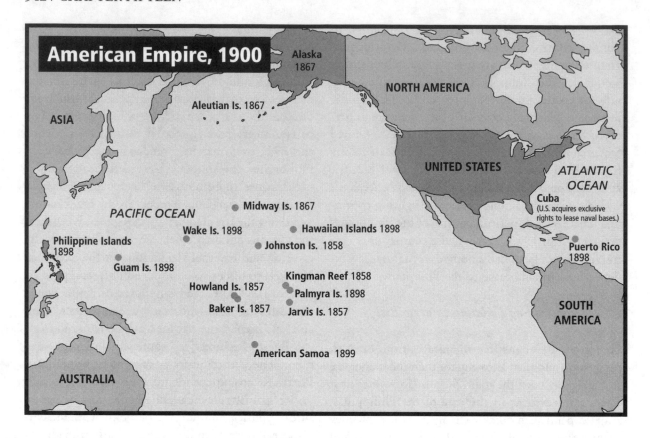

American Empire, 1900

Alaska 1867

NORTH AMERICA

ASIA

Aleutian Is. 1867

UNITED STATES

ATLANTIC OCEAN

Cuba
(U.S. acquires exclusive rights to lease naval bases.)

PACIFIC OCEAN

Midway Is. 1867

Wake Is. 1898

Hawaiian Islands 1898

Johnston Is. 1858

Puerto Rico 1898

Philippine Islands 1898

Guam Is. 1898

Kingman Reef 1858

Howland Is. 1857

Palmyra Is. 1898

Baker Is. 1857

Jarvis Is. 1857

SOUTH AMERICA

American Samoa 1899

AUSTRALIA

less annually, a figure thousands of dollars below the U.S. poverty line. In its skewed distribution of wealth and its lack of industrial development, Puerto Rico resembles the poorly developed nations of Central and South America more than it does the affluent country that took over its government in 1900.

Unlike the Philippines, very few Americans were disturbed by the subjugation of Cuba and annexation of Puerto Rico. Since the promulgation of the 1823 Monroe Doctrine, the United States, had, in effect, claimed the Western Hemisphere as its sphere of influence. With that sphere, many Americans believed, the United States possessed the right to act unilaterally to protect its interests, as well as those of the hemisphere in general, from foreign interlopers and aggressors. Before 1900, most U.S. international actions (with the exception of the Mexican War) focused on keeping the European powers out of the hemisphere—Britain, France, Russia, and Spain. After 1900, however, the U.S. assumed a more aggressive role, seizing land, overturning governments not "favorably disposed" to American interests and

exploitation—in short, forcing its economic and political policies on weaker neighbors to turn the Caribbean Sea into what policymakers called an "American Mediterranean."

CONCLUSION

The United States' emergence in a few short years from isolationism to internationalism attested to the plutocracy's overwhelming power and influence to shape both domestic and foreign policy. That is not to say that they were exclusively responsible for America's rise to international preeminence in the late nineteenth century. They were ably assisted by a wide array of individuals outside the business community, ranging from politicians to intellectuals, to journalists and military leaders, who believed for different reasons that it was time for the United States to break the chains of isolationism and claim its rightful role and destiny as a respected and feared world leader. Despite the influence of those plutocrats who promoted expansion and despite the righteous nativist and ethnocentric exhortations of men like Theodore Roosevelt and Henry Cabot Lodge, the American public initially hesitated to embrace imperialism. Thus, the imperialists/jingoists had to persuade Americans that it was morally necessary for them to abandon isolationism. They "shopped around" the hemisphere until they found a cause celebre just ninety miles off the shores of the continental United States. There, on the island of Cuba, was the "moral imperative" essential to convince enough Americans that it was time to eschew their provincialism and come to the aid of fellow "New Worlders"—the Cubans—who were trying to liberate themselves from the tyranny and brutal oppression of a decadent and decaying Old World power—Spain. With the help of newspaper magnates William Randolph Hearst and Joseph Pulitzer, both of whom were committed imperialists and plutocrats, the expansionists found in these men's respective newspapers the perfect medium through which to propagate their ideas to an increasingly receptive American audience. Unfortunately, much of the "news" Americans received from Hearst and Pulitzer papers were greatly exaggerated distortions, if not outright fabrications, of events in Cuba. Spanish atrocities were greatly magnified, if not made up, for the purpose of so morally outraging the American public that they would be willing to go to war to stop such barbarity. That is not to say that the Spanish were innocent of the propagandists' allegations; they were not. But to what degree their actions were as brutal as portrayed in the imperialists' newspapers remains debatable. Nonetheless, the imperialists' constant agitation ultimately bore the desired fruits: a war with Spain to establish American military power and the acquisition of an empire.

Despite an easy victory over a third-rate power, American chests were puffed; but now the debate raged both inside the halls of Congress and in the public forums about what to do with the acquired people and territory. To the imperialists the resolve was simple: all were to be incorporated into an American colonial empire, no different than what the other major world powers had at the time. However, many Americans, for a variety of reasons, were very uncomfortable with the idea of the United States becoming a world power in the same context as the Europeans. The United States, from its inception, was to be different—a country which had a mission to the world to spread the ideals of democracy and individual freedom; a nation committed to self-determination; a nation that valued liberty more than power. Even though some of the nation's luminaries in arts and letters, as well as labor leaders and even some capitalists like Andrew Carnegie, were anti-imperialists, they could not muster enough popular support to defeat the imperialists' momentum. By 1900, the United States had become a recognized world power, the first realization that the nation's size, economic strength, and honor required it to accept such a destiny and over the course of the next century, expand upon its role, vision, and responsibility of what it meant to be a first-rate world power.

Chronology

1868-78 Cubans revolt against Spanish rule in Ten Years' War

1875 U.S. agrees to allow Hawaii to export sugar to America duty-free

1878 U.S. gains treaty rights for base at Pago Pago in Samoa

1887 U. S. gains treaty rights for base at Pearl Harbor in Hawaii.

1889 First Pan-American Congress meets

1890 Alfred Thayer Mahan publishes *The Influence of Sea Power on History,* exhorting the government to modernize the nation's navy and through it assert American power worldwide. Also, U.S. ends favored status of Hawaii in sugar trade, damaging Hawaiian

1893 U.S. sugar planters in Hawaii foment rebellion against weak native king
Harrison signs annexation agreement with Hawaii but new president Grover Cleveland rejects it.

1894 Wilson-Gorman tariff on Cuban sugar plunges island economy into depression, exacerbating political tensions between Cubans and Spanish officials.

1895 Invoking Monroe Doctrine and asserting hemispheric hegemony, Cleveland administration intervenes in boundary dispute between Venezuela and Great Britain, demanding U.S. right to arbitrate the issue. Cuban insurrection against Spanish renews.

1898 Jingoist/imperialist newspaper magnate, William Randolph Hearst, publishes de Lome letter
U.S. battleship *Maine* explodes in Havana harbor
Congress declares war on Spain, April 25
Spanish army in Cuban retreats
Dewey captures Philippines
U.S. and Spain sign armistice August 12

Treaty of Paris (December) cedes Puerto Rico, Philippines, and other Spanish possessions to U.S. and recognizes Cuban independence
U.S. formally annexes Hawaii
Anti-Imperialist League formed.

1898-1902 Philippines revolt against American rule

1899 Senate ratifies Treaty of Paris
Hay releases "Open Door notes" on China

1900 Foraker Act establishes civil government in Puerto Rico
Hawaii granted territorial status
Boxer rebellion breaks out in China
McKinley reelected president

1901 American forces capture Filipino rebel leader Emilio Aguinaldo
U.S. establishes civil government in Philippines
Congress passes Platt Amendment making Cuba a U.S. colony/protectorate

SUGGESTED READINGS

Robert L. Beisner, *From the Old Diplomacy to the New, 1865-1900.* (1986).

———*Twelve Against Empire: The Anti-Imperialists, 1898-1900* (1968).

James E. Bradford, *Crucible of Empire: The Spanish American War and Its Aftermath* (1993).

Michael Blow, *A Ship to Remember: The Maine and the Spanish-American War.*

Paul Carano and Pedro Sanchez, *A Complete History of Guam* (1964).

Raymond Carr, *Puerto Rico: A Colonial Experiment* (1984).

Warren J. Cohen, *America's Response to China* (1971).

Graham A. Cosmas, *An Army for Empire: The United States Army in the Spanish-American War* (1971).

John Dobson, *America's Ascent: The United States Becomes a Great Power, 1880-1914* (1978).

Philip S. Foner, *The Spanish-Cuban-American War and the Birth of American Imperialism,* 2 volumes (1972).

William B. Gatewood Jr., *"Smoked Yankees; Letters From Negro Soldiers 1898-1902* (1971).

David F. Healy, *U.S. Expansionism: Imperialist Urge in the 1890s.* (1970).

Walter R. Herrick, *The American Naval Revolution* (1966).

James H. Hitchman, *Leonard Wood and Cuban Independence, 1898-1902* (1971).

Paul M. Kennedy, *The Samoan Tangle* (1974).

Walter LaFeber, *The Cambridge History of Foreign Relations: The Search for Opportunity, 1865-1913* (1993).

Patricia Nelson Limerick, *The Legacy of Conquest: The Unbroken Past of the American West* (1987).

Gerald F. Linderman, *The Mirror of War: American Society and the Spanish-American War* (1974).

William E. Livezey, *Mahan on Sea Power* (1981).

Thomas J. McCormick, *China Market: America's Quest for Informal Empire, 1890-1915* (1971).

Ernest R. May, *Imperial Democracy: The Emergence of America as a Great Power* (1961).

Stuart Creighton Miller, *"Benevolent Assimilation:" The American Conquest of the Philippines, 1899-1903* (1982).

Joyce Milton, *The Yellow Journalists* (1989).

H. Wayne Morgan, *America's Road to Empire* (1965).

Edmund Morris, *The Rise of Theodore Roosevelt* (1979).

Louis A. Perez, *Cuba Under the Platt Amendment, 1902-1934* (1986).

Julius W. Pratt, *Expansionists of 1898* (1936). *America's Colonial Empire* (1950).

Emily Rosenberg, *Spreading the American Dream: American Economic and Cultural Expansion, 18909-1945* (1982).

William A. Russ Jr., *The Hawaiian Republic, 1894-1898 and Its Struggle to Win Annexation* (1961).

Daniel B. Schirmer, *Republic or Empire? American Resistance to the Philippine War* (1972).

Peter Stanley, *A Nation in the Making: The Philippines and the United States, 1899-1921* (1974).

Merze Tate, *The United States and the Hawaiian Kingdom* (1965).

E. Berkeley Tomkins, *Anti-Imperialism in the United States, 1890-1920: The Great Debate* (1970).

David F. Trask, *The War With Spain,* (1981).

Richard E. Welch, Jr. *Response to Imperialism: The United States and the Philippine War, 1899-1902* (1979).

William Appleman Williams, *The Tragedy of American Diplomacy*

Marilyn B. Young, *The Rhetoric of Empire: American China Policy, 1895-1901* (1968).

Chapter Sixteen

PROGRESSIVE ERA

A beautiful young teenager from the slums of Chicago was thrilled to get her first job working in the local match factory. She was sure that she would not have to work there for too long; she would either get married or get a job working on the new machine, the typewriter. She would never get "phossy jaw," a degenerative disease caused by the phosphorus on the heads of the matches. No! She would not look like other girls who were old women at nineteen.

In another part of Chicago, a young immigrant boy was pleased that he had gotten a job at a meat packing plant not far from his tenement home. True, the smell was horrible; the work was dangerous. His next door neighbor had been seriously injured by an enraged bull not killed by the mallet blow to his head, and the pay was not good. But it was a start to the American dream. He was strong and young and sure that he would not have to work there so long that he would be permanently bent over like an old man by age twenty-five.

A middle-class family in Chicago looked forward to a delicious breakfast of that new deviled ham product produced locally. Then the calm of the early morning was punctuated by a scream from the kitchen. When the mistress of the house went to investigate, she found the cook lying on the floor. She had fainted after finding three bloody human fingers in the canned meat!

When the mistress went to her meeting of the Women's Christian Temperance Union, she heard first-hand reports of spousal and child abuse at the hand of a drunken husband. She decided that she, too, would join the movement for women's suffrage. How else could wives and children be protected?

Her husband's day was not much better. On the way to his office he encountered filth flowing down the streets, resulting from the lack of garbage pick-up. Political corruption prevented an efficient and clean city. Meanwhile, the newspaper that he read on the way to work reported the latest doings of the new upper class: a party where the guests rode their horses onto the expensive carpeting of one of New York's best hotels. At dinner guests ate oysters that contained perfect black pearls. After dinner they lit cigarettes rolled in one hundred dollar bills. When he got to work, he found that his company had been bought out by a huge trust, and his job was one of many to be eliminated.

It was such abuses that fueled the desire of many to join the reform movement that spanned the last years of the nineteenth century and the first twenty years of the twentieth, the Progressive Era. While often given the dates from 1900-1917, the administration of Theodore Roosevelt to the United States' involvement in World War I, the roots of the Progressive Era go back much further, and its accomplishments continued past the end of World War I.

PROGRESSIVE IDEOLOGY
AND GOALS

Progressivism was founded on the notion that social progress was possible, indeed necessary. Progressives differed in their approaches, but most of them had the same goals: to make economic life fairer and more competitive, to make political life more democratic, and to make social life more moral and more just. Some hoped to broaden opportunities for the common man, whether he was a farmer, skilled or unskilled worker, or recent immigrant. At the same time they wanted to eliminate special privileges and favoritism for the wealthy.

Their motives were not completely unselfish. Most reformers were from middle-class backgrounds and had no love for immigrants or the nouveau riche, whose over-indulgence in all things led Mark Twain to dub an earlier period the Gilded Age. Progressives believed changes were necessary to prevent democracy from moving toward either a **plutocracy**, a government of the rich, or to the socialism that seemed ready to infect the working class as a result of horrendous working conditions.

Progressives realized that, although society appeared healthy and prosperous, many problems were festering beneath the surface. The working class had more comforts, but the wealth of the nation was unequally distributed. The poorest Americans lived at a shameful level of existence.

TRUSTS AND FINANCIAL
CAPITALISM

The Second Industrial Revolution contributed to many conditions that brought the rise of heavy industries: oil, steel, and transcontinental railroads. Although the theory of capitalism is competition, the nineteenth century reality was monopoly and concentration of wealth. With the advantages brought by these new industries came problems of price-gouging, industrial poverty, greater swings in the business cycle that created periods of large unemployment, and bank failures. The amazing growth of capitalism would have been impossible without laws that favored corporations. Although joint stock companies had existed in the United States since the founding of the first colony, the Civil War and the Supreme Court's interpretation of the Fourteenth Amendment, as defining corporations as "persons," enabled corporations to grow and prosper until they were the dominant form of business organization. For example, in 1899 corporations made 66 percent of all manufactured goods; ten years later, it was 79 percent.

As the huge steel, oil, mining, and manufacturing concerns grew, so did the need for a domestic investment market where the savings of Americans could be solicited for stocks. By 1900, tens of thousands of Americans owned corporate securities; at the close of the Progressive Era in 1917, it was hundreds of thousands.

The large corporations meant that investors no longer managed their own capital; they simply owned stock in large corporations over which they had little control. Corporation officials were subject to the extraordinary temptations that arose from handling other people's money. Shrewd operators used reorganizations, mergers, and other devices, though often planned for sound business reasons, to manipulate funds for their own purposes and to eliminate competitors.

To the person of modest means, the potential investor, and the ambitious new entrepreneur, big corporations seemed to be obstacles that shut down the most profitable avenues of enterprise and confronted one with overwhelming competition. To the employee, the corporation represented a world of impersonal, mechanized, bureaucratized, and standardized relationships, rather than a world of personal employer-employee relations. Although corporations could offer employees many advantages that the small business could not, these were not yet part of the economic scene in the Progressive Era.

From 1893 to 1903 corporate consolidation increased rapidly because of the growing change from entrepreneurial capitalism to financial capitalism. Rather than an individual founding a corporation, it was the banker who provided the financing. The best-known instance of this process was in railroading. In 1893, two leading Wall Street investment houses, J. P. Morgan & Co. and Kuhn Loeb & Co.

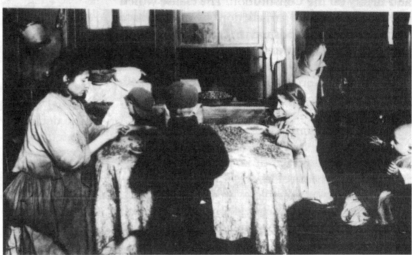

These pictures show the sharp contrast between the nouveau riche and the working class.

(a Rockefeller Company), concluded that lack of organization and excessive competition had caused much of the chaos in railroading. They began to consolidate railroads. This worked so well that Morgan next turned his attention to the steel industry. When rivalry between Carnegie and the other steel men threatened to precipitate a price war, Morgan stepped in and formed the first billion dollar corporation, United States Steel Corporation. Morgan continued to look for other fields where he might use his expertise. He acquired new industries and secured positions for his partners and representatives on many of the boards of directors.

Morgan's opportunities for consolidation arose because of cutthroat competition in some industries

that he thought endangered the industrial base of the United States. The Depression of 1893 made this kind of competition all the more severe. When prosperity returned in 1897, banks easily floated the new issues of securities needed to finance consolidations. Between 1898 and 1904 the number of consolidations reached a peak not to be equalled until the 1920s.

In John Moody's 1904 book, *The Truth About The Trusts*, he listed 318 great corporations that had been organized or were in the process of being organized that year. Such trusts included United States Steel, Standard Oil, Consolidated Tobacco, Amalgamated Copper, International Mercantile Marine Co., American Smelting and Refining Company, International Harvester, General Electric, New York Life, Mutual Life, and Equitable Life. Insurance companies were considered particular plums for financial capitalists since they represented good markets for securities. Consolidations were also taking place in the utilities: telephone, telegraph, and gas.

The public learned of the activities of financial capitalists when a fight broke out in the railroad industries over control of the Chicago, Burlington and Quincy Railroads, which would provide a Chicago link to one of the transcontinental railroads. Two major banking interests, the House of Morgan and Kuhn, Loeb and Company, backed the two top contenders. One of the results was a market crash that wiped out thousands of stockholders and brokers. It did not, however, harm either the Rockefeller or Morgan interests who compromised and emerged wealthier than ever.

The masters of the great combinations thought unity was preferable to competition. This lesson was reinforced when the two banking groups had to act together to stem a stock-market panic in 1907. After that, the two groups tended to merge through interlocking directorates and the purchase of stock in each other's companies.

For the economy as a whole, large corporations had sweeping significance for they meant that men who controlled a few strategic businesses could create vast economic empires. An investment banker like J. P. Morgan could extend his bank's control by lending money to a corporation or by selling its securities if the corporation made room for a Morgan man on its board of directors. Since the banker-director could control what new money the corporation might borrow, he played a decisive role in the corporation's decisions.

In 1913 the Pujo Committee of the House of Representatives, which had worked for two years to untangle their financial affairs, showed that persons belonging to either the Morgan or Rockefeller interests controlled more than three times the assessed value of all property in the thirteen Southern states and more than the assessed property values of the twenty-two states west of the Mississippi.

MUCKRAKERS

While congressional committees played a small role in exposing the inequities of the era, most people's source of information was a group of investigative reporters whom Teddy Roosevelt nicknamed "**muckrakers.**" Roosevelt devised the term from a character in John Bunyon's *Pilgrim's Progress,* who could not look anywhere but at the filth he was raking up. Although Roosevelt agreed with many of the muckrakers' charges, he condemned them because he feared that their widely read exposes of the "muck" or underside of the business world, government, and society to the general public would arouse dangerous discontent. The muckrakers responded that the facts they exposed would make the American people indignant enough to fight for necessary reforms.

The digging up of dirt didn't begin with the muckrakers but was aided by the growth of popular magazines and newspapers as well as an increase in the number of readers who could buy such publications. Magazines such as *McClure's, Cosmopolitan, Everybody's, Collier's,* and *American Magazine* financed the muckrakers' investigations and provided them with a built-in audience. The public wanted the inside dirt, and the publishers were willing to give it to them. With this monetary backing, reporters could dig into court records, locate witnesses, and dig up mountains of facts. The new muckrakers named names and recounted misdeeds in sensational detail, and the new national magazines gave them national influence. Nothing escaped their pens.

Often cited as the first muckraker, Henry Demarest Lloyd examined monopolies including Standard Oil and published his finding in 1894, *Wealth Against Commonwealth.* Lloyd showed how the heads of the huge corporations and trusts answered to no one and were able to exert considerable control over the government by assiduous use of their wealth to support their friends and punish those they saw as enemies. Another early muckraker was Jacob Riis, who wrote extensively on the life of immigrants in the city and exposed the disease, vice, and desperation of its residents. His expose was published in book form in 1890, *How the Other Half Lives*; in 1902 he published *The Battle With the Slum.*

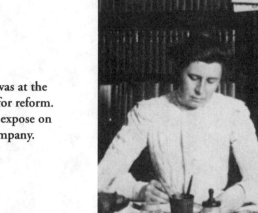

McClures magazine was at the front of the crusade for reform. Ida Tarbell wrote an expose on the Standard Oil Company.

What is considered the golden era of muckraking began with Lincoln Steffens who wrote on political conditions in American cities. These articles were republished in 1903 as *The Shame of the Cities*. With $2,000 from *McClure's* available for research, Steffens investigated city government in Philadelphia, Pittsburgh, Minneapolis, St. Louis, and other cities. They all suffered from the same ills: bribery by businessmen, corrupt and shrewd party bosses, political collusion, special privileges, organized vice, venal police, and apathetic citizens.

Ida Tarbell's expose of Standard Oil, also financed by *McClure's* for $4,000, was eventually published in 1904 as the *History of Standard Oil Company*. Tarbell, whose father had been driven out of business by Rockefeller, retold the story of the pitiless methods by which that huge combine bent other companies to its will. Her three years of research resulted in a more detailed analysis than Lloyd's and was even more damaging.

Another woman who reported on societal ills was Marie Van Vorst, a socialite-turned-muckraker, who described the life of working women in a Massachusetts' shoe factory and went undercover as a mill worker in a South Carolina textile mill where she exposed the abuses of child labor. Van Vorst's collected articles were published in 1903 as *The Woman Who Toils*. Even worse conditions of child labor abuses existed in the industrial Northern states.

In 1900 in Pennsylvania 120,000 children under fifteen worked in mines and mills while in New York in that year 92,000 children worked ten to twelve hours a day, often seven days a week, in dangerous and unhealthy conditions.

Muckrakers wrote on a variety of social problems. David Graham Phillips, a *Cosmopolitan* reporter, wrote a series about the United States Senate, a private club of millionaires who put personal interests first. These articles were also republished in 1906 as the *Treason of the Senate*. It was in response to this publication that Roosevelt had coined the term "muckraker." Gustavus Myers drew upon old court records and other forgotten materials to show the extent to which American enterprise had thrived on exploitation, dishonesty, and unearned profits. Other muckrakers included Charles Edward Russell, who exposed the beef trust, Thomas Lawson, who wrote about Amalgamated Copper, and Upton Sinclair's expose of the Chicago meatpacking industry in his novel *The Jungle* (1906).

While Ida Bell Wells Barnett, a prominent African-American woman, is not often included in the standard listing of muckraking reporters, her expose of lynching in the South was of that genre. Wells Barnett was already well known as an advocate of integration of trains and schools before she began her campaign to eliminate lynching in the South. She wrote articles in the *Memphis Free Speech* that

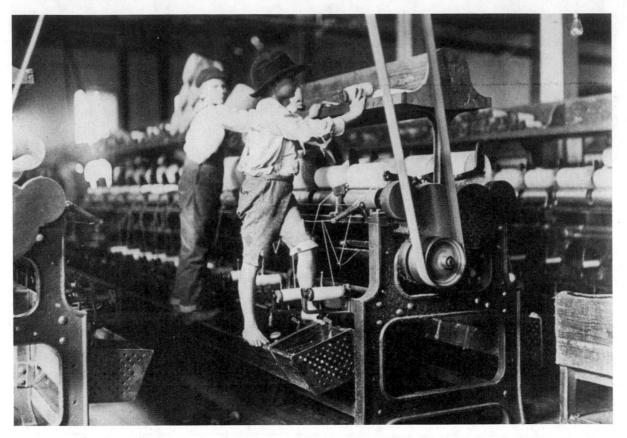

In some cities children like these boys worked in the garment industry instead of playing
with their friends.

showed how African-American males were murdered for being "sassy" or for supposed rape even when a victim testified that the rapist was a white man. These articles infuriated the white power base in Memphis who destroyed the newspaper and told her that her life would be worthless if she remained in Memphis. Wells Barnett moved to Chicago and, in 1909, co-founded the National Association for the Advancement of Colored People.

Some muckrakers' efforts did produce results. Upton Sinclair's novel, *The Jungle*, exposed conditions in the Chicago meat-packing industry that helped lead to the passage of the Meat Inspection Act and the Pure Food and Drug Act. Burton Hendrick's expose of insurance companies in *The Story of Life Insurance* resulted in the governor of New York pushing for regulation of the great insurance companies in New York State. The life of innocence was over for the American citizen.

PROGRESSIVISM ON THE LOCAL AND STATE LEVELS

The same pervasive influence of giant corporations applied at the local and state levels. The progressive movement, like the Populist Movement, began at the local level, spreading from cities to states and, ultimately, to the federal level. On the urban scene the movement for municipal reform began in New York City in 1894, when reformers overthrew Tammany Hall, and in Chicago, as an aftermath of the attention drawn to the corruption of the city during the Columbian Exposition. In 1901 a reformer was elected mayor of Cleveland. He secured tax reforms and made Cleveland one of the best run cities and a model for other reformers.

Because the state legislatures controlled the cities, political bosses often went to them in an attempt to thwart the reformers. This is how the progressives started moving into the state level of politics. One of the greatest of the state reformers was Robert La Follette who was elected governor of Wisconsin in 1900. He ousted the strong Republican state machine, established his own, made advances in the regulation of railroads and public utilities, and reformed the tax system of the state. Hiram Johnson did a similar job in California. In New York Charles Hughes fought for the regulation of railroads and utilities. Woodrow Wilson did the same in New Jersey.

Their goals were to cripple the power of the political machines, to put the control of affairs more directly into the hands of the citizens, and to increase the efficiency of government. To improve municipal government, reformers insisted that a commission of administrators without party affiliations replace the mayor and council. This advanced the idea of a city manager. There was a tidal wave in Galveston, and the city council proved completely incompetent to handle this emergency so the legislature set up a five-man commission to govern the city. This worked, and soon other cities adopted it. The final modification happened as a result of a flood in Dayton, Ohio. Here the board of commissioners hired a city manager, who was someone especially trained for the job. By 1923 over 300 cities had this form of local government.

Besides concern for economic justice as consumers, there was also a concern for economic justice for those who worked for big business whether it was the oil, railroad, or the steel industries. Nor was industry itself free from the same exploitations that the trust used on the individual. As Ida Tarbell detailed it, those railroads that served Standard Oil, which was synonymous with the oil industry, might be held up for rebates, money returned to them under the table so that they paid cheaper rates than those published. Large trusts like Standard Oil also demanded drawbacks, by which the railroad would raise the published rates to all oil companies and return to Standard Oil its regular rebate and most of the increased rates charged to its competitors. Thus, its competitors would be subsidizing Standard Oil.

Social Evils

The progressives also addressed problems women faced. Recognizing that many women and children suffered when the men in the family drank, there was a movement to prohibit the making, selling, and consuming of alcoholic beverages. The movement is most closely identified with the Women's Christian Temperance Union. It was a movement for prohibition not temperance. Although Frances Willard was the founder of the WCTU, Carrie Nation was its best-known advocate. An imposing woman six feet tall and 175 pounds, Carrie Nation was arrested thirty times for breaking up saloons with her axe. The WCTU was also involved in many other projects: members ran a hotel for working women, provided classes in stenographic skills, and campaigned for kindergartens, prison reform, and woman suffrage.

To combat the social evils of the day, the Social Gospel developed within the Protestant tradition. The idea was that Christians should conduct themselves as if Christ were alive and living in the tenements of the cities. While the Social Gospel occurred only in some Protestant churches, the majority of the inhabitants of the slums were recent immigrants from southern or eastern Europe who were primarily Roman Catholic, Russian or Greek Orthodox, or Jewish. Thus, it had little effect.

HULL HOUSE

The settlement house movement that began in Europe was a different attempt to improve life in the slums. Operating much like a latter-day Peace Corps, the volunteers lived in the worst sections of the cities. Rather than telling the residents what was wrong, settlement house workers sought to work with their neighbors to solve the problems that the community identified.

The most famous of the settlement houses was Jane Addams' Hull House in Chicago. Jane Addams was typical of the new generation of middle-class college-educated women. Financially secure, Addams did not have to work and, in fact, her family expected her to stay at home and live the passive life of the stereotypical nineteenth century woman. Her reaction to this was also typical of many women. Like the writer, Charlotte Perkins Gilman, she suffered a bout of "nervous" prostration. Her physician was Dr. S. Weir Mitchell, the same "alienist," a nineteenth century term for psychiatrists, who had also treated Gilman. Weir prescribed a rest cure of total seclusion, soft food, darkened rooms, and massages from the physician. While many women responded positively to this common prescription, it was equally ineffective for both of these active women. Gilman was eventually cured by becoming a popular author and lecturer and Addams by her involvement in the settlement house movement.

During a trip to Europe with her best friend, artist Ellen Starr, Addams visited the original settlement house, Toynbee Hall in London, and saw young college graduates living among the poor to aid them. When they returned to Chicago, Addams and Starr bought an abandoned mansion from Charles J. Hull, and thus the most famous settlement house in the United States was begun.

Although Addams began as a naive do-good-er, she was able to overcome this and learn from the immigrants who lived near Hull House what their basic needs were. Soon Hull House was offering classes in English, hosting union meetings, providing kindergartens, and other services. Although Hull House had many successes, workers also met defeats. One occasion was the attempt to get the city government of Chicago to correct the problem of raw sewage running down the streets of the Hull House neighborhood. The greatest success of Hull House and settlement houses was that it involved many upper-class women in a world outside their own and thus educated them to the inequalities of society. They also led to a new profession, that of social worker.

Over the years a host of important women came to Hull House and changed Addams' goals. Doctor Alice Hamilton, a volunteer who also was a physician, took on the match girls' problem of "phossy jaw," a disintegration of the jaw bone caused by the phosphorous used on the heads of matches. She solved the problem and saved the girls' jaws by find-

Jane Addams founded Chicago's Hull House in 1889. The settlement house brought hope to poverty-stricken slum dwellers.

ing a substitute for the dangerous phosphorous. Another Hull House volunteer, Julia Lathrop, was instrumental in the founding of the juvenile court system.

One of the most important residents was Florence Kelley. Like Addams, Kelley came from an upper middle-class home and was college-educated. A graduate of Cornell University, she was denied admission to law schools in the United States. As a result, she studied law in Zurich, Switzerland where she became a Socialist. When Kelley's marriage to a Polish-German Socialist broke up, she moved to Illinois where it was easier to obtain a divorce than in New York.

Kelley provided a contrast to Addams. While Addams was unmarried and may have been a lesbian, Kelley was a divorced mother. Addams was proper and reserved while Kelley was hot tempered and explosive. While Addams liked evening prayers, art lessons, and scholarly meetings, Kelley was an activist. In 1892 she was appointed to the State Bureau of Labor Statistics where she was asked to inspect factories in Chicago. Later, she was appointed the first factory inspector for the state of Illinois. Kelley's influence has been credited with turning Addams from a philanthropist to a reformer.

Addams' work as a reformer made her one of the first native-born Americans to recognize the importance of environment in explaining the problems of the immigrants. Addams, however, was more interested in solving the immediate problems of the poor than in a philosophical examination of the nature of capitalism. Her beliefs led her to become a leader of the Progressive Party that, in 1912, called for an eight-hour day, six-day week; abolition of tenement manufacture; improvement of housing; prohibition of child labor under sixteen; regulation of employment for women; a federal system of accident, old-age, and unemployment insurance; and woman suffrage.

WOMAN SUFFRAGE

During the Progressive Era, a new generation was coming of age in the woman suffrage movement. Members were less ideological and more focused than Elizabeth Cady Stanton and Susan B. Anthony had been. These new leaders like Carrie Chapman Catt and Anna Howard Shaw sought to win the support of middle-class women. To do that, they purged the movement of unconventional leaders and radical positions. Catt succeeded Anthony as the president of the National American Woman Suffrage Association (NAWSA). Her strategy was first to pursue suffrage on a state by state basis to get the grass roots support that would be necessary to get a federal amendment passed. She wanted the suffrage message carried into every town meeting, caucus, and primary to influence the ordinary voters who would never come to NAWSA meetings. When Catt resigned the presidency due to the illness of her husband, she was succeeded by Anna Howard Shaw, a woman of great organizational ability but a leader who lacked the people skills necessary to build unity and to secure victory. During her tenure the movement was at a standstill.

On the local level the new generation was changing the strategy from the demand for full equality to the argument that women deserved the vote because they were morally superior, an argument that fit in comfortably with Victorian notions. They truly be-

lieved that when women got the vote, they would support candidates who would solve the social and moral problems of the era. The arguments used were undemocratic but appealed to the racist and anti-immigrant feelings of the middle class: women could counteract the votes of ignorant males whether black or immigrant. By 1903 the woman suffrage movement was completely separated from the black movement, a discarding of the movement's roots in the pre-Civil War abolitionist movement.

The final push for woman suffrage began in 1910 as several states gave women the right to vote. It was accelerated when several American women, Harriot Stanton Blatch, Elizabeth Cady Stanton's daughter; Alice Paul; Lucy Burns; and others returned from England where they had learned the militant tactics of the radical wing of the British suffrage movement. Emmeline Pankhurst and her daughters who led the British movement believed in civil disobedience and confrontation with the government. Their activities included chaining themselves to buildings, burning down buildings, battling with the police, and mass marches. When they were arrested, they went on hunger strikes.

By 1915, those who were more radical grouped under the leadership of Alice Paul, who organized the Congressional Union to take advantage of the political power of four million women who already had the vote. Paul's strategy was to hold the party in power, the Democrats, responsible for women's lack of the vote. She proposed harassing the Democrats and their leader, President Woodrow Wilson, until they ceased their opposition. The NAWSA leaders disliked Paul's plan as it ran counter to their non-partisan policy. Many in NAWSA also considered Paul's tactic of mass marches and picketing improper. When Carrie Chapman Catt returned to power as president of NAWSA, Paul was expelled. After that, Paul and other members of the Congressional Union organized the Woman's Party that had one plank: winning the vote for all women. While Catt was working for a state by state strategy, Paul took more direct action.

In 1916, Paul's Woman's Party campaigned against Wilson's re-election bid. Although Wilson won, the Woman's Party had forced politicians to

A 1911 women's suffrage parade

take note of the suffrage issue. Members began to picket the White House standing in silent vigil in all types of weather holding banners that referred to Wilson as "Kaiser Wilson" or that demanded "Democracy should begin at home." After several months, police began making arrests. When the pickets returned, they were charged with obstructing traffic, found guilty, and sent to Occaquan workhouse in Virginia, a notorious hellhole. Those sentenced included Alice Paul. Like their British counterparts, they demanded to be treated as political prisoners and went on hunger strikes. The result was that they were force-fed. This turned out to be a mistake for it aroused sympathy for the women and their cause. Their convictions were overturned, and when they were released from prison, they began picketing again!

The combination of the tactics of the Woman's Party and the NAWSA worked and the Rules Com-

mittee of the House, after many years of bottling up the suffrage amendment, brought it to the floor for debate. By the war's end, it was clear that women's suffrage would eventually pass; the question was when. The antisuffrage forces had gathered strength for the final battle. They included conservatives who painted woman suffrage as a radical plot; racists who claimed enfranchising black women would mark the end of white supremacy; liquor interests who opposed it because they feared it would lead to prohibition; and northern political bosses who feared women's reformist impulses might drive them out of power. Antisuffragists had no hesitation about bribing politicians, lying about the nature of the women's movement, and producing scurrilous propaganda. One group, the National Women's Organization to Oppose Suffrage, said the vote would be a burden that woman did not want.

Finally on January 10, 1918, Jeanette Rankin of Montana, the first woman elected to Congress, introduced the suffrage amendment onto the floor of the House where it passed. It took another year and a half for the amendment to pass in the Senate. The final battle was to secure ratification by thirty-six states. The battle was won in August 26, 1920, when Tennessee ratified the Nineteenth Amendment by one vote, ensuring its addition to the Constitution. NAWSA evolved into the League of Women Voters, and the Women's Party began working on an Equal Rights Amendment.

ECONOMIC AND SOCIAL PROBLEMS

At the bottom of the economic ladder was a class of workers who were plagued by unemployment, huddled into hideous slums, and vulnerable to all sorts of diseases. Some worked 72 hours a week. Industrial accidents brought tragedy and then poverty to a large portion of the working class. Even by 1913 when numerous industries had adopted safety measures, many workers were killed on their jobs and thousands gravely injured. Women and children worked long hours in factories without any protection of laws or unions. Immigrants lived in the cities under the most trying and dangerous conditions. African Americans, victimized by a heritage of slavery, were terrorized and voteless in the South.

The newly minted millionaires were a concern of the progressives. During the 1840s there were approximately twenty millionaires; by 1892 the New York *Tribune* listed 4,047. The distribution of wealth was also a concern since in 1893, 71 percent of the wealth was owned by 9 percent of the families! The new millionaires were extraordinary rich, numerous, and often uncultivated and crude. They were the new barbarians who came from above. The mere existence of "robber barons" was provocative to the rest of society. Their swollen fortunes made men of more modest means feel insignificant. Their lack of scruples put men of principle at a disadvantage.

Even their charities and philanthropies seemed overly conspicuous and threw other men's generos-ity into the shade. The follies they and their families indulged in were in keeping with their means: ostentatious houses, squads of retainers and mistresses, and extravagances of all kinds.

The new rich were firm believers in Social Darwinism, Charles Darwin's concept of survival of the fittest applied to economic life. They also believed in laissez faire capitalism where the government kept hands off of the economy except for the enforcement of contracts. Those who had large fortunes increasingly determined public economic, social, and political philosophy through the members of Congress whom they figuratively and often literally owned. They planned to use their wealth to buy whatever was needed politically to keep it! Political leaders like Teddy Roosevelt were afraid that the life style and activities of the rich would provoke the public into dangerous political extremes. After 1900 progressives became involved in politics to see their ideas put into action.

Social Legislation

The progressives had their greatest success with social legislation, particularly in state legislatures. State laws were now passed against child labor. By 1914 every state but one had a minimum age for child labor. Other prohibitions prevented night work and employment in dangerous occupations. Efforts at the federal level were not so successful. In 1918 the United States Supreme Court declared the Keating-Owen Act, which prohibited the interstate shipment of goods made in factories, mines, or quarries employing children under specified ages, unconstitutional. The Court declared the act a violation of the police powers of the state and an attempt to use the interstate commerce clause to achieve other ends.

The campaign to protect women in industry also resulted in state laws limiting the number of hours of female labor: New York and Massachusetts had a limit of 60 hours per week. In 1908 the Supreme Court decided the case of *Muller v Oregon* in which an employer challenged the Oregon law limiting the hours women worked to 10 a day. The law was declared constitutional. By 1917 some thirty-nine states enacted new legislation governing women's

On March 25, 1911, a fire broke out on the eighth floor of the Triangle Company's building. Exit doors had been locked by the company to prevent theft and to shut out union organizers. Many terrified seamstresses jumped to their deaths on the street below. In all, 3 men and 143 women and girls died.

work. Minimum wages were also set. The Supreme Court, however, declared a law regulating the wages of women in the District of Columbia unconstitutional because it deprived them of the freedom of contract. This effectively ended the reform movement.

After 1909, a number of states adopted the accident insurance systems we call workmen's compensation. By 1920, all but five of the states and territories had fallen into line with some kind of insurance. Before that, workers and their families had to sue the company, a risky and costly business.

In 1911 states began to accept the idea that it would be better to aid dependent children in their own homes rather than putting them in institutions. States began to pass mother assistance acts that set up public agencies to grant relief or financial help to working mothers with dependent children. In 1914 some of the states began to pass legislation to help the aged poor in their own homes. Arizona began the practice although its Supreme Court found the law unconstitutional. In the 1920s, thirty states passed such legislation.

Progressives in Political Life

In the political sphere, the progressives sought greater involvement in the political life of the state and federal governments. One way to break the power of the political machines, they thought, was to institute the direct primary as the source for nominations to office. This proposal enabled the ordinary members of political parties to vote for their party's candidates rather than a political boss choosing the nominees. Progressives hoped that this would insure the selection of abler and more independent candidates. By 1916, some form of direct primary had been adopted by all states except Rhode Island, Connecticut, and New Mexico. To involve the citizens more directly in their government, referendums were added to state constitutions. Here an issue, proposed by the legislative body at a city or state level, would require the approval of the citizenry at the next election. In some states this was followed by the idea of the initiative whereby citizens can propose legislation by securing signatures on petitions. Such devices were particularly popular in the Western states.

The next task was what to do about people who were not performing in their elective offices. This led to the movement for recall in which an elective official can be recalled after sufficient signatures have been collected on a recall petition. The official then has to stand for election again. To the conservatives, the most radical and objectionable proposal of all was the recall of judges. This measure gained strength because many judges were invalidating the social reforms. Several states adopted judicial recall, although

Fire nets did not help the Triangle workers who jumped from the upper stories to escape the flames. Labor organizer Rose Schneiderman spoke out against a system that treated human beings as expendable commodities.

it was never invoked. Another plan was to push for a constitutional amendment for the direct elections of United States senators who were still chosen by the state legislatures.

The Square Deal of Teddy Roosevelt and the New Freedom of Woodrow Wilson came out of this reform impulse, as well as a host of other reforms that were, strictly speaking, not part of either program but that won the support of men in both major parties.

PRESIDENTIAL PROGRESSIVISM

When Theodore Roosevelt succeeded to the office of president in 1901, at the age of 42, he was the youngest man to hold that office. He was also one of the most interesting with his unconventional family. "Teddy" was the sickly, asthmatic son of an aristocratic New York family that traced its ancestry back to the original Dutch settlers. The Harvard graduate became an ardent advocate of physical fitness, working hard on a ranch in the Dakotas where he experienced "the strenuous life" firsthand.

The Spanish-American War made Roosevelt a national hero. He parlayed his fame as a "Rough Rider" into election as governor of New York in 1898. As a moderate reformer, he quickly clashed with the local political bosses who used their influence to "kick him upstairs" to the vice presidency, a job that buried most of its occupants. In fact, Roosevelt himself wrote, "I would a great deal rather be anything, say a history professor, than Vice President." A worried presidential adviser, Mark Hanna, implored McKinley to survive, since only he stood "between that madman and the White House." But in September 1901, McKinley was suddenly dead, the victim of an assassin. "I told McKinley that it was a mistake to nominate that wild man," Hanna reportedly declared ruefully, "Now that damned cowboy is President."

Roosevelt did not look like a president. He was short, wore thick glasses, had buck teeth, and spoke in a high-pitched voice. He did not act like a president either. Nor did his family. His sons rode their ponies into the White House. Reporters spotted Teddy and the Japanese ambassador on their knees searching for young Quentin's missing frog. His daughter, Alice, was equally unconventional and indulged her taste in smoking and making cutting remarks. At one point someone asked Roosevelt if he couldn't do something about Alice's behavior. He responded that he could control Alice or he could run the United States, but he could not do both!

His views were mostly conventional: the government should interfere in the economy only to make competition more humane; blacks and, by extension, all non-Anglo-Saxons were inferior; foreign trade was seen as beneficial because it made America strong; and Anglo-Saxons were being outbred by fecund immigrants. He deplored the social callowness of men of great wealth while at the same time fearing radicalism and agitation. He was an ardent nationalist who saw in devotion to the nation and to the public welfare an answer to the extremes of both big business dominance and radical agitation. He was shrewd in practical politics and had an ability to deal with other politicians. He also had a remarkable intuitive sense for the workings of the popular mind. He was quick to grasp concerns of the ordinary person and to express them. Few presidents have projected their personalities so vividly and with such success to the American public particularly in an era before mass media and have remained so popular for so long as Theodore Roosevelt.

Conservation

Roosevelt was dedicated to the conservation movement that then meant that natural resources be efficiently developed. Forests, for example, should be preserved because they protected watersheds, and timber production should be balanced against other uses. While forests could be exploited, it was only under the guidelines established by the Forest Service, headed under Roosevelt by Gifford Pinchot. In accordance with the Forest Reserve Act of 1891, Roosevelt set aside almost 150 million acres of unsold government timber lands in various parts of the country as forest reserve and closed about 85 million additional acres in Alaska and the Northwest to public access so that the mineral and water resources of the area could be studied. The result was that the land under Pinchot's control tripled in size. Because the Forest Service believed in efficiency, it often favored large timber companies over small ones and cattle ranchers over sheep ranchers and farmers. A significant split existed between those like Pinchot who wanted to conserve resources for continuous human use and those like John Muir who wanted to set aside wilderness areas. Muir never forgave Pinchot for endorsing a water reservoir in the wild Hetch Hetchy Valley of Yosemite National Park to supply water to San Francisco.

Trust Buster

Roosevelt thought that there was a difference between bad trusts and good trusts. Good trusts were a result of efficiency and evolution; bad trusts, like Standard Oil, became rich from illicit practices. While good trusts could be tolerated, bad ones should be broken up. Roosevelt's reputation as a trust buster rested on the actions he took in 1902 when he ordered his attorney general to bring suit to dissolve the Northern Securities Company organized by the Morgan and Rockefeller interests after their fight over the Chicago, Burlington and Quincy Railroads. It was an excellent way of dramatizing the vigor of the new administration. The announcement suggested that Roosevelt was going to battle with the mightiest of financial giants. The suit dragged on for almost two years. In 1904 the Supreme Court handed down a decision that seemed a great triumph for the president and the anti-trust principle. By a 5-4 decision the Court ruled that the combination must be broken up. This reversed a previous decision and opened the way to further prosecution. Roosevelt thought that this was the greatest achievement of his administration. "The most powerful men in this country were held accountable before the law."

Roosevelt soon ordered more prosecutions. One suit was brought against the "Beef trust," a combination of packing companies and others against Standard Oil and the American Tobacco Co. These cases dragged on and had rather indecisive results. While they did not halt the wave of business consolidation, they did keep alive the possibility that a particularly ruthless firm might find itself confronted with a costly prosecution. In 1903 Roosevelt set up a Bureau of Corporations under the new Department of Commerce to investigate corporations, and it provided valuable information on several industries that were in time made subject to prosecution.

In 1902 Roosevelt intervened in a labor dispute. In May John Mitchell of the United Mine Workers called a bitter strike in the anthracite fields. The workers got much sympathy because of a statement made by George F. Baer, president of the Reading Railroad and spokesman of the mine operators. He announced that the miners would be protected "not by the labor agitators but by the Christian men to whom God in His infinite wisdom, has given control of the property interests of this country."

As the strike wore on and it looked as if there would be real coal shortages in the cities in the winter, Roosevelt took action. In October he called Mitchell and the operators to the White House for a meeting. Mitchell agreed to arbitration, but the owners refused. Roosevelt made plans to have the United States Army take over and operate the mines on behalf of the government. He also asked J. P. Morgan to try to get the operators to arbitrate before the impending seizure became necessary. The mine operators agreed with one condition: that no labor officials be appointed to the commission on arbitration. Roosevelt did not argue the point; instead, he appointed a former president of one of the railroad unions to the board as an "eminent sociologist." Ultimately, the mine workers won a 9 hour day, a 10 cent wage increase, a permanent board of conciliation, and the right to select check-weighmen. It was the most decisive, most impartial, and most satisfactory intervention that an American president had ever undertaken in a labor dispute. It added greatly to Roosevelt's prestige and strengthened the public's perception that, at last, a man occupied the White House who could deal successfully and in the public's interest with the great masters of capital.

In 1904 Roosevelt was nominated for president in his own right and won handily. During the next four years his major achievements involved railroad regulation, protection of consumers, and the conservation of natural resources.

The Interstate Commerce Act had been a disappointment partly because previous administrations had neglected to make much use of it but also because the Supreme Court's narrow interpretation of the powers of the commission rendered it almost helpless. In 1903 Congress passed the Elkins Act, making it illegal for railroads to depart in practice from their published freight rates and making shippers, as well as railroads, liable for infractions. This measure struck at rebating fees to bigger customers, which the railroads themselves began to see as a nuisance. However, the Elkins Act failed to give the Interstate Commerce Commission any power to fix rates, which was what farmers and businessmen wanted most.

The Hepburn Act passed in 1906 was the first really effective regulation of railroads by the federal government. It failed to go as far as most reformers wanted, but it did authorize the commission, when a complaint was received, to set maximum rates and to order railroads to comply after 30 days. The Courts were instructed to assume the Interstate Commerce Commission's rulings sound until evidence was massed to the contrary. This threw the burden of proof on the railroads and its lawyers and reduced judicial setbacks for the Interstate Commerce Commission.

The Hepburn Act also extended the Interstate Commerce Commission's powers to include regulation of storage, refrigeration, and terminal facilities, sleeping cars, express, and pipe-line companies. In 1910 it was expanded to include telephone and telegraph companies.

The next businesses to be regulated were the food and drug industries to prevent undesirable additives and preservatives from being added to the nation's food supply. The *Ladies Home Journal* and *Colliers* published articles on patent medicine and their misleading and exaggerated claims. One of the most notorious was Lydia Pinkham's Vegetable Compound, which was 18 percent alcohol. In 1906 Congress responded by passing the Pure Food and Drug Act and the Meat Inspection Act, which struck at some of the worst abuses.

In 1907 a financial panic occurred. While J. P. Morgan was busy serving in the unofficial role as the nation's central banker, he advised Roosevelt that the panic could be stemmed if United States Steel was allowed to acquire control of Tennessee Iron and Coal Company. Whether this was true or not, Roosevelt gave his consent. His secretary of the treasury also released Panama Canal bonds on terms both generous and reassuring to bankers. The panic was stemmed, and prosperity returned. One result of this was the desire of financial authorities to search for ways to strengthen national finance that eventually led to the establishment of the Federal Reserve Act of 1913. Roosevelt's actions demonstrate that he was not an opponent of capitalism but rather believed that government must regulate its excesses.

WILLIAM HOWARD TAFT

At the end of his second term Teddy Roosevelt bowed to the two-term tradition and threw his support to his secretary of war, William Howard Taft of Cincinnati, Ohio. He had been a circuit court judge, governor of the Philippines, and administrator of the Canal Zone. Although Taft was not a man bitten by the presidential bug, his wife Nellie wanted to be First Lady, and so he accepted Roosevelt's support and the Republican Party's nomination. The Democrats again ran William Jennings Bryan. The progressive reforms that Roosevelt had pushed undercut Bryan, and he lost for the third and final time.

It would have been difficult for anyone to follow the flamboyant and popular Teddy. Taft, a genial man who lacked political instincts, was cautious, slow-moving, and passive. Already obese, his weight ballooned to over 350 pounds. A special oversized tub was installed for his use lending credence to the rumor that he once was stuck in a too snug tub.

Roosevelt and Taft thought their views were alike, but they were wrong. Taft was much more conservative than Roosevelt. Taft did not want to tussle with the Old Guard in the Senate with whom Roosevelt had had to bargain for every reform. His notion of the presidency was much more passive than anything Roosevelt had ever envisioned. As a result, the Republicans gradually returned to their conservative ideology.

Although Roosevelt was known as the trust buster, it was Taft who instituted twice as many antitrust actions under the Sherman Antitrust Act in one administration than Roosevelt had done in two. Taft concluded the prosecutions of Standard Oil and American Tobacco begun under Roosevelt. Taft also proceeded with antitrust cases against International Harvester and United States Steel for acquiring Tennessee Iron and Coal Company. Both were unsuccessful.

Progressives, rather than Taft, must be credited with what was accomplished in railroad regulation. The Mann-Elkins Act of 1910 represented a victory by empowering the Interstate Commerce Commission to suspend general rate increases and to take the initiative in revising rates. A Commerce Court was established to speed up the judicial process by hearing appeals directly from the commission. Railroads were also prohibited from acquiring competing lines. The Physical Evaluation Act enabled the Interstate Commerce Commission to do a physical evaluation of railroad property as a basis for rate making. Now the Interstate Commerce Commission could fix rates on the true value of operating properties rather than the watered stock that the railroads had been in the habit of issuing since the time of Daniel Drew and Jay Gould at the Erie Railroad.

Except for his antitrust policies, President Taft was not closely identified with the progressive measures that Congress enacted during his administration. He split with the progressive members of his party, known as the insurgents, over the tariff. Taft called Congress into special session in March of 1909 to lower the tariff, but when these proposals for a downward revision met with strong opposition from Senator Nelson Aldrich, who was the spokesman for special interests, Taft acquiesced in raising the tariff. When the Payne-Aldrich Bill passed, Taft signed it. He further alienated the progressives by calling it the best tariff the Republicans had ever passed.

Taft also irritated the progressives by helping to quash a rebellion of insurgents against the Speaker of the House, Joseph G. Cannon of Illinois. The progressives and a number of Democrats were trying to replace Cannon, who was a virtual dictator, but Cannon appealed to Taft, who supported him in order to get his vote. Nevertheless, early in 1910, Cannon was removed from the Rules Committee, which meant that he no longer could appoint members to standing committees thus weakening his power.

The Pinchot-Ballinger affair was the last straw for Republican unity. Chief Forester of the Department of Agriculture, Gifford Pinchot, heard from an investigator that Secretary of the Interior Richard A. Ballinger had agreed to sell to the Guggenheim mining interests several million acres of reserved coal lands in Alaska. Pinchot encouraged the investigator to appeal to Taft while he issued a statement denouncing Ballinger. Taft chose to believe Ballinger's denials rather than the investigator's charges and authorized the investigator's dismissal. Pinchot carried on with the attack until he, too, was removed. Congress now investigated and found Ballinger not guilty. However, it was obvious that he was no conservationist. Taft was a conservationist, but after his support of Ballinger, it was easy to persuade people that he wasn't.

After March 1910, open warfare erupted between Taft and the insurgents as Taft used presidential patronage to build up conservative Republicans in the Midwest, the insurgents' power base. The congressional elections that year showed that the Republicans could not succeed without the progressives. The House went Democratic for the first time since 1893, and many Democratic governors were elected. It seemed that the Democrats might even capture the White House. It also seemed that the insurgents would capture the Republican Party and repudiate Taft.

The obvious man to lead the insurgents was Robert La Follette of Wisconsin, who had been active in Republican politics since 1880. He was the first leader in American history to make use of a brain trust, most of whom were his old school friends from the University of Wisconsin. He made good use of professors at the university, and he did careful research into economic and social programs before he gave speeches. Some of the most ardent progressives wanted him to be the Republican candidate for president. Others, who felt La Follette could not be elected, supported Taft.

Election of 1912

Taft's break with the insurgents also included a break with Theodore Roosevelt, who now proceeded with caution. When Roosevelt returned to New York in 1910 from his year-long trip to Africa and Europe, he was dismayed at how Taft had allowed the party to go to pieces. At first, he refrained from making comments, but by August 1910 he gave a famous address in Kansas in which he came out for a number of progressive anti-administration reforms, including more federal regulation of business and judicial recall. His accusation that the federal judiciary was obstructing the popular will shocked conservatives throughout the nation. La Follette thought

Roosevelt was going to support him, but when La Follette, tired, ill and troubled by the illness of one of his daughters, collapsed while delivering a major speech, the more formidable progressive Republicans deserted La Follette. In February of 1912, at Roosevelt's instigation, seven Republican governors wrote him, urging him to announce his candidacy. Two weeks later, his hat was in the ring.

A savage fight followed between Roosevelt and Taft for the Republican nomination. At the convention, there were 254 contested seats; the Taft forces carried all of them, and Roosevelt's delegates stormed out of the hall, leaving Taft to be renominated by a now split party.

The Roosevelt Republicans quickly organized the Bull Moose Party, which took its name from Teddy Roosevelt's statement after an assassination attempt that he was as fit as a Bull Moose. The Bull Moose Party met in Chicago, nominated Roosevelt, and adopted a platform calling for the adoption of almost all the long-proposed social reforms: initiative, referendum, recall, popular overturning of judges, workmen's compensation and social insurance, minimum wages for women, women's suffrage, child-labor laws, and federal trade and tariff commissions to regulate business. Roosevelt's followers said, "Roosevelt bit me and I went mad."

Meanwhile the Democrats had gotten the good news that Bryan would not run again. Among the leading aspirants was Woodrow Wilson, the progressive Democrat from New Jersey. Because the Democratic Party required a two-thirds vote for nominees, it took forty-six ballots for Woodrow Wilson to receive the nod. Their platform also called for a number of reforms and was particularly outspoken in demanding business and tariff reform.

Wilson combined a flair for politics and a high respect for statesmanship. He had been educated for law but swiftly turned to academic life. He attended graduate school at Johns Hopkins University and wrote a book on congressional government, receiving a Ph.D. in 1886. In 1902 he became president of Princeton University where he began to make reforms. He was seen as a democratic spokesman at a time when people were looking for vigorous leaders. In 1910 the party bosses offered Wilson the nomination for governor of New Jersey. Once elected, he repudiated their backing, which surprised them. He then espoused a variety of reforms that brought him the ardent support of the New Jersey progressives. In the first legislative session he won a primary and election law, corrupt practices act, workmen's compensation, utilities regulation, school reforms, and an enabling act giving New Jersey cities the right to adopt the commission form of government.

As a person, Wilson was a bundle of paradoxes. Although his political career was in the North, he was the son of a Virginia minister. Outwardly cold and forbidding, he was extraordinarily intense. Despite his substantial achievements as a reformer, he also displayed a deep sense of tradition and a great reverence for the past, particularly when it involved race relations. He sought to restore a social and economic order long dead. That Wilson was successful in politics was remarkable. He was an excellent speaker with rhythmic speech, clear and dignified, an impressive campaigner. But offstage he was ill-suited to the give and take of American politics. His personality expressed itself in terms of ideals and principles, not personal loyalties. He was too rigid to compromise. To continue to be so high-principled and yet to engage in practical politics meant that Wilson had to deceive himself, a self deception that some of his critics called hypocrisy. As president, he left patronage to his Postmaster-General. Like Roosevelt his goals were those of moderation. He disliked both the plutocracy and distrusted radicals of the extreme left.

In 1912 his greatest asset was the split in the Republican ranks. The three-way fight soon narrowed down to Wilson versus Roosevelt. Since both campaigned as progressives, the issue turned on the question of how to deal with the trusts. Wilson favored regulated competition; Roosevelt favored regulated monopoly. Wilson said the trusts were too big to be regulated for they would soon control the government itself. He pointed to big businessmen who were among Roosevelt's financial backers. To Wilson, the only possible answer was to restore true competition to business and for the government to take vigorous action to suppress unfair and illicit competition.

Teddy Roosevelt countered with the claim that Wilson's ideas were archaic. To restore competition as it had once existed would be undesirable. It would deny the nation the benefits of large-scale operations, which were seen as more efficient (although that was far from always being accurate). Roosevelt claimed that Wilson was attempting to reverse the natural progress of economic evolution. For Roosevelt, trusts were regulated for the best interests of the nation.

Wilson got 6,296,547 votes, 41.9 percent of the popular vote and 435 electoral votes; Roosevelt was second with 4,118,571, 27.4 percent of the popular vote and 88 electoral votes; Taft received 3,486,720 votes, 23.2 percent of the popular vote and 8 electoral votes. The Democrats captured the House and won a working majority in the Senate, so Wilson had the prospects for a constructive administration with a united party and a large bloc of Republican progressives behind him.

WILSON'S ADMINISTRATION

The years of the Wilson administration, 1913-1921, were years of extraordinary fruitfulness in significant reform legislation. The first item on Wilson's agenda was a revision of the tariff. The Underwood Tariff, which lowered the tariff to 29 percent, passed the House with no problem but encountered problems in the Senate where special interests began their work. Wilson reacted with a public statement denouncing the lobbyists working to defeat the bill. La Follette and other progressives inquired of the senators what properties they had that the tariff would affect. The Underwood Tariff was the first downward revision since the Civil War. It also included an income tax of 1 percent on incomes over $4,000 with a graduated surtax from 1-6 percent to make up the revenues lost. This was possible because the Sixteenth Amendment added to the Constitution in 1913 provided for a federal income tax. A second progressive amendment adopted in the same year was the Seventeenth that provided for the direct election of United States senators.

Wilson's second item was banking reform. The need for a federal central bank had been made obvious in the Panic of 1907. A lender of last resort was needed for the banking system. The nation no longer could depend on having a J. P. Morgan to come to the rescue. A bill was finally developed that included twelve Federal Reserve Banks representing twelve regions of the country. These were owned by member banks of the Federal Reserve system who subscribed part of their capital to the banks. The regional banks acted as agents and servants of the member banks. The Federal Reserve system was under the direction of the Federal Reserve Board, consisting of the secretary of the treasury, comptroller, and seven others appointed by the president for fourteen-year terms. A new currency was issued known as federal reserve notes. All national banks had to join the system, and state banks were also eligible. By 1923, 70 percent of the banking resources were in the system. The Federal Reserve system created a currency that was both flexible and sound.

Corporate, Labor, and Farm Legislation

Wilson pushed two regulatory acts through Congress that reflected his philosophy regarding trusts. The Federal Trade Commission Act, passed in 1914, was designed to prevent rather than to punish unfair trade practices. It set up a five-member "watch dog" agency, the Federal Trade Commission (FTC), with the power to investigate corporations engaged in interstate commerce, to look into alleged violations of anti-trust laws, and to issue cease and desist orders. The commission could also sue corporations. Under Wilson the commission issued 379 cease and desist orders.

The second act was the Clayton Antitrust Act of 1914, which described a list of illegal activities such as price discrimination, contracts that forced purchasers to refrain from buying the products of competitors; and corporate acquisition of stock in competing concerns, interlocking directorates connecting corporations with capital of more than $1 million or banks with capital of more than $5 million. Officers of corporations were made individually liable for prosecution and victims of price discrimination could sue for compensation three times the

amount of damages suffered. Labor unions were not to be construed as illegal combinations and labor injunctions were forbidden except when necessary to prevent irreparable injury to property or property rights. Wilson's appointments to the Federal Trade Commission weakened many of its provisions. In the 1920s most of its provisions were nullified under Republican administrations.

Four important acts met the needs of farmers. In 1916 the Federal Farm Loan Act created a Federal Farm Loan Board patterned after the Federal Reserve Board. Twelve Federal Land Banks were established with a minimum capital of $750,000 and could offer farmers loans of five to forty years at 6 percent interest rates. Farm lands, buildings, and improvements for up to 70 percent of the assets secured the loans. Profits were to be distributed to the members of the association. Within fourteen years over four thousand loans were made.

The second act was the Warehouse Act of 1916, which like the old Populist sub-treasury plan authorized licensed warehouse operators to issue warehouse receipts against farm products deposited with them. The third act was the Smith-Lever Act of 1914, which provided millions in federal grants-in-aid for farm demonstration agents working under the land-grant colleges, and the fourth act in 1917 was the Smith-Hughes Act, which subsidized vocational and agricultural education and rounded out the program begun in the Civil War with the land grant colleges. Although not strictly an act for farmers, those that had cars were very interested in the Federal Highways Act of 1916, which provided dollar-matching contributions to state highway departments that met federal standards.

The inaction on labor legislation was also overcome in the Wilson administration with the passage of the Kern-McGillicuddy Bill, which provided workmen's compensation for federal employees. This was followed by the Keating-Owen Child Labor Act. The last act was the Adamson Act, which required an eight-hour day with time and a half for overtime for workers on interstate railways and appointed a commission to study the problems of railroad labor.

It was under Wilson's administration that the last two of the four progressive amendments to the

Constitution were passed: the Eighteenth Amendment that prohibited the manufacture, sale or transportation of intoxicating liquors within the United States and the Nineteenth Amendment that gave women the right to vote.

PROGRESSIVE FOREIGN POLICY

Immediately preceding the Progressive Era, the United States had become a colonial power when it obtained the Philippine Islands, Puerto Rico, Guam, and Hawaii, as well as the right to interfere in the internal affairs of the newly "independent" Cuba. It was not just a question of obtaining property that made the United States a colonial power; it was the status of the people on this property. Congress would determine their civil rights and political status without any promise of citizenship or statehood. In the Insular Cases, the United States Supreme Court ruled that the Constitution did not follow the flag. In practical terms this meant that people living in the new possessions did not have the same rights that American citizens enjoyed, such as freedom of the press and trial by jury. Even citizens of Hawaii, which was annexed to the United States, did not have the freedoms mentioned in the Bill of Rights. In effect, there were now two classes of persons: American citizens who lived either in states or territories on the continent and who enjoyed full civil and political rights and those subject peoples living in American possessions.

A further problem was created when the United States took the Philippines. The Filipinos wanted not only their independence from Spain but also from any other nation, including the United States. From 1898 to 1901 the United States fought a war in the Philippines to establish control over this new possession. The tactics in this war included forcing the natives into concentration camps, the same tactics that had led Americans to call the Spanish General in Cuba "Butcher" Weyler.

Although the United States entered the Spanish-American War with the purpose of helping Cuba gain its freedom from Spain, the United States effec-tively kept Cuba in a subservient position by insisting that the Cuban constitution allowed for direct United States intervention "for the preservation of Cuban independence, the maintenance of a government adequate for the protection of life, property, and individual liberty." It was needed often.

American involvement in Latin America and Asia continued to grow in the aftermath of the Spanish-American War and Philippine conflict. The new possessions and industrial might had catapulted America into the role of a major player on the stage of world power politics. The progressive presidents, accustomed to a positive view of the place of dynamic government, sought to create an American-influenced world order. If a combination of democracy, progressivism, trade, and capitalist expansion could create a better, stronger America, why couldn't it benefit more "backward," benighted societies?

The irrepressible Teddy Roosevelt sought to create a macho image of a president who embodied "the soldierly virtues." His motto was, "Speak softly and carry a big stick." (Although he often forgot the first part.) In practical terms, he believed that the United States had to increase its role in the world, protect its predominance in Latin America, and ensure the Open Door and power balance in Asia.

Panama Canal

Perhaps the most notable example of the United States flexing its power is in the way the U. S. obtained the Panama Canal. The idea of a canal across the isthmus had been of interest since the settlement of the Oregon boundary in the 1840s. Interest increased with the discovery of gold in California, resulting in Cornelius Vanderbilt's building of a railroad across Nicaragua that connected a lake and river to provide a shorter route to the Pacific than going around the horn of South America. A railroad had also been built across Panama as early as 1855. Both sites remained in contention for potential canals in which the United States had a vested interest.

While the Americans deliberated, a French company headed by Ferdinand de Lesseps, builder of the Suez Canal, obtained a concession from Columbia to build a canal across the Isthmus of Panama. In

1881 the work began. The United States' reaction was to charter a corporation to exploit the rival Nicaraguan route, while at the same time seeking to abrogate a previous treaty with Great Britain, so that a United States owned and controlled canal could be built. By 1890, the French company in Panama was bankrupt, and only a small portion of the canal was completed. The company set up to build a canal in Nicaragua had also failed to raise the funds for such an enterprise. It became clear that only the U. S. government had the resources and ability to build the canal wherever it was to be located.

The Spanish-American War made it clear that it was in the U. S. interest to build and control a canal across the isthmus. American pubic opinion strongly favored the construction of a canal connecting the Atlantic and Pacific Oceans and eliminating the long and costly trip around South America. The question was which route the canal would take: Nicaragua or Panama.

Although the Nicaraguan Route had some power backers in Congress, the New Panama Canal Company had key players: William Nelson Cromwell of an important New York law firm and the Frenchman Philippe Bunau-Varilla, both representing the interests of the New Panama Canal Company. They were soon able to enlist the influential Senator Mark Hanna of Ohio. When the New Panama Canal Company dropped its price from $109,000,000 to $40,000,000 and a volcano erupted in Nicaragua, the location was settled. In 1902 Theodore Roosevelt signed the Isthmian Canal Act, which made Panama the first choice.

There was only one problem. Columbia owned Panama. In January 1903, the Hay-Herran treaty was signed with the following financial terms: $10,000,000 to be paid at once, $250,000 annually. In return the United States was to have sovereignty over the canal zone, which was to be ten miles in width. The Columbian Senate rejected the treaty saying the price was too low and the loss of Columbian sovereignty in Panama too sweeping. Theodore Roosevelt was not pleased at what he saw as Columbia reneging on the deal. It was like trying to nail jelly to the wall, he raged, when you tried to negotiate with those "dagos."

Roosevelt indicated his willingness to look favorably upon a revolution by the Panamanian people. Events moved swiftly: Philippe Bunau-Varilla headed a junta in New York that fomented a rebellion in the Columbian Department of Panama. Members of the Columbian garrison in Panama were bought off for $50 a head. The commanding general received $30,000 and was nearly drowned in the buckets of champagne poured over his head. A U.S. warship prevented the Columbians from putting the rebellion down, while the U.S. government recognized Panama as independent and signed a treaty with

Theodore Roosevelt's "Big Stick" diplomacy toward Latin America

Panama, giving the U.S. even more sweeping privileges in Panama. Panama received the same amount of money once offered to Columbia. The Frenchman from the New Panama Canal Company, Philippe Bunau-Varilla, signed the treaty for Panama.

Columbia was bitterly resentful and some in the United States questioned the actions of the Roosevelt administration. Roosevelt's response was: "I took the canal zone and let Congress debate." Within ten years of the transfer of the canal from the French company to the U. S. government, the canal was opened to the traffic of the world.

The completion of the canal in 1914 was an enormous achievement. Colonel William Gorgas was able to eradicate the yellow-fever bearing mosquito by 1906, which enabled construction to begin. Companies in Pittsburgh, Wheeling, and other American cities produced the bolts, steel girders, special bearings and gears, and electrical devices needed to complete the construction. Americans were both proud and awed when the canal opened.

In 1921, after the death of Roosevelt, the U. S. paid Columbia $25,000,000 although there was no apology. It was an implicit acknowledgment that the methods used in obtaining it were not justified. The ill-will Roosevelt caused, as well as the other Latin American interventions of the progressive presidents, haunted relations for many years to come.

The Roosevelt Corollary

American involvement in the Caribbean increased with the need to protect the canal. Roosevelt feared that Latin American defaults on the debts they owed to European banks would lead to European intervention in the Western Hemisphere. Such interventions would be detrimental to our interests. To prevent this, in 1904, the president issued the Roosevelt Corollary to the Monroe Doctrine. The original 1823 doctrine had warned Europe against interference in Latin America. Roosevelt now lectured Latin Americans against "chronic wrongdoing," which, in "flagrant cases" would cause America to take on the task of "an international police power." Thus, the right to intervene in Latin American affairs became an American prerogative.

The first application of the Roosevelt Corollary occurred in 1905 when the United States took over the operation of the Dominican Republic's customs service and the management of its foreign debt. Revolutionary upheaval in Cuba in 1906 led to a three-year occupation by American troops.

The Far East

United States policy in the Far East was based primarily on the traditional notion of balance of power. It was a policy that also had repercussions in domestic affairs. Japan was rapidly becoming the dominant Asian power. In 1904 Japan began the Russo-Japanese War with a sneak attack on Port Arthur. After eighteen months the war ended with Japan becoming the first Asian nation to defeat a European nation. At the beginning of the war, Roosevelt had assumed a neutral position while making it clear that he favored Japan. In doing so, he was following the balance-of-power theory of international relations. However, as the war progressed, Roosevelt became more concerned about the rise of Japan. Because Japan was unaware of this change in sentiments, it asked Roosevelt to propose a peace conference to end the war. He did, and the delegates met at Portsmouth, New Hampshire in August of 1905.

During the conference Japan demanded a large indemnity of $600 million or more to cover the cost of the war: Russia refused. Finally Roosevelt convinced the Japanese to give up that demand, and Russia and Japan signed a treaty of peace that recognized Japan's interests in Korea and that gave her the southern half of Sakhalin Island among other things. For his work, Roosevelt received the Nobel Peace Prize in 1906. Later, Roosevelt advised Japan that the U.S. would approve a Japanese takeover of Korea, which quickly occurred.

Although the Japanese government was pleased with the peace, the Japanese public was not. Soon other problems developed. By 1906 Japan was violating the Open Door policy in Manchuria. In the United States, particularly California, anti-Japanese sentiment was growing. By 1906 one thousand Japanese a month were settling in the Pacific coastal states. The San Francisco school board banned ninety-three

Japanese children from the city's white schools and required them to attend Oriental schools established for Chinese and Korean children. The Japanese government thought this policy stigmatized Japanese Americans as inferior. There was talk of war in the Japanese newspapers, and Roosevelt intervened by inviting the members of the San Francisco school board to Washington where he pointed out that any war would most likely hit the West Coast first and the hardest. The order was rescinded.

In addition, Roosevelt concluded a "gentleman's agreement" with Japan that would continue to bar Japanese workers from coming to the United States while the U. S. barred them from entering from intermediate points such as Hawaii, Mexico, or Canada. This agreement lasted until 1924 when a new immigration law superseded it.

While these agreements did help smooth the waters with Japan, anti-Japanese feelings in California did not diminish. Although Roosevelt was able to lobby California Republicans to defeat a bill that would have excluded Japanese residents from buying land, Woodrow Wilson was not so successful, and in 1913 the California legislature passed a bill forbidding ownership of land to aliens ineligible for citizenship, i. e., the Japanese. Sensational newspapers inflamed public opinion with fears of Japanese expansionism.

In 1907, Roosevelt ordered the American fleet on an around the world "training operation" to demonstrate American naval strength and to show the Japanese that he was not afraid of them. Its first stop was Japan. Shortly after the visit, Japan signed a treaty with the United States that pledged both nations to respect the other's interests in Asia. But, even as the Japanese appeared to be impressed by the visit of the "Great White Fleet," they began to build a bigger navy of their own.

Taft and Dollar Diplomacy

Although the United States owned only a few colonies, it had amassed an empire based upon economic and political control rather than possessions. "Order" was central to the maintenance of this empire. American power was particularly apparent in the Car-ibbean area where marines landed and rearranged economies and governments. Taft's foreign policy was concerned with the promotion of American business interests overseas. Critics called it "dollar diplomacy."

American trade and investment in Latin America boomed. An American corporation, the United Fruit Company, owner of vast banana plantations and railroads, had more power than most Latin American governments. The U. S. intervened "to maintain order" in the Dominican Republic, Cuba, Haiti, Honduras, and, most provocatively, in Nicaragua. In the latter country, nationalist revolutionaries overturned an American-backed ruler who had promised that his nation would become "a field for American commerce, instead of a pest under your nose." Taft sent 2,700 marines in 1912 to "keep order" and uphold the "legally constituted government." The troops remained until 1933.

Dollar diplomacy was less successful in Asia, where Taft labored to get American bankers involved in railroad construction. The Japanese and Russians united to keep America out of Manchuria and stymied efforts to expand into the vast Chinese market.

MINORITY RIGHTS IN THE PROGRESSIVE ERA

Although many things were accomplished during the Progressive Era, it did not extend to minority Americans.

As mentioned earlier in the discussion of the women's suffrage movement, the suffrage movement and its divisions represented one example of problems related to race. Suffrage leaders ignored black women who had worked in the movement and appealed to Southern whites that the vote should be given to women so that they could join with their WASP (White Anglo-Saxon Protestant) husbands to counteract the votes of black men and ignorant immigrants. Of course, since black men had already been effectively disenfranchised in the South, there was no danger of black women joining their husbands in voting. The Nineteenth Amendment would, in reality, only enfranchise white women.

There were other examples of racism seen in this period besides the lynching in the South and the treatment of Japanese in the West. Roosevelt had been considered a friend of African Americans when he invited Booker T. Washington to lunch at the White House to consult on distributing minor federal jobs to black Republicans in the South. A storm of racist criticism ensued, including a complaint that the White House Republicans "had been painted black." It took more than thirty years before a president (Franklin Roosevelt) dared to invite a black to dine at the White House.

Teddy Roosevelt's African-American supporters were disappointed at his handling of a 1906 incident in Brownsville, Texas, which seemed to demonstrate his true feeling towards blacks. After a shootout between black troops and white townsmen, Roosevelt ordered the entire black regiment to be dishonorably discharged without any trial or even any investigation. Roosevelt's action was even more incomprehensible when you consider that it was black regiments known as Buffalo Soldiers who had rescued Roosevelt at San Juan Hill during the Spanish-American War. The 25th Regiment that had been stationed in Brownsville had an interesting history. At one point the Army considered replacing horses with bicycles and to test the idea, the 25th Regiment, known as the Black Bicycle Brigade, rode bicycles for 2,000 miles from Montana to St. Louis. Their acts of courage and endurance were for naught. It was 1972 before Congress removed the "dishonorable" from the military records of these black soldiers.

While the Taft administration began segregation in the federal department buildings, it was accelerated under Woodrow Wilson, the first Southerner to be president since the Civil War. Although the leaders seemed to have been the Secretary of the Treasury and the Postmaster General, Wilson was well aware of their policies. An additional innovation was the requirement that applicants for civil service positions include a photograph with their applications. Despite this executive action, Congress refused to adopt legislation to segregate the races in the federal departments. Nor did they enact any legislation that curtailed black rights. In response to criticism, Wilson declared that segregation was "in the interest of the Negro."

Neither in foreign affairs nor in domestic affairs did the progressive presidents extend the basic tenets of progressivism to non-whites.

CONCLUSION

Wilson's New Freedom Program represented the apex of the Progressive Movement and with it reform came to a halt. The movement was nullified by the war and the conservative reaction of the 1920s. Although many reforms were enacted, the results were not always what the reformers had wanted. Party machines found ways to manipulate the political processes despite the direct primary. Initiatives and referendums were cumbersome and often misfired. Recall was used only rarely. Money still continued to influence politics although there were more punishments for corruption. Too often the reforms lasted for only a short term and often depended upon the personality and drive of only one person. The bosses eventually came filtering back, more careful but still powerful. Reformers had to console themselves that without their efforts things might have been worse.

Chronology

1889 Jane Addams founds Hull House in Chicago

1901 U. S. Steel Corporation founded first billion dollar corporation.
Jacob Riis, *How the Other Half Lives*

1894 Henry Demarest Lloyd, *Wealth Against Commonwealth;* Tammany Hall overthrown

1896 *Wabash vs Illinois*—U. S. Supreme Court outlawed state regulation of interstate commerce

1898 Spanish-American War

1899 Thorstein Veblen, *The Theory of the Leisure Class*

1900 International Ladies Garment Workers Union (ILGWU) founded; Carrie Chapman Catt becomes president of National American Woman Suffrage Movement

1901	McKinley assassinated; Theodore Roosevelt becomes president; Colonial war fought in Philippines
1902	Roosevelt mediates coal strike; Roosevelt orders attorney general to bring suit to dissolve Northern Securities; Jane Addams, *Democracy and Social Ethics*
1903	Maria Van Vorst, *The Woman Who Toils* W. E. B. DuBois, *Souls of Black Folks* Revolution organized in Panama
1904	Roosevelt elected president; *Northern Securities Case* resolved; Lincoln Steffens, *The Shame of the Cities;* Ida Tarbell, *History the Standard Oil Company;* John Moody, *The Truth About Trusts;* Roosevelt Corollary to the Monroe Doctrine
1905	International Workers of the World (IWW) organized; Pinchot head of the U. S. Forest Service; Roosevelt mediates Russo-Japanese War settlement; At Roosevelt's urging San Francisco desegregates schools
1906	David Graham Phillips, *The Treason of the Senate;* Hepburn Act to regulate railroads; Upton Sinclair, *The Jungle;* Pure Food and Drug Act; Meat Inspection Act; Roosevelt wins Nobel Peace Prize
1908	William Howard Taft elected president
1909	National Association for the Advancement of Colored People (NAACP) founded; Ballinger controversy
1910	Push for woman suffrage increases with several new states granting women the right to vote; Mann-Elkins Act empowered; Interstate Commerce Commission
1911	Triangle Shirtwaist Company fire; Standard Oil dissolved
1912	Three way election - GOP (Taft), Progressives (T. Roosevelt), and Democrats (Wilson). Wilson elected; U. S. troops in Mexico
1913	Pujo Committee; Federal Reserve Act; Sixteenth Amendment—income tax Seventeenth Amendment—direct election of senators; 30,000 march in New York for woman's suffrage
1914	Clayton Anti-trust Act; Completion of Panama Canal; Federal Trade Commission Act
1915	Congressional Union founded to push for woman suffrage
1916	Federal Farm Loan Act; Wilson re-elected; Margaret Higgins Sanger opens birth control clinic
1918	Jeanette Rankin introduced suffrage amendment that passed the House
1919	Eighteenth Amendment—prohibition
1920	Nineteenth Amendment—woman's suffrage

SUGGESTED READINGS

John Milton Cooper Jr., *The Warrior and the Priest: Woodrow Wilson and Theodore* (1983).

Robert Morse Crunden, *Ministers of Reform; The Progressives' Achievement in American Civilization, 1889-1920* (1984).

David B. Danbom, *"The World of Hope": Progressives and the Struggle for an Ethical Public Life.* (1987).

Noralee Frankel and Nancy F. Dye, (eds.), *Gender, Class, Race and Reform in the Progressive Era* (1991).

Elizabeth Frost and Kathryn Cullen-DuPont, *Women's Suffrage in America, An Eyewitness Report* (1995).

Richard Hofstadter, *The Age of Reform: From Byran to F.D.R.* (1955).

Harold Howland, *Theodore Roosevelt (1921).*

William O'Neill, *The Progressive Years: America Comes of Age* (1975).

John Lugton Safford, *Pragmatism and the Progressive Movement in the United States: The Origins of the New Social Sciences* (1987).

Dorothy Schneider and Carl J. Schneider, *American Women in the Progressive Era, 1900-1920* (1994).

Mildred I. Thompson, *Ida B. Wells-Barnett: An Exploratory Study of an American Black Woman, 1893-1930* (1990).

Ida B. Wells-Barnett, *On Lynching: Southern Horrors, A Red Record Mob Rule in New Orleans* (1991).

Marjorie Spruill Wheeler (ed)., *One Woman, One Vote: Rediscovering the Woman Suffrage Movement* (1995).

Robert H. Wiebe, *Businessmen and Reform* (1962).

SURE!
We'll
Finish
the Job

Gerrit A. Beneker 1918

VICTORY LIBERTY LOAN

Chapter Seventeen

THE "GREAT" WAR: World War I

June 28, 1914, was a hot morning in the Bosnian town of Sarajevo, a spot on the globe virtually unknown to Americans. (Eighty years later, when it again led in the news, Americans would still be unable to locate Bosnia on the map.) The city's balconies were hung with banners and colorful carpets to welcome Archduke Francis Ferdinand—heir to the throne of the large and troubled Austro-Hungarian empire—and his wife, Sophie. The Archduke intended it to be a day of celebration and validation for his more lowly born wife on the occasion of their fourteenth wedding anniversary. He and his wife entered an open car at 10:00 A.M. for a triumphant procession.

Waiting among the milling crowds, however, were seven young Serbian nationalists. They were a disorganized and crudely armed group of conspirators, seeking a Greater Serbia. The Archduke's chauffeur, misunderstanding his instructions, took a wrong turn. When he realized his mistake, he braked and stopped the car less than five feet from Gavrilo Princip, the most determined of the assassins. Princip fired two shots. One hit Francis Ferdinand in the neck; the other struck Sophie in the abdomen. Observing his beloved wife crumpled in a

heap, the dying Archduke cried, "Sophie dear...don't die. Stay alive for our children." His last words were a response to questions about his own suffering, "Es ist nicht." (It is nothing.) By 11:00 A.M., both were dead.

As Leon Trotsky would say later, "History had already poised its gigantic soldier's boot over the ant heap." In a little over a month, a complex system of alliances would escalate the responses to the assassination into the most terrible war the world had yet seen, the "Great War."

It was three in the morning in New York when the Archduke stepped into his motorcar. Dancers tangoed at Coney Island's Castle Summer House and on the sand at Brighton Beach. Americans found Europeans difficult to understand. They seemed decadent and corrupt in contrast to American innocence and happiness. Despite lynchings, labor exploitation, and violence, Americans deeply believed that human progress was inevitable. The New York Times reported that music by wireless had actually been heard two hundred miles away! The New York Yankees and the Cleveland Indians were locked in a titanic struggle for the American League Pennant (which was ultimately won by the Philadel-

phia Athletics). In the minor leagues, Baltimore beat Buffalo 10 to 5, behind the pitching of a rookie named Babe Ruth. Jack Johnson, the controversial black boxer, won another match in Paris. Steak was advertised for thirty cents a pound, eggs for twenty-one cents a dozen, and the "Benefactor" cigar claimed that it provided a good smoke for only six cents.

It was hard to believe that "the Good Years" might be coming to an end. Even the conflagration that had engulfed Europe by August 1914 failed to dampen American optimism. Sir Edward Grey, the British Foreign Secretary, had a more realistic intimation that an age was about to end. Watching a London lamplighter at work on the evening of August 4, 1914, he commented sadly to a friend, "The lamps are going out all over Europe; we shall not see them lit again in our lifetime."

WILSONIAN "MISSIONARY DIPLOMACY"

Woodrow Wilson at first seemed less concerned with the titanic events in Europe than with democracy in the Americas. Woodrow Wilson, a minister's son, disdained his predecessors' crass commercialism and power hunger. America, he vowed, would "never again seek one additional foot of territory by conquest." He did, however, deeply believe that Latin American nations could be reshaped into replicas of the United States. "When properly directed, there is no people not fitted for self-government," he announced. "Every nation needs to be drawn into the tutelage of America" to learn "the habit of law and obedience."

Early tests of Wilsonian policy arose when bloodshed and chaos swept through Haiti and the Dominican Republic. After suffering through seven corrupt despotic governments in a four-year period, the disgusted Haitians rose up against the latest petty tyrant and dismembered him. Wilson sent the marines to bring order to both small countries. The marines crushed uprisings and remained in occupation until 1924 in the Dominican Republic and 1934 in Haiti. It is doubtful that either the marines or the local population appreciated the differences between the interventions for economic gain and the ones to "restore" democracy.

Wilson's chief foreign policy concern before 1914, however, was Mexico. Conflicts in that country between the elite large landowners and the mass of poverty-stricken peasants led to massive upheavals. In 1911, a motley combination of activists, socialists, Indians, and radical Catholic land reformers overturned the thirty-five year reign of the dictator, Porfirio Diaz. Diaz had granted many concessions to American investors. The idealistic leader of the revolutionary forces was in turn murdered by General Victoriano Huerta, who imposed a military dictatorship just before Wilson took office in 1913. The new American president declared, "I will not recognize a government of butchers," under whom "entire villages have been burned, their inhabitants...slaughtered and mutilated indiscriminately." He went on to announce that the United States would, in the future, have relations only with "republican governments based upon law, not irregular force." This reversed earlier policies of recognizing any government that was actually in power. While committing America to democratic ideals, it required the president to decide the moral purity of new governments before dealing with them. It would have fateful, and not always positive, consequences, permeating future American foreign policy with a moralistic self-righteousness.

Despite American and British pressure, the Huerta regime did not collapse. In April of 1914, Wilson stumbled into direct intervention. A group of American sailors was arrested in Tampico. Although they were released almost immediately, the American commander demanded a formal apology and a twenty-one gun salute to the American flag. When Huerta refused, Wilson ordered the occupation of Mexico's main Gulf port, Vera Cruz. The resulting heavy fighting led to some five hundred Mexican casualties and intense anti-American feeling. Huerta was forced to abdicate. He was replaced by Venastiano Carranza, a reformer favored by Wilson.

The winds of disorder did not abate so easily. Pancho Villa, an adventurous, romantic revolutionary (or bandit, depending on one's point of view),

Woodrow Wilson directs world events from the top of the Washington Monument.

THE OUTBREAK OF THE GREAT WAR

While the United States was preoccupied with Latin America, the ominous storm clouds of war loomed over Europe. Europe had had no wars involving all of the major powers for almost a century. Many "experts" predicted that war, a discreditable by-product of a "barbarous" past, would never again rear its ugly head. But below the seemingly placid surface, many young European men felt that their society had become decadent, uninteresting, and dangerously soft. They longed for the excitement of war, an experience they believed would build character and create a new "superman," sweeping away the rotting remains of a decaying civilization. (Teddy Roosevelt had held similar views of the value of the Spanish-American War in American character-building.)

Strategists argued that a balance of power in Europe would maintain the existing system because no nation would be dominant enough to risk war. The balance, however, rested precariously on competing forces of nationalism, imperialism, and an armaments race. The European powers had, through a complex system of alliances, eventually divided themselves into two camps: the Triple Entente (Allied Powers)—Great Britain, France, and Russia; and the Triple Alliance (Central Powers)—Germany, Austria-Hungary, and Italy. (Italy switched sides after the outbreak of war.) The imperial ambitions of Britain, France, and Germany clashed in the race for markets and resources in Africa and Asia.

The Turkish Ottoman Empire had become the "sick man of Europe," losing control of most of southeastern Europe where the independent nations of Romania, Bulgaria, and Serbia had arisen. The fires of nationalism burned brightly in these areas, particularly Serbia. Russia encouraged Pan-Slavism, the dream of uniting all the Slavic peoples of Europe. Russian goals conflicted with those of the Austro-Hungarian Empire, which simultaneously hoped to expand into the remains of the Ottoman Empire and to crush Slavic nationalism within its own territories. Germany had succeeded in creating a united nation out of many principalities only in 1871. Under the leadership of Kaiser Wilhelm II, it boldly

raised the banner of nationalist rebellion against Carranza. In 1916, Villa slaughtered sixteen American mining engineers he had pulled from a train. Then he burned down Columbus, New Mexico, killing nineteen of its citizens. Wilson responded to these provocations and an angry American public by ordering General "Black Jack" Pershing to cross the border in a "punitive expedition." Villa, to the embarrassment of the American military, easily eluded Pershing's forces and even launched a raid into Texas. Wilson then dispatched 150,000 National Guardsmen to seal off the border. In 1917, Wilson was able to use the increasing problems in Europe to withdraw American forces and recognize the Carranza government. With the best of intentions, Wilson had succeeded only in antagonizing the very people he professed to be helping. The United States, whether from idealism or imperialism, assumed that its goal should be to control and improve "inferior" nations. The "cloak of empire," however, seemed to be a poor fit on an uneasy America.

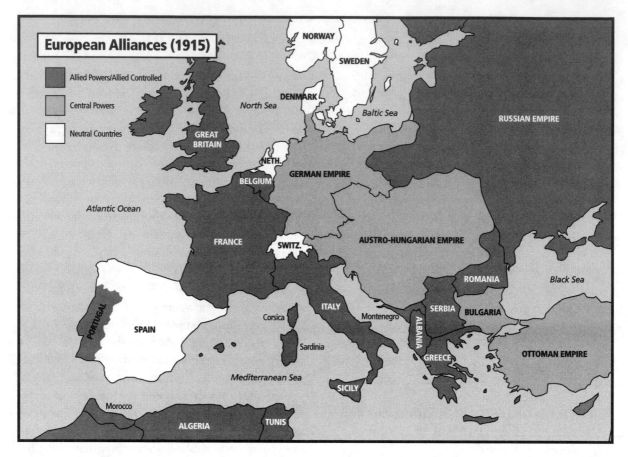

European Alliances (1915)

- Allied Powers/Allied Controlled
- Central Powers
- Neutral Countries

pursued national greatness and military might, seeking to overwhelm France's army and to challenge British naval supremacy.

All of these elements created an explosive brew, needing only a spark to set off a calamitous conflagration. The assassination of Austrian Archduke Franz Ferdinand by a Serbian terrorist supplied that spark. Austria-Hungary, fearing the consequences of Slavic nationalism, consulted its partner Germany, which urged an unyielding stance. Austria then made harsh demands on Serbia, which, in turn, called on its Slavic "big brother," Russia, for help. When Austria declared war, after announcing that the Serbian response was unacceptable, the alliance system dragged in the rest of Europe. Russia mobilized. Germany struck quickly, declaring war on Russia and then its French ally. Great Britain hesitated briefly; but when Germany invaded neutral Belgium to attack France, Britain declared war. Turkey eventually joined the Central Powers. Japan, using the European conflict to gain control of Germany's sphere in

China, joined the Allied side. An assassin's bullet had ripped apart a once-peaceful world and altered it forever.

American Neutrality

The onset of the Great War shocked and dismayed many Americans. "Civilization is all gone, and barbarism come," one writer lamented. President Wilson declared neutrality and urged Americans to be impartial "in thought as well as in action," to show "the dignity of self-control." In private he argued that the United States had to maintain neutrality "since otherwise our mixed populations would wage war on each other."

The majority of Americans favored Wilson's position. They continued to assume that the "great watery moats," the Atlantic and Pacific Oceans, would protect them from the dangers of war. Some progressives organized an anti-war group, the American Union Against Militarism. A group of suffragists founded the Woman's Peace Party. Industrialists Andrew Carnegie and Henry Ford helped finance peace groups. "If I had my way," Ford announced, "I'd throw every ounce of gunpowder into the sea and strip soldiers of their insignias." Ford backed up his words by chartering a "peace ship" that sent a group of anti-war activists, including Jane Addams, to Europe vainly to attempt to persuade the warring sides to accept neutral mediation. Each appalling report from the European battlegrounds, where the terrible toll of trench warfare was being felt, strengthened peace sentiments in the United States. Fifteen hundred women, dressed entirely in black, marched down Fifth Avenue in New York City in opposition to the war. A popular song that declared, "I didn't raise my boy to be a soldier, to kill some other mother's darling boy," showed the national frame of mind

Other factors, however, worked against idealistic appeals to neutrality. There were ethnic groups who sympathized with the Central Powers. These included millions of German-Americans and Irish-Americans. (The Irish yearned for independence from British rule.) The brutal British crushing of the Easter rebellion in Ireland added to these feelings. More Americans, however—including Wilson and his closest advisers—felt emotional ties to the British. These rested on common bonds of language, history, religion, and democratic government. The president had been forced to deal with the personal misfortune of the death of his wife, Ellen, just as the war began. Edward Grey, the British Foreign Secretary, who had suffered a similar loss, sent a moving condolence message to Wilson. The president responded, "We are bound together by common principle and purpose." Wilson was referring to more than personal tragedy. He believed that a German victory "would change the course of our civilization and make the United States a military nation."

British propaganda made effective use of these sentiments by emphasizing the "atrocities" committed by the barbarous German "Huns" against innocent civilians in neutral Belgium. Clumsy German public relations played into British hands when the German Foreign Minister supposedly dismissed the treaty guaranteeing Belgian neutrality as nothing more than "a piece of paper," a cynicism that shocked a naive American public. Documents were discovered that revealed that Germany was financing espionage and, possibly, sabotage in American factories. This further inflamed public opinion.

American economic links with the Allies also undermined neutrality. The British had long been America's chief trading partner. The war led to a tripling of American exports of manufactured goods and food supplies to the Allies. These sales pushed the American economy out of a recession and into an economic boom. Loans from American banks financed much of this trade. After initial opposition to these loans as contrary to true neutrality, Wilson's advisers convinced him that to insure American prosperity, "We must finance it." By 1917 such credit totaled more than $2 billion, an enormous sum for that time period. One consequence of this relationship was that America now had a tremendous economic interest in an Allied victory.

In spite of all the factors undermining neutrality, Wilson and the vast majority of the American public continued to believe that America must stay out of the conflict. Wilson doggedly attempted to mediate the European conflict. In 1917 he declared, "We are the only one of the great white nations that is free from war today, and it would be a crime against civilization for us to go in." Nevertheless, with substantial popular support, the president and the country did "go in." What caused this shift?

Naval and Submarine Warfare

Wilson firmly believed that international law guaranteed the rights of neutral nations to engage in trade with nations at war. Britain was determined to use its naval superiority to cripple Germany economically. The British, "ruling the waves and waiving the rules," stopped American merchant ships and seized their cargoes bound for Germany. International law defined **contraband** as goods "essential to warfare" that might rightfully be seized "by either belligerent when shipped to the other one by a neutral country." The British revised the definition to include anything, including food, which might, even indirectly, aid Germany. Wilson vigorously protested. The British actions reminded him of the War of 1812 when similar issues had arisen. "Madison and I are the only two Princeton men that have become president," he remarked ruefully to a friend. "The circumstances of the War of 1812 and now run parallel. I sincerely hope they will not go further."

Wilson's objections increased when the British, in a further departure from international law, planted deadly mines throughout the North Sea. American ships might well have been sunk if the U. S. had chosen to challenge the British by sending them into the area unescorted. The president, instead, protested in a formal note. He never entertained the notion of serious actions against the Allies. He really believed that, "England is fighting our fight." When some of his advisers suggested prohibiting exports to the British, he responded, "Gentlemen, the Allies are standing with their backs to the wall fighting wild beasts." The British were also able to deflect criticism by paying for confiscated cargoes. German violations that, unlike the British actions, destroyed both life and property aroused far more anger.

The Germans had developed a frightening new weapon: the U-boat, a submarine equipped with torpedoes. In February 1915, determined to weaken the blockade and disrupt American trade with the Allies, Germany announced a war zone around the British Isles where ships were likely to be sunk. Wilson immediately informed the Germans that he was holding them to "strict accountability" for any American losses. He insisted on an inflexible interpretation of international law under which attackers must warn merchant or passenger ships and provide for the safety of passengers and crew before sinking the vessel. The Germans felt that Wilson was unfair, denying them the chance to retaliate against the British blockade. The problem was that the submarines were fragile and so small that they had crews of only a few men. If they surfaced to give warnings, they could easily be rammed and destroyed.

In the months that followed, U-boats sank several ships, including an American tanker. On May 1, 1915, a small announcement appeared in American newspapers warning against travel on British vessels in war zones. Despite the warning, the Brit-

The German U-boat attacked silently and without warning

ish luxury liner, the *Lusitania*, the pride of the Cunard Lines, cast off with a full contingent of passengers. (Only one had canceled.) The great ship neglected to follow the precaution of a zigzag path. When it was off the coast of Ireland, a German submarine fired torpedoes. Within eighteen minutes, the *Lusitania* went to the bottom, causing the deaths of 1,198, including 128 Americans. Americans were outraged. The nation declared, "The torpedo which sank the *Lusitania* also sank Germany in the opinion of mankind." (Historians later discovered that the ship's cargo had included contraband, including ammunition.) Colonel House, Wilson's emissary in London, remarked, "We shall be at war within a month." He was wrong.

Wilson vigorously argued that, even if the ship was carrying war supplies, its sinking constituted an unjustified attack on innocent civilians. He demanded that Germany pledge to end unrestricted submarine warfare. Nevertheless, he believed that the U. S. could gain recognition of neutral rights without conflict. "There is such a thing as a man being too proud to fight," he declared.

Public opinion was bitterly divided over his actions. Secretary of State William Jennings Bryan felt that Americans should not be allowed to travel on belligerent ships and argued that the protest notes were unnecessarily hostile. "Germany has a right to prevent contraband from going to the Allies," he argued, "and a ship carrying contraband should not rely on passengers to protect her from attack—it would be like putting women and children in front of an army." When Wilson rejected his views, Bryan resigned in protest. The openly pro-Allied Robert Lansing replaced him. Wilson and his congressional supporters defeated a resolution that would have prohibited Americans from traveling aboard belligerent vessels.

Other Americans, however, believed that war with Germany was inescapable. Theodore Roosevelt loudly condemned "weasel words" from the "word-lover in the White House" who had demonstrated "abject cowardice and weakness." "Preparedness" parades to promote a military buildup countered the peace demonstrators.

For a while it appeared that Wilson's approach, resolute but restrained, was working. German Chancellor Bethmann, dismayed by the anger of the American public, wanted to abandon submarine warfare. German naval leaders opposed him. The Kaiser shifted between these views. After some further sinkings, including that of an unarmed French ferry, the *Sussex*, Wilson warned Germany that "the United States can have no choice but to sever diplomatic relations" if German attacks continued. This threat caused the Germans to back down and pledge that they would no longer sink merchant vessels without warning. A qualifying clause, declaring that the United States must also insist that the British observe "the rules of international law," was conveniently ignored. The so-called "Sussex pledge" also boxed the U. S. into a corner should Germany change its position.

The 1916 Presidential Election

The war was a crucial factor in the presidential election of 1916. Wilson, who had been elected in 1912 as a result of the Republican/Progressive split, was renominated by the Democrats. He ran on a peace platform as his followers proclaimed, "He kept us

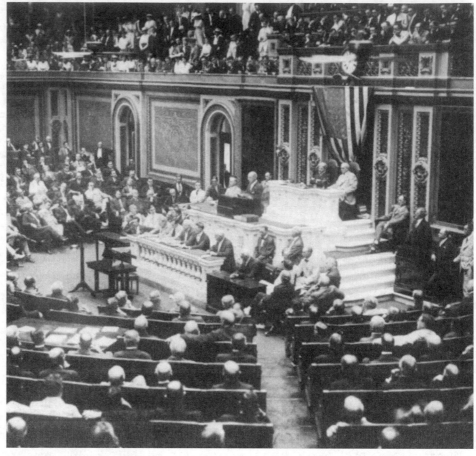

President Woodrow Wilson addressed Congress on February 3, 1917. Wilson announced that the United States was breaking diplomatic relations with Germany,

out of war." His program of domestic reforms also helped.

The Republicans nominated Supreme Court Justice Charles Evans Hughes, declared by Theodore Roosevelt to be a model of "clean-cut, straight-out Americanism." Hughes seemed unable to decide whether he should condemn Wilson for being too warlike or too passive in the face of German provocations. The election was extremely close. Hughes went to bed on election night convinced that he had been elected president. However, he lost California by a minuscule 4,000 votes, leading to a mere 23-vote victory for Wilson in the electoral college (277 to 254).

After his victory, Wilson continued his efforts to mediate the conflict. He called for a just peace, "a peace without victory," which would be maintained by a League of Nations. Most Americans were enthusiastic about his proposals, but, despite war-weariness, the belligerents ignored his suggestions.

The End of Neutrality

As 1917 arrived, the Germans planted two time bombs that would explode America out of its neutrality into full-scale conflict: submarine warfare and the Zimmermann telegram. The German military leaders were winning their argument that the U-boat, their best weapon, should be used to its fullest extent. They contended that, even if America declared war, they could defeat the British by cutting off supplies before American troops could reach the front. The German Foreign Secretary, Arthur Zimmermann, even held out hope that "America will do nothing because Wilson is for peace and nothing else." Bolstered by this advice, the Kaiser sent a secret message to his navy declaring: "I order that unrestricted submarine warfare be launched with the greatest vigor on February 1." On February 3 Wilson broke off diplomatic relations with Germany, as he had promised.

In late February, the British gave the American ambassador a message they had intercepted and deciphered. It had been sent by Zimmermann to the German ambassador to Mexico through U. S. State Department cables. The cable proposed a German alliance with Mexico should the United States enter the war. In return, Germany would agree to "an understanding on our part that Mexico is to reconquer the lost territory in Texas, New Mexico, and Arizona." In view of the revolutions and near anarchy in Mexico at the time, the proposal was absurd. Wilson released the Zimmermann telegram to the press on March 1, creating indignant headlines all over the country. The main result was a reduction of the effectiveness of the small minority in Congress who were filibustering against American preparedness. (Wilson called them a "little group of willful men.")

German policy of victory at any price appeared to be paying off. In February alone, U-boats sank 781,500 tons of Allied shipping. American war fever increased as a result. Teddy Roosevelt roared, "There is no question about going to war. Germany is already at war with us." In preparedness parades throughout the country, banners declared: "Kill the Kaiser" and "Let's Get the Hun."

In the middle of March two American ships, *City of Memphis* and *Illinois*, the latter with two large American flags and "U. S. A." painted on its side, were torpedoed by German submarines. At the same time, the March revolution in Russia toppled the Tsar and replaced him for a time with a more representative government. Now, it was easier to paint the conflict as one of democracy against tyranny. Wilson sent for Congress to meet in special session.

At 8:30 on the evening of April 2, 1917, with armed cavalry restraining the tumultuous crowd outside, Wilson appeared before a hushed Congress and packed gallery. He eloquently asked for a declaration of war. After enumerating German provocations, the president proclaimed, "There is one choice we cannot make, we are incapable of making; we will not choose the path of submission." Chief Justice White, a Civil War veteran, broke down in tears at this passage. Wilson continued, with persuasive idealism, to place the purpose of the war on a higher moral plane. If "this great peaceful people" was to be led into "the most terrible and disastrous of all wars," it must be in a fight "for the things we have always carried nearest our hearts." It must be a "People's War, a war for freedom and justice and self-government" for all nations. "The world must be made safe for democracy."

At the conclusion of his address, Wilson received an overwhelming standing ovation. Later, he remarked sadly to his secretary, "Think of what it was they were applauding. My message of today was a message of death for our young men. How strange it seems to applaud that."

Congress quickly voted to declare war, 82 to 6 in the Senate and 373 to 50 in the House. Jeanette Rankin of Montana, the first woman in Congress, cast one of the no votes. "Peace is a woman's job because men have a natural fear of being classed as cowards if they oppose war," she noted. "Mothers must protect their children." (Almost twenty-five years later she cast the only vote against entering

World War II. Fifty years later, at the age of 87 she led a march against U. S. involvement in Vietnam.)

Certainly, the resumption of submarine warfare and the implications of the Zimmerman note converged with economic and cultural factors to push a reluctant president and country into the fray. In a deeper sense, however, a moral mission to reform the world order motivated Wilson and his nation. The president hoped to promote the principles of democracy, the Open Door, and an end to aggression, at any postwar peace conference. As a neutral, he could have only called "through a crack in the door" at such a conference. As a participant, however, he could bring the ideal peace that all Americans desired.

The day after the declaration of war, an exuberant newspaper headline proclaimed, "The Yanks Are Coming." The only question was: would they arrive in time?

AMERICA AT WAR

The country, which found itself at war, was in no way prepared for its monumental task. A nation of more than 70 million people had fewer than 200,000 men in its army, 80,000 of whom were recently called-up National Guardsmen. Privates, few of whom had even attended high school, were paid a paltry $15 a month and were not allowed to marry. Officers were more accustomed to playing cards than to organizing military strategy. The War Department had become the preserve of petty bureaucrats, one of whom had managed to stockpile twelve thousand typewriters in his offices. The General Staff in Washington, limited by American suspicion of militarism, consisted of nineteen officers. They met and decided to send one Army division to France as rapidly as possible as a symbol of American commitment to its allies. They hoped to build up the army to a million men by December 1918.

The natural choice to command the troops was General John Pershing, who had just been recalled from the punitive expedition to Mexico. On his return, Pershing called a press conference to inform reporters of his desire for command: "Each of you must know some way in which you can help me." This frank ambition was typical of the blunt and iron-willed "Black Jack." The loss of his wife and three children in a 1915 fire had further steeled the personality of this son of German immigrants. The organizational task he faced was formidable.

Meanwhile, the German U-boat attacks had succeeded in reducing Britain to a six-week supply of food. When American Rear Admiral William Sims concluded, "Looks as if the Germans are winning the war," his British counterpart replied, "They will unless we stop those losses." Sims convinced the British that the way to counter this menace was to send merchant ships in swarms, guarded by circling destroyers—the **convoy** system. The convoys rapidly cut the rate of loss in half, convincing military planners that the German submarines would not be able to stop the flow of American troops to France.

Many Americans believed that the Allies were winning the war and required limited American assistance. In fact, the Allies were on the verge of collapse. The years of terrible trench warfare across France had taken its toll. Soldiers lived amidst mud, rats, and disease in "stinking trenches." When they ventured out into "no man's land" to charge the enemy trenches, they would be mowed down by newly sophisticated machine guns and artillery or poisoned by chlorine gas (first used by the Germans in 1915). In the particularly terrible 1916 Battle of the Somme, in which very little was gained or lost, the two sides suffered more than a million casualties. Mutiny was spreading through the French army. When French Field Marshal Joffre arrived in Washington shortly after America's war declaration, American officials asked him what the Allies most needed. It is hardly surprising that he replied, "We want men, men, men."

The American Army

Controversy arose over how to raise an army. Theodore Roosevelt and many in Congress preferred volunteers. Wilson insisted on **conscription**—compulsory service for every able-bodied man between 21 and 31 (later enlarged to 18 to 45). Despite one congressman's argument that, "There is precious little difference between a conscript and a convict," Congress passed the Selective Service Act in May 1917.

On June 5, more than 9.5 million young men lined up to register. Despite fears of Civil War type anti-draft riots, particularly in cities with large German-American populations, the occasion went well in a holiday atmosphere. It would be a while before registrants could be called up. First, barracks had to be built and factories had to gear up for war production. Construction of the camps themselves created major difficulties. Each camp had 120 barracks and numerous other buildings for administration, dining, toilets, etc., all of which also required water, electricity, and paved roads. A mini-army of 50,000 carpenters and 150,000 other workers largely completed the job in an amazing three months.

A symbolic division of the regular army had been rushed to France by July 1917. They arrived in time to take part in July 4th celebrations in Paris. A battalion parading through the streets of Paris was welcomed tumultuously by the French people to whom they represented the promise of an end to the war. The ecstatic crowds shouted, "Vive less Teddies!" A brief ceremony was held at Lafayette's Tomb. There, an aide of Pershing's pronounced the slogan that would capture French and American imaginations and later be attributed to Pershing: "Lafayette, we are here!" It was clear that the French army, physically and morally wounded, would require a summer of rest. There would be no great offensive for the rest of the year, giving Pershing time to build up American forces for 1918.

The American "Doughboys"

The Allies called the American troops "doughboys," because they seemed so fresh and clean. By the end of the war 24 million men registered for the draft. Of these, 2.8 million were actually called up, all from the first category—able-bodied single men without dependents. Another two million serving in the armed forces were volunteers.

Despite the superpatriotism fostered by the war, three million men succeeded in evading registration. Although a few were arrested and others fled the country, most remained in place and were never discovered. Some 300,000 who had registered and been called up never arrived for induction. Most of these "deserters" and "evaders" were working class men with limited education. Only a few thousand draftees were given conscientious objector status when they refused to serve because of religion or conscience. Military men, who regarded them as "enemies of the Republic," harassed many of them. One Mennonite who refused to take a rifle was kicked down the street with a gun tied to his shoulder. Another was court-martialed for refusing to plant flowers as a noncombatant. He was sentenced to ten years of hard labor.

Most of the two million men who served in France set forth with confidence and a sense of adventure. The only sulking was by well-known men prevented from participating. The most notable of these was Teddy Roosevelt who had enthusiastically raised several divisions of volunteers. Wilson denied him any opportunity to get in on the action, but Pershing assured him that all of his sons would be allowed to serve.

The images of the Civil War were still vivid to many older men of this era. Like Wilson, they summoned up "the old spirit of chivalric gallantry." Theodore Roosevelt, with his usual gusto, preached the notion of war as a vehicle for the revival of moral idealism. Most Americans had heard about the Rough Rider charging up San Juan Hill, flourishing his hat—it was their image of war as a romantic escapade.

Well before America's entrance into the war, young men from the social elite and leading universities had joined volunteer units with the Allies, such as the Lafayette Escadrille air unit and various ambulance services. One such volunteer was the poet, Alan Seeger, killed in 1916. The sound of the artillery was to him, "the magnificent orchestra of war." The poems of the man eulogized by Roosevelt as the "gallant, gifted young Seeger," were enormously popular. (Many years later, the young John Kennedy called Seeger's "I Have a Rendezvous With Death" his favorite poem.) Another 1917 best seller, "Over the Top," told of the real-life adventures of a New Jersey boy with the British army in France. War, in this account, was a thrilling sport. These books, poems, and preachings served to counter the stories about war's atrocities and nurture expectations of what Roosevelt had termed the "Great Adventure." Years later, one participant remembered with astonishment, "the eagerness of the men to get to France and above all to reach the front."

The typical draftee was a young (21 to 23 years old) single white male with minimal education. Almost one fifth, however, were foreign born. Young men with little experience outside their farms, small towns, or urban neighborhoods were thrown together in, "the army, the army, the democratic army," in the words of one popular marching song. It went on to declare:

> The Jews, the Wops, and the
> Dutch and Irish cops,
> They're all in the army now!

Women and African Americans in the Military

Although women were kept out of active military service, a precedent-shattering decision by the secretary of the navy permitted eleven thousand to serve in the navy and several hundred in the marines in various support services. Other women saw duty as telephone operators in the Army Signal Corps and as nurses. For the first time, women received basic training, but, to preserve their femininity, they went through all their exercises wearing long skirts.

Many black leaders, such as W. E. B. DuBois, hoped that a war fought to make the world safe for democracy would lead to an amelioration of prejudice at home. He urged young black men to volunteer for service since, "If this is our country then this is our war." Some political leaders opposed drafting any African Americans, agreeing with one racist senator that "arrogant, strutting representatives of black soldiery in every community" would cause race riots. Despite this view, almost 400,000 African Americans were drafted or volunteered for service. Almost half of those went to France, but only fifty thousand saw combat duty, mostly with the French Army, which could not understand American unwillingness to use able-bodied blacks in combat.

A marine recruitment poster in New York City with uniformed young women called "Marinettes."

Racism was as prevalent in the military as it was in the larger American society. The marines excluded blacks, and the navy used them only as "mess boys." The regular army immediately forced its highest ranking black into retirement for supposed ill health, despite his trip on horseback from Ohio to Washington D. C. to demonstrate fitness. As in the Civil War, white commanding officers led black regiments. After agitation by the NAACP and black leaders, a separate training camp for black officers was grudgingly opened. Eventually, seven hundred candidates were commissioned captains and lieutenants, despite one commander's warning that they "need not expect democratic treatment."

Black soldiers in training camps were often subjected to insults, harassment, and even beatings. In August 1917 desperate African-American troops in Houston retaliated by seizing weapons and killing seventeen local whites. After a very speedy trial, thirteen were quickly executed without being allowed to appeal. Forty-one were sentenced to life imprisonment.

Even in France white Americans tried to spread prejudices, warning the French, particularly the women, to avoid contact with black troops. One section of the American High Command persuaded the French Military Mission to inform its troops, "The kindly spirit which exists in France for the Negro profoundly wounds Americans who consider it an infringement of their national dogmas." Although the document went on to declare, "The merits of Negro soldiers should not be too warmly praised, especially in the presence of Americans," hundreds of individual soldiers and the entire 369th regiment were awarded the Croix de Guerre for their bravery under French command. Despite incessant German propaganda urging desertions to counter American racism, not one African-American combat soldier took up the offer.

Social Experimentation in the Army

Reformers agreed that it was crucial to protect innocent young men from the vices they might meet with near the training camps and, particularly, in the wicked old world of France. The army banned the sale of liquor anywhere near the bases, and men in uniform were officially barred from buying drinks. (The latter prohibition proved almost impossible to enforce.)

The army also launched a massive campaign against sexual vice. Many young men were given their first frank sex education. The military distributed Margaret Sanger's article on venereal disease, "What Every Girl Should Know," (which had twice been banned as obscene) as what every soldier should know. Another pamphlet reassured men that wet dreams were normal, and masturbation would not cause insanity, despite grandma's warnings. The implication was clear that both were preferable to dangerous sexual encounters since, "a man who is thinking below the belt is not efficient." Camps were plastered with posters declaring, "A German Bullet is Cleaner than a Whore." Another pamphlet asked, "How could you look the flag in the face if you were dirty with gonorrhea?"

This sexual purity campaign was somewhat hampered overseas by what General Pershing diplomatically described as "the difference between the French attitude and our own." French Premier Georges Clemenceau offered to provide Americans with the same type of licensed, inspected houses of prostitution available to French troops. A horrified Secretary of War Baker supposedly responded to the communiqué, "For God's sake...don't show this to the president or he'll stop the war." The army preferred to punish sternly soldiers with venereal disease. Although about 15 percent of American soldiers did contract VD, the army believed its campaign greatly reduced the rate of infection. Certainly the widespread distribution of condoms aided in the post-war birth control campaign, and the frank discussions of sexual matters helped change American mores.

The army was far less eager to cooperate with the "mental meddlers," psychologists who sought to administer intelligence tests, a novel procedure at the time. The American Psychological Association hoped to establish the legitimacy of its field through testing and classifying inductees. By early 1918, the army grudgingly permitted the testing. The testers expressed surprise that a quarter of the draftees could be classified as illiterate. Psychologists claimed that the examinations measured intelligence rather than education, but the test authors clearly demonstrated class and cultural bias. It is obvious that the native intelligence of poor rural blacks or recent immigrants could hardly be measured by such questions as who wrote "The Raven," or what was the best definition of "mauve." Not surprisingly, men from "native" or "old" immigrant backgrounds were more likely to score in the "superior" range, while half of "new" immigrants and 80 percent of blacks were labeled "inferior."

These results served to reinforce existing prejudices. While pundits deplored the supposed rising tide of imbecility sweeping the nation, the army made little use of the resulting data and ended the testing program in January 1919. In spite of this, psychologists vigorously announced that their tests "helped to win the war." The nation's educational system and many American businesses eagerly appropriated what the army had rejected. This widespread acceptance of the validity and importance of intelligence testing was a significant legacy of the war.

THE WAR FRONT

As the American army geared up and trained, Allied prospects seemed increasingly bleak. A major British offensive in November 1917 had been blocked in Belgium after gaining four miles at a cost of 100,000 casualties per mile. At the same time, in a second revolution in less than a year, the Bolsheviks, led by Lenin and Trotsky, seized power in Russia. They lost little time in signing a treaty with Germany pulling Russia out of the war. This freed thousands of German troops who had been fighting on the Eastern front to join the conflict in the West. The war was rapidly becoming a race between American mobilization and the newly invigorated German military juggernaut.

VLADIMIR LLYICH ULYANOV—LENIN

The desperate Allied commanders hoped to integrate American units into the existing armies. General Pershing, however, backed by Washington, insisted that the Allied Expeditionary Force (AEF) be "distinct and separate" under his command. Pershing deplored the reliance on deadly trench warfare, favoring a more aggressive strategy.

War in the Air

The greatest spectator sport for the soldiers of the AEF in their muddy battlefields was the "Big Show" in the air. The aviators were the chivalric knights, the romantic heroes of the war with their aerial "duels." Egged on by enthusiastic newspapers and a "thoroughly fascinated" Secretary of War Baker, Congress appropriated an unheard-of $639 million to launch a massive program to construct planes. They believed it would be a major factor in the winning of the war.

In fact, however, only thirty-seven planes were built in America. The infant Air Service was almost completely dependent upon the French for its planes. The war in the air was more of a dramatic sideshow than a main event. Nevertheless, spectacular victories and punishing losses captured the public imagination. The most publicized was that of Theodore Roosevelt's son, Quentin, who three days after outmaneuvering three German planes, was shot down and "buried by German aviators with military honors."

When the war was over, the legendary commander of the Air Service, General Billy Mitchell, was able to exult that Americans had downed 927 German airplanes and balloons while losing only 316. He concluded, "We Americans had developed the best system of air fighting that the world had ever seen." Although the significance of air power had not yet been convincingly demonstrated, Mitchell became its most vocal advocate for the future.

The AEF in France

"All hell broke loose" at the end of March 1918. German troops now outnumbered the Allies. This might be their last chance, through a major offensive, to win the war. The Allies had to hold on until

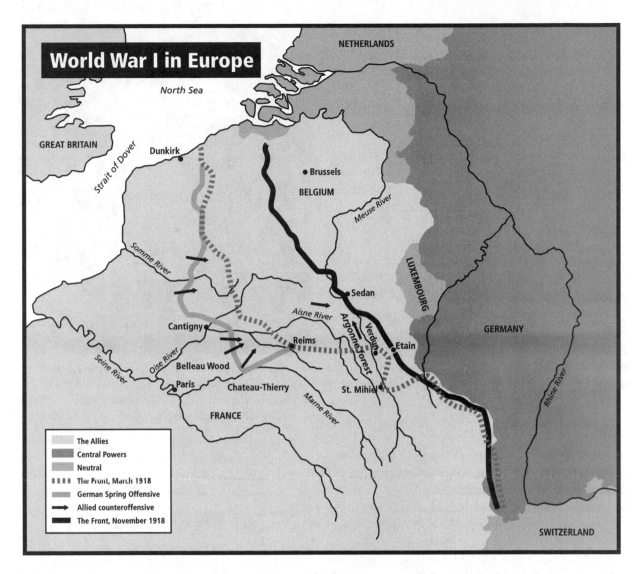

World War I in Europe

NETHERLANDS

North Sea

GREAT BRITAIN

Strait of Dover

Dunkirk

• Brussels

BELGIUM

Meuse River

Somme River

LUXEMBOURG

Sedan

GERMANY

Aisne River

Argonne Forest

Verdun

Cantigny

Reims

Etain

Oise River

Seine River

Belleau Wood

St. Mihiel

Paris

Chateau-Thierry

Marne River

FRANCE

Rhine River

SWITZERLAND

The Allies
Central Powers
Neutral
The Front, March 1918
German Spring Offensive
Allied counteroffensive
The Front, November 1918

the American troops could arrive in any substantial numbers. The Germans launched an enormous offensive in the area of the Somme River, smashing through the Allied lines. They had succeeded in winning more ground than either side had gained since the beginning of trench warfare. The mounting peril frightened the Allies into creating a unified command under French Marshal Ferdinand Foch. It also led to an enormous increase in the number of American troops arriving in France. When the German push began, there were fewer than 300,000 soldiers in the AEF. By July 1, Pershing had a million men under his command.

By the end of May, the Germans had broken through to the Marne and were an alarming 50 miles from Paris. At the same time, Americans were ready to launch their first small offensive operation at Cantigny. The American success in capturing the village (Major Theodore Roosevelt Jr. had repulsed a German counterattack.) provided a boost to the sagging Allied morale.

In June, American troops were suddenly rushed into a bloody conflict to help stem a spectacular German breakthrough in the area of the Marne. As they marched to the front, they encountered French soldiers being sent back, "broken in health and wounded," one marine recalled. "Not soldiers like our men, young and healthy, but old veterans of the war...They were broken in everything but spirit." At Chateau-Thierry and nearby Belleau Wood Americans drove back the enemy assaults. The price, in American lives, was not as high as it had been for the Allies in the earlier terrible battles of the war, but 67,000 of the 310,000 Americans who had fought in the Aisne-Marne region were either dead or wounded.

In July, the German army launched its last great drive on Paris. By July 28, one soldier was able to write to his parents, "Folks we have them on the run." The arrival of hundreds of thousands of fresh American troops caused the Allies to regain numerical superiority. (By the end of the war they had 600,000 more men under arms than the Germans.) By midsummer the great German offensive had been broken, and the Allies permanently seized the military advantage. As the summer turned to fall, American troops increasingly participated in vanquishing the Germans. The U. S. Army was assigned an expanding front of its own.

Material aid from American farms and factories was also tremendously important to the ultimate Allied triumph. By the end of the war black troops, working as stevedores, (often in 24-hour shifts) were unloading 20,000 tons of supplies per day. These included over five million gas masks, 9.5 million overcoats, and 22 million blankets, all manufactured and delivered within eighteen months!

As the Allied offensive gained momentum in the Meuse-Argonne campaign, the fighting was brutal and bloody. This last great battle took place in an area filled with trenches of past engagements, the smell of poison gas, rats feasting on corpses, a steady cold rain, and mud enveloping everything. More than 26,000 Americans died before the Argonne Forest was secured in October, though fighting continued in the larger sector. By early November 1918, German railway lines had been cut by the AEF.

Despite the stark realities of modern warfare encountered by the doughboys, their letters and diaries remained enthusiastic about the "Great Adventure." They continued to speak of "feats of valor" and of the "crusade" they were pursuing. They still believed that their cause was a righteous one against the Germans "who murdered the poor women and children on their advance through Belgium." The

Weak eyesight prevented Harry S Truman from enrolling at West Point. Truman served in the Missouri National Guard and commanded an artillery battalion in France during the First World War.

most publicized of the "crusaders" was Corporal (later Sergeant) York. He wiped out a nest of German machine gunners with his rifle, forcing the rest of the platoon to surrender. Then he rounded up the survivors with his .45 Colt and marched 132 prisoners back to the American lines. He was awarded the Congressional Medal of Honor. Later, his heroism became the theme of a popular motion picture starring Gary Cooper.

Their time in the army was unforgettable to most of the surviving soldiers. Few had been subjected to lengthy defensive warfare. Their two chief battles were mobile engagements at the end of the war. They had been awed by the splendor of an Old World few had ever experienced before. "How 'Ya Gonna Keep 'Em Down on the Farm After They've Seen Paree?" asked a popular song. Many formed lifelong friendships that were bolstered by joining the American Legion. One young lieutenant, Harry S Truman of Missouri, continued his relationship with his old wartime "buddies" when he became president of the United States.

THE HOME FRONT

Many progressives viewed the war as a wonderful opportunity to expand and centralize government operations to realize their dreams of greater efficiency in the public interest. They believed the war would bring national unity, patriotism, and real sacrifice for the greater good. They predicted the development of a "true national collectivism" that would revive moral purpose and reform the ills of society. Wilson had admonished the nation, "We must speak, act, and serve together." Efficiency became the central progressive motto, with its image of a productive war machine operating without political interference.

Organizing the Economy

The initial wartime achievements of the American economy failed to meet the progressive ideals. The government created a multiplicity of boards and commissions to supervise production. A headline in a Washington newspaper, "Ten thousand New Clerical Workers Expected This Summer," gave some indication of growing government activity. The top policy and planning positions went to leaders of Wall Street and industry who served as "dollar-a-year" men. The American government and big business leaders entered into a close relationship after years of largely unsuccessful efforts by progressive presidents to regulate business. One slogan proclaimed that the solution to production problems was, "Business as Before—Only More."

Early problems led to increased government intervention. General Pershing, anxiously awaiting the arrival of vital supplies in France, discovered he had been sent lawnmowers and obstetrical instruments. In the bitterly cold winter of 1917-18, shortages of food and coal and the inadequacy of the railroads led to civilian deaths and the closing of some war plants. War production schedules were lagging, particularly in the vital steel industry. President Wilson stepped in to nationalize the country's railroads during the war. He also appointed Bernard Baruch, "the wizard of Wall Street," to head the War Industries Board (WIB).

FOOD WILL WIN THE WAR
You came here seeking Freedom
You must now help to preserve it
WHEAT is needed for the allies
Waste nothing

Baruch hoped to increase production and reduce waste. He believed that this could be best accomplished by guaranteeing substantial profits. Baruch argued, "You could be forgiven if you paid too much for the stuff, but you could never be forgiven if you did not get it and lost the war." "Cost-plus" contracts ensured substantial profits. The government suspended anti-trust laws to encourage industrial cooperation. Corporate mergers caused big business to grow even bigger, while business profits tripled. One steel executive admitted, "We are all making more money out of this war than the average human being ought to."

The WIB had the power to allocate supplies and standardize goods to save scarce products. Halting of the production of metal stays in women's corsets was said to have saved enough steel to build two warships. Daylight-savings time was also introduced in 1918 as a wartime conservation measure.

Another self-made millionaire, Herbert Hoover, became head of the Food Administration. Hoover set prices and regulated distribution of food to ensure adequate supplies for the army and the Allies. He also proved to be a master of propaganda, appealing to patriotism with his "gospel of the clean plate." Women "Hooverized" by pledging to observe "meatless" and "wheatless" days. Posters urged them to "Serve Beans by All Means" and "Don't Let Your Horse Be More Patriotic Than You—Eat a dish of Oatmeal." All of this proved to be quite effective in assuring the necessary food supplies for the war effort. At the same time, farm production and income substantially increased. Farmers, like businessmen, experienced the war as an economic bonanza.

One unfortunate result of the high prices set by government agencies was a precipitous jump in inflation. Clothing prices tripled, while food and fuel costs more than doubled. While workers benefited from the full employment created by increased manufacturing, many of their gains were wiped out by the high cost of living.

Wilson created the National War Labor Board (WLB) to settle labor disputes. Samuel Gompers, president of the American Federation of Labor (AFL), ardently supported the war effort and was able to win concessions recognizing the right to organize and endorsing the eight-hour workday. The militant Industrial Workers of the World (IWW) continued to emphasize class warfare and to strike for better wages and working conditions. Businessmen were able to play upon patriotism to demand the suppression of the radical "Wobblies." By contrast, the AFL saw a more than 50 percent growth in membership to four million by the end of the war.

Perhaps the most challenging task of all was that of financing the war. In 1915 the total federal budget had been $1.5 billion. When a Columbia University economics professor suggested that the war might cost $10 billion, Wilson reacted "with a smile of incredibility." By 1918 the federal budget reached $35 billion. Wilson turned to the secretary of the treasury, his son-in-law, William McAdoo, to raise the necessary funds. Reformers finally won their long struggle for a more progressive tax system in which upper-income groups paid a larger share of government costs. Tax revenues, however, amounted to only one-third of the war costs. McAdoo who, according

to a popular verse, was "always up and McAdooing," launched a series of government bond drives called Liberty Loans. Giant rallies, featuring such movie stars as Mary Pickford and Charlie Chaplin, whipped up popular enthusiasm. Schoolchildren bought 25 cent stamps to be pasted in "Liberty Books," which were redeemed for bonds when filled. "Lick a Stamp, and Lick the Kaiser," they were urged. Billboards appealing to adults featured similar slogans. The five drives succeeded in paying for two-thirds of the war expenses. An increase in the national debt from $1 billion to nearly $27 billion was one unintended consequence, however.

Through trial and error, the American economy moved from early chaos to more effective bureaucratic mobilization. The war produced a booming economy and spiraling profits. Approximately 42,000 millionaires had been created. The United States was now the greatest economic power in the world. The war had also brought the government into the economy in ways Americans could hardly have imagined. Although the regulatory agencies were rapidly dismantled at the war's end, the wartime coordination and interrelationship between government and business changed American economic life and helped cause the big business domination of the 1920s.

Propaganda and Hysteria

Wilson believed, "It is not an army we must shape and train for war, it is a nation." To that end, Wilson turned to the new field of public relations to "sell" the war. George Creel, a former newspaperman, became the head of the Committee on Public Information that served as America's first official propaganda agency. At his urging, Hollywood produced popular films reinforcing the notion that the Allies were all shining heroes while the Central Powers were evil incarnates. They had such inflammatory titles as, "The Kaiser: The Beast of Berlin," the "Claws of the Hun," the "Prussian Cur," and "To Hell with the Kaiser." Creel also mobilized an army of 75 thousand "four minute men," speakers who gave some 7.5 million brief patriotic talks to audiences totaling over 300 million.

Songwriters also contributed to the effort. George M. Cohan was awarded the Congressional Medal of Honor for such patriotic tunes as "You're a Grand Old Flag." The favorite, "Over There" promised, "The Yanks are coming...and we won't come back 'till it's over, over there!" Another popular ditty darkly threatened to, "Kill another Dutchman (a slang term for Germans)—hang him from an apple tree." It was difficult to mobilize public opinion without stirring up bigotry and hysteria.

Hatred of anything vaguely related to Germans swept through the country. When German saboteurs blew up an ammunitions depot in New Jersey, paranoia increased. Angry mobs attacked German language newspapers. Schools dropped the German language from their course of studies. Orchestras dismissed German conductors and eliminated German music from their programs. Libraries removed German books and occasionally even burned them. Restaurants renamed frankfurters "hot dogs" and sauerkraut "liberty cabbage." Dachshunds became "liberty pups" and even German measles turned into "liberty measles." A German-born miner in Illinois was wrapped in a flag and lynched. A member of the jury that acquitted the mob leaders announced,

Eugene V. Debs served time in an Atlanta penitentiary for speaking out against the war.

"Nobody can say we aren't loyal now." Even the *Washington Post* saw the lynching, although unfortunate, as part of "a healthful and wholesome awakening in the interior of the country."

Hordes of vigilantes particularly targeted radicals and critics of the war. In Tulsa a mob beat up IWW members and poured tar into their wounds. In Arizona 1200 IWW miners were rounded up and stranded without any food or water in the New Mexico desert. A pacifist minister in Cincinnati was stripped and beaten. Columbia University fired an eminent professor for his anti-war opinions. A colleague, the distinguished historian Charles Beard, who favored the war, resigned. "If we have to suppress everything we don't like to hear," Beard protested, "this country is resting on a pretty wobbly basis."

Dissenters and the Suppression of Civil Liberties

Despite President Wilson's warning: "Woe be to the man that seeks to stand in our way in this day of high resolution," some courageous (or foolhardy) dissenters continued to criticize the war. These included pacifists like Jane Addams and Socialists like Eugene Debs. Debs argued that the war had been declared by the "master class" for its own gain, "while the subject class has nothing to gain and all to lose—especially their lives." The Socialists succeeded in gaining as much as 40 percent of the votes in some cities and in electing a congressman, Victor Berger of Wisconsin. One liberal journalist, Randolph Bourne, chastised reformist intellectuals who had welcomed the war as a test for their progressive ideals. "If the war is too strong for you to prevent," he argued, "how is it going to be weak enough for you to control and mold to your liberal purposes?"

Bourne proved to be prophetic as the nation moved to suppress any instances of dissent, ignoring constitutional guarantees of civil liberties. Theodore Roosevelt characterized Senator Robert La Follette, an opponent of the war, as "an unhung traitor." The House voted 309 to 1 not to allow Congressman Berger to take his seat in view of his anti-war opinions.

Federal laws and actions made repression official policy. Congress overwhelmingly passed the Espionage Act (1917) and the Sedition Act (1918). These prescribed prison sentences for anti-war activities or "statements" containing "disloyal, profane, scurrilous or abusive language" about the government, the flag, or the military.

The language of this legislation was vague enough to allow the government to prosecute more than two thousand people. Eugene Debs was sentenced to ten years in prison for his speech cited above. Even after the war had ended, a self-righteous Wilson denied him a pardon declaring, "While the flower of American youth was pouring out its blood to vindicate the cause of civilization, Debs stood behind the lines sniping, attacking and denouncing them." (A new administration of Warren G. Harding in 1921 finally pardoned him.) One woman was prosecuted for announcing to an audience, "I am for the people, and the government is for the profiteers." The government sent the army to IWW strongholds in the West to crush strikes. Most of the union's leaders ended up in jail.

The postmaster general had the power to bar questionable material from the mail. He used it to suppress socialist periodicals and even moderately leftist journals that expressed some doubts about the war. He banned one magazine when it suggested that more revenue could be raised by taxes. A judge sentenced the producer of a film about the American Revolution to ten years for questioning "the good faith of our ally, Great Britain."

Few people had the courage to object to these violations of basic rights. Senator Hiram Johnson of California complained that the result was "You shall not criticize anything or anybody in the government any longer or you shall go to jail." Protesters formed the Civil Liberties Bureau, which later became the American Civil Liberties Union. The Bureau, however, found it difficult to raise money or publicize its cause. Its leader, Roger Baldwin, was himself jailed as a conscientious objector.

The Supreme Court unanimously upheld the Espionage Act. In a famous decision in *Schenck v. United States* (1919), Justice Oliver Wendell Holmes noted that, "Free speech would not protect a man falsely shouting fire in a theater." Free speech could be restricted when it posed "a clear and present danger" to the country. Later, Holmes regretted his decision and worried about the jeopardy to the "free trade in ideas," posed by government actions. The bleak civil liberties record of the Wilson administration during the war led to a climate of suspicion and conformity. Its consequences continued long after the war was over.

Social Reform and Social Change During the War

The war did advance progressive hopes for social reform. It gave the final push to the prohibition movement. The "drys" had achieved success in many states, but Congress did not pass the Eighteenth Amendment, barring "the manufacture, sale, or transportation of intoxicating liquors," until December 1917. (It was ratified in 1919.) Prohibitionists had argued that the use of vital grain supplies to manufacture alcoholic beverages was unpatriotic. They also exploited anti-German feelings by stressing the German names on the major breweries (Pabst, Schlitz, and Anheuser-Busch). They implied that beer was part of a sinister German conspiracy to destroy America's capacity to fight.

The anti-prostitution movement also benefited. Not only were brothels near bases closed, but Congress appropriated funds to combat prostitution on the home front. The government closed down red-light districts. Among these was Storyville in New Orleans. Jazz musicians who performed in that famed district moved up the Mississippi to other cities: Memphis, St. Louis, Kansas City, and Chicago. Thus, one unintended consequence was the spread of jazz music to the North.

Leaders of the women's movement believed that the war would also lead to greater equality. Certainly it did add, as one historian has pointed out, "a few strings to the suffrage bow." Activist middle class clubwomen had enthusiastically rushed into such volunteer war efforts as selling bonds, saving food, and organizing benefits. Radicals, led by Alice Paul of the National Woman's Party, refused to support the war effort. Paul garnered national publicity by

The Nineteenth Amendment, granting women the right to vote, was ratified in 1920.

women. Such patriotic slogans as "A Woman's Place is in the War" led a million women to find employment in war-related industries. Most of these shifted from low-paying jobs to somewhat better ones. As white women workers moved up, black women took their places in some cases. Department stores began to hire black women (at least those with lighter skins) as elevator operators and waitresses.

When the war ended, women lost their jobs to returning veterans. The war did not alter the basic attitude that the proper place for women was the home. Streetcar workers in Cleveland struck to force women conductors out. Even women judges in New York were told that they had been hired only as a temporary wartime measure and were forced to resign. "During the war they called us heroines," one woman worker complained, "but they throw us on the scrapheap now." By 1920 the number of women in the workforce was less than it had been in 1910.

Blacks also hoped that the war would better their conditions. Job opportunities, created by war mobilization, did lure Southern blacks to Northern cities. During the war a half-million African Americans found their way north to the "Land of Hope," the beginning of the "Great Migration." Most were able to get only the most menial jobs abandoned by recent immigrants. But salaries of at least three dollars a day in areas of less blatant racism seemed wonderful to those escaping from sharecropping, debt peonage, and Jim Crow. Southern whites, fearing the loss of their cheap labor force, tried forcibly to stop the migration. Like their ancestors fleeing slavery, some blacks had to devise ways to "steal away" from the rural South.

Many Northern whites resented the "Negro invasion." Race riots broke out in twenty-six cities in 1917. Some blacks, who had expected a better life in the North, fought back. The worst incident occurred in East St. Louis, Illinois where ten thousand African Americans had recently arrived from the South. A white mob, opposed to black employment in defense plants, burned down black homes and shot at the fleeing residents. Nine whites and forty blacks died. These included a two-year old who was thrown into a burning house after being shot. Lynchings continued in the South. Almost four hundred blacks

her round-the-clock picketing of the White House with signs condemning the undemocratic denial of the vote by "Kaiser Wilson." The plight of jailed pickets who went on hunger strikes aroused sympathy. They also succeeded in making the more conservative mainstream suffragists of the National American Woman Suffrage Association (NAWSA) seem more reasonable.

Carrie Chapman Catt, NAWSA's president and a former pacifist, argued that the woman suffrage amendment was a "war measure." It was necessary at a time that female war work was essential and was a reward for patriotic support of the war. Wilson, a convert to woman suffrage since 1916, told the Senate that the amendment was "vital to the winning of the war." The Nineteenth Amendment, granting women the right to vote, passed the Senate in 1919 and was ratified in 1920.

Apart from the vote, however, the war did not lead to any permanent improvement in the status of

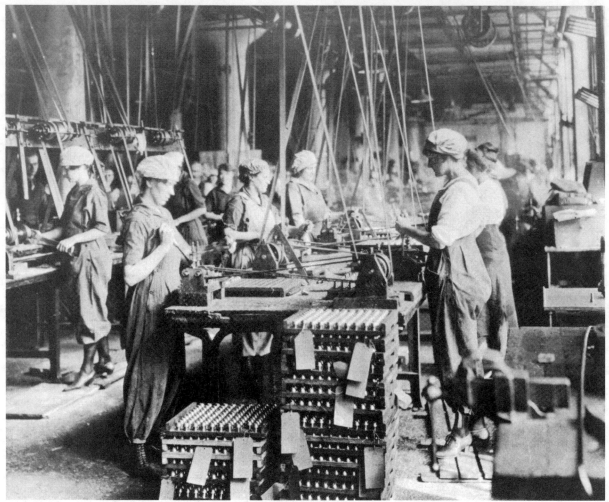

A million women found employment in war-related industries, but when the war ended, women lost their jobs to returning veterans.

were lynched between 1914 and 1920, some still in military uniform.

The NAACP organized a march down Fifth Avenue in New York shortly after the East St. Louis riot. Banners asked, "Mother, Do Lynchers Go to Heaven?" and "Mr. President, Why Not Make AMERICA Safe for Democracy?" Both the black migration to Northern cities and the resulting racial tensions continued to grow after the war ended.

The most serious emergency on the home front ignored race and gender lines. A virulent strain of influenza swept through the world in 1918-19. The flu first raged through the United States in the spring of 1918. Arriving AEF troops spread it to Europe. As many as 40 million people may have died through-

out the world from this killer disease. In the United States, some 700,000 perished, far exceeding war casualties and overshadowing any problems on the home front.

THE END OF THE WAR AND THE SEARCH FOR PEACE

Although American military successes had been relatively minimal, the demonstrated capacity of the United States to move its men overseas forced the Germans to face the prospect of an unending supply of American troops and equipment. The German war machine had collapsed. Mutiny had spread among its armed forces and starving urban dwellers. Turkey and Austria-Hungary, its allies, had sued for peace. Wilson declared that he would negotiate only with a "democratic" Germany. The unhappy Kaiser was forced to abdicate and flee to neutral Holland where he took up gardening. The new government quickly agreed to Allied terms. Firing did not cease immediately. More soldiers on both sides needlessly died in the few days left to reach the symbolism of ending the Great War at 11:00 A.M. of the 11th day of the 11th month. On November 11, 1918, precisely at 11:00 A.M., American air ace Eddie Rickenbacker flew over the war zone and watched the great guns silenced. Men broke into tears and laughter and wild cheering. Enemies cautiously approached each other and began exchanging food and souvenirs. At an American officers candidate school in France, the delirious soldiers bombed one another with live grenades. The resulting dozen flesh wounds merely added to the general merriment.

It was 6:00 A.M. in New York and Washington, and there were no radios yet to disperse the news. By word of mouth and newspapers, the story slowly spread. Cheering multitudes poured into the streets. Bands reprised, "Over there," "The Yanks Are Coming," and "Pack Up Your Troubles." Banners proclaimed, "Long Live Peace." Wilson's hopeful armistice message declared, "Everything for which America has fought has been accomplished."

There were not enough ships to return rapidly the vast AEF to America, division by division. After long waits, however, all the soldiers came home on crowded troop transports. One soldier who finally glimpsed the Statue of Liberty as his ship entered New York harbor is said to have announced: "Old girl, if you ever want to look me in the face again, you'll have to turn around on your pedestal."

Many black soldiers in stevedore units at base ports had married French women. The military gave them the unenviable choice of being discharged in France to stay with their wives or returning home by themselves. This surprised them since they had been taught that the war was fought for the brotherhood of mankind. Some remained in France, but most returned to the United States.

America lost almost fifty thousand in battle. Two hundred thousand were wounded. Still, "America had barely bloodied its nose." These numbers paled beside those of the European belligerents who, in the most deadly war ever for combatants, suffered at least 10 million deaths and 20 million wounded. As the war deaths were being estimated, an epidemic of Spanish influenza was sweeping the world, wreaking devastation among both soldiers and civilians. More American soldiers died of influenza than were killed in battle. (In the war years of 1917-18, 6,000 more Americans were killed in automobile accidents than died in the war.) As many as fifty million people may have died in the influenza epidemic worldwide. Nevertheless, an entire generation of young men had been virtually wiped out by the war. Would their sacrifice prove meaningful in the creation of a better world?

The Fourteen Points

The signing of the armistice pleased President Wilson. The combatants were not only ending the slaughter, they had also accepted his Fourteen Points as the basis of the peace negotiations. During the war Wilson had convened a group of scholars and writers, called The Inquiry, to prepare America's peace agenda. Well before America's entry into the war, the Allies had signed agreements to gain territory and indemnities at the expense of the Central Powers. The new Bolshevik government in Russia had threatened to publish the terms of these secret treaties. Wilson hoped to create a new world order in which the world "will turn to America for those moral inspirations which lie at the basis of all freedom...."

In a January 1918 address to Congress, Wilson presented his Fourteen Points, a summary of American war aims designed to ensure a world "made fit to live in." A central idea, based on the progressive belief in public awareness of government actions, was "open covenants, openly arrived at." This implied a rejection of the self-serving secret treaties that were perceived as a cause of World War I. His new, American-led, moral order also included freedom of the seas, freer trade, disarmament, readjustment of colonial claims to reflect the interests of the peoples involved, and "self-determination" for the peoples

Woodrow Wilson left for Paris to personally be involved in the peace process with his fourteen points.

of the former Austro-Hungarian and Ottoman Empires. The new boundaries would be based on the language spoken in each area. (Such "linguistic nationalism" proved difficult to achieve in the intertwining of peoples of Central and Eastern Europe and remains problematic even today.) The fourteenth point was most important of all, in Wilson's view. It called for "a general association of nations" (or League of Nations) to maintain world peace. To the idealistic Wilson, these points were "the moral climax of this final war for human liberty."

The Peace Conference and the Treaty of Versailles

Although Wilson had proven to be an effective political leader in achieving his domestic policy goals and in articulating the aspirations of the American people, he made some serious blunders in his preparations for the peace negotiations. The first was his

"October appeal," asking the voters to vote for Democrats in the 1918 congressional elections to demonstrate their support for him as their "unembarrassed spokesman." Instead, the voters, reacting more to domestic issues such as inflation, gave the Republicans a slight majority in both Houses. He needlessly aroused Republican enmity and revived the spirit of partisanship. Wilson could be portrayed as the loser in a referendum on his peace program.

Wilson further compounded his misjudgment in selecting the American Peace Commission. He decided that he would personally lead the delegation, risking his personal prestige. He neglected to include any Republican leaders in the commission. Moderate Republican internationalists, like former President William Taft or Wilson's 1916 opponent, Charles Evans Hughes, would have added essential bipartisan support to his efforts. Any treaty required the approval of two-thirds of the Senate, but the president refused to name any senator to the delegation or even to consult with the Senate Foreign Relations Committee, headed by Henry Cabot Lodge. He seemed to have lost touch with the realities of domestic politics.

In spite of this, delighted Americans lined the docks on December 4, 1918, to cheer the first president to go to Europe while in office. The war-weary people of Europe also responded enthusiastically to the eloquent prescriptions for peace offered by the American president. He was met with joyful frenzy in a march up the Champs-Elysees in Paris. At the docks in England, children threw flowers in his path. Passionate Italian crowds shouted, "Viva Wilson, king of peace." One ardent adherent even compared his arrival to the Second Coming of Christ.

The other Allied leaders who met in the peace conference at Versailles Palace, near Paris, in January 1919, were less enthusiastic about Wilson and his moralistic ideas. The war had caused their nations far more grievous damage than the United States. Britain's tough Prime Minister, David Lloyd George, had helped his party win victory with the slogan, "Hang the Kaiser." He was committed to British colonial expansion and reparations from Germany. France's "tiger," Georges Clemenceau, whose nation had suffered the most, was resolute in his conviction that Germany must be punished and prevented from ever making war again. The Italians and Japanese pressed for territorial advantage. Wilson's visions of a new world order did not impress the other world leaders. The cynical Clemenceau best expressed their views when he supposedly observed, "God gave us the Ten Commandments and we broke them. Wilson gave us his Fourteen Points—we shall see."

Wilson fought the hardest for the League of Nations, a permanent international organization that would gather to settle disputes without resorting to war. To persuade skeptical European statesmen to place the covenant of the League of Nations into the treaty, Wilson was forced to compromise the idealism of the Fourteen Points. He convinced himself that any faults in the treaty could be corrected later by the League.

The Treaty of Versailles that emerged from the negotiations was reluctantly signed by the Germans on June 28, 1919. It stripped Germany of all its colonies and awarded them to the League of Nations, which, in turn, gave them to various powers to administer as "mandates." The French, who had pushed for a permanently divided Germany, settled for a re-

The Big Four (left to right) British Prime Minister David Lloyd George, Italian Prime Minister Vittorio Orlando, French Prime Minister Georges Clemenceau, and U. S. President Woodrow Wilson.

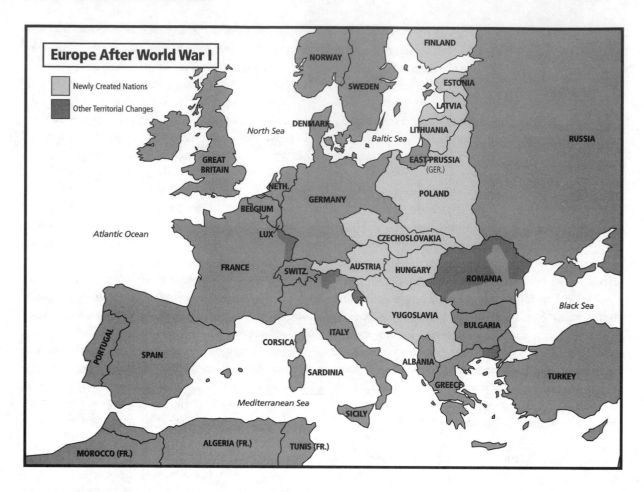

Europe After World War I

Newly Created Nations

Other Territorial Changes

turn of Alsace and Lorraine (which had been taken from them in an 1871 war), control over the coal-rich Saar Basin for fifteen years, and a demilitarized zone in the Rhineland. On the east, the newly recognized Polish state was given a corridor to the sea that cut off the bulk of Germany from its eastern section and created resentment. Wilson's plan for universal disarmament applied to Germany alone, which was limited to an army of 100,000 and forbidden any heavy armaments. Other treaties created a series of new nations in Central and Eastern Europe out of the old empires. These new entities included Czechoslovakia and Yugoslavia.

The Allies, who had been devastated by the war, wanted the Germans to pay huge, unrealistic "reparations" for war damages. The treaty did not set a total for reparations. As a compromise, it was decided that a future commission would determine the sum, which would be substantial. (The Germans ultimately paid less than one-quarter of the amount

that the commission set.) The treaty included a "war guilt" clause to justify the reparations. By this clause Germany "accepted the responsibility" for the damages of the war, caused by "the aggression of Germany." Most Germans saw this as an attack on their honor. It provided an opening for later demagogues.

If the purpose of the Treaty of Versailles was to prevent future wars and end the German menace, it was not successful. In practical terms it was either too harsh or too lenient. Certainly, it was too severe to be considered a "peace without victory." It created resentments in Germany that would help lead to the rise of Hitler. On the other hand, its terms were not nearly as onerous as those the Germans would have imposed on the Allies had they won (as shown by their treaty with Russia). The treaty did not destroy German economic and military strength as the French had hoped. Thus, it succeeded in creating the worst of both worlds—a resentful Germany that could again disrupt the peace of the world.

The unwillingness to come to terms with the new revolutionary regime in Russia was another flaw in the peace process. At the same time that the Allies were meeting at a peace conference to which Russia was not invited, they had launched a military intervention in Russia, which was engaged in a bloody civil war. Allied troops became deeply involved in a campaign to overthrow the infant Bolshevik communist government believed to be dangerous to capitalist democracy. Several thousand American troops, who had hoped to be home for Christmas in 1918, found themselves in Northern Russia where they joined other Allied contingents, including a large Japanese force. American troops remained until the spring of 1920. Despite the intervention, the subsequent economic blockade and the Wilsonian policy of nonrecognition, the Bolshevik regime survived. (The United States did not recognize the Soviet government until 1933.) The main result of this failed policy was that it contributed to the Soviet government's enduring feelings of resentment and suspicion.

The Fight for the League

Exhausted by the months of intense bargaining at the peace table and weakened by a bout of influenza, Wilson focused his attention on the "covenant" that established the League of Nations. The League represented a type of international progressive commission, free from politics and able to settle international conflicts through arbitration. Even though he had been forced to compromise many of his ideals, Wilson wrote to a friend, at least, "We are saving the Covenant, and that instrument will work wonders, bring the blessing of peace, and...it will not be difficult to settle all the disputes that baffle us now."

Wilson believed that the "backbone" of the covenant was Article X. It stated that the members of the League would preserve the "territorial integrity and existing political independence" of all other members. They would, upon the advice of the League's Council, take action against aggression. This principle of collective security, Wilson believed, was central to the creation of a new world order. The president presented the treaty to the Senate exhort-

ing them, "We cannot turn back. We can only go forward, with lifted eyes and freshened spirit to follow the vision."

The war effort had concentrated great power in the executive branch, completing the tendency that had begun in the presidency of Theodore Roosevelt. The new Republican Congress was intent on reasserting congressional influence on foreign, as well as domestic, policy. The Senate Republicans, however, were divided over approval of the Treaty of Versailles and the League. One group consisted of a dozen "irreconcilables," opposed to virtually any international involvement. Henry Cabot Lodge led the "strong reservationists." This group was willing to consider American membership in the League only with major reservations, severely limiting American responsibility to take action against aggressors. Hatred for Wilson, the upstart president, who had replaced him as Washington's preeminent intellectual, also motivated Lodge, a Harvard Ph.D. The "mild reservationists" were a large faction who supported the principle of the League but were concerned about Article X. They wanted to insure that congressional consent be required for any collective security action. This last group, combined with Senate Democrats, could have provided the necessary two-thirds vote to approve the treaty with some sort of League membership.

Lodge followed a crafty strategy of holding interminable hearings giving publicity to every League opponent and loading the treaty with modifying amendments. Although none of these reservations would have crippled the League, Wilson fell into Lodge's trap by refusing to discuss any possible compromise.

Instead, Wilson decided to take his case to the people, ignoring the warnings of his doctors. They were concerned about his deteriorating health. He had a history of arteriosclerosis (hardening of the arteries) and several minor strokes, as early as 1896. Information about his medical problems had been withheld from the American people. Although trembling and complaining of migraine headaches and insomnia, he launched a grueling 8,000 mile tour in September. In 22 days he delivered 40 speeches. The huge crowds responded warmly to his eloquent appeals: "The whole freedom of the world not only, but the whole peace of mind of the world, depends upon the choice of America." Although polls showed that most Americans supported Wilson in his fight for the League, his tour brought him further away from political realities and strategies to secure senatorial consent.

On September 25, the exhausted president collapsed, tearfully admitting, "I just feel as if I am going to pieces." He was rushed back to Washington where, a few days later, he suffered a paralyzing stroke. Had he died then, he would have become a "martyr" for peace, and America might well have joined the League. Instead, he remained an invalid for the rest of his term. His illness seriously impaired his judgment and emotions. He broke with close friends and advisers and did not meet with his cabinet for six months. There was no legal or constitutional way to remove a disabled president. Thomas Marshall, the genial vice president, (best known for his comment, "What this country needs is a good five cent cigar!") was kept from the White House. The president's true condition was concealed from the public.

Wilson's second wife, Edith, carefully shielded her ailing husband from political visitors who might have brought doses of reality. His isolation and physical condition reinforced Wilson's natural inclination to inflexibility. Although international law experts and even many of the Allies felt that the reservations would not cause major damage to the League, Wilson rejected "dishonorable compromise." Secretary of State Lansing sadly characterized the president as "a slave to vanity."

A combination of irreconcilables and loyal pro-League Democrats who followed Wilson's admonitions rejected the treaty with reservations on November 19, 1919. The following March, nearly half of the Democrats broke with the president and voted for the treaty with modified reservations, but twenty-three continued to follow his wishes. The vote was 49-35. Although a majority had voted for League membership in some form, the vote was seven short of the necessary two-thirds. The president, himself, was responsible for the failure of his deepest dreams for a new moral world order.

Postwar Racism and Red Scare

In 1919, as one historian has noted, "Domestic discord...mirrored the collapse of Wilson's moral world." The superpatriotism, engendered by the war, continued in the postwar period as fear and hysteria directed against groups that most Americans believed to be threatening.

Returning black troops paraded under New York City's victory Arch on February 17, 1919, to the cheers of thousands and cries of, "God bless you boys!" The following day an African American was brutally lynched in Georgia. Dreams of better race relations in a world "made safe for democracy" quickly died at the war's end. Southern whites feared that returning black veterans, spoiled by their experiences in France, would no longer be satisfied to stay in their "place." There, Southern politicians argued, blacks had been influenced by Bolshevism. They cited an editorial by W. E. B. Du Bois in *Crisis* that declared, "We return fighting. We make way for democracy. We saved it in France, and by the Great Jehovah, we will save it in America or know the reason why." The Justice Department investigated and reported "radical opposition" by "Negro leaders." These worrisome tendencies were demonstrated by "an ill-governed reaction toward race-rioting" and the "threat of retaliatory measures in connection with lynching." Even worse, according to the government, was "the more openly expressed demand for social equality." Southern whites responded to the new "danger" with a "reign of terror" in which seventy-six blacks were lynched, including ten returning veterans.

In the North the tensions increased as a result of the vying for housing and jobs, worsened by the return of thousands of veterans. In Chicago a banner across one street proclaimed, "They Shall Not Pass," referring to African Americans. Fifty-eight blacks who ignored that warning saw their new homes bombed. In the heat of the "red summer" of 1919 race riots swept through some two dozen American cities. The bloodiest was in Chicago where the large influx of migrating blacks had caused dangerous tension. When a black teenager drifted across an imaginary line dividing the waters of Lake Michigan into black

Tensions increased in the North between whites and African Americans for jobs and housing.

and white areas, indignant whites stoned him, and he drowned. Fighting broke out when white police refused to arrest one of the killers. This quickly escalated into a riot as wild rumors spread through the city that "Negroes were raping white women" or "Negroes were being soaked in gasoline, set afire and made to run like living torches." One anxious white city alderman warned that blacks possessed "enough ammunition for years of guerrilla warfare." It did not matter that none of these stories were true. The violence by white and black mobs raged for thirteen days, leaving thirty-eight dead, over five hundred injured, and more than one thousand families, mostly black, homeless.

Middle and upper class Americans also panicked at the upsurge in labor strikes in 1919. By the end of the year, four million workers, 20 percent of the workforce, had walked out in more than 3600 strikes. These were caused by an accumulation of grievances, particularly crippling inflation and intense job competition as veterans returned. In January, Seattle shipyard workers struck for higher wages and organized a general strike that paralyzed the city. The mayor, who charged the strikers with attempting to "duplicate the anarchy of Russia," got the federal government to send in the marines. Mill owners, denouncing "Red agitators," crushed a September strike by 350,000 steelworkers demanding an eight-hour day. (Their typical workweek averaged 70 hours.) In the same month the Boston police struck, leading to an outbreak of crime until businessmen, aided by Harvard students, restored order. State guardsmen replaced the striking policemen. All of these strikes were crushed now that unions could no longer expect government support. Organized labor suffered serious defeats and decline in membership.

Despite union weakness, the labor unrest led many Americans to fear that revolution was at hand. The Bolsheviks, whose government the U. S. fought to overturn in Russia, had organized the Third International, which called for workers of the world to overthrow their governments. A bomb scare intensified anxieties when some extremist group sent bombs through the mail to prominent businessmen and government officials.

All of these factors plunged the nation into the "Red Scare" of 1919-20 during which civil liberties fell victim to national hysteria. A gang of soldiers and sailors attacked the offices of *The Call*, a socialist newspaper, and beat up the staff. In Centralia, Washington, American Legionnaires stormed an International Workers of the World (IWW) office, losing four attackers in the fight. A mob dragged an IWW agitator from prison and, in retaliation, castrated him before lynching him. The New York State legislature expelled five socialist assemblymen in early 1920.

The ambitious Attorney General A. Mitchell Palmer, who had been a progressive reformer, sought to capitalize on this atmosphere of hysteria to further his presidential aspirations. Palmer warned that the "blaze of revolution" was sweeping the nation, "burning up the foundations of society." He created a special antisubversion division of the Justice Department, headed by the young determined J. Edgar Hoover, later the head of the FBI. Hoover had painstakingly collected thousands of names of alleged communists. Hundreds of alien radicals were arrested at the end of 1919, and 249 were deported to Russia. These included the anarchist "Red Emma" Goldman, a mainstay of the birth control movement. In January 1920 "Palmer Raids" took place in thirty-three cities. More than four thousand suspected radicals were rounded up and their homes and offices ransacked, without search or arrest warrants. In one case thirty-nine people were arrested at a meeting to discuss the formation of a cooperative bakery. In Boston hundreds were crowded into bitter cold Deer Island where two died of pneumonia. Only the courage of Assistant Secretary of Labor Louis Post, who conscientiously insisted on verifying every piece of paperwork, saved most from deportation. Ultimately, the government deported 556.

Palmer's flagrant disregard for civil liberties eventually drew protests. The distinguished former presidential candidate, Charles Evans Hughes, assailed the raids as, "violations of personal rights which savor of the worst practices of tyranny." When Palmer's preposterous predictions of widespread terrorist violence on May Day 1920 failed to materialize, he quickly lost credibility. This destroyed Palmer's presidential hopes. The fears of a "Bolshevik threat" suddenly seemed irrational. Even when a real bomb exploded, killing thirty-eight in New York in September 1920, the public dismissed it as the work of a crazy fanatic. The "Red Scare" had fizzled out. It had, of course, greatly weakened radical and even reform groups. Senator La Follette believed that it had shown the perilous "encroachment of the powerful few upon the rights of the many."

The Election of 1920

Woodrow Wilson declared that the election of 1920 would be a "solemn referendum" on the League. In times of peace, however, American presidential elections rarely turn on issues of foreign policy. The Democrats nominated James M. Cox of Ohio, a rea-

sonably progressive governor, who halfheartedly endorsed the League. They chose assistant secretary of the navy Franklin Roosevelt for vice president, mainly to try to benefit from the politically potent Roosevelt name. Teddy, the Republicans' own Roosevelt, had died in 1919, so they had to look elsewhere for a candidate. The Republicans selected Senator Warren Harding, also of Ohio. Harding had few qualifications to be president apart from his willingness to be easily manipulated and his card-playing prowess. As his running mate, they picked Governor Calvin Coolidge of Massachusetts, whose sole accomplishment appeared to be his role in helping to break the Boston police strike.

While Cox vigorously barnstormed, Harding's managers limited him to a "front porch" campaign, fearful of possible blunders if they allowed him out. "Keep Warren at home," one adviser insisted. "If he goes out on a tour somebody's sure to ask him questions." Harding blurred the controversy over the League, announcing that he favored some sort of "association of nations." For most voters the League was no longer an issue. Instead, voters were drained by years of reform and war and anxious about inflation, unemployment, labor violence, and high taxes. They responded to Harding's vague but reassuring call for a return to "normalcy."

Harding won in one of the greatest landslides in American history, amassing 64 percent of the popular vote (16 to 9 million). Almost a million voters cast protest ballots for Socialist Eugene Debs, still serving time in prison. After the election, Harding announced that America's entrance into the League was "dead." Six years earlier Wilson had declared the progressive era as "the high enterprise of the new day." Its goal would be to "cleanse, reconsider, correct the evil" and bring about a higher moral order. Abruptly and completely, his new day had ended.

CONCLUSION

The war had taken a tremendous toll of human life, particularly in Europe. It failed to live up to the eloquent rhetoric of Woodrow Wilson. The United States became the leading economic power in the world. America, however, declined to accept the responsibilities that its new role implied when it refused to ratify the Treaty of Versailles or join the League of Nations.

Domestically, the legacy of the war was division and strife, fueled by fears of radicals, immigrants, and blacks. The federal government became a central factor in the economy. Wartime policies also contributed to the continued dominance of big business. Although the war furthered such progressive aims as woman's suffrage and prohibition, it, in a deeper sense, undermined the basic humanitarian spirit of progressivism. The America that emerged after the Great War was very different from the optimistic reform-minded nation that had entered the war.

Chronology

1914   Wilson sends U.S. troops to occupy Vera Cruz, Mexico
Archduke Franz Ferdinand assassinated by Serbian nationalist
World War I begins in Europe; Wilson declares American neutrality

1915   U.S. marines occupy Haiti and the Dominican Republic
German submarine sinks British liner, *Lusitania*, killing 1200 (128 Americans)
Jane Addams and others form Women's Peace Party
Wilson begins preparedness program

1916   After sinking the *Sussex*, Germany promises to cease unannounced U-boat attacks
General Pershing leads military expedition into Mexico in pursuit of Pancho Villa
Wilson wins re-election

1917   Germany resumes unrestricted submarine warfare
British inform Wilson of Zimmerman telegram, proposing Mexican alliance with Germany
United State enters war (April 6)
Selective Service Act sets up military draft
Wilson creates War Industries Board and Committee on Public Information
Espionage Act limits rights of freedom of speech, press, and assembly
Bolshevik revolution leads Russia to leave the war

1918   Wilson outlines his Fourteen Points
Armistice ends World War I (November 11)
Worldwide influenza epidemic claims more than 20 million lives

1919   18th Amendment added to the Constitution
Treaty of Versailles signed
Racial violence erupts in Chicago and elsewhere
Wilson launches speaking tour to support Versailles Treaty, but suffers paralyzing stroke.
Versailles treaty rejected by Senate
Wave of labor strikes hits nation

1920   Justice Department launches "Palmer Raids;" "Red Scare" hits nation
Nineteenth Amendment (Women's Suffrage) added to Constitution
Senate again rejects Treaty of Versailles
Warren G. Harding elected president

1924   Woodrow Wilson dies

SUGGESTED READINGS

Arthur E. Barbeau and Florette Henri, *The Unknown Soldiers: Black American Troops in World War I* (1947).

Robert H. Ferrell, *Woodrow Wilson and World War I, 1917-1921* (1983).

Frank Freidel, *Over There* (1964).

Martin Gilbert, *The First World War: A Complete History* (1994).

Maurine W. Greenwald, *Women, War and Work* (1980).

Ellis W. Hawley, *The Great War and the Search for a Modern Order: A History of the American People and Their Institutions* (1992).

David M. Kennedy, *Over Here: The First World War and American Society* (1980).

Arthur S. Link, *Woodrow Wilson: Revolution, War, and Peace* (1979).

Carole Marks, *Farewell—We're Good and Gone: The Great Black Migration* (1989).

Barbara Tuchman, *The Guns of August* (1962).

William Tuttle Jr., *Race Riot: Chicago and the Red Summer of 1919* (1970).

Chapter Eighteen

THE ROARING TWENTIES

In 1926 a young midwestern son of a radical Progressive politician, Charles Lindbergh Jr., was earning a modest living as an air mail pilot on the St. Louis-Chicago route. Commercial aviation was a new and still hazardous occupation in which pilots were often forced to land in emergency fields, lit only by an occasional kerosene lantern (when they could find any field). "Slim," as his friends called him, supplemented his income by stunt flying at county fairs.

One night, while flying his mail route, Lindbergh formulated a plan to try for a long-standing $25,000 prize offered for the first successful non-stop flight from New York to Paris. Several famous and well-financed aviators were vying for the reward. Their plans required elaborate designs of three-engine planes with crews of at least two men. Lindbergh believed that a single-engine plane of lighter aluminum construction with a larger fuel reserve would be better able to cross the ocean successfully. And he proposed to fly the plane by himself! He persuaded some St. Louis businessmen to back him financially and supervised the building of a monoplane to his own specifications. He named it The Spirit of St. Louis. On the morning of May 20, 1927, the little plane took off a rain-soaked runway in Roosevelt Field, New York, ahead of his highly publicized competitors.

Struggling against sleep and dreadful weather, and without a radio that he felt would add too much weight, Lindbergh crossed the lonely ocean in 33 and a half hours. "In flying I tasted the wine of the gods," he said many years later. Lindbergh, who understood the benefits of good publicity, had notified reporters of his take-off. Both sides of the Atlantic featured the news, including photographs of the youthful (25-year-old) daredevil who was bravely defying the elements alone in a single-engine plane. When he landed at Le Bourget airport in Paris, he found 100,000 delirious French people waiting. It was the wildest demonstration since the Great War had ended.

Lindbergh, with unassuming manners and innocent good looks, was a press agent's dream. His references to himself and his plane as "we" also fascinated Americans. (That was the title of the quickie book he completed three weeks after his flight.) The concept of the unity of man and machine was entrancing to a public *mesmerized by the wonders of the new age of transportation. Lindbergh's reception in America eclipsed anything he had experienced in Europe. The normally taciturn President Coolidge effusively praised "this wholesome, earnest, fearless, courageous product of America" whose plane represented "American genius and industry." Before a wildly approving crowd, Coolidge awarded him the Distinguished Flying Cross and a promotion to colonel in the Officers Reserve Corps.*

The greatest show of all was a ticker tape parade down Fifth Avenue in New York City. Four million people lined the streets to cheer and shower the hero with more than 1800 tons of shredded paper. Song writers wrote about "Lucky Lindy" and a new dance, the Lindy Hop, was named for him. He received 3,500,000 letters, including 14,000 gifts and 7,000 job offers. Vaudeville circuits and movie companies offered him huge contracts that he modestly declined.

The nation was truly in the grip of a Lindbergh cult. In an age of cynicism, political scandals, anxiety about morals, racial and religious prejudices, the ascendancy of gangsters, and deep divisions in society, the public longed for a genuine, pure hero. At a time of mass production and growing anonymity, he was a "Lone Eagle" who represented the best of American individualism. As stated by F. Scott Fitzgerald, "In the spring of 1927, something bright and alien flashed across the sky. A young Minnesotan who seemed to have nothing to do with his generation did a heroic thing, and for a moment people set down their glasses in country clubs and speakeasies and thought of their old best dreams."

"Lucky Lindy" did not remain the unscathed hero after the era of the 1920s. When one has the world at his feet at the age of 25, what can one do to top that at age 35 or 45? Perhaps, as a reporter shrewdly remarked at the time, "Too much supermanning can hardly help one." When Lindbergh's first born child was kidnapped and murdered in 1932, the public was appalled. But the ghoulish fascination and overwhelming publicity drove the Lindberghs from America. In Europe Lindbergh became enthralled by the "new order" in Nazi Germany. He returned to America as the poster boy for isolationist and anti-Semitic forces. In the 1920s, however, Lindbergh remained the greatest symbol of the yearning for individual heroism.

DIVISIONS IN AMERICAN LIFE

The American obsession with Lindbergh and his exploits also illustrated the duality of American life in the Twenties. On the one hand, his achievement represented the triumph of American technology in the new field of aviation. On the other, it exemplified the supposed virtues of a simpler, more innocent, small-town America. Many historians portray the Twenties as the beginning of modern America— "the first decade of the twentieth century." The Great War, they argue, provided the final blow to the nineteenth century. Yet, there were still many areas of American life firmly in the grasp of that presumably dead Victorian past. The tensions between the "two Americas"—the one exhilarated at the possibilities of a limitless future, the other longing for "traditional values"—typified the Twenties.

The Scopes Trial

Protestant fundamentalists believed in the divine inspiration and literal truth of every word in the Bible. Their numbers had grown, particularly in small towns and rural America, in reaction to the skepticism and irreverence they felt resulted from America's infatuation with scientific theory. The growth of the big bad cities, with their hordes of Catholic and Jewish immigrants, reminded them of the Biblical Sodom and Gomorrah, destroyed by God for their evil ways. By the early 1920s fundamentalists decided that the increasing acceptance of the theory of evolution (first propounded by Charles Darwin in 1859) symbolized an alarming rejection of Christian ideas and Biblical truth. They worked for the passage of legislation prohibiting the teaching of evolution in several southern states.

One such state was Tennessee. A new law, passed in 1925, made it a crime to "teach any theory that denies the story of the Divine creation of man as taught in the Bible." A 24-year-old science teacher in the drowsy little town of Dayton agreed to test the law by reading a sentence from a biology textbook to his class. He was promptly prosecuted. A team of American Civil Liberties Union (ACLU) lawyers, headed by the noted Chicago criminal defense lawyer, Clarence Darrow, arrived to defend Scopes. William Jennings Bryan, three-time presidential candidate, populist reformer, and defender of the true faith, rushed to the scene as a volunteer prosecutor.

The "Monkey Trial" became a media sensation, attracting throngs of reporters and interested bystanders and live coverage from the new medium of radio. In the resulting carnival atmosphere, banners were strung across the streets declaring: PREPARE TO MEET THY MAKER, WHERE WILL YOU SPEND ETERNITY? and READ YOUR BIBLE DAILY. Below them hot-dog vendors, Bible salesmen, lemonade stands and stores featuring little cotton apes and pins reading "Your Old Man's a Monkey" competed for business with street evangelists.

The judge opened each session with a prayer over the objection of "the greatest infidel of his age," Darrow. He moved the proceeding to the lawn to accommodate the hordes of curious people and mitigate the oppressive heat and humidity. The greatest drama lay in the confrontation between Bryan, the defender of "revealed religion," Darrow, the urban intellectual, and the two Americas they represented. Stymied in his attempt to summon scientific experts to testify, Darrow, in a brilliant stroke, called upon Bryan to take the stand as a "Biblical expert." In answering a series of remorseless questions, Bryan affirmed his beliefs that a big fish had swallowed Jonah and Joshua had made the sun "stand still." He added that when, "The Bible states it; it must be so." Bryan protested that the questions had "no other purpose than ridiculing every Christian who believes in the Bible." Darrow replied, "We have the purpose of preventing bigots and ignoramuses from controlling the education of the United States." While Darrow had easily held Bryan's "fool ideas" up to ridicule and scorn, it took the local jury only a few minutes to find Scopes guilty. (The State Supreme Court later threw out the case.) Scopes subsequently went on to graduate school, became an eminent geologist, and never returned to Tennessee.

Although the prosecution had officially won, a tired and ill Bryan retreated to a friend's house to read the derision heaped upon him by the nation's press. "Do they have a law to keep a man from making a jackass of himself?" Will Rogers mockingly inquired. One reporter more sympathetically wrote, "To see this wonderful man...whose silver voice and majestic mien had stirred millions...humbled and humiliated before the vast crowd which had come to adore him, was sheer tragedy, nothing less." Less than a week after the trial, Bryan died. They buried him at Arlington National Cemetery where his tombstone read, "He kept the faith." The issues raised by the Scopes trial have endured. They have resurfaced in recent years in fundamentalist attacks on "secular humanism" and demands to teach "creationism" in public schools. Bryan was dead, but fundamentalism survived.

New denominations, independent churches, and roving evangelists took up the cause. They had their roots in the long American tradition of revivalism that dated back to the colonial Great Awakening. Billy Sunday, a former professional baseball player who threatened to close down Chicago, was, perhaps, the most successful. Father Divine attracted urban blacks. His large following of "children," with such names as Glorious Illumination and Heavenly Dove, went into ecstatic trances and "holy rolling" on the floor. The Reverend Bob Shuler, "the Lord's avenger," gained fame by surprising the Los Angeles police chief in bed with a woman who had married into an infamous crime family.

Aimee Semple McPherson was the most spectacular of all. In her flowing white satin robes, she

Aimee Semple McPherson blended religious fundamentalism, faith healing, and show-biz glitz.

exuded sexuality and unlimited energy as she spread her message of "joy, joy, joy," highlighted by colored lights and Hollywood productions. Her "International Institute of Foursquare Gospel" prospered to the point of building a large Angelus Temple in Los Angeles to accommodate 5,000 and mounting a successful radio show. Sister Aimee gained her greatest fame in 1926 when she disappeared, only to emerge in the desert with an elaborate tale of kidnapping and heroic escape. The skeptical noted that her shoes were unscuffed and her dress clean. Evidence that the disappearance was a hoax grew with testimony about a fling with a married man. Her reputation was tarnished, but thousands of the faithful hysterically welcomed her survival from her "ordeal." When she died of an overdose of sleeping pills in 1944, her church had six hundred branches. She was the forerunner of a later generation of televangelists.

Prohibition

Protestant crusaders saw the passage of the Eighteenth Amendment, outlawing the manufacture, sale, and importation of alcoholic beverages, as a great victory. On the night of January 15-16, as Prohibition went into effect, there were midnight services in thousands of Protestant churches and joyous victory bells chimed. Billy Sunday confidently predicted, "The slums will soon be only a memory. We will turn our prisons into factories...." Many urban middle class reformers agreed. They believed that liquor helped cause poverty, worker inefficiency, dysfunctional family life, and political corruption.

At first, it seemed as though the reformers' expectations would be realized. Saloons closed; arrests for public drunkenness fell, and alcohol consumption by the lower classes declined. Poorer Americans could not afford illegal liquor. The increasing resistance of urban Americans, however, crippled the crusade.

Enterprising "businessmen," known as bootleggers, quickly stepped into the void. They produced dreadful concoctions of hard liquor such as Jackass Brandy, which caused internal bleeding, and Soda Pop Moon, which contained poisonous alcohol. According to one story, when a suspicious customer

sent a sample of his bootlegger's liquor to a chemist for analysis, the reply began, "Dear Sir, your horse has diabetes." In 1927, the death toll from ingesting these potent brews was 11,700. Adulterated Jamaican ginger extract left 20,000 people in "jake paralysis."

Only the prosperous could afford to drink regularly without jeopardizing their lives. But they greatly increased their alcohol consumption as "rum runners" regularly smuggled good quality liquor from Canada and Europe. "Speakeasies" openly operated in cities throughout America. Neither Congress nor the states provided adequate money to enforce the prohibition law. Reporters noticed Harding's bootlegger delivering cases of liquor to the back door of the White House. Prosecution, despite some colorful agents, was erratic, judges uninterested, and juries unwilling to convict. Journalist H. L. Mencken noted that, "The business of evading Prohibition and making a mock of it has ceased to wear any aspects of crime, and has become a sort of national sport."

As whiskey took on the taste of "forbidden fruit," speakeasies became the "in" places to be seen. There were, supposedly, thirty-two thousand in New York City with a mere two hundred agents assigned to close them down. "Texas" Guinan, who greeted her customers with a cheerful, "Hello suckers," presided over the most famous establishment. She was celebrated for hurling humorous insults at raiding federal agents as the band broke into "The Prisoner's Song." While earlier saloons had barred women customers, speakeasies welcomed them, in a rather odd step forward for women's rights. Alcoholism increased among the affluent for the first time.

The public willingness to evade prohibition provided unforeseen opportunities for organized crime. One observer noted, "Because bootlegging provided such resources in money and organization, an unprecedented consolidation and centralization of organized crime occurred." Big-time criminals expanded, and, like businessmen, rationalized their operations. The age of the gangster as city businessman began. In cities like Chicago, "the only completely corrupt city in America," competing gangs engaged in open combat to control liquor operations. One article estimated that 1,291 people were murdered in mob warfare in the late 1920s, 500 in Chicago alone. Few of these cases were ever solved. The bloodshed rarely endangered ordinary citizens. "It is a war in which the non-combatants are safer than they were in Belgium," remarked one observer.

Al Capone seized control of Chicago's crime network after years of relentless conflict. A lavish funeral and huge crowds of mourners followed each gangland slaying. The climax occurred on St. Valentine's Day, 1929, when Capone's men trapped seven members of a rival mob in a garage and executed them with submachine guns. Capone ruled Cicero, a Chicago suburb, once kicking the mayor down the steps of City Hall for not following orders. At his height, Capone's network of rackets was earning him over $100 million a year. He had become a hero to many, a modern Robin Hood. Organized crime became a means for immigrant inner-city young men to achieve social mobility. Capone argued that he was nothing but an ordinary businessman: "All I do is to supply a public demand. I do it in the best and least harmful way I can." Despite the untiring efforts of a ten-man Justice Department squad ("the Untouchables") to destroy his operations, it was a conviction for income tax evasion that finally brought Capone down. Although he was widely publicized and celebrated, his reign was relatively brief.

The growth of organized crime and the open flouting of the law seemed to many to prove the futility of Prohibition. The "drys," however, felt confirmed in their belief that cities had demonstrated the decline of morals. All that was required, they argued, was more zealous enforcement of the law. The issue continued to divide American politics and public discourse.

The Ku Klux Klan

Throughout the country in the 1920s, people joined organizations promising fellowship and devotion to true Americanism. These included the Rotary, Moose, Elks, Lions, and American Legion. The Ku Klux Klan was the fastest growing of these fraternities, easily surpassing the newly formed American Legion. The Klan's revival (It had been a powerful factor in the Reconstruction era.) began with the showing of D.W. Griffith's spectacular motion picture, *Birth of a Nation*, in 1915. This movie epic, which revolutionized the nature of films, depicted the heroic knights of the Klan saving the South from brutish black tyranny and lust, after the Civil War. The film helped inspire "Colonel" William Simmons to revive the Klan as a "100 percent pure American," white Protestant fraternity. The group did not take off until 1920 when Simmons hired two expert fund raisers from the Southern Publicity Association to recruit members. They hired an army of salesmen (called "kleagles") to sell memberships at ten dollars each, which Simmons, the promoters, and the salesmen would split. Sheets, horse robes, and initiation water bottles were additional costs. What had begun as an elaborate con game rapidly grew to a potent organization with four million or more members.

Its success was partly a result of its ideology, which was "at once anti-Negro, anti-Alien, anti-Red, anti-Darwin, anti-Modern, anti-Liberal, Fundamentalist, vastly Moral, militantly Protestant" in the words of a distinguished historian. It also enabled the Klansman to relieve his personal frustrations by becoming a crusader "for White supremacy, religion, morality, and all that had made up the faith of the Fathers...." The revived Klan was flexible in its use of local hatreds and fears, expanding its anti-black base. In Texas it appealed to anti-Mexican feelings, in California to fear of the Japanese, in the Northeast to anti-Semitism and anti-foreign sentiments, in the South to racism and anti-Catholicism. While Klansmen rationalized that they wanted to bring about a return to a fantasy world of small-town virtues, free of pre-marital sex, marital infidelity, and disrespect for authority, their actions showed their fear and hatred of anyone who was different from them in race, religion, or ethnicity. The Klan, with its parades and burning crosses, added color and excitement to dreary small-town life. It also grew rapidly among newly urbanized people, particularly those less well educated and economically marginal.

A part of the Klan's excitement, especially in the Southwest, was its violence, a heritage of its Reconstruction days. "Night-riders" flogged or tarred and

Members of the Ku Klux Klan terrorized blacks and other minorities.

feathered accused prostitutes, bootleggers, gamblers, adulterers, and lawyers with black clients. In the summer of 1922, in Mer Rouge, Louisiana, the bodies of two outspoken opponents of the Klan were found in a lake, horribly mutilated. Despite the imposition of martial law, witnesses were afraid to testify, and the jury acquitted all eighteen men accused of the ghastly crime. In Kokomo, Indiana, in response to Klan propaganda that the "Pope was finally pulling into town...to take over," a mob stoned the southbound train from Chicago.

Although the Klan even gained a foothold in the industrialized Northeast, more opposition arose there. In 1923 some ten thousand New Jersey Klansmen demonstrated and burned a 62-foot cross not far from Manhattan. But when the Klan tried to organize in Perth Amboy, New Jersey in the same year, local Catholics and Jews joined forces to mob their meeting place and forcibly drive out the "Ku Kluxers." Immigrant Catholic workers in Pennsylvania coal and steel towns attacked Klan demonstrators who came in chartered trains "to give the micks something to think about." Crusading reporters won awards for exposing the activities of the Klan.

Despite this opposition (or perhaps because of it), the political power of the Klan continued to grow.

The governor of Oklahoma, who sought to curb Klan lawlessness by calling out the National Guard, was impeached. The Klan was instrumental in electing governors in states as diverse as Georgia, Ohio, Colorado, Oregon, Maine, and six others, as well as fourteen senators. (At least five of the senators and four of the governors were Klan members.) Up-and-coming young politicians, like Hugo Black of Alabama (later to become a very liberal Supreme Court justice), felt they had to join the Klan to succeed. In 1925, thousands of hooded Klansmen marched twenty abreast down Pennsylvania Avenue to demonstrate their strength to an astonished national capital.

There was no state in which the Klan seemed more secure in its power than Indiana. There, the Klan had elected a governor and boasted more than 400,000 members. David Stephenson, the "Grand Dragon," bragged, "I am the law in Indiana." He had amassed a personal fortune from his Klan activities and expected to be elected to the Senate in 1926. In 1925, however, he and his bodyguards forced a reluctant secretary on a train to Chicago. There he raped and brutally bit her, leading her to poison herself with a lavatory cleanser. She survived long enough, however, to give a complete statement to doctors and police. Stephenson was sentenced to life imprisonment. When the pardon he had confidently expected from his "pal" in the governor's seat failed to develop, he gained his revenge by implicating many of Indiana's political leaders in a web of pervasive corruption. These sensational events and revelations badly tarnished the Klan's pretensions as moral guardians of America. The remaining leaders struggled over the spoils. By 1930, the Klan's membership had fallen to 50,000. The "Imperial Wizard" of the Klan sold its Peachtree Street Palace to the Roman Catholic Church.

Nativism and Immigration Restriction

Klansmen were not the only Americans hostile to foreigners. The growing numbers of foreign-born deeply troubled many old stock Americans. They worried about the "undesirable" Catholics and Jews from southern and eastern Europe who flocked to the already problematic big cities. Two well-known psychologists declared, "The intellectual superiority of our Nordic group over the Alpine, Mediterranean and Negro groups has been demonstrated." Other "experts" agreed with the *New York Times* that our nation was in danger of becoming "mongrelized." Besides their supposed intellectual inferiority, the "new" immigrants were labeled as dangerous Bolsheviks and anarchists and more likely to be crazy or paupers.

Americanization committees tried to enforce cultural conformity. In some cases, feelings reached a fever pitch. In 1920, in West Frankfort, Illinois, mobs formed to drive every foreigner (in this case Italians) out of town. For three days they raged through the streets, burning all Italian homes and stoning and beating their inhabitants.

Eventually, the Americanization movement lost its momentum. Its followers shifted their efforts to immigration restriction. The vast majority of Americans agreed that immigration had to be curbed. The first efforts, literacy tests, succeeded only in setting higher standards, rather than in restricting the numbers of immigrants. Woodrow Wilson had vetoed efforts to impose quotas, but in 1924, Calvin Coolidge signed the National Origins Act, announcing that "America must be kept American."

The new law cut the total number of immigrants in any one year to 164,000 (compared to the million who entered in 1921). It also limited each nation to 2 percent of the number of people of that "national origin," living in the United State in 1890. Since most southern and eastern European immigrants had arrived after 1890, the not-very subtle aim was clearly to keep those "undesirables" out. Under this system, for example, 66,000 immigrants could come from Great Britain, but only 5,800 from Italy and 2,700 from Russia. To satisfy California nativists, the law completely excluded Asians. This needless slight deeply angered the Japanese. (They had earlier agreed to limit Japanese migration to America in the Gentleman's Agreement of 1907.) One protester committed harikari (suicide) in front of the American Embassy in Tokyo and relations with Japan worsened.

One, perhaps unintentional, result was the soaring rate of unrestricted immigration from the Western Hemisphere. Thousands of Mexicans poured across the border to seek a better life in the Southwestern United States. Many became migratory farm workers, earning very little and living in dreadful conditions.

The Case of Sacco and Vanzetti

The trial, conviction, and execution of Sacco and Vanzetti vividly demonstrated both the powerful currents of anti-foreign feeling and the deep divisions in American society. In 1920 a five-man band of robbers held up a shoe factory in South Braintree, Massachusetts, seizing the payroll and killing the paymaster and guard. Witnesses described the killers as Italians. A few weeks later the police arrested Nicola Sacco and Bartolomeo Vanzetti, two Italian immigrants, a shoemaker and a fish monger, well known in the area for their anarchist activities. Both were carrying loaded pistols.

The trial took place in 1921. The testimony on both sides was far from conclusive. Neither the money nor the getaway car was ever traced to the two men. Eyewitness descriptions changed to fit the defendants more closely as the date of the trial arrived. Historians have since analyzed, dissected, and redissected the evidence. Some have suggested that ballistic tests on Sacco's gun point to his involvement. Few, however, have argued that the trial was fair. Judge Thayer, who presided, was clearly hostile to Sacco and Vanzetti whom he described to friends as "those anarchist bastards." In the atmosphere of the time, it was easy for an Anglo-Saxon New England jury to feel that foreigners were suspicious types who could not be believed. Anarchists were probably also murderers. Aliens who had dodged the draft in World War I were undoubtedly guilty of something.

Judge Thayer found the men guilty of murder in the first degree and sentenced them to death. This was not the end of the case. It was, instead, the beginning of a worldwide outcry. Prominent liberal and radical intellectuals and Italian-Americans took up their cause. For six years they secured stays of execution and uncovered new evidence, including a confession by a convicted killer and recantations by prosecution witnesses. In 1927 the governor of Massachusetts appointed a distinguished advisory commission, headed by the president of Harvard, (a member of the Immigration Restriction League) to review the evidence. While noting "a grave breach of official decorum" by Judge Thayer, the commission upheld the conviction. Demonstrations erupted throughout the world. A famous newspaperman wryly commented, "What more can the immigrants from Italy expect? It is not every person who has a president of Harvard throw the switch for him." The words of the eloquent Vanzetti further convinced his supporters of the two men's innocence: "Never in our full life could we hope to do such a work for tolerance, for justice, for man's understanding of men as we do by accident...That last moment belongs to us—that agony is our triumph." They were electrocuted on August 23, 1927.

Five days later, enraged police broke up a funeral march by fifty thousand mourners. To Sacco and Vanzetti supporters, the death of "these two good men" proved that justice and change could never be achieved through the "system." Intellectuals and reformers moved sharply to the left. In *The Big Money*, John Dos Passos bitterly expressed their views. The narrator, thinking of the early settlers who hated oppression, reflects on recent events:

> America our nation has been beaten
> by strangers...who have taken the clean
> words our fathers spoke and made them
> slimy and foul...
> they have built the electric chair and hired
> the executioner to throw the switch.
> All right we are two nations......

No event reflected the cultural divide between the two Americas more than the Sacco and Vanzetti case.

POLITICS AND GOVERNMENT IN THE TWENTIES

The politics of the 1920s did not reflect those deep divisions. Instead, the Republican presidents and congresses mirrored the admiration of big business that most Americans felt. After the disillusionment caused by years of reform and war, Americans yearned for stability. They wanted a leadership that would turn the clock back to an earlier time when government and business were partners. (Business would be the senior partner.) H.L. Mencken, whose cynical commentary defined the Twenties, noted, "Today no sane American believes in any official statement of national policy...Tired to death of intellectual charlatanry, he turns despairingly to honest imbecility." The comment of famed lawyer, Clarence Darrow reflected the mediocre (or worse) quality of leadership: "When I was a boy I was told that anybody could become president; I'm beginning to believe it."

President Harding and His Scandals

Warren G. Harding, the first president of the 1920s, was a handsome man who looked as though central casting had sent him to play the role of president. He was a kindly, good-natured moderate whose ignorance of issues and unconcerned lack of savvy horrified the White House press. "I can't hope to be the best President this country ever had," he once admitted, "but if I can, I'd like to be the best loved." In the White House, Harding remained the same small-town politician he had always been. He enjoyed playing cards with his "Poker Cabinet" and relished his cigars and illegal cocktails. He also seems to have maintained a small house for his mistress and their child. (In 1927 she wrote a best selling account of the relationship, *The President's Daughter*.)

Harding made some well-received appointments to his cabinet. These included Charles Evans Hughes, the 1916 presidential candidate as Secretary of State; Henry Wallace, a well-respected authority, as Secretary of Agriculture; and Herbert Hoover, the wartime food administrator as Secretary of Commerce. Some also cheered the appointment of "the world's second richest man," Andrew Mellon, as the Secretary of Treasury. Hoover, who in many ways dominated the cabinet, pushed for voluntary business associations to cooperate in building a prosperous economy. Mellon opposed government regulations and urged slashing taxes on the wealthy.

"Uncle Warren" could be generous and tolerant. He spoke out against mistreatment of Southern blacks to an astounded segregated audience in Birmingham, Alabama. His civil liberties record compared favorably with Wilson's repressiveness. Wilson had twice refused to free the imprisoned socialist leader Eugene Debs after the war was over, while Harding pardoned Debs on Christmas Eve, 1921. At Harding's invitation, Debs even visited the White House for a talk and declared, "Mr. Harding appears to me to be a kind gentleman." Harding also freed virtually all the two hundred federal political prisoners who remained from the war and the subsequent Red Scare.

Harding worked hard to fulfill the obligations of office. He labored at personally answering routine White House mail. He struggled to make the right decisions about intricate economic and legislative questions. But his intellectual limitations and inability really to understand the issues drove him to despair. He went for treatment of his nervous disorders to a sanitarium in Battle Creek, Michigan, run by the eccentric Dr. Kellogg, the cereal king.

The president's most tragic flaw was his tendency to persuade himself that the political cronies he enjoyed as pals must be honest and able. "Warren, it's a good thing you wasn't born a gal," his father supposedly once remarked, "You'd be in the family way all the time—you can't say no." Virtually everyone in the know warned Harding against appointing as attorney general the wheeler-dealer who had helped make him president. To Harding, loyalty was the prime virtue. "Harry Daugherty has been my best friend from the beginning of this whole thing," he informed one protester. "He tells me that he wants to be Attorney General and by God he will be Attorney General." The result: Daugherty and his friends set up a "little house on K street" to buy and sell pardons, appointments, licenses, and government surplus.

Upset by the plight of disabled war veterans, Harding was proud of his creation of the Veterans Bureau to help them. As its head, he appointed Charles Forbes, a supposed Medal of Honor winner who was also a hustling go-getter. The bureau became the major spender in the government and its head renowned for his lavish life style. Cleanliness seemed to be his fixation. He bought enough floor cleaners to last a hundred years and paid 98 cents a gallon for cleaner that usually cost a nickel. Forbes' chief assistant, informed of an impending senate investigation, committed suicide, as did a close associate of Daugherty.

As evidence of the scandals and mismanagement reached him, the despondent president confessed to a journalist, "I have no trouble with my enemies....But my friends, my God-damned friends...they're the ones that keep me walking the floor nights." The president complained of chest pains and faintness. His doctors urged rest and approved an unhurried rail tour of Alaska. Instead, Harding brought his card-playing buddies along and played bridge compulsively for hours on end. He also insisted on making dozens of speeches along the way. By the time the train reached San Francisco, the president had collapsed. After some inept medical treatment by his doctor/crony, Harding's death (probably from a heart attack) was announced on August 2, 1923. The public was unaware of the brewing scandals. Millions waited along the tracks in silence or softly singing hymns as the casket passed by, reacting as though they had lost a latter-day Lincoln. Harding, in his death, was lavished with the love he had always wanted.

The Teapot Dome Scandal, the worst of the Harding administration disgraces, surfaced shortly after Harding's death. Secretary of Interior, Albert Fall, had been a senator from New Mexico known for his hostility to conservation. He had gained control of federal naval oil reserves. He promptly granted drilling rights to two millionaire oilmen in return for almost $400,000 in "loans." Fall became the first cabinet member in American history convicted and sentenced to prison for crimes in office. His disgrace and the publicity given to the other scandals forever blemished the image of the until-then beloved president.

Silent Cal

The public was entranced when Colonel John Coolidge administered the oath of office by the light of a lantern at the family farm to his son, Calvin Coolidge. The farm was in a part of Vermont that had remained, in the words of William Allen White, journalist and Coolidge biographer, "like the interior of some cool museum preserving colonial life." As vice president, Coolidge had been virtually unknown to the public. One of his most ambitious efforts had been an article entitled "Are the Reds Stalking our College Women?" (The answer was yes.)

The new president was a quiet, private man, a Puritan in an age of excess. White called his biography of Coolidge, *Puritan in Babylon*. The commonplace virtues of "silent Cal" reassured the public. He attempted to sit on the front porch of the White House in a rocking chair, but when crowds gathered, he gave up that small-town pleasure. He opened the doors of the oval office at 12:30 each day and, for a half hour, he shook more than 1,000 hands. He believed in as little government as possible, rarely worked more than four hours a day, and slept 12 hours or more each night. As one writer noted, "He aspired to become the least President the country had ever had; he attained his desire."

Sophisticated observers sneered at the dour little man with his obvious limitations. Alice Roosevelt

This cartoon pictures the Teapot Dome spewing out oily crooks.

Longworth said he "looked as if he was weaned on a pickle." When informed of his death, the author Dorothy Parker asked, "How could they tell?" The public, on the other hand, admired his integrity and assumed that his "curious shell of sardonic silence" was evidence of deep thought. He made them forget the earlier Republican scandals. His personal honesty and frugal life style made the people feel secure.

On a more serious level, Coolidge combined his belief in minimal government with a reverence for big business. "The business of America is business," he declared. "The man who builds a factory builds a temple. The man who works there, worships there." Mellon, the millionaire Treasury Secretary became his chief adviser, lowering taxes for the wealthy and increasing the widening gap between rich and poor, while balancing the budget. Tariff rates climbed to all-time heights to aid manufacturers. At the same time, Coolidge twice vetoed efforts to provide government aid to farmers noting, "Farmers have never made much money. I don't believe we can do much about that." He even turned down aid to victims of one of the worst Mississippi River floods in history (500,000 homeless and 500 dead). The government, Coolidge lectured, had no responsibility to protect people "against the hazards of the elements." He sincerely believed that government's main goal should be "not to embark on any new ventures." Earlier progressive reforms had brought high costs, complications, and thousands of deaths in the war. The public embraced the Coolidge view of limited government.

The Election of 1924

In February 1924 the ghost of a different activist America vanished with the death of Woodrow Wilson. The official Republican slogan in the 1924 election was, "Coolidge or Chaos," but most Americans preferred, "Keep Cool with Coolidge." The nation was enjoying the "Coolidge prosperity." Even farm discontent had eased, seeming to vindicate the policy of doing nothing. During the campaign Coolidge characteristically remained in Washington allowing Charles Dawes, his energetic running mate, to do all the campaigning.

A bitterly divided Democratic Party met at New York's Madison Square Garden in the midst of a devastating heat wave. Differences over Prohibition and the Klan tore the party apart. (A resolution to condemn the Klan failed 543-542.) The most dramatic event of the convention was the reappearance of Franklin Roosevelt whose promising political career had seemingly been destroyed by a devastating attack of polio some years earlier. When Roosevelt painfully pulled himself erect and, in his ringing voice, nominated Al Smith, (New York's governor) as the "Happy Warrior," the convention erupted in wild cheers. Roosevelt seemed to some observers to be "the real hero of the convention." His "adversity" had made him "the one leader commanding the respect and admiration of delegations from all sections of the land." That would prove to be the case in the future. In the meantime, the convention remained deadlocked for 102 ballots between Smith, the urban Catholic, and William McAdoo, Wilson's Treasury Secretary who represented Southern rural Protestant interests. Finally, the weary delegates compromised by nominating John W. Davis, a gentlemanly Wall Street lawyer who was almost as conservative as Coolidge.

Progressives attempted to regroup by nominating the elderly ailing "Fighting Bob" La Follette who sought to revive earlier progressive ideas of activist government reform. Barely half the public bothered to vote. Coolidge won a lopsided victory with almost 16 million votes, nearly twice that of Davis. La Follette received 17 percent of the vote, an impressive total compared to that of other third party candidates in our history. The voters had, however, basically endorsed the status quo.

Foreign Policy

The people seemed to believe that by rejecting Wilson's League, they could safely ignore the world. President Coolidge reinforced that view in 1925 when he declared, "The people have had all the war, all the taxation, and all the military service they want."

In Russia, Lenin died, and an unknown, Stalin, ruthlessly seized power. In Italy, Mussolini brutally eliminated all opposition. Magazines wrote enthusiastically about how this unusual Italian actually made the trains run on time. These events barely penetrated American consciousness.

Although American investments and exports skyrocketed in the Twenties, the nation refused any commitment outside the Western Hemisphere. America even rejected membership in the World Court. Two rare exceptions were the Washington Naval Conference of 1922 and the Kellogg-Briand Pact of 1928. In the first, the United States, Britain, Japan, France, and Italy agreed to reduce somewhat battleship tonnage to a fixed ratio. In the Kellogg-Briand Pact, sixty-one nations piously resolved to renounce aggressive wars. Everyone seemed to have gotten something for nothing. It was, as one writer has observed, "painless, toothless, and gutless."

A nation that had suffered neither defeat nor destruction decided that only European dishonesty stopped the Germans from paying reparations to the Allies and the Allies from repaying their debts to America. Few realized that these issues were intertwined and related to the economic well-being of the world. They agreed with Coolidge who concluded, "They hired the money, didn't they?" Although America eventually produced plans to lower debt demands, high tariffs made it virtually impossible for the Europeans to earn enough money to repay even the reduced amounts. Continued American insistence led to European resentment of an America described by Winston Churchill as "Uncle Shylock."

Unwillingness to fund adequately the American armed forces further illustrated the distaste for any foreign involvement. General Billy Mitchell, the foremost exponent of air power, demonstrated conclusively in 1923 that planes could sink battleships. Military and political leaders totally ignored his crucial lesson. Mitchell was eventually court-martialed and forced to resign.

The government, Americans felt, should help find foreign markets for American business and might intervene in the Western Hemisphere, but it should avoid any international commitments. The famed critic, George Jean Nathan, reflected the attitude of the Twenties when he wrote that millions of deaths overseas, "would not matter to me in the least. What concerns me alone is myself, and...a few close friends. For all I care, the rest of the world may go to hell at today's sunset."

Business Influence and the Decline of Progressivism

The results of the 1924 election marked the high water mark of the triumph of business influence in government. Mellon was able to win even further reductions in taxes on the wealthy, arguing that the benefits would "trickle down" to the less fortunate. A skeptical Nebraska progressive remarked, "Mr. Mellon himself gets a larger personal reduction than the aggregate of all the taxpayers in the state of Nebraska." The leaders of the very industries they were supposed to regulate ran the main regulatory agencies.

Former President William Howard Taft was appointed Chief Justice of the Supreme Court. The role of the Court, he announced, was "to prevent the Bolsheviki from getting control." Under his direction the Court held a national child labor law unconstitutional, struck down minimum wages for women, and softened anti-monopoly rulings. Encouraged by the favorable attitude of courts and government agencies, big business went on a merger

binge. Organized labor, by contrast, suffered a precipitous decline. Courts routinely granted injunctions against picketing or boycotts and sanctioned mass arrests of strikers.

The decline of the Teddy Roosevelt wing of the Republicans and the disorder among the Democrats seemed to signal the final collapse of progressive reform. The voters, however, did elect a core of determined, though often frustrated, reformers. These included old style Western progressives and new urban liberals such as Senator Robert Wagner and Congressman Fiorello LaGuardia of New York. Their successes at the federal level were minimal, but they did better at the state and local level where the ideology of progressive Republicans shifted to the more urban Democratic Party. Progressive-led campaigns resulted in workmen's compensation programs and aid to women with dependent children in many states. Governor Al Smith in New York started the first public housing program.

Most Americans were uninterested in reform. One young woman exemplified the attitude of many: "We're not out to benefit society...or to make industry safe. We're not going to suffer over how the other half lives." Coolidge's comments in his inaugural address reflected the general satisfaction, "No one can contemplate current conditions without finding much that is satisfying and still more that is encouraging."

PROSPERITY AND THE CONSUMER SOCIETY

The booming prosperity of America in the 1920s dazzled visitors from abroad. One English observer noted, "In the world's history can there have been such a display of wealth, power and energy as is spread out across the whole continent; never such feverish activity...." The visitor was troubled, however, by the cost: "the ruthlessness, the concentration, the unsleeping demand for efficiency." Americans did not seem to have any such doubts. They believed that a new age of unending affluence was at hand.

The great boom era began with a bust. The sudden cancellation of government contracts and the

France demanded war reparations from Germany.

rapid return of veterans to the labor market made the adjustment from war to peace time very difficult. A sharp recession, characterized by steep declines in production and employment, struck from 1920-21. Recovery came by 1922, confirming the faith many economists had in the inevitability of regular business cycles. The economy then entered a "new era" of dramatic economic growth. Unemployment fell to as low as 3 percent and national income grew at an annual rate of 5.6 percent. (That growth rate has never been matched in any comparable era in American history.)

Technology and the Consumer

Technological advances were at the root of this spectacular growth. Industrial output almost doubled, with remarkable increases in worker productivity. Mass production techniques, utilizing the moving-belt assembly line, made this possible.

A new age of electricity had dawned. Electricity powered 70 percent of American industry by the end of the era. Although many parts of rural America remained untouched, more than 60 percent of American homes were also wired for electric power. This made possible the production and sale of an amazing array of new electric appliances including refrigerators, washing machines, vacuum cleaners, fans, and mixers, as well as phonographs and radios, and a huge stimulus to the economy.

An extensive chemical industry also arose. Its efforts led to new alloys, synthetic materials such as rayon, and preserved foods. The quantity of gasoline that could be refined from one gallon of crude oil tripled.

Corporate structures "modernized" as well. Corporations continued the wartime consolidations that a friendly government still encouraged. A handful of big firms dominated major industries. By 1929, the two hundred largest companies owned half of the nation's corporate assets. Within the corporations, management was "rationalized" and "professionalized." Unlike the old-fashioned individualistic and autocratic style of Henry Ford, the day-to-day activities of most modern corporations were in the hands of trained professional managers. It was the beginning of the "organization man."

The old progressive fears of big business expansion and domination disappeared. The prospects of unending economic growth and prosperity, fueled by continuous technological advances, dazzled Americans.

The Automobile Age

Above all, American prosperity rested on the automobile. At the turn of the century, the automobile had been a toy of the rich. Woodrow Wilson once complained, "Nothing has spread socialistic feeling in this country more than the automobile; to the countryman it is a picture of arrogance and wealth, with all its independence and carelessness." Henry Ford had revolutionized the industry by 1914 when he had offered his workers an unprecedented wage of five dollars a day in return for a speed up in the assembly line. By 1925, the Ford plant turned out one enormously popular Model T every ten seconds. The price fell to $290, about three months wages for a typical worker.

The "Tin Lizzie," as the Model T was lovingly called, was the object of many affectionate jokes. You didn't need a speedometer, ran one, because at 15 mph the windshield rattled; at 20 the fenders shook;

and at 30 your fillings fell out. But as Ford's production was merrily rolling along, a new style executive, Alfred P. Sloan, had taken control of General Motors. Unlike Ford, an eccentric self-taught "tinkerer," Sloan was an M.I.T. graduate. He reorganized GM so that each division was a self-contained entity, run by expert managers. Sloan used modern marketing methods to introduce annual model changes, "planned obsolescence," and a variety of colors. (Ford had said that you could have the Model T in any color you liked, "so long as it's black.") For $90 more, the Chevrolet offered such conveniences as a self starter (no more standing in the rain cranking and swearing) and head lights that did not depend on the speed of the engine to work. GM also encouraged installment buying, creating the General Motors Acceptance Corporation to provide credit. By 1927, two-thirds of all automobile sales were bought on time payments, and Chevrolet had overtaken Ford in sales.

Suddenly, in May 1927, Ford shut down the Model T plant. He and his son, Edsel, drove the last (15,007,003rd) Model T off the line into the pouring rain. Ford and his men had to retool completely his giant factory to create a new car. One historian has written, "The magnitude of the reorganization which had to be completed within the calendar year...was something new in American industry." Without planning or any research department, Ford produced the new Model A by November 1927. Buyers had already ordered half a million cars, sight unseen. Huge crowds poured into the showrooms around the country, requiring mounted police to control them. It was a great public event. The new model, with its clean lines and improved convenience, proved to be enormously popular. One song declared, "Henry's Made a Lady out of Lizzie." Automobile registrations grew from 9 million to over 26 million in the decade. The United States was manufacturing about 85 percent of the world's automobiles.

The automobile industry had a tremendous impact on the American economy and lifestyle. It stimulated the growth of such related industries as steel, rubber, glass, and petroleum. It led to America's oil dependency. It created the national highway system and its resulting spread of restaurants, motels, and service stations. America's love affair with the automobile caused the neglect and ultimate decline of the railroads. Suburban development increased, as well as real estate booms in distant Florida and California.

While one working class woman enthusiastically announced, "I'll go without food before I'll see us give up the car," critics blamed the automobile for the decline of family togetherness and private morals. The enclosed cars, they argued, were nothing more than "portable bedrooms." For most Americans, however, the rapid growth of motor-vehicle registrations created an optimistic faith in technological progress.

The Age of Advertising

The demand for automobiles and the other goods upon which the consumer economy rested was stimulated by the flourishing advertising business. By 1929, advertising earnings had jumped to $3.4 billion, more than all expenditures for formal education put together. Many advertisers followed the behaviorist theories of the psychologist John Watson. Watson believed that human beings could be easily manipulated. The authors of *What About Advertising?* argued that the advertiser "must recognize the extreme mental stupidity of the vast majority of his audience." They believed that the average American had the mental capacity of a twelve-year-old and would believe anything, presented in the right way. That way would be to aim at the emotions with a hard-sell approach.

Advertisers often played on the public's deepest anxieties. The hazards of life could destroy the unwary. "Halitosis," a new term for bad breath, was discovered to sell Listerine. "B.O." (body odor) could destroy any relationship unless the afflicted used Lifebuoy soap. The menace of pyorrhea (gum disease) seemed worst of all, hitting "four out of five" Americans. Those who failed to use Forhan's gum treatment were depicted wearing white masks to hide their hideous mouths. Even the Encyclopedia Britannica claimed that it could save the marriage of a dull young woman, "one year married and all talked out."

Other products trumpeted their benefits. Cigarettes could make you slimmer, promised Lucky Strikes with its slogan, "Reach for a Lucky instead of a sweet." The heroism of the crew of the *S. S. America* in saving thirty-two Italian sailors was a result of their smoking Luckies. Fleischmann's discovered that its yeast was a "health food," which could cure constipation, lack of energy, and even acne. Famous people willingly accepted money to give testimonials for such dubious products as useless "nerve tonics."

Advertising also worked to advance a new era of consumption. It would be a world of luxury and pleasure. A GE refrigerator could be a magnet for envious guests to admire in your kitchen. ("The owning of such a refrigerator is a form of health and happiness insurance.") Shiny new plumbing fixtures would show that you had arrived. Albert Lasker, often credited as the father of modern advertising, was able to skirt prohibitions against using words like "menstruation" or "sanitary napkin" and successfully launch the newly invented Kotex. When American orange growers produced far more fruits than Americans ate, Lasker began a campaign to get people to drink orange juice every day.

To many Americans, advertising was the new gospel. Bruce Barton, an advertising executive (founder of the giant firm B.B.D.& O.), wrote *The Man Nobody Knows*, the number-one best seller of 1925 and 1926. In it Barton discovered that "the real Jesus" was an outgoing organization man who had forged "twelve men from the bottom ranks of business" into "an organization that conquered the world." Christ, had he lived in the Twenties, would certainly have been an advertiser. Advertising, Barton explained, "as a force...is as old as the world. The first four words ever uttered, 'Let there be light,' constitute its charter." The success of advertisers made spending a major national pastime.

Farmers and Workers: The Limits of Prosperity

"The rich get rich and the poor get children," a 1921 song snickered. The booming economy left many behind. Spurred on by the all-time high prices during World War I, farmers had greatly expanded production. They had gone into debt to finance increased mechanization. After the war, prices and land values collapsed, leaving debt-ridden farmers with no chance to recover. As they increased productivity, prices fell even further (wheat, corn, and hay by more than 50 percent). For most American farmers, the 1920s was more a decade of depression than of prosperity. Foreclosure signs appeared on the fences of thousands of deserted farms. The owners had loaded their rickety Model Ts with their meager possessions and headed to the highways. The Department of Agriculture estimated that 19 million rural Americans had given up and gone to live in the cities.

The story for workers was mixed. Real wages for factory workers rose modestly and hours decreased. Business profits, however, increased seven times as much as wages. The wages of unionized workers rose rapidly. They generally earned twice as much as the unorganized. Nevertheless, union membership declined from over 5 million to 3.4 million by the end of the decade. The increase in mass production techniques accelerated the trend away from skilled hand labor where union labor had predominated. With the approval of a sympathetic government and courts, business-men, like Henry Ford, discouraged union organizing by using hired thugs and friendly police forces to intimidate physically union organizers.

"Welfare capitalism," based on the idea that the interests of workers and employers were identical, was even more effective in obstructing unionization. The General Electric Company pioneered in the view that workers should not be treated like machines. The cooperation of the workers, gained through better treatment, would increase production. With the growth of the industrial relations movement, companies began to hire personnel managers, trained to deal with workers. Some giant corporations introduced stock purchase plans, medical programs, group insurance, and credit unions. Companies like U. S. Steel saw no contradictions between welfare capitalism and the continued use of anti-union spies and strict controls in company-run towns.

Scientific management introduced more efficient machinery and speedups in production. Many workers complained that the new work disciplines required by these machines stripped the employees of their humanity. In nineteenth century factories, for all their evils, workers and bosses were often able to establish personal relationships. Visitors to the factories would meet the laborers. Now, as one worker complained, visitors were brought in to admire the new machinery. Charlie Chaplin's film, *Modern Times*, brilliantly satirized the plight of the modern workman.

The large number of workers who did not share in the general prosperity was even more worrisome. The wages of the unskilled barely increased at all. The textile industry was in dire straits. Textile mills had abandoned their historic homes in New England to seek nonunion labor and considerably lower wages in the South. Many New England mill towns were devastated. By the mid-1920s, the Southern textile industry was, itself, suffering serious decline as a result of foreign competition, the new "miracle" fabric, rayon, and the reduced demand due to shorter skirts. Hours rose and wages fell below the poverty level. Even employed factory workers in more prosperous industries lived in constant fear of plant shutdowns or layoffs. Miners, particularly in coal-producing areas, also suffered from the competition of oil. Despite a series of bitter strikes, neither their wages nor their working conditions showed any signs of improvement.

Almost 42 percent of American families had annual incomes of less than $1,500, the poverty level. Of the 26 million American families in the mid-1920s, 6 million were listed as "chronically destitute." Less than half the homes in America met *Fortune* magazine's "minimum standards of health and decency," which included electricity, inside toilet and running water, and regular garbage removal. There was, indeed, poverty amidst the prosperity. Chief Justice Taft expressed the view that the country was fortunate to have a government committed to allowing "the people to work out for themselves the prosperity they deserved." Many Americans agreed with his assumption that the rich and successful merited their wealth, while the distressed farmer or poorly paid worker received precisely what each "deserved."

LIFE IN THE TWENTIES

In many ways the Twenties represented a better life for millions of Americans, particularly those in the ever-increasing middle class. Life expectancy, as a result of public health programs, rose from 55 to 60, the greatest increase ever in one decade. Tuberculosis, once called "the Great White Plague," was now an illness confined to the very poor. Other infectious diseases also declined.

Other health news was not so positive. Heart disease and cancer replaced the older diseases as the leading causes of death. Cigarette consumption had gone from 15 billion to 100 billion. Sugar use tripled. Drug addiction increased with the growth of cities. Doctors and pharmacists filled increasing demands for opium and morphine. With the support of the American Medical Association, the authorities arrested doctor-suppliers, criminalizing drug addiction.

American education was transformed. Only one-fourth of the high school-age population attended secondary school at the end of World War I. By 1930, more than half attended high school. Every state now had compulsory education laws. Even colleges and universities experienced enormous growths in enrollment.

These healthier, better educated Americans, above all, wanted to enjoy life. They did not want to be troubled by problems and issues. Ernest Hemingway's hero in *A Farewell to Arms* expressed their views when he declared, "I was always embarrassed by the words sacred, glorious and sacrifice...." The attitudes of the young led the way in this "Age of Flaming Youth."

Cities and Suburbs

The 1920 census marked a great turning point in American history. For the first time, a majority of the nation's people were counted as living in cities. Although the definition of what constituted a city was somewhat questionable (2,500 or more inhabitants), the announcement had symbolic importance. It seemed to confirm the demise of the rural way of life. There were now a dozen cities with populations of more than 600,000. During the 1920s this trend continued. Steel, oil, automobile, and commercial and service centers boomed. Even greater growth took place in warm climate resort cities like Miami and San Diego.

An increase in corporate administrative and service headquarters led to an enormous boom in the construction of downtown skyscrapers. By 1929, there were 377 buildings at least 20 stories tall. City and state governments were spending large sums of money in constructing new roads, improving streets, and regulating traffic with such amazing new equipment as the traffic light.

Ironically, just as America was officially described as an urban nation, suburban development, which would ultimately undermine the cities' growth, was also increasing. By 1920, the growth rate of suburbs was greater than that of cities for the first time. Industries began to move out of the central city. Increased use of electric power made greater flexibility in location possible. The assembly line required sprawling single or two-story plants in areas where cheap land was available. Many white workers moved out of the cities to be near their work. The newly available inexpensive automobiles made it possible for workers to move out into areas lacking mass transportation. Retail establishments followed the movement to the suburbs. In 1923 Kansas City, Missouri developed the nation's first suburban shopping center. Others quickly followed.

The growing decentralization of industry and retailing led to increased building of roads. The construction of "parkways" began in the 1920s, stimulating automobile commuting and recreational trips. Decisions to pave gathering places and stress easy movement destroyed nineteenth century city neighborhoods. The new suburban expansion, coupled with continued growth of cities and rising automobile use, caused the formation of metropolitan districts (cities and their suburbs). By 1930 there were 93 such areas with populations over 100,000.

African-American Life in the Twenties

A substantial portion of the migrants into the nation's cities was African American. Conditions in the rural South worsened as the boll weevil destroyed cotton farms and the rebirth of the Ku Klux Klan reinvigorated racial repression. "I'm tired of this Jim Crow, gonna leave this Jim Crow town," one blues song proclaimed. Black newspapers spread word of job opportunities in growing industries, encouraged by Ford's expressed willingness to hire black workers on the assembly line. This "Great Migration," in which some 1.5 million African Americans moved into America's cities, was a remarkable and unprecedented redistribution of American population

In reality, they met rising tides of prejudice. They were forced to squeeze into overcrowded slums, restricted by fearful whites from moving to better housing. In addition, despite Ford's example, few factories or construction firms were willing to hire blacks.

The Empire State Building had 102 stories and space for 25,000 tenants. In 1950, 222 additional feet were added.

(In Philadelphia less than 1 percent of the 43,000 factory workers were blacks, 15 percent of the population.) Most employed black women worked as domestics. The church was the central institution in the lives of African Americans who had moved from the rural South. Barbershops and beauty parlors were also significant social institutions for urban blacks. Hairdressers were part of the black elite that also included doctors, lawyers, teachers, and ministers. In fact, Madame C. J. Walker, considered the first American woman self-made millionaire, became rich by manufacturing skin creams, "whiteners," and hair-straighteners for black women. As black ghettoes spilled into adjoining neighborhoods, they often met bitter, even violent, resistance.

One response to this discrimination was an up-surge in black protest organizations. The conservative Urban League attempted, with limited success, to find jobs for blacks in the cities. The National Association for the Advancement of Colored People (NAACP) fought school segregation in the North and worked hard for a federal anti-lynching bill. After a bitter debate (one Southern congressman declared, "When these black fiends keep their hands off the throats of the women of the South the lynch-

The Brotherhood of Sleeping Car Porters was one of the few unions with black members.

ing will stop."), the House voted to make lynching a federal crime by a 2-1 margin. Southerners filibustered the bill to death in the Senate. The threat of possible federal action, coupled with the NAACP publicity campaign, did succeed in bringing about an enormous decline in the number of lynchings.

A. Philip Randolph was far more radical and militant than the two mainstream organizations. He decided to organize a black union, the Brotherhood of Sleeping Car Porters. Although their work was largely menial—making beds, attending to passenger comforts—porters were comparatively well paid and were among the elite of the community. College-educated black men often found that jobs as Pullman porters were all they could get. (In one deadly train wreck, his Dartmouth Phi Beta Kappa key identified the porter.) The union had its setbacks and advances, but it gave Randolph and, through him, black workers a "Harvard-accented voice" in the labor movement.

West Indian immigrants who lived in black communities in American cities tended to be more confident, enterprising, and ambitious than Southern migrants, as a result of their history. Marcus Garvey, who came from Jamaica, preached pride in blackness. He formed the Universal Negro Improvement Association (UNIA) to further black separatism, capitalism, and eventual migration to Africa. The UNIA newspaper refused to accept ads for skin whiteners or hair straighteners. Garvey's colorful costumes and charismatic personality appealed to working class people, many of whom bought stock in his Black Star shipping line. Eventually, undermined by crooked officers, the line went bankrupt. Garvey was convicted of mail fraud on very dubious evidence, sent to jail, and then deported. His message of "race and color consciousness," however, remained a potent one for many years to come, having a profound impact on later black nationalism.

In the 1920 census there were less than 50,000 blacks living in New York. By the end of the decade, there were 300,000, two-thirds of whom crowded together in Harlem. As Harlem became a black ghetto, it also developed into the center of African-American intellectual and cultural activity. The "Harlem Renaissance" bloomed in the 1920s, the

Marcus Garvey offered black pride to the urban blacks of the eastern cities.

black version of the cultural dynamism of the era. Nearly every important black writer and intellectual flocked *Home to Harlem*, the title of a Claude McKay work. Writers and poets explored the lives and often contradictory role of black people in America. "Yet do I marvel at this curious thing: To make a poet black and bid him sing," declared Countee Cullen. Langston Hughes, less ironically and more defiantly, professed pride in being "Negro," "Black as the night is black, Black like the depths of my Africa."

Nightclubs and theaters also demonstrated the variety and vitality of black culture. Bessie Smith sang her plaintive blues. Jazz had moved up the Mississippi from the whore houses of New Orleans to Memphis and Chicago. From there it came to Harlem clubs through Duke Ellington and many others. Langston Hughes recalled the Twenties as "the period when the Negro was in vogue." Whites had discovered Harlem as a place to escape from dull

upper and middle class life. They crowded into places like the Cotton Club where white-only audiences watched black performers. The more daring went to "black and white" night spots where the races actually mixed. Broadway even featured its first all-black review, *Shuffle Along*.

Rebellious white intellectuals, youths, and bored society people were part of the fad for everything black. They felt the pull of the exotic and "primitive." White patrons supported many aspiring black writers and artists. The whites expected confirmation of their stereotypes about "African soul" from their proteges. When Langston Hughes insisted on writing about black American workers, his generous patron dropped him. Once the Depression struck, Harlem was "no longer in vogue." White supporters departed and, as Langston Hughes ruefully remarked, "The ordinary Negroes hadn't heard of the Negro Renaissance. And if they had, it hadn't raised their wages any."

The Jewish Experience

Jews from Eastern Europe were among the flood of "new" immigrants who had arrived in America from 1890-1914 and crowded into American cities. By 1920, Jews were 20 percent of the population of New York City. The restrictive immigration laws, aimed at all eastern and southern Europeans, led to a drastic decline in Jewish immigration. Only 73,000 Jewish immigrants entered the country from 1924-31. The children of the earlier immigrants wanted to become a part of American society. They aspired to the American dream as defined in the 1920s.

They met with discrimination in employment, particularly in such white collar areas as banking and commercial offices. (The New York Telephone Company announced that it could not hire Jewish women as operators since their arms were too short for the switchboards!) Better housing, resorts, and country clubs were also restricted. Despite these obstacles, Jews succeeded to a remarkable degree. Although most remained working class, a substantial number moved up to the middle class, particularly the second generation Americans. Many were small businessmen in light manufacturing or sales. Barred from the major heavy industries, the more adventurous entrepreneurs entered the riskiest new ventures, particularly the film industry. A cultural stress on education and study led others into the professions: medicine, law, and teaching.

In spite of these successes, intensified anti-Semitism appeared to threaten the hopes and security of American Jews. Major American universities, such as Harvard, and most professional schools instituted quotas to limit the number of Jews in their student bodies. Jews were startled when police in the small town of Messina, New York in 1928, rounded up the local rabbi to question him about the disappearance of a little girl. The police had heard that Jews used the blood of Christian children in a religious ritual. This was an alarming appearance of the European medieval "blood libel" on American soil. (The child was found the next day.)

What is more important, the eccentric Henry Ford had turned his attention to the promotion of anti-Semitism. In the 1920s Ford became increasingly autocratic and distrustful of others. He purchased the newspaper, the *Dearborn Independent*, and increased its circulation to 700,000 by requiring his auto dealers to distribute it. The paper launched a lengthy anti-Semitic campaign, arguing inconsistently that Jews were both radical Bolshevik revolutionaries and Wall Street capitalist conspirators. It ran such "exposes" as "The Jewish associates of Benedict Arnold." The paper also serialized a Czarist Russian forgery, *The Protocols of the Elders of Zion* to "prove" an international Jewish conspiracy and then distributed it in book form, *The International Jew*. In 1922, a *New York Times* correspondent reported from the headquarters of a young politician in Munich: "The wall beside his desk in Hitler's office is decorated with a large picture of Henry Ford....there is a large table covered with books, nearly all of them are a translation of *The International Jew*...published by Henry Ford." After losing a libel suit by one Jewish victim of the paper's rantings, Ford released a public apology. He declared that he did not know about the nasty slanders issued in his name for seven years and asked for forgiveness. By 1929, Ford was paying tribute, in a radio address, to "the great benevolence of the Jewish people....their eager-

ness to make this world better...stamps them a great people." Although Ford never again returned to his earlier obsession, the ugly forces of hate he had helped release remained and led to far more serious consequences in the thirties.

The New Woman—Sexuality and Consumerism

"Cigarette in hand, shimmying to the music of the masses, the New Woman and the New Morality have made their theatric debut upon the modern scene," one observer proclaimed in the middle of the decade. Increasing sexual permissiveness, as symbolized by the independent, self-indulgent flapper, was an enduring image of the 1920s. There was a new mood of sexual emancipation, particularly among young urban middle class women. The idea of the great Austrian psychoanalyst, Sigmund Freud, that sex was central to the human experience, gained widespread acceptance. Popularizers oversimplfied his theories to mean an end to all sexual restraint. Popular culture reinforced this view in "hot" movies, songs with titles like, "I Need Lovin'," and cheap books such as, *One of Cleopatra's Nights*. The young flapper was a "liberated" woman who showed her assertiveness and rebelliousness by bobbing her hair, wearing cosmetics (used only by prostitutes a generation earlier), smoking cigarettes in public, raising her hemline, and dancing the Charleston uninhibitedly.

"If all the girls at the Yale prom were laid end to end, I wouldn't be surprised," Dorothy Parker wrote. Other observers were more distressed than amused. The flapper's defiance of rules, such as a willingness to "pet" in her boyfriend's car and other assertions of female sexuality, was worrisome to traditionalists. Alarmist articles with such titles as, "These Wild Young People," filled magazines.

There was some validity to the view that sexual behavior was changing. Later exhaustive studies by Dr. Alfred Kinsey showed that women of the 1920s generation were twice as likely to have premarital sex as their mothers' generation. The sexual revolution aided in the dramatic decline of prostitution. The institution of "dating," marked a substantial

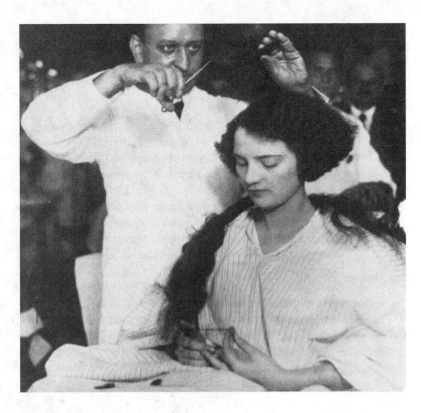

The "bob" symbolized the breezy independence of the 1920s woman.

change from the era of adult-supervised "calls" paid at home by male suitors. Now that women were conceded to be sexual beings, they expected romantic and sexual gratification in marriage. "Companionate marriages" were promoted as the ideal. Perhaps as a result, the divorce rate tripled from 1890 to 1930, rising to 18 out of every 100 marriages.

Margaret Sanger, who had launched the birth control movement in the Progressive era as a radical form of direct action by working-class women, reshaped her program to fit the new era. She won the support of academics and physicians by stressing eugenics arguments that birth control would keep the unfit poor from reproducing. She reinvented the birth control movement as a middle class reform by emphasizing the possibilities of transforming sex from "biological necessity" to "a psychic and spiritual avenue of expression." Now women could be liberated from "loathing, disgust, or indifference to the sex relationship" and from "involuntary motherhood," to experience sexual satisfaction in marriage. Middle class women, able to obtain illegal diaphragms from physicians, became the main advocates of birth control. Abortion rates also grew. New York City was the site of a thriving abortion clinic industry protected by payoffs to police and politicians. It has been estimated that there were almost one million criminal abortions each year, with perhaps as many as 50,000 deaths.

The apparent liberation of women in the Twenties was, in reality, severely limited. The "new woman" used her increased sexuality to find a hus-

Margaret Higgins Sanger was the founder of the American Birth Control League (1921).

A 1920 flapper poses beside her roadster, December 1927.

band, rather than to follow an emancipated life style. Far from identifying with other women, as Progressive-era feminists had, she regarded them as potential competitors and avoided the traditional female friendships. Same-sex relationships declined in the race to attract the opposite sex. Colleges increasingly began to prepare women for their appropriate roles. Business and home economics emerged as new fields for male and female specialization. New courses with titles like, "Motherhood" and "The Family as an Economic Unit" encouraged traditional roles. In contrast to the earlier era when about half of women's

college graduates never married, in the 1920s college women were marrying at increasingly earlier ages, often before they completed their degrees.

Most women willingly abandoned being flappers to become wives and mothers. The responsibility of keeping "the thrill in marriage" rested with the wife. Advice manuals sternly informed women that marriage was their "vocation." Only marriage could satisfy all their needs, and any outside activities could pose a danger. Women's magazines exhorted them to reject careers and devote themselves to running the home. Dorothy Dix, a widely syndicated columnist, informed her readers, "A man's wife is the show window where he exhibits the measure of his achievement." The first edition of Emily Post's *Etiquette* appeared in 1923 to advise the newly prosperous about proper behavior. "Infant and Child Care," the most widely read government publication, disseminated Dr. John Watson's behaviorist theories on raising children. Children were to be fed strictly by the clock and taught that crying would be rigorously ignored. Anxious wives and mothers could relieve anxieties by following the French guru, Coue, reciting twenty times a day, "Every day, in every way, I am getting better and better."

Women could also fulfill their roles by becoming avid consumers. Even flappers were defined by the products they purchased like silk stockings, cosmetics, ready-made clothing, and cigarettes. Advertisers stressed that household appliances, canned goods, and other products would "liberate" women from "constant drudgery." Toastmaster trumpeted, "The Toaster that FREED 465,000 homes." Modern studies have demonstrated that most of the new conveniences did not cut time spent in housework because of increasing demands for cleanliness.

Unmarried women did continue to work while waiting to find husbands. Some young married women attempted to combine careers and marriage for the first time. The numbers of working women increased, although their proportion in the work force remained the same. More women entered lower levels of the business world as office clerks, secretaries, switchboard operators, and saleswomen. The more than forty thousand beauty parlors, which opened in the decade, provided a new vocational option. Protective progressive measures that limited women's working hours and regulated conditions added to male/female income gaps by making women less desirable employees. Wage gaps between men and women increased. Working-class women, the majority of whom were immigrants or blacks, continued to labor at dismally low levels of pay.

While more educated women became professionals, they surged into traditionally female "service" professions, such as teacher and librarian. Social work, a new profession, began to replace upper-class settlement house volunteers. By the end of the

1920s, there were twenty-five thousand trained social workers, largely women. Male professions increasingly closed ranks against women. With strict quotas on female applicants and the refusal of most hospitals to appoint women interns, the number of female physicians fell by one-third. The proportion of women graduate students also declined as a result of tighter quotas. The press celebrated such examples of female achievement as women in aviation, like Amelia Earhart, and successful entrepreneurs, like Helena Rubenstein. These, however, were exceptions, rather than the vanguard of a new era.

Suffragists had believed that the passage of the Nineteenth Amendment, granting women the right to vote, would permanently transform American politics. After some mild efforts to win the expected "women's vote," the political parties quickly realized that no voting bloc existed for "women's issues." Women seemed to vote just as men did. (The "gender gap" would not appear until much later.) Feminist reform groups of the Progressive era languished or disappeared. Alice Paul and her National Woman's

Alice Paul and her National Woman's Party compaigned for an equal rights amendment to the Constitution.

Party continued the struggle by proposing an Equal Rights Amendment to the Constitution in 1923. She attracted few supporters and quickly got into conflict with those who favored protective laws for women. Most younger women were turned off by both the equal rights and social reform branches of feminism. They associated feminism with loneliness and spinsterhood, not the "fun" of the brave new era. An article in *Harper's* in 1927 noted that young women felt contempt for those "who antagonize men with their constant clamor about maiden names, equal rights, woman's place in the world, and many another cause."

LEISURE TIME AND AMERICAN CULTURE

A popular song of the Twenties proclaimed, "'Aint We got Fun!" This reflected the image of a decade in which spending on amusement and recreation rose by 300 percent at a time when prices of other things remained relatively stable. White collar workers, whose numbers were growing, generally had two days a week off and received annual vacations. Even industrial workers saw their workweek decline to five-and-a-half days. The availability of increased leisure time led city dwellers, in particular, on a frantic search for "fun" and escape. The United States became the entertainment leader of the world.

There seemed to be an unending appetite for fads and "ballyhoo." New games and activities attracted middle class families with increased incomes. Mahjong, a tile game imported from China, became the rage of middle class women. The crossword puzzle craze launched Simon and Schuster, which became one of the nation's major publishing houses. Some thirty thousand miniature golf courses were built to accommodate the new enthusiasts of this activity. Camping became the most popular vacation activity, causing visits to national parks to rise from 5 million to 40 million per year. The new Miss America contest helped revive the fortunes of Atlantic City. Daring dances, like the Charleston and Black Bottom, attracted "Flaming Youth." The marathon dance mania tested the health of many. For some strange reason, people liked to stand around and watch others dance for endless days and nights until the dancers dropped from exhaustion or even heart attacks. "Shipwreck" Kelly introduced a particularly silly fad, flagpole sitting. The sitter would perch on top of a flagpole for as many as ten days, as thousands looked on.

The Movies

Mass entertainment was provided in many forms. Vaudeville shows drew family audiences with magic, animal, and juggling acts; song and dance performers; and, most of all, comedy that rested heavily on ethnic and racial stereotypes. As popular as vaudeville was, the extraordinary growth of the motion picture industry rapidly surpassed its appeal. The new industry was, in the words of one of its pioneers, a "Marvel of science, mirror of art, product of the ingenuity of man....You are King in the Land of Mechanical Wonders.... You are great. You are the agent of the age...."

The first Miss America was Margeret Gorman of Washington D. C. crowned in 1921.

Enormous crowds flocked to the movies. From 1927-29, weekly movie attendance was estimated at 110 million when the total population was 120 million and weekly church attendance was 60 million. People could find refuge from their daily lives in ornate movie "palaces." In the big cities these dream palaces had crystal chandeliers, plush carpets, velvet-covered seats, huge organs, even stuffed peacocks and stars glittering on ceilings. In smaller towns the movie theater was often the most recognizable building. Since it was expected that everyone in a community would go at least once a week, some three or four times, it was not uncommon for a town of ten thousand to have a theater that seated three thousand.

Comedy predominated in the era of the silent film, an intensely visual medium. Charlie Chaplin, the tramp-clown, was the most famous and best loved star of the age. His comedy satirized middle class pretension and materialism. There were other great slapstick comics like Buster Keaton, Harold Lloyd, and "Fatty" Arbuckle. (Fatty was the victim of the first great Hollywood sex scandal and was driven from films despite a jury acquittal in the death of a "starlet.")

Sexuality quickly became a potent draw. Clara Bow, the "It girl," replaced Mary Pickford, the more Victorian "America's sweetheart," as the leading female star. Lurid ads promoted films with titles like, *Forbidden Fruit, Ladies of Pleasure, The Golden Bed*, and *Women Who Give*. These promised, "beautiful jazz babies, midnight revels, petting parties in the purple dawn" and "pleasure-mad daughters, sensation-craving mothers...." When women's clubs complained, Cecil B. DeMille, the most influential film director, switched to Biblical spectacles like *The Ten Commandments*. There, he managed to find a Biblical setting for his sexual revelry.

In 1927 filmmaking was revolutionized. Warner Brothers, a film company whose fortunes seemed to be declining, released the first full-length feature film with sound, *The Jazz Singer*. The film was a tremendous hit, despite the warnings of critics that Hollywood was self-destructing by eliminating "the soul of the film—its eloquent and vital silence...." The public formed long lines to see the "talkies" and broke

Walt Disney left behind an enduring legacy.

into applause when they ended. The increase in Warner Brother profits from $30,000 to $17 million led other companies to follow suit. Some of the old stars were destroyed when their voices or accents were unsuitable to their images. New stars, like Greta Garbo, Gary Cooper, and Jean Harlow, were discovered. Mickey Mouse made his debut in 1928 in a short film by the young Walt Disney. Movies were more popular than ever as Hollywood offered "its great bargain sale of five and ten cent lusts and dreams," in the words of John Dos Passos.

Radio

Americans were willing to pay well to avoid boredom. Despite its tinny tones, the Gramophone enabled the listener to crank a handle and dance to popular music or even enjoy the soaring notes of Enrico Caruso (probably the most popular opera singer ever). The radio extended these pleasures. "Tin Pan Alley" in New York became the center of a burgeoning song-writing industry featuring such composers as Irving Berlin, the son of immigrants, and Cole Porter, the sophisticated WASP (White, Anglo-Saxon Protestant). People could now enjoy the music of the big bands on a regular basis. They could thrill to the play-by-play calls of baseball games and the blow-by-blow descriptions of boxing matches. They could learn election results and hear speeches by political leaders. (Franklin Roosevelt was the first American president to understand this potential.)

The phenomenon began in 1920 when KDKA in Pittsburgh, the first commercial station, transmitted news of Harding's election. In 1921 a Newark station broadcast the Giants' win over the Yankees in the World Series. By 1922, there were 576 licensed stations. They began hiring announcers whose rich syrupy voices were equally comfortable introducing variety programs or reporting sports spectacles or major disasters. The first network, the National Broadcasting Company (NBC), began in 1926. The Columbia Broadcasting System (CBS) followed in 1927. Each attempted to outdo the other in its appeal to the largest possible number of listeners.

Few enterprises have succeeded as rapidly. Radio sales had increased from $1 million in 1920 to $400 million in 1925. Radio's reach transcended class and regional boundaries. A 1929 presidential commission reported, "On the roof of practically every tenement house on the lower East Side numerous radio antennae are in evidence." By 1930, 40 percent of American homes owned radios. Advertisers soon realized the potential of having their messages reach millions of homes. They began to sponsor programs where their "commercials" could be repeated over and over again.

Like the movies, radio contributed to the standardization of American culture, surmounting the divisions in American society. Throughout the nation, families followed serials like "The Green Hornet." Housewives never missed "Portia Faces Life" and other daily "soaps." "Amos'n' Andy" was the most popular show of all. It ran five nights a week for 15 minutes. It followed the adventures of two black stereotypes who were proprietors of the "Fresh-Air Taxicab Company of America, Incorpulated." In the tradition of stage "burnt-cork" humor two whites wrote and acted the parts. Everybody seemed to listen and rearrange schedules to hear the show. Even

President Hoover was a buff, inviting its stars to the White House. Pepsodent toothpaste, the show's sponsor, realized millions in sales.

Radio had brought the country together, but not everyone applauded the results. Lee DeForest, whose invention of the vacuum tube made the whole thing possible, was dismayed by what had happened to his "child." "You have debased this child" he complained, "you have sent him out on the streets...to collect money from all and sundry for hubba hubba and audio jitterbug. You have made him a laughing stock to intelligence...."

In 1927, the image of Herbert Hoover's face was transmitted from Washington to New York on a tiny screen. Television had made its first tentative American appearance. Its challenge to both radio and movies remained in the future.

Mass Sports

The emergence of the modern consumer culture, a result of rising incomes, led to the growth of organized sports. Sports mania gripped almost every city in the nation. Organized sports offered cities and groups within them a feeling of community and special identity. At a time of the ascendancy of technology and the assembly line, Americans yearned for the dramatic and unpredictable.

Millions jammed parks and stadiums to view athletic events. Intercollegiate football contests brought in $21 million by the late 1920s. In the era of the revived Klan, Catholics in the cities became fervent fans of the "Fighting Irish" of Notre Dame and their renowned coach, Knute Rockne. The attendance of 130,000 at the Dempsey-Tunney heavyweight championship fight in 1926 broke all records.

Above all, baseball became "the National Pastime." The sport had been seriously shaken by the "Black Sox" scandal that broke in 1920 and pushed every other story off the nation's front pages. It was revealed that eight Chicago White Sox players had taken bribes to fix the 1919 World Series. The scandal caused the reorganization of major league baseball through the appointment of Judge Kennesaw Mountain Landis as commissioner with unlimited powers. (Despite the subsequent acquittal of the players, Landis banned all of them from organized baseball for life.) Landis gave baseball a new image of integrity. (The movies followed this successful example by appointing a "czar" to censor films.) The sport also gained a new legal foundation when the Supreme Court ruled that it was exempt from antitrust laws. Baseball's rise in popularity was even more attributable to the phenomenal rise in batting averages and home runs. In 1923, a record 300,000 fans watched the New York Yankees defeat the New York Giants in six games.

Large numbers of Americans used their added leisure time to participate in sports. Tennis was the favorite of many. Golf became an obsession for millions. By 1927, there were five thousand golf courses, most of them built in the 1920s.

Currents of Culture

The growth of universal secondary education meant that most American adults read more regularly. Many new magazines appeared in the Twenties, several with circulations over a million. *Reader's Digest* and *Time* were among the most successful. Intellectuals were more likely to read H.L. Mencken's *American Mercury* and his attacks on the materialistic middle class whom he called the "booboisie." The sophisticated *New Yorker* may well have been the best-written of all. Book sales also increased enormously as the newly founded Book-of-the-Month Club and the Literary Guild competed with the quaint old-fashioned book store. The number of new book titles doubled in the decade.

The anguish felt by many in the developing intellectual class vividly demonstrated the split between the "two Americas." They rejected both the old rural fundamentalist values and the newer middle class embrace of materialism and self-satisfaction. Many felt so alienated that they fled the country for Paris where they were known as "the Lost Generation." Ironically, this was a decade of unequaled creativity.

There was probably more outstanding writing in the Twenties than in any other single decade of American history. The decade began with the 1920 publication of Sinclair Lewis' *Main Street*, "the most sensational event in twentieth-century American publishing history." The novel, an unsparing portrait of the bleakness and conformity of small-town middle America, sold an astounding 3 million copies. *Babbitt* (1922), Lewis's next novel, was an even greater success. Babbitt, the "hero" of the book, became a synonym for the small businessman who unthinkingly embraces the middle class obsession with material success. F. Scott Fitzgerald became the symbol of the lost generation in his reckless life style, as well as his novels. His works depicted "flaming youth" and their "vast carelessness" that would ultimately destroy "the greatest, gaudiest spree in history."

Ernest Hemingway was probably the most important of this group of American writers. His spare, uncluttered prose, in books like *A Farewell to Arms*, perfectly captured the disillusioned spirit of the times. He coupled a rejection of the moral values of war with a fascination with its violence. Eugene O'Neill was the towering playwright of the era. His passionate plays lifted American theater from silly melodrama to worldwide prominence. American fiction has since followed many of the themes of the Twenties—rejection of small-town mores, preference of the young to the old, preoccupation with sex and violence.

The other arts also expressed the creativity of the 1920s. Adventurous architects transformed cities with ever more daring skyscrapers. Artists, like Georgia O'Keeffe, boldly experimented with audacious colors and forms. Serious composers drew upon American folk music and the rich tradition of black jazz. (George Gershwin's *Rhapsody in Blue* was the best example of the latter.) Despite their cynicism, most American writers and artists reflected rather than rejected the dynamism of the era.

Heroes and Other Celebrities

As the Victorian value system continued to erode, individuals felt increasingly powerless in a complex and bureaucratic society. They longed for heroes who had achieved individual fame outside the "system." That explains the phenomenal popularity of Lindbergh. The media helped create other celebrities who quickly surpassed the traditional heroes of business or politics. The media in a consumer society helped create these "stars" of movies and sports.

In their films, Hollywood heroes defeated sword-wielding villains or saved innocent whites from "savage" Indian attacks. In the nineteenth century theater, heroes had been depicted as winning the rich man's daughter through good character. In silent films, Rudolph Valentino prevailed through his personal allure. The early movie stars earned enormous salaries and lived glamorous lives, promoted by the new profession of press agent and relentlessly covered by magazines and newspapers.

Rudolph Valentino, star of *The Sheik*, was the undisputed male sex symbol. Men throughout the nation attempted to emulate his appeal by growing sideburns, greasing their hair, and batting "bedroom eyes" at their girlfriends. When the "Great Lover" died suddenly at the age of 31 in 1926, his funeral caused a frenzied outbreak of mass hysteria. A famous actress arrived with four thousand roses and a song solemnly announced, "There's a New Star in Heaven Tonight."

Just two days after the great Valentino delirium in New York, enormous crowds turned out to cheer for 18-year-old Gertrude Ederle. "Trudy," as she was affectionately called, was the first woman to swim the English Channel and had done so in a time that broke the old male record by two hours. The parade in her honor was the greatest ever seen in the city, surpassing Pershing's reception at the end of the war. (Lindbergh's welcome would soon overtake Trudy's ceremony.)

Above all, sports idols dominated the public eye and heart in the 1920s. "Never before, or since, have so many transcendent performers arisen contemporaneously in every field of competitive athletics as graced the 1920s," according to two long-time sports journalists. Part of the acclaim was due to the efforts of public relations men and the exaggerated images created by sports reporters and radio broadcasters. A good deal, however, was the result of the public need for heroes who projected images of power and immediate success.

The 1920s was the "Golden Age" of American boxing. Tex Rickard, the "King of Sports Promot-

ers," understood the public craving for heroes. He found his man in Jack, "the Giant-Killer" Dempsey. Dempsey was quickly bringing in million-dollar gates. He loved his life as a celebrity with its movie contracts, product endorsements, and vaudeville performances. The two fights pitting Dempsey, the ruthless brawler, against Gene Tunney, the "scientific" boxer, were each dubbed, "The Battle of the Century." Public excitement was so great that approximately 60 million Americans listened to the rematch on eighty-two radio stations. Seven collapsed from heart attacks during the seventh round with its legendary "long count." Tunney, the victor, an educated man who relied on defensive finesse, did not fit the public image of hero. Boxing's appeal declined.

The media found the perfect football player in Red Grange, the "Galloping Ghost." His specialty was the long run, often culminating in a touchdown. He quickly capitalized on his fame at the University of Illinois by hiring an agent and turning professional

"Red" Grange of the University of Illinois

Babe Ruth was adored by millions of baseball fans. Between 1926 and 1931, Ruth averaged 50.3 home runs a year.

in the middle of his senior year. Professional football, up to that point, had received little respect since it was associated with immigrants and working-class people. Grange was able to attract huge crowds to the Chicago Bears' games and made enormous sums of money from various endorsements. "Kid," Babe Ruth warned him, "don't believe everything they write about you."

The great British playwright, George Bernard Shaw, supposedly once asked, "Who is this Baby Ruth? And what does she do?" There were few Americans in the 1920s who would have asked such a question. Babe Ruth was "The Sports Hero" of the era. (Only Lindbergh exceeded his popularity.) Ruth represented the ultimate fulfillment of the American dream of success; the natural, unrestrained man who revolutionized baseball with his power. He had overcome a grim and neglected childhood to rise, by the age of 19, to the big league Boston Red Sox, first as an outstanding pitcher, then a great hitter. The high-living Red Sox owner, needing money to finance a Broadway show, sold Ruth to the New York Yankees. (The Red Sox subsequent lack of post-season success became known as "the curse of the Bambino.") In his first year with the Yankees, 1920, Ruth hit 54 home runs, more than any other **team**. The public responded to his awesome power with great enthusiasm. His mammoth blasts seemed to challenge the dominant world of the organization man and scientific rationality. He loved to play the game, and he also loved incredible quantities of bootleg liquor, junk food, and casual sex. The public forgave his excesses and adored his love of children and visits to their hospital beds. They marveled at his childlike delight. Yankee attendance doubled. In 1923 they were able to move into their own ball park, Yankee Stadium, "the house that Ruth built." Newspapers all over the nation ran a syndicated box, "What Ruth Did Today." Home run production and batting averages soared throughout the game and, with them, public excitement. In 1927 Ruth hit 60 home runs on what was probably the best team ever, "Murderer's Row." Not only did Ruth revive and save the game of baseball, he remains the nation's premier athletic hero to this day.

Public obsession with celebrities often extended to the far-from-heroic. Organized crime kings, like Al Capone, received celebrity status through images of forceful success. The press fueled popular fascination with the marriage of 51-year-old "Daddy" Browning and his 15-year-old bride, "Peaches." Their breakup even made the front page of the normally sober *New York Times*. Clarence Darrow got as much publicity for saving thrill killers Leopold and Loeb from execution as he later did for the Scopes trial. Jimmy Walker, the flamboyant mayor of New York, became a folk hero by spending all his time and energy living the good life, writing songs, selling favors, visiting speakeasies, and flaunting his mistress. He won reelection overwhelmingly against Fiorello LaGuardia (who would later become the city's greatest mayor). The showman, Earl Carroll, gave the most famous party of the time, which was to culminate in a champagne bath by a nude chorus girl with the guests drinking champagne from her tub. When she fainted, the party ended, but the publicity led to Carroll being sentenced to a year in jail for serving illegal liquor.

The press fed the national fixation on sensational crimes. In the Hall-Mills case, a well-respected minister was found shot to death with a married church choir singer at his side. Passionate love letters were discovered near them. Despite frenzied newspaper coverage by over three hundred reporters, the jury acquitted Mrs. Hall and her brothers. In the Snyder-Gray case, Ruth Snyder and her married lover bludgeoned her husband to death. The sleazy little murder vied with Lindbergh's flight for headlines in 1927. The public was startled that such an act could take place in a middle class home by a woman, "so like the woman across the street that many an American husband was soon haunted by the realization that she also bore an embarrassing resemblance to the woman across the breakfast table," as one observer noted. The grim picture of Ruth Snyder dead in the electric chair was a widely displayed cautionary image.

THE END OF AN ERA

The most discussed event in college sports in 1929 may well have been the emblem of the end of the "Roaring Twenties." At the annual Rose Bowl game, when Georgia fumbled the football, Roy Riegel, California's center, picked it up. Eluding his opponents, twisting away from tackles, Riegel ran for 60 breathtaking yards towards the wrong goal line! (One of his own team mates finally intercepted him at the three-yard line.) "Wrong Way" Riegel, one of the "heroes" of 1929, symbolized, perhaps, the direction in which the nation was also heading.

The Election of 1928

Coolidge had been even more gloomy than usual towards the end of his term. The strange death of his son from a foot infection devastated him. On vacation in the Black Hills of South Dakota, he summoned reporters to a press conference. There, he handed each a slip of paper on which was typed: "I do not choose to run for President in nineteen twenty-eight." He offered not a single word of explanation to the baffled reporters.

Few elections in American history have more graphically demonstrated the divisions in American society than the election of 1928: Rural America vs. Big City; "Wet" vs. "Dry"; Protestant vs. Catholic Irish. Both candidates were self-made men, but they were "as far apart as Pilsner and Coca Cola." Secretary of Commerce Herbert Hoover easily won the Republican nomination. A Quaker from a small

Herbert Hoover, the Republican candidate, stressed continued economic prosperity.

Al Smith campaigned from a train platform in his familiar brown derby.

town in Iowa, Hoover was orphaned at the age of ten. He was the embodiment of the ideals of self-reliance and rugged individualism so admired at the time. He had worked his way through Stanford University to become a millionaire mining engineer. Before entering the cabinet, he had dedicated his life to public service and humanitarian activities as wartime food administrator and leader in food relief efforts abroad. In contrast to Harding and Coolidge, he was considered somewhat progressive, a believer in the president as leader of a modern economy. He was a strong advocate of the cooperation of government and business.

The Democrats turned to Al Smith. Smith, the son of Irish immigrants, had gone all the way from a Lower East Side tenement in New York to the governor's mansion. He was the first Roman Catholic ever to run for the presidency. Although personally conservative, he had amassed a record of effective progressive reforms as governor. He was also an outspoken opponent of Prohibition. Smith launched a spirited campaign throughout the country but turned

off many small town voters with his New York City accent, style, and wisecracks. ("My opponents couldn't get elected on a laundry ticket.") As a Roman Catholic and a "wet," he represented everything rural Americans believed was evil in a rapidly changing urban America.

The intensity of the anti-Catholic campaign that was launched against him stunned Smith. A flood of pamphlets and newspapers swept across the South and other areas, claiming that Smith was building a tunnel to connect to the Vatican; that the Pope would set up a White House office; that Protestant children would be forced to go to Catholic schools. Eleanor Roosevelt later wrote, "If I needed anything to show me what prejudice can do to the intelligence of human beings, that campaign was the best lesson I could have had." (Thirty-two years later, John F. Kennedy would again have to face the forces of anti-Catholic intolerance.)

The conclusive issue of the campaign was undoubtedly the "Coolidge prosperity" for which Republicans took the credit. "We in America today,"

Hoover announced, "are nearer to the final triumph over poverty than ever before in the history of any land. The poor-house is vanishing from among us." The Republican ad campaign promising "A chicken in every pot, a car in every garage," was topped by some enthusiasts who confidently predicted *two* chickens and *two* cars. In the resulting sweep, Hoover had 21 million votes to Smith's 15 million, cracking the solid Democratic South and even carrying Smith's own New York. Franklin D. Roosevelt, a reluctant candidate for governor of New York, was one of a small number of leading Democrats to survive the Republican landslide. There were a few other positive signs for the Democrats. So many more people voted, that Smith received twice as many votes as Davis had in 1924. What was more important, Smith carried all twelve of the nation's largest cities whose significance would increase in the future.

Calvin Coolidge left office convinced that he had achieved his goals. "The country," he informed Congress, "can regard the present with satisfaction, and anticipate the future with optimism." As he departed, many people firmly believed that he was one of the greatest presidents ever. That view did not last a year.

The Crash of an Era

Despite rising signs of problems, the Coolidge boom continued into 1929. Much of its momentum depended on spiraling speculation. As one observer noted, "Everybody speculated, everybody believed 'prosperity' was eternal...." From newspapers and business journals, to Wall Street, and even to university theorists, speculation was widely defended. It was argued that Columbus and the western pioneers who built the nation had been speculators and even "Christ himself took a chance." Greed had become the defining feature of the era. Stories, largely untrue, circulated about scrubwomen now riding to work in chauffeured limousines, fueling the frenzy to get rich as quickly, and with as little effort, as possible. The 1925-6 Florida land boom was a cautionary tale ignored by most Americans. Land prices had risen to dizzying heights as lots in swamp areas sold for $20,000 or more. Miami grew so fast that it

was known as "the Magic City." Then, in September 1926, a hurricane devastated the area, leaving four hundred dead and fifty thousand homeless. The land boom collapsed, leading to thousands of bankruptcies, foreclosures, and shattered dreams. By 1928, Miami was one of the most inexpensive cities in America.

Few people learned a lesson from the Florida disaster. In August 1929, a millionaire industrialist, in an interview in *Ladies Home Journal*, declared, "I am firm in my belief that anyone not only can be rich but ought to be rich." He recommended investment in the Stock Market as the means to achieve that goal. Many joined in the speculative frenzy known as the "Great Bull Market." Contrary to popular myth, the ordinary American was not involved. Most shareholders came from the wealthy or urban upper middle class. New securities, in the words of one historian, "were manufactured almost like cakes of soap" to make quick profits from their sale. Stock prices soared through the stratosphere. In four years the market value of all stocks had risen from $27 billion to $87 billion in paper value. Brokers willingly lent speculators as much as 75 percent of a stock's price, leading to increased buying on "margin." By 1929, brokers' loans had risen to $8.5 billion. Mellon's tax cuts for the rich gave them more money to speculate on the market. By the fall of 1929, the average stock was selling at more than 100 times its earnings value.

The Crash finally came on "Black Thursday," October 24, 1929. Panicky selling orders jammed the lines of the Stock Exchange, but it was difficult to find buyers. Leading bankers collected a pool to buy millions of dollars worth of stocks to instill confidence in the market. For a few days, it seemed to work. "The worst is over....General conditions are good," one leading broker announced. On "Black Tuesday," October 29, the bottom fell out. A guard described the bedlam on the Stock Exchange floor: "They roared like a lot of lions and tigers....It was like a bunch of crazy men. Every once in a while when Radio or Steel would take another tumble, you'd see some poor devil collapse and fall to the floor." The panic demolished $30 billion in market stock value. By mid-November, stock prices were

Crowds gathered on Wall Street in response to the stock market crash of October 1929.

half their October highs. Some millionaires, like Joseph Kennedy and John D. Rockefeller, began buying stocks at bargain prices. "Sure he's buying," said comedian Eddie Cantor of Rockefeller, "Who else has any money left?" Many of the "new" rich, like Cantor and Jack Dempsey, America's first millionaire athlete, lost their entire fortunes. Will Rogers, the era's most beloved humorist, complained, "You stand in line to get a window to jump out of."

Many people believed that the Crash was a necessary correction that would not change American life very much. At the end of 1929, the *New York Times* chose the expedition of Richard Byrd to the South Pole as the most memorable event of the past year. As for the economy, the paper's editorial noted with relief, "the patient" was on the road to a complete recovery. Henry Luce of *Time* magazine, picked this moment to launch his new business magazine, *Fortune*, convinced that the "business slump" would last no longer than a year. President Hoover proclaimed that there was no reason to panic: "The fundamental business of this country, that is, production and distribution of commodities is on a sound and prosperous basis." He was wrong.

The market crash would not have led to the Great Depression had there not been fundamental flaws in the economy of the 1920s. We have seen that farm-

ers, textile workers, and miners were already in a virtual depression. Wages of workers lagged far behind profits. Tax policies favoring the rich had increased the uneven distribution of income. (By 1929, the 24,000 richest families had incomes three times as great as the 6 million poorest.) Much of the added income of the wealthy went to luxurious living and speculation. (The income of the wealthiest 1 percent had risen 75 percent in the decade.) Remarkable gains in productivity led to a need for increasing consumption. But demand was leveling off, and businesses refused to give workers wage increases that might have created new consumers for their products.

Spending on durable goods, like housing and automobiles, began a precipitous decline. By the end of 1928, the key construction industry had gone into a serious descent. Automobile sales seemed to have reached their "saturation" point. By August of 1929, automobile factories began laying off thousands of workers. One culprit was installment buying. Millions of American families were deeply in debt for the first time in American history. While they carried much less debt than people do today, they were far more worried about it. Noticing the slowdown in the economy and the market crash, they felt particularly vulnerable and further cut down on spending. The resulting 10 percent decline in consumer spending led to further reduction in production and layoff of workers. These, in turn, had still less to spend and the cycle continued its downward spiral. Unlike Europe, the United States had no unemployment insurance to cushion the blow.

Other factors also helped cause the Depression. The banking system was shaky at best. Rural banks, dependent on farmers, failed at alarming rates (1,000 in 1926 alone). Even stronger urban banks were caught up in the prevailing obsession with risky speculation. When stock prices disintegrated, brokers demanded that their loans be repaid, and buyers tried to remove their savings from banks. Bankers, in a bind for cash, called in loans to brokers. The banking system collapsed under the burden of impossible-to-meet obligations. European economic difficulties, which were worsened by higher American tariffs, also contributed to the depression. High tariffs destroyed foreign trade and left America with no place to sell its overprotected goods. The unwillingness of the government to regulate unchecked speculation or dubious banking practices added to the problems. Most experts firmly believed that the business cycle was an inevitable part of capitalism. They waited for the depression to "bottom out" and the cycle to rise again.

CONCLUSION

The Twenties have been labeled the "era of excess," as a result of its emphasis on consumerism, entertainment, speculation, and "fun." It was also a genuinely "new era" in American life, characterized by mass production, technological change, bureaucratization, and the rise of cities and suburbs. In grappling with the forces of change, the nation was bitterly divided. The old rural Protestant America struggled with the new urban secular society. Prejudices and intolerance surfaced amidst the strains but so did a rich cultural dynamism. Despite the huge national identity crisis, a modern society emerged. As the decade ended, however, some observers worried that the system, so carefully constructed, was nothing more than a house of cards. "May we not

fear," the critic Edmund Wilson wrote at the end of 1929, "that what this year has broken down is...the capitalist system itself?—and that even with the best will in the world, it may be impossible for capitalism to guarantee not merely social justice, but even security and order." As the nation entered the Thirties in the grip of the most devastating depression in American history, many Americans felt similar misgivings about the nation's future.

Chronology

1915   Ku Klux Klan is revived, reaches heights in 1920s

1917-1925   Great migration of Southern blacks into Northern industrial cities

1920   Eighteenth Amendment, prohibiting alcoholic beverages, goes into effect
Nineteenth Amendment, granting women suffrage, ratified
KDKA, first commercial radio station, begins broadcasting in Pittsburgh
Sinclair Lewis publishes *Main Street*; F. Scott Fitzgerald, *This Side of Paradise*
Warren G. Harding elected president on pledge of "return to normalcy"

1921   First Miss America beauty pageant held in Atlantic City, New Jersey

1922   High tariff rates restored
Sinclair Lewis publishes *Babbitt*; T. S. Eliot, *The Wasteland*
Supreme Court declares child-labor law unconstitutional

1923   Equal Rights Amendment written by Alice Paul
Harding dies
Calvin Coolidge becomes president
Teapot Dome and other scandals revealed

1924   National Origins Act passed, imposing quotas on immigration
Calvin Coolidge re-elected president

1925	Scopes trial on teaching of evolution takes place in Tennessee
	F. Scott Fitzgerald publishes *The Great Gatsby*
	Ku Klux Klan scandal in Indiana destroys its power
1926	Ernest Hemingway publishes *The Sun Also Rises*; Langston Hughes, *The Weary Blues*
	Further reduction in tax rates for high incomes demonstrates "trickle down" theory
1927	*The Jazz Singer*, first sound motion picture, released
	Henry Ford retools and introduces Model A
	After long struggle, Italian immigrant anarchists, Sacco and Vanzetti, are executed
	Charles Lindbergh completes first successful solo transatlantic flight
	Babe Ruth hits 60 home runs
1928	Herbert Hoover defeats Alfred E. Smith, first Catholic candidate for president
	Walt Disney releases first Mickey Mouse cartoon
1929	Robert and Helen Lynd publish *Middletown*, pioneering sociological study
	William Faulkner, *The Sound and the Fury*
	Ernest Hemingway, *A Farewell to Arms*
	Stock market crashes (October 24)

SUGGESTED READINGS

Frederick Lewis Allen, *Only Yesterday* (1931).

Lois Banner, *American Beauty* (1983).

Loren Baritz, ed., *The Culture of the Twenties* (1970).

Edith L. Blumhofer, *Aimee Semple McPherson* (1993).

Ellen Chesler, *Woman of Valor: Margaret Sanger and the Birth Control Movement in America* (1992).

Stanley Coben, *Rebellion Against Victorianism: The Impetus for Cultural Change in 1920s America* (1991).

Robert Creamer, *Babe* (1974).

Kenneth S. Davis, *The Hero: Charles A. Lindbergh* (1959).

Ann Douglas, *Terrible Honesty: Mongrel Manhattan in the 1920s* (1995).

Susan J. Douglas, *Inventing American Broadcasting* (1987).

Lynn Dumenil, *The Modern Temper: American Culture and Society in the 1920s* (1995).

Paula Fass, *The Damned and the Beautiful: American Youth in the 1920s* (1977).

James J. Flink, *The Car Culture* (1975).

Neal Gabler, *An Empire of Their Own: How the Jews Invented Hollywood* (1988).

John Kenneth Galbraith, *The Great Crash, 1929* (1955).

Ray Ginger, *Six Days or Forever?* (1958).

Allen Guttmann, *A Whole New Ball Game* (1988).

Ellis W. Hawley, *The Great War and the Search for a Modern Order* (1979).

John Higham, *Strangers in the Land: Patterns of American Nativism, 1860-1925* (1955).

Kenneth T. Jackson, *The Ku Klux Klan in the City, 1915-1930* (1967).

William Leach, *Land of Desire: Merchants, Power and the Rise of a New American Culture* (1993).

Daniel L. Lewis, *When Harlem Was in Vogue* (1981).

Fred J. Macdonald, *Don't Touch That Dial: Radio Programming in American Life 1920-1960* (1979).

Nancy MacLean, *Behind the Mask of Chivalry: The Making of the Second Ku Klux Klan* (1994).

Daniel Pope, *The Making of Modern Advertising* (1983).

Joan Shelley Rubin, *The Making of Middlebrow Culture* (1971).

Francis Russell, *Tragedy in Dedham: The Story of the Sacco-Vanzetti Case* (1971).

___ , *The Shadow of Blooming Grove* (1968).

Arthur M. Schlesinger Jr., *The Crisis of the Old Order* (1957).

Chapter Nineteen

THE DEPRESSION AND THE NEW DEAL

European immigrants eventually became assimilated, and once that process was complete, they quickly proved themselves to be "worthy "citizens," whose contributions were especially noteworthy in the nation's cultural and social life. One "immigrant" who gained such acclaim during the 1930s was motion picture director Frank Capra. Today, he is probably best remembered for his last successful picture, **It's a Wonderful Life***, shown ever year at Christmas—sometimes in its new "colorized" version—to millions of American viewers. In the movie, George Bailey, a kind and compassionate small-town savings-and-loan officer (played by Jimmy Stewart, one of Capra's "regular" stars) is almost destroyed by a wealthy, greedy, and malicious banker. So distraught by his impending ruin, George was on the verge of committing suicide when he is visited by an angel who shows him what life would have been like in Bedford Falls—his town—had he never been born. Taking a page out of the Dicken's classic,* **Mr Scooge***, which was also made into a movie in the 1930s, Capra shows George, accompanied by his angle/guide, wandering through a coarse, corrupt, degraded town as he realizes that his life does indeed have value. He returns to the real Bedford Falls to find that his family, friends, and neighbors have*

rallied together to rescue him from his financial woes and affirm his value to them and theirs to him.

When **It's a Wonderful Life** *premiered, Frank Capra was already one of Hollywood's most popular and successful directors. Virtually every one of his 1930s films were critical and commercial successes. They had won two academy awards for best picture (and Capra himself won best director in 1934). Capra's artistic and creative talents were undoubtedly remarkable; equally impressive was his vision. His pictures were enthusiastically embraced by Depression-era Americans because Capra's personal social and political views resonated clearly with those of his fellow citizens as they struggled through a decade of unprecedented uncertainty and anguish.*

Capra, a Sicilian immigrant, came to the United States with his family in 1903. The Capras made their way to California where young Frank grew up. After working his way through college, Capra found a job in the still-young movie industry in his home state and eventually became a director of feature films. His great breakthrough came in 1934, with the romantic comedy, **It Happened One Night***, which has since become a classic in that particularly film genre. The picture,* *starring Clark Gable and Claudette Colbert, won five Academy Awards, including best picture and best director. Over the next seven years, Capra built on that success by making a series of poignant sociopolitical commentary pictures, which helped to establish the director as a powerful voice of an old-fashioned vision of democracy and American life. Capra's pictures expressed his romantic notion of small town America and the virtuous and noble common man who came from such an environment, while simultaneously revealing his distaste for cities, his contempt for opportunistic politicians and demagogues, and his condemnation of what he considered the amoral (often immoral) capitalist marketplace. In* **Mr. Deeds Goes to Town**, *(1936) a simple man from a small town inherits a large fortune, moves to the city, and—not liking the greed and dishonesty he finds there—gives the money away and moves back home. In* **Mr. Smith Goes to Washington**, *(1939), a decent man from a western state is elected to the U.S. Senate, refuses to join in the self-interested politics of Washington, and dramatically exposes the corruption and selfishness of his colleagues. The rugged Western's actor, Gary Cooper, played Mr. Deeds, while the epitome of small town innocence and virtue, Jimmy Stewart, played Mr. Smith. In 1941, as the United States was about to enter World War II, Capra made* **Meet John Doe**, *once again starring Gary Cooper. In the picture, Cooper plays an ordinary man manipulated by a fascist cartel to dupe the public on their behalf. He comes to his senses just in time and by threatening suicide, rallies ordinary people to turn against the evil plans of the fascists. He then disappears into the night.*

Capra was entirely conscious of the romantic populism that he brought to his pictures. "I would sing the songs of the working stiffs, of the short-changed Joes, the born poor, the afflicted," he once wrote, in an apparent allusion to one of his creative heroes, the great American chronicler through poetry of the common folk, Walt Whitman. "I would fight for their causes on the screens of the world." He was intensely patriotic, a characteristic of many successful immigrants, and he believed passionately that the United States stood for individual opportunity and was defined by the decency of ordinary people. He was not, he said (in an effort to distance himself from the communists) a "bleeding heart with an Olympian call to 'free the masses.'" Indeed, he loathed the term "the masses" and found it "insulting, degrading." He saw the people, rather, as a "collection of free individuals. . .each an island of human dignity."

When the United States entered World War II, Capra collaborated with the government (and the Walt Disney studios) to make a series of pictures designed to explain to new soldiers what the war was about—a series known as **Why We Fight**. *Capra contrasted the individualistic democracy of the American small town with the dark collectivism of the Nazis and Fascists. He poured into them all his skills as a filmmaker and his romantic, patriotic images.* **It's a Wonderful Life**, *released a year after the war, continued his evocation of the decency of ordinary people. In the decades that followed, Capra, although he was still a relatively young man, and although he continued to work, ceased to be an important force in American cinema. The sentimental populism and comic optimism—the two central themes of his 1930s pictures—no longer appealed to post-war audiences. Post-war filmmakers and their audiences wanted harder, more realistic movies, and thus Capra faded into motion picture obscurity by the 1960s. A romantic to the end, Capra was never fully able to adjust to the vagaries of the post-war film industry. In a time of crisis, however, Capra had helped his viewers find solace in his romantic vision of the American past— in the warmth and goodness of small towns and the decency of common folk.*

THE DEPRESSION

As discussed in the last chapter, the soaring hopes of the 1920s abruptly vanished with the October 1929 stock market crash. The decade of the 1930s thus became one of the most traumatic and critically important eras in the Republic's history. Indeed, many would conclude that after the Civil War, the Great Depression marked the second most pivotal crisis in the nation's history. However, under the leadership of Franklin Delano Roosevelt and his "New Dealers," the Republic met the crisis with unprecedented activism, ultimately changing the course of domestic history down to the present. Indeed, to many Americans the New Deal represented "The Third American Revolution"—as much a pivotal turning-point in the nation's history as Independence and the Civil War.

Herbert Hoover, the personification of the 1920s business ethos, was humiliatingly rejected by a desperate and disillusioned electorate in the 1932 presidential election. Under the leadership of his successor, FDR, the national government implemented bold, innovative programs and policies, which offered material and emotional relief to millions of suffering and distraught citizens. Perhaps more important than such solicitude was FDR's determination to create a new relationship between the federal government and the Republic's citizens. Included in that new dynamic was also a reformation of the executive branch of government. In many ways, as will be illustrated in this chapter, FDR, like his beloved cousin, Theodore Roosevelt, and like Abraham Lincoln and Andrew Jackson, will significantly augment the power, prestige, and expectations of that office. In many ways, FDR was the inaugurator of the modern presidency, establishing during his four terms much of what we expect from our presidents down to the present moment. FDR will set the criteria by which we will judge all future executives, and if they fall short of those standards or hopes, then, like Herbert Hoover and many others, they will be historically relegated to that most undistinguished category of being one term presidents.

In the end, as will be seen, the New Deal did not end the Great Depression; World War II ultimately did. However, FDR's and the New Deal's importance lies in the fact that from the 1930s on, the American people could turn to their government not only as the guarantor and protector of their liberties but as a source of assistance in time of need and provider of equal opportunities for all. In short, the New Deal laid the foundation for postwar liberalism (the welfare state), which as will be seen in later chapters, will become the new American creed, replacing by the 1960s the conservative, laissez faire business ethos (rugged individualism) that had dominated the American value system since the end of the Civil War. FDR and his New Dealers will make it the federal government's responsibility to henceforth ensure that all Americans would have a minimum standard of well-being during their lives.

President Herbert Hoover's belief in limited government hurt his programs to deal with the Depression.

HERBERT HOOVER

The Technocrat as President

At his 1929 inauguration, Herbert Hoover told the American public that, "We in American today are nearer to the final triumph over poverty than ever before in the history of any land. The poorhouse is vanishing among us." The nation had not yet reached that goal, he acknowledged, "but given a chance to go forward with the policies of the last eight years, we shall soon with the help of God be in sight of the day when poverty will be banished from this nation." Those words came back to haunt Hoover, for in eight short months after making that speech, the nation's economy began its declension, ultimately collapsing into the worse financial crisis in the Republic's history. Hoover and his reputation were among the first casualties, along with the reverence for business that had been the hallmark of the New Era.

In one of the cruelest ironies in twentieth-century United States history, Herbert Hoover was inaugurated president only eight months before the nation's greatest economic calamity struck. Coming into office in March 1929, Hoover possessed all the requisite credentials for a successful and popular tenure. He embodied the rags-to-riches ideal, having risen from poor orphaned beginnings to graduating from Stanford University with an engineering degree. By the age of thirty Hoover had become one of the world's most successful mining engineers. Before the United States' entry into the Great War, Hoover directed a private American relief agency that fed millions of civilian victims of a war-ravaged Europe. For his efforts, Hoover was acclaimed the "Great Humanitarian," and such status led Woodrow Wilson to name him head of the Food Administration once the United States entered the war. Under his directorship, the Food Administration was responsible for feeding and aiding in a variety of other ways hundreds of thousands of dispossessed postwar Europeans. As a reward for his achievements, Hoover was appointed Secretary of Commerce by the 1920 Republican victor, Warren G. Harding, and remained at that post until becoming president in 1928. Indeed, in an era of lackluster presidents with equally mediocre cabinets, Herbert Hoover was a paragon of professionalism and competence.

Because he favored efficiency and growth, Hoover thought of himself as a progressive, but his reluctance to use the government as an agency of change and reform alienated him from prewar progressives, still committed to the reform ethos of early twentieth-century progressivism. Having lived most of his adult life abroad, he had never even voted in a presidential election. Aware of his political limitations, Hoover confided to a friend: "I have no dread of the ordinary work of the presidency. What I do fear is the exaggerated idea that I am sort of superman, that no problem is beyond my capacity." He added prophetically, "If some unprecedented calamity should come upon the nation I would be sacrificed to the unreasoning disappointment of a people who expected too much."

Hoover's initial responses to the depression were clear and firm. If the cooperative principles behind the modern economy were correct, as everyone seemed to embrace, Americans should then use them to stabilize the economy and then recover prosperity. "Progress is born of cooperation," the president reminded citizens. "The Government should assist and encourage these movements of collective self-help by itself cooperating with them." During the first two years of the crisis, Hoover turned to the "associational" principles he had followed as secretary of commerce, with its emphasis on "voluntary cooperation." For business, Hoover sponsored meetings and forums, hoping to convince the heads of the major corporations that his idea was the best approach to recover the economy. Hoover made it clear to these individuals that they need not worry about the possibility or specter of direct government intervention, nor was there a need for a massive overhaul or reform of the American industrial corporate system. In short, Hoover believed that the industrial chieftains were altruistic enough and savvy enough to embrace his ideas, realizing that his proposal was the only way of not only eventually restoring employment and prosperity but of saving American capitalism as well. Unfortunately, as will be seen, American businessmen disappointed Hoover, and their refusal to accept his ideas helped to plunge the economy ever deeper into depression.

For labor, Hoover won a promise from business leaders to spread the work in their firms rather than simply fire a percentage of their employees. For agriculture, the new Federal Farm Board issued large amounts of credit so that the commodity cooperatives could keep their products off the market and halt the decline in farm prices. For hard-pressed Americans everywhere, Hoover made the president's office the coordinator (but not the provider) of private, voluntary relief. Between 1929 and 1932 donations for relief increased about eightfold, a remarkable accomplishment by any previous standard. Viewing the economy as a national system, Hoover was the first president in history to attack depression systematically.

The Deepening Depression

But Hoover, like the economy, took a grim downturn in the middle of 1931. As his sense of control over affairs began to slip, he became more rigid, more isolated, more disillusioned, and frustrated by his inability to deal with the vast specter of oppressive forces. Particularly disturbing was big businesses' refusal to cooperate and enact his policies. Most only paid lip-service to the president's idea of cooperation, while others—too many—flat-out refused to acknowledge, let alone implement, any of his suggestions. As a consequence, unemployment in the industrial sector continued to rise as corporations continued to cut costs by laying off workers, something Hoover did not want to happen and believed would not if his advice had been heeded. So overwhelmed and despairing did Hoover become by 1932, that the White House became a funeral parlor. The president, never a charmer, looked, as one visitor remarked, as if a rose would wilt at his touch. In that mood, Hoover called together the villains of Wall Street who, in the president's view, had fed the Great Bull Market instead of facilitating legitimate business. When he demanded that they make massive new investments, they stalled. Finally, Hoover accepted the inevitable: the necessity of government intervention, as least as far as offering federal funds for credit. Thus, in 1932, the Reconstruction Finance Corporation was created, which, in that year, invested $1.5 billion in private enterprise, ranging from loans to ailing banks and to corporations willing to build low-cost housing, bridges, and other public works. The RFC was the biggest peacetime federal intervention in the economy to that point. The Home Loan Bank Board, set up that same year, offered funds to savings and loans, mortgage companies, and other financial institutions that lent money for home construction. Meanwhile, to ease the pressures on international finances, Hoover issued a moratorium on the payment of war debts owed to the United States by its former allies against Germany.

Unfortunately, Hoover refused to offer the same generosity to suffering Americans. Still devoted to the concept of rugged individualism, Hoover believed it an anathema to even contemplate the possibility of offering Americans in dire need direct federal relief. The idea of inaugurating the concept of the welfare state was an idea that never crossed Herbert Hoover's mind. Every citizen, he believed, must rely for survival on his or her own efforts. To give money to the poor, he insisted, would destroy their desire to work, undermine their sense of self-worth, and erode their capacity for citizenship. Critics pointed to the hypocrisy in such an attitude by reminding the president that in 1930 he refused a request of $25 million to help feed Arkansas farmers and their families but approved $45 million to feed the same farmers' livestock. And in 1932, shortly after rejecting an urgent request from Chicago for aid to help pay its teachers and municipal workers, Hoover approved a $90 million loan to rescue that city's Central Republic Bank.

By 1932 the president's policies lay in shambles. The exceptionally high Hawley-Smoot Tariff, which Hoover had signed in 1930, was intensifying worldwide depression by cutting off the flow of international trade, virtually locking out of American markets foreign manufactured goods. Employers discarded their programs for spreading the work, and unemployment shot above 12 million. Local relief funds, both public and private, evaporated. As commodity prices fell, the Federal Farm Board simply ran out of credit. Farmers burned their crops or left them unpicked as with cotton because it no longer paid them to market the crop. In some Midwestern county seats, silent men with hunting rifles closed the courts so that their mortgages could not be foreclosed. It was no wonder that by the spring of 1932, there had emerged a groundswell of protest and resentment toward the president and his uncaring policies and attitude.

The Death Knell of Herbert Hoover: The Bonus Army March

In the spring of 1932, a group of World War I army veterans mounted a particularly emotional challenge to the Hoover administration and its policies. In 1924, Congress had authorized a $1,000 bonus for Great War veterans in the form of compensation certificates that would mature in 1945. But now veterans were demanding the bonus immediately. Spearheaded by a group from Portland, Oregon, veterans decided to take action. Starting from that city and calling themselves the Bonus Expeditionary Force, they hopped onto empty boxcars of freight trains heading east, determined to stage a march on Wash-

Veterans of the Bonus Army camped outside Congress in Washington, D. C., demanding bonuses promised to them during World War I.

ington. As the impoverished "army" traveled east-ward, many surviving on handouts from sympathetic citizens, their ranks swelled, reaching 20,000 vets, including wives and children. Upon their arrival in Washington, the Bonus Army encamped in the Anacostia Flats, southeast of the Capitol, and peti-tioned Congress for early payment of the promised bonus. The House of Representatives agreed to al-locate the funds, but the Senate rejected the bill. Hoover supported the Senate, and, more importantly, refused to meet with any of the Army's emissaries. To Hoover, the gathering represented not a plea for help but, rather, a sign that potential revolution was on the horizon. Nothing could have been further from reality. By July 1932, after two months in Wash-ington, the Bonus Army was becoming desperate for help. Hoover, however, was intransigent; a "siege mentality" now overcame the president as he secluded himself in his fortress, the White House, with the

Potomac serving as his "moat" of protection. After a group of veterans who had been staying in abandoned Washington apartments scuffled with police (who many claim were sympathetic to the veterans' plight), Hoover called on federal troops led by Army Chief of Staff Douglas MacArthur and 3rd Cavalry Com-mander George Patton to drive the veterans out. The troops attacked the veterans' Anacostia encampment, razed their tents and shacks, and dispersed with rather brutal force the "protestors." In the process, more than one hundred veterans were wounded, and one infant was killed.

News that impoverished veterans and their fami-lies had been attacked in the nation's capital intensi-fied an already growing anti-Hoover sentiment. Those who suspected that Hoover never cared in the first place about the plight of the poor and dispos-sessed were now convinced that Hoover was a cal-lous, paranoid man, willing to use force to suppress cries for help. His days in the White House were numbered.

During the years 1921-29 relatively little was expected of the president as an individual. The modern political economy was, after all, a complex impersonal system, not the product of a particular administration, and it appeared to operate on its own momentum. But when the thoroughly national system broke down, only the national government had the scope and authority to repair it. Because the executive branch dominated the national government, people naturally looked there for help. However, only a handful of past presidents infused the Oval Office with the energy and personality essential for its sustained vitality and preeminence within the federal structure. Consequently, throughout much of the nation's history, Congress actually dominated the national government because few presidents possessed either the willingness or the ideological inclination, or personal requisites, to assert executive authority and power. That was definitely true for both Warren G. Harding and Calvin Coolidge. Herbert Hoover certainly had the academic background to be an effective president, but he lacked both the personality and the willingness to use the full power of his office to address the crisis. The longer the depression, the more the American people turned to Hoover, not to Congress, to lead them out of the wilderness. Hoover was judged by new, demanding standards, and because he failed to deliver the people from the crisis, the popular verdict condemned him. By 1932 millions who had no other place to turn were blaming Hoover in a bitter, personal way for their troubles. A humane man with great administrative skills, Hoover lacked the flexibility, political instincts, and inspirational leadership required by the ordeal. Millions of Americans wanted desperately to believe that a brave new leader with a magic touch might still transform the toad of depression into a dazzling prince of prosperity. Thus, though knowing very little about their new "prince," the American electorate turned completely against the Republicans and their president in the 1932 election. In that year, the Republicans were voted out of office after having dominated national politics (excepting Woodrow Wilson's two terms) for 36 years. Hoover received only 39.6 per-

FRANKLIN DELANO ROOSEVELT

cent of the popular vote and just 59 (of 531) electoral votes. FDR and the Democrats won a resounding, landslide victory. When he left the presidency in 1933, Hoover was a bewildered man, reviled by the people for what they took to be his indifference to suffering and his ineptitude in dealing with the economy's collapse. FDR's overwhelming victory, however, should not be viewed as a mandate for him or his "New Deal." Americans were desperate for hope and change and were simply willing to give the man with a "magic" name a chance, and if he proved to be as ineffective as his predecessor, then four years from now, they would turn to someone else as the hopeful "messiah."

THE LORD OF THE MANOR: FDR

It is hard to believe today that Franklin Delano Roosevelt was a man of mystery to many Americans in 1932. Though no doubt name recognition helped his credibility—he was the distant cousin of Theodore Roosevelt, a strong leader and exceptional president—few Americans, outside of his native New

York, knew much about his background and experience. FDR was born in 1882 into a patrician Anglo-Dutch family whose pedigree on both sides dated back to the colonial period. By the time of his birth, the Hyde Park manor where he was raised had been in the family for over 200 years. In short, FDR grew up among people who were convinced of their superiority in matters of ancestry, intelligence, and leadership. His education at Groton, Harvard College, and Columbia Law School was typical of the path followed by the sons of America's blue-blood elite. Though wealthy, the Roosevelt clan's holdings paled in comparison with that of some of their friends and neighbors, such as the Rockefellers, Carnegies, and Harrimans, whose fortunes ranged between $50 and $100 million or more. Interestingly, the Roosevelts disdained the nouveau riche parvenus, which many of the industrial elite were. Particularly galling to the older elite like the Roosevelts was the new elite's vulgar displays of wealth, their lack of taste and etiquette, their indifference to the natural environment, and their hostility toward those less fortunate than themselves. In short, the behavior and attitudes of the new-wealth industrial capitalists lacked that most impor-

tant ingredient of quality rearing: a sense of noblesse oblige. In FDR's view, his cousin, Theodore, was the embodiment of this virtue and thus worshipped him and wanted to emulate his political career. Thus, in 1907, FDR began his ascent, following almost verbatim in the tracks of his beloved "Uncle Teddy." Like TR, FDR envisioned first a seat in the New York State Assembly, then he would be appointed assistant secretary of the navy, and then he would become governor of New York, vice-president of the United States, and then president of the Republic. Incredibly, this is almost exactly what happened (except that FDR became a state senator rather than an assemblyman, and he lost his 1920 bid for the vice presidency).

The governorship of New York and the presidency might have eluded him had he not been transformed by personal calamity. In 1921, at the age of 39, FDR was stricken by one of the most deadly afflictions of the time, polio, which luckily did not kill him but instead took away the use of his legs. Before becoming paralyzed, FDR's career, both professionally (the practice of law) and politically, was not that outstanding. He owed his political ascent

First Lady Eleanor Roosevelt played an active role in her husband's administration. She became a prominent figure in high-level decision making. This was a sharp change from the roles of previous First Ladies. Eleanor had an unwavering commitment to social justice. She and Franklin had six children, however, she eventually found time for her own political career. She became the eyes and ears for her wheelchair-bound husband and traveled extensively, touring the depression-scarred nation.

more to his famous name than to actual acumen or hard work. He was charming, gregarious, and popular among associates in the New York Democratic Party. He was quite the bon vivant, a playboy in many ways, who devoted more time and energy to socializing and sailing, partying and, unfortunately, womanizing, than he did developing a devotion to career and family. However, after his illness, FDR spent the next two years bedridden, and while confined to his bed, he seemed to experience an Ignatian revelation, a reformation of character and spirit, a desire to eschew his past life and forge a new one with a determination and seriousness of purpose conspicuously absent during his earlier years. He developed a sense of humility and compassion for those suffering misfortune that would later enable him to reach out to the millions caught in the Great Depression. FDR's physical debilitation also transformed his relationship with his wife, Eleanor, with whom he shared a testy and increasingly loveless marriage. Eleanor's dedication to nursing FDR back to health forged a new bond between them. More conscious of his dependence on others, FDR now welcomed his wife as a partner in his career. Eleanor soon displayed a talent for political organization and public speaking, a gift that surprised those who knew her only as a shy, awkward woman. She would become an active, eloquent First Lady, her husband's trusted ally and political confidant, and a key player in the formation of American liberalism. Indeed, many regard her as this nation's greatest First Lady.

Roosevelt Liberalism

During his four years as governor of New York, FDR initiated various reform programs, many of which reflected his attachment and homage to progressivism. Other programs, however, seemed to embody a new reform impulse called liberalism, which called for government intervention in economic matters while maintaining libertarian views on questions of personal behavior. As the 1932 election approached, FDR appeared to be increasingly gravitating toward this new ideology. By the time of his nomination, FDR seemed wholly committed to implementing this new ethos after his election. In a rousing call to ac-

Speaking from his campaign train in 1932, FDR conveyed his message of optimism to a weary nation.

tion, the future president told his supporters in his acceptance speech at the Chicago Democratic convention, "Ours must be the party of liberal thought, of planned action, of enlightened international outlook, and of the greatest good for the greatest number of citizens." He promised "a new deal for the American people."

In his campaign, however, FDR did not always emphasize this call to activism. Always searching for a middle ground between conservatism and liberalism, FDR, at least during the hustings, appeared more of a moderate than a liberal. He was too shrewd of a politician to embrace an ideology that most Americans either did not understand or were, at best, uncertain of. Moreover, within his own party, the conservatives, especially those from the South, still wielded significant power, and the majority of them

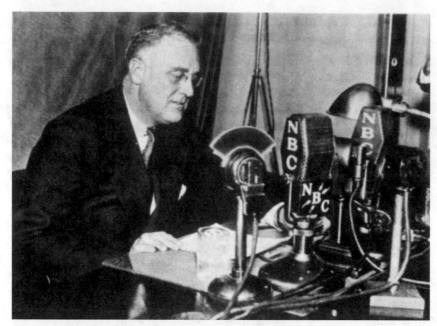

Roosevelt used the radio to reassure the American people.

were not all disposed toward liberalism. FDR thus sometimes spoke of using the powers of the federal government to stabilize the economy but in the same breath he reassured the conservatives that he was at heart a non-interventionist who had no intention of destroying all that was "sacred" in American life: the preservation of rugged individualism, which was code for maintaining adherence to the principles of laissez faire and the conservative ethos. Though FDR started his presidency as a "moderate conservative," as will be seen later in the chapter, as the New Deal evolved and became more popular and defined, FDR moved both himself and his agenda to the left. By the time of his 1936 reelection, the New Deal no longer reflected its initial conservative restraints. By that time, the influence and ideas of the liberal coalition in his cabinet had prevailed, and thus the New Deal would become the progressive reform foundation upon which subsequent Democratic presidents, most notably Lyndon Johnson, would attempt to build the most ambitious liberal edifice: The Great Society.

In point of fact, FDR made only two outright promises during the campaign: to repeal Prohibition and to balance the budget. Thus, the nation had to wait until March 4, 1933—the day FDR was sworn in as president—to learn what the New Deal would bring.

"President Roosevelt"

The reversal in presidential character and personality between Hoover and FDR could not have been more striking. Hoover, one associate remarked, "didn't like the human element." FDR reveled in it. Not only did he mix easily with all kinds of people, but he also made them feel that intuitively he sympathized with them. Hoover, taking no one's counsel, thought he knew what the nation wanted. Unlike Hoover, FDR welcomed the challenge of selling his programs to a demoralized nation. A master of popular phrasing, simple analogies, and, most important, the media, especially the radio, FDR had a strong, warm voice that reached into millions of American homes through his famous "fireside chats," which began on the second Sunday after his inauguration, were bits of genius in the use of a mass medium. Whereas Hoover had behaved like a distant autocrat, upbraiding the American people for their lack of fortitude, FDR projected the image of a kindly grandfather, gathering his children around him to read them a soothing bedtime story called the New Deal. He always spoke in a plain, friendly, reassuring voice that went far to calm the fears and anxieties of the forlorn and discouraged. In his first chat, he explained the banking crisis in simple terms but without condescension. "I want to take a few min-

Harold Ickes, was a serious-minded man with a reputation for absolute incorruptibility. Reporters dubbed him "Honest Harold."

visers. For secretary of the treasury, FDR selected his close friend and Hyde Park neighbor, Henry Morgenthau, whose conscientiousness and loyalty made him indispensable to the president. For secretary of agriculture, FDR appointed Henry Wallace, the son of Harding's secretary of agriculture, whose broad liberal vision compensated for his occasional inattention to practical matters. Another liberal Republican, Harold Ickes, became secretary of the interior and watched over his domain with a fierce jealousy and a scrupulous honesty. From his New York administration, FDR brought both the first woman to hold a cabinet post, Frances Perkins, to become secretary of labor, and the tough, dedicated administrator of relief, Harry Hopkins. All of these individuals served to the end of FDR's presidency.

The administration also drew people who had never before influenced government policy: an obscure Montana professor named M.L. Wilson with a proposal for limiting agricultural production; Raymond Moley, Rexford G. Tugwell, and Adolf

utes to talk with the people of the United States about banking," he began. An estimated 20 million Americans listened. To hear the president speak warmly and conversationally—as though he were actually there in the living room—was riveting. An estimated 50,000 Americans wrote letters to FDR within days of his inaugural address. Millions more, many of them barely literate, would write to him and Eleanor over the next few years, thanking them for all they had done, or simply writing to them to air their troubles. Americans, regardless of party affiliation, began to hang portraits of FDR in their homes, often next to a picture of Jesus or the Madonna. Where Hoover cast somber eyes downward, the tilt of FDR's chin and the cocky angle of his cigarette holder invariable gave the sense of a man looking upward; an individual filled with confidence and optimism, which his perpetual public smile radiated.

Urging "bold experimentation" for a devastated land, FDR attracted a swarm of newcomers to Washington, a curiously mixed but effective group of ad-

Harry Hopkins was the head of FERA, the Federal Emergency Relief Administration. He was a longtime Roosevelt colleague. He became so closely associated with Roosevelt and the New Deal that reporters called him the assistant president. In his first two hours in office, Harry Hopkins distributed $5 million of relief.

Secretary of Labor Frances Perkins was the first woman cabinet member. She was one of several women appointed by FDR to posts previously held only by men.

Berle of Columbia University, the "brains trust" of FDR's 1932 campaign, with ambitions to improve the economy's organization; social workers with plans to aid the unemployed, disabled, and the aged; and many more. Together, this polyglot of human intelligence, vision, and a zeal for change composed the "New Dealers." During FDR's long tenure this term became part of the nation's everyday language—used with affection by some with hatred by others to express their strong feelings about FDR and his administration.

Behind FDR's easy public style and gracious private manner lay a keen, calculating politically savvy mind that always sought to direct—control—people and events. Indeed, FDR was never the benign father figure he made himself out to be. Behind closed doors, he was arrogant, temperamental, and often vituperative beyond description when dealing with individuals who dared question or criticize his ideas or policies. Always looking to expand the power of

the presidency, as well as the Democratic Party, FDR often used the New Deal for those ends rather than for the nation's welfare. His public image was skillfully crafted. Compliant, if not intimidated, news photographers agreed not to show him in a wheelchair or struggling with the leg braces and cane he used to take even small steps. For his part, FDR often sought to hide the true purpose of much New Deal legislation behind the façade and rhetoric of "for the good of the people." Such manipulation and media control worked. Policy failures rarely seemed to adversely affect his appeal.

The din of demands around his powerful office never ruffled him. Moreover, reflecting his progressive background, FDR brought to office a firm faith in the principles of his "Uncle Teddy's" New Nationalism: He wanted business to organize, industry by industry; and agriculture, commodity by commodity. He believed that an efficient labor, with rights protected by the federal government, not forced by

Banks closed during the depression. One of FDR's first moves as president was to close all of the banks, allowing only those that were solvent to reopen.

unions, and private financial institutions working with industry and agriculture could restore prosperity. The government had only to assist them in regaining their strength and finding their proper places in the system. FDR would experiment—but within these boundaries. Not surprisingly, the new president selected equally orthodox or conservative men for the crucial administrative posts of the early New Deal: Hugh Johnson and Donald Richberg in business affairs, George Peek and Chester Davis in agriculture, and Jesse Jones for the RFC, and Lewis Douglas for the Bureau of the Budget. All of these individuals were known conservatives; indeed, some of them, like Jones from Texas, notoriously so. FDR never wanted to appear to be too far left, and thus with men like Jones in his cabinet, he was able to deflect much criticism from the right, which often accused him of trying to move the country toward socialism. FDR's conservative appointees' influence was more than checked by the imaginative, liberal appointees, among them Ben Cohen and Tom Corcoran, who set the long-term tone and direction of the New Deal.

To his credit, FDR used his popularity and executive power to strengthen American democracy at a time when democracy was crumbling around the world. However, during his thirteen years in the White House, he set in motion tendencies that would long plague American politics: a shift in overwhelming power to the executive branch, a steady expansion of the size and reach of federal bureaucracies, and a widening gap between political appearance and political reality and substance.

The "Hundred Days"

FDR's most pressing priority upon assuming office was to try to remedy the nation's banking system, which had collapsed by March 1933. The president responded with his fine sense of style and an instinctive moderation. By inauguration day several states already had closed their banks as accumulating panic spread from banks in the agrarian regions toward America's financial centers, principally in the cities of New York and Chicago. On March 4, 1933, the day FDR took his oath of office, the major banking houses in both those cities finally succumbed and closed as well. As a result of those doors closing, the entire system stopped functioning. FDR immediately declared a nationwide "Bank Holiday," dispatched expert teams to investigate and classify all banks as either strong, wavering, or hopeless, and started a transfusion of over a billion dollars from the RFC into the banking system. The president spoke soothing words; in less than two weeks 90 percent of the frozen deposits were again available to customers, and all over the country money came out of mattresses to fill the banks. It was an exemplary performance in the service of a free-enterprise system, and Wall Street joined Main Street in cheering the president. "In one week," the journalist Walter Lippmann declared, "the nation, which had lost confidence in everything and everybody, has regained confidence in the government and itself."

Only after the financial crisis eased did FDR turn to the structural reform of banking. A second Glass-Steagall Act (1933) separated commercial banking from investment banking. It also created the Federal Deposit Insurance Corporation (FDIC), which assured depositors that the government would guarantee up to $5,000 of their savings. The Securities Act (1933) and the Securities Exchange Act (1934) imposed long overdue regulation on the New York Stock Exchange, both by reining in buying on the margin (and other speculative practices) and by establishing the Securities and Exchange Commission to oversee the stock market's daily operation and enforce the new regulations and laws, as well as authority to investigate improprieties and punish the violators with fines, loss of licenses, and imprisonment if the infraction was especially egregious. FDR wanted to ensure Americans that from this point on the market would never "crash" again because of the activities of nefarious, greedy speculators.

FDR's treatment for the banking emergency and subsequent policies to regulate the stock market revealed the broad strategy of the New Deal's first months—"The Hundred Days." Among the many popular prescriptions for halting an apparently endless economic decline, none appealed more to the president's spirit than a nationwide surge of activity that headed upward instead of downward. Mobilize confidence, synchronize energy, and prosperity would return because throughout the land people would suddenly behave as if it *were* returning. To a president who told Americans "that the only thing we have to fear is fear itself," that kind of grandiose bootstraps operation made perfect sense. As Roosevelt took office, he called Congress into special session, plied it with proposals, and during a whirlwind hundred days, guided through fifteen major laws, the greatest outburst of far-reaching legislative activity

in United States history—and most of it emanating from the Oval Office, not Congress.

SAVING THE PEOPLE

Although a fiscal conservative at heart, FDR understood the need to temper financial prudence with compassion. Congress responded swiftly in 1933 to the president's request to establish the Federal Emergency Relief Administration (FERA), granting it $500 million for relief to the poor. To head it, FDR appointed a brash, young liberal reformer, Harry Hopkins, who disbursed $2 million during his first two hours on the job. True to his Roosevelt heritage, FDR was as much a conservationist as his beloved "Uncle Teddy" and was thus as interested in expanding the national park system and preserving the nation's natural beauty. The creation of the Civilian Conservation Corps (CCC) would be a logical and natural compliment to this interest. Also inspiring FDR to create the CCC was a less altruistic concern: the rise in juvenile delinquency and crime, especially in the urban areas. What better way to "nip this problem in the bud" than to transport the potential offenders hundreds if not thousands of miles (primarily to the Far West and Southwest) from temptation and put them to work in the outdoors, doing something not only constructive but aesthetically pleasing and physically and spiritually fortifying as well. Functioning like an army boot camp, the program provided full room and board, as well as a paycheck, of which they were allowed to keep only a small portion of. The lion's share of the money went into a "savings account" so when they finished their tenure (a maximum of two years) they would have something to start their new life with. A percentage of their pay was also sent home to help out there. During its existence the CCC put 2.5 million single young (primarily ages 18-25) white males (not until 1937, thanks largely to the admonishments of Eleanor Roosevelt, did FDR create a CCC for young African American men) to work planting trees, halting erosion, building national parks, putting out forest fires, and otherwise improving and protecting the environment. The CCC became

Begun in 1933, The Civilian Conservation Corps (CCC) contributed to the development of the nation's natural resources.

one of the most successful and popular of the work programs.

In the winter of 1934, FDR launched the Civil Works Administration (CWA), an ambitious work-relief program, also under Harry Hopkins's direction, that hired 4 million unemployed at $15 a week and put them to work on 400,000 small-scale infrastructure government projects. This particular work program focused on providing jobs for working class or blue-collar Americans. For middle class Americans threatened with the loss of their homes, FDR won congressional approval for the Homeowner's Loan Corporation (1933) to refinance mortgages. These direct subsidies to millions of jobless and home-owning Americans lent credibility to Roosevelt's claim that the New Deal would set the country on a new course.

The NRA and AAA

From this array of legislation, two programs formed the heart of the early New Deal. The Agricultural Adjustment Act (AAA) and the National Industrial Recovery Act (NIRA). During his first year in office, FDR was confident he could recover the economy, not from relief but through agricultural and industrial cooperation. He regarded the AAA, passed in May 1933, and the NIRA, passed in June, as the most important legislation of his Hundred Days. Both were based on the idea that curtailing production would trigger economic recovery. By creating scarcities in both agricultural and manufactured goods, FDR's economists reasoned, they could restore the balance of normal market forces. In short, FDR and his advisers believed, and to a degree, rightly so, that overproduction in both economic sectors had contributed to the depression. By artificially creating shortages, demand for goods would then exceed supply, prices would rise, and revenues from massive sales would climb. Farmers and industrialists, earning a profit once again, would increase their investment in new technology and hire more workers, and prosperity and full employment would be the final result.

The NIRA represented a continuation of Hoover-inspired government-sponsored business co-operation. Its most important provisions authorized each specialized segment of business to prepare a code of self-governance and established the National Recovery Administration to supervise the process. As director of the NRA, FDR appointed the brash, loud World War I veteran, General Hugh Johnson, an experienced public affairs man, who immediately launched a circus of a campaign to enlist all Americans behind his program. Through parades—a massive one down New York City's Fifth Avenue— public rallies—he staged an elaborate NRA celebration in Yankee Stadium— evangelical speeches, and assorted hoopla, Johnson made the Blue Eagle, the NRA's emblem of cooperation, synonymous with the New Deal itself, and he counted on public opinion to make it correlative with Americanism. Indeed, blue eagles soon sprouted everywhere—on storefronts, at factory entrances, and on company stationary— usually accompanied by the slogan "We Do Our Part." Americans everywhere joined the campaign, and morale soared.

Johnson's first task was to persuade industrialists and businessmen, large and small, to raise employee wages to a minimum of 30 to 40 cents an hour and to limit employee hours to a maximum of 30 to 40 hours a week. The intent was to reduce the quantity of goods that any factory or business could produce. Next, Johnson brought together the largest producers in every manufacturing sector and asked them to prepare codes of fair competition. In the NRA's first four months, business groups wrote over seven hundred constitutions to govern their affairs. Where one or more large firms dominated an industry, the NRA relied on them to prepare the codes; where no company controlled an industry, the NRA turned to a trade association. Although these "blue codes" varied from industry to industry, they usually included some agreement on prices, wages, and the acceptable limits of competition. The only integration among them was a common commitment to stabilization, a common freedom from antitrust prosecution, and a common dependence on the industrial groups themselves to regulate their own members. Johnson exalted the spirit of cooperation and swore at the "slackers" but never coerced businessmen into joining "the club" nor of having to adopt the "blue codes." Johnson's policy of non-coercion was backed by his boss, FDR.

Section 7a of the NIRA authorized workers to organize and bargain in their own behalf, and some labor leaders, most notably John L. Lewis of the United Mine Workers, exulted that the government was now their sponsor. "THE PRESIDENT WANTS YOU TO JOIN THE UNION!" Although the NRA did not actually encourage an independent labor movement, it provided labor with other important benefits: it fostered a national pattern of maximum hours and minimum wages, and it eliminated child labor and the sweatshop.

In the summer and fall of 1933, the NRA codes drawn up for steel, textiles, coal mining, garment manufacture, rubber, and other industries seemed to be working. The economy picked up, and people began to hope that an end to the depression was near. However, in the winter and spring of 1934, economic indicators plunged downward once again, and manufacturers, blaming the NRA, began to evade the provisions of the codes. Also contributing to the growing anti-NRA sentiment was the fact that from the program's beginning, small businesses felt left out of

The government's purpose for creating the NRA, to benefit both factory owner and workers, is depicted in this 1933 cartoon.

the grand plan and discriminated against because of their size. Moreover, small businesses could not adopt the minimum wage guarantees nor any of the other codes because they simply could not afford to do so. Their profit margins were already slight, and to have to pay a minimum wage to workers and other benefits, while simultaneously cutting back on production, was something they could not do without going out of business. Thus, by 1934, many small businessmen cried out against the NRA, asserting that it violated free enterprise and that the New Dealers responsible for it were conspiring to eliminate the small businessman altogether. In short, small businessmen believed that the real intent of the NRA was to consolidate industrial production, ensuring that in the future only a handful of major producers would supply the nation's manufactured goods. Though such was not the planned intent of the program, there was nonetheless sentiment in the White House among some New Dealers that the industrial sector would be better off if there was less "competition."

Government committees set up to enforce the codes were powerless to punish violators. By the fall of 1934, it was clear that the NRA had failed. When the Supreme Court declared the NRA codes uncon-stitutional in May 1935, FDR allowed the agency to die. By then, New Dealers had given up on the idea that limiting production in the industrial sector would promote recovery.

The other cornerstone of the early New Deal was the May 1933 Agricultural Adjustment Act. The fundamental objective of this program was to increase farm income by artificially creating shortages. By decreasing supply and increasing demand, it was hoped that farm income would rise to a level of "parity," or equality, with the farmers' purchasing power just before World War I, the supposed "golden years" of farm production and income. The act was a veritable grab bag of alternatives. It included provisions from almost every farm program proposed in the twentieth century: marketing agreements, commodity loans, export subsidies, government purchases, and—reminiscent of William Jennings Bryan—even currency inflation. To these familiar devices, the government added the New Deal favorite of production restrictions, aimed at reducing agricultural surpluses at the source. During its first months the Agricultural Adjustment Administration (the AAA) used production cutbacks as a way of getting emergency cash relief to the countryside. In midseason farmers

Many black tenant farmers and sharecropprs were evicted from the land and pushed deeper into poverty.

AAA made no provisions for the countless sharecroppers, tenant farmers, and farm laborers who would be thrown out of work by acreage reduction. In the South, the victims were disproportionately black. A Georgia sharecropper wrote Harry Hopkins of his misery: "I have Bin farming all my life But the man I live with Has Turned me loose taking my mule [and] all my feed. . . .I can't get a Job so Some one said Rite you."

The AAA programs also proved inadequate to the plight of Great Plains farmers whose economic problems had been compounded by Mother Nature. Just as the depression rolled in, the rain stopped falling on the plains. The land, stripped of its native grasses by decades of excessive cultivation, dried up and turned to dust. And then the dust began to blow, sometimes traveling 1,000 miles across open prairie. Dust became a fixed feature of daily life on the plains, which soon became known as the "Dust Bowl." The dust covered furniture, floors, and stoves, as well as penetrating people's hair and lungs. The worst dust storm occurred on April 14, 1935, when a great mass of dust, moving at speeds of 45 to 70 miles an hour, roared through Colorado, Kansas, and Oklahoma, blackening the sky, suffocating cattle, and dumping thousands of tons of topsoil and red clay on homes and streets. Despite government assistance via the Soil Conservation Service, which helped instruct Plains farmers with new cultivation techniques and subsidies, hundreds of thousands of dispossessed, desperate Plains farmers left the region, primarily migrating to California via the now famous Route 66.

were paid to plow under their crops and slaughter livestock, a bitter expedient with so much hunger in the nation. After 1933 the AAA expected each farmer growing a particular crop to reduce production by a nationally fixed percentage.

From the moment it was promulgated, the act was guaranteed to arouse farmer opposition and thus destined to fail. Many farmers, proud of their work ethic, did not readily accept the idea that they were to be paid more money for working less land and husbanding fewer livestock. Most egregiously, the

These sharecroppers are leaving their farm in Missouri after being evicted.

A young mother from Oklahoma sits in a California migrant camp in this 1937 photo.

This exodus of humanity was the most significant and largest internal movement of citizens in the history of the nation. This "Okie" migration (They were called that because most, but not all, of these migrants came from Oklahoma.) made famous in John Steinbeck's *The Grapes of Wrath,* disturbed many Americans, for whom the plight of these once-sturdy yeomen became a symbol of how much had gone wrong with the American dream.

In 1936 the Supreme Court, as it did a year earlier with the NRA, declared the AAA unconstitutional because its mandated limits on farm production were considered an illegal restraint of trade. Thus, in a matter of one year's time, the two most important programs of the New Deal were shot down by the judicial branch. As will be seen later in this chapter, FDR did not take these defeats lightly. Indeed, he took them as personal affronts to both his power and agenda to uplift the nation. He was so angry at the Court—"those nine old men" as he referred to the justices—that he decided it needed to be "reformed." But he was too shrewd of a politician to challenge the Court before being reelected. Once that was accomplished, he went full-steam ahead with his plan to "reform" the judicial branch of the federal government.

The use of subsidies, begun by the AAA, did eventually bring stability and prosperity to agriculture. But the costs were high. Agriculture became the most heavily subsidized sector of the nation's economy, and the Department of Agriculture grew into one of the government's largest bureaucracies. Rural poor, black and white, never received a fair share of federal benefits. Beginning in the 1940s and 1950s, they would be forced off the land and into the cities of the North and West.

REBUILDING THE NATION

In addition to establishing the NRA, the NIRA also launched the Public Works Administration (PWA). The PWA was given a $3.3 billion budget to sponsor internal improvements that would both refurbish and expand with new construction the nation's infrastructure of roads, bridges, sewage systems, hospitals, airports, and schools. The labor needed for these projects would shrink the relief rolls and reduce unemployment, especially among the industrial working class. The projects themselves could be justified in terms that conservatives approved: economic investment rather than short-term relief.

The PWA authorized the building of three major Western dams—The Grand Coulee, Boulder, and Bonneville—that opened up large stretches of Arizona, California, and Washington to industrial and agricultural development. It funded the construction of the Triborough Bridge in New York City and the 100-mile causeway linking Florida to Key West. It also appropriated money for the construction of thousands of new schools and public libraries between 1933 and 1939.

The Tennessee Valley Authority

If there was one piece of legislation passed during the First New Deal that represented a strategy for economic recovery different from the one promoted by the NRA it was the Tennessee Valley Authority Act of 1933. Simply called the TVA, this particular approach called for the government—rather than private corporations—to directly foster economic development throughout the vast watershed area of the South known as the Tennessee Valley. This vast river basin winds through parts of six southern states and in the areas where these rivers flowed poverty was widespread because of the inhabitants' inability to control these rivers, especially during the rainy season. Flooding was endemic, and thus the towns and farms along the rivers were destroyed every year by the surging rivers. Thus the primary objective of the TVA was to control the flooding of the Tennessee River while simultaneously harnessing its water power to generate electricity, develop local industry (such as fertilizer production), improve river transportation, and, in the process, ease the poverty and isolation of the region's inhabitants. In some respects the TVA's mandate resembled that of the PWA, but the TVA had greater authority over economic development, which reflected the influence of New Dealers such as Rexford G. Tugwell, who were committed to statism: the creation of government-planned and government-operated enterprises. Although advisers such as Tugwell never publicly admitted so, they were drawn to certain socialist ideas such as public ownership of key industries and utilities.

The TVA's accomplishments were impressive. The program built, completed, or improved more than twenty dams, including the massive Wheeler Dam near Muscle Shoals in Alabama. Hydroelectric generators were also constructed at many of the dam sites, providing the region's population with electricity for the first time. Indeed, the TVA became the nation's largest producer of electricity, and the low rates it provided consumers forced private utility companies to reduce their rates as well. The TVA also constructed waterways to bypass unnavigable stretches of the river, reduced flooding, and taught farmers how to prevent soil erosion and use fertilizers. In short, the project, with all of its different permutations, brought the Tennessee River Valley and its inhabitants into the twentieth century with a massive, government-planned and operated rural reclamation project.

Although the TVA was one of the New Deal's most touted successes and boldest experiments in government planning (as well as coming dangerously close to socialism), it generated little enthusiasm for more ambitious programs in national planning. Only a handful of New Dealers—and most of them equivocated when pressed on the issue—wanted FDR to nationalize established industries. Though it had never been done before, the TVA made it acceptable for the government to intervene to bring prosperity to an impoverished region. However, neither FDR, the majority of Congress, or the American people favored any further extension of governmental power that such programs would necessitate. Contrary to what many conservative critics of the era asserted, and even after the depression was over, neither FDR or the New Deal embraced the idea of the federal government as a substitute for private enterprise. Nonetheless, when FDR wanted to sum up his proudest domestic achievement as president, he often cited the TVA. Today, delegates at a Democratic National Democratic Convention would snicker in baffled disbelief if a speaker saluted FDR for his greatest accomplishment: rural electrification. But the symbolic significance of the TVA and similar projects can hardly be exaggerated. They were thought of as not mere public utility companies but as the pilot projects of a new and "futuristic" way of life. FDR, many of his allies and supporters, believed the TVA provided a model for a new kind of

PWA workers began construction of Boulder Dam in 1933. The Public Works Administration's projects created new jobs for skilled workers.

technological civilization superior to that of the early industrial era. In 1937, Baker Brownell, a professor at Northwestern University, wrote that the TVA was "building more than a dam. It is building a civilization. The visitor here [at Norris Dam] is looking into the next century."

Power-generating dams were to New Deal state capitalists what steel mills were to communists and what stock exchanges were to the neoliberal free-marketeers of the late twentieth century—not just institutions but icons. Here is a song from *Power,* a 1937 pro-New Deal play: "All up and down the valley/They heard the great alarm;/The government means business/Its working like a charm/Oh, see them boys a-comin'/Their government they trust/Just hear their hammers ringin'/They'll build that dam or bust."

The region that underwent the most dramatic transformation thanks to New Deal-state-capitalist development projects was the West. There, dam construction and other infrastructure ventures brought agrarian societies, which had been bypassed by the age of steam power, directly into the second industrial era of electricity and internal combustion engines in tractors, trucks, and cars. Between 1933 and 1939, per capital payments for public works

projects, welfare, and federal loans in the Rocky Mountain and Pacific Coast states outstripped those of any other region. When FDR assumed office, the United States, in many ways, was still two countries—an industrialized country, the Northeast, surrounded by a backward agrarian country, the Southern/Western periphery. As already seen, FDR's task in industrialized America was to get the factories going again by putting money into the pockets of the industrial working class, among other initiatives. But in the South and West, there were hardly any factories and only a small urban, industrial working class. These regions had more in common with the Northeast of the 1830s, before it industrialized, than with the Northeast of a hundred years later. FDR had to revive existing industries in the Northeast and build them from nothing in the West and the South.

Central to Western development and inspired by the success of the TVA was the program of dam building that became one of the New Deal's most enduring legacies, especially in the West. For decades Western land and agricultural capitalist developers wanted to dam the region's major rivers to provide water and electricity for urban and agricultural development. The costs, however, were prohibitive, even to the wealthiest entrepreneurs, until the New

Deal offered to help with federal dollars. Via the dispensing of funds through the Bureau of Reclamation, a previously underutilized federal agency, the bureau oversaw the building of the Boulder Dam (later renamed Hoover Dam), which brought drinking water for southern California, irrigation water for California's Imperial Valley, which eventually became the fruit and vegetable "basket" of the nation, and electricity for Los Angeles and southern Arizona. The greatest construction project of all was the Grand Coulee Dam on the Columbia River in Washington, which created a 150-mile long lake. Together with the Bonneville Dam (also on the Columbia), the Grand Coulee gave the Pacific Northwest the cheapest electricity in the nation and created the potential for significant economic and population growth. The Bonneville and Grand Coulee Dams made the state of Washington the largest per capita recipient of New Deal funds. The benefits of this dam building program, in terms of economic development and population growth, did not come to fruition until the post-World War II years. Also, dam building in the West was not seen as a threat to established capitalist businesses because the government did not actually build the dams itself (as it did under the TVA) but rather hired private contractors to do the work, who became rich in the process. In short, Western dam construction was meant to aid primarily agricultural development—agribusiness as it turned out—not the poor, and it was intended to aid private enterprise, not bypass it.

It must be remembered that unlike post-World War II liberals, FDR and his contemporaries were less concerned with the redistribution of income from one group to another than with using the new technology and organizational techniques to develop the nation's productive human and natural resources. Instead of rejecting modern industry (as many agrarians did) or modern corporations (as socialists did), New Deal liberals, true to their Progressive heritage, wanted to regulate industrial capitalism to the degree that they could guide it to promote democratic social and political goals. Their main objective was geographic decentralization of both productive industry and people. Industry, concentrated in the Northeastern manufacturing belt, should be dispersed throughout the country. Population, too, should be relocated, especially from the crowded urban areas of the Northeast to the South and West. The working classes of that region, living in crowded, unsanitary conditions, should be encouraged to move to low-density suburbs and village-like "garden cities." The decentralization of industry and population would tend to promote both equality among regions and classes in the United States. The nation would no longer be a collection of resource-producing regions functioning as colonies of a single industrial area, the Northeast. Instead, the country would become a federation of balanced regions, each with a mix of manufacturing and agriculture. As the population left the crowded Northeastern industrial cities for the small, spacious, planned communities in the South and West, the wages of the urban workers who remained would rise. New Dealers believed that the key to accomplishing that vision was to implement a comprehensive infrastructure projects program, utilizing the technologies of the second industrial revolution: electricity (hydroelectric dam networks) and the internal combustion engine (highways for cars and trucks). New Deal liberals believed their "planning policies represented a "third way" between laissez faire capitalism and state socialism. While they experimented with production quotas in certain economic sectors like agriculture and to a lesser degree in industry, one could not equate their policies with Soviet-style economic planning. By planning, the New Dealers meant a flexible and eclectic combination of zoning, public works, and the providing of public credit that would attract private enterprises to develop certain regions of the country, particularly the South and the West, in a desired direction. Though this conception began with programs like the TVA, its full realization did not occur until after World War II and, more precisely, not until the 1970s and 1980s.

POPULIST OPPOSITION TO THE NEW DEAL

In their desire to rally popular support for such New Deal programs as the NRA, FDR and the New Deal-

Louisiana Senator Huey Long founded the Share Our Wealth Society. The society advocated a redistribution of wealth to lessen the gap between the rich and poor in America.

ers unleashed new political forces that they would have to reckon with by 1935. Though opposition to the New Deal emerged from both the Right and the Left, initially it was a group of left-leaning dissidents who defied easy ideological classification, who posed the greatest threat to FDR and the New Dealers. The great fanfare created to boost popular support for key programs, such as the NRA, raised the people's expectations that recovery was on its way. Perhaps more important, it freed them from their torpor; the people now believed that if they came together en masse (which the NRA encouraged), they could effect significant changes, or at the very least their clamors for reform would be heard, and FDR and his Brains Trust would implement the desired policies. This politicized electorate also made it clear to the New Dealers that if they could not achieve economic recovery, in the name of *all* the people, then the people would turn to others who could. Early popular criticism of the New Deal was not directed at FDR but at his advisers and at the Democratic Congress. Still, the president worried that the breadth and depth of the insurgency threatened his political survival. However, once FDR overcame his initial trepidation, his political instincts and shrewdness "kicked in," and he was able to defeat these poten-

tial usurpers by embracing or "co-opting" many of their ideas. In the end, FDR had little to fear from these individuals, for the people, though attracted to these men's programs, were not going to forsake the man who already had delivered to them so much more than anyone in history had to date.

Some critics were disturbed not only by the New Deal's failure to bring recovery but also by what they perceived as the conservative orientation of many early New Deal programs. Banking reforms, the AAA, and the NRA, they asserted, all favored large economic interests, an assessment that was not unfounded or that inaccurate. In their opinion, FDR had failed in his promise to uplift the ordinary people, the "forgotten Americans," whom they claimed was their principal concern.

The Rise of the Demagogues: Huey Long and Father Charles Coughlin

Of the above individuals, the most alarming to the Roosevelt administration was the "Kingfisher," Senator Huey P. Long of Louisiana. Long had risen to power in his home state by engaging in demagoguery: that is, by exploiting the fears, prejudices, and general feelings of alienation and hostility of middle and lower class Louisianans toward the conservative political oligarchy that controlled the state. This powerful coterie of bankers, oilmen, sugar planters, and utility company owners, primarily located in the southern part of the state, ruled Louisiana with an iron grip. Long's strident attacks on these interests won him the governorship in 1928, and from that office, he launched an all-out war on these individuals and their various enterprises. Long's purge of these men was so thorough and forceful that they were left with virtually no political power whatever. Many claimed that Huey had become a dictator, which in effect, he had. Long, however, remained popular with the Louisiana electorate, in part because of his flamboyant, charismatic personality and captivating oratory, and in part because he "delivered the goods." He built roads, schools, and hospitals; revised the tax codes, distributed free textbooks; and lowered utility rates. To pay for his progressive programs, which he boasted were for the benefit of the common people, Long taxed wealthy Louisianans into the "poor house." Barred by law from succeeding himself as governor, Long ran in 1930 for a seat in the United States Senate and won easily. Huey was now ready to take his ideas, first introduced in Louisiana, to Washington and to the American people in general.

Long supported FDR for president in 1932, but within six months of the president's inauguration, Long broke with Roosevelt, believing that FDR had broken his promise to deliver the American people from the plutocracy's continued abuse. Long lampooned the rich as "pigs swilling in the trough of luxury." In attacks on New Deal programs, he alleged that "not a single dime of concentrated, bloated, pompous wealth, massed in the hands of a few people has been raked down to relieve the masses." Long, like FDR, mastered the use of the radio, which contributed most directly to his growing national popularity. But demagogic rhetoric would not be enough to get people to turn against FDR and the New Deal; he needed to offer them something significantly more.

As an alternative to the New Deal, he advocated something he had introduced as governor: taxing the wealthy to force a redistribution of wealth "down to

the people." He named his program the Share-Our-Wealth Plan. The government, he claimed could end the depression easily by using the tax system to confiscate the surplus riches of the wealthiest men and women in the nation and distribute these surpluses to the rest of the population. That would, he claimed, allow the government to guarantee every family a minimum "homestead" of $5,000 and an annual income of $2,500. Long's mastery of the radio helped to create a membership in his Share-Our-Wealth Clubs of 10 million Americans, or so the senator claimed. Regardless of the accuracy of the number, Long's idea was popular with millions of unemployed, suffering, and disillusioned Americans, searching for a scapegoat for their woes. A majority of the clubs' rank and file came from middle-class people: independent proprietors who operated their own farms, businesses, and shops; self-employed doctors and lawyers; and plumbers, carpenters, electricians, and other contractors. Many members of these groups perceived the apparent big business favoritism of the New Deal programs as a direct threat to their future economic and social well-being. Substantial numbers of Share-Our-Wealth Club supporters also came from highly-skilled and white collar sections of the working class—railroad workers, bricklayers, postal workers, teachers, department store sales clerks, and others who aspired to a middle class income and status. By 1935 FDR considered Long as the most likely challenger to his presidential reelection bid. Indeed, in the spring of 1935, a poll by the Democratic National Committee disclosed that Long's popularity might be enough to attract more than 10 percent of the vote if he ran as a third-party candidate, enough to tip a close election to the Republicans. But before that campaign began, Long was assassinated. In an act of revenge for his wronged father-in-law by the Long machine, a young physician, Carl Weiss, shot Huey on the night of September 8, 1935 as the "Kingfisher" stood chatting with aides outside the Capitol in Baton Rouge. Though not instantly killed by Weiss' one shot, which lodged under Huey's ribs, two days later, largely as a result of poor surgery, the "Kingfisher" died.

Meanwhile in the Midwest, Father Charles Coughlin, the "radio priest," delivered a message similar to Long's. At first a warm supporter of the president and the New Deal, which he called "Christ's Deal," by 1934, Coughlin had become a harsh critic. In his weekly sermons broadcast nationally from his home parish in Royal Oak, Michigan, Coughlin proposed a series of monetary reforms—remonetization of silver, issuing of greenbacks, and nationalization of the banking system—that he insisted would restore prosperity and ensure economic justice. Coughlin's sermons were listened to by an estimated 30 to 40 million Americans. By late 1934, Coughlin had become disheartened by what he claimed was FDR's failure to deal harshly with the "money powers," which he contended were running the New Deal. The NRA was a program to resuscitate corporate profits. Coughlin called for a strong government to set national priorities and force, if necessary, business, labor, agriculture, and even white-collar professionals to do its bidding to help recover the economy and usher in a more "just" capitalist system. In 1934 Coughlin founded the National Union of Social Justice as a precursor to a political party that would challenge the Democrats in the 1936 election. By 1935, Coughlin began moving to the right, endorsing in his "sermons" fascists like Benito Mussolini and his corporative state, as well as Il Duce's ruling by decree rather than by democratic consent, which Coughlin believed FDR should be doing as well "in the name of the people." As Coughlin's disillusionment with the New Deal intensified, his admiration for the fascists dictators grew more pronounced. Most disturbing and alarming was his increasing anti-Semitism, which permeated his radio talks. Reflecting his growing approval of Hitler and Mussolini, Coughlin claimed that Jewish bankers were master-minding a world conspiracy to suppress the toiling masses. Although Coughlin was a spellbinding speaker, he failed to build the NUSJ into a viable political entity. After the 1936 election, Coughlin, embittered, moved further and further right, denouncing both Jews and democracy with incredible vituperation. His condemnations were so extreme and outright vicious that many radio stations refused to allow him airtime. Despite his fanaticism, millions of ordinary citizens continued to believe that the "radio priest" was their savior.

Another popular figure was Francis Townsend, an elderly California physician who claimed that the way to end the depression was to give every citizen over the age of sixty $200 a month, provided they retired (thus freeing jobs for younger, unemployed Americans) and spent the money in full (which would pump needed funds into the economy). By 1935, the Townsend Plan had attracted the support of more than 5 million older men and women. While the plan itself made little progress in Congress, the idea's popularity helped build support for the Social Security system, which Congress did approve in 1935.

None of these self-styled reformers showed much skill at transforming his popularity into disciplined political parties that could compete with either of the two major parties in elections. Moreover, though all three individuals—Long, Coughlin, and Townsend—were appealing orators with large public followings and masters of the new medium of radio, their speeches or sermons were more tirades or rantings against the established order than offering realistic, viable alternatives. Though Long's taxation scheme sounded good on paper and to desperate ears, in reality, there was no way the federal government would or could implement, or Americans in general support, such a blatant violation of the sanctity of private property that such a confiscatory program of taxation represented. Coughlin's initial ideas of government protection of labor's rights was sound, but his drift to the far right with his embracing of fascism and anti-Semitism negated what legitimate message he might have had. Townsend, the "mildest" of the three dissidents, whose idea of aid to the elderly was not seen as "crackpot" or "hairbrained" or even "radical" but sound and decent, for if any group of Americans were in need and deserved some sort of federal assistance it was the nation's elderly. This was why Congress eventually enacted the Social Security Act and perhaps would not have acted as swiftly had it not been for Francis Townsend.

Members of the Roosevelt administration considered dissident movements— and the broad popular discontent they represented—a genuine threat to the president. An increasing number of advisers were warning FDR that he would have to do something dramatic to counter their strength.

THE "SECOND DEAL"

The populist insurrections of 1934-35 forced a reluctant FDR to move to the left. Though personally and ideologically hesitant to move the New Deal down that path, the people had moved that way, and being the consummate politician, FDR knew that if he hoped to be reelected, he had to shift the New Deal in that direction as well. FDR's rhetoric (in which could be heard some of the tirades of Huey Long), suddenly took on an anticorporate tone. He called for the "abolition of evil holding companies." He attacked the wealthy for their profligate and unpatriotic ways. He clamored for new programs to aid the poor and the downtrodden. In short, FDR wanted to "connect" with the people and turn them away from radical solutions and, in the process, to win reelection. Thus, in the spring of 1935, Roosevelt launched the so-called Second New Deal.

The new programs represented both a new focus and direction in New Deal policy. To help him develop programs reflecting this new direction, FDR turned to reform-minded businessmen, investment bankers, lawyers, economists, and labor leaders who embraced a new theory and thus advocated a new approach to hopefully ending the depression: underconsumptionism. Supporters of this idea believed that underconsumption, or an endemic weakness in consumer demand, had caused the Great Depression. Individual consumers simply had not had enough money during the twenties to buy what the nation's industries produced. Thus, the key to recovery was not to limit production as the First Deal had implemented but rather to increase Americans' purchasing power through a variety of government policies. These policies included government support for strong labor unions to force up wages; higher social welfare expenditures to put more money in the hands of the poor; and a significant increase in public works projects to increase the number of Americans working and thus earning and spending money. The underconsumptionists did not worry about a federal deficit that increased public works programs would create. The government could always borrow funds from private sources and, in fact, considered such an approach a crucial antidepression device. Those who received government assistance would have additional income to spend on consumer goods; and producers would profit from increases in consumer spending. In short, government borrowing would increase the money supply or "inflate" a deflated economy and eventually would put an end to the depression. This "fiscal" approach to economic downturns, which the depression in effect was, represented a reversal of traditional thinking that a government should always maintain a balanced budget. In the 1940s this new theory became known as Keynesianism, named after its originator, the British economist John Maynard

Franklin Roosevelt appointed Mary McLeod Bethune as director of the Division of Negro Affairs of the National Youth Administration in 1936.

Keynes. From 1935, the United States' economy became essentially Keynesian; that is, the government would henceforth do whatever was deemed necessary through various fiscal and monetary policies to revitalize a sluggish or "depressed" economy. Many politicians and economists rejected this new approach, believing that deficit spending would only create a debt-ridden government. FDR himself remained a fiscal conservative but was willing to give the new idea a try.

One of FDR's first actions reflecting his change in attitude toward big business was his proposal to finally break up the great utility holding companies and spoke venomously of monopolistic control of their industry. Indeed, at the time, thirteen utility companies controlled 75 percent of the nation's electric power. The Holding Company Act of 1935 was passed, but frantic lobbying by the utilities led to revisions that sharply limited its effects. A companion measure to the Holding Company Act was the Congressionally-created Rural Electrification Administration, which oversaw the bringing of electricity at reasonable rates to hundreds of thousands of rural households. This New Deal agency was especially important to the South and West, largely rural regions where few inhabitants had electrical power. Indeed, the REA along with the Western dam projects mentioned earlier were the cornerstones of Western modernization. Finally, Congress passed the Emergency Relief Appropriation Act, a $5 billion measure that dwarfed similar legislation passed during the first New Deal. FDR gave part of this sum to the PWA and CCC so those work-relief programs could continue and used another portion to create yet another work and guidance program for primarily high school and college students, the National Youth Administration (NYA), which in Texas was directed by a future president and liberal, Lyndon Baines Johnson.

FDR, however, directed most of the new relief money to a new agency, the Works Progress Administration (WPA). This new work program was headed by the irrepressible Harry Hopkins, who was now referred to as "Minister of Relief." Though much of the WPA's money and focus continued or expanded infrastructure refurbishing and new construction, significant funds were funneled into an entirely new

The Federal Art Project employed these artists to work in a New York City gallery. Many of the project's paintings and murals depicted scenes of American life during the Depression.

direction for the first time: the arts. Thanks largely to the exhortations of Eleanor Roosevelt, the WPA was largely responsible for not letting American cultural life die during the Great Depression. The WPA funded a vast program of public art, supporting the work of thousands of painters, architects, writers, playwrights, actors, and intellectuals. Beyond extending relief to struggling artists, it fostered the creation of art that reflected and spoke of and to the values, customs, and lifestyles of ordinary Americans. All across the land, WPA artists adorned public buildings with colorful, story-telling murals, usually with a theme that showed how thanks to FDR and the New Deal, people were working and happy again. Photographers also traversed the nation, capturing with their cameras the suffering of hundreds of thousands of especially rural Americans. In many ways FDR used the WPA not only as a major work-relief program but also as a means of boosting morale. FDR also used the program to ensure, by the use of various artistic mediums, that future Americans would never forget how Depression-era Americans overcame the trauma of the second most severe crisis in the Republic's history, thanks largely to FDR and his New Deal. By the time the decade of the 1930s ended, the WPA, in conjunction with an expanded RFC and the PWA, had brought about the building of 500,000 miles of road, 100,000 bridges, 100,000 public buildings, and 600 airports. The New Deal transformed the nation's urban and rural landscapes. Everywhere they turned they found concrete examples of its accomplishments.

Equally alarming to the upper classes was FDR's tax reform proposals, a program conservatives labeled as a "soak-the-rich" scheme, which, when compared to all previous taxation policies, it indeed did seem to "discriminate" against more affluent citizens. Politically, FDR's intention with his tax reform bill was to slow Huey Long's Share-Our-Wealth momentum, which it did by establishing the highest and most progressive peacetime tax rates in history. Unfortunately, as is still true today, the actual impact of these rates was limited, and many wealthy individuals found ways to escape them altogether. In retrospect, FDR's tax reform bill was put into "effect" not because he wanted to see a genuine redistribution of wealth, which he opposed, but rather for purely political reasons: he hoped to curtail the "Kingfisher's"

growing popularity by stealing "his thunder." If FDR could present to the people a more realistic and viable plan than Long, then, come 1936, the president could win back those wayward voters.

Without question, the most momentous piece of legislation to come out of the Second New Deal was the 1935 Social Security Act. From the beginning of the New Deal, important cabinet members such as Secretary of Labor, Frances Perkins, had been pressuring FDR to create a system of federally sponsored social insurance for the elderly and the unemployed. FDR had consistently opposed such a measure until now. Like with his tax reform bill, FDR was responding politically rather than with any great conviction that such assistance was the right thing to do for such individuals. Regardless of FDR's motivation, the Social Security Act laid the foundation of the modern welfare state. The act established several distinct programs. For the elderly, there were two types of assistance. Those who were presently destitute could receive up to $15 a month in federal aid. More important for the future, many Americans presently working were incorporated into a pension system, to which they and their employers would contribute by paying a payroll tax; it would provide them with an income on retirement. Pension payments would not begin until 1942, and at that time, eligible persons would receive only $10 to $85 a month.

This cartoon criticizes the Social Security Act for identifying people by their assigned social security number. The program was financed by both the employers and the employees, and the money was placed in a combined account controlled by the government. A negative criticism was that this payroll tax would take money out of the economy and reduce the amount of money in circulation.

Broad categories of workers (including domestic servants and agricultural laborers, occupations overwhelmingly dominated by African Americans and women) were excluded from the program. Nonetheless, the act was a crucial first step in building the nation's most important social "net" for the elderly.

Labor Resurgent

The emergence of a powerful trade union movement in the 1930s was one of the most important political and social developments of the decade. It occurred partly in response to government efforts to enhance the power of unions, but it was also a result of the increased militancy of American workers and their leaders. During the 1920s most workers rarely challenged their employers or demanded recognition of their unions. Moreover, shrewd employers such as Henry Ford, with their promotion of "welfare capitalism" in their industries, were able to greatly curtail the appeal of unionization among their workers. Also affecting unionization during the 1920s, especially among ethnic/immigrant workers, was the trend toward Americanization at school, at work, and in popular entertainment, which not only made unions appear unnecessary but also anti-American at a time when working class ethnic Americans wanted to "fit in" and be accepted. The Depression, however, rapidly changed working class sentiment toward both unions and labor militancy. The Depression heightened the sense of awareness and shared experience among workers as few working-class families escaped the distress and despair of the early 1930s. The increased politicization of the working class first became apparent in the 1932 election when many workers voted for FDR. The NRA helped to transform their despair into hope. As already noted, it set guidelines for wages and work hours that if implemented by employers would improve working conditions. Moreover, clause 7(a) of the NIRA granted workers the right to join unions of their choosing and bound management to recognize unions and bargain with them in good faith. As a result, millions of workers, encouraged by such government promotion and protection, joined unions in 1933 and 1934.

Initially, union members' demands were quite modest. They wanted employers to observe the provisions of the NRA codes. They wanted to be treated fairly by their foremen, and they wanted management to recognize their unions. Few employers, however, were willing to give them any say in their working conditions. Most ignored the NRA's wage and hour guidelines and even used their influence over the program's code authorities to get worker requests for wage increases and union recognition rejected. Workers appealed directly to FDR and Hugh Johnson for a redress of their grievances, but their pleas went unanswered. Workers now decided to take matters into their own hands. In 1934 they staged 2,000 strikes across the country and in virtually every industry. Most of the strikes attracted little attention and were peaceful; some, however, were not, as they escalated into violent, bloody confrontations between workers and police. Such became the situation at the Electric Auto-Lite plant in Toledo, Ohio, in May 1934 when 10,000 surrounded the place and blocked all entrances and exits until the company agreed to shut down operations and negotiate a union contract. Management refused, called out the police to "remove" the striking workers, and the inevitable occurred: for seven bloody hours a pitched battle raged between strikers and the police as the latter resorted to the use of fire hoses, tear gas, and gunfire to disperse the workers. Worker resistance, however, was more resilient than anticipated, forcing the governor to call out the National Guard, which succeeded in forcing the workers to disband but not until after more gunfire was exchanged and two workers lay dead. More violent and prolonged confrontations between police and striking workers occurred in Minneapolis and San Francisco. In the former city, from May through July 1934, National Guardsmen, police, and private security forces fought striking truckdrivers and warehousemen that in the end left four dead and hundreds wounded. In the City by the Bay, striking longshoremen fought employers and police in street skirmishes throughout the month of July, in which two were killed and scores wounded. Employers there had hoped to break a two-month old strike with the use of force, but their attempt at intimidation only succeeded in gaining sympathy for the longshoremen, who were able to rally to their cause 100,000 additional workers in the transportation, construction, and service industries, who all walked off their jobs in a secondary supportive strike. As a result, for two weeks the city of San Francisco was virtually shut down. In the end, in both cities, politically astute municipal and state authorities intervened and eventually helped the workers win important concessions from employers.

The above strikes and confrontations between workers and police paled in comparison to the largest and most violent strike of 1934, which began on September 1, 1934, when 400,000 textile workers from Maine to Alabama, went on strike. Workers previously unwilling to unite because of ethnic and religious differences threw all that aside and bonded together against a common foe: textile mill owners. All of a sudden, New England Catholic Europeans joined with white Protestants from the Southeast to battle their respective employers. Both groups insisted that they were Americans first, bound together by class and national loyalties that transcended ethnic and religious identities. In the first two weeks of September striking workers brought cotton production to a virtual standstill. Mill owners tried to bring in replacement workers and hired private security forces to protect them but that only caused greater anger among the workers and the result was violent confrontations between strikers and the police. In northern communities such as Saylesville and Woonsocket,

Rhode Island, full-scale riots erupted, causing several deaths, hundreds of injuries, and millions of dollars in property damage. Similar encounters took place in the South, where local vigilante groups, claiming workers to be communists, sided with the police and National Guardsmen to beat up strikers, kill union organizers, and help to incarcerate hundreds of strikers in barbed wire camps.

The often brutal suppression of strikes and other labor protests made workers more determined than ever to organize and use such unity to combat management's obvious refusal to accept the right of their workers to join unions. For that purpose, in 1935, John L. Lewis of the United Mine Workers, Sidney Hillman of the Amalgamated Clothing workers, and the leaders of six other unions that had become alienated by the AFL's lack of support seceded from that organization and formed a new consortium called the Committee for Industrial Organization, later renamed the Congress of Industrial Organizations. The new union's priority was to organize the millions of nonunion workers, regardless of skill level, gender, or race, into effective unions that would strengthen labor's political power. Hillman and Lewis made it clear that their new organization was pro-FDR and pro-New Deal and thus would vote *en masse* for the president and his party. Lewis and Hillman also pledged their union's financial support for FDR and pro-labor Democrats. Needless to say, FDR was euphoric about such support, and by his next cam-

Workers strike at an auto body plant in 1937. Labor unions gained in number and power during the 1930s.

paign labor had become part of the New Democratic coalition. The passage of the Wagner Act and the creation of the NLRB in 1935 enhanced the labor movement's status and credibility. Because of the CIO's platform, labor union membership skyrocketed, and in short order union members began flexing their new muscles.

In late 1936 the United Auto Workers, a CIO affiliate, took on General Motors, considered by many the most powerful corporation in the world. Determined to improve wages and hours, as well as recognition of their union, workers in the Flint, Michigan plant took over the operation by employing a new tactic, the "sit-down strike," which saw workers simply, literally sit down at their job site and remain there until their grievances were redressed. For the first time in 50 years, a governor refused to call out the National Guard to end the strike. Frank Murphy, the governor of Michigan, wanted to avoid the violence and bloodshed he knew would ensue if he did and instead urged GM management to recognize the UAW and its right to collectively bargain on behalf of its workers. General Motors capitulated after a month of resistance. The CIO-UAW victory was followed up by another major triumph over a notorious anti-union corporation, United States Steel, which also announced that it too was ready to negotiate a contract with the CIO. In short order, the CIO successfully took on and won recognition and concessions from two of the most notorious anti-union corporations in the country.

As the CIO triumphed over big business, labor's stature in the nation grew along with its size. Many writers and artists, funded through the WPA, used their respective mediums to further popularize and establish the labor movement as America's first and best hope—the voice of the people and the embodiment of the nation's best and truest values—community, cooperation, and ethical individualism. Murals sprang up in post offices and other public buildings depicting blue-collar Americans at work, with faces reflecting a sense of pride and dignity as a result of their new status. Broadway's most celebrated play in 1935 was Clifford Odett's classic *Waiting For Lefty*, a raw drama about taxi drivers who confront their bosses and organize an honest union. Audiences were so inspired by the play that they often spontaneously joined in the final chorus of "Strike, Strike, Strike," the words that ended the play. *Pins and Needles*, a 1937 musical about the hopes and dreams of garment workers that was performed by actual members of the International Ladies Garment Workers Union (the play-within-the play, a new, Depression-era genre used by both Broadway and Hollywood during this time, especially in musical productions), became the longest-running play in Broadway history until *Oklahoma* broke its record of 1,108 performances in 1943.

Movies and novels also reflected the change of values brought forth by the labor movement. Both mediums celebrated the decency, honesty, and patriotism of ordinary Americans. In *Mr. Deeds goes to Town* (1936) and *Mr Smith Goes to Washington* (1939) director Frank Capra delighted audiences with stories of simple small-town heroes vanquishing the evil forces of wealth, corruption, decadence, and the abuse of power. Likewise, John Steinbeck's classic, *The Grapes of Wrath*, the best selling novel of 1939, told the story of an Oklahoma family's fortitude in surviving eviction from their land, migrating westward, and their exploitation in the "promised land" of California. In 1940, famed Hollywood westerns' director John Ford put Steinbeck's novel on the screen and made one of that year's most acclaimed pictures. Moviegoers found special meaning in the declaration of one of the story's main characters, Ma Joad: "We're the people, we go on." In themselves and in one another, Americans seemed to discover the resolve they needed to rebuild a culture that had surrendered its identity to corporations and businesses.

THE DEPRESSION, THE NEW DEAL, AND A CHANGE IN VALUES

As reflected in labor's platform, as well as in the above mentioned movies and plays, many New Deal liberals and intellectuals were harsh critics of what conservatives believed should dictate the marketplace—amorality and its concomitant tenets of individualism, acquisitiveness, and egoistical behavior. These values informed the American political economy from the nation's founding through the 1920s. The Great Depression, however, destroyed much of the myth surrounding classical economic thought and its attendant values. As the 1930s progressed, Americans increasingly rejected those values and embraced instead the ideals of "moral economics"—the promotion of cooperation, justice, and compassion, especially a humanity inherent in a government's policies of protecting workers' rights and interests, as well as those of middle class consumers. Broadly stated, historically Americans have been torn by two opposing sets of values. Both are individualistic but one emphasizes cooperation, the other competition. Worker organizations have tended to promote cooperative individualism while businessmen have been the strongest advocates of acquisitive individualism. Middle class support of one or the other of these ideals is determined largely by historical/economic conditions. For example, during times of relative prosperity, many in the middle class have tried to emulate the upper classes and so adopted their values—the acquisitive ethic. The 1920s, 1950s, and 1980s serve as the best examples of such value acculturation in the twentieth century. During hard times, on the other hand, like the 1930s, many in the middle class identified with the working class cooperative ethos and thus, along with the working class, looked to the government—the embracing of liberalism—to ameliorate, if not rectify, the economic and social inequities caused by the amoral marketplace—unfettered capitalism.

Often American intellectuals and academics have found themselves in conflict with the popular mood. Such was the case for many of the nation's intelligentsia in the 1920s. However, during the 1930s, (and to some degree again in the 1960s), intellectuals and the common folk found enough social and economic commonality that they momentarily found themselves traveling ideologically parallel courses. Intellectuals and Depression victims alike criticized the effects of capitalism, though the latter not as explicitly or as harshly as the former. The Depression rapidly forced millions of Americans to rethink their devotion to traditional values, especially those associated with laissez faire capitalism. Even the American Dream itself was questioned by many citizens.

The economic collapse of the 1930s, at the very least, called for a readjustment in values. Searching for new values, some intellectuals found hope and inspiration in the idealization of peasant societies or regional agrarianism in the United States. More turned to the legacy of Marxist socialism or other manifestations of socialist thought. What 1930s intellectuals and common folk had in common was a search for a life of community and sharing as opposed to the acquisitive individualism of modern industrial capitalism.

The Rise of the Radical Third Parties

One of the most important repercussions of labor unrest was the emergence of left-leaning third party movements. In Wisconsin, for example, Philip La Follette, son of "Battling Bob" La Follette of Progressive-era fame, was elected governor in 1934 and 1936 as the candidate of the radical Wisconsin Progressive Party, which advocated, among other things, unemployment compensation and farm loans. Perhaps more disturbing to New Dealers was his antiliberal rhetoric. Indeed, La Follete publicly proclaimed in 1934 that "We [the Progressive party] are not liberal!" he further announced that "liberalism is nothing but a sort of milk-and-water tolerance. . . . I believe in a fundamental and basic change. I am a radical." La Follette believed there was "no alternative to conscious distribution of income," and thus in his opinion and that of his party, "this American principal of popular government, and the constitutions conceived to secure it, were not designed to sustain any particular economic system." Just what La Follette had in mind as an alternative to capitalism, he never really articulated. Yet, his rhetoric found receptive ears in his home state as former Wisconsin Democrats and even some Republicans embraced La Follette's attack on New Deal "liberalism" and voted for his party rather than for Roosevelt's Democrats.

In Minnesota, the Farmer-Labor Party, a fusion of discontented farmers and urban laborers, rose to challenge and defeat Democratic New Dealers. Led by Governor Floyd Olson, who was elected in 1930, the party completely dominated state politics from that year until the end of the decade. The party's platform echoed that of Wisconsin's Progressive Party, with Olson using the same radical rhetoric of La Follette, declaring that capitalism was "on trial for its life," and that it was "steeped in the most dismal stupidity." Olson's relief agenda for his citizens far outstripped FDR's modest early approaches, with Olson threatening conservatives in the legislature that if they did not enact his relief bills he would declare martial law. Olson stated that those who opposed his measures "because they happen to possess considerable wealth will be brought in by the provost guard. They will be obliged to give up more than they are giving up now." Olson further announced that as long as he was governor there was "not going to be any misery in the state if I can humanly prevent it." "I hope," Olson told wildly cheering crowds, that "the present system of government goes right down to Hell." Like La Follette, Olson took great pride in being a "radical," using that term constantly to describe his ideology and that of his party's. Olson announced he was a "radical," not a liberal, because he wanted "definite change in the system. I am not satisfied with tinkering, I am not satisfied with hanging a laurel wreath upon burglars and thieves and pirates and calling them code authorities or something else." Olson went even so far as to intimate that he was a closet-socialist, when again, to a rousing ovation, he declared that "When the final clash comes between Americanism and fascism, we will find a so-called 'red' as the defender of democracy." As the rise to power of both La Follette and Olson indicated, the overwhelming majority of Minnesotans and Wisconsinites wanted more drastic change than the New Deal was producing.

The same message emanated from California in 1934-36. Instead of forming a third party, discontented Californians took over the Democratic Party. In the Golden State, former Socialist Party candidate and famous author Upton Sinclair led the anti-New Deal charges. In a book titled *I, Governor of California, And How I Ended Poverty: A True Story of the Future,* Sinclair outlined his plan. The novelist described how he would be nominated and elected, and how as governor he would create a production-for-use economy in the midst of capitalist California. Sinclair predicted that he would totally eliminate poverty in the state in less than four years. The central feature of Sinclair's End Poverty in California (EPIC) was the concept of production-for-use. The profit system, the writer argued, had produced itself into a depression. Under it, increased productivity was a curse because workers were not paid enough to buy what they made. This "fact" led to unemployment, idle factories and farms, and storehouses full of goods, especially food products people desperately needed but were destroyed while millions went hungry. To remedy this, Sinclair proposed that the state take over the idle land and factories and permit the unemployed to use the land and machines to provide for their needs. Sinclair also advocated the establishment of land colonies to produce food for the hungry and state-owned and operated factories to meet other needs. Suffice it to say, Sinclair's "new socialism" terrified California conservatives because it amounted to the old concept of a "moral economy of provision" as opposed to the political economy of the free market. Despite conservative opposition, which became vicious in its falsehoods and accusations labeling Sinclair an atheist (actually he was a Christian Democrat) and a free lover—he was a devoted husband—and of course a communist—the only thing Sinclair had in common with the communists was mutual animosity—his EPIC swept the Golden State like an old-fashioned Awakening. However, come election time, the conservative coalition and its massive propaganda campaign against Sinclair, which included "newsreels" with Hollywood actors portraying Okies and people with putative Russian accents endorsing the novelist, was too much for EPIC to overcome. Sinclair was defeated by a closer-than-anticipated margin. However, like elsewhere in the mid-thirties, Sinclair's defeat confirmed the leftward drift of American attitudes in another way. In order to win, the Republican Acting Governor, Frank Merriam, a borderline reactionary, felt constrained to speak favorably of the New Deal, calling for a thirty-hour workweek and endorsing the Townsend Revolving Pension Plan. Conservatives had to pose as progressives to have a chance of winning at this time. The American political structure as a whole had tilted definitely leftward.

This is a meeting of the Communist Party in Detroit, Michigan. The Communist Party organized women and men into neighborhood organizations to fight evictions and gain relief for the unemployed.

Surprisingly, the American Communist Party (CP) at this time never became strong enough to pose a real political threat either in any of the states or nationally. In the early thirties, especially during Hoover's administration, the party had success in rallying to its platform homeless urban African Americans in the North, southern white and black sharecroppers, and Latino and Filipino agricultural workers in the West. Among those individuals the party mobilized them into unions and unemployment leagues. The CP also played significant roles in the Minneapolis and San Francisco strikes. The party reached its zenith of membership (80,000 by 1938) when it stopped preaching world revolution in 1935 and, instead, began calling for a "popular front" of democratic forces against fascism. Despite its new "popular front" ideology, the party remained a dictatorial organization that took its orders from Moscow. Membership turnover was high, as many left the party after learning about its authoritarian character. Interestingly, like the other movements noted above, the party's most important contribution to thirties politics was to channel popular discontent into unions and other political parties that, in turn, would force New Dealers to respond to the demands of the nation's dispossessed and forgotten.

THE 1936 ELECTION: FDR Reelected and Democratic Party Ascendancy

Despite the "thunder from the left" and the anxiety it caused FDR and the New Dealers, in the end, come election time, the president had little to fear from the populist insurgents. FDR was simply too shrewd a politician to allow an upstart, no matter how popular they or their rhetoric was, to unseat him. By moving the Second New Deal to the left, he not only silenced the populists, by "stealing their thunder" as it was, but also ensured both a victory for himself and his party. In his 1936 reelection campaign, FDR labeled the conservatives and corporate moguls and "economic royalists" who had "concentrated into their own hands an almost complete control over other people's property, other people's money, other people's labor—other people's lives." He called on citizens to strip the economic royalists of their power and "save a great and precious form of government for ourselves and the world." Voters responded by giving FDR the greatest popular mandate—for himself and his New Deal—in the history of American politics to that time. "The Messiah" received 61 percent of the popular vote; his hapless Republican challenger, Alf Landon of Kansas,—who even lost his own state—received only 36 percent. Only two states, Maine and Vermont, having between them a "whopping" 8 electoral votes went for Landon.

FDR's landslide represented not only overwhelming endorsement for the president and his New Deal but the beginning of Democratic/liberal ascendancy. From this moment forward, the Democratic Party became the party of reform and the party of the "forgotten American." Perhaps more important for the Democratic Party's future, FDR, via the New Deal, began to assemble the various interest groups or coalitions that would sustain the party and keep it the majority party for the next five decades. Not until the 1980s would the New Deal coalitions dissolve, allowing conservative Republican candidates such as Ronald Reagan to capture the presidency. But until that decade, these various groups kept the Democratic Party in power. For example, one of the party's key future "blocs" were African Americans, especially northern urban black folk, who deserted the Republican Party en masse and voted Democrat. African Americans calculated that their interests would best be served by the "Party of the Common Man." Also, ethnic, working class Americans, especially those of Italian, Irish, and Jewish heritage, voted overwhelmingly Democratic. And finally, FDR did well among the Anglo-Saxon middle class, many of whom were grateful to him for pushing through the Social Security Act.

As noted above, FDR's move to the left was politically motivated—to get himself and his party reelected. Upon closer examination of the Second New Deal's "concern for the common people" legislation, many of the most important measures fell far short of their supposed intention of uplifting the downtrodden and the oppressed. For example, the Holding Company Act did little to break-up the big trusts, and FDR's promise to deliver the nation's poor, like farm workers, were not covered by the Social Security Act or by the National Labor Relations Act. Consequently, thousands of southern black sharecroppers and Mexican-American farm workers in the Southwest were excluded from their protections and benefits. Not until the late 1960s did Southwestern and California farm workers achieve any such benefits. As will be seen, they will attain such status

largely by their own initiative and by the perseverance of their leaders such as Cesar Chavez. No white southern Democrat was going to vote for a bill that would improve the economic or social condition of southern blacks. Moreover, FDR only fleetingly mentioned, and with great hesitation, the possibility of anti-lynching legislation or voting rights or any guaranteeing or protecting black folks' basic civil rights.

FDR's populist rhetoric also obscured the fact that many big business enterprises throughout the nation, but especially in the West, where corporations such as Kaiser of California and Brown and Root of Texas, enthusiastically supported the Second New Deal because it gave them such massive and lucrative infrastructure contracts to build dams and other projects. In the Midwest and East, FDR's corporate supporters included real estate developers, mass merchandisers (such as Bambergers and Sears, Roebuck), clothing manufacturers, and the like. All of these New Deal supporters were convinced that prosperity depended on high, stable levels of consumer spending and were thus willing to tolerate labor unions, welfare programs, and high levels of government spending. They had no intention, however, of surrendering either economic or political power. Though on the one hand the Democratic Party definitely became the party of the common people, on the other, it also became the party of big business. From one constituency came the votes; from the other came money to finance the campaigns. The conflicting interests of these two groups often led to great strife and disunity in the party, especially in the latter decades of the twentieth century, and ultimately helped contribute to the party's loss of majority status.

Forgotten Americans

As alluded earlier, the New Deal was designed to ameliorate conditions for white middle and working class Americans. By the 1930s, this category included (because of their sheer numbers and potential political "value"), southern and eastern European ethnic groups—Italians, Slavs, Poles, and other previously discriminated groups from those European regions. Indeed, by the 1930s, a very high percentage of individuals from these groups had been assimilated, or at least acculturated, into mainstream WASP society, and, perhaps more important, as they became politicized, they joined the Democratic Party almost en masse. By the early 1930s, their potential political power was realized, especially in the urban North and West where no Democratic politician could afford to ignore their power. FDR understood their importance well, for he was a product of New York Democratic politics where such men as Al Smith and Robert Wagner, and others had organized the "ethnic vote" even before 1920. Thus, after becoming president, FDR made sure that New Deal largesse—PWA and CWA infrastructure projects and other relief measures—found their way into the urban enclaves where these "voters" lived. As a result, Jewish Americans and Catholic Americans, especially those descended from southern and eastern European stock, voted for FDR in overwhelming numbers. Though FDR and many of his WASP New Dealers were closet anti-Semites and anti-Catholic, and did nothing to alleviate such sentiment in the nation, they at least helped to promote the belief among these ethnic Americans that they were overcoming the stigma of their heritage and would someday soon no longer be considered second-class citizens. Such would not occur, however, until after World War II.

More important to the rise in status and importance for southern and eastern Europeans was their strong working class presence. In many of the mass production industries in the Northeast, Midwest, and the West, they formed the majority of the workforce and thus made crucial contributions to the labor movement's rebirth and especially to the CIO's formation in 1935. Ever the astute and ambitious politician, FDR realized this early on in his presidency and thus accommodated their demands because he understood and feared the power they wielded through their labor organizations.

Unfortunately, the New Deal, on the whole, paid little attention to the needs of African Americans and Mexican Americans. New Dealers believed that the issues of capitalism's viability, economic recovery, and the inequality of wealth and power in white society took precedent over the social problems of racial and ethnic discrimination. Few 1930s liberals were ready or willing to address these deep-seated social issues; their priority remained saving American capitalism and if along the way the quality and quantity of life for minorities could be improved with a modicum of resistance then that was fine. Because they were disproportionately poor, most minority groups did not benefit from the populist and pro-labor New Deal reforms. In many ways, the New Deal did more to intensify racial discrimination than it did to ameliorate it. This was especially true for African Americans living in the South. Their northern counterparts, however, benefited somewhat from New Deal legislation, especially those black folk living in northern industrial centers. There, they joined unions, particularly the CIO, which welcomed them, and voted. As alluded earlier, beginning in the 1936 presidential election, large numbers of northern blacks voted Democratic instead of Republican because they had received some attention from the New Deal. Yet, even in the North, in programs like the CWA, black workers received less pay than whites for doing the same work. In the South, black folk were barred from voting, excluded from AAA programs, and denied federal protection from white reprisals when they tried to form their own farmer unions. Perhaps most unsettling was FDR's refusal to support anti-lynching legislation, a key objective of the decade's civil rights activist.

Not all New Dealers ignored the plight of African Americans. Particularly concerned for their welfare was the First Lady, who almost single-handedly did more to help black folk than any New Dealer, including her husband. Eleanor Roosevelt spoke out frequently against racial injustice. In 1939 she resigned from the Daughters of the American Revolution when the organization refused to allow black opera singer Marian Anderson to perform in its concert hall. With the support of another civil rights advocate, Secretary of the Interior, Harold Ickes, Eleanor "pressured" her husband to sponsor the idea of permitting Anderson to sing from the steps of the Lincoln Memorial. On Easter Sunday, 1939, 75,000 people gathered at the memorial to hear Anderson sing while demonstrating their support for racial equality. FDR did not attend.

Though FDR succumbed to his wife's admonishments to appoint a few African Americans to second-level posts in his administration, he was never willing to make the fight for racial justice a priority—it was just too risky politically. FDR was not about to alienate white southern senators who controlled key congressional committees for the sake of even the most modest of civil rights proposals. Like the rest of his white cabinet, FDR believed that economic issues far outweighed in importance the racial ones. As already established, FDR was the consummate politico who was always calculating potential political loss or gain. In his mind, support of civil rights legislation would be a definite political loss, not a gain, and thus only with the greatest of reservation would he expend any political capital on supporting even the most circumscribed civil rights bills. Unlike other groups, such as northern ethnics, African Americans at this time were not yet strong enough as an electoral constituency or as a reform movement to force FDR to accede to their wishes.

Perhaps more adversely affected by the Depression years than African Americans were Mexicans and Mexican Americans. The plight of Hispanic folk was especially harsh in the Southwest, where at this time the majority lived. The most devastating manifestation of racial prejudice toward Mexican and Mexican Americans was repatriation, which actually began during the Hoover administration but was continued during the early New Deal years. Repatriation meant the returning of immigrants to their land of origin. As the depression worsened, and white Americans in certain regions looked for scapegoats for their woes, the Hoover administration in 1931 announced a plan for repatriating illegal aliens and giving their jobs to American (white) citizens. This policy focused on Mexican immigrants in the Southwest, especially those in California and Texas, the two western states with the largest Hispanic population at the time. Local governments in those two states were more than willing to enforce the law for they were eager to eliminate the minority poor from their relief rolls. Between 1929 and 1935, the federal government repatriated 82,000 Mexican immigrants in "raids" that occurred on businesses and homes. Those unable to prove his or her legal status

with the necessary documentation were deported. California and Colorado authorities went even further than what was intended. Threatening to remove them from the relief rolls, California officials "persuaded" 12,000 unemployed Mexicans in the Los Angeles area to leave, offering them free railroad tickets to Mexico as a further "inducement." Colorado authorities secured the departure of 20,000 Mexicans through similar techniques. Suffice it to say, such a dragnet by federal, state, and local governments created a climate of fear within the Hispanic community and consequently 500,000 more returned to Mexico voluntarily. This total equaled the number of Mexicans who had come to the United States in the 1920s. Most revealing was the fact that in the ranks of the repatriated were a significant number of legal immigrants who were unable to produce their immigration papers, the American-born children of illegals, and most egregious, thousands of Mexican Americans who had lived in the Southwest for generations.

Life grew more difficult for those immigrant Mexicans who stayed behind. Harassed by government officials, Mexicans everywhere sought to escape public attention and scrutiny. In Los Angeles, where their influence had been felt and accepted in the 1920s, they now retreated into the separate community of East Los Angeles. To many, they became the "invisible minority." Mexican Americans did receive some benefit from the New Deal, especially from the program's pro-labor legislation. Those Chicanos living in urban areas and who worked in blue collar industries, such as in the cannery and garment sectors, joined CIO-affiliated unions in large numbers and won concessions from their employers. But most Chicanos lived in rural areas and thus were agricultural workers. The National Labor Relations Act did not protect their right to organize unions, while the Social Security Act excluded them from the new federal welfare system. The New Deal, in short, offered the rural Chicano majority virtually nothing.

Interestingly and ironically, the only group of truly "forgotten Americans" whose lives were significantly improved by New Deal liberalism were Native Americans. From the 1880s to the 1930s, the

This Native American mother and child rest in a Minnesota blueberry camp sponsored by the Farm Security Administration.

federal government had pursued a policy of removing Native Americans to reservations, and once they were confined there, they were egregiously neglected in hopes they would all soon die off. As noted in a previous chapter, the 1887 Dawes Act called for the dismemberment of tribal lands and the parceling out of such domain to individual owners in the hope of transforming a nomadic, hunting people into docile and sedentary farmers. Such a policy would have been welcomed most enthusiastically by black Americans, but it was totally rejected by Native Americans. By 1933 nearly half the Indians living on reservations whose land had been allotted were landless (They had been swindled out of their land by greedy white land speculators.), while those who still had their land were living in deserts or on land so marginal that no white person would want it. The shrinking land base in combination with a growing population intensified Native American power. Compounding this growing problem was the desire of "assimilationists" in the 1920s who put pressure on the Bureau of Indian Affairs (BIA) to outlaw all Indian religious ceremonies, to take Indian children from tribal communities and place them into federal boarding schools, and impose limits on the length of men's hair. This draconian policy was finally redressed during FDR's presidency, especially by John Collier, whom the president appointed to run the BIA. Collier brought to his agency the same kind of energy and efficiency that Harry Hopkins had injected into New Deal relief programs.

Collier was one of the few New Dealers who shared Eleanor Roosevelt's genuine humanitarianism and altruism. He was determined to improve the life of one of the nation's most "forgotten" citizens. No sooner was he in office that he pursued a policy of relentless pressuring of other New Deal agencies to include Native Americans. For example, a full Native American CCC was created, and Indians also were employed in numerous other agencies on projects to improve reservation land, as well as to educate Native Americans in land conservation methods. Collier also exhorted Congress to pass the Pueblo Relief Act, which compensated the Pueblo Indians of Colorado for land taken from them in the 1920s. The 1934 Johnson-O'Malley Act was also passed, which gave federal money to states to provide for Indian health care, welfare, and education. Collier also pushed for the repeal of the once-mandatory federal boarding schools for Indian children and instead promoted their enrollment in local public schools. Perhaps one of his most important accomplishments was the allowing of Native Americans to once again practice their traditional religions. He also created the Indian Arts and Crafts Board, which promoted Indian artists and helped them to market their works.

The centerpiece of Collier's agenda was the Indian Reorganization Act of 1934 (also known as the Wheeler-Howard Act). This act revoked the allotment provisions of the Dawes Act by restoring tribal lands and granting Indians the right to establish constitutions and bylaws for self-government. It also provided support for new tribal corporations that would regulate the use of communal lands and appropriate funds for the economic development of the reservation. This was a landmark act that ended the assimilationist policy pursued by previous administrations. The act recognized that Native American tribes possessed the right of self-determination and self-government, as well as the right to control their own cultural and economic well-being. It reflected Collier's commitment to what we would call today "cultural pluralism," a doctrine which celebrates and accepts diversity in American society and seeks to protect that diversity from those who believe in "Americanism"—code for the belief that all peoples living in the United States should acculturate WASP values, mores, and norms. This was the assimilationist position. Collier hoped that his policy of cultural pluralism would invigorate traditional Indian cultures and tribal societies and sustain both for generations. Cultural pluralism was not a popular idea in depression America, for too many white Americans believed it only caused greater division and the potential for racial or class warfare. Collier thus encountered opposition everywhere: from Protestant missionaries and cultural conservatives who wanted to continue the assimilationist policy; from white farmers and businessmen who feared that the new legislation would protect Indian lands from their acquisition; and even from some Indian groups who

had embraced assimilation, while others viewed the IRA as one more attempt by the federal government to impose the "white man's will."

One such tribe that believed the IRA was another white conspiracy against Native Americans was the Navajo, the nation's largest tribe, who voted to reject its terms. For a variety of reasons, other tribes joined with the Navajo in rejecting the IRA, but a majority of the tribes—181—nearly 70 percent of the total—supported Collier's agenda and organized new tribal governments under its auspices. Thanks to Collier and the BIA many Native American tribes gained significant measures of freedom and autonomy. The New Deal, then, showed considerably more sensitivity to the needs and aspirations of Native Americans than had previous administrations. FDR's approval and support of Collier's reforms is interesting because for once there was no political gain to be had. Does that mean FDR was genuine in his concern and support for a truly neglected and oppressed people? Unlikely. Because Native Americans had been abused and oppressed for so long, and had become a truly invisible people, FDR probably saw that little political harm would result if he came to their rescue. They would still remain a marginalized people, despite his help, and thus still forgotten. Not until the 1970s would Native Americans demand their tribal rights and thus finally realize Collier's dream of cultural pluralism.

The New Dealers

For the academics, policymakers, advisers, counselors, and bureaucrats who designed and administered the rapidly expanding programs and agencies of the New Deal, the years 1936-1938 were heady ones. Never before had the federal government employed so many individuals to carry forth its policies and programs. Even the activisim of Theodore Roosevelt and his coterie of progressives paled compared to the flurry of activity and passion that emanated from the Oval Office during these years. Fired by idealism and dedication, they were confident they could make the New Deal work. In the euphoria that set in after FDR's 1936 landslide victory, which the New Dealers interpreted as a popular mandate for their ideas, they devised countless schemes to expand the government's role especially in the nation's economic affairs. For example, the Farm Security Administration was created, an agency designed to help improve life for tenant farmers, sharecroppers, and farm laborers. In 1938, they drafted and got passed the Fair Labor Standards Act, which finally outlawed child labor, set minimum wages and maximum hours for adult workers, and put the federal government on its way to providing a home for all Americans by initiating low-cost housing projects in many urban areas.

Although the New Dealers proclaimed that all their efforts and ideas were for the "people," in reality the New Dealers were members of a new technocratic elite that had little in common with the nation's plain folk. Few were genuine humanitarians determined like a Collier to uplift and protect the truly downtrodden and oppressed. Most were motivated by the prospect of building a strong state committed to prosperity and justice but, concomitantly, to order and stability. They delighted in the intellectual challenge and technical complexity of social policy. They did not welcome interference from those they regarded as less intelligent or motivated by outworn ideologies. In short, the majority of the New Dealers were well-educated, university graduates, often animated to do the right thing for the people by an inherent sense of noblesse oblige. Many were the progeny of some of the oldest, wealthiest, most prestigious families in America upon whom it had always been incumbent to serve the public and protect the commonweal from the excesses of democracy as well as from the abuse of power by big business. They were social conservatives at heart and by temperament, but they were willing to experiment with socioeconomic reform (or social "engineering" if such efforts could guarantee a more prosperous and stable society and economy).

Not all of the New Dealers had been raised among wealth and privilege as was the case generally with earlier generations of reformers. To his credit, FDR was the first president since his cousin Teddy to welcome Jews and Catholics into his administration. Some became members of the president's inner circle of advisers, men such as Thomas "Tommy the Cork" Corcoran, Jim Farley, Ben Cohen, and Samuel Rosenman. These were men who had struggled from immigrant beginnings; they were "street smart," ambitious, politically savvy young men who brought to the Oval Office quick minds and mental toughness.

Though the New Deal offered opportunity to ethnics, a few blacks, Catholics, and Jews, such was not the case for women. The New Deal offered American females very little, especially when it came to the issues of greater economic opportunity, sexual freedom, and full equality. One reason why the issue of women's rights found few supporters was that the suffrage movement, after its 1920 triumph, had lost its momentum. Another was that prominent New Deal women, such as Frances Perkins, did not vigorously promote equal rights. They concentrated instead on "protective legislation"—laws that safeguarded female workers, who were thought to be more fragile than men. Those who insisted that women had "special" needs in the workplace could not easily argue that women were the equal of men in all respects. The most significant deterrent, however, to feminism was the general, pervasive male hostility that the depression only exacerbated. Men of all classes experienced a degree of emasculation during the Depression years because so many had lost their identity as the "bread winner" and provider of economic security for their families. For such men, being unemployed and then having to accept relief—the dole—unleashed feelings of inadequacy. The unemployment rates of men, especially among the ranks of blue-collar workers, tended to be higher than those of women, many of whom worked in white collar occupations, which were less vulnerable to job cutbacks. This fact only made unemployed men feel even more emasculated and useless. Resentment toward women, particularly those with jobs, intensified. The American male was not ready to accept the possibility that his wife or daughter could be a breadwinner.

This male anxiety had political and social consequences. Several states passed laws forbidding the hiring of married women. New Deal relief agencies were reluctant to authorize aid for unemployed women. The labor movement, even the more egali-

In the 1930s, most factory jobs were divided into women's work and men's work. Women's work, such as sewing clothes, usually paid less than the jobs done by men.

tarian CIO, made the protection of the male wage earner one of its principal goals. The Social Security pension system did not cover waitresses, domestic servants, and a host of other female-dominated occupations. Male fears of being emasculated and the venting of such anxiety became so intense during the 1930s that many artists, especially those involved in cartoon/comic strip production, started to project a strident "masculinism" in their work. Mighty Superman, the new comic-strip hero of 1938, reflected this male fretfulness. Superman was depicted as a working-class hero who, on several occasions, saved workers from mine explosions and other disasters caused by the greed and negligence of villainous capitalists. Superman's greatest vulnerability, besides kryptonite, was his "fatal" attraction to the sexy and aggressive working woman, Lois Lane. He was never able to resolve his dilemma by marrying Lois and then making her a kept woman because the continuation of the comic strip demanded that Superman repeatedly be exposed to kryptonite and female danger. However, in other media, such as the movies, producers faced no such technical obstacles. Anxious men could go to the local motion picture theater and find comfort from the conclusions of such

pictures as *Woman of the Year*, in which Spencer Tracy (in many ways the epitome of masculinity) persuades the ambitious Katherine Hepburn to exchange her successful newspaper career for the bliss of motherhood and domesticity. From a thousand different points, 1930s politics and culture made it clear that woman's proper place was in the home. Faced with such intense, sometimes virulent opposition to breaking the confines of domesticity, it is not surprising that female activists failed to make feminism a part of New Deal reform.

Stalemate, 1937-1940

By 1937-38, the New Deal began to lose momentum and popularity, especially among increasing numbers of middle class Americans. Though initially supportive of the working class and its cooperative ethos, labor's increasing militancy, exemplified by the CIO's rise to prominence, began alienating the middle class. After the UAW's victory over General Motors in 1937, other workers began imitating the successful tactics pioneered by the Flint, Michigan auto workers. The sit-down strike became ubiquitous across the nation. Many middle class Americans were becoming disturbed by labor's growing power and apparent radicalism. To many members of the middle class, FDR had taken the New Deal too far to the left and thus wanted him and the party to "calm things" done. This was the moment the right had been waiting for since 1936 to regain power. Prior to this time, the conservatives had been unable to stop the Rooseveltian juggernaut. Now, with the middle class support waning for the New Deal, the right resurrected itself and began to aggressively assault both the president and his program as having gone too far to the left and endangering democratic republican government. Though the conservatives' criticisms found receptive ears, ultimately forcing FDR to move back to the center and curtail the more ambitious, left-leaning social reform programs of the New Deal, at really no time was the president ever in jeopardy of losing favor with the American people nor of being denied a third term.

"The Arrogance of Power": The Court Packing Debacle

Unfortunately for the fate of New Deal liberalism, its allegedly greatest proponent, FDR, helped to cause its final demise. One year after receiving the greatest electoral landslide in American political history and an apparent mandate for his New Deal, FDR committed what proved to be one of the greatest political blunders of his career: his attempt to "pack" the Supreme Court by adding a new justice for each sitting justice who, having served at least ten years, did not resign or retire within six months after reaching the age of 70 (with a proviso that no more than six additional justices would be appointed). FDR's stated reason for his plan was that the current justices were too old and feeble to handle the large volume of cases coming before them. It became rapidly apparent to many Americans that it was not the justices who were "feeble" but that FDR's excuse to expand the Court was "feeble" at best. What prompted one of the savviest political presidents in history to commit such a mistake? Simply put, in FDR's mind, for the New Deal to move forward, that is to further the advance of the welfare state, he had to find a way of "removing" the last obstacle to that end. He believed the most effective way of doing that without arousing too much opposition was to propose the idea of simply adding more justices to the bench. Naturally they would be liberals and thus no further New Deal leg-

This cartoon depicts the Democrat's mascot, the donkey, abandoning Roosevelt after his proposal to change the number of justices. Congress had changed the number of justices several times in the previous century. However, the "Court packing" would load the Court in Roosevelt's favor.

islation would go the way of the NIRA, the AAA, and Guffy Coal Act—all shot down by the Court in 1935-1936 largely because they reflected an improper delegation of power to the executive branch. In that assessment, the Court was "strictly" correct; however, FDR had believed he did have such power and that the Court was wrong in denying him the exercise of that prerogative, which he insisted came under the "necessary and proper" clause of the Constitution.

Much to FDR's amazement, few Americans bought his "plan." It was perceived by many to be a high-handed attempt to concentrate even greater power in the executive branch, removing the last check on his already immense control of the government. Congress, in the eyes of many Americans, had become nothing more than a rubber stamp for the president's agenda. Southerners were especially aroused by the plan for they read into it a "conspiracy" by FDR and his Yankee New Deal liberals, led by "That Woman," Eleanor Roosevelt, to secretly appoint liberal justices who would upset their region's racial order.

Throughout the nation, the Court packing crisis proved to be the beginning of the end of New Deal liberalism and the conservatives' ascendancy. Conservatives had made little headway a year earlier by denouncing the welfare state but now found Americans more receptive to attacks on Court reform. The president's plan, they maintained, proved that he was dangerously power-hungry and that he aspired to be a dictator. The charges, though wildly exaggerated, resonated well with many Americans who were troubled by the advance of the European dictatorships. *The Dallas Morning News* expressed these fears when it editorialized: "Perhaps it is a little difficult for Mr. Roosevelt, who is entirely self-convinced as to the integrity of his motives, to see that the objection is not giving the particular present executive unlimited power but to giving it to any President. The objection is to a practical dictatorship which Mr. Roosevelt seeks in his conviction that the purity of his motives will overcome the drawbacks of a nation in political servitude. Unfortunately, the obsession in the case of all dictatorships is the same."

Very few Americans supported the packing plan because they did not associate it with immediate, tan-gible, or direct benefits, as they did earlier New Deal measures such as relief programs, agricultural price supports, old-age pensions, and unemployment insurance. As conservative attacks on the bill mounted, FDR's motives assumed a darker hue. As the editor of the conservative *Texas Weekly* declared, "His [FDR's] proposal to subjugate the judiciary strikes at the roots of the American constitutional form of government, and the people have the right to know precisely why he proposes so drastic a step. If there is to be a Newest Deal, some further incursion into the political unknown, we should like to know what he has in mind."

Needless to say, FDR was stunned by the widespread opposition to his plan. Once he realized the blunder he had made, FDR decided to back down and allowed the plan to go down to defeat in the Senate in July 1937. From this point on, FDR's earlier zeal to push the New Deal further to the left by expanding the welfare state seemed to dissipate with each passing month. To be sure, there were a few more social welfare programs left in the New Deal, but they were not as enthusiastically, nor as adamantly, pushed as they were earlier. FDR's hesitant behavior contrasted sharply with the impression of energy and purpose he had conveyed in 1933. The administration became less committed to restructuring the economy and more interested in stabilizing it and producing growth. Historian Alan Brinkley maintained that by 1938 New Dealers "were no longer much concerned about controlling or punishing 'plutocrats' and 'economic royalists,' an impulse central to New Deal rhetoric in the mid-1930s. Instead, they spoke of their commitment to providing a healthy environment in which the corporate world could flourish and in which the economy could sustain 'full employment.'"

That FDR's once supposed passionate devotion to social welfare programs should decline so precipitously after 1937 was not surprising when one remembers that he was never as committed to social reform or to championing organized labor as he publicly let on. FDR was not a left-wing social democrat. Pressured by leftists in his party and by populist demagogues like Huey Long, FDR reluctantly supported the 1935 Social Security Act on the con-

Franklin and Eleanor Roosevelt greeting Americans during a parade. Roosevelt believed that every citizen deserved a decent standard of living and that the government had an obligation to help those in need.

dition that it be solvent and designed according to "insurance principles." Nor was he as pro-union as his rhetoric led many to believe. He despised the "dole" for able-bodied citizens, preferring work programs like the CCC to welfare checks for non-workers. FDR was also a late convert to Keynesian economic theory, which only became the foundation of liberal political economy after his death. Most interesting, he resisted to the end leftist pressure to sponsor anti-lynching and civil rights laws, partly because he did not want to alienate southern white Democrats, but also because, unlike Eleanor, he shared the racial prejudices of most white Americans of his time—a fact illustrated by his support of Japanese-American internment during World War II.

THE RECESSION OF 1937-1938

Whatever hope FDR may have had for a quick recovery from the court-packing fiasco was dashed by a sharp recession that hit the country in late 1937 and 1938. FDR had mostly himself to blame for the

downturn. The expanded work program of the Second New Deal helped stimulate the economy to the degree that in 1937 production surpassed the highest level of 1929, and unemployment dropped to 14 percent. Confident the depression was easing, FDR made the mistake of cutting back on the federally sponsored work relief programs that sustained the supposed "recovery." The Federal Reserve tightened credit, and new payroll taxes took $2 billion from wage earners' income to subsidize the Social Security pension fund. That withdrawal would not have hurt the economy had the money been returned to circulation as pensions for retirees. Instead, the money was held with no pensions scheduled to be paid until 1941. Once again, the economy lacked a sufficient money supply, and, once again, the stock market crashed. By October 1937, the market fell by almost 40 percent from its August high. By March 1938, the unemployment rate soared back to 20 percent.

The widespread distress resulting from the 1938 recession badly hurt Democrats in the 1938 midterm elections. Republicans won a smashing victory, gaining 81 House seats and 8 seats in the Senate. The Congress that assembled in January 1939 was the most conservative of the New Deal years. Since all the Democratic losses had taken place in the North and West, particularly in such key states as Ohio and Pennsylvania, Southerners were now once again in a strong position, and they were in no mood to see any further extension of the welfare state, in any capacity. The House contained 169 non-southern Democrats, 93 southern Democrats, 169 Republicans, and 4 third-party Representatives. For the first time, FDR could not form a majority without the help of Southerners and Republicans. Most observers agreed that the president could, at best, hope to consolidate but certainly not extend the New Deal. FDR admitted as much when he delivered his annual message in January: "We have now passed the period of internal conflict in the launching of our program of social reform. Our full energies may now be released to invigorate the processes of recovery in order to preserve our reforms."

By the end of 1938 it had become clear that any new ambitious goals faced an uncertain future: the New Deal had essentially come to an end as congressional opposition now made it difficult, if not impossible, for FDR to enact any major new programs. More important, perhaps, in ending the New Deal was the threat of world crisis, which hung heavy in the political atmosphere. FDR was gradually growing more concerned with persuading a reluctant nation to prepare for war than with pursuing new avenues of reform. With such retrenchment at the national level, the way was now open for conservatives to mount an all-out attack on New Deal liberalism. FDR would continue through the war years to say that the New Deal was not dead but on the "backburner." But everyone knew the New Deal had run its course.

CONCLUSION

Elected in 1932, Franklin Roosevelt dominated the nation's history for the next thirteen years. He had few qualms about using the powers of the federal government to combat the Depression and reform society. Dire economic problems gave him unprecedented opportunities to redefine the federal government's relationship with the American people.

Americans' expectations created opportunities for FDR, but he faced serious constraints as well. Crisis or not, there were political and ideological limits on how much the president could change and how much he wanted to change. Many on the political left saw FDR's election as a chance to reform society, to achieve social justice for all, and to restructure American capitalism to make it more human and responsive to the needs of the common people. But FDR had no intention of abandoning corporate capitalism or restructuring American society. Roosevelt's choices were thus shaped by public and political expectations and constraints as they intersected with the economic and social needs caused by the Depression. The result was the New Deal, a three-part barrage of legislation designed to bring about economic recovery, relief for Depression victims, and reforms to better regulate the economic sector. In the end, the New Deal did not end the Depression nor did it even provide adequate relief for the most destitute. However, the New Deal's legacy saw the emergence of the federal government, especially the executive branch, as the most powerful and important level of government in the nation. Before the 1930s, people had looked to local, county, and state governments for help. After the New Deal, people looked to Washington for assistance, and government and politics were forever changed.

Thanks to the New Deal's extension of public relief to millions of Americans, we have come to accept the legitimacy of the welfare state. We recognize that many individuals in our society need such assistance to survive. In sharp contrast to progressivism, the reforms of the New Deal endured. Voters returned FDR to office for an unprecedented third and fourth terms. And these same voters remained wedded for the next forty years to FDR's central idea: that a powerful state could enhance the pursuit of liberty and equality.

Chronology

1929 Herbert Hoover assumes the presidency
   Stock Market crashes on "Black Tuesday," October 29

1930. Congresses passes Hawley-Smoot tariff, raising
   duties to all-time high on many foreign goods

1931 2,000 U.S. banks fail
   Austrian bank failure triggers European depression.

1932 Unemployment rate reaches 25 percent
   Reconstruction Finance corporation established
   Bonus Army marches on Washington
   FDR defeats Hoover for presidency

1933 FDR assumes presidency
   Hundred Days legislation defines First New Deal
   Roosevelt administration recognizes the Soviet Union
   "Good Neighbor" policy toward Latin America
    launched
   Reciprocal Trade Agreement lowers tariff

1934 Father Charles Coughlin and Huey Long attack
    conservatism of First New Deal
   2,000 strikes staged across the nation
   Democrats overwhelm Republicans in off-year election
   Radical political movements emerge in Wisconsin,
    Minnesota, California, and Washington
   Indian Reorganization Act restores tribal land,
    provided funds, and grants limited right of self-
    government to Native Americans.

1935 Committee for Industrial Organization (CIO) formed
   Supreme Court declares NRA unconstitutional
   FDR unveils his Second New Deal
   Congress passes Social Security Act
   National Labor Relations Act (Wagner Act)
    guarantees workers' right to join unions
   Holding Company Act breaks up utilities' near
    monopoly
   Congress passes Wealth Tax Act
   Emergency Relief Administration Act passed, funds
    WPA and other projects
   Rural Electrification Administration established
   Number of Mexican immigrants returning to Mexico
    reaches 500,000

1936 FDR defeats Alf Landon for second term
   Supreme Court declares AAA unconstitutional
   Congress passes Soil Conservation and Domestic
    Allotment Act to replace AAA
   Farm Security Administration established

1937 United Auto Workers defeat General Motors in
    sit-down strike
   FDR attempts to "pack" the Supreme Court
   Supreme Court upholds constitutionality of Social
    Security and National Labor Relations acts
   Severe recession hits.

1938 Conservative opposition to New Deal does well in
    off-year election
   Superman comic debuts
   Fair Labor Standards Act passed

1939 75,000 gather to hear black opera singer Marian
    Anderson perform at Lincoln Memorial.

1940 FDR reelected for unprecedented third term
   New Deal is over as nation engages in military
    preparedness and begins aid to Great Britain, only
    nation still standing against Hitler's attempt to
    conquer Europe

SUGGESTED READINGS

Anthony Badger, *The New Deal: The Depression Years* (1989).

Barton J. Berstein, ed. *Toward a New Past; Dissenting Essays in American History* (1968).

Michael Bernstein, *The Great Depression: Delayed Recovery and Economic Change in America, 1929-1939,* (1987).

Alan Brinkley, *The End of Reform: New Deal Liberalism in Recession and War* (1995).

___, *Voices of Protest: Huey Long, Father Coughlin, and the Great Depression* (1982).

David Burner, *Herbert Hoover: A Public Life* (1979).

Lizabeth Cohen, *Making a New Deal: Industrial Workers in Chicago, 1919-1939* (1990).

Paul K. Conklin, *The New Deal* (1975).

Cletus E. Daniel, *Bitter Harvest: A History of California Farmworkers, 1870-1941* (1981).

Roger Daniels, *The Bonus March* (1971).

Michael Denning, *The Cultural Front: The Laboring of American Culture in the Twentieth Century* (1997).

Melvyn Dubofsky and Warren Van Tine, *John L. Lewis: A Biography* (1977).

Martin L. Fausold, *The Presidency of Herbert Hoover* (1985).

Sidney Fine, *Sitdown: The General Motor's Strike of 1937-1937* (1967).

Steve Fraser and Gary Gerstle, eds. *The Rise and Fall of the New Deal Order, 1930-1980* (1989).

Frank Friedel, *Franklin D. Roosevelt: A Rendezvous With Destiny* (1990).

Colin Gordon, *New Deals: Business, Labor and Politics in America, 1920-1935* (1940).

Linda Gordon, *Pitted But Not Entitled: Single Mothers and the History of Welfare* (1994).

Ellis Hawley, *The New Deal and the Problem of Monopoly* (1967).

Dorothy Ray Healey and Maurice Isserman, *California Red: A Life in the American Communist Party* (1990).

Abraham Hoffman, *Unwanted Mexican Americans in the Great Depression: Repatriation Pressures, 1929-1939* (1974).

Herbert Hoover, *Memoirs: The Great Depression* (1952).

Irving Howe and Lewis Coser, *The American Communist Party, 1919-1957* (1957).

Barry D. Karl, *The Uneasy State, the United States from 1915-1945* (1983).

Lawrence C. Kelley, *The Assault on Assimilation: John Collier and the Origins of Indian Policy Reform* (1983).

Robin D.G. Kelley, *Hammer and Hoe: Alabama Communists During the Great Depression* (1990).

David Kennedy, *Freedom From Fear: The American People in Depression and War, 1929-1945* (1999).

Harvey Klehr, *The Hyeday of American Communism: The Depression Decade* (1984).

Joseph P. Lash, *Eleanor and Franklin* (1981).

William E. Leuchtenberg, *Franklin D. Roosevelt and the New Deal*.

Nelson Lichtenstein, *The Most Dangerous Man in Detroit: Walter Reuther and the Fate of American Labor* (1995).

Richard Lovitt, *The New Deal and the West* (1984).

William F. McDonald, *Federal Relief Administration and the Arts* (1968).

Robert S. McElvaine, *The Great Depression* (1984).

Richard D. McKinzie, *The New Deal for Artists* (1973).

Barbara Melosh, *Engendering Culture: Manhood and Womanhood in New Deal Public Art and Theater* (1991).

Greg Mitchell, *The Campaign of the Century: Upton Sinclair's EPIC Race for Governor of California and the Birth of Media Politics* (1992).

Mark Naison, *Communists in Harlem During the Great Depression* (1990).

James T. Patterson, *The Struggle Against Poverty, 1900-1980* (1981).

Richard Pells, *Radical Visions and American Dreams: Culture and Social Thought in the Depression Years* (1973).

Albert V. Romasco, *The Poverty of Abundance: Hoover, the Nation, the Depression* (1965).

____, *The Politics of Recovery: Roosevelt's New Deal* (1983).

Vicki Ruiz, *Cannery Women/Cannery Lives: Mexican Women, Unionization, and the California Food Processing Industry, 1919-1950* (1987).

George J. Sanchez, *Becoming Mexican American: Ethnicity, Culture, and Identity in Chicano Los Angeles, 1900-1945* (1993).

Lois Scharf, *Eleanor Roosevelt: First Lady of American Liberalism* (1987).

Arthur M. Schlesinger Jr. *The Age of Roosevelt: The Crisis of the Old Order* (1957).

____, *The Coming of the New Deal* (1958).

____, *The Politics of Upheaval* (1960).

Jordan Schwarz, *The New Dealers: Power Politics in the Age of Roosevelt,* (1993).

Bruce Shulman, *From Cotton Belt to Sunbelt* (1910).

Harvard Sitkoff, *A New Deal for Blacks* (1978).

Graham D. Taylor, *The New Deal and American Indian Tribalism: The Administration of the Indian Reorganization Act, 1934-1935* (1980).

Studs Terkel, *Hard Times.*

Richard M. Vallely, *Radicalism in the States: The Minnesota Farmer Labor Party and the American Political Economy* (1989).

Geoffrey Ward, *Before the Trumpet: Young Franklin Roosevelt, 1882-1905* (1985).

____, *A First Class Temperament: The Emergence of Franklin Roosevelt* (1989).

Susan Ware, *Holding Their Own: American Women in the 1930s* (1982).

Harris G. Warren, *Herbert Hoover and the Great Depression* (1959).

T. H. Watkins, *The Great Depression: America in the 1930s* (1993).

____, *Righteous Pilgrim: The Life and Times of Harold Ickes, 1874-1952* (1990).

Nancy J. Weiss, *Farewell to the Party of Lincoln: Black Politics in the Age of FDR* (1983).

Blanche Wiesen, *Eleanor Roosevelt*, vol. 1 (1992).

Joan Hoff Wilson, *Herbert Hoover: Forgotten Progressive* (1975).

Chapter Twenty

THE "GOOD" WAR:
World War II

It was a Sunday morning, December 7, 1941. Americans were home relaxing, listening to the radio and reading the Sunday papers. The children were absorbed in the comics: Popeye was being bashed in the head for trying to make Olive jealous; Flash Gordon was in trouble for stealing an "enemy" plane suspiciously resembling a Japanese model. The newspapers reported conflicts overseas and exchanges of threats and ultimatums. Few were concerned. We were having problems adequately caring for our own people. Under no circumstances should we be involved in disputes between "Chinks and Japs" or in trying to solve the problems of Europe. "We had already solved Europe's problems in World War I, and what good had that done?" It was inconceivable that anyone would dare to attack us. Hadn't Admiral Clark Woodward, in a syndicated newspaper column, assured us that the Japanese armed forces were inferior fighters and our economic restriction would deter any possible military ambitions?

So when the distinctive voice of H.V. Kaltenborn, the radio commentator, interrupted regular programs to inform Americans that the Japanese had attacked the American fleet in Pearl Harbor, most Americans were

astounded. "This shouldn't have happened to us. We were Americans, they were Japanese...Jesus Christ, how the hell'd this happen," one man wondered. To a seventeen-year-old girl, the seriousness did not sink in. The thing that really bothered her about Pearl Harbor Sunday was that they weren't playing dance music on the radio. To most Americans, however, the attack created a new atmosphere—a tremendous surge of excitement and patriotism. In Seattle, a band of young people roamed the city smashing windows and lights to insure total blackout that evening. A Princeton junior rushed to the recruiting office and found a line so long that he had to wait until the next morning to enlist. Americans rushed off to fight the war, "a good war, a war we could understand." No wonder those who survived it call it "the last of the good wars."

THE WORLD DRIFTS TO WAR

It might seem odd to us today that Americans had so resolutely refused to acknowledge the ominous events taking place in other parts of the world. While

The *San Francisco Chronicle* for December 8, 1941.

Americans turned inward, struggling with the effects of the Depression, totalitarian Italy, Germany, and Japan were becoming increasingly aggressive and dangerous. Mussolini had gained control of Italy back in 1922 by taking advantage of economic and social discontent. He continued to suppress all opposition and create a one party fascist state, proclaiming, "We have buried the putrid corpse of liberty."

Fanatic militarists seized power in Japan and launched a systematic policy of expansion in Asia. In 1931, using a flimsy cover story of assault by Chinese railroad workers, the Japanese occupied the vast Chinese province of Manchuria and installed a puppet government. A lengthy investigation by the League of Nations came to the not-very-surprising conclusion that Japan had indeed committed aggression, and the League voted to "condemn" Japanese actions. Japan demonstrated its contempt for the toothless international organization by simply withdrawing from the League. Although Japan's actions were a clear threat to the Open Door policy, President Herbert Hoover refused to consider economic sanctions. Instead, he embraced the Wilsonian notion of "nonrecognition." The American and international powerlessness emboldened the dictators to further aggression. Within a month of the U. S. warning, Japanese cruisers were shelling Shanghai and preparing to invade China.

Adolf Hitler, who took power in Germany in 1933 at virtually the same time as Franklin Roosevelt in the United States, posed an even greater menace. (The lives of these two men were ironically and inextricably intertwined for the following twelve years until they died in April 1945, within two weeks of each other.) Hitler swiftly established a brutal dictatorship, boasting that the German master race would rule the inferior "mongrel" races of Europe in a thousand-year empire. First, however, the nation must be purged of the "subhuman" Jews whom he blamed for Germany's defeat in World War I. A series of racist laws severely limited the civil and economic rights of German Jews. The world stood by silently, allowing the 1936 Olympics to take place in Nazi Germany. The American Olympic Committee, to avoid antagonizing the Nazis, even removed the American Jewish track star, Marty Glickman, from his running events.

"Today Germany, tomorrow the world," the Nazis had proclaimed. They rapidly moved to make their boast a reality. They rearmed in open violation of the Treaty of Versailles. In 1936 Nazi troops reoccupied the "demilitarized" German-speaking Rhineland. Earlier, Mussolini had attacked the North African country of Ethiopia where his tanks and planes barely prevailed against the spears and flintlock rifles of the native troops. In alliance with Mussolini, Hitler intervened to aid Francisco Franco in his rebellion against the elected government of Spain. The dictators used the vulnerable civilian population of Spain to test new weapons and techniques of air warfare. The three aggressor nations, Germany, Italy and Japan, signed treaties of alliance and defense in 1936. This ultimately led to the creation of the Rome-Berlin-Tokyo Axis, binding them together in destruction and war.

In 1938 German storm troopers marched into Vienna, annexing Austria, in yet another violation of the Treaty of Versailles. Not to be outdone, the Japanese had begun a full-scale invasion of China in 1937. The democratic nations of Europe were reduced to hand wringing at these various acts of aggression and the League of Nations to unenforceable declarations of sanctions. The United States remained aloof from the troubles of others.

Bolstered by his easy successes, Hitler turned his attention to democratic Czechoslovakia and demanded that he be ceded a strategic region, the Sudetenland, the home of many ethnic Germans. A conference was held in Munich in September 1938. The Czechs and their potential Russian allies were excluded. The British and French agreed to all of Hitler's demands in return for his promise not to ask for anything else. A triumphant British Prime Minister, Neville Chamberlain, returned to cheering throngs of his countrymen to announce that he had achieved, "Peace in our time." Within six months, however, his words became a mocking symbol of the futility of appeasement (giving in to dictators) as Nazi troops marched into the rest of a greatly weakened Czechoslovakia. The United States had played no role at Munich. "It is always safest and best to count on nothing from the Americans but words," Chamberlain noted. Finally, the British and French resolved that they could not allow Hitler to continue his unopposed conquest of Europe and warned him that the consequences of any further aggression would be war.

Not surprisingly, Hitler was unimpressed with the new found Western backbone. In August 1939 he dropped a bombshell by signing a nonaggression pact with his arch-foe Joseph Stalin of the Soviet Union, ensuring that he would not have to fight on two fronts. On September 1, 1939, a hot Saturday, the German armed forces surged into Poland. When he was informed, Roosevelt understood the significance immediately, "It's come at last. God help us all," he sighed.

The British and French honored their commitments by declaring war. They were not, however, able to save Poland. The Poles fought gallantly, using cavalry and antiquated weapons against twentieth century military technology. The German *blitzkrieg* or "lightning war" coordinated tank, plane, and troop movements with ruthless efficiency. The Russians attacked Poland from the East, and the doomed country fell to superior forces in three weeks.

After a few months of nervous quiet in the dark winter that followed the fall of Poland, Germany suddenly struck at Denmark and Norway and easily subdued them in April 1940. The *blitzkrieg* knifed through Belgium and Holland in twenty-three days and launched an attack on France. Only an heroic effort by the Royal Navy and an unlikely flotilla of English pleasure and fishing vessels were able to save over 300,000 British soldiers from total annihilation at the beaches of Dunkirk. Their equipment and the field were left to the Germans.

A few weeks later, on June 22, 1940, the Nazis piled humiliation on top of defeat. They forced the demoralized French to sign a document of surrender in the same railroad car where the Germans had signed the armistice in 1918 ending World War I. Only Britain stood against Hitler's total triumph. Thousands of Nazi planes dropped bombs on British cities. Sympathetic radio and news reports chronicled the heroic British resistance. Winston

Employing *blitzkrieg* tactics, a motorized division of German troops drives through a ravaged town.

WINSTON CHURCHILL

Churchill, the new British Prime Minister, asked for American assistance, "Give us the tools, and we will finish the job." How would the American public respond to the stunning events of 1939-1940?

NEUTRAL IN WORD AND DEED

For many Americans, during those years of anxiety and conflict, as the world crashed toward the abyss, events in Europe and Asia might as well have been taking place on Mars. Americans were uninterested in the early years of the rise of fascism. As more Americans began to understand the significance of events unfolding in Europe and Asia, most passionately believed that we should avoid involvement in another war at almost any cost.

Novelists and poets of the 1920s had expressed the increased American revulsion against war. A series of popular "exposes" in the 1930s, with titles like *Merchants of Death*, had argued that America had been dragged into World War I through the evil machinations of arms dealers and bankers. A series of Senate committee hearings from 1934 to 1936,

led by Gerald Nye of North Dakota, "revealed" the obvious—that munitions' makers had made a great deal of money in World War I. Although the committee failed to discover any sinister conspiracy, an angry public was only too ready to believe the worst. The same rich manufacturers who had brought the Depression must have reaped enormous profits over the bodies of innocent young men.

Led by the American Student Union, a peace movement spread through the nation's college campuses. In the spring of 1936 half a million students joined a "peace strike" in which they stayed out of classes to attend antiwar activities. A 1937 Gallup poll showed that 70 percent of Americans now believed that the U. S. should not have entered World War I, and an astounding 95 percent believed we should stay out of any future world war.

From 1935-37, applying the supposed "lessons" of 1917, Congress passed a series of Neutrality Acts. These were designed to prevent the kind of circumstances that had "dragged" us into World War I. They outlawed arms sales and loans to nations at war and declared that Americans traveling on ships of such nations would do so at their own risk. By failing to distinguish between victims and aggressors, these laws benefited the fascist powers who had already armed themselves. A provision, added in 1937, allowed nations at war to buy "nonmilitary" supplies, if they paid in advance and carried them on their own ships. This had the potential to favor the British with their naval superiority. Congress hoped that this would enable American manufacturers to sell their goods overseas without involving us in any conflict.

President Roosevelt was unwilling to get ahead of American public opinion. In 1936 he declared, "I hate war. I have passed unnumbered hours...thinking and planning how war may be kept from this nation." While he sincerely desired peace, he never worked to educate the public about the growing fascist menace.

When the Japanese overran North China in 1937, Roosevelt appeared to move cautiously toward a more activist policy. In a speech in Chicago he suggested that the peace-loving nations should act collectively to "quarantine" aggressors because "we cannot have complete protection in a world of disorder in which confidence and security have broken down." Although he gave no concrete suggestions of what measures should be taken, the public reaction was decidedly mixed. Roosevelt remarked, "It's a terrible thing to look over your shoulder when you are trying to lead—and to find no one there." He quickly retreated into silence. When Japanese planes bombed Standard Oil tankers and a U. S. gunboat, *Panay*, killing three, the U. S. government accepted a Japanese apology for the "accident." Most Americans supported this meek response. Over 70 percent believed that we should withdraw from the Far East completely.

One group of Americans, American Jews, watched world events with increasing trepidation. The intensifying brutality of Hitler's anti-Semitic policies was a matter of grave concern. Like most Americans, Jews were more concerned with the domestic economic issues of the depression than with events abroad. They were against the neutrality laws and believed that the appeasement at Munich was a serious mistake. They were fearful, however, of causing an increase in American anti-Semitism if they overplayed "the Jewish hand in America as it was overplayed in Germany before the present suppression." Fully two-thirds of the American public already believed that Jews had "too much power" in the country. The very visible presence of such Jews as Treasury Secretary Henry Morgenthau among Roosevelt's circle of close advisers led to snide remarks about the "Jew Deal."

Hitler's remorseless war against the Jews reached its culmination of violence on November 9, 1938, with *Kristallnacht*, the "Night of the Broken Glass." Using the pretext of the assassination of a minor German embassy official in Paris by a grief-stricken young Jewish man, the Nazis unleashed a rampage of destruction. Thousands of Jewish-owned shops were looted and destroyed, homes were vandalized, and two hundred synagogues were burned. In addition, thousands were thrown into camps, and Jews were barred from virtually all occupations. This was a foreshadowing of the "final solution," Hitler's extermination policy, carried out during World War II.

American Jews reacted by organizing protests, picking up support and sympathy from the general public who believed it was unsporting to bully a defenseless minority and burn down its "churches." The American government responded with a mild protest and the recall of its ambassador to Germany "for consultation." Josef Goebbels, the German Minister of Propaganda, sardonically replied to the protests, "If there is any country that believes it has not enough Jews, I shall gladly turn over to it all our Jews." Roosevelt expressed his shock that "such things could occur in the twentieth century," but he evaded the issue of allowing any more German Jewish refugees.

Jews fled Germany by the thousands, seeking haven from the rising brutality. Hundreds of famous and distinguished Jewish scholars, writers, and scientists were welcomed in America, including the cadre of physicists who were instrumental in creating and building the atomic bomb. The masses of ordinary refugees, however, were not so lucky. Immigration quotas were not liberalized to admit them. Led by a bitterly anti-Semitic Assistant Secretary of State, Breckinridge Long, consular officials blocked the desperate petitioners from even filling the German quota.

American Jews feared that requests for government intervention on behalf of German Jews would be seen as special pleading. Although most Americans claimed to deplore the German persecution, 75 percent opposed allowing any more "Jewish exiles from Germany." Congress in 1939, reflecting overwhelming public sentiment, refused even to relax the quota to admit 20,000 Jewish refugee children. The wife of the Commissioner of Immigration commented, "20,000 children would all too soon grow up to be 20,000 ugly adults." The result of such a policy, of course, was that the children would never be able to grow up at all.

A graphic demonstration of these attitudes occurred in June 1939. The ship *St. Louis*, carrying nine hundred desperate Jewish refugees who were refused expected landing permits in Havana, was denied permission to unload its passengers in Florida. A Coast Guard cutter even stood by to foil any attempt to jump off the vessel and swim ashore. Although it had come within sight of the lights of America, the *St. Louis* was forced to sail back across the Atlantic to deliver most of its hapless passengers to certain death.

FROM NEUTRALITY TO WAR

The outbreak of war in Europe led to a gradual retreat from isolationism in America. With the backing of most of the American public, Roosevelt called a special session of Congress to revise the neutrality laws. Munitions could now be sold to the Allies on a "cash and carry" basis. Arms began to flow across the Atlantic to Britain and France. The public had come around to favoring aiding the Allies short of war, but less than 30 percent agreed that we should enter the war if the Allies seemed on the verge of defeat.

The fall of France was particularly sobering to many Americans. The United States had many sentimental ties to a romantic Paris, now blighted by the image of Nazi storm troopers marching in triumph down the *Champs Elysees.* Jerome Kern expressed this anguish in his popular song, "The Last Time I Saw Paris." Some active interventionists joined the "Committee to Defend America by Aiding the Allies," chaired by William Allen White, a famed Kansas editor and a Republican. White warned that it was "impossible for a free country and a free people to live beside Hitler's world enslaved."

As German bombs rained down on England, Congress considered a proposal for the first peacetime draft in American history. Outside a thousand protesters sang, "Ain't Gonna Study War No More." The regular army numbered only 137,000 in 1939, but ultimately Selective Service processed some twenty million men and funneled eleven million into the armed services. Service in the peacetime army was limited to one year and confined to men aged 21 to 35. A Gallup poll showed that most young men were willing to accept a year of compulsory military service. The first mass registration went through with few hitches. Only a small number of Indian tribes (Seminole and Hopi) boycotted registration claiming they were still at war with the United States or not obliged to obey any American law.

(During the war, most Native Americans fought bravely in the armed forces.)

At the same time that he pledged to keep our country out of the war, Roosevelt abandoned any pretense of impartiality to strengthen defenses and aid the beleaguered British. Radio reporters, such as Edward R. Murrow, broadcast vivid descriptions of the bombing of London and the heroism of the Royal Air Force to the public. Their reports helped convince most Americans that we should assist British war efforts. In September of 1940, Roosevelt dared to issue an executive order transferring fifty "old" destroyers to the British in exchange for leases on British bases in the Western Hemisphere. He was also able to obtain an increase in appropriations for airplanes and other defense needs.

This "tilt towards the British" angered anti-interventionists and led to the formation of America First. Although they represented a minority of Americans after the fall of France, isolationists remained strong in the Midwest, particularly among Republicans and old-time progressives such as Senator Robert LaFollette Jr. of Wisconsin. They also appealed to German-Americans and Irish-Americans. Charles Lindbergh, the famed flying hero, was their most renowned spokesman. Reflecting the persistent anti-Semitism of the era, Lindbergh concluded that the three main groups pressing for war are "the British, the Jewish, and the Roosevelt administration." He warned the Jews not to push too hard because "they would be among the first to feel its consequences." His wife added that while fascism might well be evil, it was the "wave of the future" that could not be defeated. Others, like Joseph Kennedy, American Ambassador to Great Britain, simply believed the European war did not concern us. "This is not our war," he declared. Roosevelt privately complained that Kennedy was an appeaser and "a pain in the neck to me."

During these months of crisis in 1940, Roosevelt decided to break with tradition and run for a third term. The Republicans passed over their front runners, all of whom were isolationists. Instead, they nominated a dark horse liberal Republican, Wendell Willkie, a utilities executive. Although Willkie was an internationalist who favored aid to Britain, he pro-

Women from various mothers' groups conducted a pray-in to protest the passage of the Lend-Lease Act.

claimed, "I will never send an American boy to fight in a European war." Roosevelt, in turn, assured American parents, "Your boys are not going to be sent into any foreign wars." Both men, thus, underplayed the possible military consequences of the crisis in Europe. Americans seemed to agree with Mayor Fiorello LaGuardia of New York that they preferred "Roosevelt with his known faults to Willkie with his unknown virtues." Roosevelt won with a reduced, but still substantial, majority, 27 to 22 million.

Once the election was safely over, Churchill notified FDR that Britain could no longer afford to pay for necessary equipment. America, Roosevelt informed the people, must become "the great arsenal of democracy." A bill, introduced in January 1941, allowed the president to "lend, lease, or otherwise dispose of" war supplies to nations whose defense was vital to the United States. Roosevelt argued that the policy was similar to offering a garden hose to a neighbor whose house was on fire. You don't ask your distressed neighbor to pay you in advance (cash and carry). You just expect the hose to be returned once the fire is out. Others agreed with the view of Senator Robert Taft of Ohio that a better analogy would be to "chewing gum. You don't want it back." Senator Burton Wheeler, in a more vicious comparison, described lend-lease as similar to the

AAA crop destruction of the 1930s: "It will plow under every fourth American boy."

Despite the intense debate that included a Capitol prayer meeting by the "Mother's Crusade" against lend-lease, Congress passed the measure in March 1941 with considerable public support. American aid proved to be of vital assistance to the British war effort and in bolstering British morale.

In June of 1941 Hitler astounded the world by breaking his alliance with the Soviet Union and launching a surprise invasion, hoping to gain control of vast Soviet resources. Most experts expected a rapid Soviet collapse. But, like Hitler, they greatly underestimated the Soviet ability to fight back. When the Soviets mounted an effective resistance, Roosevelt extended lend-lease to the Soviet Union. Anti-Communists were angered, but Churchill supported the decision, concluding, "If Hitler invaded Hell, I would make at least a favorable reference to the Devil...."

In August Roosevelt met with Churchill off the coast of Newfoundland to discuss strategy. Although Eleanor Roosevelt fretted over Churchill's night owl proclivities that denied her husband adequate sleep, the two world leaders hit it off famously. They established the closest relationship ever held between an American president and foreign leader. They also drew up the Atlantic Charter, an unofficial statement of war aims. These included a peaceful, disarmed world that embraced the "Four Freedoms"—freedom of speech, freedom of worship, freedom from want, and freedom from fear. The United States and Great Britain had clearly become allies.

By this time, in the fall of 1941, American destroyers were escorting convoys as far as Iceland and stalking German submarines thereafter to report their whereabouts to British commanders. Incidents at sea were inevitable. The president deliberately deceived the public when the Germans attacked the tracking destroyer, *Greer*. Stating that the *Greer* was an innocent vessel carrying only passengers and mail, and that the Nazis were "the rattlesnakes of the Atlantic," Roosevelt ordered the navy to "shoot on sight" any hostile ships.

At the end of October a German submarine sank the destroyer *Reuben James,* causing the death of 115 American sailors. At Roosevelt's urging, Congress authorized the arming of American merchant ships and the transport of lend-lease supplies directly into war zones. Nothing remained of the 1930s neutrality legislation that had been designed to keep us out of war. The United States was already involved in a limited war. Roosevelt declared to a concerned public in a fireside chat, "Never before since Jamestown and Plymouth Rock has our American civilization been in such danger."

Isolationists at the time, as well as later historians, have argued about Roosevelt's European policies. They insisted, with some validity, that he gradually increased American involvement and did not tell the whole truth to the American public. Recent sources confirm, however, that he really did hope to stay out of the conflict until the last possible minute. In 1941 America obtained German codes and used the German naval messages to avoid, rather than provoke, incidents. Roosevelt had been proven right in his belief that first Britain, then the Soviet Union, would successfully hold on against the Nazis. He hoped to aid the Allies, but keep America from the fighting, remarking, "The time may be coming when the Germans and the Japs will do some fool thing that would put us in. That's the only danger of our getting in."

TOWARD PEARL HARBOR

Roosevelt was preoccupied by events in Europe. Since Hitler seemed by far the more dangerous enemy, the president hoped to avert any showdown with Japan. He particularly sought to avoid provoking Tokyo into any conflict before the completion of the "two-ocean navy" Congress had authorized. "I simply do not have enough navy to go around," he remarked to an aide in mid-1941. Earlier in 1941, a large portion of the fleet was fortuitously transferred from the Pacific to the Atlantic to protect shipping.

Hitler had always given as an excuse for his aggression the need for **lebensraum**—"living space" to expand. Encouraged by his success, the Japanese also insisted on the need for a "Greater Asia Co-Prosperity Sphere" where they could obtain raw materials and food for their rapidly growing population and modernized economy. Their determination was matched by American insistence on the Open Door Policy. At the same time, Japanese pillaging of Chinese cities, including the slaughter of 300,000 in Nanking, alienated the American public. The United States pursued a gradual policy of economic pressure, hoping to give the Japanese time to reconsider their actions and to encourage moderate leaders. America eventually instituted embargoes on scrap iron, steel, industrial chemicals, and oil and ultimately froze Japanese assets in America. However, Hitler's conquest of Europe led Japanese leaders to believe that the raw materials of French Indochina and the Dutch East Indies could replace embargoed goods.

By the fall of 1941, the Japanese had decided on war. They would seize Southeast Asia and talk with the United States but proceed with war if Americans did not concede all demands. They expected to win great victories in the early stages of the war, to be followed by a stalemate and a peace reaffirming Japanese conquests. Grim militant expansionists, led by General Hideki Tojo, toppled the more "moderate" Japanese government. The government kept its decision for war from its own diplomats, so they could seem to be negotiating in good faith. The one thing they did not want was any settlement that would interfere with the rush to war. On the night of December 6, American experts deciphered an unyielding message from Tokyo to the Japanese ambassador to Washington. "This means war," Roosevelt concluded upon reading it.

Military experts had expected the Japanese to attack British and Dutch possessions in Southeast Asia and were debating how to respond. Instead, the Japanese gambled that a surprise air raid on the U. S. naval base at Pearl Harbor, Hawaii, would destroy the American Pacific fleet. That would enable them to solidify their Asian conquests by neutralizing the United States.

The Japanese attack came at dawn, Hawaii time, on December 7, 1941. Waves of Japanese dive-bombers and torpedo planes soared across the harbor to bomb the anchored ships and strafe the planes parked wing tip to wing tip. Luckily, the two American aircraft carriers, still with the Pacific fleet, were out at sea. But the damage was devastating. In less than three hours most of the aircraft and many of the unprotected naval vessels were destroyed or damaged. More than 2400 Americans were dead, and 1100 were injured.

The next day, the Japanese attacked General Douglas MacArthur and his troops in the Philippines and pounded Malaya and Thailand. Roosevelt appeared before a stunned joint session of Congress where he called on the American people to avenge "a date that will live in infamy." Congress passed a Declaration of War against the Empire of Japan with only one dissenting vote (Jeanette Rankin who had also voted against entry into World War I).

These events have led "revisionist" writers to claim that the government knew of, or even invited,

Japan launched a surprise attack on the United States at Pearl Harbor on December 7, 1941. Hitler declared war on America four days after the Pearl Harbor attack.

Franklin D. Roosevelt signed a war declaration against Japan after the attack on Pearl Harbor.

the attack beforehand to push America into the war. Why, these writers asked, were the battleships and planes so close together and open to attack? Why had Roosevelt sent the Pacific fleet from the West Coast to the more vulnerable base in Hawaii? Why didn't junior officers report last minute warnings of blips on their radar screens?

There were serious errors. These were, however, human, rather than conspiratorial. The planes and ships were so close together to guard against possible sabotage. The fleet was sent to Hawaii as a warning to Japan. In addition, all the so-called experts allowed racist presuppositions to color their evaluations of Japanese abilities. Admiral Gene LaRoque remembered, "We were so proud, so vain, and so ignorant of Japanese capability. It never entered our consciousness that they'd have the temerity to attack us." Americans believed that "nearsighted" Japanese couldn't see well enough to bomb targets accurately. They also "knew" that the makers of "junky equipment" could never build good weapons. "We thought," concluded Admiral LaRoque, that "they were of a lesser species."

As for Roosevelt's supposed maneuvers to get America into war, it is hardly likely that he would deliberately destroy elements of the very navy he was working so hard to rebuild. The president was trying to avoid a war in Asia that would have likely led to a war on two fronts. He clearly believed that the Germans were the greater danger. The Japanese, however, had been determined to follow a course of inevitable conflict.

As it turned out, the great Japanese "success" at Pearl Harbor ultimately proved to be a strategic and tactical disaster. The navy repaired and returned to service all the supposedly "sunk" battleships, except the *Arizona* and the *Oklahoma*. Several played key roles in subsequent American naval victories. What is more important, as anyone familiar with the history of the *Maine* or the *Luisitania* could have predicted, an unprovoked attack could only unite the American people behind the war effort. Even Senator Burton D. Wheeler, a leading isolationist, proclaimed, "The only thing to do now is to kick hell out of them." Thus, the Japanese surprise attack destroyed its basic strategy of neutralizing the United States and, ultimately, guaranteed defeat.

Roosevelt briefly worried that he would not be able to fight the greater menace of Nazi Germany. Hitler solved this dilemma, even though the Tripartite Pact required him to help only if Japan was attacked. Despite the pleas of his advisers, on December 11, he declared war against "half Judaized and the other half Negrified" America. Mussolini quickly followed suit. Americans now united behind the massive effort needed to defeat the Axis powers. Isolationism and appeasement were discredited for a long time to come.

In 1942 the military situation seemed hopeless. In the Battle of the Atlantic German submarines destroyed Allied ships at a faster pace than workers could produce new ones. The Japanese conquered Hong Kong, Singapore, the Dutch East Indies, and the Philippines and seemed well on their way to realizing their imperial ambitions in Asia. Could a society as determinedly nonmilitary as the United States was at the time meet the challenge of totalitarian militarism?

THE CITIZEN-SOLDIER

Increased draft calls and enlistments enormously enlarged the armed forces. By the end of the war 15 million men and 350,000 women had served. Local draft boards, which determined who was to go to war, often took the heat from people who suspected them of favoritism, especially as casualties rose. Deferments were granted to married men, particularly "Pre-Pearl Harbor Fathers." Many boards were suspicious of marriages entered into, and children conceived, after that pivotal date.

Boards also received letters from "patriotic Americans," pointing out people they might have overlooked. One woman urged consideration of her "shiftless" son-in-law who would benefit from military discipline. Another begged, "Please locate Enoch Calhoun and put him in the service. He has deserted his family and took another woman with him."

After 1943 deferments were based mainly on the importance of one's occupation to the community or to the war effort. Physicians, dentists, defense plant workers, and, most particularly, farmers and farm workers could gain exemptions. Actors and professional athletes had the highest proportion of draftees, largely for symbolic reasons. The public tended to be suspicious when seemingly healthy celebrities gained deferments, so the army began to waive defects that might have disqualified others "to satisfy public opinion." Jimmy Stewart, the actor, won great public approval when he went on a weight-gaining diet to meet army requirements.

The GI, so-called because everything he was given was government issue, received four to six months of physical training and indoctrination. The citizen-soldier tended to hold a firmly negative attitude about army life, despite efforts to improve morale. He cynically joked about "SNAFU—situation normal, all fouled up." A report to the army warned that the 1940 man was "a different breed of cat" from his 1917 counterpart. "The present breed (mark well) is questioning everything from God Almighty to themselves." Perplexing authorities, he would ignore a new post recreation hall for a scroungy town pool hall to "get away from the Goddamn Army." The typical soldier was an infantryman, as repre-

sented by Willie and Joe—craggy, unshaven, and disheveled. These were the characters of a syndicated cartoon first drawn by Bill Mauldin when he was an 18-year-old GI. These remain forever symbols of the World War II soldiers.

The army spent a great deal of effort to improve morale, especially for overseas troops. Entertainers, like Bob Hope, were encouraged to tour overseas. The American military even filled cargo space on flights to North Africa with hundreds of crates of Coca-Cola, to the dismay of the British. Soldiers received cigarettes at almost every turn, leading, perhaps, to increased addiction. Five million pictures of actress Betty Grable, the most popular "pin-up," were distributed to fighting men. Interestingly, she represented the wholesome, supportive girlfriend or wife many men dreamed of meeting when they returned from war, rather than an overtly erotic sex goddess. When she became a mother in 1943, it only seemed to add to her appeal.

The American armed forces were given constant reassurance of their superiority, leading to self-confidence, even in adversity. One striking photograph shows grim German guards leading American prisoners-of-war through Rome. The captured Americans are waving, smiling, and making V-for-victory signs. The novelist, Robert Kotlowitz, recalled how he, like most soldiers, truly believed that the war was a struggle between "good and evil...Right and wrong. Us and them." He saw the world "in simple adolescent terms, for I was still an adolescent. And that is why it was easy for me to hate the enemy."

The men came from small towns or farms or city neighborhoods. Most had never been anywhere else. Now they found themselves in strange places, running into exotic people, "as well as into one another, whom they found equally exotic." They learned to depend on one another and that became the most important thing. "The reason you storm the beaches," one remarked, "is not patriotism or bravery. It's that sense of not wanting to fail your buddies. There's sort of a special sense of kinship."

The experiences of the fighting men in the European theater were very different from that of the Pacific. The number of killed and wounded in combat was higher in Europe, due to the larger quantity and superior quality of German artillery. Psychological casualties were greater in the tropical jungles of the Pacific. There malaria often claimed more victims than the Japanese. The climate and terrain of Europe generally compared to that of the United States. In 1944 many soldiers in Europe would go AWOL (absent without leave) for short periods as self-prescribed treatment for combat exhaustion. (When the American army first crossed the Seine near Paris, ten thousand GIs took off to see the city.) By contrast, the Pacific islands were strange and forbidding. There were few AWOLs, since there was no place to go. Venereal disease rates were only a tiny fraction of those in Europe. The heat, mosquitoes, and rain led one soldier to cry, "It's hell living here in the Pacific."

Despite denunciations of Nazi "barbarism," letters home show a lack of deep hatred towards German soldiers. Unlike the Japanese, Germans surrendered when the situation was hopeless. They were "exactly our age. They were boys like us." There was little real dislike of German soldiers who fought an "honest fight and lost." On stationary fronts firing often stopped when ambulances appeared or when food was brought. Both sides followed "Tacit rules of conduct."

The mood was very different on the other front. *Yank* magazine ran an article about tossing grenades into caves where Japanese troops hid, shooting anyone who came out, whether armed or not. One soldier-reader expressed the view that it was an inhumane practice. His comment drew hundreds of responses. "We are fighting back-stabbers," said one. Our motto, another suggested, should be, "Kill the bastards." Interestingly, this attitude did not come only from experiences fighting the Japanese. Men serving in Europe or still at home exhibited the same feelings about the Japanese. The roots of these attitudes came from a sense of racial and cultural superiority, reaffirmed by the attack on Pearl Harbor. It was reinforced by the belief that the Japanese themselves violated rules of warfare, as shown by the Bataan Death March in which thousands of American and Filipino prisoners died. It was true that the Japanese military took a dim view of surrender, which they regarded as dishonorable. In retaliation, many

American outfits took no prisoners. This made intelligence officers, who had hoped to obtain information from prisoners, very unhappy.

There was a widely held belief that Japanese soldiers, who lacked Western "feelings," were better suited to jungle warfare and night fighting. But American intelligence officers who read the letters of Japanese troops knew that, like American GIs, the Japanese soldier wrote of the jungle as a sinister place, complained about American snipers and tricks, and had similar gripes about food, officer privileges, and men with soft jobs at home.

The heaviest fighting took place in the last fourteen months of the war. In the last six months of 1944, 12,000-18,000 Americans were killed each month, and 40,000-60,000 were wounded. Death by friendly fire, called "amicide," was rarely discussed. Attacks by U. S. aircraft were common enough that soldiers dubbed the U. S. 9th Air Force, "the American Luftwaffe." One investigation in the Pacific estimated that 12-16 percent of the deaths had been caused by American weapons.

If a man was wounded, his odds for survival were excellent. Only 3.5 percent of the wounded who survived to reach medical facilities subsequently died. The use of transfusions and the development of penicillin helped to bring about this substantial improvement over earlier wars.

Prisoners of War

Some ninety-five thousand Americans became prisoners of war in Europe, and twenty-five thousand in the Pacific. Both Axis powers routinely violated the Geneva Convention in their treatment of enemy prisoners, particularly in forcing them to aid in the manufacture of war supplies. Despite Hitler's stated preference for executing prisoners, the German record was generally better than the Japanese. The Germans, however, did use prisoners as miners under terrible conditions. In December 1944 an SS unit murdered many American prisoners in the Malmedy Massacre. Prisoners of the Germans, nevertheless, did receive letters from home and packages from the Red Cross. Prisoners in the Pacific were not given any letters or parcels, even those with medical supplies.

The Japanese regarded those who allowed themselves to be captured as contemptible. The prison guards tended to be misfits who deliberately mistreated and humiliated their charges. The Japanese displayed airmen, shot down over Tokyo, in a cage in the zoo. More than 90 percent of the Pacific POWs had been beaten, one in three died, and half of the survivors qualified for veteran's disability after the war.

In contrast, there were nearly 500,000 German POWs held in more than 500 camps in the United States, including old CCC camps, gyms, and even the Santa Anita race track. Farmers and businessmen used some of them to fill labor shortages. They were employed in lumber production, road and farm work, and, ironically, at a kosher meat packing firm in New Jersey. One proposal, seriously considered, then rejected, was to recruit a POW "German Volunteer Corps" to fight the Japanese. The POWs at Fort Lewis held a huge party for Hitler's birthday, complete with a Nazi banner. Several others escaped and joined American society. The last one surrendered in 1985.

African-American G.I.s

In Salina, Kansas, a black soldier, refused service at a local restaurant, watched in disbelief as six German POWs were accommodated at the lunch counter. This was typical of the contradiction inherent in fighting a war against racism with a segregated army. Black American servicemen had to fight dual enemies—Hitler and Jim Crow. In many training camps blacks were not allowed to use white servicemen's clubs or recreational facilities and were not given their own. German POWs rode in the front of streetcars in the South, black soldiers in the back. Even the blood supply was segregated—plasma from blacks and whites stored separately. Ironically, the process for storing plasma had been invented by Dr. Charles Drew, an African-American physician.

The newsreels spoke lyrically about "Legions of colored troops, dramatic evidence of American solidarity and the fight for freedom." In reality, numerous clashes resulted from the use of MPs to make sure blacks stayed "in their place," enforcing Jim Crow laws in the South and establishing a color line

in England. At least fifty black soldiers were killed in these racial conflicts.

Some 1.2 million African Americans served in the armed forces in World War II. As in 1917, blacks were, originally, almost exclusively in labor battalions—loading, cleaning up, digging, working as "domestics abroad as well as at home." Despite earlier American history (the Civil War, the Indian wars, San Juan Hill), most military experts believed the myth that blacks could not be trusted in combat. Secretary of War Stimson stated, "Leadership is not embedded in the Negro race yet and to try to make commissioned officers to lead men into battle—colored men—is only to work a disaster to both."

One of the tasks of some black naval units was to load ammunition on ships under conditions that violated all safety standards. In July 1944, in the worst home front disaster of the war, two ships, a pier, 202 black men, and some whites were blown up at a California naval depot. Ten days later, the remaining men were ordered back to the same work, and fifty were court martialed for refusing to do so. The white officers, responsible for the fiasco, went unharmed and unpunished.

In 1944, as war casualties rose, a few black units were permitted to go into combat. This was partially a result of a "Fight for the Right to Fight" campaign, launched by the NAACP and the black press, and supported by Eleanor Roosevelt. These units proved themselves in battle. General Patton exhorted the 761st Tank Battalion to "establish a record for yourself and...for your race" and to "make a liar out of me." (He once said that blacks were incapable of the technical abilities needed in tank warfare.) They were awarded 293 Purple Hearts, 60 Bronze, and 11 Silver Stars in a unit of 750 men.

General Arnold, of the Army Air Corps, said that blacks could never be fighter pilots, since they could not withstand "high g forces," because of "the simpler configuration of their brains." The 332nd Fighter Group, better known as the Tuskegee Airmen, proved him wrong. They were carefully screened and trained, creating an elite group of the brightest and most fit. Generally, they flew escorts for bombers. After more than 15,000 sorties and 1500 missions, they were able to brag that they never lost a bomber, while destroying or damaging 409 enemy aircraft. The group won 95 Distinguished Flying Crosses. Included were men who later became a Mayor of Detroit, a Manhattan Borough president, a congressman, a Secretary of Transportation, and a college president. The last, one of the first Americans to shoot down a German jet, later concluded, "Our success ended segregation."

While civilian America continued to maintain segregation, the military began to change. Although somewhat halfheartedly, an effort began in 1944 to integrate training camps. As early as mid-1942, black officers were graduating from integrated Officer Candidate Schools at a rate of two hundred a month. Three years after the war, under the order of President Truman, the armed forces became the first American institution to integrate.

The war also gave black veterans greater self-esteem and increased expectations, as they understood the irony of "fighting fascism and letting racism run rampant." This change was exemplified by the experience of a young black lieutenant who boarded a military bus at Fort Hood, Texas, and was ordered to "get to the back of the bus where the colored people belong." Since the army had already officially desegregated its bases, he refused to move. The Officer of the Day called him "uppity," and he was tried for insubordination. The military tribunal took only a few minutes to find him not guilty. His name was Jackie Robinson and, a few years later, he became the first black major league baseball player, integrating American professional sports.

Women in the Military

In World War II, for the first time, the military ceased to be an exclusive male club, in which the women worked only as nurses. Female leaders like Eleanor Roosevelt had pressed for a military role for women. In May 1942 the military formed the Women's Auxiliary Army Corps (WAACs) to perform four traditional jobs at reduced pay—secretarial, telephone, driving, and cooking. By the following year, "Auxiliary" was dropped from the title. WACs gained equal ranks and pay and were allowed to perform 406 jobs, almost all traditionally female. The navy began its own corps, the WAVEs. One woman, who rose to Master Sergeant, recalls that she had to overcome a threat by her father to "kill himself" if she was so unfeminine as to enlist. Harassment by resentful men and the restrictiveness of an olive drab girdle were part of her daily routine. But, despite these and other limitations, she remembers, "You felt enthused, just like the men who signed up."

From 1942 to 1944, 1800 WASPs (Women Air Force Service Pilots) were trained. They flew every type of plane, including the B29 Super Fortress, which they were allowed to fly to demonstrate to balky men that "even women could fly" it. The women constantly worried about sabotage. In one case sugar was found in a gas tank. When a utility plane crashed, the army sent the male pilot's body home with honors, but the WASPs themselves had to take up a collection to send home the unacknowledged body of his female copilot. A great deal of hostility was directed against the nontraditional activities of "Jackie Cochran's glamour girls." One magazine article sarcastically suggested that "these 35 hour female wonders" trade flying outfits for nurse's uniforms. "But that would be downright rub and scrub work—no glamour there." On December 22, 1944, the army disbanded the WASPs without any public commendation. Their efforts were not officially acknowledged until 1977.

Gays in the Military

The war also had a great impact on another minority group in the military—gay men and women. Before the war, the armed forces neither excluded nor discharged homosexuals, unless they were convicted of performing homosexual acts. As the war began, psychiatrists "reformed" military policy so people diagnosed as homosexuals would be given undesirable discharges, rather than going to prison. They developed screening procedures to discover "medical problems" of suspect "unfit" personality types. Recruits were asked if they "liked girls" or were curious about masturbation. Examiners evaluated whether each man seemed effeminate or "too sensitive" or was interested in being a dancer or interior decorator. While the psychiatrists saw these

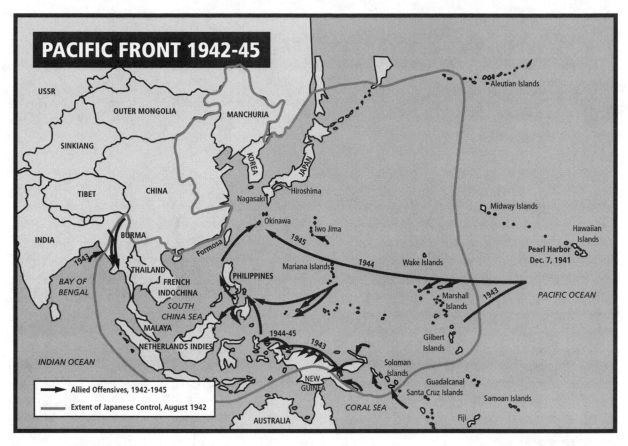

PACIFIC FRONT 1942-45

USSR

OUTER MONGOLIA

MANCHURIA

SINKIANG

KOREA

JAPAN

TIBET

CHINA

Nagasaki

Hiroshima

INDIA

BURMA

Okinawa

Iwo Jima

1945

Aleutian Islands

1943

Formosa

1944

Midway Islands

THAILAND

FRENCH
INDOCHINA

PHILIPPINES

Mariana Islands

Wake Islands

Hawaiian
Islands

BAY OF
BENGAL

SOUTH
CHINA SEA

Pearl Harbor
Dec. 7, 1941

MALAYA

1943

Marshall
Islands

PACIFIC OCEAN

NETHERLANDS INDIES

1944-45

1943

Gilbert
Islands

INDIAN OCEAN

Soloman
Islands

NEW
GUINEA

Guadalcanal
Santa Cruz Islands

Samoan Islands

CORAL SEA

Fiji

AUSTRALIA

→ Allied Offensives, 1942-1945

— Extent of Japanese Control, August 1942

policies as being more humane, the new emphasis on homosexuality led some officers to conduct witch hunts and imprison suspected homosexuals in "queer stockades." Gays awaiting discharge filled the psychiatric wards of some military hospitals.

Thousands of patriotic homosexuals faced the dilemma of weighing the sacrifices inherent in military service against those of remaining civilian at a time of national crisis. Most took the chance of being eventually discovered and stigmatized in the service. "Everyone in my age group went into the service that year—and you would have been ashamed if you didn't go in," said one. Those who made it in realized that "you had to form relationships very discreetly and privately."

Ironically, the war mobilization helped loosen restraints that had once isolated gays and lesbians. The draft placed thousands of homosexuals in gender-segregated barracks where, for the first time, they could find each other and discover the gay life in the cities. Like other GIs, they fought and died in all theaters of the war. The Veterans Benevolent Asso-

ciation, founded in 1945, was the first significant gay membership organization in America. The homosexuals who served in World War II fought one war for their country and another to protect themselves against their own government. Fifty years later, the issue of the role of gays in the military still causes controversy.

THE WAR FRONTS

While Winston Churchill was shocked by the news of Pearl Harbor, he was also excited. "We have won the war," he thought and then slept "the sleep of the saved and thankful." Within two weeks, he was in America to discuss strategy with Roosevelt. To most Americans Japan was the number one enemy because of its sneak attack. Outside the big cities, in America's heartland, many people neither knew nor cared about the European conflict. A March 1942 opinion poll showed that 70 percent wanted to crush Japan first.

WORLD WAR II: EUROPEAN THEATER

Allied Powers
Axis Powers
Neutral Nations
Allied Offensives

The two Allied leaders, however, reaffirmed their earlier plan to assign the highest priority to the European theater, since Germany was seen as the more dangerous enemy.

Although the Allied military situation appeared grim in 1942, there were glaring weaknesses in the Axis alliance. Both Germany and Japan were fighting two front wars without any strategic coordination. They had to commit huge armies to Russia and China at great costs of supplies and manpower.

Both were so brutal in their occupation of conquered countries that they made implacable enemies of local populations. Valuable resources had to be used to maintain control.

The Allies, also, had important strengths, particularly Soviet manpower and American productive capacities. In 1940, FDR astounded the country by calling for the unheard-of production of 50,000 planes per year. By the end of the war, American factories had turned out more than 300,000 planes.

The Allied forces faced the German General Rommel in North Africa.

The big Three Allied leaders—Stalin, Roosevelt, and Churchill, despite differences,—were able to focus their efforts on the common goal of defeating Hitler. Stalin, whose people were suffering catastrophic losses, demanded that the Allies relieve the pressure by opening a second front in Western Europe. (It was said that the Soviet Foreign Minister knew four English words—"yes, no, and second front.") Churchill persuaded Roosevelt that there were not enough men and equipment to mount such an attack. Despite the objections of some American generals, FDR agreed to Churchill's idea of starting the offensive in North Africa. The postponement of the second front to 1943, and later until mid-1944, helped to increase Stalin's paranoia about the motives of his capitalist partners.

In spite of the early concentration on defeating Germany, the first successes came in the Pacific. In mid-1942, the American navy won a surprisingly decisive victory at the Battle of Midway, breaking Japanese Pacific naval superiority, sinking aircraft carriers, and destroying hundreds of enemy planes. By August 1942, American forces began to mount an offensive against Japanese-held islands. The grim and costly six-month struggle by the marines at Guadalcanal was the precursor of the bloody "island hopping" campaign to come.

In November 1942, American and British troops, commanded by General Dwight D. Eisenhower, landed in North Africa in "Operation Torch." They swept eastward, defeating the "Desert Fox," the famed German commander, General Erwin Rommel, by May 1943. Despite orders to fight to the death, more than 300,000 Axis troops surrendered. By drawing substantial German forces into a new theater of war, the African campaign provided significant relief to the beleaguered Soviet army.

At the same time, German and Soviet armies, each with more than a million men, faced each other at Stalingrad in the Soviet Union. In the four months of this battle, the Soviets lost more men than the Americans did in the entire war. However, at the end of the battle, the Germans had lost an entire army, and the Red Army was able to go on the offensive along a thousand mile front.

By the end of 1942, the Allies were also beginning to turn the tide in the Battle of the Atlantic. They sank two-thirds of the German submarines by incorporating modern radar into an increasingly sophisticated antisubmarine warfare campaign. In early 1943, the American and British air forces began round-the-clock bombing of Germany. The hundreds of tons of bombs dropped on Hamburg de-

American soldiers land on the coast of France.

stroyed a good part of the city, killing some sixty thousand people.

In a meeting at Casablanca in January 1943, Roosevelt and Churchill agreed to invade the Axis' "soft underbelly," Sicily and Italy, after victory in North Africa. They also declared that they would accept only the "unconditional surrender" of the Axis powers. Despite later criticism that this demand was a tragic mistake that steeled the enemy resolve and prolonged the conflict, at the time most Americans believed that Germany and Japan had to be totally defeated. No other option would have been politically or emotionally acceptable. In any case, no policy, no matter how generous, could have swayed the leaders of Germany and Japan from their self-destructive course. Within two months of the land-

ing on Sicily, Italy surrendered. But Mussolini fled to German troops who had poured into the country. It took the Allies eight more months of painful, bloody fighting to drive the 150 miles to Rome. They were still fighting in Northern Italy when the war ended.

The Big Three met again in Teheran, Iran, late in 1943. There the Allies agreed to launch the often delayed "second front," Operation Overlord, the invasion of Normandy, France in mid-1944. Stalin also again agreed to enter the war against Japan, once Germany was defeated.

Under the command of the new Supreme Allied Commander, General Eisenhower, D-Day, the greatest amphibious (land and water) landing in the history of warfare, began on June 6, 1944. Hitler real-

MacArthur lived up to his pledge to return to the Philippines.

ized that the Allies were coming, but encouraged by deliberate Allied misdirection, he had decided they would land at Calais, the port closest to Britain. Dummy parachutists were dropped on several locations to confuse the Germans further, causing Hitler to delay sending two available reserve divisions. On June 6, the first assault troops established beachheads along the coast of Normandy. Over the next few days, 1.5 million soldiers landed. Hedgerows on the Norman farms, which served as effective barriers for the German defenders, slowed the Allied offensive. However, Allied tanks were able to break through German lines. The retreat turned into a rout. On August 25, a Free French division, accompanied by the American Fourth Infantry, liberated a Paris "mad with joy." By mid-September, the Germans had been driven out of France and Belgium.

In December 1944, in the deluded hope that a military setback would lead the British and Americans to realize that their true enemy was the Soviet Union, Hitler ordered a final desperate winter offensive in southern Belgium. The Germans succeeded in pushing the Allied lines back 50 miles, trapping the 101st Airborne. (Its commanding officer gave the famed reply, "Nuts," to a German demand for surrender.) American troops, initially surprised, fought tenaciously and stood fast in the "biggest, most stunning and confusing battle of the Western Front." The Battle of the Bulge delayed the in-

vasion of Germany by about a month and cost 77,000 American casualties, but Hitler lost 200,000 irreplaceable men and hundreds of tanks. Both in the West and the East, little stood in the way of Allied conquest of Germany.

The battles for the control of the Pacific and its island groups were fought preeminently by Americans. Here, there was no battle front or clear line between opposing forces. Both sides relied on carrier-based aircraft.

As late as 1943, only about 15 percent of Allied resources were allotted to the Pacific war, which, thus, proceeded more slowly. After the fall of Guadalcanal in early 1943, a series of naval engagements and amphibious operations succeeded in destroying Japan's carrier air power and the offensive capabilities of its fleet. American forces seized airfields within bombing range of Japan. By January 1945, the flamboyant General MacArthur had kept his earlier dramatic promise to return to the Philippines. He became, with the help of a public relations campaign, America's most recognizable military hero.

Although Japanese leaders realized that the war was lost, they refused to consider surrender, with disastrous consequences. Beginning in March 1945, B29s launched bombing attacks on major Japanese cities. The firebombing of Tokyo swept destruction through its wooden structures and killed 100,000 people. But the Japanese fought on.

THE HOME FRONT

The massive war effort required a total mobilization of American society by the government. A week after Pearl Harbor, Congress granted the president extraordinary authority in the War Powers Act. Soon, hundreds of wartime agencies were regulating most aspects of American life. These included the War Production Board, the War Labor Board and the Office of Price Administration. At the end of 1942, the OPA imposed strict price controls to prevent the runaway inflation experienced in World War I.

Roosevelt explained that "Dr. New Deal" had given way to "Dr. Win the War." After Republicans won additional seats in Congress in 1942, a conservative coalition was able to kill WPA, CCC, and new bills designed to aid education and introduce national health insurance. However, basic New Deal reforms, such as Social Security, remained in place. The war actually led to a tremendous growth in the size of government and in the power of the presidency, which had already been significantly increased during the Depression. Federal spending and the deficit both increased ten fold. To win the war, the federal government had almost doubled the total that the government had spent since its founding in 1788!

The government had to increase taxes to meet those expenses. The number of Americans required to file returns and pay taxes quadrupled. Total tax revenues increased more than twenty times. In 1943 the payroll deduction system was introduced to make tax collection more efficient. It became a permanent feature of the tax structure. In a widely seen cartoon short, the OWI enlisted Donald Duck to explain the new system and convince the public that it was their patriotic duty to comply. The Treasury Department commissioned the great American composer, Irving Berlin, to write, "I Paid My Income Tax Today" to reinforce a willingness to share the burden of fair taxation:

> I never felt so proud before
> To be right there with the millions more
> Who paid their income tax today.

> You see those bombers in the sky,
> Rockefeller built them,
> So did I!
> I paid my income tax today!

Bugs Bunny, as well as human celebrities, helped sell war bonds to the public with the slogan, "Buy a share of freedom today." Their efforts and the limitations on consumer spending made it the most popular way to save. Bonds paid almost half the costs of the war.

The miracle of production may well have been America's most significant victory. Within two years, American factories were producing twice as much as the combined output of the three Axis nations. It was, as one observer noted, "a case of Scripture turned upside down, plowshares were beaten into swords (or their twentieth century equivalents: tanks, mortars, planes, bombs)." Two-thirds of all industrial production was war production. Much of the astonishing increase was the result of connections between big business and the military. Large corporations had more experience producing the huge volume needed. They were given generous contracts, loans, tax write-offs, and suspension of antitrust rules. Henry J. Kaiser, for example, used government loans and prefabrication techniques in his giant West Coast ship yard. He lured workers with superior wages and benefits, including child-care facilities. He managed to reduce the production time of a Liberty cargo ship from six months to twelve days. Corporate profits rose 70 percent, and large corporations increased their dominance over the economy. Some people worried about the rise of what was later called, "the military-industrial complex."

To an extent unimaginable under the New Deal, the war created prosperity for ordinary Americans as well. The hard times of the Depression "as though by some twentieth century alchemy were transmuted into Good Times." It even caused the only major improvement in income distribution in modern times. The rich certainly did not grow poorer, but, because of more regular employment and overtime pay, real wages of industrial workers rose almost 50 percent. As a result, the income share of the richest 5 percent declined from 24 to 17 percent. The war aided in the development of an expanding middle class.

Organized labor grew more rapidly than at any other time in its history. Except for a dramatic and unpopular coal miners' strike, labor unrest was limited and had little impact. As the worst of the war ended, more strikes occurred, particularly of the "wildcat" variety. Many people condemned the strikers with the slogan, "There are no strikes in fox holes." They replied, "There are no profits either."

At the beginning of the war, one Iowa farmer told another, "What we needed was a damn good war and we'd solve our agricultural problems." The other, who had a son about to enter the service, later killed in combat, replied, "Yes, but I'd hate to pay with the price of my son. It's too much of a price to pay." Because of the war, farmers finally did overcome the hard times they had experienced in the 1920s and 1930s. Farm production rose dramatically, even though farm population had fallen. Output per worker and farm income both doubled. On the radio, listeners could hear the words of a nursery rhyme parody, "The farmer's in the dough." The use of scientific advances and consolidations created "agribusinesses" and changed the face of American farming.

Science and the Atomic Bomb

The government created the Office of Scientific Research and Development to use the talents of scientists, particularly refugees from Axis countries. They produced improved radar, sonar, anti-aircraft guns, and other military devices. They also saved lives with the development of insecticides, pesticides, drugs to stop the spread of malaria and syphilis, and mass production of miracle drugs like penicillin. One result was a three-year increase in the average life expectancy.

The atomic bomb was the most sensational and lethal development. German scientists had discovered fission, releasing energy by splitting a uranium atom. Late in 1939, the great physicist, Albert Einstein, convinced FDR of the importance of atomic science and the danger to humanity if the Nazis developed atomic weapons. Within a few years,

the largest research and development effort in history was underway, code named the Manhattan Project. General Leslie Groves, a tough, wily administrator, was placed in charge. The original purpose was to beat the Nazis in the race for atomic weapons, a grim goal clearly understood by the refugees from fascism, who were the leading scientists on the project. As far as they knew at the time, Japan was never in this race. The government committed more than $2 billion in federal funds and 160,000 people in 37 facilities to the top-secret effort. Despite major technical breakthroughs, scientists were still working feverishly to produce a usable weapon as 1945 and the war's conclusion approached.

Consumers, Advertisers, and Entertainment

The wartime stimulation of the economy was marvelous for the American consumer. Despite taxes, rationing, and wage and price controls, people found themselves able to buy amenities long denied to them. Wartime shortages created frustrations, but the average family income climbed well above 1938 levels. People moved about to find better jobs in defense industries or to follow servicemen to their camps. Buses were filled with passengers. Railroads made money on passenger travel for the first time in 15 years. The "sunbelt" cities of the South, Southwest, and Pacific Coast boomed. Women, with $8 billion more in their purses, spent freely. The sales of women's clothing doubled despite shortages. With restrictions in many areas, Americans spent their extra money on entertainment and recreation, particularly motion pictures and night clubs. During the war, New York was known as "fun city." Even scarce and rationed goods could be bought for the right price on the black market. Jewelry sales mounted because as one jeweler noted, "People are crazy with money. They purchase things...just for the fun of spending." On December 7, 1944, the third anniversary of Pearl Harbor, Macy's had the biggest selling day in its history.

Advertisers tried to encourage the urge to spend and to prepare the public for a postwar of plenty. Formfit urged the purchase of its bras "for the *sup-*

port you need in these hectic days of added responsibility." Western Electric predicted, "Some day Johnny...will climb out of his foxhole into a world freed from the fear of dictators. When that day comes, the telephone...will help to place all peoples...on friendly speaking terms." In a Nash Kelvinator refrigerator advertisement, a woman with her chin held high addressed her heroic soldier-husband, "I know you'll come back to me...and when you do...you'll find...everything your letters tell me you hold dear. I will be wearing the same blue dress I wore the day you went away....Everything will be here, just as you left it," except, of course, for the shiny new refrigerator in the kitchen. Another ad asked, "Is This Worth Fighting For?" It showed a typical American living room with a fireplace and the western pine walls of the advertiser. That, in fact, did symbolize what many Americans felt the war was about. The *Saturday Evening Post*, addressing Admiral Yamamoto, the planner of the Pearl Harbor attack, declared, "Your people are giving their lives in useless sacrifice. Ours are fighting for a glorious future of mass employment, mass production, and mass distribution and ownership."

Now that Americans had more money than ever, there were restrictions on spending it. People could afford steak every night, but they could not buy it. It was frustrating enough, joked a shipyard worker, "To make you want to save money." The slogan was, "Do with Less so They'll Have Enough." Americans practiced consumer patriotism. "Save newspapers, save scraps, save America." They improvised. Cigarettes went to servicemen, so civilians rolled their own. Twenty million families planted "victory gardens," which eventually produced 40 percent of the food grown. As nylon supplies dropped, nylon stockings were unavailable (except on the black market for $5 a pair). Women made do with liquid leg make-up. When the government ordered a 10 percent reduction in the cloth in women's bathing suits, the desired result was achieved by replacing the full 1930s style suit with a skimpier two-piece model. "The difficulties and damages of the situation are obvious. But the saving has been effected—in the region of the midriff," noted the *Wall Street Journal*.

For all the mistakes and bureaucratic bumbling, the system of controls worked. The OPA's 5600 boards registered every American family for rationing and generated five billion forms a year. It was remarkable that everything worked as smoothly as it did. Few people were badly inconvenienced, and, certainly, nobody starved. Americans accepted cuffless trousers and "imitation chocolate that tasted like soap and imitation soap that did not lather." Having survived the Depression, meatless Tuesdays and other aspects of rationing did not seem so difficult to the average American.

The Office of War Information was designed to help shape public opinion and to protect the American myth, so Americans could "tell the good guys from the bad guys." The mass media cooperated. *Time* magazine entitled an article about Iwo Jima, "Rodent Extermination." The author concluded, "The ordinary Jap is ignorant. Perhaps he is human. Nothing...indicates it."

Hollywood churned out scores of films showing the brave struggle against Japanese barbarism and German viciousness, movies like *Bataan, Wake Island, Thirty Seconds Over Tokyo, Purple Heart, Sahara*, and *Lost Patrol*. All of these featured a clean-cut valiant young middle-American fighting man or a grizzled, no-nonsense "sarge" surrounded by his ethnic buddies—the Irish cop, the Jew and/or Italian from Brooklyn, the Southern farm boy, a cross section of America (except for blacks). Their unity enabled them to withstand enemy soldiers or even torture. (A similar view was expressed in the song about "The Little Yellow Bellies who Meet the Cohens and the Kellys.") Other films presented the lesson that even your German or Japanese friend could not be trusted. In *Lifeboat*, a "serious" film, only the tough American workingman is able to deal with the immoral Nazi sneak.

Billboards warned Americans that "Loose Lips Sink Ships" and "Carelessness is the Enemy Fifth Column." Some movies reflected the same concerns. Fifth columnists, spies, and saboteurs could be everywhere, disguised as ordinary Americans. In the Hitchcock film, *Saboteur*, the enemies are spoiled idle rich folk who refer to the masses as the "moron millions." The hero, an innocent American worker, declares that the issue is "love and hate," and "the world's choosing up sides." Some longed for the simpler past depicted in escapist, nostalgic films like *Meet Me in St. Louis*. The big hit on Broadway was *Oklahoma*, where the singer belts out, "The land we belong to is grand."

Captain Midnight, Jack Armstrong: All American Boy, and Hop Harrigan, all radio heroes, fought the enemy and spies. Superman and other comic strip heroes also went to war. Radio and juke boxes played numbers like, "We Did it Before and We Can Do it Again," "Let's Put the Axe to the Axis," "Praise the Lord and Pass the Ammunition," and "Goodbye Momma, I'm Off to Yokohama," the first hit of 1942. As the war went on, songs reflected the longings and feelings of lonely women and of love interrupted. These included, "They're Either Too Young or Too Old," "Don't Sit Under the Apple Tree With Anyone Else But Me," and the melancholy, "Saturday Night is the Loneliest Night of the Week."

The hunger for wartime news increased the circulation of popular magazines. Radio audiences reached record levels, as people sought the latest information. The voices of Edward R. Murrow and Eric Severeid, reporting from the battle fields, became as familiar as old favorites Jack Benny and Fred Allen.

The war had a major impact on the national pastime, baseball. One paper declared, "Baseball is more than a National Game. It is America's anchor...American boys play ball. 'Play ball' is their battle cry, not 'Heil Hitler.'" Baseball Commissioner Kennesaw Mountain Landis asked Roosevelt if he wanted the game to shut down for the duration of the war. FDR, who was a huge baseball fan, replied, "I honestly believe it would be best for the country to keep baseball going." He warned, however, that individual players would have to go into the service, even if it hurt the quality of the game. Eventually, 340 major leaguers and 3000 minor leaguers served in the war. Hank Greenberg, the first major leaguer called in the peacetime draft, re-enlisted when Pearl Harbor was attacked. The great pitcher, Warren Spahn, survived the Battle of the Bulge. Bob Feller, chief of a gun crew, kept in shape by jogging around the deck between Japanese air attacks. Most stars

★ SILENCE MEANS SECURITY ★

Propagandists ordered security posters because of worries about spies.

played baseball for the army or navy to boost morale and raise funds. The public continued to come to games, even though most of the remaining players were well past their prime. The St. Louis Browns even employed Pete Gray, a one-armed outfielder. The 1945 World Series was so bad that one observer said it reminded him of "the fat men against the tall men at the company picnic." In 1943 an "All-American Girls' Professional League" was formed to appeal to baseball-deprived fans. Even though the players were coached on femininity and wore skirts, the league drew one million fans in one year.

People who were children during the war remember it as an exciting era. They watched movies in which the Allies always won. Favorite candy bars disappeared; weird-tasting gum replaced Wrigley's; ice cream gave way to orange and vanilla sherbet; and Spam sandwiches replaced rationed meat. The Green Hornet's Japanese pal became Filipino. The Dragon Lady in "Terry and the Pirates," after a long criminal career, was now urging her band to "Follow me against the invader who threatens to engulf China." Comic heroes fought in the war against "Japs who looked like monkeys with their thick glasses."

Children ducked under desks in air raid warning drills. They participated in the war effort by buying ten cent savings' stamps, as classes competed against each other. They became "Uncle Sam's Scrappers" and "Tin-Can Colonels." They collected "old tires, old rubber raincoats, old garden hoses, rubber shoes, bathing caps, gloves," as the president had requested. They saved "tin foil" from packages and rolled it into balls. One 13-year-old collected more than 100 tons of paper in three years. One girl recalled that they were encouraged "to pray that a lot of Germans and Japs got killed." In her Catholic girls' school, "We were taught, in no uncertain terms, that God was on our side." Children believed that every contribution they made was important in defeating the Axis.

The nation's schools felt the impact of the war. Thousands of teachers quit to join the armed forces or find a better paying defense job. Schools in rural areas and new boom towns were particularly shorthanded. High school enrollments plummeted as teenagers were now able to find work. Colleges admitted more women to fill empty seats. The military sent almost a million servicemen to college to acquire needed skills. At one point, Harvard granted four military certificates for every bachelor's degree it awarded. Higher education became increasingly dependent on federal government grants, subsidies, and contracts.

Ordinary civilians were involved in the war in other ways. There were constant fears of invasions by enemies who were "spotted" everywhere. (German submarines, along the Atlantic coast, did manage to put some spies ashore on Long Island and Maine. All were captured in New York City.) Twelve million Americans were involved in Civil Defense. Many took part in crash courses in firearms. Some manned positions on top of light houses, church steeples, and hill tops to spot enemy aircraft. Families whose sons were serving in the war put a blue star in the window. If the serviceman was killed, the star became gold.

The war often forced young couples to make immediate decisions whether to marry or wait and see if their love could survive the war. Everything was sped up. It was not surprising that the divorce rate jumped. Marriage and birth rates also soared. More surprising was the number of quickie marriages that lasted. Wives of servicemen often waited weeks or months without getting letters. Some men were gone two years and were never able to get home. Young wives volunteered, donated blood, prayed, and worried. Mostly, they waited. A poignant popular song, "I'll Be Seeing You," captured their emotions.

Women on the Home Front

No event had a more revolutionary effect on the lives of women than World War II, although views about gender roles hardly changed. Reversing the Depression-era efforts to keep women out of the labor force, the federal government suddenly discovered "the vast resources of womanpower." With so many men in uniform, the government tried to persuade women to go into defense jobs to "help save lives" and "release able-bodied men for fighting." Songs like "We're the Janes Who Make the Planes," and "Rosie the Riveter...She's making history, working for victory," appealed to women's patriotism. Women were assured that these jobs were no more difficult than housework and, therefore, no challenge to traditional female roles. "If you've sewed button holes...on a machine, you can learn to do spot welding on airplane parts. If you've used an electric mixer in your kitchen, you can learn to use a drill press," a government publication declared.

More than 6.5 million women did enter the workforce during the war. Many performed highly skilled jobs that had been always considered "male." Most of the new workers were married and middle-aged, unlike earlier female workers. Gains were particularly striking for black women. Some 300,000 of them were able to leave domestic and farm labor for better paid factory jobs. Women found great satisfaction in their work and in its importance to their country. "We were happy to be doing it....Workers from other ships would look at us and see that we were welders and it was a terrifically wonderful thing," one recalled. She felt great joy at the "beautiful, beautiful ships" she helped build. They were also thrilled by their new income that gave them, for the first time, a chance at a middle class life style. It was truly a miracle!

Most Americans believed this change was a temporary war time situation. A War Department brochure maintained, "A woman is a substitute, like plastic instead of metal." Companies found ways of getting around regulations requiring equal pay for equal work. One way was to classify jobs as "heavy" and "light." Women were placed in the latter category and earned about 65 percent of what men did for the same work. The reluctance to supply day-care centers for the children of war workers was evidence of the persistence of traditional expectations. Most agreed with Mayor LaGuardia of New York that even the worst mother was better than the best facility. There were fears of worsening juvenile delinquency as women worked, and the term "latch-key child" was coined at this time.

One woman remembered, "They were hammering away that the woman who went to work did it to help her man, and when he came back, she'd cheerfully leap back to the home." Although women did lose their defense industry jobs when the war ended, they enjoyed the money and the feeling of self-worth it gave them. As the same woman observed, they got a taste for independence. "Like that of Wrigley's chewing gum found in the pack of every GI, its flavor was longer lasting." Despite expectations, women remained in the work force after the war, although in more traditional female jobs at lower pay levels. The war had expanded their world. "I feel," said one "Rosie," "that was the beginning of women's liberation—we showed we could do it."

African Americans at Home

African Americans experienced a similar revolution of rising expectations, as their lives were substantially altered by the war. In 1940 three-quarters of the black population still lived in the rigidly Jim Crow South. The pull of jobs in the cities of the North and West caused more than a million to leave the South. It was the beginning of one of the greatest mass migrations in American history. The portrayal of the war as a fight against Nazi racism led to greater black self-awareness and militancy. Black leaders advocated the "Double V—victory over our enemies at home and victory over our enemies in the battlefields abroad." Most black Americans fought loyally for their country, agreeing with the great heavyweight

"Rosie the Riveter," a song extolling women workers, was popular during the war. This photograph is by Margaret Bourke-White.

During World War II many African Americans used nonviolent direct action against prejudice.

The membership of the largest civil rights organization, the NAACP, grew from 50,000 to 500,000, as it pushed for voting rights. A new organization, the Congress of Racial Equality (CORE), was founded in 1942 to use nonviolent direct action against prejudice. One of their demonstrations was a sit-in at a Chicago restaurant that had refused to serve blacks. Pickets at Yankee Stadium carried signs saying, "If we are able to stop bullets, why not balls?"

The shortage of labor may have opened factory doors, but intolerance and racism remained. The federal government accepted "local standards" in housing and education, including segregation. A government documentary, *War Town*, unwittingly illustrated this. It showed defense plant workers as they left the gates separating into two groups—whites to go to their houses and blacks to theirs in a different direction.

Thousands of blacks came into Detroit, the capital of the defense industry. Most lived in a crowded, filthy rundown ghetto known, ironically, as Paradise Alley. Interracial tensions grew when blacks tried to move into a new housing project built for them at the edge of a Polish neighborhood. A strike of 25,000 Packard workers, to stop the promotion of three blacks, made the situation worse. The strikers shouted, "We'd rather see Hitler and Hirohito win than work beside a nigger." *Life* magazine characterized wartime Detroit as "a keg of powder with a short fuse." Finally, on a steamy hot Sunday in June 1943, racial war erupted. White mobs dragged African Americans out of trolleys and movie theaters to assault them, and blacks smashed and looted white stores. Federal troops arrived to bring peace, after twenty-five blacks and nine whites were killed, and seven hundred people were injured. When the federal government told the city of Philadelphia to solve its shortage of streetcar drivers by hiring blacks, the union rebelled, arguing, "The next thing they will be marrying our sisters." Other race riots broke out in Los Angeles, Mobile, and New York.

Nevertheless, as the war went on, even in Detroit, jobs and living conditions improved for African Americans. The new baseball commissioner, a Kentucky politician named "Happy" Chandler, reflected the beginning of changing attitudes, "If a

champion, Joe Louis, "America's got lots of problems, but Hitler won't fix them."

A. Philip Randolph, head of the Brotherhood of Sleeping Car Porters, the most powerful black labor union, wanted blacks to be able to share equally in the new prosperity. In 1941, he threatened to bring 100,000 blacks to a March on Washington right to "the White House lawn" if the president did not eliminate bias in federally subsidized employment. After procrastinating to avoid offending Southern Democrats, Roosevelt compromised by issuing an executive order to prohibit racial discrimination in defense industries. The Fair Employment Practices Commission (FEPC) was established to enforce the policy. Although the understaffed FEPC was not able to do much about complaints, labor shortages caused more than two million blacks to obtain jobs in industry. The average wage of black workers quadrupled during the war, rising to 65 percent of white wages.

Some Hispanics were nicknamed "Zooters" because of their suits. Police arrested the Zooters, who were often the targets not the causes of violence with white sailors.

black boy can make it on Okinawa and Guadalcanal, hell, he can make it in baseball." The new opportunities in the North created hope. In 1944, for the first time, black votes played a significant role in the re-election of Roosevelt. Gunnar Myrdal, the Swedish author of the 1944, *An American Dilemma*, a pioneer study of race relations, believed that "not since Reconstruction had there been more reason to anticipate fundamental changes in American race relations."

Other Minorities

In the West, Mexican Americans also experienced new opportunities and serious difficulties. Wartime shortages led American growers to import **braceros** (temporary workers) from Mexico, under contract. There were also thousands of illegal Mexican immigrants working under substandard conditions on large farms. Thousands of other Mexican Americans left agriculture to improve their living standards in defense industries.

In Los Angeles, young Mexican Americans asserted their own culture by wearing "zoot suits"— long, large-lapelled, broad shouldered jackets and baggy, tapered pants in vivid colors. Servicemen were angry at the young "draft dodgers" who roamed the streets. When the rumor spread, in June 1943, that a sailor had been stabbed by a **pachuco** (Mexican American), thousands of sailors and soldiers rioted through the streets of Los Angeles. They grabbed residents wearing zoot suits, ripped off their clothes, and beat them up. Mexican Americans, with their clothes in shreds, filled the jails. Los Angeles officials praised the rioting servicemen, and the city council made it a misdemeanor to wear a zoot suit. However, a disproportionate number of Mexican Americans served bravely in the armed forces and, like blacks, anticipated a better life after the war.

American Jews also discovered that fighting a war against Nazism did not automatically doom prejudices. A poll showed that 47 percent of Americans thought that Hitler had picked on the Jews because they were too powerful in Germany. Forty-six percent believed that Jews "have too much power in America." When a few Jewish refugees were rescued and put up at a fort in Oswego, New York, locals, angry at "Eleanor's folly," called them "refujews." (Eleanor Roosevelt had led the rescue effort.) One Jewish soldier was taken aback when a fellow GI read a poem over the post loudspeaker: "When we finish with the Germans and the Japs, we'll come back and kill the Jews and the blacks." When he confronted the bigot with "I'm the Jew you're gonna kill," he was assaulted. He later noted wryly, "The experience gave me another interpretation of World War II."

Franklin Roosevelt had been appalled by the violations of civil liberties he had witnessed during World War I, when he was Assistant Secretary of the Navy. He wanted to avoid the mob attacks on foreigners, the spying on neighbors, and the suppression of dissent that had characterized the earlier conflict. In World War II, conscientious objectors were scorned by the public as "damn yellow bellies." Some were sent to Civilian Public Service camps, where they received no pay. The Mennonites became the nation's first smoke jumpers. Jehovah's Witnesses, who refused to serve in any capacity and, worst of all to the public, refused to salute the flag, were sent to prison. (They were executed in Nazi Germany.) In general, however, the government treated dissenters more fairly than they had in World War I.

"Enemy aliens" also had fewer problems than in the earlier war. At first, German and Italian immigrants, who were not citizens, were somewhat restricted in traveling and urged not to "speak enemy languages." However, German and Italian Americans looked like everyone else. The public may have seen Italians as a little darker skinned, but they did produce great ball players like DiMaggio. Roosevelt was eager to retain the support of Italian voters, so he lifted the restrictions on Italian aliens on Columbus Day, 1942. Many Americans sympathized with the plight of these German and Italian Americans and "treated the war led by their native countries as a source of embarrassment, something like an uncle who had become a petty crook." The Japanese, on the other hand, could not blend in so

readily, "Our relations had not married their children."

Japanese Americans During the War

A woman recalls the image of Japanese in films. "They sure as heck didn't look like us. They were yellow little creatures that smiled when they bombed our boys....The Japanese were all evil." Years of warning about the "Yellow Peril" combined with superpatriotism when the war began. In the hysteria that followed the attack on Pearl Harbor, people believed that the Japanese had attacked the Golden Gate Bridge. The *San Francisco Examiner's* headline screamed JAPANESE INVADE WEST COAST. Almost immediately, people turned on Japanese Americans living on the West Coast. Rumors spread that they were setting forest fires as arrows pointing to military installations. Milkmen refused to deliver milk to them. A funeral parlor proclaimed, "I'd rather do business with a Jap than with an American."

These popular feelings, and some evidence that onshore shortwave operators may have assisted Japa-

A Nisei toddler waits to be taken to a detention camp.

The 442d Regimental Combat Team fought some of the bloodiest battles of the war.

nese submarine shellings on the coast, helped persuade Roosevelt to agree to an executive order allowing the roundup and relocation of Japanese Americans on the West Coast. Two-thirds of the 120,000 living on the coast were **Nisei**, born in the United States. "A Jap's a Jap," declared the Commander of West Coast Defenses. "It makes no difference whether he's an American citizen or not....The Japanese race is an enemy race." The lack of evidence of any Japanese acts of disloyalty, merely confirmed his suspicions, "The fact that no sabotage has taken place to date is just a disturbing...indication that such action will be taken."

Japanese Americans were told to report to assembly centers and given 48 hours to pack their things and dispose of their property. "We are going into exile as our duty to our country," one Japanese-American leader announced. Most lost everything, as whites made the rounds, looking for "fire sale prices." A newspaper columnist wrote, "I am for immediate removal of every Japanese...to a point deep

in the interior....Herd 'em up, pack 'em off....Let 'em be pinched and hungry....Personally, I hate the Japanese. And that goes for all of them." The detainees were sent hundred of miles to desolate Western areas. The conditions in the detention camps were primitive. Detainees lived in crude black tar paper barracks, lacking any privacy. They were surrounded by barbed wire and guard towers with machine guns and searchlights. Internees were asked to sign a humiliating loyalty questionnaire in which they agreed to "forswear any form of allegiance to the Japanese Emperor." Eventually, many showed their resilience by forming bloc organizations, constructing swimming pools, planting gardens, and building educational institutions.

When given a chance, thousands of Nisei enlisted in the armed forces. "We wanted to show the rest of America that we meant business," said one. The all-Japanese 442nd Regimental Combat Team, which served in Italy and France, became the most decorated military unit in World War II: the 4500

Prime Minister Winston Churchill of Great Britain, President Franklin D. Roosevelt of the United States, and Premier Joseph Stalin of the Soviet Union (seated left to right) during the Yalta Conference in February 1945.

men amassed 18,000 individual decorations. Their slogan, "Go for Broke," was well demonstrated by their breaking through German lines to rescue a besieged Texas unit, the "Lost Battalion." Parents, still in prison camps, were awarded combat medals for their sons who had died for their country.

In *Korematsu v. United States* (1944), the Supreme Court upheld the constitutionality of the relocation as a wartime necessity. Justice Murphy, who dissented, characterized the removal as "one of the most sweeping and complete deprivations of constitutional rights in the history of the nation." By this time, the hysteria had lessened, and those who could find jobs were allowed to leave the camps. As a result, the Japanese-American population scattered throughout the country to areas where anti-Japanese prejudice was less pervasive. When one family returned to California after the war, their shed was dynamited, and shots were fired into their house. The older people were devastated by their experience. "They not only lost their homes, they lost the sense that they belonged," a grandson wrote. They became dependent on their children who were able to prosper in postwar America. Only a tiny trickle elected to go to Japan after the war. In 1982 the government condemned the relocation as "race prejudice" and "war hysteria" and apologized for a "grave injustice." A few years later, Congress voted to compensate each interned Japanese American with $20,000.

POLITICS AND DIPLOMACY

The war did not cause a suspension of domestic politics. Franklin Roosevelt appeared to be noticeably weakened by his years of fighting the depression and war. Although only 62, he seemed years older, and many wondered whether he would seek a fourth term in 1944. One week before the Democratic Convention, Roosevelt announced, "As a good soldier...I will accept and serve." Conservative Democrats forced him to drop his liberal vice president, Henry Wallace, in favor of a little-known Missouri Senator, Harry S. Truman. The Republicans nominated the moderate young New York Governor, Thomas E. Dewey. Dewey, who had few disagreements of substance with FDR, emphasized the president's failing health. But the improvement on the military front, and the feeling of many that, if Roosevelt was worn out, it was in service to his country, resulted in a fourth term for the president. It was the closest of his victories—he gained 53 percent of the popular vote. The New Deal coalition may have been showing cracks, but the weary president had to turn his attention to international diplomacy.

In February 1945 Roosevelt met with Churchill and Stalin for the last time at Yalta on the Black Sea. He was tired and ill. Roosevelt's aims were to set up a viable international organization, redeeming the promise of Woodrow Wilson and, above all, to make sure that the Soviets would enter the war against Japan. American military leaders felt that Soviet participation was essential to avoid a blood bath in the invasion of Japan. Stalin did reaffirm his commitment to enter the Pacific war "two or three months" after the defeat of Germany. In return, he would regain territory lost to Japan 40 years earlier and concessions in Manchuria. Stalin also agreed to a United Nations Conference to be held April 1945 in San Francisco. He insisted, however, on Soviet preeminence in Eastern Europe, particularly Poland, the pathway in both world wars for German invasions of Russia. Roosevelt and Churchill reluctantly accepted a vague Soviet promise to hold "free elections" in Poland "as soon as possible."

Later, critics charged that a sick, dying Roosevelt was duped by Stalin or, perhaps, even "soft on communism." The faultfinders, however, forgot that military realities favored the Soviets, whose armies had already overrun Eastern Europe. They stood 50 miles from Berlin at the time. There was no way, short of war, to dislodge them. Roosevelt was realistic in this regard. When an aide complained of the vagueness of Stalin's promises for Poland, FDR replied, "I know. But it's the best I can do for Poland at this time." It also may well be that Roosevelt was more correct than his critics in his assumption that Stalin was more interested in protecting Soviet security than in stirring up world revolution.

A weary president appeared before Congress to declare that the new world organization would "provide the greatest opportunity in all history to achieve real peace." His increasing frailty was apparent to a shocked public. For the only time in his political career, he delivered the speech seated and commented on the weight of the steel braces on his legs. In March, American troops crossed the Rhine, capturing Cologne and surrounding the Ruhr industrial heartland of Germany. The end was near. Roosevelt went to his vacation home in Warm Springs, Georgia, to rest for the upcoming United Nations Conference. On April 12, 1945, while sitting for a portrait, he complained of a "terrific headache." He died within two hours of a cerebral hemorrhage. Most Americans, old enough to remember, can recall exactly where they were when they learned of the president's death. Although some die-hard Roosevelt-

haters expressed delight, the nation, as a whole, had not been so grief-stricken since the assassination of Lincoln. Roosevelt represented a wise leader and father figure, the only president many Americans had ever known. "We're finally winning this war, and now he'll never know," one GI remarked sadly. Eleanor Roosevelt said that people told her, "They missed the way the president used to talk to them."

Harry Truman now faced the overwhelming task of replacing Roosevelt. In the short time he had been vice president, Truman had rarely met with Roosevelt and knew virtually nothing about FDR's plans. No one had bothered to tell him about the top-secret work on the atomic bomb. "Boys," Truman told reporters, "if you ever pray, pray for me now...I feel like the moon, the stars, and all the planets have fallen on me." Truman did display remarkable decisiveness in office, some believed to cover his inadequacies. He quickly got into disagreements with Stalin whom he profoundly distrusted. Some historians feel that his decision to reduce economic assistance to a devastated Soviet Union was the opening salvo of the cold war. Averill Harriman, a diplomat and public official, believed, "If FDR had lived, the cold war wouldn't have developed the way it did, because Stalin would have tried to get along with Roosevelt. FDR had a facility of keeping negotiations open...."

This serviceman, as well as the entire nation, mourned the death of FDR, a man who had tried to meet the challenges of the Depression and a global war.

THE FINAL DAYS OF TRIUMPH AND TRAGEDY

Although Hitler had danced when he learned of Roosevelt's death, believing it might change the tide of the war, by the last week of April American and Soviet troops met in Germany and embraced at the Elbe River. One Jewish American captain had the pleasure of accepting the surrender of a German general to whom he insisted on speaking in Yiddish. The Soviets had overrun Vienna and were arriving in the suburbs of Berlin. On April 30, Hitler committed suicide in his bunker far beneath the streets of Berlin—he wanted to avoid the fate of Mussolini whose body had been mutilated by angry partisans. His last order, which was ignored, was to flood the Berlin subways filled with Germans seeking shelter from the bombardment. On May 2, Berlin fell to the Soviets. Germany surrendered on May 7.

V-E Day brought great jubilation. "V-E Day, oh such a joyous thing....I was ecstatic...when the GIs and Russian soldiers met, they were all knights in shining armor saving humanity," one woman fondly recalled. "To see fascism defeated, nothing any better could have happened to a human being," said a Jewish soldier. "I always felt very lucky to have been a part of it." But the joy was short-lived as Americans had to turn to the Pacific war, and word began seeping out of the horrors Allied troops were encountering in their liberation of Europe.

The Holocaust

The advancing armies were dumbfounded at the indescribable barbarism of the concentration camps. The Nazis had implemented the "final solution," an attempt to exterminate all of Europe's Jews, as wel as Gypsies, homosexuals, and other "inferior" peoples. Extermination centers were constructed to kill people in gas chambers and burn them in ovens. The Nazis murdered six million Jews (including 1.5 million children) and five million other people. Western officials had known of the slaughter since 1942. The State Department attempted to keep information about the "final solution" from reaching the public. By 1943 word had leaked out, and hun-

dreds of church sermons and newspaper articles informed Americans of the terrible butchery. A mass protest rally was held in Madison Square Garden in New York. Concerned Jewish leaders desperately sought intercession from the American government. The president and his advisers responded that the best way to save the Jews was to win the war as rapidly as possible. While European Jewry was being destroyed by the Holocaust, American Jews were divided over whether to press for a homeland in Palestine. By 1944, Henry Morgenthau, secretary of the treasury and the only Jew in the cabinet, had grown increasingly alarmed by the actions of the State Department. He sent Roosevelt a report, "The Acquiescence of this Government in the Murder of the Jews." This led to the creation of the War Refugee Board and to the erection of refugee centers in Europe, saving thousands, but coming too late to save millions. Although the United States had aerial photographs of Auschwitz and other camps by 1944, the

Prisoners look from their bunks at the Buchenwald concentration camp. Many died from disease, maltreatment, and starvation. The camp was opened in July 1937 and liberated by American troops on April 11, 1945.

A row of ovens reveals the cremated remains of the bodies of Jews sent to their deaths in gas chambers.

Allies refused to bomb either the rail lines to the camps or the gas chambers to interrupt the murders.

American troops, who liberated the camps, had seen a great deal of combat, but they "couldn't believe human beings could treat other humans this way." They saw skeletal corpses, stacked like cordwood, shorn of recyclable clothing, hair, glasses, and gold teeth. At Dachau, they came upon a garage filled with human bone dust from the crematorium, which was to be used as fertilizer for nearby farms. "You heard these things, but you never believed 'em. It's typical of American people I guess. You don't believe it until you see it," one soldier commented. Those who saw never forgot. A doctor in command of an Armored Division Medical Company remembered Buchenwald fifty years later. He saw ovens with human bones in them and lampshades made from tattooed human skin. The commanding general ordered local city officials and their wives to clean the camp so they could see the results of Nazism. At the time, the doctor noted, "I was dulled. I can't recall any particular effect...but over the years, I am driven to relive what I saw. Every time there are films about the camps, I have to see them and then I cry."

Only about 110,000 of Europe's Jewish population had been able to find refuge in America, a number so meager that it haunted American Jews. Graphic photographs and films, and the testimony of survivors who arrived in America, seared the Holocaust into the consciousness of American Jews. Although they lacked any real power to change government policy, they felt enormous guilt at not having done enough. As a result, they began to organize to become more effective advocates and to make sure that such horror could never happen again.

The Dropping of the Bomb and the End of the Conflict

Meanwhile, the bloody conflict in the Pacific ground on. Marines had received a foretaste of the struggle to come in 1944 on Saipan. There, both Japanese soldiers and civilians hid in caves. Told that the marines had achieved status by killing their own parents and would torture and murder them, the Japanese committed suicide by leaping to their deaths from cliffs. (Some who balked were beheaded by Japanese troops.) Of forty thousand on the islands, only one hundred survived. Japanese extolled the "glorious acts," while Americans saw only fanaticism.

Early in 1945, a marine assault force invaded the tiny island of Iwo Jima, a place that "looked like nothing that belonged on earth. It looked like another planet." It took six weeks and thousands of casualties to dislodge the Japanese soldiers from tunnels and concrete bunkers in "eight square miles of

Unimaginable atrocities of the death camps shocked Americans

unadulterated hell." The famous photograph of the marines planting the American flag on Mt. Suribachi became a symbol to all Americans of the valor of American fighting men.

Between April and June 1945 on Okinawa, 370 miles from Japan, determined defenders, including 3500 **kamikaze** (suicide pilots), inflicted 50,000 American casualties. (The kamikaze brought terror to the American psyche, convincing many that the Japanese would always fight to the bitter end.) The battle degenerated into a yard-by-yard, cave-by-cave flushing out of soldiers and civilians with artillery and flame throwers. It was "a netherworld of horror" in which "life had no meaning." Over 100,000 Japanese soldiers died, including their commander who disemboweled himself in his command post cave rather than surrender. Fire, suffocation, and sword also took the lives of 100,000 civilians. An invasion of Kyushu, the southernmost of Japan's home islands, was scheduled for November 1, 1945, with the main island of Honshu targeted for March 1946. If the

resistance on these small islands had been so fierce and costly, what would an assault on Japan itself have entailed?

Just before sunrise on July 16, 1945, a fireball arose from the desert in Alamagordo, New Mexico with "the brightness of several suns at midday." Scientists of the Manhattan Project had finally detonated their first atomic explosive device with the force of 20,000 tons of TNT. The mind-boggling sight inspired J. Robert Oppenheimer, the scientific director of the project, to quote Hindu texts about Shiva, god of destruction, "Now I am become death, the destroyer of worlds."

Truman learned of the successful bomb test on his way to his first meeting with Stalin and Churchill. The Allied leaders met from July 17 to August 2 in a palace in the elegant city of Potsdam, just 15 miles from the heart of shattered Berlin, and down the road from Wannsee, where the "final solution" had been planned. (Churchill, whose party lost an election, was replaced in the middle of the conference.) The world leaders agreed to a plan for occupying Germany. Stalin was not impressed with Truman, "that noisy little shopkeeper," but he did agree to enter the Pacific war within a month. "Fini Jap when that happens," Truman noted in his diary. However, Truman also had his "ace in the hole," the bomb, which was to be dropped if Japan did not surrender by August 3. Truman casually informed Stalin that he possessed a weapon of "awesome destruction." Stalin appeared uninterested, probably because he already knew about the bomb from his spy network and was working on one of his own. On July 26, a rather vague ultimatum was issued to Japan, threatening "inevitable and complete destruction," using the "full application of our military power" if Japan did not surrender unconditionally. Tokyo ignored the Potsdam Declaration, perhaps unaware of its true meaning.

In the darkness at 2:45 A.M. on August 6, 1945, a B29 bomber, called the *Enola Gay*, left Tinian Island in the Pacific. At 8:15 A.M., it arrived over the city of Hiroshima and dropped its cargo, an 8900-pound uranium bomb nicknamed "Little Boy." When the bomb exploded, it filled the plane's cabin with an intensity that one crew member likened to a "photographer's bulb going off." When the plane turned to look, the city seemed "like a pot of black boiling tar." On the ground human beings were vaporized where they stood or suffered agonizing burns. One 12-year-old saw charred bodies "laid down like in a fish market, all burned black. They could hardly be recognized as male or female." Her father could not identify her in the hospital because, "My skin had hardened like stone, my lip was pulled up, my chin was adhered to my neck." A huge firestorm erupted in the center of the business district. Nearly 100,000 were killed instantly, and 50,000 were dead by the end of 1945. The scientists had not known about radiation poisoning.

The Japanese government did not send any messages to the Allies acknowledging the catastrophe. Two days later, as scheduled, the Soviet Union entered the war and quickly steam-rolled over Japanese forces in Manchuria.

On a humid sunny August 9, early in the afternoon, in the city of Nagasaki, an "all clear" had been sounded after earlier false alarms. People were emerging from bomb shelters. One 13-year-old looked up and saw two parachutes floating down. This was followed by "a blinding flash, the sky filled with fire." He was thrown across the road. When he regained consciousness, he looked down and realized that his "skin had peeled away in sheets." A second atomic bomb (a more powerful plutonium bomb called "Fat Man") had been dropped from the belly of another B29, the *Bock's Car*. In the blink of an eye, the center of the port city was obliterated. Two-thirds of the 240,000 residents were killed or horribly injured.

The Tokyo regime was badly split over what kind of peace offer, if any, to accept. An American pilot, shot down over Japan on August 8, had lied to his Japanese interrogators, telling them that the United States had 100 more bombs and Tokyo would be the next target. At the same time, the Soviet entry into the war was an enormous blow to the Japanese who had hoped that Stalin would remain neutral. The Minister of War and top military leaders wanted to continue the struggle. However, for the first time, the Emperor intervened, warning his ministers that a continuation of the fight "means nothing but the destruction of the whole nation." Despite an at-

tempted coup and a mutiny by die-hard militarists, the Emperor prevailed. He spoke directly to his people on the radio on August 15, urging acceptance of the peace terms. Truman, who had confided that he did not want to kill any more women and children, approved terms that implicitly accepted the retention of the Emperor. These terms might have been politically impossible for the president to accept before the bomb had repaid the "treachery" of Pearl Harbor. The famous surrender ceremony took place on September 2 on the battleship *Missouri*.

The servicemen, preparing to be shipped over to the conflict, felt, as Churchill put it, that the bomb was "a miracle of deliverance." Said one, "We're sitting on the pier in Seattle sharpening our bayonets when Harry dropped that beautiful bomb. The greatest thing ever happened. Anybody sitting at the pier...would have to agree." Some cried with relief, "We were going to grow up to adulthood after all." One unit went so wild with joy at the news of the surrender that every soldier took a gun and started shooting. With all the bullets flying, "32 men out of our outfit were killed that night by stray celebrating bullets." To civilians as well, V-J day was "the biggest party in the history of the nation." There was an orgy of drinking, kissing, screaming, and having fun without feeling guilty. It took San Francisco "about a week to recover from the hangover." Americans felt good about the war. Evil had been defeated. The forces of light had prevailed.

In 1945, 85 percent of the public supported what seemed to be Truman's unassailable decision to drop the bomb. Fifty years later, a Gallup Poll showed that only 44 percent of the public supported that decision. Critics later noted that, even at the time, other options had been suggested. Some of the atomic scientists signed a petition urging that the United States demonstrate the bomb on a desert or uninhabited island first, giving the Japanese a chance to surrender before the bomb was used on civilians. Military leaders like Generals George Marshall and Dwight D. Eisenhower and Admiral Leahy questioned or opposed the use of the bomb without warning.

Revisionist historians have argued that American officials knew at the time that, even without the bomb, the Japanese government was prepared to surrender soon. The Japanese were waiting for Truman's reassurance that they could keep the Emperor. These revisionists have argued that there is little historical basis for the often-cited assertion that up to a million Americans would have died invading Japan. They suggest that a racist tendency to see the Japanese as subhuman "monkeys" or "rats" made it easier to drop such a destructive weapon on them. These critics also contend that the real purpose of using the bomb was to demonstrate American power to intimidate the Soviet Union and crowd it out of potential gains in the Pacific war.

While it is undoubtedly true that some of the president's advisers saw the bomb as an implied threat to the Soviet Union, many people feel that the speedy end to the war and the saving of American lives were foremost in Truman's mind. He believed the Japanese would ignore any warning and might concentrate on shooting down the plane carrying the bomb. Military experts worried that a demonstration might not work. America and its president would look ridiculous, particularly since there were only two bombs ready for use at the beginning of August.

Japanese revisionist historians have pointed out that it is not so clear that Japan was prepared to surrender, even if concessions were granted on the Emperor's role. In August 1945, a senior Japanese naval officer proposed a huge suicide attack on the Allies that might "sacrifice 20 million Japanese lives." The Emperor's top adviser later said that the peace faction in the government had been "assisted by the atomic bomb in our endeavor to end the war."

Once the moral threshold of deliberately killing civilians had been crossed in the firebombings of Dresden and Tokyo, the A-bomb seemed nothing more than an easier, less risky way of conducting strategic bombing. (Of course, the Germans and Japanese had obliterated those lines long before.) Certainly, after years of research and billions of dollars spent, once the bomb was successfully tested, it is hard to imagine any American president refusing to use it or opting to invade Japan. "For what sane power, with atomic weapons in its arsenal," sociologist Kai Erikson has asked, "would hurl a million more of its sturdiest young men on a heavily fortified mainland?"

A half century later, the issues posed by the bombing had not been resolved. One psychiatrist has argued that the bomb plunged America into fifty years of troubled denial of the nation's capacity to "inflict and...ignore mass death." Philip Morrison, an A-bomb physicist, believed, sadly, that Hitler had created the legacy of war, "When we beat the Nazis, we emulated them...I became callous to death." Perhaps, the ultimate legacy was that all the world did as well.

CONCLUSION

World War II left death and destruction in its wake. Civilian casualties greatly exceeded the number of soldiers who died. The death toll probably reached 60 million, of which 25 million were in the Soviet Union. As the war memorial in Dresden declared, "How many died? Who knows the number?" Approximately 300,000 American fighting men and women died. Protected by two oceans, alone among the combatants, few American civilians were killed, and American cities were not destroyed. The costs in lives, suffering, destruction, and dislocation in the rest of the world, however, were on a scale never seen before. Some have asked whether such a price could ever be worth paying. The alternative of a fascist victory in which, as one historian has noted, "a new dark age was to descend on the earth...a world dominated by evil," would have been even more appalling.

"World War II changed everything," a retired admiral declared. The structure of the American economy was affected as trends towards bigness and centralization accelerated in business and agriculture. The size of the national debt guaranteed that the role of the federal government in the economy would continue to grow. The power of the presidency, as well, was greatly enhanced. The placement of training facilities and defense industries in the South and West played an important role in rearranging the American economy and population. The development of science and technology during the war showed their potential for creating a better world in the future, as well as the possibilities of mass annihilation.

Many Americans worried about how returning veterans would adjust to a peacetime world. "They Won't All be Psycho-Neurotics," was the dubious reassurance of an article in the *Saturday Evening Post* in April 1945. Although there may have been some small shocks, the reabsorption turned out to be relatively easy. The average GI had never been attracted to the military way of life. He came home to a genuine welcome, "the sort any home town accords to members of a winning team after a well-played game." He was aided by continued economic expansion and prosperity. He benefited from the bounty of government programs, such as education benefits and low-cost home loans. Statistics showed that veterans did very well economically, moving up rapidly. Despite the horrors many had faced, most had fond memories of their service. One rifleman observed, "In a short period of time, I had the most tremendous experience of all, of life, of fear, of jubilance, of misery, of hope, and of endless excitement. I honestly feel grateful for having been a witness to an event as monumental as anything in history."

Black GIs were the exceptions. They had come from being welcomed warmly as liberators abroad and expected more dignity and respect at home. One black soldier, stopping in Georgia on his way home by bus, made the mistake of reaching inside a white waiting room to fill a cup with water. Although he was in uniform, local whites beat him unconscious for his effrontery. This experience turned the GI, Hosea Williams, into a civil rights leader. The conditions to which the black servicemen returned led not only to bitterness but also to a revived struggle for human rights.

Many believed that the experience of Rosie the Riveter was nothing more than a "cultural hiccup." It wasn't. The nature of women's roles had been altered forever even though obstacles remained. Japanese Americans regained, and even improved, their place in American society. The stark images of the face of evil as revealed in the Holocaust made anti-Semitism far less acceptable, and both political parties pledged to support the establishment of a Jewish homeland in Palestine. Americans had become a

This man returns to his family in 1945. He was wounded in the invasion of Normandy.

more mobile people. The necessities of rebuilding a war-torn world helped maintain growing American productivity and prosperity.

On the world scene, the United States assumed a role that would have been unimaginable only five years earlier. An article in *Harper's* in the 1970s explained:

> In 1945...the United States inherited the earth...what was left of Western civilization passed into the American account. The war had also prompted the country to invent a miraculous economic machine that seemed to grant as many wishes as were asked of it. The continental United States had escaped the plague of war, and so it was easy enough for the heirs to believe that they had been anointed by God.

But, there was also another new superpower. The Soviet Union was as intent as the United States on reshaping the postwar world in its image. The European colonial empires in Africa and Asia rapidly dissolved and became centers of contention. People worried that the fragile new peace could disintegrate, just as it had after Versailles. Above everything loomed the shadow of the atomic bomb, bringing fear as well as caution. It was all too clear that another world war would be the last. The "good war" that "had to be fought" was over. Americans declared, "We'll never have to do it again." Perhaps the new United Nations would see to that. But, as one observer noted, "Liberty, like truth, is a piece of unfinished business."

Chronology

1922   Mussolini grabs power in Italy

1928   Kellogg-Briand pact renounces war

1931   Japan invades Manchuria

1933   Hitler seizes power in Germany
United States recognizes Soviet Union
Franklin Roosevelt declares Good
    Neighbor policy in Latin America

1935   Neutrality Act seeks to shield America from
    world conflicts
Italy invades Ethiopia

1936   Germany reoccupies Rhineland
Spanish Civil War begins
Second Neutrality Act passed

1937   Japan invades China
Roosevelt urges "quarantine of aggressors" in
    speech
Third Neutrality Act passed

1938   Germany annexes Austria
Munich Conference gives Hitler
    Sudetenland in Czechoslovakia

1939   Nazi-Soviet non-aggression pact signed
Germany's invasion of Poland starts World
    War II (September 1)
Cash-and-carry agreement concludes between
    U. S. and Britain

1940   German *blitzkrieg* conquers most of Western
    Europe, including France
Isolationists, like Charles Lindbergh, form
    America First
Roosevelt re-elected to unprecedented third term
U. S. agrees to destroyers-for bases deal with
    Britain
America institutes first peacetime draft

1941   Lend-lease plan enables Britain to obtain
    needed war materials on credit
Germany invades Soviet Union
Roosevelt establishes Fair Employment
    Practices Commission (FEPC)
American ships skirmish with German
    submarines in North Atlantic
Atlantic Charter, signed by Roosevelt and
    Churchill, states war aims
Japan attacks Pearl Harbor (December 7) and
    U. S. enters World War II

1942   Japan captures the Philippines
Japanese-Americans interned in camps
U. S. navy wins first victories in battles of
    Coral Sea and Midway
Top secret Manhattan Project started to
    develop atomic bomb
War Production Board and Office of Price
    Administration created
Allies invade North Africa
First news of the Holocaust reaches United
    States

1943   Soviets win victory at Stalingrad
Allies invade Italy—Mussolini overthrown and
    Italy surrenders to Allies
Race riot breaks out in Detroit
"Zoot suit" riots erupt in Los Angeles

1944   Allies launch D-Day invasion of Normandy
    (June 6)
GI Bill of Rights passed
Roosevelt wins fourth term as president
U. S. recaptures Philippines

1945	Big Three meet at Yalta
	Roosevelt dies (April 12); Harry Truman becomes president
	Germany surrenders (May 7) V-E Day
	U. S. drops atomic bombs on Hiroshima (August 6) and Nagasaki (August 8)
	Japan surrenders (August 14); V-J Day ends World War II

SUGGESTED READINGS

Michael C.C. Adams, *The Best War Ever* (1994).

Stephen E. Ambrose, *The Supreme Commander: The War Years of General Dwight D.Eisenhower* (1970).

Allan Berube, *Coming Out Under Fire: The History of Gay Men and Women in World War II* (1990).

Michael Beschloss, *The Conquerors: Roosevelt, Truman and the Destruction of Hitler's Germany, 1941-1945* (2002).

John Morton Blum, *V Was for Victory* (1976).

David Brinkley, *Washington Goes to War* (1988).

Tom Brokaw, *The Greatest Generation* (1999).

A. Russell Buchanan, *Black Americans in World War II* (1977).

James McGregor Burns, *Roosevelt: The Soldier of Freedom* (1970).

Peter N. Carroll, *Odyssey of the Abraham Lincoln Brigade: Americans in the Spanish Civil War* (1994).

John Costello, *Virtue Under Fire: How World War II Changed Our Social and Sexual Attitudes* (1985).

Robert Dallek, *Franklin D. Roosevelt and American Foreign Policy, 1932-1945* (1979).

Roger Daniels, *Prisoners Without Trial: Japanese Americans in World War II* (1993).

Lewis A. Erenberg and Susan E. Hirsch, *The War in American Culture: Society and Consciousness During World War II* (1996).

Carlo D'Este, *Eisenhower: A Soldier's Life* (2002).

Bill Gilbert, *They Also Served: Baseball and the Homefront* (1992).

Sherna B. Gluck, *Rosie the Riveter Revisited* (1987).

Doris Kearns Goodwin, *No Ordinary Time: Franklin and Eleanor Roosevelt: The Home Front in World War II* (1994).

John Hershey, *Hiroshima* (1946).

Lee Kennett, *G.I.: The American Soldier in World War II* (1987).

Richard Lingeman, *Don't You Know There's A War On?* (1970).

Deborah E. Lipstadt, *Beyond Belief: The American Press and the Coming of the Holocaust* (1993).

Mauricio Mazon, *The Zoot Suit Riots* (1984).

William O'Neill, *A Democracy At War: America's Fight At Home and Abroad in World War II* (1993).

Geoffrey Perrett, *There's a War to Be Won* (1991).

___ , *Days of Sadness, Years of Triumph: The American People, 1939-1945* (1974).

Richard Polenberg, *War and Society* (1972).

Gordon W. Prange, *At Dawn We Slept: The Untold Story of Pearl Harbor* (1981).

Leila Rupp, *Mobilizing Women for War* (1978).

Leon Sigal, *Fighting to a Finish* (1988).

William Tuttle Jr., *"Daddy's Gone to War": The Second World War in the Lives of America's Children* (1993).

Gerhard Weinberg, *A World At Arms: A Global History of World War II* (1994).

Allen M. Winkler, *Home Front U.S.A.* (1986).

David S. Wyman, *The Abandonment of the Jews: America and the Holocaust, 1941-1945* (1984).

Chapter Twenty-one

THE COLD WAR: The Truman-Eisenhower Years

"But I don't want to lose my job as a machinist. This is the best money that I have ever made. I don't want to go back to clerking in a department store." Many Rosie the Riveters echoed this sentiment as industry quickly forced women out of their jobs when the men returned home from World War II. The women's experience of knowing that they could do "difficult" but well-paid work just as well as men was but one of many war experiences that helped to shape the cold war era. Black men, who had served in the segregated armed forces and were made officers of all black units, expressed similar sentiments. Having experienced leadership in the army, many were determined not to go back to segregated menial life again. Finally, there were the changes made possible by the GI Bill. As young men from Turtle Creek, Pennsylvania, neither Bill Norris nor his best friend, Layman Allen, expected to be anything but laborers. World War II and the GI Bill changed all that for them and a generation of Americans. Looking back on a career as a U.S. Circuit Judge, Bill Norris said about himself and University of Michigan law professor Layman Allen, "Princeton opened all those doors for us. But the GI Bill opened the doors to Princeton." If only those were the only memories of this period. But there was that other war. "Kiddies, send a stamped self-addressed envelope to WCVI radio Connellsville, Pennsylvania and get your free map of Korea. Use your crayons to trace the daily advance of American forces as we beat back the Godless Communists!" Leading the nation at the beginning of this period of intense changes was the man who had succeeded to the presidency: Harry S Truman.

TRUMAN PRESIDENCY

After twelve years of the leadership of Franklin Roosevelt, Americans wondered what their new president was like and if he would be equal to the tasks of post-war America. Some said he looked and talked like what he was: a failed haberdasher. Without question, he was a contrast to the beloved FDR.

FDR came from a comfortable background with inherited wealth. Truman had grown up on a small farm outside Independence, Missouri in relative poverty. FDR was a Harvard graduate who had been educated at private schools; Truman could not afford a college education. FDR had never served in the military even though he was Assistant Secretary of the Navy in World War I. In contrast, what changed Truman's life was his service in World War I as a captain. There he found that he had leadership skills.

When Truman returned from the war, he and a partner began a haberdashery business. They were soon bankrupt. Although it took him many years, Truman eventually paid back every debt incurred in the bankruptcy. With business closed to him, Truman became a professional politician beginning his career as a county judge.

He was next elected to the United States Senate where he chaired a committee to investigate war mobilization. His relentless search for evidence of price gouging brought him national attention. Truman was decisive, feisty, and loyal. He was also profane and had a temper. The most famous example of these last traits was the letter he wrote during his presidency to a music critic, Paul Hume, who had panned the singing of his daughter Margaret. Hume had written a critical review for the *Washington Post* of Margaret Truman's first Washington concert as a coloratura soprano. In his letter Truman wrote, "Some day I hope to meet you. When that happens you'll need a new nose, a lot of beef steak for black eyes, and perhaps a supporter below!"

Truman's presidency began with a myriad of problems in both domestic and foreign affairs. The most pressing was foreign affairs. Our old war time ally, the Soviet Union, now opposed the United States. While our support of the Soviets in World War II was a partnership of convenience, Roosevelt had thought the United States could work with the Soviet leader, Joseph Stalin, to prevent future wars. It soon was obvious that this was not possible. The factors that influenced the development of this new

form of conflict, the cold war, can only be understood if the nature of Soviet Communism is clear.

Karl Marx, the father of Communism, based his theories on class conflict that he thought was inevitable. He believed that capitalism was the last stage in the evolution to a utopia where the proletariat, the workers of all countries, would control the government. Marx fully expected that the proletarian revolution would begin in one of the most heavily industrialized nations; instead, it began in one of the more backward, Czarist Russia. Under Lenin, the leader of the revolution, and his successor, Stalin, the Soviet Union followed a foreign policy that was a mixture of world revolution and the old czarist policy of expansionism. The United States was prepared for neither.

UNITED NATIONS

Roosevelt had obtained a consensus among the war-time allies to establish a new international organization to replace the defunct League of Nations. Accordingly, on April 25, 1945, delegates from fifty nations met in San Francisco to draw up the charter of the UN. The UN could admit additional members by a two-thirds vote of the General Assembly, which included delegates from all member nations.

The other permanent agency was the Security Council, which had five permanent members (United States, Union of Soviet Socialist Republics, Great Britain, France, and China) and six elected members. Each permanent member had veto power over any action. The Security Council might investigate any dispute, recommend settlement or refer the dispute to the International Court, and take measures including a resort to military force. The UN was lodged at Lake Success, New York with a permanent home planned in New York City.

There was also a consensus that those responsible for the atrocities of World War II should face trial and punishment. The Potsdam Conference gave final approval to the principle of war-crime trials. Both German and Japanese officials went on trial for crimes against peace, against humanity, and against the established rules of war. Out of twenty-two Nazis tried at Nuremberg, twelve were sentenced to death, three to life imprisonment, and four to shorter terms. In Tokyo, twenty-five Japanese were tried with seven sentenced to death, sixteen to life imprisonment, and two for short term imprisonment. Thousands of others were tried in national courts. The accused offered the excuse that "they were just following orders." It was not accepted. Fifty years later it was revealed that many Japanese who had conducted biological experiments on allied prisoners had escaped punishment even though the United States knew of the experiments. There were also many Nazi scientists whom the U. S. protected because they could be helpful in the new cold war against the Soviets.

POSTWAR PROBLEMS: EUROPE AND THE MIDDLE EAST

Americans hoped that the Yalta and Potsdam agreements with the Soviet Union would stand. The Yalta agreement had divided Germany and Berlin into occupation zones with a divided Berlin within the Soviet Zone. At Potsdam, Truman accepted the reality of the border that the Soviets had established between themselves and their satellite Polish state. When the Americans, British, and French successfully blocked any Soviet claims to reparations from their western zones, the Soviets stripped $3 billion a year from East Germany. It soon became clear that the Soviets were not going to keep the agreements but instead were intent on keeping what they had. To the Soviets, this was just providing a buffer zone between them and the Germans who had invaded them twice in less than twenty-five years. They also thought that it paralleled American control in Japan and Western control in most of Germany and Italy.

As early as 1946, Stalin had pronounced international peace as impossible "under the present capitalist development of the world economy." His statement impelled George Kennan, a foreign service officer, to spell out the roots of Soviet policy and to warn that the Soviet Union was "committed fanatically to the belief that with the United States

there can be no permanent *modus vivendi*, that it is desirable and necessary that the internal harmony of U.S. society be disrupted, the traditional way of U.S. life be destroyed, the international authority of the U.S. be broken, if Soviet power is to be secure."

The turning point in the relationship came with the Moscow Conference of 1947. The foreign ministers met to discuss the question of German political and economic unification. The Soviet Union would agree to economic unification on two conditions: that they share in the control of industry of the Ruhr Valley and the recognition of their claims for ten billion dollars in reparation. The West rejected this. Nor was there any agreement on political unification. This conference ended any hope of friendly cooperation between the Communist and non-Communist worlds. It also marked the beginning of the policy of containment.

By 1947 Kennan was back at the State Department and presented his ideas for a proper response to the Soviets in *Foreign Affairs* under the pseudonym "X." "...it is clear that the main element of any United States policy toward the Soviet Union must be that of a long-term, patient but firm and vigilant containment of Russian expansive tendencies." Kennan thought that there was a strong possibility "that Soviet power, like the capitalist world of its conception, bears within it the seeds of its own decay, and that the sprouting of those seeds is well advanced." This became America's basic foreign policy stance during the cold war. While Kennan later wrote that his recommendation applied only to Europe, future administrations applied it world-wide.

The first action under the policy of containment was the Truman Doctrine: the policy of the United States to support free peoples who were resisting attempted subjugation by armed minorities within or by outside pressure. The first application of this doctrine was in Greece and Turkey.

For centuries the Russian Empire had sought a warm water port to give them access to the Mediterranean. The Soviet Union continued this policy by pressuring Turkey to yield control of the Dardanelles, as well as areas on the Black Sea. The pressure on Greece was less direct, but it had been fighting Communist forces within Greece, who were receiving aid from Communists in three neighboring states since 1945. Great Britain had been aiding both Greece and Turkey, but in 1947 informed Truman that it could no longer continue this aid. Truman asked Congress for $400,000,000 in military and economic aid to Greece and Turkey. After two months of debate, Congress authorized all that the president requested, as well as sending military and civilian experts. By 1949, U. S. aid had saved Greece and Turkey. It was the first success for containment.

While the problems in Greece and Turkey required military and monetary aid, the problems in the rest of Europe were economic. By 1947, a severe drought and a harsh winter made Europe a "rubble heap and a charnel house, a breeding ground of pestilence and hate" in Winston Churchill's words. Amid the chaos, the Communists were flourishing. While aid from the United Nations had prevented starvation, it did nothing to aid economic recovery.

The American answer was the Marshall Plan. George C. Marshall, the former general who had coordinated U.S. wartime planning, was now secretary of state. In May 1947 Marshall unveiled the plan in a commencement address at Harvard University. American aid was offered to any European nation who would coordinate its efforts for recovery and present the United States with a program and specification of its needs. Marshall stated: "Our policy is directed not against country or doctrine, but against hunger, poverty, desperation and chaos."

This promise of economic assistance included the Soviet Union and the eastern European nations that comprised the Soviet bloc. Some members of the Soviet bloc did turn up at the planning meeting but were ordered home "from the imperialist" scheme. In December Congress passed the European Recovery Program and in June 1948 funded it with an initial $4 billion. The total cost of the program that saved Europe was $10.25 billion. We also poured money into rebuilding Japan. Since the U. S. was the only major economic power after World War II, the Marshall Plan also benefited the United States.

With the failure of the Moscow Conference, the United States, Great Britain, and France decided to unify their three zones to create West Germany and West Berlin. Unification proceeded with the creation of a representative government that would control its domestic affairs and have limited control over foreign affairs. The ban on rearmament remained, and the military occupation would continue. The U. S. then invited the West Germans to participate in the Marshall Plan.

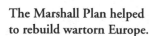

The Marshall Plan helped to rebuild wartorn Europe.

Berlin Airlift

The Soviets tried to shut off ground access to Berlin in June 1948. The plan was to force the Allies from West Berlin, which was in Soviet-controlled East Germany. Truman responded with a massive airlift that delivered 4,500 tons of food and coal a day! It operated for eleven months. The strain of the blockade was not without its humorous encounters. The Soviet commander's gas main ran through West Berlin so the Americans shut it off. When the Soviets attempted to move his furniture through the American zone to another home, the Americans seized the furniture. There was also the spectacle of the Berlin children who waited outside the fence at the airport for the candy bars thrown to them by American pilots as they waited for their planes to be unloaded. Eventually the Soviets lifted the blockade. The first major encounter of the cold war showed that neither side wanted to turn it into a "hot" war.

As the change in the world order became clearer in 1948, Congress authorized the president to develop collective defense pacts under the UN charter. This was the beginning of the **North Atlantic Treaty Organization** (NATO), a defensive alliance of Britain, France, United States, Belgium, Netherlands, Luxembourg, Canada, Denmark, Iceland, Italy, Norway, and Portugal. It later included Greece, Turkey, Germany, and Spain. It marked the first treaty of alliance the United States had had since the Franco-American Alliance of 1778 during the American Revolution.

The last big foreign policy decision with long term consequences came in the Middle East. In 1947 the United Nations proposed to partition Palestine into Jewish and Arab states. The Arab states fiercely resisted to no avail. May 14, 1948, Jewish leaders proclaimed the independence of Israel. The United States, disregarding its oil interests in the Arab states, recognized it in minutes. The Arab states immediately went to war. A temporary truce and peace were worked out in May 1949, and Israel was admitted to the United Nations.

The Berlin airlift provided food and fuel for West Berliners. Children waited for candy that American pilots dropped in tiny parachutes.

A domestic policy decision that was destined to have long-range effects on foreign policy was the National Security Act of 1947. Passed in response to the Pearl Harbor intelligence debacle, the National Security Act of 1947 created a National Military Establishment headed by the secretary of defense. It also created a Joint Chiefs of Staff and, most importantly, the Central Intelligence Agency (CIA). The CIA, which was the replacement for the wartime Office of Strategic Services (OSS), was designated to coordinate intelligence gathering. It was permitted neither covert actions nor any domestic activities. But the act contained a big loophole that would in time allow the CIA to engage in both: authority to perform "such other functions and duties related to intelligence" as the National Security Council might direct. While the activities under the Truman administrations were limited, the CIA would enter a new era of activity under succeeding administrations.

THE COLD WAR: JAPAN, CHINA, AND VIETNAM

Japan

A Far Eastern Commission, speaking for the eleven powers that had fought against Japan, existed to make policy. In reality, however, it was the Supreme Commander for the Allied Powers, General Douglas MacArthur, who controlled Japan. Under MacArthur's administration the Japanese docilely accepted the changes that revolutionized their nation. These included the shrinking of Japan to four islands; the renunciation of war; the punishment of war criminals; and the institution of a constitutional monarchy with woman suffrage. There was also an attempt to institute a more democratic economy. These last changes ended when the occupation ended.

China

U. S. policy was not so successful with other major Asian powers. During World War II, both the Nationalist Chinese (Kuomintang) and the Communist Chinese had worked together to defeat the Japanese. American foreign policy was based on the erroneous belief that this situation would continue and that the two could join together in a post-war democratic China. What the United States did not know was that during the final months of the war when the Communists were retaking the interior in the Northwest and North, the Soviets were sending them assistance. It was soon clear that only action by the United States could save China from a civil war.

In November 1945 Truman sent newly retired General George C. Marshall to China with two instructions: seek a truce in the fighting; and obtain political unification through a conference of the Nationalists, Communists, and other groups. The underlying assumption was that the only legal government in China was the Nationalist government. After spending a year in China, Marshall returned home and reported to Truman that there was no hope of compromise because of extremist elements on both sides. It was a situation that the United States would find often: dedicated Marxists on one side and the criminal element of corrupt elite on the other.

While the United States continued to recognize the government of Chiang Kai-shek, it had lost faith in Chiang's ability to solve China's problems and, therefore, did not supply the massive military aid that Chiang would have needed to win. The United States undertook a progressive disengagement from the Chinese situation as the Truman administration concentrated on the problems in Western Europe. The expectation was that eventually the nationalist interests of the Chinese would overcome their Communist ideology so that they would, like Marshall Tito in Yugoslavia, go their own way and not be dominated by the Soviet Union. At that point, the administration thought, China, like Yugoslavia, would want to establish good relations with the United States. In the midst of this, the United States ascertained that the Soviet Union had exploded an atomic bomb. A week after this news, the People's Republic of China was inaugurated; Chiang was in Formosa and Mao Zedong and his Chinese Communists were in control of mainland China. In future years, Republicans would charge the Democrats with losing China. Historians still disagree on the issue of whether China could have been saved.

Soon after the Communist take over in China, Truman decided to build the "Super" hydrogen bomb that would have ten times the destructive force of the bombs dropped on Hiroshima and Nagasaki. In fact, its "trigger" was a nuclear explosion!

Vietnam

At the settlements at the end of World War II, Churchill had prevailed on Roosevelt to return Indochina to France, its former colonial master. In 1945 Ho Chi Minh, the leader of the Communist Vietnamese, declared Vietnamese independence using the stirring phrases of Jefferson's Declaration of Independence. Nevertheless, the Allies gave France their approval to reassert dominance in the area. By 1946, the French were fighting Ho Chi Minh and his Independence League, the Viet Minh. Few natives of either Vietnam, Laos, or Cambodia supported the French who had been too slow in fulfilling their promises of independence. The French choice for a ruler of Vietnam, the Emperor Bao Dai, did not gain an enthusiastic response like that given to Ho Chi Minh. While the United States did not send troops, American money supported the French effort.

DOMESTIC POLICY

As soon as the war ended, Americans began to demand the return of their men. Accordingly one of Truman's first acts was the demobilization of 9 million men and a few women from the army and navy. This reduced the military to 1.5 million, with Congress asking for more reductions. By 1950 there were 600,000 men in the military. In his memoirs Truman termed this "the most remarkable demobilization in the history of the world, or disintegration if you want to call it that."

The return of the men from war presaged social and economic changes whose repercussions have not yet ended. The first result came in 1946 with a baby boom that continued until the early 1960s. The second result took a bit longer since it was tied to the GI Bill of Rights passed in 1944 by a margin of one vote. This act provided veterans with money for education, vocational training, and medical treatment, as well as loans for homes or business.

Despite predictions by opponents of the bill that the educational benefits would be ignored, American colleges and universities were flooded with 2.2 million veterans taking advantage of the higher education provisions. This group included 60,000 women and 70,000 African Americans. Many veterans were married, so the colleges had to establish married housing or vetvilles. At a cost of $5.5 billion this first GI Bill produced 450,000 engineers, 240,000 accountants, 238,000 teachers, 91,000 scientists, 67,000 doctors, 22,000 dentists, 17,000 writers, and thousands of other professionals of all types. Estimates of the return on this investment range from $3-$4 for every dollar spent. Along the way, it enabled new millions to enter the middle class and led to the most equitable distribution of wealth in American history. In 1949 the richest 5 percent owned only 19.3 percent of the wealth. By comparison in 1998, 97 percent of the wealth was controlled by 5 percent of the people. The GI Bill also fueled the economy, helped to prevent a post-war depression, and led to inflation.

Unions, which had not gotten much of an increase in wages during the war, now began to strike. When the mine owners refused to accept the United Mine Workers' demands, Truman, using war powers, took over the mines. In the railroad strikes, it was the workers who refused the agreement, so Truman took over the railroads until the strike was settled.

Such decisive actions made it obvious that Truman was not going to be just a caretaker president. He next sent a program to Congress that called for an enlarged New Deal. It included expansion of unemployment insurance, extension of the Employment Service, a higher minimum wage, a permanent Fair Employment Practices Commission, slum clearance and low rent housing, regional development of the nation's river valleys, and a public works program.

This is a post World War II housing project established on the edge of a metropolitan area.

Although there were the usual fights with the Congress, the Employment Act of 1946 was passed that set up a Council of Economic Advisors to advise the president on employment needs. There was also the Atomic Energy Act, which gave civilians power over the new force and authorized only the president to use it in war.

In the off-year election of 1946, people voted for a Republican controlled Congress, which was anti-labor, and passed the Taft-Hartley Act of 1947. This banned the closed shop, which required that only union workers be hired, but permitted a union shop, which required that workers must join a union within a short period of time after they are hired. While it included provisions against unfair union practices, it also required union leaders to take oaths that they were not Communists. Truman's veto restored his credit with labor, but the bill was passed over his veto. Its biggest effect was that Southern states passed right-to-work laws that banned union shops.

The Republican Congress also passed a tax cut that Truman vetoed on the grounds that while production and employment were high, the federal deficit should be reduced. Congress overrode his veto.

Truman recommended and Congress passed a law changing the order of presidential succession so that the Speaker of the House and the President Pro-tempore of the Senate, both elected officials, came before the secretary of state and other cabinet officials. In a swipe at FDR, Congress passed and the states ratified the Twenty-second Amendment, limiting presidents to two terms or not more than a total of ten years should they serve out part of a previous president's term. It did not apply, however, to Truman.

Civil Rights

On February 2, 1948, Truman sent a civil rights message to Congress, the first in American history. He called for anti-lynching laws, anti-poll tax laws, the establishment of a Fair Employment Practices Commission to prevent discrimination by employers and unions alike, an end to discrimination in interstate travel, and a request that the claims of Japanese Americans who had lost their property and had been confined because of their racial origin be acted upon. (The latter was not approved until the Reagan administration.) Truman also announced that he had ordered the secretary of defense to end segregation in the armed forces. When asked to soften his civil rights views, Truman, whose ancestors were Confederates, replied, "...my stomach turned over when I learned that Negro soldiers, just back from overseas, were being dumped out of army trucks in Mississippi and beaten....as President I know this is bad. I shall fight to end evils like this."

ELECTION OF 1948

Republican successes in the 1946 election seemed to indicate that the Republicans could take the presidency, especially since the Democratic Party was divided. Henry Wallace, who had served as one of FDR's vice-presidents and who wished for closer relations with the Soviet Union, ran on the Progressive Party ticket. Truman ran for the Democrats, and Thomas E. Dewey ran for the Republicans. The Republican platform was conservative and international; the Democrats included a civil rights plank and the enactment of federal anti-lynching and anti-poll tax laws. When the Democrats met in convention, the Southern Democrats, or Dixiecrats, bolted and nominated Strom Thurmond, later a Republican Senator from South Carolina, for president. The Dixiecrats wanted to split the electoral vote so that no one would have a majority. This would result in the presidential race being thrown into the House of Representatives, which the Republicans controlled. Under this scenario a deal could be struck to prevent any attempt at civil rights.

With the Southern Democrats alienated from the national party, Truman's strategy was to appeal to the black vote in the North. With a strong civil rights platform and his executive order to desegregate the military, Truman was well positioned to gain the black vote. The four party race also benefited Truman since it put him right in the middle of the political

spectrum. With the Progressives putting forth a leftist campaign and the Republicans and Dixiecrats a rightist one, Truman became the moderate in the ideological middle.

Thomas Dewey, the GOP candidate, had run for president against Roosevelt in the 1944 election. He had an admirable record as an anti-Mafia prosecutor and a competent governor of New York. However, he seemed to think that he was automatically going to win the election. He followed the conventional belief that Truman was a bumbler and a sure loser. Not all Republicans were enamored of Dewey. Teddy Roosevelt's daughter, Alice, derided him as, "The little man on the wedding cake."

As Truman traveled around the country on a whistle-stop train tour, criticizing the "do-nothing" Republican 80th Congress, a man yelled out, "Give 'em hell, Harry." Truman replied that he just told the truth, and they considered that hell. Whatever the case, it reaffirmed Truman's image as a fighter.

On November 1, 1948, the Gallup organization published the results of their last poll taken between October 15 and 25. It gave Dewey the winning edge of 49.5 to Truman's 44.5. To the surprise of everyone but Truman, Truman won the election, the greatest upset in American political history. We now know that in close elections, voters make their decision the weekend immediately before Election Day. Thomas E. Dewey and his supporters were so confident of winning that the *Chicago Tribune* even published a headline issue announcing "Dewey Defeats Truman." It was an issue of the *Tribune* that Truman delighted in holding up for photographers. One congratulatory telegram to Truman was from General Dwight Eisenhower. In it he stated: At no point in the political history of the United States was there a "Record of greater accomplishments than yours, that can be traced so clearly to the stark courage and fighting heart of a single man." Along with the presidency, the Democrats also carried both houses of Congress.

Truman worked with Congress to increase the minimum wage to $.75 an hour and to increase coverage under the Social Security Act. A National Housing Act, extension of rent control, farm price supports, slum clearance, and support for the

Tennessee Valley Authority also passed. The Dixiecrats, however, gave the cold shoulder to civil rights, national health insurance, federal aid to education, and subsidies for farm incomes rather than farm prices.

Truman's next four years in the White House were ones of declining popularity and increasing problems. Shortly after the election, the Trumans moved from the White House to Blair House while the White House was totally gutted and rebuilt with the exterior walls still standing. This was necessitated when a leg of daughter Margaret's piano came through the ceiling of the room beneath it! While they lived in Blair House in 1950, two Puerto Rican nationalists attempted to assassinate Truman. In the ensuing gunfire, a White House policeman was killed along with one of the Puerto Ricans. Had the assassins waited a few hours, they might have had a better chance of killing Truman at an outdoor speech.

SECOND TERM

Foreign policy issues became paramount during Truman's second administration, and the worst problems were in Asia. Here the issue of China had been bubbling away for all the years that Truman had been president. The problems with U. S. policy were two-fold. Chiang had retired to Formosa, an island 100 miles off the coast of China, where he set himself up as a government in exile. The second problem was that Mao was more of a Communist than a pragmatist and was vociferously anti-American. The Chinese knew that it was more important for them to have a good relationship with the Soviets with whom they shared a border than with the distant United States. On February 14, 1950, Red China and the Soviet Union announced the signing of a mutual-defense treaty. Soon the administration would face the Republican charge of "losing China."

Harry Truman displays the headline on the front page of the *Chicago Tribune*, which had declared Dewey the winner.

In the midst of these foreign policy concerns were highly interrelated domestic concerns. One was the trial of Alger Hiss with the accompanying rise of a young Republican representative from California, Richard Milhous Nixon, a member of the House Committee on Un-American Activities (HUAC). The other was the beginning of a phenomenon called McCarthyism. Both were concerned with the subversive activities of Communists or Communist sympathizers called fellow travelers. One danger was that any one who disagreed with the ideology of their accusers could be called a Communist, fellow traveler, or comsymp (Communist sympathizer).

Alger Hiss was a former mid-level State Department official who had become president of the Carnegie Endowment for International Peace. Whittaker Chambers, an editor from *Time* and admitted former Communist, accused Hiss of Communist sympathies. Nixon was a HUAC supporter of Chambers. When Chambers testified before the HUAC where he was backed by Nixon, he enlarged his charges and accused Hiss of espionage. At a crucial point in the investigation Chambers produced microfilm documents that he claimed Hiss had passed to him in 1937 and 1938. The documents that had been hidden in a pumpkin on Chambers' farm were known as the Pumpkin Papers. In December 1948 Hiss was charged with perjury for denying these allegations under oath. He could not be charged with espionage because the statute of limitations had expired. After two trials, a federal jury convicted Hiss in January 1950, and the judge sentenced him to five to ten years in a federal prison. To his defenders, Hiss was the victim of a conservative conspiracy led by Richard Nixon. To his accusers, he was a symbol of a naive government policy that was leaving the United States vulnerable to its worst enemy. Although Hiss is now dead, as are Chambers and Nixon, the case is still discussed and, while Hiss denied it to his dying day, all available evidence points to his guilt. The case did help propel Nixon to the United States Senate and from there to the vice-presidency.

HUAC also conducted a series of investigations on Communist infiltration of the film industry. This resulted in the imprisonment of a group of writers,

Alger Hiss, who had been a prominent State Department official, was convicted in January 1950.

directors, and producers known as the Hollywood Ten. One of the people who testified before the committee was Ronald Reagan, a six-time president of the Screen Actors Guild, the union for film actors. As union president, Reagan tried to remove suspected Communists from the movie industry and made strong anti-Communist statements to HUAC.

HUAC also investigated one of the most popular stars of the 1950s, Lucille Ball. Ball had once registered to vote as a Communist to please her elderly grandfather. When her husband defended her before their popular TV show, *I Love Lucy*, he said the only thing red about Lucy was her hair and even that was dyed.

The other politician who rode the issue of communism to fame was Joseph McCarthy, the junior senator from Wisconsin. Friendless and generally considered a failure, he was looking for an issue that might raise him out of obscurity. Communist subversion was that issue. In February 1950 in a speech to Republican women in West

Virginia, McCarthy waved a piece of paper on which he said were the names of 205 known Communists in the State Department. Later he made essentially the same speech but said it was fifty-seven "card carrying" Communists. This speech made the headlines and soon gave birth to a new term in American political history, "McCarthyism." In a follow-up speech to the Senate, which went on for five hours, he claimed eighty-one names.

Although McCarthy had no evidence that there was even one Communist, he soon was no longer obscure. Despite his hard-drinking recklessness, moderate and liberal Republicans did not reject him. Many conservative Republicans gave him unconditional support including Senator Robert Taft from Ohio, son of President William Howard Taft, who was planning a run for the presidency in 1952. The only Republican to challenge McCarthy was Senator Margaret Chase Smith, the only woman in the Senate. She declared that she did not want to see the Republican Party ride to a midterm victory in 1950 on the "four horses of calumny—fear, ignorance, bigotry, and smear."

As early as 1947, Truman had been concerned about the political issue of Communists in the government. Partly as a reaction to HUAC, Truman issued an executive order establishing an elaborate Federal Employees Loyalty and Security Program. It did serve to pull the rug out from under his Republican detractors in Congress. However, years later in private conversations with friends, Truman conceded that it had been a mistake. The Truman administration also indicted and convicted eleven leading Communist Party officials under the Smith Alien Registration Act of 1940. The Supreme Court upheld the constitutionality of the act, and they were sent to prison.

However, these programs did not provide any cover against the charges that McCarthy made. Truman showed his ethical standards when he refused to leak a huge file on McCarthy's bedmates to the press. As author John Hersey has reported, Truman said, "You must not ask the President of the United States to get down in the gutter with a guttersnipe. Nobody, not even the President of the United States, can approach too close to a skunk, in skunk territory, and expect to get anything out of it except a bad smell." His only defense against McCarthy's charges would be the truth.

KOREAN WAR

Korea was Truman's biggest foreign relation problem in his second administration. To facilitate the surrender of Japanese troops in Korea, it had been divided at the 38th parallel into a Soviet zone and an American zone. Just as the Soviets would not agree to political or economic reunification in Germany, they would not agree to it in Korea. Although the United Nations set up a Temporary Commission to hold elections, they were excluded from North Korea. In South Korea a constitution was written for the Republic of Korea with Syngman Rhee, a ruthless man, elected as the first president in 1948. In the North the Soviets organized a Democratic People's Republic with Kim Il Sung as president. Each government aspired to control the entire peninsula, but North Korea was better equipped with tanks and heavy artillery. The United States had equipped the South with defensive weapons only. When the Soviet and American armies left, military might belonged to the North. Saturday, June 24, 1950, Truman received the news that North Korea had invaded South Korea. It was a complete surprise.

Within a few hours Truman asked for a meeting of the United Nation's Security Council, which declared the North Korean aggressors by a vote of 9-0 and called for the cessation of hostilities and the withdrawal of North Korean forces. It was 9-0 because the Soviet ambassador was boycotting UN meetings to protest the non-recognition of Communist China. While fifteen nations responded to the call for troops, the military was heavily composed of South Korean and American troops. The response of the American public was that, of course, we could easily defeat a third rate power such as North Korea. Radio stations even offered free maps of Korea so that American children could follow the advance of American forces.

Because of their superior fire power and training, the North Koreans pushed the South Korean forces

The Korean War was a war of containment.

to the extreme southeast corner of Korea at Pusan. MacArthur notified Truman that a complete collapse of South Korea was imminent and that combat forces must be used, Truman discussed the matter with congressional leaders who advised against a war resolution. Accepting their advice, Truman used his presidential authority to send troops. He also called for the support of the UN. Since the Soviets were still absent and therefore unable to veto it, the resolution to use armed force to stop the invasion in a "police action" passed. One caution came from the Secretary of Defense Olin Johnson: to give MacArthur detailed instructions "so as not to give him too much discretion." The immediate response was positive: Truman was praised by Democrats and Republicans alike for his bold action.

MacArthur showed his military brilliance when he unveiled a plan to stage an amphibious invasion at Inchon on the western coast of Korea and within easy distance of the southern capital at Seoul. Although military odds makers gave the chances of success as 5,000 to 1, Truman backed MacArthur. The invasion took place on September 15, and the North Koreans were soon routed. Truman now gave MacArthur permission to liberate the North. Containment seemed to be giving way to liberation. On October 2 Chinese Prime Minister Zhou En-lai sent a warning to Washington via the Indian Ambassador to China: Peking did not object to South Korean troops entering North Korea. However, if American troops crossed the border, China would enter the war. In the flush of the Inchon invasion success, the momentum of events could not be stopped. The State Department, Pentagon, and White House all considered the warning to be a bluff. However, Truman made clear that MacArthur was only authorized to cross the 38th parallel if there was no sign of major intervention in North Korea by the Chinese or the Soviets.

October 7 the first American troops crossed the 38th parallel. A week later Truman flew to Wake Island to meet with MacArthur about the final phases of the war. MacArthur indicated that the formal resistance would end by Thanksgiving and that by Christmas the Eighth Army would be back in Japan. He expected that the United Nations would hold elections in January 1951 and that a military occupation would end shortly after that. When Truman asked about the possibility of Chinese or Soviet intervention, MacArthur reported very little chance of either. While Truman and MacArthur talked, the first Chinese troops had crossed the Yalu River, the Korean-China border.

By the end of October, MacArthur, in direct violation of his orders that only South Korean forces were to be allowed near the Chinese and Russian frontiers, ordered all his forces to drive northward at full force. UN forces first encountered the Chinese on October 26. By November 6 MacArthur was calling the Chinese response wanton aggression. On November 24 MacArthur announced an "end the war offensive." Rather than formal resistance ending on Thanksgiving, the day after Thanksgiving 250,000 Chinese Communists swarmed across the Yalu River. Within two days, MacArthur's forces were fleeing south in what became the longest retreat in American military history. The UN forces retreat involved some of the worst and most tragic fighting of the war in sub-zero temperatures for which they were totally unprepared. So disastrous was the retreat that it has been compared to Napoleon's withdrawal from Moscow, which destroyed the French army in the winter of 1812-1813.

MacArthur now wanted to fight a total war even if it meant taking on China directly. Since China had a defensive treaty with the Soviet Union, this would have meant the start of World War III. Omar Bradley, the Chairman of the Joint Chiefs, said it was the wrong war at the wrong place with the wrong enemy. Newly appointed Secretary of Defense General George Marshall favored getting out of Korea with honor. There must be no all out war with China.

The press, which had long glorified MacArthur, now went on the attack. *Time* charged him with being responsible for the worst military disaster in history; the New York *Herald Tribune* said that MacArthur could no longer be accepted as the final authority on military matters. MacArthur soon began to rewrite history by saying that it was not his fault. He denied that his strategy had been the cause of the Chinese intervention. He blamed his lack of success in combating the Chinese forces on Washington-imposed restrictions.

While MacArthur was waging war in the media, a new commander, Matthew Ridgway, took command of the Eighth Army in the field and, after some consolidation, began to push forward. Soon the Americans were again at the 38th parallel. Meanwhile in Tokyo, MacArthur's utterances became increasingly bizarre: he proposed massive air attacks on Manchuria. This was followed by a new twist: depositing radio-active wastes from atomic manufacture along the Yalu River. When MacArthur learned that Truman planned a statement about negotiations to end the war, MacArthur released his own declaration in which he threatened to expand the war into China and offered to meet with the Chinese commander-in-chief to reach a settlement that sounded very much like Chinese unconditional surrender. When MacArthur wrote to Republican House Minority Leader Joseph Martin that there was no substitute for victory and that the Nationalist Chinese of Chiang Kai-shek should join the battle, it was the last in a series of acts of insubordination. Despite the fears of Truman's advisers that there would be vicious attacks on Marshall, Bradley, and Truman himself, April 11, 1951, Truman fired MacArthur and replaced him with General Matthew Ridgway.

There was an immediate political and public outcry over MacArthur's firing. The Republican congressional leaders called for Truman's impeachment. One Republican Senator declared that the U. S. was in the hands of Russian spies who were directing "a secret coterie." Opposition ranged from longshoremen who walked off their jobs in protest to a Baltimore women's group who wanted to march on Washington. Truman was even burned in effigy in Massachusetts and California. Probably the most extreme reaction was that of a Protestant minister from Houston. He became so upset dictating a telegram that he died of a heart attack. Despite this, most newspapers, including some staunch Republican papers, praised Truman for asserting civilian control of the military. Nevertheless, when MacArthur returned home for the first time in fourteen years, he received a hero's welcome including parades and a chance to address a joint session of Congress. We know today that Truman had received information from American spies that made it all too clear that MacArthur's rhetoric on the Nationalist Chinese and war with China was actually more than that. He was determined to start World War III, a nuclear war in Asia, with himself as the American commander.

By June 1951, negotiations began on an armistice that the Eisenhower administration would finalize in June 1953. One problem that turned up during this conflict was the brainwashing of American prisoners who then turned against their own government. This was accomplished by sleep deprivation. Americans at home could not understand how in the few short years between World War II and the Korean War, American soldiers had so changed that they would cooperate with the enemy. Questions were raised to determine the responsibility for such moral failures. One answer was to blame it on the soldiers' mothers.

Another problem that remained hidden for fifty years was, at least, one atrocity Americans committed that seemed like a precursor of events at My Lai in Vietnam. American infantry and pilots massacred Korean civilians hiding under a bridge at No Gun Ri. For years the Army rejected claims by Korean survivors that American troops were involved. In the fall of 1999, however, three hundred witnesses including former G.I.'s came forward to support the victims' accounts.

During his last year and a half in office, Truman was beset by revelations that some in his administration were involved in influence peddling and other scandals. He seemed incapable of realizing that any of his people would dishonor the offices they held by illegal acts.

ELECTION OF 1952

Although the Twenty-second Amendment did not bar Truman from running for re-election, a 23 percent approval rating marked the end of any thoughts of such a run and, in truth, Truman was ready to return to Independence. The problem was to decide what Democrat would run in 1952.

The man Truman wanted to succeed him was Adlai Stevenson, the governor of Illinois, who, to Truman's distress, was playing the role of reluctant candidate. In July Stevenson finally decided to run against Estes Kefauver, a senator from Tennessee who held the lead in committed votes. After the second ballot, Truman intervened to see that support would go to Stevenson. Senator John Sparkman of Alabama ran with Stevenson. Problems quickly arose between Stevenson and Truman when it seemed that Stevenson agreed with the Republicans that there was a "mess" in Washington.

The Republicans were expecting a landslide victory on the issues of Communists, corruption, and Korea, no matter who their candidate was. As the year progressed, the GOP nomination turned into a battle between Dwight Eisenhower, who represented the Eastern moderate wing of the party, and Robert Taft, who was the darling of the conservative wing. Despite many scurrilous rumors about Ike and his wife, Mamie, he won the Republican nomination on the first ballot. To balance the ticket, ideologically, geographically, and demographically, Ike chose as his vice-president Senator Richard M. Nixon from California.

In September the press revealed that wealthy southern California businessmen had established a secret trust fund for Nixon. Many of Ike's advisers counseled him to dump Nixon from the ticket. Instead, Nixon went on TV to explain the fund. He then asked people to wire their verdict to the Republican National Committee. When Ike refused to say when he would make his decision about Nixon's future, Nixon used an unfortunate choice of words to push Ike. "There comes a time in matters like this when you've either got to shit or get off the pot." Ike never forgot the phrase. No one had ever presumed to speak to him like that. Later Ike told Nixon, "You're my boy!"

One of the low points in the campaign was Eisenhower's October speech in Wisconsin with Joe McCarthy sitting behind him on the stage. Ike's aides had been telling the press all that day that Ike planned to give a tribute to George Marshall, whom McCarthy had labeled a traitor over the fall of China. When he made the speech, Ike omitted the tribute to Marshall. Instead, Ike charged that the Reds in Washington had caused the fall of China, as well as the surrender of the nations in Europe. Many criticized Eisenhower who seemed to be so intimidated by McCarthy that he directly criticized the man who had recommended him for the post of Supreme Allied Commander in World War II.

The high point of Ike's campaign was also in October when he promised that, immediately after his election, he would go to Korea. Those who favored winning the war thought Ike meant he would go to see how this could be accomplished. Those who favored an armistice thought Ike meant that he would go to Korea to end the war. In either case, Americans were certain that Ike would take charge and end the war. Ike's lead at the polls increased in response to this. Two weeks later the election results followed predictions with the Republicans sweeping both the presidency and the Congress, although by slim majorities. When Ike was inaugurated, the frosty relationship between the president-elect and Truman was clear to all.

EVALUATION OF TRUMAN

The total renovation of the White House was one of the things that Truman was most pleased with completing during his second term. In April 1952 the White House was again open to the public. Truman took the American public on a television tour that all three networks covered. They were the only television broadcasters in 1952. Truman's love of the history of the White House was obvious to all, and it helped to raise his standing with the American people.

When Truman retired from the presidency and wanted to make arrangements to move his personal family belongings to Independence, a Washington, D.C. bank refused to give him a loan without a co-signer. His former Secretary of State Dean Acheson, who was a wealthy man, agreed to co-sign the loan. Truman's wife's family even owned the house in Independence that Truman lived in. In 1953 there was no pension for former presidents or congressmen; Truman's only source of income was his pension from his service as a captain in World War I. A man of honor who had no intention of selling his fame as president by serving on corporate boards or giving speeches, Truman faced some hard financial times. Five years later in 1958 Congress agreed to provide all former presidents with a pension of $25,000 a year, which was one fourth the annual presidential salary, money for staff, office space, and free mailing privileges.

Truman stepped into the presidency with almost no briefings from FDR. Despite this, he successfully ended World War II, resisted Soviet expansionism, extended the ideals of the New Deal, and confronted the issue of segregation. In the years since his presidency, Truman's stature has increased. Historians have consistently rated him one of the near-great presidents.

EISENHOWER YEARS

The Eisenhower years are often seen today as a golden time of peace and prosperity, family values, and traditions—a time when everything was right in America. Such is not the case. For example, teenage pregnancy was at an all time high with many out of wedlock births. While the economy was good and many Americans were prosperous, it was a prosperity that left many Americans in poverty. Twenty-five percent of the population was poor, and there were no food stamps, Medicare, and few federal housing programs. One third of American children lived in poverty, as well as 60 percent of the elderly. The prosperity that existed was directly related to federal policies such as the GI Bill with its easy access and low down payments for homes. Before World War II banks required 50 percent down and financed homes for only 5-10 years. By the 1950s you could buy a home with 10 percent down under the Federal Housing Administration and pay for it over 30 years at an interest rate of 2-3 percent. If you were a veteran, it was possible to get a mortgage for one dollar down!

Although most families were still intact in the 1950s, there were problems below the surface. For example, the problem of battered wives was blamed on the wives, not the husbands. Psychoanalysts like Helen Deutsch said such a wife was a "masochist who provoked her husband into beating her." She also proclaimed that a "feminine" woman left the initiative to the man and renounced her own needs to experience herself through her identification with her man. Another family problem hiding beneath the surface was incest. When Marilyn Van Derbur became Miss America in 1958, most thought she

Dwight D. Eisenhower

came from a typical American middle class family. No one suspected her respectable successful father of sexually molesting her from ages 5-18. Years later, she discovered that he had done the same to her sisters. Her mother, like many wives of the times, denied that the incest had occurred.

The roots of such passivity on the part of women can be traced back to society's view of women in the post-war period. A 1947 best seller was *The Modern Woman: The Lost Sex* by Marynia Farnham, a psychiatrist, and Ferdinand Lundberg, an historian. They declared that feminism was an illness and that an independent woman was a contradiction in terms. The authors also claimed that war and depression were a result of women leaving homes and families. In their view the women's rights movement had caused women to reject their natural, sex-based instincts in a futile attempt to become imitation men.

Most of the problems of society were blamed on women. Dr. Benjamin Spock in his best selling *Baby and Child Care* cautioned that mothers who wanted to work and leave their children should seek counseling. The good mother was the one who was always there for her children while at the same time never being overprotective. This last was to guard against the condition called "Momism." After World War II, author Philip Wylie castigated women as evil mothers who smothered and devoured their children

by keeping them dependent and immature because there was nothing else in their lives. Such mothers created men who could not function in wartime as soldiers. Adding fuel to this debate about the role of women were such cold war icons as J. Edgar Hoover, head of the Federal Bureau of Investigation (FBI), who saw mothers as the first line of defense against the "twin enemies of freedom—crime and communism."

WOMEN'S ROLES

For a while it did seem that women were returning to the life of domesticity with enthusiasm. Early marriages and a rising birth rate characterized the 1940s and 1950s. Suburbs bloomed, and woman as consumer became an increasingly popular concept.

Post-war fashions also showed a new feminine image as the Dior silhouette took hold: long full skirts, defined bustlines, and tiny waists. In the 1950s the "baby doll" style was introduced with greater emphasis on the feminine image: belted waists, padded brassieres, and full skirts over layers of crinoline petticoats. Shoes had three inch heels that had to be reinforced with steel to avoid breakage. The idea was to emphasize slim beautiful legs. In reality the shoes worked to make women more passive and contributed to many sprained ankles, as well as foot and back problems.

While the emphasis was on the typical American suburban housewife, the truth was that this applied to only a minority of American women. Millions lived either in cities or farms. Many suffered from poor health, unemployment, and poverty. Poor women could not remain at home; they had to work. This was especially true of African-American women. Despite 40 percent of African-American women having small children at home, they had to work outside their own homes for survival. The only good news was that, with the labor shortage, department stores began to hire black saleswomen and office managers began to hire black clerical workers. Most black women, however, remained in the domestic sphere.

Living the ideal suburban life was difficult for most African-American women. They found employment in menial, low-paying jobs, such as this woman cleaning a Greyhound bus.

While it was possible to get jobs in the traditional female occupations, other jobs were closed to women, a fact made evident by the gender separated listings in the want ads. An agent for a large insurance company reported that his company did not recruit female college graduates for jobs since they did not expect to have a career and the few that did changed their plans in a few years. Because the only jobs left open were more tedious and allowed no room for ambition, college women often quit them in a few months. It was a double bind because they were not hired for "women's work" since they would become bored and leave, and they were not hired for "men's work" since they might marry and leave.

The technology that dominated the 1950s was not an unmixed blessing for women either. Since they had all of these machines to save time, society thought women should be able to do more. By the end of the 1950s although labor saving devices proliferated, the women's housework time actually increased from slightly less than fifty-two hours per week to fifty-four.

Life magazine in 1956 had a special issue on the ideal American woman: mother of four, wife, hostess, volunteer, and home manager but, above all, a conscientious mother who spent hours with her children helping them with their homework and listening to their problems. In essence, she was a sweet and innocent homebody. Television had a different view and showed the American housewife in "I Love Lucy" where Lucille Ball played a lovably comic but ditzy Lucy Riccardo. The irony is that Lucille Ball was the brains behind the success of "I Love Lucy" and its production company, Desilu. Even the sex sirens of the day such as Marilyn Monroe and Elizabeth Taylor combined aggressive sexuality with a certain artlessness and naivete that made them less threatening and more of a sex object. Monroe's wide-eyed charm, physical voluptuousness, and natural sex appeal made her the most famous international sex symbol of the twentieth century.

SUBURBAN LIFE AND THE AUTOMOBILE

With the end of World War II, Americans were able to renew their love affair with the automobile. While Congress had passed the Interstate and Defense Highway Act in 1944, which provided $1.5 billion for road building and improvements in the first three post-war years, it soon proved inadequate. Very little of it was spent for limited access highways like the Pennsylvania Turnpike, which had proved its worth during the war in carrying shipments of Pittsburgh steel east to the Atlantic ports. While California began building the much admired freeways, tollways continued to be the answer in the East. By the end of the 1950s it was possible to drive from New York to Chicago via tollways, which included links to Philadelphia, Pittsburgh, Cleveland, and Toledo. Few people thought of what these limited access highways would do to the Mom and Pop businesses that were soon consigned to oblivion.

The growth of highways at the same time spelled the end of the other major mode of transportation: rail. The first to go was the Pacific Electric Railway (PER) that served the Los Angeles area. Although it was probably always doomed by Angelenos' love of their cars, a General Motors led consortium including Firestone, Standard Oil of California, and Philips Petroleum hastened its demise. The consortium bought up rail systems and replaced them with bus service. In all, over one hundred transportation systems were involved in the West and Midwest with the PER being the largest. In 1949, in federal court, the members of the consortium were found guilty of anti-trust violations because GM produced buses in their Yellow Coach Division. Some suggested that the purpose of the consortium was more sinister. Since profits on the bus lines were minimal, the real purpose may have been to get local governments to improve highways to the benefit of all members of the consortium. It seems clear that, with or without the aid of GM and its associates, the interurbans, rail lines connecting urban areas, would have declined if for no other reason than their lack of flexibility.

The demise of the interurbans isolated those who lived in the poverty areas of large cities such as the Watts neighborhood of Los Angeles. It also made possible the exurbs, as the distant communities surrounding core communities were named. While the suburbs sprang up because of the rail system, the exurbs were dependent on the car. That changed the nature of the life of the commuter who could easily spend fifteen to twenty hours a week just traveling to and from work. Nor were exurb women excluded from this since most shopping, schools, and other services also required a car. With people spending so much more time in their cars, automotive manufacturers began to put greater emphasis on comforts to keep the driver happy: radios to make the traffic congestion more bearable; improved heating and air-conditioning to even out the extremes in the American climate; and automatic transmissions and power steering to reduce the strain of stop and go driving.

To lure buyers into the showrooms and to break the back of the minor car manufacturers, the Big Three (General Motors, Ford, and Chrysler) put an emphasis on styling. The first of their products to show this was the Chevrolet Corvette, unveiled in 1953. Described as one of the sexiest looking vehicles to come off an assembly line, the 'Vette was sold primarily on styling rather than engineering and went on to become the most successful sports car made in America. The accent was on aviation type styling, which often included aviation type names. For example, the 1950 Oldsmobile 88 had a "Rocket" engine; the Mercury had a "jet-scoop hood." The minor car companies never caught up, although Studebaker-Packer did come out with some designs that were on par with the Big Three. Their lack of chrome and fins, however, defined their lack of success with the public.

The automobile also included sexual images in a way to make them a fetish. The body of the car was curvaceous, with a symmetry that was like the female human form. It was designed to create an erotic whole. No one did it better than Cadillac. A 50s sex symbol, Jayne Mansfield, not only owned and died in a Cadillac, she was one. Other companies followed suit, and the ads showed this. The car was desirable, something to be possessed, and then transformed into a slave to man's desires. Some historians report that this was all unconscious to the consumer and to most of society, but teenage boys in the 50s often described their girlfriends as a car model. Just as Jayne Mansfield was a Cadillac and Doris Day a Lincoln Continental Mark IV, so were their girlfriends.

As the car population increased, the need for improved national highways became more evident. In 1954 Eisenhower established a committee to look into the issue of creating a network of limited access highways. Ike had been in charge of an army convoy that had crossed the country in 1918. He knew well the military value of such a network of roads. In addition, the construction of such a network would stimulate the economy. In 1956 Congress passed the Interstate Highway Act, which provided for the construction of 41,000 miles of toll-free highways. The federal government would provide 90 percent of the funds and establish standards for their construction, while leaving administration and maintenance to the individual states. Levies on trucks, tires, gasoline, and related products would raise money and channel it through a Highway Trust Fund. These limited access highways were part of a system called the National System of Interstate and Defense Highways. The expectation was that vehicles on these limited access highways would move at 70 miles per hour, although many went much faster.

While the interstate highway system was a boon to the tourists and the truck industry, there were some humorous stories involving the first motorists who encountered the cloverleaf pattern that provided the access and egress from the highway. There were jokes about commuters who never reached the main lanes of the interstate but spent hours trapped in the cloverleaf going on and off, on and off, on and off.

The construction of the interstate system had unforeseen effects in both cities and rural areas. In cities, the webs of urban expressways often destroyed long-established neighborhoods. While this problem existed throughout the nation, the work of Robert Moses in New York City produced some of the worst examples of such destruction. In the rural areas, the interstate spelled the end of the Mom and Pop businesses that were on the side roads. In both areas, urban and rural, there was the growth of the strip

mall often located near the new motels like Holiday Inn and Howard Johnson's, a cross between the urban hotel and the auto-court. They also propelled the growth of franchises such as Harland Sander's Kentucky Fried Chicken and Ray Kroc's McDonald's. Travelers appreciated the efficiency, cleanliness, and guarantee of a product that was the same across the entire nation. The strip mall evolved into the enclosed shopping mall that encouraged year round shopping. The first was opened in 1956 in Edina, Minnesota, a suburb of Minneapolis. And that, in its turn, marked the demise of the shopping center in the central city.

EISENHOWER ADMINISTRATIONS

During the Eisenhower years, technology became an important element in the lives of American citizens. It was seen in the new cars they drove down the interstate highway system, the television that showed them the civil rights struggle and Elvis, the airplanes that transported them across the country in record time and protected them from attack as part of the Strategic Air Command, the computers that made missiles possible, and the atom and hydrogen bombs that added to the anxiety of modern life.

It was also during the supposed placid years of the 40s and 50s that sexual activities became a focus of academic study at Indiana University. Here, in 1942, Alfred Kinsey, a world authority on gall wasps, founded the Institute for Sex Research to investigate human sexual behavior. Kinsey and his associates collected data by interviewing some 18,000 men and women. Kinsey published his results in *Sexual Behavior of the Human Male* in 1948 and in *Sexual Behavior of the Human Female* in 1953. Both books caused considerable controversy over the subject matter and the methodology. Nevertheless, Kinsey made the study of human sexual behavior a respectable field of study. In recent years sociologists have criticized his methods of data collection, which they believe gave inaccurate and misleading data.

To fight all of these changes as well as "Godless Communism," there was a new emphasis on so-called traditional religion and traditional values. Congress

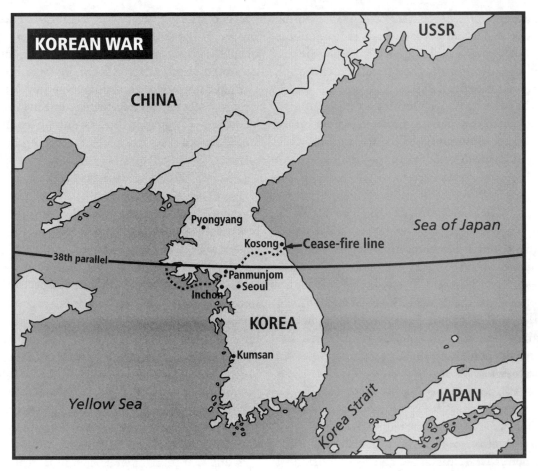

KOREAN WAR

responded by inserting the phrase "under God" in the Pledge of Allegiance. June 14, 1954, Flag Day, CBS carried the ceremony of the first use of the "under God" phrase on its morning show. Religious programming was on the television not only on Sunday but also in prime time with the Baptist Reverend Billy Graham and his evangelical crusades and Roman Catholic Bishop Fulton J. Sheen whose show rated higher than the popular comedian Milton Berle who was in the same time slot. Although religion seemed to many to be a prop for the status quo, there was still that kernel of the social gospel that would re-emerge in the 1960s in the civil rights movement.

Americans generally thought that they knew the new president well. Dwight Eisenhower was the third of six sons born to a religious farm family in Abilene, Kansas. Ike was a star athlete but an average student. Despite this, both Ike and his older brother, Milton, wanted to attend college. However, the family could

not afford it. The brothers agreed to alternate helping each other through school. For a few years Ike worked at a dairy with his father so that he could provide money for Milton's college expenses. Then Ike learned that he could attend West Point for free if he scored high enough on the entrance exam. Before this point, Ike had shown no interest in a military career.

Ike gained the appointment to the United States Military Academy. At West Point Ike continued his athletic career until he injured his knee. From the beginnings of his military career, his superiors recognized his superior ability as an organizer. This served him well and eventually led General Marshall to promote him over many others to lieutenant general and eventually to recommend to FDR that Ike be the Supreme Allied Commander in World War II.

After the war ended, Ike served as president of Columbia University in New York City and later as the first Supreme Commander of NATO. During all these years, Ike had stayed so far away from politics that no one knew whether he was a Democrat or a Republican. Both parties had tried to draft him to run on their ticket in 1948.

While Ike had a wonderful disarming grin, he was also a man who had a temper. In that regard, he had a lot in common with his predecessor. Still, Americans had no problem in saying "I Like Ike" and voting that preference.

The End of the Korean War

The first item that Eisenhower had to deal with was a resolution of the Korean War. During the 1952 campaign, Ike's Secretary of State John Foster Dulles had condemned the Truman policy of containment and said that it would be replaced with one of liberation. In reality, the policy of liberation was nothing but domestic campaign rhetoric. Rather, the new policy could be summed up in these watchwords: domino theory and brinkmanship. The domino theory was just a spin on containment. Defense of a nation might be required because if that nation fell, all the other nations in that area of the world would fall just like a line of dominos. Brinkmanship involved using the threat of nuclear attack or bringing the United States to the brink of war.

In Korea Ike faced two problems: dealing with the Red Chinese and dealing with Syngman Rhee and the South Koreans. The Chinese had to be convinced that it was in their interests to settle the issue of repatriation of prisoners of war and agree to an armistice. That was accomplished by brinkmanship. John Foster Dulles told the Indian Prime Minister Jawaharlal Nehru, who was a conduit to the Communist Chinese, that the United States might feel compelled to use atomic weapons if a truce could not be arranged. Even without this, the Chinese certainly knew that the United States could deliver bombs to the Chinese mainland from the island of Okinawa. This "threat" is particularly interesting in view of a letter that Ike wrote after the bombing of Hiroshima and Nagasaki in which he criticized Truman's use of the bomb.

The issue with Rhee was to get him to keep an armistice. Ike sent an emissary to Rhee to tell him that if he did not cooperate, all American troops and aid would be withdrawn. Rhee finally realized that it was futile to try to go it alone. On July 26, 1953, the truce was signed, and the war in Korea came to an end. Ike regarded this as one of his greatest achievements.

CIA and Foreign Policy

Ike appointed John Foster Dulles' brother, Allen, head of the CIA, which now became very active in covert operations around the world. The first overthrow of a government took place in Iran in 1953 under the leadership of Kermit Roosevelt, Teddy Roosevelt's grandson. The plan was to depose Iranian Prime Minister Mohammed Mossadegh and replace him with the former leader Shah Mohammed Reza Pahlavi. Mossadegh had seized the British owned Anglo-Persian Oil Company. The British and American oilmen told Ike that Mossadegh was a Communist. Here was the perfect place to use the CIA to implement American policy. As Ike's biographer Stephen Ambrose has written, "Eisenhower's fundamental belief [was] that nuclear war was unimaginable, limited conventional war was unreasonable, and stalemate was unacceptable." That left only covert activities.

In Iran the CIA used what became its traditional methods: bribery of army officers, use of paid rabble rousers to manipulate public opinion, and the installation of someone who would agree with Western economic policy even if having no interest in the establishment of a democratic government. It was very successful; Mossadegh was removed, the previously deposed Shah was reinstalled, and American oil companies were given 40 percent of Iranian oil. During the time that Roosevelt was planning the overthrow, Brigadier General H. Norman Schwarzkopf, who had reorganized the Shah's police force in 1940, arrived in Iran and became part of the operation. The police force was the Shah's agency of suppression. Despite over a billion dollars in American aid, there were no social or economic reforms, which were greatly needed.

The successful events in Iran set a precedent for presidents to use the CIA as a quick fix for foreign policy problems. Soon the CIA would perform a similar task in Guatemala where the Communists dominated the government. The worst crime was the expropriation of 225,000 acres of the best land of United Fruit Company, an American owned company and the major economic power in Guatemala. United Fruit had powerful connections in the United States, including the Dulles' brothers. John Foster Dulles' old law firm, Sullivan and Cromwell, had long represented United Fruit, and Allen Dulles had served on the United Fruit board.

The CIA chose a leader for the *coup d'etat* and provided an air force and American pilots. It took less than two weeks for the overthrow. The first thing the new leaders did was to disenfranchise illiterates who were 70 percent of the population. When a "free" election was held, it was to vote yes or no on the question of Castillo-Armas continuing as president. It was no surprise when he won. The government soon took 800,000 acres of land from the peasants, returned to United Fruit Company the land it had lost, and repealed laws guaranteeing worker rights and the rights of labor unions. This was just the first of many military dictators.

The rationale for the CIA's activities in Latin America goes back to recommendations made by George Kennan in 1950. From Kennan's viewpoint it was better to have a strong regime in power than a liberal government that might be penetrated by the Communists because of the freedoms that it permitted its people. Kennan wanted U.S. policy in Latin America to protect the United States' source of raw materials; to prevent military exploitation by the Communists; and to prevent the Latin Americans from being turned against the U.S. through psychological mobilization. By 1954, thirteen of the twenty countries in Latin America were under military dictatorships. To protect United States interests in Latin American nations, the U.S. Army operated the School of the Americas, first in Panama and later at Fort Benning, Georgia. Here, army officers and police were trained in repression, torture, and murder that they then went home and carried out. The United States Army has consistently denied

Secretary of State John Foster Dulles frequently took a hard line stand in foreign affairs.

that the School of the Americas taught torture, but the activities were confirmed in the 1990s.

FOREIGN POLICY CRISES

In October 1956, just in time for the fall presidential election, which was a rematch of Eisenhower versus Stevenson, two foreign policy problems moved to the fore: a revolution in Hungary and the Anglo-French-Israeli attack on Egypt. During the 1952 campaign John Foster Dulles had preached liberation, and over the almost four year administration the United States had encouraged people in the satellite nations to push for their freedom. The Hungarians took the U. S. at its word, but there would be no liberation. Instead, Soviets moved in to crush the revolt leaving poignant pictures of unarmed men throwing stones at Soviet tanks. The U. S. did permit thousands of the Hungarian refugees to enter the country.

The situation in Egypt was more complicated. Gamal Abdel Nasser had overthrown the Egyptian king and taken control of the country. In December 1955 the United States and Great Britain offered to help Nasser build the Aswan Dam, which was his pet project. In April 1956 Egypt joined with other Arab nations to form an anti-Israel alliance and then recognized Red China and withdrew its recognition of Nationalist China. As a result of congressional pressure, John Foster Dulles had to withdraw the Aswan offer. The Soviets moved in quickly to replace the United States. Now the British, French, and Israelis decided to secretly coordinate attacks on Egypt with Israel attacking the Sinai and France and Britain moving in to "protect" the Suez Canal. At the UN both the U.S. and U.S.S.R. condemned the Anglo-French action, and it was abandoned December 22, 1956.

U-2 Spy Plane

During the second Eisenhower administration, the CIA hit the top of its technical expertise with the building of the U-2 reconnaissance plane. Built in 1956 in seventeen months at $19 million ($3 million under budget), it was designed for the latest cameras, which used high resolution film. U-2s would fly over the Soviet Union filming whatever areas interested the CIA.

These were not the first flights over the Soviet Union. Strategic Air Command (SAC) under General Curtis Le May had sent SAC bombers, which were loaded with nuclear and thermonuclear weapons, in unauthorized flights over the Soviet Union. In May 1956 alone, SAC had flown twenty-seven flights over Soviet airspace in an attempt to intimidate the Soviets. In part because Ike did not completely trust the military, he gave control of the U-2 to the CIA. Before each flight, Eisenhower had to give permission for the use of a ten-day period. From the first, the Soviets had tracked the U-2 and had complained through diplomatic channels about the flyovers. It was clear that eventually the Soviets would develop the capabilities to bring a U-2 to earth. Sooner came in 1960 when Eisenhower was preparing for a Big Four (the Americans, British,

French, and Soviets) meeting in Paris. Ike hoped that he could get Soviet Premier Nikita Khrushchev's agreement on a nuclear test ban treaty as a first step toward arms control and an agreement on Berlin.

There had only been two overflights in 1960, and those were primarily because the Soviets had fired their first intercontinental ballistic missile. Eisenhower approved the final flight as long as it was completed by May 1. The CIA thought that even if the Soviets shot down a U-2, they would never admit it because they would have to admit that the flights had been going on for a while and that they had been unable to stop them. In any event, the CIA was sure that neither a plane nor its pilot would survive a downing. A contract pilot, Francis Gary Powers, left the U-2 base in Turkey for his flight. The Soviets shot down his U-2 and arrested him. The CIA knew something was wrong and reported the plane as "lost." The Soviets kept quiet about the capture of Powers and the plane until May 5 when Khrushchev made a speech denouncing the U. S. for its aggressive provocation. Eisenhower had the National Aeronautical and Space Administration (NASA) issue a release that it was a weather plane that was lost. On May 6 Khrushchev released a photo of a wrecked plane that was not the U-2. The U.S. stuck to its weather story, and Khrushchev sprung his trap by showing part of the U-2 and its still alive pilot, Powers. Next, Eisenhower authorized the story that Powers had not been authorized to fly over the Soviet Union. When the summit finally took place, Khrushchev lambasted Eisenhower for the overflights and demanded that he apologize. Then the Soviets walked out of the meeting. Any hope Eisenhower had for détente or peace had been ruined by his decision to authorize the U-2 flights. The Soviet Union tried Powers and sentenced him to prison. The U. S. later traded a Soviet spy for Powers.

Cuba

The CIA also played a role in Cuban affairs after Fidel Castro gained power. The United States had supported the rightist dictator, Fulgencio Batista. On January 1, 1959, he fled Cuba as Fidel Castro entered Havana. Castro was soon executing Batista's officials after public trials that were more like Roman circuses. It became clear that Castro planned a socialist revolution and opposed foreign control of the Cuban economy. When he began land reform and nationalization of foreign owned property, relations with the U.S. worsened. Some believe that by rejecting Castro's requests for loans and other aid, the United States lost its chance to influence the revolution and pushed Castro further to the left.

The United States did not like Castro's seizure of British-American refineries, which would not process Soviet oil. Although Eisenhower was never able to determine to his satisfaction whether Castro was a Communist, he did determine that he wanted to get rid of him. In July Ike ordered economic sanctions against Cuba by reducing the sugar quota for 1960 and eliminating it for 1961. Sugar was the main Cuban crop.

In August 1960 Eisenhower met with the CIA to see what progress had been accomplished on a

A young Fidel Castro lead his followers in the early stages of the Cuban Revolution.

four-point program that he had approved in March. On point one, no leader for a government-in-exile could be found because the Cubans who were anti-Castro could not work together. Point two, which was a propaganda offensive, was underway. Point three, a resistance movement within Cuba, was a total failure. Progress was being made on point four, which was the creation of a para-military force in Guatemala from Cuban exiles. These four points formed the basis of the later Bay of Pigs invasion.

The other anti-Castro activity that the CIA directed was the assassination attempts that involved the American Mafia. Castro had shut down the American Mafia's gambling, dope, and vice dens in Havana. Some of the assassination plans can only be described as bizarre. They included using Mafia hit men, poisoning his cigar or coffee, and giving him something to make his facial hair fall out. None of the plots succeeded, but they kept on trying. It is unclear whether Eisenhower directly ordered such attempts. Since he was the author of the "plausible denial concept," either case could be true. Certainly, the CIA thought they had approval.

Eisenhower had appointed General Jimmy Doolittle chair of a committee to investigate the CIA. The 1954 report concluded: "It is clear that we are facing an implacable enemy whose avowed objective is world domination by whatever means and at whatever cost. There are no rules in such a game. Hitherto acceptable norms of conduct do not apply." Whether this was the way it should have been, this was definitely the reality as far as the CIA was concerned. Shortly after Allen Dulles took the realm, the Agency began a program of covert use of biological and chemical weapons. The purpose was to turn humans into robots that could be programmed to kill on command. The guinea pigs would be Americans. Some like the addicts at a drug treatment center in Lexington, Kentucky were informed and asked to consent to the use of experimental drugs. Most were not. The agency was mainly interested in d-lysergic acid diethylamide, more popularly known as LSD. When the tests showed that the addicts did not respond to control for long periods of time or at long range, LSD was tested on "normal" people rather than drug addicts.

Numerous Cubans emigrated to the United States after World War II.

Some died from these experiments. Others had long term mental problems. These activities did not come to public notice until the 1970s.

One man who died was Frank Olson, an Army scientist from Fort Detrick, Maryland, the Army's biological research center. Unknown to his family Olson worked for the CIA and had done research on LSD and the spreading of anthrax and other toxins. He was found dead 10 stories below his hotel room in New York City. The death was ruled a suicide, but the story is much more complicated than it appeared.

In 1975 Olson's family discovered part of the story when a commission headed by Vice President Nelson Rockefeller revealed that the CIA had given an Army scientist LSD with the result that he jumped from a hotel window. A later congressional investigation identified that Army scientist as Frank Olson. The family decided to sue the federal government for damages and to find out the truth. To prevent the suit, the Ford administration proposed that Congress pass a Private Bill of $750,000 to settle the claim. This was done to keep other information from becoming public, such as the CIA's assassination manuals. One of the preferred assassination methods de-

scribed in the manual was to drug or stun victims and then throw them from 75 feet or more to a hard surface.

Over the years Frank Olson's son, Eric, discovered bits and pieces of the story, and in 1993 he had a forensic pathologist perform an autopsy on his father's exhumed body. The autopsy concluded that Frank Olson had been struck on the head and then thrown from his hotel window to his death.

The last tantalizing piece of the story was the discovery in late 2002 of a memo in the Gerald Ford Presidential Library from Vice President Dick Cheney, then a White House Aide, to Secretary of Defense Donald Rumsfeld, then serving as Ford's chief of staff. This memo warned that a lawsuit might require revealing highly classified national-security information and the illegal activities of the CIA. A second memo from the White House counsel that was routed through Cheney and Rumsfeld suggested the need to settle the case to prevent any court settlement appearing as money to cover up CIA activities.

The agency was also interested in biological warfare, and, in 1960, Dr. Sidney Gottlieb, who was head of the Agency's Technical Services Staff, was on his way to Africa to assassinate Patrice

Lumumba, the Congolese national leader, with bacteria that would cause a fatal disease. Before Gottlieb could succeed, Lumumba was captured and killed by a rival.

One of Eisenhower's strengths as president was his knowledge of the military and the politics and ploys it used to increase its budget. It was much harder to contest an Eisenhower military budget cut than it was other president's. It was, however, not impossible, as Curtis Le May proved, when he created the notion of a "bomber gap" and went to Congress to lobby for more bombers for SAC. It also did not protect Ike from charges that there was a missile gap after the Soviets had beaten the United States into space with the launching of their satellite, Sputnik, in the fall of 1957.

Nuclear War Threats

Eisenhower used the threat of nuclear war more often than any president before or since. Whether he was bluffing, no one knows for sure. Ike reportedly told Lyndon Johnson, when Johnson became president, that he had let the Chinese know that he would not hesitate to bomb China. He also threatened atomic warfare over Quemoy and Matsu, two islands off Formosa. Eisenhower saw no difference between atomic warfare and conventional warfare. For this reason he ordered the deployment of nuclear weapons as close to the Soviet Union as possible. This included loading SAC bombers, which were on standby twenty-four hours a day, with both nuclear and thermonuclear weapons.

By 1954, both the United States and U.S.S.R. had exploded hydrogen bombs and achieved a "balance of terror," as Churchill called it. The United States had tested the first hydrogen bomb, "Big Mike," on Bikini Atoll in the Pacific Ocean. It was much larger than expected. The cloud formed a canopy that was over one hundred miles wide on a stem that was thirty miles high. The fireball had vaporized the entire island and lifted into the air over 80 million tons of solid material. It left a circular crater two hundred feet deep and more than a mile across. It was, indeed, a balance of terror.

After the Soviets launched Sputnik in 1957, Americans feared possible attacks and focused on civilian defense. Drills were routinely held in the schools.

Another problem of the nuclear age was the Pentagon's loss of thermonuclear weapons, Hydrogen Bombs. In 1958 the Air Force had four major accidents involving H-bombs. Two of them have never been recovered.

In February 1958, two Air Force jets crashed off the Georgia coast, and the bomber pilot was told to jettison his H-bomb. He dropped it near the mouth of the Savannah River where he thought it could be easily recovered. This was a primitive version of the H-bomb that weighed four tons and had 100 times the explosive force of the A-bomb dropped on Hiroshima. It was equipped with a plutonium trigger and armed with 400 pounds of TNT. The big danger was not that there might be a thermonuclear explosion but rather that the TNT might explode on contact and send radioactive debris across the area where it fell. The H-bomb jettisoned near the Savannah River did not explode and rescue efforts ceased on April 16, 1958 as the Pentagon reported to the Atomic Energy Commission in a request for a replacement. That bomb is still buried off Warsaw Sound, and there are no plans to recover it.

A second H-bomb was accidentally dropped in March 1958 in Florence, South Carolina, and the TNT in this one exploded causing extensive damage on the ground and several injuries, as well as spewing radioactive debris across the area. The remainder of the H-bomb was recovered.

Vietnam

In 1954 the United States also began the long trek to Vietnam. That year, the French lost the battle at Dien Bien Phu and were preparing to leave. Ike did consider American intervention via a single air strike using three atomic bombs, which we would then deny ever using. It was also at this time that the domino theory was enunciated. On April 7, 1954, Ike said at a news conference: "You have a row of dominos set up, you knock over the first one, and what will happen to the last one is the certainty that it will go over very quickly." In July, the Geneva agreements were signed calling for nation-wide elections in Vietnam in two years. The United States did not sign the Geneva agreements and instead worked to get the South East Asian Treaty Organization (SEATO) organized to establish a defensive line in Asia. By September, SEATO included France, Britain, Australia, New Zealand, Thailand, the Philippines, Pakistan, and the United States. A special protocol was added to the treaty extending coverage to Indo-China

Soon the CIA was running the policy in Vietnam. When Ho Chi Minh took over in North Vietnam, the United States helped those who wished to get to South Vietnam and pushed Ngo Dinh Diem, who had been in exile at a Catholic seminary in New Jersey, as the next premier. Because the Communist leader of North Vietnam, Ho Chi Minh, would be the winner in any free elections in 1956, Eisenhower effectively blocked them. He next agreed to assist Diem "in developing and maintaining a strong, viable state, capable of resisting attempted subversion or aggression through military means." In return for United States aid, Diem was to institute needed reforms. When the French left, Diem ousted the emperor and had himself installed as president. By 1957, when the North Vietnamese guerrilla forces, the Vietcong, began attacking South Vietnam, the United States was stuck with Diem. Later, as a past-president, Eisenhower advised both Presidents Kennedy and Johnson to declare all out war in Vietnam and seek victory, not negotiations, threatening nuclear war if necessary.

DOMESTIC POLICY

Although Eisenhower saw McCarthy as a problem, it was one that he did not address until McCarthy began attacking Eisenhower's own appointees rather than Truman's. The battle ground was the United States Army. McCarthy was investigating it for the promotion of supposed Communists. Ike remained behind the scenes having his press secretary leak negative information on McCarthy and sending Richard Nixon to challenge McCarthy for television coverage. The Army-McCarthy televised hearing served only to humiliate McCarthy. Eisenhower hastened the destruction

Televisions became popular in American homes by the late 1940s. It became the center of family life in prosperous households.

by encouraging Republican senators to push for a formal censure vote against McCarthy that spelled the end of his career.

Economic Policy

Eisenhower's economic policies were focused on limiting the federal government's role in the economy, lessening governmental regulation, fighting inflation, and balancing the budget. To achieve these, Ike fought for lower taxes for industry and capital and turned over the tideland oil reserves to the states. While he tried to hold down the increase in individual social security benefits, he also expanded the number of workers covered so that, at the end of his administrations, five-sixths of the paid work force were under Social Security.

Eisenhower promoted new and stronger forms of government-business cooperation, which harkened back to the approach of Herbert Hoover in the 1920s.

Businessmen were also the most frequent invitees to the stag dinners that Ike held. Antitrust prosecutions declined and were replaced by more cooperative arrangements, such as pre-filing conferences, consent decrees, and pre-merger clearances. Even these did not completely please his business colleagues. In addressing the national housing shortage, Ike set up a national advisory committee that was composed of realtors, builders, bankers, and pro-administration politicians hostile to the competition of the federal public housing. The result was the Housing Act of 1954, which did little for the poorest segments of the population. New federal policies did clear slums, but they provided no alternative housing for the poor who were now permanently displaced from their former urban homes. In his second administration Ike pushed for the passage of the Landrum-Griffin Act of 1959, which had anti-union provisions that pleased his corporate backers. A small but important favor to some of his backers was the repeal of the penny tax for each label placed on the top of a whiskey bottle. This saved Seagrams and other distillers millions of dollars.

Health Issues

In his first term Ike had two serious health problems. In September 1955 he suffered a heart attack while on vacation in Colorado. Unlike the ailments of his predecessors, Ike's heart attack was revealed to the American public. By Christmas Ike was fully recovered and back in Washington. In early June 1956 Ike had an attack of ileitis, a severe inflammation of the lower intestine, which was described in detail. These health problems did nothing to shake the faith of the American people in Ike's ability to serve as president.

Television

One of the technological advances of great importance was the growth of television. Its importance in the post-war year cannot be over emphasized. TV changed how Americans received their news, helped to homogenize the nation, and affected the cost of presidential campaigns.

The number of households with television grew from several thousand in 1946 to over fifteen million in 1952. By 1955 more than two-thirds of all American homes had television. Advertising dollars were tremendously increased in the 1950s rising from a mere $170 million in 1950 to passing $1 billion by 1955. While the first television shows included the documentary series, Edward R. Murrow's "See It Now," it soon degenerated into a bland menu of situation comedies that pictured women as zany madcaps or saccharine sweet housewives. Fathers did not do much better. They were often pictured as stumbling incompetents. Much of the media was saturated with violence, either in the Old West or in police dramas and even children's shows.

In no case did television deal with the Other America of the poor, the homeless, and the dispossessed. Blacks, Native Americans, and Hispanic-Americans were invisible on TV. The media did, however, depict teenagers but in the worst possible light as zip gun toting hoodlums with hair slicked back into ducktails. And TV gave American adults the first look at rock and roll. White performers such as Buddy Holly, Bill Haley, and others had adapted the rhythm-and-blues of the black community into the new rock and roll. The first major hit was Haley's "Rock Around the Clock." No performer, however, had the magic of Elvis Presley, an ex-truck driver from Tupelo, Mississippi. Between January 1956 and his induction into the armed forces in 1958, Presley recorded fourteen consecutive million-selling records. His popularity was so great that he was asked to appear on the "Ed Sullivan Show," which was the mecca for entertainers. However, to maintain respectability, his gyrating pelvis, which was his trade mark, could not be shown. Millions of American teenagers tuned in only to be disappointed to see Elvis from the waist up.

Television did, however, show Americans how black Americans were being treated when they peacefully protested for their civil rights whether it was attending school or boycotting buses. For the first time many white Americans outside of the South saw how blacks were treated.

CIVIL RIGHTS

Ike was not committed to civil rights although he did believe in law enforcement. He confessed to aides that, while he believed in legal and economic equality of opportunity, he opposed social mingling. After the Little Rock crisis Eisenhower backed completely away from the civil rights struggle in the South. He thought the *Brown* decision was a mistake and would require thirty to forty years to implement in the more moderate Upper South and border states. He was quite disgusted with the decisions of the Supreme Court under Chief Justice Earl Warren and referred to Warren's appointment as "the biggest damn fool mistake I ever made." Under Chief Justice Earl Warren the Supreme Court entered an activist phase where the Court began to make decisions with social implications. Such decisions were against Ike's idea of a limited government.

Brown Decision

Pauli Murray had an unpublicized effect on the *Brown* decision. Murray, who found sexual discrimination at Howard Law School and labeled it "Jane Crow," began work at Howard on a paper later completed at Berkeley, which would be important in the *Brown v. Board of Education of Topeka* decision of 1954. In 1946 Murray urged NAACP lawyers to work to overturn *Plessy v. Ferguson* (separate but equal) on the basis that segregation was a violation of the Fourteenth Amendment's equal protection clause. She argued that separate but equal put blacks into both a social and legal position that was inferior and that did violence to the personality of the individual who was affected. To support her position, she used social science data. This was the tactic that Thurgood Marshall employed in developing the strategy in the *Brown* case. By using black and white baby dolls, Dr. Kenneth Clark and his wife Mamie Phipps Clark were able to show that black children would always choose the white baby dolls because segregation had made them feel inferior. The *Brown* decision declared in words similar to Murray's that to separate Negro children from others of their age and qualifications created "a feeling of inferiority as to their status in the community that affect their hearts and minds in a way unlikely to ever be undone" and thus violated the equal-protection clause of the Fourteenth Amendment. Separate but equal was inherently unequal. A year later the Court ordered the states to desegregate with "all deliberate speed."

Emmett Till Case

In 1955 white men were still killing blacks in Mississippi with impunity, but now a case came to the attention of the whole nation. Emmett Till was a fourteen-year old Chicago boy visiting his grandfather, Mose Wright, outside Money, Mississippi. On a dare, he entered Byrant's Grocery and Meat Market and told Carolyn Bryant, "Bye Baby" after he had purchased some candy.

Three days later, Roy Bryant, a truck driver, and his brother-in-law, J.W. Milam, came to Wright's cabin and took Till away. When his body was found in the Mississippi River, it had been weighted down with a cotton-gin fan. He had a bullet in his skull, one eye gouged out, and his forehead was crushed on one side. The mutilation was so bad that the body could only be identified from a ring. *Jet* magazine published pictures of Till to ensure that all of black America saw what happened. Further publicity came when the national media covered the trial of Bryant and Milam. Some compared the expected acquittal to the Holocaust in Nazi Germany. The publicity increased again two months after the trial when Bryant and Milam sold their story for $4,000. In the story they admitted the murder and tried to justify it because Till had not begged for mercy or seemed repentant.

Montgomery Bus Boycott

One of the papers that had given a prominent display to the Till case was the *Montgomery Advertiser*. Three months later three women, two black and one white, pushed the civil rights movement forward in Montgomery, Alabama. They were Rosa Parks, Jo Ann Robinson, and Virginia Foster Durr. Parks and Robinson were granddaughters of slaves while Durr was the granddaughter of a slave owner.

Virginia Foster Durr had grown up in Birmingham, Alabama, the outspoken daughter of a racist preacher. She was educated at Wellesley College where she first associated with blacks on the basis of equality. After she married Clifford Durr they moved to Washington, D.C. where they had become active in the National Association for the Advancement of Colored People (NAACP), an involvement that they continued when they moved to Montgomery, Alabama.

Two of the Durrs' friends in Montgomery were Mr. E. D. Nixon, the head of the local NAACP, and Rosa Parks, secretary of the NAACP. Parks was a woman who had the bearing and demeanor of a middle-class woman even though she was from a working class background and earned her living as a seamstress. In 1955 Virginia Durr arranged for Parks to attend the Highlander Folk School in Tennessee on a scholarship. It was one of the few places in the

South where blacks and whites mixed freely, and for that reason bigots called it communistic. Parks returned from the school more committed than ever to the civil rights movement.

The third woman, Jo Ann Robinson, was the youngest of twelve children and the first member of her family to graduate from college. After getting an MA in English, she moved to Montgomery where she taught at the black Alabama State College and became active in the Dexter Avenue Baptist Church. Because Robinson owned a car, she did not experience the segregation on busses in Montgomery and elsewhere in the South until she took a bus to Cleveland to visit relatives. Her experience in being forced to the back of the bus helped lay the foundation for the decision to overturn Montgomery's law governing segregation on buses.

The opportunity to do so came December 1, 1955, when Rosa Parks refused to give up her seat in the black section to a white person. She was arrested and jailed. When Nixon could not bail her out, he called upon the Durrs to aid him. After Rosa was out on bail, Parks and the others discussed whether they should have the charge dismissed on a technically. The other alternative was to test the constitutionality of segregation. Parks' husband was very afraid and chanted in the background, "Rosa, the white folks will kill you. Rosa, the white folks will kill you." But Rosa Parks was determined to test Montgomery's Jim Crow laws.

Jo Ann Robinson had also been at work. As soon as she heard of Park's arrest, she called some of her trusted students, and they ran off tens of thousands of flyers, which were distributed by the Women's Political Caucus. The flyers asked Montgomery blacks to stay off the city busses. That Monday no blacks rode the busses, and Parks was tried and convicted but decided to appeal. It was at this point that Martin Luther King, Jr. entered the scene. There was a mass meeting at Holt Church where King gave an impassioned speech that spoke of the power of non-violent resistance. The boycott continued, and King became the leader of the movement that eventually gave birth to the Southern Christian Leadership Conference (SCLC). The foot soldiers, however, were the women who walked for months rather than ride the segregated busses. The boycott led the Supreme Court of the United States to rule in 1956 in favor of a lower court decision striking down the city's segregated seating practices.

In 1999, Parks was honored for her contributions to the civil rights movement with the prestigious Congressional Gold Medal of Honor, the highest civilian award bestowed by the United States government.

Little Rock

The next major civil rights crisis was in Little Rock, Arkansas, where in 1957 nine black teenagers were chosen to integrate Central High School. Governor Orville Faubus called out the Arkansas National Guard to bar them from entering the school. After attempting to reason with Faubus, Eisenhower was forced to send in the 101st Airborne Division and the federalized Arkansas National Guard to protect the nine teenagers. Each student was assigned a soldier to protect him or her, but the soldiers could not blunt the forces of terrorism that were loosed upon these nine teens. There were organized campaigns of terrorism: telephone threats, insults and assaults, groups of attacking mothers, restroom fireball attacks, rogue policemen, acid-throwers, stalkers, economic blackmail, and even a price upon the head of one student, Melba Pattillo Beals. An uncle, who was a deputy sheriff passing for white and a member of the Ku Klux Klan, warned Beals that the KKK planned to skin Beals alive. This was meant literally. Beals' family got her out of town and out of Arkansas to save her life.

Not all whites were opposed to integration. One friend of Beals was a white student, whose true identity is still hidden by the pseudonym Link. Link came from a prominent family and was part of a gang who came to attack Beals. Instead, he saved her by throwing her his car keys which enabled her to escape. He also became her spy. Another was the white soldier assigned to protect her. Finally there was the Quaker family in California who took her in so that she could finish her high school education in safety.

Whites protested the integration of their junior high school in Little Rock, Arkansas. They did not want change and charged that many of the civil rights workers were really communist infiltrators who stirred up the local black communities. Resistance was especially strong in states in the Deep South where a majority of whites still clung to a belief in white supremacy and staunchly favored states' rights over those of the federal government.

Sit-Ins

The last civil rights action in the Eisenhower years took place in Greensboro, North Carolina and was led by four freshman college students from North Carolina Agricultural and Technical College. All four were members of the NAACP Youth Council and had discussed what they could do about segregation. They decided to go to the local F.W. Woolworth Company and ask to be served at the all white lunch counter. Before approaching the lunch counter, the four had made purchases. When the white waitress refused service, they pointed out that another counter in the same store had served them. The students sat there until the store closed. Unsure of what to do next, they sought assistance from the Congress of Racial Equality (CORE), which sent a representative to organize more sit-ins. The SCLC also lent its support. Soon there were sit-ins all across the country organized and led by both black and white college students. Eventually the students founded their own organization, the Student Nonviolent Coordinating Committee or SNCC.

While African Americans made progress in the 1950s through the *Brown* decision and the Montgomery boycott, other minority groups did not fare as well. Only Asian Americans began to move into the middle class primarily due to the heavy use of the educational benefits guaranteed under the GI Bill. Both Hispanic Americans and Native Americans made little headway in ending discrimination against them. One third of Hispanic Americans lived below the poverty line. The Native Americans were the poorest of any minority group. The Seminole Indian Tribe sent a petition to Eisenhower in which they stressed that they were neither inferior nor superior to white men; they were Indians who had a different outlook from white men and wished to retain that. The plea was unanswered.

ASSESSING THE COLD WAR AND EISENHOWER

American and Soviet misunderstandings of each other were virtually unavoidable. American principles, such as self-determination and democracy, conflicted with the Soviet ideals of spheres of influence. Soviet leaders wanted buffers to protect them from another invasion by Germany. The only other principle that the Communists held to was world revolution. The United States wanted them kept out of the Western Hemisphere so the Monroe Doctrine was now made multinational. All states in the Western Hemisphere eventually agreed that an attack on one was an attack on all, whether the attack was from outside or inside the hemisphere. There was some misinterpretation of Kennan's containment. He later said that he listed five regions of the world: United States, United Kingdom, Rhine Valley with adjacent industrial areas, Union of Soviet Socialist Republics, and Japan, where military strength could be produced in quality and only one of those was Communist. Containment was to see that none of the four others fell into communism.

The cold war was a huge change for the United States. It became a nation committed to a major and permanent National Military Establishment with a National Security Council, CIA, and later National Security Agency for monitoring media and communications for foreign intelligence. The United States had entered into peacetime alliances for the first time. It was a far cry from 1796 when George Washington warned against "those over-grown military establishments which...are inauspicious to liberty" and advised that the United States "steer clear of permanent alliances with any portions of the foreign world."

Eisenhower had wanted his legacy to be one of peace. This was clear from a 1953 speech, "The Chance for Peace," given before the American Society of Newspaper Editors. In it he welcomed the Soviets post-Stalin offer to limit the arms race.

Every gun that is fired, every warship launched, every rocket fired signifies... a *theft* from those who hunger and are not fed, those who are cold and not clothed. This world in arms is not spending money alone. It is spending the sweat of its laborers, the genius of its scientists, the hopes of its children....We pay for a single fighter plane with a half million bushels of wheat. We pay more for a single destroyer with new homes that could have housed more than eight thousand people. This is not a way of life at all, in any true sense. Under the cloud of threatening war,...it is humanity hanging from a cross of iron.

His farewell address carried out this theme when Eisenhower warned about the dangers of the military-industrial complex. "This conjunction of an immense military establishment and a large arms industry is new in the American experience....In the councils of government, we must guard against the acquisition of unwarranted influence, whether sought or unsought, by the military-industrial complex. The potential for the disastrous rise of misplaced power exists and will persist." With the new importance of technology, Ike warned of the dangers of a "government contract becom[ing] virtually a substitute for intellectual curiosity" in directing university research. The new circumstance created the dual danger "of domination of the nation's scholars by Federal employment" and the shaping of policy by a scientific/technological elite.

Rated by historians as a high average president, his two greatest legacies are the building of the interstate highway system, the largest pubic works project in American history, and his work for peace.

Although not a boaster, Eisenhower once summed up his presidency: "The United States never lost a soldier or a foot of ground in my administration. We kept the peace. People asked how it happened— by God, it didn't just happen, I'll tell you that."

ELECTION OF 1960

The Democrats had met in Los Angeles and had nominated Senator John F. Kennedy from Massachusetts who in a surprise move chose Senator Lyndon Johnson from Texas as his running mate. The first surprise was that Kennedy wanted him and the second was that Johnson accepted, trading in his power as Majority Leader in the Senate for the vice-presidency. In recent years Kennedy's long time secretary, Evelyn Lincoln, has revealed that she was present when Kennedy discussed the issue with his brother, Robert. Johnson wanted the nomination and had some of J. Edgar Hoover's secret FBI files on Kennedy's extensive womanizing. According to Lincoln, Johnson used this as leverage to secure the vice-presidential nomination despite the opposition of both Kennedy brothers.

The Republicans nominated Nixon who had no serious opponents. For his vice-president Nixon chose Henry Cabot Lodge, Jr., the man Kennedy had defeated in his first senatorial campaign. A problem arose between Nixon and Eisenhower because Nixon was stressing his eight years of experience as vice-president and wished to show himself as having a leading role in the decision making process of the administration. This, however, was precisely the area in which Ike was the most sensitive because of Democratic charges that he reigned rather than ruled. Ike also saw the election as a referendum on his eight years as president, while Nixon saw it as Nixon vs. Kennedy. While Nixon wanted Ike to campaign for Nixon as indispensable and a leader, Ike campaigned in defense of his own actions. Another problem arose when Nixon separated himself from the administration on the issue of defense spending. Ike could not help but interpret that as a rejection of all that he had stood for.

Neither candidate seemed an embodiment of the national purpose. Nixon had served as vice president under Eisenhower for eight years and was famous for a kitchen debate with Nikita Khrushchev. Here Khrushchev said "we will bury you" and Nixon replied that the U. S. makes more color TVs. Nixon had also developed a reputation for duplicity and was popularly known as "Tricky Dick," who concealed his true self under a series of masks. Kennedy seemed equally calculating. His record in the Senate was undistinguished although he was an author of a Pulitzer Prize winning book, *Profiles in Courage*, which caused some pundits to say that his career showed more profile than courage.

Three events helped to shape the election: religion, the debates, and civil rights. As the first Catholic to run since Al Smith lost to Herbert Hoover in 1928, Kennedy sought immediately to dispel the religious issue by giving a speech before the Houston Ministerial Association in which he said that "the separation between church and state is absolute." This helped to neutralize the religious issue.

Nixon made a key mistake when he agreed to a series of TV debates with Kennedy, the lesser known of the two candidates. Nixon's strong suit had been his experience. The first debate turned out to be the most important. Nixon had just come out of the hospital where he had been treated for an infected knee. He looked wan while Kennedy was tanned and seemed the epitome of vigor. The results of the first debate showed that Kennedy could hold his own. His poise made him seem the equal if not the superior of Nixon to the TV audience but not the people who had listened to the debate on radio. He was a candidate made for the television media; it brought out his charisma. In the words of one bemused southern senator, Kennedy combined the "best qualities of Elvis Presley and Franklin D. Roosevelt!"

During the campaign Martin Luther King, Jr. was sent to jail during a sit-in in Atlanta. Both Nixon and Kennedy were working behind the scenes to help King, but it was only Kennedy who called Mrs. King to express his sympathy. His brother, Robert, also called a judge in Atlanta and the mayor to see if they could expedite King's release. The day after John Kennedy's phone call, King was released on bail. His father, Martin Luther King, Sr., said, "It's time for all of us to take off our Nixon button." According to the Gallup poll, Kennedy received 68 percent of the black vote, more than a 7 percent increase over what Stevenson had gotten.

Ike was no help to Nixon either. In answer to a press conference question as to what idea of Nixon's Ike had adopted, Ike responded that if given a week, he might think of one. Although he called Nixon to apologize and express his regrets, it was too late. The damage had been done. Even though Ike campaigned for Nixon in October, his focus was still on his own administration rather than what Nixon might do in leading the U.S. in the 1960s. November 8, 1960, one of the closest elections in American history was decided by less than 120,000 popular votes: John Kennedy would be the 35th President of the United States.

CONCLUSION

Post World War II Americans felt good about their many accomplishments. In foreign affairs they had held the line against the Communist menace in Europe and Asia, rebuilt Europe and sustained military dominance. Domestically the middle class had grown as a result of the G.I. Bill and the economy was good. Beneath the accomplishments, however, were signs of upheaval. There was now a communist nation in the Western Hemisphere: Cuba; twenty percent of Americans were not benefiting from the good economy; minorities and women had begun demanding their rights; teenagers were listening to Elvis. Nevertheless, the average American little suspected that an era was ending and that what would follow would change the nation and their lives forever.

Chronology

1945
Franklin Roosevelt dies; Harry Truman becomes president
United Nations established
Indochina returned to French control

1946
Iron Curtain speech—Winston Churchill
Coal miners' strike
1,000,000 GIs to college
GOP wins Congress
Spock's *Baby and Child Care Book* published
Vietnam declares its independence
Baby Boom begins

1947
Truman doctrine
Taft-Hartley Act
Marshall Plan
Levittown development started
Containment policy developed by George Kennan
Central Intelligence Agency (CIA) established
Marynia Farnham and Ferdinand Lundburg, *The Modern Woman: The Lost Sex*

1948
Israel founded
Berlin blockade and Airlift
Truman orders end to segregation in the armed forces and sends the first civil rights message to Congress
Truman-Dewey election with Truman victor in greatest upset in American history

1949
NATO established
Communist victory in China
Soviets detonate atomic bomb

1950
Truman authorized hydrogen bomb
Joseph McCarthy announces that there are Communists in the government
Korean War begins
China enters Korean War and U. S. begins the longest retreat in U. S. military history

1951
MacArthur fired for insubordination
Rosenbergs convicted of espionage
Armistice talks begin
Twenty-second Amendment—limits on presidential term of office

1952	First hydrogen bomb exploded
	Eisenhower elected
	White House renovation completed
1953	Korean Truce signed
	CIA supported coup in Iran
	Earl Warren appointed Chief Justice
1954	Army-McCarthy hearings
	Brown v. Board of Education of Topeka
	CIA intervention in Guatemala
	"Under God" inserted in Pledge of
	Allegiance
	U.S.S.R. explodes hydrogen bomb
	South East Asian Treaty Organization
	(SEATO) established
1955	Emmett Till murder
	Montgomery Bus Boycott
1956	Interstate Highway Act
	Suez Crisis
	Eisenhower re-elected
	Hungarian Revolution
	U-2 spy plane built
	Eisenhower agrees to support Diem in
	Vietnam
1957	Eisenhower Doctrine
	Civil Rights Act (first since Reconstruction)
	Little Rock desegregation of schools crisis
	Sputnik launched
1958	Halt of atomic tests by U. S. and U.S.S.R.
	National Aeronautical and Space
	Administration (NASA) founded
1959	Castro comes to power in Cuba
	Landrum-Griffin Act passed
1960	U-2 incident
	Second Civil Rights Act
	Sit-ins begin
	Election of John Fitzgerald Kennedy
1961	Eisenhower's farewell address—
	military industrial complex

SUGGESTED READINGS

Stephen E. Ambrose, *Eisenhower: Soldier and President* (1990).

Melba Pattillo Beals, *Warriors Don't Cry: A Searing Memoir of the Battle to Integrate Little Rock's Central High School* (1994).

Christopher Finch, *Highways to Heaven: The Auto Biography of America* (1992).

Alonzo Hamby, *Man of the People: A Life of Harry Truman* (1995).

George F. Kennan, *American Diplomacy, 1900-1950* (1951).

_____, *Memoirs 1925-1950* (1967).

David McCullough, *Truman* (1992).

John Ranleagh, *The Agency: The Rise and Decline of the CIA from Wild Bill Donovan to William Casey* (1986).

Richard Rhodes, *Dark Sun: The Making of the Hydrogen Bomb* (1995).

Lisle A. Rose, *The Cold War Comes to Main Street: America in 1950* (1998).

Stanley Sandler, *The Korean War: No Victors, No Vanquished* (2000).

Sam Tannehaus, *Whittaker Chambers, A Biography* (1997).

Warren A. Trest, *Air Commando One: Heinie Aderholt and America's Secret Air Wars* (2000).

Stanley Weintraub, *MacArthur's War: Korea and the Undoing of an American Hero* (2000).

David Wise and Thomas B. Ross, *The Invisible Government* (1962).

Chapter Twenty-two

HOPE TO DESPAIR:
Kennedy-Johnson Years

Inauguration day in 1961 was crisp and cold with snow piled everywhere in Washington. Matching the untypical weather was the address that John F. Kennedy gave that day. It was at once a call to patriotism and selfless dedication to the good of the nation. As Kennedy called the nation to ask "what you can do for your country," he set the youth of all races afire with the notion that they could change the nation and even the world. The drama of this beginning was matched three years later with the drama of its end. The shock of the assassination was such that over thirty years later, 300,000 Americans wrote to advice columnist, "Dear Abby," to answer the question, "Where were you when President Kennedy was shot?"

"I was in the Peace Corps and had been teaching English in a small town in Thailand for just two months. The shy young Thai student who lived with me came and told me in Thai that President Kennedy had died. I couldn't imagine why he would die suddenly, and said, 'Oh, you must mean that his father has died.' No, no, she said, and kept explaining in Thai what had hap-

pened. I didn't know the Thai word for 'assassinate' so I couldn't understand her. Finally she got her English lesson book and pointed to a drawing of a fellow shooting a gun, next to the sentence, 'He fired a shot.' Then I knew."

M.J.B. Van Nuys, CA.

"I still feel the loss as if a member of my family had been killed. I was twenty years old that year and just about idolized John Kennedy. I don't think I will ever forget."
M.B. Gadsden, AL.

"My husband and I were working in the yard as it was a beautiful November day. I could hear the telephone ringing and ringing. I finally went in to answer it, and it was Mrs. L., a woman who liked to be first with any news. She told me that John Kennedy had been killed. I yelled for my husband to come in as I turned on the TV. We spent the next four days in front of the TV crying and wondering what would happen next."
MGK, Ruffs Dale, PA.

THE KENNEDY ADMINISTRATION

The thousand days of the Kennedy administration that began the 60s with the "High Hopes" of Kennedy's campaign song turned to a decade of hopelessness, distrust of the federal government, and despair over the war in Vietnam. Not even the passage of civil rights legislation in the fallen president's honor could assuage these feelings that grew as the decade passed into history.

The two men whose presidencies comprised these years were as different in background, personality, and goals as any two presidents could be. John Fitzgerald Kennedy came from a privileged Boston background. The Roman Catholic Kennedy was also a Harvard graduate, a hero in World War II, and a U. S. Senator. In contrast, Lyndon Baines Johnson was a Texan from a family that had lost the money it once had. He had worked his way through a state college and trained to be a schoolteacher. Johnson had served as Majority Leader in the U. S. Senate for nearly a decade where he had displayed the greatest gift for compromise since Henry Clay. It was a shock to political observers and his friends when he accepted the Democratic nomination for vice president.

John F. Kennedy became the youngest elected president in American history.

Where Kennedy was seen as cool and intellectual, Johnson was viewed as earthy and volatile with an in-your-face style of confrontation. Kennedy's goals were limited while Johnson sought to outdo his hero, Franklin D. Roosevelt. Kennedy, one journalist wrote, was the first of all the presidents to be a Prince Charming. Johnson was described as Machiavelli in a Stetson. While Kennedy described his administration as the New Frontier and put an emphasis on sending a man to the moon and returning him safely to earth, Johnson named his programs the Great Society, which would eliminate poverty. Kennedy had an intellectual interest in the problem of poverty, while Johnson's political career displayed a long-standing concern for humble people and the cause of civil rights. As one of his biographers has described Johnson, he was a man of both light and dark impulses. The Great Society programs showed his light side while the involvement in Vietnam showed his dark.

Domestic Affairs

When Kennedy was choosing his cabinet, he put the accent on youth and Eastern Establishment. His most controversial appointment was his younger brother, Robert, for attorney general, who many people believed did not have the qualifications for the position. Robert immediately began to pursue the Mafia and those members of American unions who were involved with the Mafia. Years later, Kennedy's cabinet and advisers were described as "the best and the brightest."

Kennedy's appointment of Adlai Stevenson to the post of U. S. Ambassador to the United Nations gave J. Edgar Hoover, head of the FBI, one more chance to denigrate Stevenson and mischaracterize his record. Although Republicans and Democrats alike lauded him, the FBI chose to conclude its report by calling him "a controversial figure."

Although the Congress was overwhelmingly Democratic, it was firmly in the grip of the Southern conservatives who blocked Kennedy's efforts to increase federal aid to education, provide health insurance for the aged, and create a Department of Urban Affairs, as well as initiatives for unemployed youth, migrant workers, and mass transit. It also blocked a tax cut.

There were some successes with Congress: defense appropriations increased even more than requested; a Developmental Loan Fund to help Latin America called the Alliance for Progress; a new housing act; raising of the minimum wage from $1 to $1.25 an hour; an increase in Social Security benefits; and the Peace Corps. The biggest success was the Trade Expansion Act, which led to the Kennedy Round of Negotiations and a 35 percent reduction in tariffs between the United States and the European Common Market.

Space Program

When Kennedy took office, the United States was still sensitive to its failures in the Space Program and the success of the Soviets, first into space with the launching of Sputnik in 1957. To counteract this, Kennedy sought to make the United States first on the moon. By 1962, criticisms of the goal began to surface about the lack of military value of the Apollo program. Ike wrote an article for the *Saturday Evening Post* in August 1962 in which he endorsed space research but not a crash program to the moon. If prestige was sought, why not through industrial and agricultural productivity. "...[W]hy let the Communists dictate the terms of all contests?" he asked. Despite the criticism, the program continued until its successful conclusion under the presidency of Richard Nixon. One positive impact of the space program was that it helped to stimulate the economy. At the time, the economy sustained a growth rate of 6 percent while inflation was under 1.3 percent. This was a remarkable accomplishment.

THE GREAT SOCIETY

After the Kennedy assassination, Johnson used his legislative skills to push a torrent of legislation through Congress. Johnson was aware that "every day I'm in office, I'm going to lose votes. I'm going to alienate somebody." Using his honeymoon period, Johnson pushed through the Great Society leg-

The United States competed with the Soviet Union in the space race.

islation, working the Congress at a pace unseen since the First 100 Days of the New Deal. Virtually the entire agenda of liberalism was enacted from poverty programs to Medicare and Medicaid. The interest in poverty was a combination of Johnson's own interest and a legacy of the Kennedy administration.

Michael Harrington in his book, *The Other America*, detailed the problem: "40-50 million people were mired in a culture of poverty hidden from sight and passed on from one generation to another." Television made the problem vivid to the public by accentuating the relative deprivation of the poor. The poor saw how different they were from middle-class Americans, and this revelation left many fatalistic about their condition. Harrington described the poor as hopeless and passive, yet prone to bursts of violence; lonely and isolated, yet often rigid and hostile. Kennedy read the book and asked his advisers to investigate the problem and suggest a plan of action. When Johnson became president, he was determined to act in a big and bold way. In January of 1964 the Council of Economic Advisors reported that 9.3 million American families, about 20 percent of the population, were below the poverty line of $3,000 a year for a family of four.

Passed partly as a memorial to the slain Kennedy, the anti-poverty programs included the Economic Opportunity Bill, Job Corps, Head Start, work-study, and Volunteers in Service to America (VISTA). The Job Corps trained young people in marketable skills. Head Start was a program for pre-schoolers from poor families. Work study was a program for poor people who were either in high school or college. VISTA was a domestic version of the Peace Corps, encouraging community action. These programs were the basis of the Great Society. The revenues generated by the 1964 tax reduction of over $10 billion would pay for these programs. This tax cut generated one of the longest sustained economic booms in American history. In theory it was liberalism triumphant but Johnson, unlike his hero, Franklin Roosevelt, had no Harry Hopkins to monitor activities, and many programs were plagued with administrative snafus.

One example is the Economic Opportunity Act, which sought to train and place the hard-core poor in jobs. This was a new clientele for the State Employment Services. When new incentives were given, the State Employment Services often grabbed anyone off the street, even criminals or drug addicts, so that they could meet their quotas. There were cases where criminals and addicts were given advances once they entered the training programs, which they then used to support their habits. Meanwhile, the Civil Service employees could report another successful placement. Such activities almost guaranteed that the programs would not last.

Two priorities of the Great Society were health insurance and aid to education. The American Medical Association had long been opposed to health insurance, but now that Johnson had the votes, they got on the bandwagon. Johnson signed the final bill, which was broad and included both Medicare, a federal program for those over 65, and Medicaid, a state-federal program for the poor.

Johnson's proposed $1.5 billion in federal aid to elementary and secondary education was directed at poverty-impacted school districts regardless of whether they were public or parochial. With his first-grade teacher looking on, Johnson signed it in the dilapidated one-room schoolhouse he had attended.

Because many of the pockets of poverty were found in the southern Appalachian Mountains, the Appalachian Regional Development Act was passed to provide $1.1 billion for programs in remote mountain coves. The Housing and Urban Development's low cost 240,000 units and $2.9 billion for urban renewal were to remedy urban poverty. There were also funds for rent supplement for low-income families added in 1966.

The biggest domestic concern of both administrations, however, was the Civil Rights movement, which could not be controlled from Washington.

CIVIL RIGHTS

Under the first Reconstruction in the 1860s, it was the Radical Republicans in Congress who had ensured the passage of the three great civil rights amendments: Thirteenth, Fourteenth, and Fifteenth. The Second Reconstruction was quite different. The presidents and the Congresses were in the position of reacting to rather than leading the Second Reconstruction.

This Second Reconstruction was the work of ordinary Americans who sought to change the conditions under which all minorities in America were forced to live. Obtaining rights guaranteed in the Constitution was difficult if you were black, Chicano, Indian, or female. The new movement began with Rosa Parks in 1955 and built up with the sit-ins in Greensboro, North Carolina, in February of 1960.

While black leaders had some hopes that the Kennedy administration would be willing to move on civil rights legislation, activists did not wait. In May of 1961 freedom riders from the Congress of Racial Equality (CORE) began to test a 1946 U. S. Court decision that prohibited discrimination against interstate travelers. While national groups, such as CORE, organized parts of the movement, much progress was made due to acts of individual Americans demanding freedom.

One of these was black veteran James Meredith who asserted his right to attend the University of

Mississippi in 1962. Governor Ross Barnett refused to allow Meredith to enroll. Kennedy had to send federal marshals to enforce the law. Angry white mobs attacked the federal marshals, and two people were killed in the melee. Kennedy then had to send in federal troops to restore order. Although the president was willing to send federal forces to maintain order, he was not yet ready to call for additional federal legislation to protect the rights of black Americans.

By 1963 Martin Luther King, Jr. had decided to force Kennedy to act and called for federal legislation by launching non-violent demonstrations in Birmingham, Alabama. To combat the peaceful demonstrations, the Police Chief Eugene "Bull" Connor used attack dogs, tear gas, and electric cattle prods that millions saw on TV. In June Governor George Wallace stood in the doorway of the University of

Alabama to prevent two blacks from enrolling. The National Guard was called, and Wallace was forced to obey a Court desegregation order. That evening Kennedy spoke to the nation: "If an American, because his skin is black, cannot enjoy the full and free life which all of us want, then who among us would be content to have the color of his skin changed and stand in his place? Who among us would be content with the counsels of patience and delay?" That night Medgar Evers, head of the Mississippi branch of the National Association for the Advancement of Colored People (NAACP), was murdered. After four hung juries, his accused murderer, Byron De La Beckwith, was finally convicted of the crime in 1995.

The culmination of the 1963 drive was the August March on Washington by over 200,000 peaceful marchers singing "We Shall Overcome." In the afternoon Martin Luther King, Jr. gave his "I Have a

The work of the Congress of Racial Equality (CORE) drew on the talents of whites as well as blacks. Members participated in voter registration drives and the Freedom Rides on interstate buses. The sign at the left refers to the 1964 murders of three civil rights workers, including two whites, Andrew Goodman and Michael Schwerner.

Dream Speech" from the Lincoln Memorial. In the cadence of the Baptist minister that he was, King chanted over and over again, "I have a dream," and then listed his vision for the future of a land where "all of God's children, black men and white men, Jews and Gentiles, Protestants and Catholics, will be able to join hands and sing in the words of that old Negro spiritual 'Free at last! Free at last! Thank God almighty, we are free at last!'" One result of the march was that Kennedy endorsed a pending omnibus civil rights bill.

After Kennedy's death, Johnson called for the passage of the Civil Rights Act as a memorial to Kennedy. July 2, 1964, Johnson signed the most far-reaching civil rights measure ever enacted by Congress. It outlawed discrimination in hotels, restaurants, and other public accommodations. It required that literacy tests for voting be administered in writing and defined anyone who finished the 6th grade as literate. The attorney general could bring suits for school desegregation. An Economic Opportunity Commission was established that administered a ban on job discrimination by race, religion, national origin, or sex. In the same year the Twenty-fourth Amendment was ratified outlawing the use of the poll tax to deny people the right to vote in

federal elections. A 1966 Court decision later ruled that it also applied to state elections.

College students became active in the movement in 1964 in the Mississippi Freedom Summer Project where one thousand students helped blacks to register to vote in Mississippi and to become members of the Mississippi Freedom Democratic Party (MFDP). For many African Americans it was the first time they realized that they could vote. This work was dangerous both for the students and for those registering to vote. One student recorded that July 18: "...Four of us went to distribute flyers announcing the meeting. I talked to a woman who had been down to register a week before. She was afraid. Her husband had lost his job. Even before we got there a couple of her sons had been man-handled by the police." Fanny Lou Hamer was one of the women who lost her job and saw her husband also lose his because they had the temerity to register to vote. Undeterred, Hamer joined the MFDP and sought representation at the 1964 Democratic Convention. Although she was not seated at the 1964 convention, she was the chair of the Mississippi delegation in 1968.

Mississippi in 1964 was not much different from the Mississippi of the 1950s when Emmett Till was

Black citizens picketed schools in St. Louis, Missouri, in the United States in 1963 protesting the policy of school segregation.

Birmingham, Alabama firefighters used high intensity fire hoses to knock down civil rights demonstrators. The hoses were powerful enough to tear bark off trees. These pictures aroused sympathy for the civil rights movement.

killed and dumped into the Mississippi River. A college student recorded in Tchula, July 16: "Yesterday while the Mississippi River was being dragged looking for three missing civil rights workers, two bodies of Negroes were found—one cut in half and another without a head. Mississippi is the only state where you can drag a river any time and find bodies you were not expecting. Things are really much better for rabbits—there's a closed season on rabbits." Despite the threats of violence and actual violence, the civil rights workers remained undeterred in their quest for justice.

In 1965, King and the Southern Christian Leadership Conference (SCLC) announced a drive to register 3 million blacks in the South. The center of the activity was in Alabama. Here the state police, rather than protecting the peaceful marchers, violently sought to disperse them. They even used high intensity fire hoses to knock down the demonstrators. Johnson had to send in the National Guard and army military police to protect them. Several days after the march concluded in Montgomery, Johnson went before Congress to ask for a Voting Rights Act that suspended state literacy tests and authorized federal examiners to register voters. Where

states or counties had fewer than half the adults voting, literacy tests were suspended and the attorney general was authorized to dispatch federal examiners to register voters. He climaxed his speech with "And we shall overcome." The Voting Rights Act became law.

Black Power

In 1964 only 34 percent of Americans thought that blacks were trying to move too fast but by 1966 the percentage was 85. One of the things that caused this change was the Watts Riot in Los Angeles in August 1965, which came at the end of the week in which Johnson had signed the Voting Rights Act. The Watts riot was the first of more than one hundred riots that took place over the next three summers. These riots broke the coalition of organized labor, intellectuals, minorities, and the poor that had united in the Democratic Party. Johnson's appointment of Thurgood Marshall, a former NAACP attorney who had argued the *Brown* case, as the first black justice on the U. S. Supreme Court did nothing to ease the situation. By 1967 Americans saw tanks in Detroit rolling through the streets and

The Watts riot of 1965 was one of more than 100 urban riots in the 1960s.

soldiers from the 101st Airborne using machine guns to deal with snipers. Blacks now used violence and destruction on themselves and the areas in which they lived.

Black Power became the new rallying cry. King was now seen as an "Uncle Tom," someone who worked too closely with the white power structure to be trusted. Stokeley Carmichael became head of the Student Non-Violent Coordinating Committee (SNCC) in 1966 and ousted whites from the organization. H. Rap Brown, who succeeded Carmichael, urged blacks to "Get you some guns" and "Kill some honkies."

The most articulate spokesman was Malcolm X. Malcolm was born in Omaha, Nebraska as Malcolm Little. His father was a Baptist minister who was a follower of Marcus Garvey, a black nationalist of the 1920s. When Malcolm was six, his father was murdered by the Ku Klux Klan in Lansing, Michigan. When his mother suffered a nervous breakdown, the state welfare department took eight Little children. Malcolm soon was sent to a reform school and began a life of crime that lasted until he was imprisoned for burglary in 1946. While in prison, he became interested in the teachings of

Malcolm X , a militant black nationalist, urged African Americans to get their freedom "by any means necessary."

An African American being attacked by a police dog during the protest demonstrations in Birmingham in 1963

Elijah Muhammad, the leader of the Black Muslims, who taught that Christianity was the "religion of white devils." One result was that Malcolm spent the rest of his time in prison educating himself.

Malcolm left prison in 1952, joined a black Muslim temple, and took the name of Malcolm X. In 1964 he made a pilgrimage to the Islamic holy city of Mecca in Saudi Arabia. He then renounced his previous teaching that whites were evil and began to advocate racial solidarity. He adopted an Arabic name and became El-Haji Malik El-Shabazz. When Malcolm broke with Elijah and founded his own organization, Black Muslim assassins gunned him down.

A positive outcome of the Black Power movement was a pride in culture and color. An Afro became the hair style, and the chant was "black is beautiful." This last was doubly important since there was color prejudice within the black community itself. Those who were lighter in skin tone

were given more prestige than their darker hued brothers and sisters. This was also the time when black studies programs were established with African-American history as their centerpiece.

WOMEN AND THE CIVIL RIGHTS MOVEMENT

Much of the civil rights movement believed that racism's effect was more pervasive on the black male who was emasculated by his lack of economic power and thereby lost "control" of his wife and children. This resulted in black men losing their self-respect. Many civil rights leaders saw strong black women as a detriment to the black community and socially destructive. Civil rights leaders often called black women traitors to the greater cause of civil rights.

At first, black women saw their lives shaped more by racism than sexism and often distrusted the feminist movement, which seemed more for white women. This situation changed as, increasingly, black women pursued higher education and entered the professions. Now, besides racial discrimination, they also faced sexual discrimination.

"Jane Crow"

During the 1960s there was a rebirth of the feminist movement that had stagnated since the 1920s. As was true in other periods of our history, women who were involved in the Civil Rights movement soon came to realize that there was a link between racism and sexism. Before this awakening, women had responded to the same arguments used after the Civil War that black rights were more important than the rights of women. One battlefield for the new movement was equal rights.

Alice Paul's Equal Rights Amendment from the 1920s had not received political support from groups except conservative Republicans and southern Democrats, who opposed the protective legislation for women that it would outlaw. Across the country married women faced restrictions in their ability to sign contracts, sell property, have access to credit, and to serve on juries. In many states women who

The women's liberation movement of the 1960s

became pregnant had to quit their jobs. That all began to change with the election of John Kennedy and his appointment of Esther Peterson as head of the Women's Bureau in the Department of Labor.

Peterson had discovered the labor movement at college in the 1920s and soon became a labor advocate. Through her lobbying work, she met Kennedy when he was a freshman congressman from a blue-collar district in Boston. She supported Kennedy's career and was rewarded with the directorship of the Women's Bureau. From here she played a key role in the women's movement.

Because the Kennedy margin of victory was so narrow, Peterson suggested that he and the Democratic Party needed to expand their base by winning over women. Kennedy appointed her executive vice-chair of his Presidential Commission on the Status of Women (PCSW), which was chaired by former first lady and former ambassador to the U.N., Eleanor Roosevelt.

The PCSW wanted the federal government to serve as a model by leading the assault against discrimination based on sex. Before the commission filed its report, Kennedy ordered an end to separate civil service listings for men and women. The PCSW decided that the answer to the question of protective legislation for women was to extend the same protection to men.

The final report was a mixture of liberation and tradition. It stuck with the idea that it was the responsibility of men to support their wives, and it refused to change social security legislation to allow a widowed man to stay home to care for his children as women did. But it did recommend paid maternity leave, an increase in widow's benefits, and extensive child-care services for all income levels.

Women's median income dropped from 63.9 percent of that earned by men in 1955 to 60 percent in 1960. In 1963, Congress passed the Equal Pay Act, which applied only to businesses actually engaged in interstate commerce rather than the broader definition of "affecting" interstate commerce. It mandated equal pay for equal work rather than the broader equal pay for comparable work. Despite the narrowness of its application, in ten years 171,000 employees won $84 million in back pay under the act.

Rather than supporting the ERA, Peterson agreed with Pauli Murray that women could win equality by pursuing cases under the "equal protection" clause of the Fourteenth Amendment. Murray wanted to demonstrate that "Jane Crow" sexual discrimination was just as abhorrent to the Constitution as the racial discrimination of Jim Crow.

The first Jane Crow case was filed by the American Civil Liberties Union (ACLU) in 1965 in Lowndes County, Alabama. Lowndes was known as "blood Lowndes" because a clique of white men terrorized black men and kept all women, black or white, in their place by killing anyone who challenged the status quo. The ACLU lawyers, including Murray, challenged the jury selection system that barred all black men through discrimination and all women by statute. In 1966 the federal court in Montgomery ruled in *White v. Crook* that the Fourteenth Amendment applied to women as well as blacks.

New Feminists

The middle class became conscious of the women's movement in 1963 when Betty Friedan, a college-educated housewife, published *The Feminine Mystique*. One of her questions was: "What kind of a woman was she if she did not feel this mysterious fulfillment waxing the kitchen floor?" Friedan examined the role of the media in propagating the

Feminists demonstrated at the Miss America pageant in Atlantic City, New Jersey, in 1968. They protested the conditioning of women to "beauty" standards to get male approval. Bras, girdles, and hair curlers were thrown into a "freedom trash can."

idea that the only happy woman was the house-wife and that women who worked outside the home always came to a bad end. She noted that training women to be appropriate mates for ambitious men seemed to be the real goal of women's education. *The Feminine Mystique* also indicted Freudian psychology because it equated the impulse to achieve with masculine striving, bad mothering, and sexual maladjustment. It was a best seller with all the major women's magazines publishing excerpts. At times the media distorted Friedan's message into an attack on housewives, which was untrue.

Women's Rights in the Johnson Years

Alice Paul saw her chance to push for equal rights when civil rights legislation was being discussed in 1964 as one of the results of the Kennedy assassination. At Paul's urging, the word "sex" was inserted into the civil rights bill that prohibited discrimination in employment.

Many liberals opposed the bill because it would remove protective legislation. Women legislators like Martha Griffiths of Michigan rallied support for it, and it won 168-133 with most of the support coming from Southerners and Republicans. Pauli Murray got the Johnson administration to drop its opposition by pointing out that the omission of "sex" would weaken the civil rights bill by neglecting black women. They also persuaded Johnson to include "sex" as one of the grounds for prohibiting discrimination. He did this in Executive Order 11375, which governed policies for businesses with government contracts. Such contracts affected one-third of the labor force.

The Civil Rights Act of 1964 set up an agency to enforce the provisions of the act, the Equal Employment Opportunity Commission (EEOC). The first head publicly declared that he would not enforce the sex provision. To force the issue, a civil rights group for women was needed, and the informal Washington network prevailed on Friedan to start it. Thus, the National Organization for Women (NOW) was born in October 1966.

NOW called for a fully equal partnership of the sexes as part of the human rights revolution. It demanded a national system of health care and an end to all practices that denied women opportunities even if they were under the guise of protective legislation.

The passage of the Civil Rights Act of 1964 did not mean that the battle was over. An EEOC commissioner told Friedan that he was interviewing "girls" for the position of Assistant General Counsel. Friedan informed him that since the lawyers applying for the job would surely be over twenty-five, calling them girls was like calling a forty-five year old black man a "boy." The days of the "girls" were over, and the days of women were beginning.

As expected, NOW's first target was to force the EEOC to follow the law. NOW supported a sex discrimination suit brought by stewardesses against the airlines' policy of forcing them to retire when they married or reached age thirty or thirty-five. NOW also fought an EEOC ruling that sex-segregated newspaper ads did not constitute discrimination. Television networks were invited to cover a small demonstration that forced EEOC to hold hearings. The result was new rulings favoring the NOW position.

At the 1967 NOW convention, the abortion rights issue was added to its agenda. Some women split from NOW over this and in 1968 formed the Women's Equity Action League (WEAL), which considered abortion too divisive an issue for a woman's group to take a stand on. Instead, WEAL concentrated on educational and economic issues. NOW and WEAL were soon joined by the National Women's Political Caucus (NWPC), which was a bipartisan organization of women who would work on women's issues on the state level.

MEXICAN AMERICANS

Mexican Americans and others of Latin American heritage constituted another group that began to push for more rights. Many Mexican Americans had been brought into the U. S. during World War II in the

César Chávez organized Mexican-American farm workers to boycott against grape and lettuce growers who practiced discriminatory practices.

bracero (hired hand) program and made up about 10 percent of the agricultural workers. As the war ended, both the U. S. and Mexico considered the program successful. During the Korean War, a new law was enacted to bring workers in again. It was in effect from 1951 to 1964. When it was brought up for renewal in 1960, there was a seven-month debate over its extension. Finally, in December 1964, the bracero program was over. This ending had important consequences for the organizing of Mexican-American field workers since it would no longer be easy to import strike breakers.

The first Chicano (Mexican Americans) to receive national recognition was César Chávez who headed the National Farm Workers' Association (NFWA). In May 1965 the NFWA joined in the Delano Grape Strike in the San Joaquin Valley of California.

Chávez grew up as a typical Mexican-American migrant. He attended about thirty different schools before he eventually completed the seventh grade. After service in the U. S. Navy, Chávez became involved in the organizing of farm workers. Two years

after the founding of the NFWA, that was more a cooperative than a union, there were 1,000 members in the southern San Joaquin Valley.

Chávez believed the Delano strike had a chance of success because it would now be more difficult for the companies to bring in strikebreaking workers from Mexico. By presenting the strike as a broad movement for social justice, rather than just a wage-and-working-conditions issue, Chávez was able to build broad public support. He also made full use of a wide range of civil rights and religious groups, including the California bishops of the Catholic Church. This was brilliant since it effectively deprived the union's opponents of the chance to charge the union with being communist.

Chávez was also able to get the Democratic governor of California, Edmund "Pat" Brown, and the Democratic senator from New York, Robert Kennedy, to support the grape strike. After a five-year struggle, 50 percent of the table-grape growers had signed agreements with the union. In acknowledgment of his contributions, California in 2001 made César Chávez Day a state holiday.

Latina women were also being liberated. In Los Angeles and New York, they began to raise civil rights issues. One California Chicana informed her friends that times have changed. "We can stand up! We can talk back! It's not like when I was a little kid and my grandmother used to say, 'You have to especially respect the Anglos.'"

NATIVE AMERICANS

As the civil rights movement gained strength, Indian organizations became active participants. Indians wanted their rights not only as American citizens but also to maintain distinct political and cultural communities. They met success in both goals.

Indians were routinely made beneficiaries of civil rights legislation, such as the Fair Housing Act, the Equal Opportunity Act, and the Voting Rights Act, which created special protections for them as persons whose primary language was not English. The status of their tribes as distinct political communities was also recognized in civil rights legislation of the New Frontier and Great Society, which included Indian tribes as governments eligible for participation. The result was a renewal of Indian confidence and pride as they learned that they could assert their rights without worry about termination, the dismantling of tribal government, the redistribution of tribal assets to tribal members, and the end of federal services to individual Indians.

The most interesting piece of legislation was the Indian Civil Rights Act of 1968, which required tribal governments to afford to persons under their jurisdiction the civil rights guaranteed in the Constitution. The freedom of religion provision, however, did not prohibit a state religion. This protected the rights of a number of theocratic tribes. It also protected the tribes against states that sought to exercise jurisdiction over the tribal lands.

Once their rights as American citizens were firmly established, they sought to assert their rights as tribal citizens. Treaty rights and the right of tribal self-government would become the new focus. Against all odds, Indians prevailed in federal court in protecting rights that were recognized over a century earlier in various treaties. Although the final resolution of some of the cases took until the 1980s, the Indians did succeed in curtailing state power in the areas of taxation, civil court jurisdiction, and Indian child welfare proceedings.

FOREIGN POLICY

When Kennedy took office after winning the closest presidential election since 1888, he was immediately faced with a foreign policy problem: Cuba.

Though a small island, Cuba consumed more of Kennedy's time than any other area of the world. The first concern was a covert Central Intelligence Agency (CIA) operation conceived under the Eisenhower administration to overthrow Castro. The plan involved the use of the American Mafia. In September of 1960, Robert Maheu, an ex-FBI agent and free lance CIA agent, approached Johnny Roselli, Santos Trafficante, and Sam Giancana with a deal to kill Fidel Castro for $150,000. All three were high-powered men in the Mafia and could see economic benefits to eliminating Castro and regaining control of the drugs, gambling, and prostitution in Cuba that they had previously run under Castro's predecessor. There were a number of unsuccessful high tech assassination attempts. Planning for the invasion of Cuba began at the same time and soon developed into a full-bodied World War II model underground-movement plan with an amphibious invasion.

Before leaving office, Eisenhower severed American-Cuban relations and briefed Kennedy on the CIA plan for 1,500 anti-Castro Cubans to invade their homeland. The Joint Chiefs of Staff assured Kennedy that the plan was feasible. Diplomatic advisers assured him that the invasion would inspire indigenous uprisings against Castro. Few expressed doubts about the plan before it was executed. Later a book, *Group Think*, was written about the phenomena of individuals fearing to speak against what they perceive to be the group norm. The planning for the Bay of Pigs invasion was the most infamous example of group think in our history.

The scheme was poorly planned and poorly executed. Failures in intelligence, operations, deci-

President Kennedy and his brother, Attorney General Robert F. Kennedy, confer during the Cuban missile crisis. The entire world was frightened over the possibility of a nuclear conflagration that could be so devastating.

sion-making, and judgment doomed the invasion. The CIA overestimated the effectiveness of the opposition to Castro, while at the same time underestimating the effectiveness of the Cuban military. CIA planners, such as agency head Allen Dulles, were less than candid with Kennedy out of fear that he would cancel the operation. While Kennedy did not cancel the operation, he refused to support it with U. S. air cover once its failure was apparent. When the invasion force landed, Castro subdued it in three days and captured 1,200 men. A *New York Times* columnist said the United States "looked like fools to our friends, rascals to our enemies and incompetents to the rest."

Later that year, Castro began negotiations for the release of the Cuban exile brigade members in exchange for food and medicine. At the same time Castro's chief lieutenant, Ernesto "Che" Guervara, initiated contact with a Kennedy aide, Richard Goodwin, to see if a *modus vivendi* (temporary agreement) could be achieved with talks on trade, compensation for nationalized property, and the question of the Guantanamo Naval Base. The Kennedy administration rejected the overture.

The fiasco at the Bay of Pigs led, in turn, to problems with the Soviet Union and, ultimately, the Cu-ban Missile Crisis of 1962. Instead of driving the Soviets and the Communists from Cuba, the botched invasion drove the Cubans and the Soviets closer. Fearing another invasion, Castro sought military aid from the Soviets. The U. S. response was CIA sabotage: contaminating goods leaving European ports for Cuba and bribing foreign manufactures to supply faulty equipment and parts. All of these simply pushed Cuba more toward the Soviets. The CIA next renewed its efforts to kill Castro. They tried poisonous cigars, pills, and needles. Nothing worked.

At the Pentagon some people were calling for a first strike nuclear policy regarding Cuba. By September 1962, the CIA reported that the Cuban military buildup with Soviet aid was in response to a belief that the United States would attempt to overthrow Castro by one means or another. The CIA saw the buildup not as a Soviet initiative but as a response to Castro's request for help. The Soviets began to install missiles in Cuba. On October 14, 1962, CIA U-2 spy plane photographs showed the missiles. Kennedy was determined that they had to go. The choices eventually narrowed down to a so-called surgical air strike and a blockade of Cuba. The blockade was renamed "quarantine" since a blockade is an act of war. Monday, October 22 the president announced to members of Congress and then the public the discovery of the missiles and the quarantine.

Nikita Khrushchev, the Soviet Premier, blustered that Kennedy was pushing mankind to the abyss of a nuclear war. There were some tense days as five Soviet ships steamed to Cuba with supplies. At the last minute, they stopped short of the quarantine line, and World War III was avoided. October 28 Khrushchev agreed to remove the missiles and added, "We should like to continue the exchange of views on the prohibition of atomic and thermonuclear weapons, general disarmament, and other problems relating to the relaxation of international tension." The entire world breathed a sigh of relief. What was unknown to the general public in 1962 was how close we were to nuclear war because of actions of U.S. military personnel. The Commander of the Strategic Air Command (SAC) issued an alert on an open radio so that he could impress the Soviets that planes were in the air loaded with nuclear and thermonuclear bombs. During the alert an American airplane strayed into Soviet airspace over Siberia. In another instance a navy commander dropped a depth charge on a Soviet submarine. Unknown to the U.S. Navy was that the Soviet submarines were carrying nuclear-tipped torpedoes. One that patrolled in the area around Pearl Harbor had orders to attack the U.S. base if war broke out.

The positive results of the crisis were: the establishment of a "hot line" between Washington and Moscow to prevent the accidental beginning of war and the negotiation of a treaty to stop nuclear testing in the atmosphere. As Kennedy put it, "A journey of a thousand miles begins with one step."

Other peace initiatives followed. On June 10, 1963, Kennedy gave a speech at American University in which he renounced the *Pax Americana*, a peace enforced by weapons of war. Some historians judge this the most important speech of the post-1945 era. He asked Americans to re-examine their attitudes toward the Soviet Union and its citizens. Kennedy concluded the speech with the announcement that both the British and Soviets had agreed to talks to limit nuclear testing and that the U. S. would unilaterally halt atmospheric testing. Both the Brit-

ish and the Soviets hailed the speech, which was published in total in both Soviet papers *Izvestia* and *Pravda*. Kennedy seemed willing to end the cold war. The sale of surplus American wheat to the Soviets and Kennedy's September speech to the U.N. proposing that the U. S. and U.S.S.R. do the big things together, such as the trip to the moon, were two additional indications of this change. Khrushchev turned down the offer. Nor was the offer well received in the Senate, which kept funding for the space program while putting a rider on the bill forbidding a joint lunar landing without the consent of Congress.

The ending of the Cuban Missile Crisis, however, was not the end of problems related to Cuba. By March of 1963, Kennedy realized that Cuban exiles had developed links with right-wing political groups in the U. S. as well as criminals who were professional gun runners stealing armaments from the U. S. military. Kennedy ordered restrictions on unauthorized exile activities including training camps in the United States. At the same time, Castro tried to seek some accommodation with the U. S. In the fall of 1963 Kennedy authorized a member of the U.N. staff to work up an agenda with the Cubans. There is evidence that Kennedy was also pursuing non-formal contacts through a French journalist who was going to Cuba to interview Castro. During this interview both men received word of the Kennedy assassination. There have been no attempts at a détente with Cuba since then.

Europe

Two months after the Bay of Pigs, Kennedy met Soviet Premier Khrushchev in Vienna where the Soviet leader sought to intimidate the young American president. When Kennedy returned home, he called up the Reserve and National Guard units and asked Congress for $3.2 billion more in defense funds.

Shortly after this meeting, Khrushchev built the Berlin Wall thus making the Iron Curtain in East Germany a concrete reality to prevent East Germans from fleeing communism. On his last trip to Europe in 1963, Kennedy gave a speech in front of the

Berlin Wall pointing out that the West did not have to build a wall to keep its own people in; only the Communists had to do that. In what became a memorable phrase Kennedy stated that the proudest boast a free man could make was that he was a Berliner. He then repeated it in German to mass cheers, applause, and some confusion since the phrase in German meant that he was a German pastry.

Peace Corps

One of Kennedy's foreign policy initiatives that still remains today was the Peace Corps, whereby young and old Americans went to various second and third world countries to provide assistance to the people. Although many of the members were recent college graduates, some were like Lillian Carter, the mother of future president Jimmy Carter, who, at age 65, went to India to use her nursing skills.

One of the requirements of the Corps was that the volunteers had to learn the language of the country to which they were being sent and to live like the natives of the area. Although the Peace Corps was

not overtly political, there was often an ideological battle for the peoples of the third world. When volunteer Tim Scanlon asked a Peruvian Indian chief how Scanlon could be of help to his people, the chief replied, "Will you be willing to come here when it snows and you have to leave your jeep and walk twenty miles in five foot snows? The Communists will."

Vietnam

Vietnam was the foreign policy area that had the most military and domestic repercussions. The whole of Southeast Asia was a simmering caldron of conflict during the 1960s. Laos and neighboring Cambodia had been declared neutral in the Geneva Accord of 1954, but both were involved in their own struggles while at the same time serving as a conduit for troops and supplies going from North Vietnam to South Vietnam.

The focus was on Vietnam, which represented both a political and economic prize to whatever interests dominated it. As the decade opened, the two major forces were the Communists under Ho Chi

Ho Chi Minh (left) meets China's Chairman Mao during his travels in Asia.

Minin in North Vietnam and the South Vietnamese under American-backed Premier Ngo Dinh Diem.

A religious conflict added to the usual conflict between competing ideologies. The population of North Vietnam was originally heavily Catholic. However, after the Communists gained power, many Catholics fled to the primarily Buddhist South. Premier Diem was a Catholic with one brother a prominent Catholic Bishop and another the head of the secret police, a position that included CIA involvement and drug running.

Kennedy demanded that Diem begin to resolve some of the economic and social problems of South Vietnam in return for American support. Diem did not deliver on his promised reforms, and Kennedy refused to increase the American military presence, although he sent more and more advisers. Between 1961 and 1963, the advisers increased from 2,000 to 16,000.

By 1963 things were coming to a head over the Diem regime. Buddhist monks began committing suicide by setting their gasoline-soaked bodies afire. American TV news showed films of this immolation. When dissident generals proposed a *coup d'etat*, Henry Cabot Lodge, the American ambassador, assured them that Washington would not stand in the way. The U. S. offered to fly Diem into exile, but he chose to stay and was killed in the *coup*. The new government was not an improvement, as the generals were no more interested in reform than Diem.

In September 1963 Kennedy declared, "In the final analysis it's their war. They're the ones who have to win it or lose it. We can help them as advisors but they have to win it." Documents declassified in December 1997 prove that shortly before Kennedy's death, military leaders were proceeding with plans to withdraw American advisors from Vietnam. An October 4, 1963 memo from Maxwell

An American soldier on patrol along the Mekong Delta

Taylor, then chairman of the Joint Chiefs of Staff, declared that, "all planning will be directed toward preparing Republic of Vietnam forces for the withdrawal of all United States special assistance units and personnel by the end of the calendar year 1965." It continued that the plan was to withdraw 1000 military personnel by the end of 1963. The Joint Chiefs, unhappy with the plans, were pushing for war against North Vietnam. The first one hundred advisors had returned to the U. S. when Kennedy was assassinated on November 22, 1963. The following day, Johnson, the new president, reversed Kennedy's policy of withdrawal.

After JFK's death, Johnson sank the United States into the most disastrous war in our history. How this happened is partly explained by LBJ's obsession with failure. His personal history permitted him no retreat, and he saw Vietnam as a test. He also be-

lieved in the domino theory first stated by Eisenhower: "You have a row of dominos set up, you knock over the first one, and what will happen to the last one is the certainty that it will go over very quickly." If the Communists overran South Vietnam, Ike had reasoned, communism would then take over in other countries of Southeast Asia. Johnson thought the answer in Vietnam was to get in and out quickly. Led by some of the so-called "best and brightest" of the Kennedy administration, Johnson soon committed American combat forces.

The road to making the civil war in Vietnam into an American war began in 1964 with the authorization of the bombing of North Vietnam in retaliation for the death of nine American advisers. Johnson thought the bombing would boost South Vietnamese morale and get them to enact reforms. For the North it was an attempt to drive them to the bargaining table. Johnson was trying strategies that had worked for him as majority leader in the U. S. Senate: the carrot and stick of compromise. Neither Johnson nor his advisers seemed able to grasp that the Vietnamese were playing by rules that admitted no compromise or bargaining.

Gulf of Tonkin

The decision to send combat troops came out of one of the most unusual encounters of the period. The U. S. had military ships in the Gulf of Tonkin off the coast of North Vietnam. In August 1964 a novice sonar man on the *U.S.S. Maddox* reported to his captain that he had seen torpedo runs and that the ship was under attack. The *Maddox* fired its own torpedoes, although they could not see any ships, and began evasive action. The sonar man continued to report torpedo runs. Navy flyers, including Commander James Stockdale, later an admiral and 1992 vice presidential candidate with Ross Perot, flew over the area searching for North Vietnamese ships. He reported: "Not a ship, not the outline of a ship, not a wake, not a reflection, not the light of a single tracer bullet. Nothing." The first reports were immediately sent on to Washington. Later reports advising that caution be exercised since the whole report may have been in error were ignored. The truth is that there were no ships and no attack.

Nevertheless, Johnson told the American people on national TV that the North Vietnamese had attacked two American destroyers, the *U.S.S. Maddox* and *U.S.S. C. Turner Joy* on August 2 and 4 in the Gulf of Tonkin. Congress passed the Gulf of Tonkin Resolution, which authorized the president "to take all necessary measures to repel any armed attack against the forces of the United States and to prevent further aggression." Only two senators voted against it. Years later, when the full story was known, many senators, who supported the resolution because they believed the president, said they would have voted against it had they known the full story. In 1995 former Defense Secretary Robert McNamara visited Vietnam and asked General Vo Nguyen Giap of North Vietnam if there had been an attack. He confirmed that there had not.

Years later, Johnson told one of his biographers that if he hadn't gotten Congress to back him on the Gulf of Tonkin Resolution, the "commies" would have seen it as a sign of weakness, and his Republican opponents would have cut his heart out in the 1964 presidential election. The recent release of Johnson tapes reveal that he wondered "how we get the hell out of there."

Under Johnson, the war took on all the aspects of total slaughter. The line between military targets and civilians ceased to exist. When General William Westmoreland was challenged about bombing civilian targets, his response was that "it does deprive the enemy of a population." An American commander justified the shelling of the village of Ben Tre by saying that it "had to be destroyed to be saved."

The emphasis on the numbers game, where the military was constantly inflating casualty figures, was one of the problems. In previous wars, success or failure was determined by the capturing of military objectives. In Vietnam it was measured by body counts. The following conversation between Major General William E. Dupoy, Joint Chiefs of Staff, and Arthur Goldberg, Johnson adviser, illustrates the problem:

Dupoy: "There were 230,000 enemy in the order of battle. We have killed approximately 80,000 of them."
Goldberg: "...how many seriously wounded, would you say there were for every one killed?...what's the ratio of seriously wounded to killed?"
Dupoy: "About ten to one. sir."
Goldberg: "...can we agree three to one as a conservative figure for those rendered ineffective by wounds? Is that all right, General?"
Dupoy: "Yes, sir, that's all right."
Goldberg: "...by my count if you have 240,000 seriously wounded plus 80,000 killed, for a total of 320,000 out of an order of battle of 230,000, General, who the hell are we fighting out there?"

American support for the war eroded faster than the will of the North Vietnamese to tolerate casualties. Opposition began on college campuses in 1965. The rise of a New Left movement was one reason for the opposition. This included the Students for a Democratic Society (SDS) founded at the University of Michigan by Al Haber and Tom Hayden. At a 1962 meeting in a United Auto Workers' Hall in Port Huron, the SDS issued its Port Huron Manifesto, touching on most of the themes of the 1960s except for the Vietnam War that was added later. They stressed opposition to human degradation, as symbolized by racism in the South, and the threat of the cold war.

The University of California at Berkeley was another center for student activity, where the main issue became free speech. In the early 1960s Berkeley residents cared about two issues: peace and race. By 1960 the town of Berkeley was one fifth black, but blacks were almost invisible on campus or in town. In 1964 the Berkeley student chapter of CORE attacked job discrimination in the area. Recruitment for their activities took place at card tables set on city property along the edge of the campus. The students passed out leaflets, solicited funds, and gathered names.

Some of the students had worked in 1964 for civil rights in Mississippi where their eyes had been further opened to injustice. When they returned to campus, they expected to recruit more students to this cause. The president of the University of California system banned the recruitment tables. The students demanded an end to the regulation forbidding political activity on campus. They demanded the rights of free speech guaranteed by the First Amendment.

The regulations shifted many times so that no one really knew what was banned and what was legitimate. When the students moved their recruitment tables into the heart of the campus, the Berkeley administration called the police. The students then staged a sit-down and got police permission to use the roof of the police car as a podium to address the crowd. One speaker called the administrators a "bunch of bastards" who were exercising illegitimate authority.

To emphasize the "fascist" aspects of the university administration, the students planned a sit-in in one of the major halls on campus. They occupied all four floors. The college president became desperate and after getting a false report that a student had broken into an office, Governor Pat Brown ordered that the students be arrested. Seven hundred and seventy-three students were arrested, the largest number of arrests in one day in California history.

As sit-ins took place at other prestigious universities across the nation, they helped to cause a break between parents of the World War II generation and their children. Parents, who had made sacrifices in World War II and who had scrimped and saved so that their children could be educated, could not understand their ingratitude and their rebellious ways. The draft resistance movement further enlarged this break. Fathers who had fought in World War II or the Korean War could not understand why their sons had become draft dodgers.

Draft Resistance

In 1965, individuals began joining together to resist the Vietnam draft. For some it meant a break with their families as they contemplated going to Canada. Others asked their fathers to "save" them from the draft by getting them a safe post in the National Guard. Some were more confrontational and joined with their friends to burn their draft cards while chanting: "Hell no! We won't go." Momentum gathered slowly, and in July 1966 anger at the Vietnam buildup resulted in a New Haven group returning their draft cards to the local board.

While individuals and groups were protesting the war, some governmental officials were having second thoughts, too. In 1966 William Fulbright, chairman of the Senate Foreign Relations Committee, began a congressional investigation. George Kennan, the author of the containment policy, said containment was not the proper policy for Asia. General James Gavin said General Westmoreland's military strategy had no chance of achieving victory. By May 1967 even Secretary of Defense Robert McNamara seemed to be losing his faith in the war when he said, "The picture of the world's greatest superpower killing or injuring 1,000 noncombatants a week, while trying to pound a tiny backward nation into submission on an issue whose merits are hotly disputed, is not a pretty one."

As was true of the Civil War, the Vietnam War was turning into a rich man's war and a poor man's fight. Black Muslims felt the full force of the law when they refused on the ground of religion to fight in any war not declared by Allah. In 1966 Muhammad Ali, who had become heavyweight champion of the world under the name Cassius Clay, asked his draft board in Louisville, Kentucky for Conscientious Objector (CO) status. They said his beliefs were insincere. Ali replied that if he was not sincere, why would he give up millions of dollars and lose his public image? If Ali had accepted the draft, he would have been sent into armed services boxing exhibitions in Vietnam. Instead, he was convicted in 1967 for refusing induction, sentenced to five years in prison, and stripped of his heavyweight championship. Four years later, while he was free on bond, the Supreme Court reversed the conviction on technical grounds.

While the government could prosecute a few individuals, it could not deal with masses. That was the goal of the draft resisters: 100,000 acts of defiance. This resistance was organized in the fall of 1967 with scores of educators and religious leaders supporting it. These included the famous pediatrician Dr. Benjamin Spock and the head of campus ministry at Yale, Rev. William Sloane Coffin. Attorney General Ramsay Clark chose to prosecute both Spock and Coffin. Their convictions were reversed, but the Justice Department did convey a public image of vigorous enforcement of the draft law.

Congress reacted by making the burning of draft cards a crime with punishments ranging up to five years. Resisters defied the law and were promptly jailed. Once the movement gained momentum, the Justice Department became more selective in its prosecution. During the height of the resistance in 1967-1968, fewer than fifty were indicted, and forty were convicted.

Some draft boards were over zealous in their prosecutions. Robert Craig received mail at home while he was away at college. His father had recently died, and his mother did not want her only son to go to Vietnam so she returned all letters to the draft board without telling her son. He was prosecuted and convicted of draft evasion.

In the South the induction notices were often sent to "trouble makers" who were active in the civil rights movement. Mrs. Jeanette Crawford of New Orleans was a civil rights activist with three draft-age sons. When she refused to testify before the Louisiana House Committee on Un-American Activities, her three sons were ordered to report for induction. The oldest, James, who had already served thirteen years in the army, was accused of not registering for the draft. The FBI staked out the Crawford home in hopes of capturing him. This was impossible since he was serving with the U. S. Army in West Germany. His brother Warren refused induction and received the highest penalty in the Vietnam Era— six concurrent five-year sentences.

Not all draft resisters remained anonymous. Many of the leaders of the Baby Boom generation that came to power in the 1980s never served in Vietnam. These men were from both political parties. They include former Republican Vice President Dan Quayle and President George W. Bush, who obtained much sought after slots in the National Guard; Republican Newt Gingrich, former Speaker of the House, who got a family man deferment; former Republican Senator Phil Gramm from Texas, who had an educational deferment; and former Democratic President William Jefferson Clinton, who used a number of maneuvers to escape the Vietnam War. Some of those who served include Republican Senator John McCain of Arizona, who was a prisoner of war caged like an animal; former Democratic Senator Robert Kerrey of Nebraska, who lost a leg in the war; Democratic Senator John Kerry of Massachusetts, who founded Vietnam Vets Against the War; and former Democratic Vice President Albert Gore, Jr., who served as an Army journalist.

Tet Offensive

On November 24, 1967, the CIA warned that an enormous flood of Vietcong infantry was coming down the Ho Chi Minh Trail. The military ignored the warning and, thus, the January 1968 Tet Offensive came as a total surprise. The shock of the Tet Offensive, the sight of an enemy swarming all over the American Embassy in Saigon and indeed all over Vietnam, forced a public reckoning. Soon college campuses exploded with more than two hundred major demonstrations in the first six months, involving forty thousand students. Walter Cronkite of CBS News, deemed the most trusted man in America, announced that the U. S. was involved in a stalemate with no hopes of victory. Although the result was a major military defeat for the Vietcong, the American people had already turned. Johnson's popularity fell to 35 percent. Each day Johnson could hear the protesters outside the White House chanting, "Hey, hey, LBJ. How many kids did you kill today?" Other protesters shouted obscenities. In February 1968 the CIA, Clark Clifford the new Secretary of Defense, and Johnson's advisers all concluded that the war could not be won. The best that could be achieved was a stalemate. They advised disengagement and withdrawal.

Johnson's worst nightmares were beginning to come true: loss in Vietnam, Richard Nixon emerging as his GOP opponent, and Robert Kennedy thinking of challenging him for the Democratic nomination. In March of 1968 the voters in New Hampshire gave Eugene McCarthy, a little known Democratic Senator from Minnesota, 42 percent of the vote in the presidential primary. Four days later Robert Kennedy entered the race. On March 31, three days after the final meeting with his advisers, Johnson announced at the end of a televised speech: "Accordingly, I shall not seek and I will not accept, the nomination of my party for another term...." Instead, Johnson pledged to devote the rest of his term to finding a way to end the war.

At the same time the draft resistance movement became more violent. The Catonsville Nine led by the Berrigan brothers, one a priest and the other a former priest, used the same napalm the army was using in Vietnam to destroy 378 draft files. Government reaction was swift and severe. The Berrigans were caught, tried, convicted, and sentenced to prison.

What really crippled the draft process was not the resisters but the lawyers who were working within the system. The case of Daniel Seeger of New York began the unraveling of the system. Seeger had asked for an exemption as a conscientious objector. His draft board refused, since Seeger did not belong to a pacifist sect. The case went to the Supreme Court, which ruled that he qualified because of his personal religious beliefs. That did not mean that draft boards would begin to abide by this change in law; they didn't. Increasingly lawyers told their clients that they should challenge the legality of the draft board decisions, and the resisters began to win. In 1968 a small group of Washington lawyers established the *Selective Service Law Reporter,* which published decisions, regulations, and legal analysis.

The demands of the Vietnam War did not increase the safety record of the Pentagon, which continued to lose H-bombs in the 1960s. In 1966 a bomber carrying four H-bombs crashed off the Spanish coast. Three of the bombs landed near the coastal village of Palomares. The TNT charges in two of them exploded and showered the area with uranium and plutonium. The fourth bomb landed eight miles off shore and is still there in 2,850 feet of water. In 1968 a B-52 caught fire on a flight above Greenland and crashed into North Star Bay near Thule Air Base. The impact detonated the TNT in all four H-bombs and scattered uranium, tritium and plutonium over a 2,000 foot radius. The thermonuclear assembly was encapsulated in the ice and the rescue crew had to work in -70 degrees to recover it. Showing their sense of humor, the recovery work crew called it "Dr. Freezelove."

Another effect of the Vietnam War was the Johnson administration's use of the U.S. Army to spy on civilians. The Army employed more than 1,500 plainclothes agents to watch any anti-war demonstration of twenty people or more. They infiltrated civil rights protests, set up phony news organizations, and misdirected busloads of anti-war demonstrators. They were seeking to prove that communists were responsible for opposition to racial segregation and the war in Vietnam. When it was over, the Army had collected information on more than a million law-abiding American citizens. Its nefarious activities were revealed when Christopher H. Pyle, former Army Captain in Army intelligence, testified before the Senate Subcommittee on Constitutional Rights in 1971.

The Beatles were one of the most popular groups in modern music.

POPULAR CULTURE

Popular culture changed dramatically in the 1960s as the first wave of the baby boom generation entered college. Many rejected what they saw as the materialistic life style of their parents. Some became hippies and lived in communes. Others experimented with drugs and sex. Many did all three. The center for the hippie movement was the Haight Ashbury district of San Francisco, although groups were found throughout the nation.

Surveys indicated that half of the college students had tried marijuana. A minority followed the lead of Harvard Professor Timothy Leary who urged students to experiment with hallucinogenic drugs like LSD or "acid," telling them to "turn on, tune in, drop out."

Some of the rock groups like the Grateful Dead and the Jefferson Airplane popularized a new style called "Acid Rock," which had a heavy beat and lyrics that promoted the youth agenda of radical politics, sexual promiscuity, and drugs.

In 1964 a change came into popular music with the British invasion of the Beatles who appeared on the popular television program, the Ed Sullivan Show.

At first, the Beatles seemed like angelic choirboys whose hair was a bit too long and who sang lovely romantic songs. That soon changed, and their music, too, took on all the aspects of the youth culture. There seemed to be drug messages in their songs whether it was "I want to turn you on" or a hidden message about LSD in "Lucy in the Sky with Diamonds." It was, however, their 1967 album, *Sergeant Pepper's Lonely Hearts Club Band*, that ignited a summer of emotional release and youth unity. In contradistinction there was the hard rock of Mick Jagger and the Rolling Stones, another British group.

The 60s also saw soul music moving into the popular mainstream with the Motown sound of the Supremes from Detroit. Music now became part of the resistance movement as the young listened to Bob Dylan, Arlo Guthrie, Pete Seeger, and Joan Baez sing songs about draft resistance and peace.

Sexual experimentation was made easier with the marketing of oral contraceptives in 1960. The Pill freed women from the dangers of unwanted pregnancies but not the dangers of sexual diseases.

The festival held at Woodstock, New York in August 1969 was the symbol of the counter culture. Hippies, Vietnam War protestors, civil rights sup-

Woodstock festival in New York, 1969

porters, and those who experimented with sex and drugs attended. Surprisingly the festival was planned by four young executives who were interested in venture capitalism. The partners expected somewhere between 50,000 and 100,000 people so they rented a field from a local dairy farmer as the site. It soon became clear that the event was going to draw a much larger crowd. On August 15, when the festival began, an estimated 400,000 people were in attendance. The band scheduled to open the festival could not get to the site because of the traffic jams. Some of the greatest performers of the 1960s performed there, including Janis Joplin, Ravi Shankar, Arlo Guthrie, and Joan Baez, as well as bands including The Who; Crosby, Stills, Nash and Young; the Jefferson Airplane; The Grateful Dead; Sly and the Family Stone; and Creedence Clearwater. Jimi Hendrix ended the three-day event with a freeform solo guitar performance of "The Star Spangled Banner." In spite of the large numbers, the event was peaceful. It was later documented in the motion picture, *Woodstock*.

There was also a theological component of pop culture: the new consciousness movement of the "Death of God." This was an anti-theology that said the evils of Auschwitz and Hiroshima meant there was no God. Hopeful theologians like Harvey Cox expounded not that "God Is" but that rather "He Is Not Yet." There was also a reborn interest in Eastern religions, fueled by the Beatles who made their own trip to India.

Of course, people who were hippies, sexually promiscuous, or tried drugs were a minority of the baby boomers. Many saw all of this as a sign of moral decay, a beginning of the end. Questions of social and moral behavior soon entered the political arena where they remain today.

A DECADE OF ASSASSINATIONS

The three political assassinations were perhaps the most troubling aspect of the 1960s. The first was the assassination of John F. Kennedy, followed in 1968 by the killing of Martin Luther King, Jr., and then Kennedy's brother, Robert.

In November 1963 John Kennedy with his wife Jackie and Vice President Lyndon Johnson made a trip to Texas. In preparation for the 1964 election, JFK wanted to settle an internal dispute in the Texas Democratic Party. While riding through the streets of Dallas in an open car, Kennedy was hit in the throat and brain by rifle bullets that caused his death. Very quickly, the Dallas police arrested a suspect, Lee Harvey Oswald, who worked in the Texas Book Depository Building on the square where the president was murdered. No one knew the immediate implications of the plot, nor who else might have been targeted. Matters became more unsettled when Jack Ruby killed Oswald on live TV while Oswald was being moved from one jail to another.

To ease the fears of the American people, newly sworn-in President Lyndon Johnson set up a commission headed by the Chief Justice of the United States Supreme Court, Earl Warren. Members of the commission also included former CIA Director Allen Dulles and future president Gerald Ford. The commission did not have an investigative arm but instead only reviewed the information that was presented to it by the FBI and other agencies. Despite requests from Jack Ruby that he be brought to Washington, D. C. to testify, no attempt was made to secure his story. The commission accepted that Lee Harvey Oswald was the lone assassin who was killed by Jack Ruby, another lone assassin. The most persuasive presentation of the Warren Commission theory can be found in Gerald Posner's *Case Closed*,

Robert F. Kennedy, **campaigning for president before his murder.**

which some members of the media and some historians have endorsed.

Both the FBI and the CIA had their own secrets that they wished to protect. FBI head J. Edgar Hoover's confidential sources linked Oswald to organized crime and Cuban exiles and indicated that he should have been placed on the Security Index. Hoover did not want to reveal that this had not been done. The CIA did not want the news out that it had been working with the Mafia to assassinate Castro. At the first meeting ex-head of the CIA, Allen Dulles, provided the commission with copies of an article claiming that most political assassinations resulted from lone madmen.

Within a short time the reaction to the Warren Commission Report went from praise to condemnation and generated a flood of critical books, which has not yet ended. One result was the 1978 House Select Committee on Assassinations, which surmised that the most likely conspiracy involved Cubans associated with anti-Castro organizations in the United States and that it might have included the criminal element. The committee documented the ties Mafia Boss of New Orleans Carlos Marcello's had with Jimmy Hoffa, ex-head of the Teamster Union whom Attorney General Robert Kennedy had sent to prison; Santos Trafficante, Mafia Head of Miami whom Castro had jailed in Havana for a time; and Oswald, Ruby and members of the New Orleans Cuban community. While the committee was meeting, and before he could testify, Sam Giancana was killed in what had all the earmarks of a gangland hit. Johnny Roselli, a lower level Mafioso who testified to the committee, was killed and his body stuffed into a drum. He was later found off the Florida coast. In the 2001 *Science & Justice*, the journal of Britain's Forensic Science Society, D. B. Jones detailed a new analysis of recorded police radio transmissions that provided new confirmation that there were shots fired from the grassy knoll, an indication of more than one shooter, which put Kennedy in crossfire. With such revelations coming on a regular basis, it is no surprise that thirty-five years after the assassination, 80 percent of the American public believed that Kennedy's and Oswald's deaths were part of a huge conspiracy.

Vice President Lyndon Johnson took the oath after the murder of John Kennedy.

The Conspiracy Case

Some people maintain that there is evidence of interconnections between the Cuban exile community, Jack Ruby as gun runner, organized crime bosses, the CIA, the FBI, drug traffickers, leaders of the military-industrial complex, and the Dallas Police Department.

The Cuban exile community was very anti-Kennedy since the unsuccessful invasion of Cuba at the Bay of Pigs and the agreement not to invade Cuba made with Khrushchev during the Cuban Missile Crisis. The CIA's rejection of the Cuban exiles' military plan in the Caribbean, intended ultimately to goad the U.S. into war with Cuba, had leaked between November 8, 1963, and its official announcement on November 19. In the same interval the FBI received reports of a plot to assassinate the president in Dallas. It was verified in 1964 that Oswald had many associations with the militant CIA-funded Cuban exiles.

The predecessor to the CIA, organized crime, and the United States military had a history of working together since World War II. The military obtained Lucky Luciano's release from prison to work with the navy in the invasion of Sicily. This had continued with the CIA's plans to use the Mafia to assassinate Castro.

FBI head J. Edgar Hoover also had questionable ties to Meyer Lansky, the Mafia boss who organized the syndicate that controlled a large proportion of the crime in the United States and turned Las Vegas into a gambling mecca.

Some believe that Oswald's three years in Russia and activities on behalf of Castro prove that the Communists killed Kennedy. Others maintain that the original Warren Report was basically correct and the conspiracy theory is unproven. That is the argument of Gerald Posner in *Case Closed*.

And actions of the Kennedy family helped to fuel conspiracy theorists. There was contention about the casket in which Kennedy's body had been placed in Dallas and the casket it was in when it arrived at Bethesda for the autopsy. The Dallas mortician swore that he had placed the body in a bronze casket. The Navy corpsman present at the autopsy said that it had arrived in a different one. When Kennedy's body lay in state it was in a casket of mahogany.

In 1999 the National Archives released information that the casket had been damaged in transport and had been loaded aboard a military plane and dropped into 9,000 feet of water off the Maryland-Delaware Coast. This was done because the family feared that it might become an object of morbid curiosity and because the Mayor of Dallas did not want it to become a public focus.

Upon Kennedy's assassination there was a dramatic change in U. S. Vietnam policy. From a slow withdrawal of advisers to active participation with ground troops, the change in presidents marked a dramatic reversal of policy.

Since 1961, Johnson had been an ally of Air Force General Curtis LeMay, and both had been unrelenting in their efforts to get Kennedy to introduce combat troops in Vietnam. Members of the defense industry joined them in this lobbying effort. Hoover's sexual dirt on the Kennedys began to surface in late June 1963 after the president's peace speech at American University. Such tidbits as "What high American official was involved with Marilyn Monroe?" appeared in the Drew Pearson-Jack Anderson column of June 29, 1963. On the same day the Hearst paper in New York linked "one of the biggest names in American politics" to the Ward sex-ring in Great Britain, which had brought down a member of the British cabinet. It was John Kennedy.

For decades the national press had ignored the private sexual affairs of national politicians. However, not many were as active as John Kennedy. His most serious indiscretions were with women who had ties to organized crime. Judith Campbell was involved with Mafia Don Sam Giancana at the same time that she was having an affair in the White House with Kennedy. And Hoover was aware of every move that Kennedy made.

There were also some questions about Oswald, whom Johnson described as a "curious fellow." Oswald had served in the U.S. Marines and had been stationed for a time at Atsuge Air Base in Japan where the U-2 spy planes were based. He eventually defected to the Soviet Union and then reclaimed his citizenship after living in the U.S.S.R. for a few years. At the time of his arrest, Oswald was carrying a Department of Defense ID, which was only issued to those injured on active duty who needed medical privileges or those who were civilian employees overseas. This last tidbit of information was uncovered as a result of the demand for the release of more assassination information after the Oliver Stone movie, *JFK*. It had been buried for years in the files of the Dallas Police Department. In preparation for the 40th anniversary the Muchmore film, which shows the fatal head shot much better than the more famous Zapruder footage, is being remastered and restored with digital technology. Although it has been forty years since the assassination, the issues it raised have not been put to rest nor has the distrust in the federal government to which it gave rise. When the Clinton-appointed Assassinations Committee announced the release of the Kennedy Assassination files in the fall of 1998, they stated that one result of the government secrecy was an increased distrust of the federal government.

Election of 1964

When Johnson came to the presidency, it was as a man committed to the space program as a model of the role government should play in society and the role technology should play in government. To LBJ the space program was the beginning of the revolution of the 60s. It showed what could be done with proper organization and dedication, which could then be applied to other problems such as education and Medicare. This became clear in the 1964 campaign when Johnson promised a technocracy that would free U. S. from poverty and create the Great Society. His opponent, Barry Goldwater, a conservative Republican Senator from Arizona, was firmly behind individual initiative and a balanced budget, as well as behind the government's involvement in the military-industrial complex that Ike had warned against in his farewell address. While the priorities were debated, the basic premise of a technocracy where the state would direct change was not. While Johnson supported the Apollo program, Goldwater wanted the space program under the military with the race to the moon abandoned in favor of the development of antiballistic missiles and laser weapons.

Johnson was elected in his own right in 1964 against Goldwater, who scared Americans with his proposals to abolish the income tax, sell the Tennessee Valley Authority, and overhaul Social Security. He also seemed trigger-happy with his plans to bomb North Vietnam. Goldwater had voted against both the nuclear test ban and the Civil Rights Act. He claimed there was a silent majority who would vote Republican if only they quit having "me-too" candidates. He had one convert, Strom Thurmond, a former Dixiecrat who had run against Harry Truman in 1948, who became a Goldwater Republican. During the campaign, Johnson promised that "We are not about to send American boys nine or ten thousand miles from home to do what Asian boys ought to be doing for themselves." Johnson won with 61 percent of the total vote, the largest landslide given any preceding modern president. The Democrats also controlled the House and the Senate.

Evaluation of JFK

John Kennedy remains one of the most powerful, complex, and controversial actors in American history. In a long series of Gallup Polls a majority of Americans still regarded Kennedy as the greatest of all American presidents.

With Kennedy's murder, all peace initiatives ended. The ascension of Lyndon Johnson led to one of the most crucial reversals in American foreign policy. All the unanswered questions about the murder from who had actually killed him and why resulted in a cynicism in the American worldview that has yet to end.

Much of Kennedy's appeal can be attributed to his good manners, vitality, wit, self-deprecating humor, and disarming casualness, which made him the most attractive man of his generation. He articulated a sense of hope and connected the young people to the government in a way not seen since the death of his brother Robert. He conveyed a lofty standard of excellence and yet his own tastes were mundane. He could be vindictive and petty and seemed to have an enormous ego and vanity. Those traits, however, were not evident to the public.

Just like Kennedy's womanizing was unknown to the general public so was the state of his health. He looked like a strong vigorous man, and his only known ailment was back trouble. In truth he suffered from adrenal insufficiency, colitis, and osteoporosis. All of this was uncovered by historian Robert Dallak who was given access to Kennedy's medical records as he researched a new Kennedy biography to be published in 2003, *An Unfinished Life: John F. Kennedy, 1917-1963.*

Dallak described the medical records as revealing the "quiet stoicism of a man struggling to endure extraordinary pain and distress." The records revealed he had so much pain from three fractured vertebrae from the osteoporosis that he could not put a sock or shoe on his left foot unaided. Despite the constant pain, presidential tapes of Kennedy during the Cuban missile crisis and at other times show him lucid and in complete command.

The final analysis of Kennedy must be based on whether the country was in better shape as a result of his presidency and to what extent he achieved his stated goals. In the area of foreign policy he accomplished several significant goals including the strengthening of the military and the atmospheric test ban treaty. Of the major foreign policy crises facing Kennedy in 1961, only Vietnam remained at his death. Furthermore, he did much to improve the image of the United States in the newly emerging nations of Africa and Asia. Kennedy also emerged as the father of the space program.

In the domestic sphere, he promoted economic growth, provided on-the job training, updated Social Security and the minimum wage, and reduced job discrimination against women. He eased farm problems, responded to the problem of juvenile delinquency and the needs of mental retardation, implemented the first significant housing program since 1949, and began urban renewal. Under his administration the Twenty-third Amendment was passed, giving residents of the District of Columbia the right to vote in presidential elections. The fight against organized crime, which he and his brother Robert had begun, ceased upon his death.

The Kennedy administration had few scandals, and the men he appointed were an exceptional group of public servants. To the end Kennedy remained a positive role model: charming, optimistic, and positive. Historians have consistently ranked him as an above average president.

Evaluation of Johnson's Presidency

Johnson saw himself as the executor of John Kennedy's legacy, a legacy that Johnson saw himself creating. Kennedy had defined a key core of goals for his presidency: tax cuts, a civil rights bill, federal aid to education, improving life in the cities, medical care for the aged, and a poverty program. Johnson worked to have legislation in these areas passed, and it was here that he was at his best.

With the Civil Rights Act of 1964, the Voting Rights Act of 1965, and the Supreme Court's decision in 1964 in *Reynolds v. Sims* (one man, one vote), the administration completed the crucial work of the abolitionists, which had been left undone after the Civil War. This was one of Johnson's greatest accomplishments.

Johnson's strength was his knowledge of how to get legislation through Congress. A good example of this is how he got his federal aid to education bill passed. He saw to it that both the National Education Association and the National Catholic Welfare Conference were on board for the program, which gave assistance to the impoverished child and not to the school attended. It was passed four months after it went to the Congress.

Despite his strengths, Johnson also had a turbulent and infantile nature. He was prone to bullying his staff and advisers with verbal tirades, fits of temper, and even physical abuse. He kicked Vice President Hubert Humphrey in the shins so often that Humphrey once showed the scars to a newsman.

In 1965 Johnson took the U. S. into a war that turned out to be the longest in our history. He became personally involved in the war even to the extent of choosing bombing sites. He also took the involvement on a personal level. "...if I got out of Vietnam and let Ho Chi Minh run through the streets of Saigon, then I'd be doing exactly what Chamberlain did in World War II..." [And then] "there would be Robert Kennedy...telling everyone that I had betrayed John Kennedy's commitment to South Vietnam.... That I was a coward. An unmanly man. A man without a spine." Once LBJ took a thing personally, his pride and vanity knew no bounds. Despite sending more than half a million troops into Vietnam and dropping more explosives than were used by all sides in all theaters of World War II, the military was unable to win.

His undoing was the cost of the Vietnam War, hidden from both the American people and Congress. He finally was forced in September of 1967 to ask Congress for an increase in taxes in the form of a 6 percent surcharge. To get this, he had to agree to a decrease in domestic spending, ending expansion of the Great Society programs.

Johnson has not received the rating from historians that he so much wanted. He has consistently been rated as an average president. Johnson was a larger than life figure with great gifts and tragic flaws.

Assassinations of Martin Luther King, Jr. and Robert Kennedy

During the presidential election year, 1968, two more assassinations took place. The first occurred in April when Martin Luther King, Jr. was assassinated in Memphis, Tennessee. He had gone there to support sanitation workers striking for union recognition. Although James Earl Ray was soon arrested and confessed to the murder, he later recanted in prison. The King family had questions about his guilt and was seeking a trial for Ray when he died in prison in 1998. However, they were successful in getting Attorney General Janet Reno to take another look at the assassination.

Some believe that it was King's speech in 1967 against the Vietnam War that brought his end. After the speech in which he said the greatest purveyor of violence in the world is "my own government," J. Edgar Hoover wrote to Johnson that it was clear King "was an instrument in the hands of subversive forces

Violent confrontation occurred between the police and the antiwar protesters at the 1968 Democratic National Convention in Chicago on August 28 when the protesters attempted to march to the convention site. The police attacked the demonstrators with nightsticks and mace. Mayor Richard J. Daley tried to limit the television coverage; however, the evening news broadcast the events.

seeking to undermine our nation." Hoover had been tapping King's phones and keeping him under surveillance since the Kennedy administration.

King announced a new campaign in April 1968 that would use civil disobedience to force Congress to help the poor. The Poor People's Campaign wanted Congress to pass a comprehensive anti-poverty act with full-employment, guaranteed annual incomes, and a half million units of low cost housing a year. The intelligence community knew from their listening devices that King had broadened his campaign to include a peace movement to shut down the Pentagon.

When King was assassinated, Robert Kennedy was campaigning for the Democratic Party presidential nomination in Indianapolis. Thanks to his efforts, there was no riot in Indianapolis. Other cities were not so lucky. The King assassination set off riots in over sixty American cities with the worst in Chicago and Washington, D. C.

On June 6, Robert Kennedy, who had just won the California Democratic presidential primary, was assassinated as he went through a Los Angeles hotel kitchen after celebrating his victory. The assassin was a Palestinian immigrant, Sirhan Sirhan, who was captured at the scene. Robert Kennedy was the sole candidate who appealed to whites and blacks, the less privileged, and the middle class. With Kennedy

gone, the idealism of the early 60s was dead, and the presidential nomination was open for Johnson's vice president, Hubert H. Humphrey.

ELECTION OF 1968

August 1968 the Democratic convention was held in Chicago to nominate Hubert Humphrey. Richard Daley, the Mayor of Chicago, remembering the riots after the King assassination, determined that nothing like that would happen at the convention. Daley had called for twenty-four thousand police and National Guardsmen to keep order. It was a disaster. The New Left was there to protest the Vietnam War. The additional police soon added to the chaos as they arrested people indiscriminately and behaved in a savage and ruthless manner. Millions watched on TV as the police bashed the heads of the protesters and others. One of those arrested was a conservative Republican county coroner from Indiana who was in Chicago on business. Like many others, he was in the wrong place at the wrong time.

Richard Nixon who had reinvented himself since his disastrous loss of the governorship of California in 1962 was running hard for the nomination. Ike, who had been ill, finally endorsed Nixon right before the convention. By that time, Nixon did not need his endorsement since he was on a roll toward the nomination.

For his vice president Nixon chose Spiro Agnew, the governor of Maryland, in part because of his harangue of black leaders over the riots in Baltimore. In essence, Agnew blamed them for not being out on the streets stopping the riots.

Nixon said that he was listening to the great silent majority of Americans who did not protest and break the laws but instead paid their taxes and went to work—those who loved their country. The main issue of the election, however, was the Vietnam War. Nixon claimed that he had a secret plan to stop the war in Vietnam. It was so secret that it was never revealed, even after the election.

The election was full of tricks from both sides. In October Johnson was moving toward a bombing halt and peace. Nixon used Anna Chan Chennault to get President Thieu of South Vietnam to refuse to cooperate. It was truly overkill, as Thieu had no intention of committing political suicide for either Johnson or Humphrey. The Johnson-Humphrey administration found out about the Nixon plan because they were using an illegal wiretap on his phones.

When it was falsely reported that an agreement had been reached, Nixon moved to undercut Johnson. He did this by mounting a campaign to convince the American people that Johnson had sold out the people of Vietnam, and he kept this up right to Election Day.

On October 31, five days before the election, Johnson announced that Hanoi had agreed to expanded peace talks and he had therefore ordered a bombing halt. The expanded talks would resume November 6, the day after the election. On a nationwide television broadcast the Monday before Election Day, Nixon said that he had heard a report that in the last two days "the North Vietnamese are moving thousands of tons of supplies down the Ho Chi Minh Trail, and our bombers are not able to stop them." He made the whole thing up keeping to the political tactics that he had used in his very first election campaign. On November 2 the Government of Vietnam announced that it would not sit down with the Vietcong.

On the other side, Johnson and Humphrey were not being honest that serious peace talks were to be held on Wednesday. The politicians were all playing their own games and lying to the American people while American men and money were spent with abandon.

George Wallace, the governor of Alabama, became a third party candidate who appealed to people on the issues of welfare, growth of the federal government, and race. His running mate, retired General Curtis LeMay, however, scared many Americans when he said that the U. S. should just "nuke" Vietnam. Despite this, Wallace got 13.5 percent of the popular vote.

Nixon and Agnew won by a narrow margin of 800,000 votes. Nixon won in 1968 with less votes than he had gotten in 1960 when he lost! He was the first president since Zachary Taylor in 1848 to win the presidency while his party failed to carry either the House or the Senate.

CONCLUSION

The election of 1968 marked the end of the liberal consensus in American politics, which had supported government activism at home and abroad. The American people wanted calm after the chaos of their last eight years; they wanted the end of the Vietnam War. Government was now seen as an enemy that could not be trusted and that needed to be restrained. It was the beginning of the conservative resurgence.

Chronology

1960	Sit-ins at lunch counters John Kennedy elected president
1961	Peace Corps Alliance for Progress Bay of Pigs Berlin Wall erected
1962	Cuban Missile Crisis James Meredith enrolls at Old Miss
1963	Civil Rights demonstrations in Birmingham March on Washington Test Ban Treaty Diem Assassination Kennedy Assassination Betty Friedan, *The Feminine Mystique*
1964	Job Corps Head Start Mississippi Freedom Summer Civil Rights Act Economic Opportunity Act Gulf of Tonkin Incident War on Poverty Johnson-Goldwater Election
1965	Americanization of Vietnam War Assassination of Malcolm X Medical Care Act Civil Rights March: Selma to Montgomery Voting Rights Act Watts Riot Grape strike in California Opposition to draft
1966	Black Power National Organization of Women (NOW)
1967	Anti-War Demonstrations Race riots in Newark, Detroit March on Pentagon Thurgood Marshall, first African-American appointed to the U. S. Supreme Court
1968	Tet Offensive Indian Civil Rights Act Johnson not to seek re-election Martin Luther King, Jr. assassinated Robert F. Kennedy assassinated Violence at Democratic Convention Vietnam Peace talks Nixon elected president

SUGGESTED READINGS

Stephen Ambrose, *Nixon: The Truimph of a Politician 1962-1972* (1989).

James N. Giglio, *The Presidency of John F. Kennedy* (1991).

Doris Kearns Goodwin, *Lyndon Johnson and the American Dream* (1991).

Paul R. Henger, *In His Steps: Lyndon Johnson and the Kennedy Mystique* (1991).

Frederick E. Hoxie, *Indians in American History* (1988).

Ray LaFontaine and Mary LaFontaine, *Oswald Talked: The New Evidence in the JFK Assassination* (1996).

Alfred McCoy, *Politics of Heroin: CIA Complicity in the Global Drug Trade* (1972).

Myra MacPherson, *Long Time Passing: Vietnam & the Haunted Generation* (1984).

Matt S. Meier and Feliciano Rivera, *The Chicanos: A History of Mexican Americans* (1972).

John Newman, *JFK and Vietnam* (1992).

Thomas G. Paterson, *Kennedy's Quest for Victory: American Foreign Policy, 1961-1963* (1989).

Glenda Riley, *Inventing the American Woman: A Perspective on Women's History 1865 to the Present* (1986).

W. J. Rorabaugh, *True Stories from the American Past* (1993).

Peter Dale Scott, *Deep Politics and the Death of JFK* (1993).

Harvey Wasserman, *America Born and Reborn* (1983).

Where were you when President Kennedy was shot? Memories and Tributes to a Slain President as told to DEAR ABBY (1993).

Chapter Twenty-three

THE SEVENTIES: The Crisis of Confidence

Early in the morning of June 17, 1972, five men broke into the Democratic Party headquarters at the Watergate apartment and office complex only a mile from the White House. They wore surgical gloves and carried lock-picking tools, camera, mace, and wire-tapping devices to replace faulty bugs installed in an earlier break-in. The techniques used by the burglars were so primitive and the equipment so shoddy that they would have "appalled the CIA, the Mafia, the New York Police Department or the KGB," in the words of one observer. The incompetent criminals carefully placed tape across the latches of the spring locks on the door to the Democratic headquarters. A guard on a routine inspection noticed the tape and removed it. The burglars, noting that the tape was no longer in place, re-installed it in the same conspicuous way. The guard, returning an hour later, alertly observed the reappearing tape and summoned the police.

The Nixon administration had targeted Washington to demonstrate its commitment to law and order. The newly effective Washington patrol system rushed a car to the scene at 2:00 A. M. On the sixth floor of the Watergate building, the police burst in to discover the culprits who pleaded, "Don't shoot, we give up." The

inept criminal band included four Cuban-Americans who thought they were striking a blow against Castro, and James McCord, the "wire man." McCord was a former CIA agent and current security chief for the Committee to Re-elect the President (CREEP). The cash they carried in $100 bills could be easily traced through serial numbers to CREEP. Papers found on the perpetrators linked them to two CREEP officials: E. Howard Hunt, a former CIA agent, and G. Gordon Liddy, a former FBI employee.

The logic behind the break-in was difficult to discern. Apart from the size of its considerable debts, it is hard to figure out what possible secrets of any significance could have been discovered by tapping the phone of the Democratic National Committee. The burglars, undoubtedly, were comfortable in the belief that their superiors in CREEP (who now included John Mitchell, the former attorney general) could easily cover up the episode and arrange for their release.

Despite these expectations, a grand jury indicted the five burglars, as well as Hunt and Liddy. The administration quickly developed a cover story to ensure that any links to criminal activities stopped at Hunt and Liddy. The break-in, according to this tale, had been "deplorable, an excess of zeal, unauthorized, illegal, regrettable." Neither the media nor the public picked up Democratic cries of a cover-up in the 1972 election campaign. There was nothing to link the White House to this "third-rate burglary." President Nixon won a landslide re-election victory. After thanking White House Counsel John Dean, for his role in containing the damage, the president darkly threatened all of those he believed "have tried to do us in." All his enemies were "asking for it and they are going to get it." A lawyer for the Washington Post was "a guy we've got to ruin...We are going to fix that son-of-a-bitch." How had such an intoxicating victory turned into such a dark moment? Would the beleaguered White House staff be able to contain what Dean described as a "cancer on the Presidency?"

NIXON THE MAN

Historian Garry Wills recalled his feelings at a 1968 George Wallace rally:

> We have now a vast middle range of the comfortable discontented. They are not as Nixon knows, the kind who march or riot. They just lock their doors. And they vote. They do not, most of them, go to Wallace rallies, but those who do go speak for them in growing measure. This is the vague unlocalized resentment that had such effect in the 1968 campaign, tainting all the air around talk of law and order. America itself, like her major cities, has blight at the core, not in the limbs and extremities. As I stood bewildered like most reporters, in the insane din of that Wallace rally, saw a crowd of eight thousand tormented by a few hundred, I realized at last what had not sunk in at Miami's riot, or Chicago's. I realized this is a nation that might do anything. Even elect Nixon.

Indeed Nixon's life-long ambition was finally achieved. Did this victory symbolize the death of liberalism? Many "silent Americans" believed liberalism had scarred the nation's cities and college campuses and propelled the seemingly unending bloody carnage in the jungles of Southeast Asia.

Few politicians in American history have been so well prepared but so ill-suited to occupy the Oval Office as Richard Milhous Nixon. Born in 1913 to Quaker parents, he grew up in the small southern California town of Yorba Linda. World War II interrupted his plans to start a law practice in Whittier, California. After serving as a naval supply officer in the Pacific, Nixon returned to his native state, where he enjoyed a meteoric rise in the national political arena. Elected first to the House of Representatives and then to the Senate, he went on to serve eight years as Dwight Eisenhower's vice president.

From the outset his was a political life of enormous contrasts. It was a career marked by great promise but undermined by equally great character flaws. Richard Nixon was the quintessential outsider, who somehow always needed to define himself in this manner, even when he became the ultimate insider. At his second inauguration in 1972, despite his overwhelming victory, Henry Kissinger wrote, "Nixon moved as if he were himself a spectator, not the principal....There was about him this day a quality of remoteness, as if he could never quite bring himself to leave the inhospitable and hostile world that he inhabited...." John Ehrlichman, an aide who loved the president, recalled, "There was another side to him, like the flat, dark side of the moon."

Even in his first campaign for Congress in 1946, Nixon did not hesitate in capitalizing on the strongly anti-Communist post-war sentiment by questioning the loyalty of his Democratic opponent. His innuendoes about the incumbent's supposed associations with subversive elements led to a surprise Nixon victory. He achieved considerable national prominence as a member of the House Un-American Activities Committee. His greatest public visibility came from his role in the investigation of accused spy Alger Hiss. When he ran for the Senate four years later against Helen Gahagan Douglas, he continued to rely on insinuations about loyalty by labeling Douglas "the Pink Lady."

Nixon survived revelations of a "slush fund," established by California businessmen to keep him in "financial comfort." He remained Eisenhower's

Richard Milhous Nixon

vice president, despite Eisenhower's evident distaste for him. During the 1952 campaign, Nixon had continued his "redbaiting" by charging that a Democratic victory would bring "more Alger Hisses, more atomic spies." After a close defeat by the Kennedy machine in the 1960 presidential election, Nixon went on to lose his bid for the governorship of California in 1962. His political career seemed over. He even announced to the press, "You won't have Dick Nixon to kick around any more." But working hard behind the scenes, occupying the center of his party, and declaring himself to be a "New Nixon," he succeeded in resurrecting himself from political death. He campaigned vigorously for Republican candidates, accumulating political IOUs. He went on to win the presidential nomination and election in 1968. Despite his triumph, Nixon remained insecure, angry, and paranoid in his conviction that enemies, particularly the "eastern liberal establishment," were conspiring to get him.

Nixon surrounded himself with hard-working, clean-cut looking, ambitious, tough, and unswervingly loyal aides. They reflected his identification with the "silent majority" who had grown weary with the lawlessness and "moral permissiveness" of the Sixties. In his first inauguration, Nixon promised to work on behalf of national unity, pro-mote fiscal conservatism, support minority rights, fight crime, and bring peace to Southeast Asia. In many ways this very solemn and lonely man was attempting to steer a moderate Eisenhower-like course. It was a course he would never find. As one historian who has studied both those men wrote, "Eisenhower was a man full of love for life and for people, while Nixon, sadly, was a man who all too often gave in to an impulse to hate."

At first, however, the celebration of the first man on the moon symbolized the unity promised by the new president. On July 21, 1969, only seven years after President Kennedy had announced a gigantic program to counter the Soviet space challenge, astronaut Neil Armstrong stepped out of Apollo 11's lunar module to walk on the surface of the moon. Armstrong declared to the enthralled millions who were watching on television, "That's one small step for man, one giant leap for mankind." Americans were thrilled and proud when Armstrong and fellow astronaut Buzz Aldrin planted an American flag on the moon. A plaque declared, "Here men from planet earth first set foot on the moon, July 1969 A. D. We came in peace for all mankind." Many hoped that the peace announced in space might also come to earth, particularly in the continuing morass of Vietnam.

AMERICA'S LONGEST WAR

Nixon, who viewed himself as the consummate expert in foreign affairs, recognized that the war in Vietnam was his most immediate international problem. Vietnam was, in fact, the driving force behind virtually every other issue. He chose his old friend William P. Rogers, Eisenhower's second term attorney general, to be Secretary of State. Rogers remained in that position until 1973, when Henry Kissinger, the national security advisor from 1968 to 1973, replaced him. Kissinger, almost from the beginning, was Nixon's real ally in implementing his grand design in foreign policy. Kissinger, a refugee from Nazi Germany, had a distinguished academic career and was widely viewed as a highly respected expert on military and foreign policy.

Kissinger came to recognize that he and Nixon were pragmatic realists who wished to reshape cold war policies. Vietnam was their chief obstacle. It prevented détente with the People's Republic of China and, most importantly, the Soviet Union. Furthermore, the war fueled inflation, stimulated domestic disorder, and drained U. S. military might. Ending American involvement in Vietnam without loss of international credibility was the central issue Nixon and Kissinger had to address.

Vietnamization and the Nixon Doctrine

In the spring of 1969, Nixon and Kissinger began implementing a strategy of "Vietnamization." This de-escalation of American involvement was intended to achieve a number of objectives, including continued protection of the South Vietnamese government by intensifying U. S. bombings. In addition, South Vietnam was to become more militarily self sufficient by assuming a larger role in the fighting. The president understood that both the public and the troops had grown increasingly weary with the seemingly unending conflict. "I'm not going to end up like LBJ," Nixon swore, "holed up in the White House afraid to show his face on the street. I'm going to stop that war." By 1972, only 50,000 American troops remained in that war-ravaged part of the world.

In July 1969, the president announced the Nixon Doctrine. The Nixon Doctrine, reflecting the president's characteristic pragmatism, acknowledged that the United States could no longer maintain its current level of overseas commitments. America had to rely much more heavily on regional allies to prevent the further spread of communism. Nixon declared, "this approach required our commitment to helping our partners develop their own strength. In doing so, we must strike a careful balance. If we do too little to help them—and erode their belief in our commitments—they may lose the necessary will to conduct their own self-defense or become disheartened about the prospects of development. Yet, if we do too much and American forces do what local forces can and should be doing, we promote dependence rather than independence."

Escalation

The peace talks, which Henry Kissinger continued in great secrecy between 1969-71, reached a stalemate. This led the administration to exert more military, economic, and diplomatic pressure on the North Vietnamese. Nixon hoped this intensified pressure would end the conflict and win the acceptance of the Saigon government. He achieved this by undertaking bombing excursions into the neutral nations of Laos and Cambodia, where the enemy supposedly maintained supply bases. Nixon concealed these operations from the public from March 1969 until he announced the invasion of Cambodia in April 1970.

The strategy did not succeed. The Paris Peace Talks soured further as the North Vietnamese government remained implacable. The seemingly inactive United States anti-war movement came alive, when in October of 1969 the Vietnam Moratorium Committee brought over 250,000 protesters to a Washington, D. C. demonstration. As they marched past the White House, they demanded an end to the hostilities. The Cambodian invasion, which seemed to many to be reescalating the conflict, ignited the most extensive college protests in American history. Tragedy struck on May 4, 1970, when National Guardsmen shot and killed four Kent State University students. Ten more were wounded. Although Nixon regretted the deaths, he told Americans that "when disaster turns to violence, it invites tragedy." Only ten days later police on the Jackson State College campus in Mississippi killed two African-American students and wounded another twelve.

The country's mood did not improve after the 1970 revelations about American atrocities at My Lai. This episode brought to question not only the morality of the war itself but that of United States ground forces. How was it possible that an American platoon could have obliterated a small Vietnamese village of several hundred men, women, and children? Led by the inexperienced lieutenant William Calley, the unit had lined up women and old men in front of ditches and mowed them down, gang-raped young girls, and blown babies apart with hand grenades. Could the war have disintegrated to the kind of blood bath the United States had supposedly intervened to prevent in the first place? At Calley's trial, his commander declared, "Every unit of brigade size had its My Lai hidden some place."

The Cambodian invasion also brought out strong responses on Capitol Hill. What had happened to the congressional power to declare war? Was the checks and balances system no longer working? Congress, determined to recapture its lost powers, repealed the Gulf of Tonkin Resolution. Congress also tried to design proposals to restrict the commitment of additional U.S. troops.

When the United States withdrew its forces from Cambodia at the end of June 1970, none of the invasion's objectives had been achieved. In fact, the situation considerably worsened. The invasion ended

Cambodia's doggedly preserved neutrality. This provoked a civil war in which hundreds of thousands died and led to the rise to power of the horrifying Khmer Rouge rebels who massacred at least a million more. When the failure of the South Vietnamese Army denied him further expansion of the war into Laos in February 1971, Nixon determined to protect the survival of South Vietnam with air power. But hopes to cut the Ho Chi Minh trails through repeated bombing proved no more successful for Nixon than it had for Lyndon Johnson.

Problems continued to mount for the administration when, in June of 1971, the *New York Times* published the so-called *Pentagon Papers*. This was a top-secret official investigation of U. S. policies in Vietnam prepared in the Johnson administration.

Dr. Daniel Ellsberg holds an impromptu news conference outside federal building in Boston while his wife, Patricia, waits behind him after he was released on bond. Mrs. Ellsberg accompanied her husband in court for the arraignment.

Leaked by a former Defense Department official, Daniel Ellsberg, the *Papers* were politically damning. Although they contained nothing about the Nixon years, Nixon feared they would undermine public trust in the government and tried to prevent their further publication by securing an injunction. The Supreme Court overturned the order. The *Pentagon Papers* revealed extensive government duplicity, including covert U. S. activity in Southeast Asia as well as the depth of deception and intrigue of three previous administrations. Clearly, as 1971 ended, Nixon and Kissinger were deeply frustrated.

The End at Last

Vietnamization was not working as expected. Television broadcast the routing of South Vietnamese forces in the Laos venture of February 1971. Its failure was clear for all to see, as desperate South Vietnamese soldiers tried to grab on to retreating American helicopters. Encouraged by this success, the North Vietnamese government mounted an Easter Offensive in 1972. It was their largest military campaign since 1968. Not willing to abandon Vietnamization, Nixon responded with increased military action. The American military mined North Vietnam's major harbors and B-52s pummeled its cities. Although this revived the antiwar protest movement, the White House reported a public outpouring of more than five to one in favor of the president's actions. Later insiders revealed that the Committee to Re-elect the President had paid for thousands of phony telegrams of support. A public opinion poll in 1971 revealed that 71 percent of Americans thought it had been a mistake to send American troops to Vietnam, and 58 percent believed the war was immoral. The Communist offensive, however, stalled by mid-June 1972. This led the North Vietnamese to reassess their position at the negotiating table. By October, both sides were willing to be more conciliatory.

In fact, on October 26, 1972, Henry Kissinger announced, "Peace is at hand." The presidential election was only days ahead. Secretly Kissinger and Le Duc Tho, the North Vietnamese foreign minister, had agreed to a cease-fire. All remaining United States troops were to be withdrawn. All U. S. prisoners of war were to be released. And, most importantly, from the North Vietnamese perspective, their troops were allowed to remain in the South.

Henry Kissinger's October announcement was unfortunately premature; except for the effect it may have had on the outcome of Nixon's 1972 landslide. No one seemed to have anticipated the reaction of South Vietnamese President Thieu, who obdurately rejected the offer. Nixon decided to back him and ordered the Christmas bombing of Hanoi and the North. After eleven days, the bombing stopped. Large sections of Hanoi lay in ruins, a hospital had been leveled, and over two thousand civilians were dead. Thieu was now informed he would have to accept the next proposal offered or go it alone. The talks resumed for another week, at which time President Thieu did agree to a settlement little different from that proposed in October. Ironically, the United States of America ended its active involvement in the war on the very day that Lyndon Baines Johnson died of a heart attack—January 23, 1973.

But neither peace nor democracy came to Southeast Asia. The cease fire, itself, collapsed. In November of 1973 the United States Congress passed the War Powers Act, over Nixon's angry veto. The act established a sixty-day limit on any presidential commitment of American troops to foreign campaigns, unless the Congress voted to continue the action. Meanwhile, the fighting resumed in Vietnam. At last, in the spring of 1975, the South collapsed. President Thieu fled his faltering nation on April 21 and on April 30, the South officially surrendered. After thirty years of turmoil many wondered what, if anything, had been accomplished.

Despite being elected largely on the wave of disillusionment with the Vietnam War, it had taken Nixon four years, massive destruction in Vietnam, Laos and Cambodia, and 20,000 additional American lives to end the conflict. Overall, the war cost over $150 billion and 58,000 American lives. More than a million Vietnamese had also lost their lives. Despite the warnings of a "domino effect," other Asian nations, outside of Vietnam, Laos and Cambodia, did not fall to a resurgent Communism. Vietnam and China, supposed allies, soon returned to their historic animosity.

One result of America's defeat, the deeply held opposition to the war and the brutality of guerrilla combat, was that returning veterans did not receive public recognition for their sacrifices. At best, a public, that wished to forget the painfulness of Vietnam, ignored them. At worst, Americans thought of them as brutalized, dangerous, or drug-crazed. One veteran bitterly recalled the "feelings of rejection and scorn that a bunch of depressed and confused young men experienced when they returned home from doing what their country told them to do." Eventually, most were able to readjust to civilian life (although one-sixth of the three million who served suffered from posttraumatic stress disorder). One worried years later, "We have adjusted too well. Too many of us have lost touch with the horror of war...we lose the intensity...I wish we were more troubled."

A New Direction in World Affairs

If the president and his chief foreign policy expert and ally, Henry Kissinger, could not rightly proclaim a "Peace with honor" in the Vietnamese war, they could correctly claim to have dramatically changed international affairs in other arenas. They charted a course all succeeding administrations have followed.

As the war in Southeast Asia ground on, Nixon and Kissinger worked behind the scenes to reshape foreign policy worldwide. Henry Kissinger continued the well-established Kennedy and Johnson administrations' trend of moving the control of foreign policy into the White House, rather than relying on international organizations like the United Nations. The policy was a reflection of Kissinger's and Nixon's shared world view that the post World War II world, ruled over by the United States and the Soviet Union, was gone. Growing nationalism, coming from the Third World, was directed at the United States in its sphere of influence in the world and at the Soviets in theirs. As a result, both superpowers found the freedom to flex their muscles increasingly restrained.

Both Richard Nixon and Henry Kissinger understood the growing split between China and the Soviet Union. Several bloody border clashes demonstrated the rapidly worsening relations between these two communist nations. The split provided the U.S. with a diplomatic window of opportunity, as each of the communist powers felt compelled to draw nearer to the United States. In his first inaugural speech Nixon had spoken of a new "era of negotiation" rather than another "era of confrontation." What could be more surprising to all than a reversal of two decades as the world's chief anti-Communist by being the president "to open China," and cause "an arms-control agreement with Russia?" The timing was ideal. Unlike Presidents Truman, Kennedy, and Johnson, Nixon had no Nixon to accuse him of selling out to the communists.

Proceeding cautiously, Nixon began to refer to China as the People's Republic rather than Red China. Following the suggestion of the President of the International Table Tennis Federation, Premier Zhou En-Lai invited American players to visit China. In April 1971 an American table tennis team arrived. In receiving the players at the Great Hall of the People in Beijing, Mr. Zhou declared, "We have opened a new page in the relations between the Chinese and American people." So-called "Ping-Pong diplomacy" underlay serious diplomatic negotiations between the two nations. Within two months, Henry Kissinger secretly visited China and set up Nixon's extraordinary trip to China in February-March of 1972. (At the same time a delegation of Chinese table tennis players toured the United States.)

The president's plane landed in the People's Republic on February 22, 1972. He remained there for nearly a week—the longest state visit ever made by a president to a foreign country. No other modern American president had visited China. American television cameras showed a smiling Nixon and his entourage on escorted trips to the Great Wall and the Imperial Palace. Images of official rice-liquor toasts and Nixon learning to eat with chopsticks signaled a true historic milestone. Over twenty years of hostility had ended. Although full diplomatic relations between these countries would have to wait for the Carter administration, Nixon's visit was undoubtedly the single key event in relations between the United States and the People's Republic of China.

This also proved to be true for relations between the Soviet Union and the United States. Russia, apprehensive about rapprochement between China and the U.S., maneuvered closer to America as well, just as Nixon and Kissinger had hoped. As he had with the Chinese, Kissinger made a secret visit to Moscow. Soviet President Leonid Brezhnev and Kissinger discussed improving relations between their respective countries. Late in May of 1972 Nixon himself traveled to Moscow and signed an arms control treaty with Brezhnev. The Strategic Arms Limitation Treaty (SALT I) froze International Ballistic Missile (ICBMs) deployment. The two powers were limited to two hundred antiballistic missiles (ABMs), and two ABM systems each. The treaty limited the number of strategic missile launchers each nation could have for a five-year period. It did nothing, however, to slow down the buildup of the far more dangerous Multiple Independent Re-entry, or MIRVs. Clearly SALT I could not have prevented a future nuclear war. It was, however, a very real beginning to a thaw in the cold war. It also enhanced Richard Nixon's standing as a man of peace.

Détente progressed on other fronts as Nixon and Brezhnev concluded agreements on trade and technological cooperation. The Soviet government even agreed to purchase $750 million worth of grain from American farmers over three-years. Numerous athletic and cultural exchanges followed. The world appeared to have become a safer place. Nixon and Kissinger's diplomatic revolution was complete, albeit limited.

Other Foreign Initiatives

The Nixon-Kissinger diplomatic revolution did not apply to all other American overseas commitments. By 1971 while both Nixon and Kissinger viewed much of the rest of the world as a kind of footnote to Sino-Soviet-U.S. relations, they were certainly aware of the economic significance and potential in resources and markets elsewhere. Politically, they recognized a potential Third World challenge to American influence in organizations such as the United Nations. Therefore, they determined not to let affairs in Latin America, Africa, and the Middle East disrupt détente.

Foreign policy in Latin America was, consequently, very much a continuation of quite traditional cold war practices. Like Lyndon Johnson before him, Nixon continued to isolate Castro's Cuba and ensure that there were no additional communist regimes in the Western Hemisphere. Using tactics he had learned in his Eisenhower years, the president approved covert operations designed to topple the Marxist, but democratically elected, government of Salvador Allende in Chile. The CIA worked to disrupt the economy and, at the same time, fund opposition groups. The strategy worked. In three years the Chilean economy was in a shambles. In 1973 the military overthrew and killed Allende, replacing him with the oppressive military administration of General Augusto Pinochet. The United States quickly denied any role in the coup but just as quickly recognized the new government.

Nixon had also indicated that United States policy would retaliate against governments that nationalized U. S. owned companies, unless they were adequately compensated. The United States government might withhold aid or influence multilateral institutions, for example the World Bank, to veto aid. Policies such as these did little to enhance the image of America in the rest of the Western Hemisphere.

Policy in Africa also deviated little from the past. Like its predecessors, the Nixon administration sought to strengthen and broaden its relationships with white governments, including Rhodesia, South Africa, and the Portuguese-run Mozambique and Angola. In troubled Angola, for example, the CIA financially supported both the Portuguese and those fighting to gain their independence from Portugal. This sowed the seeds for the civil war that erupted in 1975, following Angolan independence. The United States, along with South Africa, covertly supported one faction in the conflict. The Soviet Union supported the other. Congress, maintaining that the United States should not be actively cooperating with racially oppressive governments like that of South Africa, cut all funding. Eventually, a leftist leaning administration assumed power in Angola causing the

An American oil shortage occurred in the early 1970s.

Nixon administration to rethink its policies. Thereafter the administration distanced itself from South Africa and Zimbabwe (the former Rhodesia). America established stronger economic ties and supplied arms to other black African nations.

Perhaps no place outside the Sino-Soviet-U.S. orbit was more volatile, and thus more likely to upset détente, than the oil rich Middle East. President Nixon, himself, had referred to this area as a "powder keg." The situation had worsened after the 1967 Six-Day War. Victorious Israel had agreed to cede most of the territory they occupied in return for peace and direct negotiations, but the Arab states refused. The Palestine Liberation Organization, or PLO, organized in 1964, had pledged to destroy Israel and regain all the land lost by Arab Palestinians in successive conflicts. Their so-called "war of attrition," using terrorist tactics, exacerbated an already tense situation. Their terrorism included hit-and-run raids on Jewish settlements, hijacking jets, and even murdering Israeli athletes at the 1972 Olympics in Munich, Germany.

In this atmosphere of continued tension, war erupted again in October 1973. Syria and Egypt launched a surprise attack on the Jewish holy day of Yom Kippur. Moscow backed the Arab states and the United States, Israel. Israel was able, with some American assistance, to hold on and begin a counterattack. The Nixon administration forced its ally into accepting a cease-fire, rather than pursuing its advantage. The oil-rich Arab states sought to avenge Arab defeats by imposing an embargo of crude oil on the United States and her allies through the Arab influence within the Organization of Petroleum Exporting Countries (OPEC). The embargo, which lasted from October 1973 to March of 1974, resulted in a major energy crisis.

Henry Kissinger, concerned about the Soviet influence in militant Arab nations and the impact of ongoing oil shortages, spent the two years following October 1973 in so-called "shuttle diplomacy." He succeeded in negotiating two Israeli-Egyptian disengagement agreements and one between Israel and Syria. The Arabs also agreed to end the oil embargo. Of course, the larger objective of Kissinger's diplomacy was to firmly establish the United States as a major Middle East peace broker, while diminishing the Soviet Union's role. This policy proved successful for the most part. In general, the Nixon administration had helped to create a new, more pragmatic era in American foreign policy.

DOMESTIC POLICY

The president-elect was never truly interested in domestic policy. In 1968 Nixon reportedly said he "always thought this country could run itself domestically without a President." To his political intimates, he confessed domestic issues bored him. Yet, like all presidents before him and since him, Nixon wished to be portrayed favorably in history as a reformer. How tragic, then, that this paradoxical politician would eventually be destroyed on his least favorite of battle fields.

Perhaps this is not as surprising as it first appears. Despite his many years in national public life, the new president mistrusted government and was profoundly suspicious of all those he considered political insiders. Nixon despised the so-called liberal eastern establishment so intensely that he needed not just to discredit them but rather to obliterate them. Adlai Stevenson once characterized "Nixonland" as "the land of smash and grab and anything to win."

The ever embattled Nixon preferred not to work with either the Congress or his cabinet. Instead, he surrounded himself in an almost fortress-like way with a small cadre of personal aides accountable only to Richard Nixon. None held cabinet titles. Thus Henry Kissinger, national security advisor, not secretary of state William Rogers, had the major voice in key foreign policy decisions. In domestic affairs, the president consulted almost exclusively with H. R. "Bob" Haldeman and John Ehrlichman labeled by the White House press corps as the "Germans."

"Nixon's Nixon," Vice President Spiro Agnew, a former governor of Maryland, became the administration's hatchet man. His role was to be the president's mouthpiece on domestic issues. Perhaps the most divisive voice in the administration, Agnew took on all those segments of American society that the administration held responsible for national domestic woes. These included educators, so-called defeatists, the news media, student protesters, and liberal Supreme Court justices. Like a ferocious warrior with clever speech writers, he attacked with alliterative verbal assaults. To the great delight of political conservatives, he depicted the power structure as "sniveling," "hand-wringing," and "deserv[ing] the violent rebellion it encourages." Intellectuals were "an effete corps of impudent snobs." He characterized the media as "nattering nabobs of negativism" and television newscasters as "a tiny and closed fraternity of privileged men."

The new president faced a formidable obstacle in the Democratic control of Congress. Nixon was the first president since 1849 to face both Houses of Congress dominated by the opposition in his first two years in office. Despite this, Nixon began his first term as the thirty-sixth president of the United States on a positive note, promising to "bring us together." In his first inaugural address, the president stated, "We cannot learn from one another until we stop shouting at one another...."

The New Federalism

This tone of moderation was as Eisenhower-like as it was politically pragmatic. Nixon called for a new kind of conservatism, that he described as a new federalism. The new federalism acknowledged and accepted the basic outlines of a welfare state. It did not propose a massive undoing of Lyndon Johnson's Great Society social programs but hoped to make federal programs much more accountable to state and local governments. In the Revenue Sharing Act federal tax funds would be released to states, counties, and cities to better meet local priorities. Federal controls and restrictions were reduced. Conservative Republicans objected to the plan because it did not significantly decrease federal spending. Nevertheless, in October of 1972, Congress passed the act. In its twelve-year existence the program dispersed some $83 billion to state and local governments. This represented the first major shift in political power, responsibility, and accountability from the national to the local level since the New Deal.

The administration also sought to confront the complex dilemma of the nation's welfare system by calling upon Daniel Patrick Moynihan, a Democrat who had helped Lyndon Johnson shape many of the Great Society programs. The Nixon administration proposed the Family Assistance Plan that Nixon hoped would revolutionize the welfare system and assure his place in history. Under this program, a family living in poverty would receive an annual guaranteed income of $1,600 plus $860 in food stamps. At the time, the payments to many welfare recipients were actually below this amount, as was the income of many of the working poor.

Democrats criticized the proposal, considering the benefits excessively low. Other liberals objected to its provision that required mothers of young children to accept substandard employment. Overwhelmingly, conservatives opposed the plan because of its costs and the potential of increasing the numbers receiving welfare. One Southerner worried that poor African Americans would be unwilling to work low paid jobs: "There's not going to be anybody left to roll those wheelbarrows and press these shirts." Interestingly Michael Harrington, whose book *The Other America* had virtually begun the 1960s war on poverty, referred to the plan as perhaps "the most radical idea since the New Deal."

Philosophically, Richard Nixon did not entirely oppose the basic concept of welfare. Yet he and Moynihan shared the view that the existing system destroyed personal initiative and esteem. Many others also held the system responsible for the destruction of families. Concerns about the welfare system grew out of a very real increase in the number of those on some kind of government assistance, primarily in Aid to Families with Dependent Children (AFDC). In 1970 the AFDC caseload was about 2.2 million families, a 30 per cent increase in that year alone. Overall, by 1972, about 6 per cent of all Americans were receiving welfare.

The proposal to revolutionize the welfare system went down to defeat on Congress in both 1969 and 1971. Nixon's commitment to the plan seemed to fluctuate, especially as the election approached. Of it he said, "I did not want to be in a losing fight with conservatives...in an election year." However, in the 1972 State-of-the-Union address, the president offered the nation "a New American Revolution." Components of the package included revenue sharing, health care and anti-pollution programs, a major reorganization of the executive branch of government, and, again, welfare reform. Administrative interest waned once more as the plan bogged down in the Democratic Congress. The revolution was aborted.

Despite the failure of welfare reform, the Nixon administration enhanced governmental regulatory powers in many areas. Much of what was done dismayed staunch conservatives, especially in the president's own Republican Party. Nixon expanded the Job Corps, supported federal subsidies in housing for low and middle income families, made food stamps more accessible, allowed for direct federal assistance to the handicapped and elderly, and increased Medicaid and Medicare benefits. In his first term, the Twenty-sixth Amendment was ratified, granting eighteen-year-olds the right to vote.

The Environment

Nixon's actions in vital environmental issues were, perhaps, most controversial. After the Cuyahoga River in Cleveland, Ohio caught fire in 1969 and a major oil spill occurred off the coast of Santa Barbara, California, Americans became increasingly alarmed about the despoliation of the environment and the wanton plundering of natural resources. Major cities like Los Angeles choked with smog. Lake Erie and other major bodies of water were declared dead. Many believed that action was essential.

Nixon sided with the nation's corporate leaders. They maintained that establishing environmental standards would increase the prices of American products and thereby decrease their world-wide competitiveness. But the Democratic-controlled Congress moved ahead and enacted numerous laws to protect the environment against the further abuses. These restricted the use of pesticides, protected endangered species, safeguarded coastal lands, and controlled strip-mining activities. Other legislation assured consumers of product safety. Regulations established maximum levels for the amount of pollutants released into the air and water.

Americans celebrated their first Earth Day on April 1, 1969. Demonstrations advocating strong government action led the ever pragmatic Nixon to understand that his administration needed to respond. He supported the National Environmental Act (1969), requiring federal agencies to prepare an analysis of the environmental impact of proposed projects, and the establishment of the Environmental Protection Agency (EPA) in 1970. Its task was to enforce all environmental regulations. In 1970, Congress also created the Occupational Safety and Health Administration (OSHA) to safeguard workers against work-related accidents and disease. Although he never really sympathized with the environmental movement, Nixon nevertheless signed the Clean Air Act in 1970, establishing strict national standards for air quality. He also agreed to the Clean Water Act and the Pesticide Control Act in 1972.

Civil Rights, the Supreme Court, and Other Americans

Richard Nixon's presidential victories in 1968 and then again in 1972 rested, in part, on his appeal to the so-called Silent Majority. These Americans, considered the heart of the Nixon-Agnew constituency, were fed up with policies they believed catered to minorities and societal malcontents through social experimentation. They complained about rising crime rates, domestic unrest, increasing drug use, oppressive taxation, pornography, and minority protests. By supporting them, Nixon and the Republican Party attempted to establish a strong political foundation with the middle class and its supposed values. These were the Americans who would prove to be the essence of a revitalized Republican Party for many decades to come.

The president appointed his friend, former law partner, and campaign manager, John Mitchell, as attorney general. An avowed conservative and outspoken proponent of law-and-order, Mitchell helped the administration pass a very tough new criminal justice law for the District of Columbia. He worked to isolate radical and student groups through infiltration and prosecution under a newly passed anti-riot law. Holding African Americans and other civil rights advocates responsible for much domestic disorder, Mitchell testified against the extension of the

Voting Rights Act, due to expire in the summer of 1970.

The administration also moved against another favorite conservative target—the Supreme Court, as part of a larger plan, called the Southern Strategy. It was a bold attempt to establish a new Republican stronghold in the once solidly Democratic South. Nixon and Mitchell succeeded in many of their political objectives. The Johnson administration and the Democratic Congress had made sure massive racial desegregation of southern schools would finally occur when Richard Nixon took office. But Mitchell and Nixon decided to shift responsibility for forced integration to the federal courts. In the summer of 1969, the United States Justice Department asked for a federal judge to delay desegregation of some thirty-three school districts in Mississippi. When the Supreme Court responded by ruling against the Justice Department, white Southerners could not hold the president responsible. Instead, they focused their vitriol on the already despised Court. At the same time, Nixon would not appear responsible for thwarting the course of civil rights.

The president also had opportunities to reshape the Court into a much more conservative body. The first such occasion occurred when Nixon's old California Republican rival, Earl Warren, retired as Chief Justice. Perhaps no single individual was held more responsible for the perceived loosening of social restraints during the preceding decades than Earl Warren. In replacing him, Nixon could strike back on behalf of the Silent Majority and perhaps begin to undo the civil rights and civil liberties activism Warren had so ably defended.

Nixon's choice, who met with little opposition, was Warren Burger. He was a man of moderately conservative views and considerable federal court experience. Real opposition mounted when the next Court vacancy occurred. The Senate rejected both of Nixon's nominees, one for obstruction of civil rights and conflict of interest and another for being clearly unfit to serve on the Court. (One senator actually defended the latter by declaring that "there are lots of mediocre judges" and that mediocre people also deserved representation on the Court.) Despite the failures of these appointments,

Nixon had enhanced himself and his party in the South.

Eventually, Harry Blackmun, a respected conservative from Minnesota (who ultimately proved to be not so conservative at all) filled the vacancy. Two more appointments followed: a distinguished jurist from Virginia, Lewis Powell, and the uncompromisingly conservative William Rehnquist of Arizona. Despite these changes, the Court upheld forced busing to advance integration, allowed the death penalty only under very circumscribed situations, and restricted the government's right to wiretap suspected subversives. In 1973, this supposedly more conservative Burger Court affirmed a woman's right to abortion in the landmark case of *Roe v. Wade*. The failure of Nixon's Court to do his bidding was a demonstration that the tides of history could not be turned back. It also showed that the decisions of justices, appointed for life, cannot be predicted or controlled.

Nixon vowed in his 1968 campaign to eliminate many of the programs of the Great Society as wasteful and symptomatic of an excessively strong centralized federal government. His administration eliminated the Office of Economic Opportunity and the Model Cities Program. A Nixon spokesperson proposed that the time had come "when the issue of race could benefit from a period of benign neglect," rather than governmental activism. To this end, the administration considerably reduced the number of federal investigations intended to determine how well communities in the nation were complying with school desegregation rulings. When the Court ruled in favor of busing students to integrate schools, Nixon used television to demand, unsuccessfully, that Congress enact legislation to prevent forced busing. And yet, in his characteristically contradictory way, in 1970 Nixon orchestrated the desegregation of school systems in seven defiant states (Alabama, Arkansas, Georgia, Louisiana, Mississippi, North Carolina and South Carolina). One not particularly sympathetic observer noted that the Nixon administration had "accomplished more to desegregate Southern school systems than had been done in the 16 previous years." He characterized Nixon's actions in this matter as "the outstanding domestic achievement of his administration."

The Economic Crisis

From his predecessor, Lyndon Johnson, the new president inherited not only the messy protracted Vietnam war but an ever spiraling rate of inflation. Johnson's economic policy of "guns and butter" (the war and an ambitious program of social reform) had created a serious economic situation. Nixon faced an inflation rate of 5 percent and a budget deficit of $25 billion. As prices rose at an alarming rate, workers demanded higher wages. The result was an economic vicious cycle.

Because of his faith in the private sector's power to turn around the economy and the Republicans' distrust of government intervention, Nixon initially seemed unable to take direct action to stop the spiral. Instead, he focused on balancing the budget by reducing government expenditures. Simultaneously he strongly encouraged the Federal Reserve Board to maintain a tight money and high interest rate policy. His hoped this would lessen inflation.

The immediate consequence of what the president called his "game plan," was a deepening economic crisis, the first recession since 1958. The Dow-Jones average dropped about three hundred points; the sharpest drop in over thirty years. As businesses failed, the Democratic Party coined a new term—"Nixonomics." Unemployment reached 5.8 percent by 1970. This was a 2.5 percent increase in less than two years. The Gross National Product (GNP) also declined. But, even worse, inflation did not subside. Internationally, this translated into overpriced American goods coupled with a weaker dollar. For the first time in almost one hundred years, the United States had a deficit in the balance of trade of nearly three billion dollars.

Besieged by critics and facing a worsening economic downturn, the president at first held fast to his "game plan." But, by the summer of 1971, Nixon realized his hand was forced. "Stagflation" (economic stagnation and inflation), as it came to be known, did not let up. Nixon announced Phase I of a new economic policy. This included devaluing the dollar, ending the old international monetary system based on gold-dollar convertibility. A 10 percent surtax on all imported goods accompanied this action. Finally, Nixon imposed a ninety day freeze on all wages and prices.

Conservative Republican voices like those of Senator Barry Goldwater from Arizona and California governor Ronald Reagan decried this new direction of their party. Nonetheless, Phase I seemed to be somewhat successful. During the first part of 1972, industrial production rose, as did the stock market. On the eve of the 1972 election campaign, the economy was the healthiest it had been since Nixon assumed office, and it contributed to his landslide re-election.

Phase II began in the summer of 1973 with a new sixty day price freeze, but prices soared again as soon as the freeze was removed. This resumption of inflation was not necessarily the result of a failed Nixon economic policy. Higher prices had much more to do with major increases in the cost of imported oil. The United States purchased about 36 percent of its crude oil supply from OPEC nations who raised oil prices by almost 400 percent from 1970 to 1973. Beginning with the winter of 1973-74, OPEC nations imposed an oil embargo on the United States and the other Western nations who had allied themselves with Israel in the Yom Kippur War of 1973. Uncontrollable inflation was only one consequence of OPEC's action. The other was unprecedented-long lines of angry Americans waiting at their neighborhood filling stations in the following administrations.

THE FINAL CRISIS

Never forgetting his losses or even his narrow victories, like the 1968 election, Richard Nixon quickly moved against his perceived political enemies. This was part of his strategy to appeal to the Silent Majority and emphasize law and order. Indeed, to liberals, law and order became code words for Nixon's antipathy toward social progress and his innate distrust of the intellectual elite. It came, as well, to play a large role in his re-election campaign in 1972.

The president was more than willing to use all the powers at his disposal to oppose all those ele-

ments he either feared or distrusted. These included civil rights activists, minorities, anti-war protesters, the government bureaucracy, and various radical groups. To achieve his ends, Nixon ordered the all-powerful Internal Revenue Service to audit tax returns and the Small Business Administration to deny loans. The president directed the Central Intelligence Agency to investigate and compile dossiers on dissidents in direct violation of the law limiting its activities to the international area. He enlisted the Federal Bureau of Investigation in illegal wire tapping and bogus arrests, based on highly questionable charges. Playing on the nation's fears, Nixon cajoled the Justice Department to prosecute political dissenters in media enhanced trials.

But his profound distrust did not stop there. Beginning in the spring of 1969, shortly after the bombing of Cambodia, Nixon ordered the wiretapping of phones following press leaks concerning the new direction of the war. The taps included not only telephones of members of the press but also those of members of his National Security Council. The following year, Nixon convened a meeting in the White House of top officials to propose methods of dealing with "the leak problem." Suggestions included increased electronic surveillance, additional legal "mail coverage," and a relaxing of restrictions on illegal mail coverage; increased number of informants on college and university campuses across the country; removal of all restrictions on "surreptitious entries" (meaning break-ins and burglaries); and the creation of an International Group on Domestic Intelligence and Internal Security. FBI director, J. Edgar Hoover, blocked the plan, largely because he believed it would undercut his power.

In June of 1971, the *New York Times* began to publish the *Pentagon Papers*. Nixon determined that there would be no further leaks of secret government information. To that end, he established a special "plumbers" unit within the White House, headed by E. Howard Hunt, a long-time veteran of the CIA, and G. Gordon Liddy, a former FBI agent. They were specifically directed to discredit anyone who leaked information to the media. Their initial target was the man responsible for releasing the *Pentagon Papers*—Daniel Ellsberg. Failing to find the expected discrediting information, they pursued their search by breaking into the office of Ellsberg's psychiatrist and searching his files, to no avail.

White House aides prepared an "enemies list." It came to include several hundred Americans who were prominent in various social and political arenas. The list ranged from liberal movie stars like Paul Newman to university presidents. The type of mentality involved in creating the list was well characterized by a White House aide, who said, "Anyone who opposes us, we'll destroy. As a matter of fact, anyone who doesn't support us, we'll destroy."

Although he failed to secure a Republican majority in Congress in the 1970 election, Nixon acted aggressively to assure his re-election in 1972. He didn't want to simply win, he wanted to humble his opposition. To assure this outcome, the attorney general, John Mitchell, formed the Committee to Re-elect the President, ominously, or appropriately, best known as CREEP. Staffed with people who were experts in political "dirty tricks," CREEP both harassed potential Democratic contenders and spied on them. White House "plumber" Liddy eventually generated the elaborate scheme to spy on the Democrats. His plans included the bugging of their national headquarters in the Watergate complex that led to the arrest of all five men who had broken in.

The Election of 1972

As amazing as it is in retrospect, the break-in and subsequent arrests did not figure significantly in the 1972 election. Too many layers removed Nixon from the bungled burglary at this juncture of history. Nonetheless, he immediately took action to cover-up the evidence. Nixon soon learned many of his top aides had been involved in some way in the crime. Publicly he adamantly proclaimed that no one in his administration "was involved in this bizarre incident." Although the public believed him, Nixon took the initial steps down the path of self-destruction. He ordered staff members to pay off those arrested with CREEP hush money. He warned the CIA to keep the FBI out of the investigation on the bogus grounds that national security issues were at stake. Finally, Nixon told those around him to lie under oath should

it prove necessary. The president privately insisted, "I don't give a [expletive deleted] what happens. I want you all to stonewall it, let them plead the Fifth Amendment, cover-up, or anything else...."

One of the most remarkable things regarding the Watergate break-in is that it was so totally unnecessary. Nixon's re-election in 1972 was assured. Candidates that might have posed the most serious opposition to Nixon either destroyed themselves or were wrecked by "dirty tricks." An assassin shot the most serious spoiler of all, former Alabama governor George Wallace. As a result of his wounds, the paralyzed Wallace had to abandon the race. This removed an opponent who might have taken some right-wing support from Nixon.

The result was as expected. Nixon received almost 61 percent of the popular vote and captured the electoral college 520 to 17. His well-meaning opponent, Senator George McGovern of South Dakota, was soundly defeated. The "prairie populist," as some called McGovern, was a long-time and strong opponent of the war in Vietnam. Although he captured the peace movement advocates, many Americans regarded McGovern's promise to end U.S. involvement and reduce the defense budget by $30 billion with suspicion. Although they wanted the war to end, they did not want to abandon the nation's role in international affairs.

McGovern's other issue of his own personal integrity as compared to Richard Nixon's was weakened by public perceptions that he was a politically inept radical. The Democratic National Conven-

The dove on George McGovern's campaign button symbolized his opposition to the war in Vietnam. He also became a symbol of other liberal causes, including women's rights.

tion of 1972 reinforced this image. After the 1968 Chicago convention debacle, a new more liberal and activist element captured control of the party, a change McGovern had aided. In 1972, the old New Deal coalition of big city bosses, organized labor and its leaders, and southern politicians was gone. The youthful and non-traditional, particularly women and minority groups, replaced it. Images of McGovern as a supporter of busing and legalized marijuana helped doom his candidacy. One traditional labor leader who normally supported Democrats denounced McGovern as "the candidate of amnesty, acid, and appeasement."

Yet the 1972 Nixon landslide bears closer examination. Voters may well have been rejecting McGovern, rather than embracing Nixon. Outside of the presidency, the Republicans gained little elsewhere in the election: twelve seats in the House—while the Democrats gained two Senate seats. In addition, voters demonstrated a pronounced tendency toward ticket splitting. Only 55.7 percent of all those eligible to vote did so, a tendency toward public disinterest that has continued to the present time. This rather sad commentary on the electoral process was all the more serious as the most critical political crisis since the days of the Civil War was about to unravel.

Watergate and the Undoing of the Nixon Presidency

Despite the public's tendency to ignore the Watergate break-in and the initial success of the cover-up, *Washington Post* reporters, Bob Woodward and Carl Bernstein, kept the case on the front pages. They exposed the direct connection between CREEP, "dirty tricks," and the break-in.

In a 1973 trial, Hunt, Liddy, and the five burglars were convicted. The hard-nosed federal trial judge, John Sirica, refused to believe that the burglars had acted on their own and threatened them with long prison sentences. As a result, one of the conspirators admitted that he and the others had committed perjury during the trial and testified about the role of well-placed White House aides in the break-in.

A grand jury was convened to examine the charges. At the same time, the Senate created its own special investigating committee, chaired by the crafty Sam Ervin of North Carolina. White House counsel John Dean, who feared that he was the designated administration scapegoat, admitted there had been a cover-up and that Nixon had ordered it. In a vain attempt to distance himself from the growing scandal, Nixon announced the firing of Dean and the resignations H.R. Haldeman and John Ehrlichman, both of whom were involved in the cover-up. Next, the president appeared on television and promised the American public there would be no "white wash." Nixon seemed to be true to his promise when he made Elliot Richardson his new attorney general. Richardson, in turn, named Archibald Cox of Harvard Law School as the special Watergate prosecutor. Both men were well known for their unquestioned integrity.

At the televised Senate hearings, John Dean in a demonstration of an almost photographic memory, revealed sensational details about "enemies" and cover-ups. His assertions seemed impossible to prove until another presidential aide almost casually revealed, "Well...yes, there's a recording system in the President's office." It seemed that there was an extensive cache of Oval Office tapes, recorded regularly since 1970. Both Ervin and Cox asked for any tapes discussing Watergate. Nixon refused to comply, citing Executive Privilege. When Cox attempted to secure the tapes through a court order in October 1973, the president ordered Richardson to fire Cox. Richardson resigned rather than comply. The deputy attorney general, who also rebuffed the president, met the same fate. Only the solicitor general, Robert Bork, would comply in what became known as the "Saturday Night Massacre." These actions outraged the public and the president's popularity rating fell to an unprecedented 27 percent.

Nixon's situation was dire. In the middle of the tape struggles, he had to confront reports that he spent $10 million of federal money on his own homes and paid federal income taxes of less than $1,000 in 1970 and 1971. (Later, it was revealed that Nixon owed a half million dollars in back taxes.) It certainly did not help that, at the same time, Vice President Spiro Agnew had to resign from his office. Agnew pleaded no contest to charges of income tax evasion and the acceptance of bribes while governor of Maryland. The president nominated the popular House minority leader, Gerald R. Ford of Michigan, to replace the dishonored and disgraced Agnew. Ford became the vice president under the provisions of the Twenty-fifth Amendment to the Constitution, ratified in the wake of the Kennedy assassination of 1963.

Cox was gone, but Nixon had an equally formidable opponent in his new special prosecutor, Leon Jaworski, a prominent Texas attorney. Jaworski eventually took Nixon to court to force surrender of the tapes. In the interval, the president released a laundered version of transcripts. While still not directly linking him with the cover-up, even these highly censored documents revealed Nixon at his worst. They contained large gaps of information and frequent references to "expletive deleted." The president exposed himself as narrow-minded and vengeful. Even the Republican newspaper, the *Chicago Tribune,* wrote of Nixon, "We have seen the private man and we are appalled."

In June 1974, the Supreme Court unanimously ruled the tapes had to be turned over to Judge Sirica. The decision stated that although there were "constitutional underpinnings" for executive privilege, such privilege "cannot prevail over the fundamental demands of due process of law in the fair administration of justice." The Court went on to declare that neither "the doctrine of the separation of powers nor the need for confidentiality of high-level communications...can sustain an absolute, unqualified presidential privilege of immunity from judicial process under all circumstances."

Shortly after the Court ordered Nixon to surrender the tapes, the House Judiciary Committee adopted its first article for the impeachment of Richard Nixon. After several painful days of testimony, the majority voted to impeach the president for obstruction of justice and presidential abuse of power. Hoping against hope that he might still be able to remain in office, Nixon went on television on August 5, 1974, to admit he had made "mistakes" by withholding relevant evidence. He surrendered three tapes that confirmed Dean's

testimony and vividly demonstrated Nixon's role in the cover-up. This was, indeed, the "smoking gun." Even diehard Nixon supporters reluctantly favored impeachment. They did so because, as one expert wrote, here was abundant evidence of a "systematic obstruction of justice for more than two years....a weapon so redolent of powder, so smeared with prints that no defendant could hope for acquittal."

Watergate involved more than a break-in and its subsequent cover-up. It was the most serious abuse of presidential power in American history. In the twentieth century the presidency had become the central institution in the federal government, establishing the legislative agenda, creating the national budget, and even circumventing congressional power to declare war. Nixon had carried the "Imperial Presidency" to its most extreme. He refused to spend moneys appropriated by Congress, constantly invoked executive privilege to avoid questions about his decisions, and even attempted to create a colorfully uniformed "palace guard." But the fall-out from Watergate brought his bid for unbridled executive power to a crashing end. The American system of checks and balances did work, as the creators of our Constitution had envisioned.

Key Republican congressional leaders, led by respected conservative Senator Barry Goldwater, told Nixon that impeachment and conviction were inevitable. Finally, on August 8, 1974, Richard Nixon announced his resignation. The following morning, he bade a tearful and revealing farewell to his cabinet and staff. "Never get petty," he advised them, "always remember, others may hate you, but those who hate you don't win unless you hate them, and then you destroy yourself." This complex man, who had so abused presidential powers, fell because of his inability to practice his own advice.

THE INTERREGNUM YEARS: 1974-76 GERALD FORD

The surprising elevation of Gerald Ford to the vice presidency following the resignation of Spiro Agnew

On Aug. 8, 1974, facing expected impeachment over the Watergate cover-up scandal, President Richard Nixon went on nationwide television and announced his resignation, the first American president to do so. The next day he left office after an emotional farewell to members of his staff and cabinet. With him are wife Pat and daughter Tricia.

in October of 1973 was surpassed by his ascendance to the White House only eleven months later. It was an unprecedented time and place for a man who had never been elected to national office. A major economic recession, energy shortages, and the final collapse of the South Vietnamese government all compounded the crisis of leadership that confronted him.

A long-time Congressman from western Michigan, Ford was a very different character than Richard Nixon. He was an amiable and well-liked man, personally conservative, and regarded as honest, trustworthy, and humble. Lyndon Johnson had once noted, cynically and unkindly, that Ford's problems resulted from having played football at the University of Michigan without a helmet! Well aware of his unique role under unique circumstances, as well

as of his own personal limitations, he informed the American people they had "a Ford, not a Lincoln" as their president. "Our long national nightmare is over," the new president declared. For many Americans his more open temperament seemed a refreshing change from Nixon's arrogance, cynicism, and paranoia.

Ford's honeymoon with the nation, however, was short-lived. On September 8, 1974, he granted a full pardon to Nixon saying, "My conscience tells me that only I, as president, have the constitutional power to firmly shut and seal this book." Instead, angry Americans believed that Ford and Nixon had struck some kind of a political deal, despite the lack of evidence to support this charge. By pardoning Nixon, the new president unintentionally linked

Members of the White House staff watch from the balcony as Gerald Ford and his wife, Betty, escort resigning President Richard Nixon and his wife to a helicopter on the White House lawn.

himself to the Watergate scandals. Ford did replace most of what was left of Nixon's White House staff but retained Henry Kissinger. In fact, Kissinger held two positions in the Ford years—National Security Advisor and Secretary of State. The public clearly demonstrated its discontent by overwhelming Democratic victories in the congressional elections of 1974.

If the pardoning of Nixon had been intended to heal the nation's wounds, so too was the September 16, 1974 proclamation offering clemency to approximately 28,000 Vietnam War era draft evaders and military deserters. A form of limited amnesty would be granted in return for a sworn oath of allegiance and performance of twenty-four months of alternative public service. As for those already convicted

for draft evasion or desertion, the president created a nine member clemency board to review their cases. Although Ford's proclamation never used the controversial term "amnesty," it was a step toward what the president called the "reconciliation...and restoration of essential unity of Americans within which honest differences of opinion do not descend to angry discord and mutual problems are not polarized by excessive passion."

Domestic Policy

Although Ford prided himself on his good relations with both Houses of Congress, he had difficulties in working with a Congress controlled by Democrats.

As a congressman, Ford had voted against virtually every Great Society initiative. In the White House, he vetoed a variety of social welfare, environmental, and public-interest bills—fifty-three vetoes in just over two years. He called bills to provide federal aid to education and federal laws to regulate strip-mining too expensive or inflationary. He also vetoed the 1974 "freedom of information" proposal, which would have granted American citizens greater access to government documents. To the great dismay of civil-rights supporters, Ford was an outspoken opponent of Court mandated school busing. Congress overrode many Ford vetoes.

The satire of comedian Chevy Chase on the popular television program, *Saturday Night Live*, bolstered the public perception of President Ford as an inept bungler. The president's propensity to bump his head when disembarking from Air Force One and to hit spectators with golf balls reinforced this image. His handling of the economic situation did not inspire greater confidence. When Ford came to the White House, the inflation rate was already more than 10 percent and the unemployment rate was 7 percent, largely as the result of rising oil costs. Consumer prices rose 12 percent in 1974 and 11 percent more in 1975.

Ford, far less flexible than Nixon, responded to rising inflation in a much more traditional Republican fashion by tightening the money supply, reducing government spending, and raising interest rates. Ford also launched his voluntary "Whip Inflation Now" (WIN). American refusal to buy overly expensive goods and willingness to stop demanding higher wages would supposedly defeat inflation. The president announced the program at a national press conference with WIN buttons for the press corps to wear in their lapels. WIN proved to be totally inadequate in dealing with the economic crisis. The nation plunged into the most severe economic recession since the Second World War as unemployment rates reached 11 percent.

Although congressional insistence on tax cuts, greater benefits, and public works projects somewhat alleviated the problem, economic woes continued for the duration of the Ford presidency and then lingered into the Carter years. These weaknesses were part of a larger American crisis that manifested itself most dramatically as urban decay. For a "people of plenty," as historian David Potter had once characterized Americans, this was a difficult reality to comprehend. The hallmarks of the 1950s and early 1960s—steady growth rates of over 3 percent per year, relatively stable prices reflected in low inflation rate, and unemployment rates of only 4.5 percent a year—were long gone.

As early as the late 1950s, the postwar economic boom enjoyed by most Americans was winding down. The United States had helped rebuild the industrial infrastructure in Europe and Japan with the latest technology. Meanwhile, in the "Rust Belt" of Ohio, Michigan, and Pennsylvania, obsolete plants and outmoded production systems meant American industries were no longer competitive. Corporations failed to invest in outmoded plants, preferring short-term profits. Highly paid unionized workers, expecting lifetime employment, suddenly found that their jobs had permanently disappeared. The consequence of the combination of these factors was that the United States was outproduced at exactly the same time American markets were opening up to foreign imports. During the 1970s, Japanese production increased by some 7 percent, while U.S. productivity was on the decline. Fundamental shifts in the structure of the economy and manufacturing system further eroded American manufacturing capability. America's economic productivity had once been based on the manufacturing sector, particularly heavy industry such as railroads, steel, and, later, automobiles. By the 1950s, the economy was beginning to shift from the manufacturing to the service sector, based on high technology, especially computers and information.

Energy shortages added to these alterations. Americans were energy gluttons who consumed about one-third of the world's fuel supply, although only 6 percent of its population. The United States came to rely all too heavily on foreign oil that, by 1973, was one-third of all oil consumed. That is why the OPEC price increase and embargo, driving the price of a barrel of oil from $5 to $12 in about three months, had such a severe impact

The Johnson administration's escalation of the Vietnam conflict in 1965 made this situation worse. Combined with domestic spending for the Great Society programs and no tax increases, the war led to a growing national debt. Especially during the late 1970s, the American penchant for living beyond one's means greatly accelerated. Household and business borrowing increased more than three-fold. The great credit expansion helped drive up prices on everything. Although most Americans suffered as a result, the crisis was most visible in the nation's cities. One factor in the decline of American cities was the deterioration of their economic essence, manufacturing.

In the cities, working class people experienced increasing difficulties in finding jobs. At the very bottom were those minorities, African Americans and Hispanics, who lived in blighted inner cities. Their unemployment rate was often three times as high as that of the rest of the work force. These people formed a virtually permanent underclass.

In Youngstown, Ohio and Pittsburgh, Pennsylvania steel mills stood idle. In Detroit, Michigan the largest automobile manufacturer in the world, General Motors, laid off 6 percent of its domestic work force. Thousands of others were put on temporary leave. Chicago lost 326,000 manufacturing jobs between 1967 and 1987. New York City lost more than half a million. By late 1975, New York was near financial collapse. It was unable to meet its payroll and pay its bonds. President Ford let it be known that it would veto any federal bailout bill passed by Congress. A headline in a New York newspaper ruefully summarized his attitude: "Ford to City: Drop Dead." After Congress agreed to grant the city a loan, however, he backed off, and the city survived. Cleveland, Ohio was less fortunate as it became the first major American metropolis to default since the days of the Great Depression.

Foreign Policy Under Ford

A long-time supporter of the war in Vietnam, Gerald Ford had the misfortune of occupying the White House during the debacle of the final days of that conflict. In April 1975, as the network television cameras recorded the scene, the public watched the pathetic evacuees scramble for helicopters attempting to flee Saigon. Ford blamed Congress for the sorry spectacle.

Two weeks later he achieved a small victory of sorts. The communist regime in Cambodia captured an American cargo ship, the Mayagüez. Ford authorized a military rescue. Americans reacted favorably to this macho response, ignoring that 41 men died to free the ships' 39 crew members. One proud senator gloated, "It shows we've still got balls in this country."

The retention of Henry Kissinger signaled Ford's initial support of Nixon's détente policy with the Soviet Union and China. The new president met with Soviet leader, Leonid Brezhnev, in 1974 and made some advances towards further arms-limitations. This led to the Helsinki Accords the following year where the two superpowers and other European leaders accepted the existing post-World War II boundaries of Europe, including Soviet-dominated Eastern Europe. Both also agreed to a rather lengthy list of human rights and freedom to travel.

Election 1976

As the bicentennial year of American independence grew nearer, Ford decided he wanted to govern in his own right. Even though he had the advantage of incumbency, his record did not inspire enthusiasm. Furthermore, the Republican Party was badly divided. Opposition came from the well-organized right-wing, which supported the former California governor, Ronald Reagan. In primaries across the nation, Reagan attacked détente with the Soviet Union, lamenting the "collapse of the American will and the retreat of American power." But, in the end, the president weathered the assault and barely prevailed.

The Democrats were also divided in 1976. Massachusetts Senator Edward Kennedy, the brother of the late president, might well have been the strongest candidate, but the terrible 1969 incident on Chappaquiddock Island hovered over him. Kennedy was driving a car involved in an accident in which a young woman drowned and was never able to provide a satisfactory explanation of his actions. Since the Democrats seemed unable to find a suitable candidate with nationwide support, a most unlikely individual emerged, James Earl (Jimmy) Carter, Jr. This "born-again" Christian was a graduate of the U. S. Naval Academy who served in the nuclear submarine fleet. When he returned to Plains, Georgia, Carter entered his father's peanut business that he successfully rebuilt. His entire political career consisted of a one term stint in the Georgia Senate and one successful term as the Governor of Georgia. This total lack of national political experience, however, was exactly what the American public seemed to want after the imperial presidencies of Lyndon Johnson and Richard Nixon and the perceived ineptness of Gerald Ford.

Sensing that Americans wanted something very different, this intelligent and ambitious Georgian swept the Democratic primaries by offering himself as a political outsider. He argued that, "the vast majority of Americans are outsiders. We are not going to get changes by simply sifting around the same groups of insiders,...the same unkept promises." He emphasized the very things that post-Watergate weary Americans wanted to hear—honesty in government and traditional values. Appearing in campaign ads dressed in blue jeans, he introduced himself to the voters as Jimmy and promised them in his soft spoken southern accent that he would "never tell a lie to the American people."

Jimmy Carter was an excellent representative of the "new" South. This was a South that accepted racial integration. Carter once told a member of the powerful racist White Citizen's Council that rather than pay them the $5 membership fee, he would flush the money down the toilet. But he was equally well rooted in the old South of evangelical faith. Carter considered himself a man of principle, honesty, human decency, and family values.

Carter began the campaign against Ford with a whopping 33 point lead. Neither candidate, however, generated much enthusiasm from the electorate. Less than 54 percent of them turned out at the polls. Carter's early lead dwindled, but he held on to win a very narrow victory (49.98 per-

James Earl Carter

cent of the popular vote and 297 electoral votes to 240 for Ford).

The 1976 election revealed significant trends in race and class. Remarkably, almost 90 percent of African Americans voted for Carter, the native Georgian. They represented his margin of victory in seven southern states and pivotal northern states like Ohio and Pennsylvania. Carter also carried the overwhelming majority of Mexican-American votes. In general, the new president appealed most strongly to the alienated and disaffected segments of society. On the other hand, Ford received most of his support from more affluent, white, better educated Americans, particularly suburbanites. Although native son, Carter, carried the South, the solid South was a phenomenon of the past. This once political monolith had become increasingly industrialized, urbanized, more heavily populated, diverse, and Republican. As the 1980 federal census would subsequently reveal, the new population center of the nation was now in the Sunbelt. The long time power base of the Democratic Party, in big labor, was gone as well. As the economic infrastructure of the country underwent massive changes, so too had the membership and power of America's unions. These changes were to have profound meaning collectively, not only for the Democratic Party, but for the nation as a whole.

THE "OUTSIDER" AS PRESIDENT

Avoiding the bullet-proof limousine used since the Kennedy assassination, Jimmy Carter, his wife Rosalynn, and their daughter, Amy, walked the 1.2 miles hand-in-hand from the Capitol to the White House. On that bitterly cold day of his inauguration, the new president wore an ordinary blue suit. Symbolically, he was rejecting so many of the trappings of the not too distant past. Even the politically savvy editor of the *Washington Post* felt moved, encouraged, and hopeful about the future. But good intentions and appearances were not enough. The complexity of the problems confronting the nation, combined with Carter's inexperience, and lack of direction or clear political philosophy, soon put his administration in trouble.

Although hard-working, decent, and very intelligent, Carter could also seem inflexible and suspicious of federal "insiders." His administration was a reflection of the man. The president selected well established and experienced Democrats for his cabinet. Those closest to him, however, were personal friends, known as the "Georgia Mafia," who had no more national experience than Carter did. At lower administrative levels, Carter appointed many liberal activists, Kennedy and McGovern supporters. Many of them were women and African Americans. The problem was activists, party insiders, and close friends were not likely to work well with one another. And they did not. Carter largely ignored the Democratic Congress, which was furious when it saw the first Carter budget. Carter eliminated projects dear to many congressmen without consultation. The ensuing budget battle established the pattern of the relationship between Carter and Congress. By the middle of 1977, most of the president's proposals were buried in the legislature.

Domestic Programs—Energy

The economy and energy costs were the most immediate problems confronting the new president on the domestic front. Of the two, energy took top priority with Jimmy Carter. He believed that excessively high energy costs caused the nation's economic woes, due to the simple fact that Americans were consuming far more energy than the nation was producing.

Calling the energy crisis the "moral equivalent of war," Carter appealed to the American public by urging them to lead more simple lives. Small individual reductions in energy consumption would yield large savings. To that end, the president proposed that more people use public transportation, wear sweaters, and lower their thermostats. He also introduced major energy legislation in the Congress, advocating increased domestic production along with conservation. The program included requiring energy savings in auto engineering, the creation of the cabinet Department of Energy, funding for the research and development of alternative fuels, and regulation and taxation to curtail excessive profit making in the energy industry.

The Department of Energy was operating by October 1977, but the other proposals were bogged down as lobbyists for oil, natural gas, and automobile industries besieged Congress. Eventually, Congress did pass legislation to allow for increases in the price of natural gas, encourage home energy conservation, and provide for increased automobile fuel efficiency. New increases in oil prices beginning in 1978, a result of serious oil shortages, finally led to funding for the development of alternative energy sources. Again, Americans waited in long lines at their nearby gas station.

Use of alternative energy sources was very controversial. Nuclear energy use fell under serious scrutiny after an almost catastrophic nuclear power plant accident at Three Mile Island in Pennsylvania. Nuclear power advocates had long argued that it was the energy source of the future. They maintained it was safe, cheap, clean, and abundant. The serious energy problems of the 1970s increased the emphasis on this alternative. Opponents argued that nuclear power was very likely dangerous to the environment and humans.

Their dire predictions seemed to be coming true when, on March 28, 1979, the power plant on Three Mile Island had a serious accident. A thousand citizens had to be evacuated from the area after the plant released a radioactive gas cloud. Although the experts prevented a meltdown, it took them more than two weeks to shut the plant down. President Carter continued to speak favorably about continuing the commitment to nuclear energy, but the disaster clearly complicated his energy problems. The incident seriously damaged the credibility of nuclear energy as an alternative energy source.

Domestic Programs—The Economy

Carter first tried to deal with the "stagflation" he inherited from the Ford and Nixon years by reducing unemployment. In his first year in office, he cut federal tax rates and initiated a public works program. National unemployment rates did fall to about 5 percent by the end of 1978. He met with no success in reducing inflation, however. Some of this failure was the result of the president's lack of leadership skills, especially his inability to work with Congress even though it was controlled by Democrats. For the most part, however, the problem of inflation was structural and beyond his control.

The United States was not yet prepared to compete in the emerging global economy. West Germany, Taiwan, Japan, and Korea all cut into American markets. The near bankruptcy of one of the big three automobile manufacturers, the Chrysler Corporation, reflected this most dramatically. In 1980, Congress agreed to save the company by granting it a $1.5 billion loan that the company eventually repaid.

The continuing rapid increases in energy prices set by OPEC helped cause rising inflation rates. During Carter's last two years as president, prices continued to rise at rates well in excess of 10 percent. Nothing seemed to work. Neither the appointment of conservatives to head the Federal Re-

Another shortage of oil occurred in 1979.

serve Board and institute high interest rates nor the call for voluntary citizen restraint proved effective. By 1980, an election year, inflation rose more than 13 percent while interest rates climbed to an unprecedented 20 percent.

As the situation worsened in the summer of 1979, the president went on a retreat to Camp David, Maryland. For ten long days he reflected on the situation and returned to address the nation. In his bleak sermon he seemed to be blaming the American people for the nation's "crisis of confidence." Following what the press derisively called the "national malaise" speech, Carter asked for the resignations of some of his cabinet members. Neither of these actions solved the nation's problems—problems which more and more Americans were coming to believe were beyond the capabilities of the president. Carter's approval rating fell to 26 percent, lower than Richard Nixon's during the depths of the Watergate scandal. Overseas events at the same time undermined the public's confidence in Carter even further.

Foreign Policy

Foreign policy provided some of the greatest triumphs of the Carter administration, but it also helped cause his ultimate defeat. Just as the United States was struggling to find its place in the new global economy, there was a similar struggle to redefine its role in international affairs. The end of the war in Vietnam seriously diminished American prestige and position. Public opinion surveys revealed an increasing lack of support for foreign intervention. One expression of this disengagement was the passage of the War Powers Act of 1973. Revolutionary nationalist movements in other parts of the world, especially in Latin America and the Middle East, seemed to limit American ability to take charge of events.

Carter's expressed foreign policy objectives included: continued détente with both the Soviet Union and China; the elimination of nuclear weapons; the eradication of poverty in the Third World through social and economic development; and fostering human rights worldwide. Unfortunately, he was not always clear about how he planned to implement these goals. Furthermore, because Jimmy Carter lacked experience in foreign affairs, he relied very heavily on others. The problem was he chose two experienced foreign policy experts whose basic outlooks were considerably at odds with each other. His secretary of state, Cyrus Vance, and his national security advisor, Zbigniew Brzezinski, were often in conflict. Vance was an establishment man and Washington insider, who wanted to pursue social, economic, and human rights objectives. Brzezinski, a Polish refugee, from Communist dominated Eastern Europe, was an uncompromising Cold Warrior. He cared little about social and economic goals outside of Europe and the Soviet Union and possessed virtually no knowledge about or interest in the Third World. Jimmy Carter recognized the differences that these two men brought to the foreign policy of his administration but felt he could build the necessary bridges to bring them together. The consequence was a foreign policy that often seemed inconsistent.

At the outset, these problems were not apparent. Building on foundations established in preceding administrations, Carter achieved a number of foreign policy successes. The death of long-time dictator Mao Zedong in 1976 opened the door for further improvements in relations with China. Carter reestablished full formal diplomatic relations with China as of January 1, 1979, opening the door for further commercial and cultural exchanges. This completed U.S./China détente begun by Richard Nixon in 1972. A few months later, Carter also met with the clearly ill Soviet leader, Leonid Brezhnev, to complete the drafting of a SALT II arms limitation agreement to restrict missiles, bombers, and nuclear warheads.

His deeply-held moral principles were the foundation of Carter's approach to foreign affairs. He believed that the United States must foster human rights throughout the world. He spoke out against repression of dissidents and Jews in the Soviet Union and against apartheid in South Africa. The administration used economic sanctions, with some success, to pressure a number of countries, such as Argentina and Chile, to stop oppressing their citizens. Sometimes, however, pragmatic security considerations took precedence over the cause of human rights as in China and Iran.

Carter and Vance worked hard to negotiate two treaties to relinquish control of the Panama Canal to the government of Panama by 1999. Both men believed the United States would be acting in the best spirit of a good neighbor, fostering human rights, and improving America's strained relations with Latin America. Carter stood firm despite the 80 percent public disapproval and criticism from Ronald Reagan and other conservatives that this was another example of U. S. loss of nerve. After a bitter debate, the Senate approved the treaty with only one vote to spare.

Carter's greatest foreign policy victory occurred when he applied his moral authority to the troubled Middle East. Despite the shuttle diplomacy efforts of Henry Kissinger in the Nixon/Ford years, the state of war between Egypt and Israel had not ended. Kissinger, however, established the foundations for the United States to be the major power broker in the area. Surprising everyone, the President of Egypt, Anwar Sadat, announced in 1977 that he was traveling to Israel to negotiate directly with the Prime Minister of Israel, Menachem Begin. This was an amazingly courageous act. It raised the very real possibility that Egypt would become alienated from all the other Arab states. Not only did this happen, but in 1981 Islamic extremists would assassinate Sadat for his pragmatic and far-sighted vision.

Sensing a real opportunity in the wake of Sadat's visit to Israel, Carter invited both Begin and Sadat to join him at Camp David, Maryland in September 1978. After a thirteen day retreat, the three men emerged with a framework for future negotiations. Begin and Sadat agreed to a future peace treaty in which Israel would return the Sinai Peninsula, seized in the 1967 war, to Egypt. In return, Egypt would recognize Israel's right to exist. When talks broke down again, Carter flew to Cairo and Jerusalem to nail down the agreement. On March 26, 1979, Carter presided over a special White House ceremony for the signing of the first peace treaty between Israel and an Arab state. Later both Begin and Sadat received Nobel Peace prizes for their efforts. The peace settlement was far from perfect. It left many major issues unresolved, particularly those concerning Palestine refugees and the claims of Palestinians for nationhood. In addition, many Arabs, led by Syria, and the Palestinians condemned the treaty. Despite these limitations, hopes for a final peaceful settlement in one of the most volatile places in the world now appeared possible. This was Jimmy Carter's finest hour in office.

Shortly after this greatest success, however, the foreign policy of the Carter administration began to unravel. Carter's insistence on human rights already jeopardized détente. On this issue the Russians reacted with considerable outrage. It was at this time that Soviet repression against dissidents like nuclear physicist, human-rights advocate Andrei Sakharov was intensifying. There was also the issue of restricting the emigration of Soviet Jews.

Nowhere was the conflicted nature of the Vance vs. Brzezinski and Carter foreign policy more evident than in relation to the Soviet Union. Working quietly behind the scenes to reverse détente, Brzezinski persuaded Carter to undertake the construction of new high tech weapons—MX missiles to replace the Minutemen ICBMs and Trident sub-

marines. Thus, whatever the fate of SALT II, a new arms race would be a certainty. The new SALT II agreement reached with the Soviets and signed by President Carter pleased very few people in the United States. Liberals thought the armament cuts were not deep enough, while conservatives thought too much had been given away. Conservative groups, many of whom were supporting presidential hopeful Ronald Reagan, demanded a massive arms buildup. Reagan claimed a "window of vulnerability" existed in the United States.

The president withdrew SALT II as it came up for a vote in the Senate in December 1979. The Soviets had invaded Afghanistan, a mountainous country on the southern border of the USSR, where a pro-Soviet government was in danger of collapsing in the face of Muslim opposition. Carter proclaimed that the invasion was "the gravest threat to peace since 1945." Apparently he interpreted it as a Soviet move toward the Indian Ocean and the Persian Gulf. The president followed words with tough action by reinstituting the draft, banning the sale of high tech materials to the Soviets, and embargoing the export of grain to the Soviets. He followed this with a boycott of the 1980 Moscow Olympic Games.

These measures did not bring an end to the Russian invasion of Afghanistan, an invasion that resulted in a protracted guerrilla war. In time, that war proved as disastrous for the Soviet Union as Vietnam had been for the United States. They too learned a lesson on the limits of military power. For President Carter, Afghanistan meant the renewal of the cold war, the death of détente, and the ruin of much of his foreign policy.

If Jimmy Carter's finest hour had been his role in the settlement of the Middle Eastern conflict between Israel and Egypt, he was to suffer his greatest humiliation in the Middle East. It took place in Iran, an oil rich state that had once provided a barrier against Soviet influence in the area. That nation was ruled by the Shah of Iran, a loyal American ally who had been restored to power through CIA intervention in 1953 to thwart Marxist nationalists. The Shah repaid his allies by allowing the United States to install electronic listening equipment along the border his country shared with the Soviet Union.

He bought huge stashes of the most sophisticated weapons available from the United States. The Shah's enormous purchases helped America deal with the balance-of-payments' crisis. Unlike other countries in the region, he continued to sell the United States oil during the 1973-74 embargo (although at inflated prices). But the Shah also ruled autocratically, using SAVAK, the brutal secret police, to suppress any dissent. Many Iranians blamed the United States for training the torturers.

Like other presidents before him, Carter mistakenly believed that the Shah was a popular leader. Beginning in the 1960s, the Shah had undertaken a massive modernization program intended to improve both social and economic conditions in his nation. Its consequence was widespread political and social unrest. The Shah had alienated every sector of his country, apart from his military and westernized middle and upper class citizens. The continuing oppression angered leftist intellectuals. At the other end of the social spectrum, reactionary Shiite Muslim ayatollahs (religious leaders) and mullahs (priests) indoctrinated the devout Iranian peasantry. They taught that the Shah was a blasphemous ruler who had contaminated Iran with Western values and sold out to the "Great Satan," the United States.

By the late 1970s the Shah's government teetered on the edge of disaster. The once mighty ruler vacillated between intensified terror and liberalization. In Washington, Carter waffled between standing fast with the Shah and preparing for a new Iranian government. Carter tried to do both.

After months of turmoil and uncertainty, the Shah left the country in January of 1979 for a "vacation." He never returned. Ayatollah Ruhollah Khomeini, the central figure of the Shiite Muslim resistance, returned from Paris where he was living in exile and established a repressive Islamic republic. Hundreds of the Shah's supporters were executed. Westernization in Iran not only ended, it was undone. More than anything, this new fundamentalist Islamic state asserted that the United States was the major source of evil in the world. Khomeini's hatred of the West was so intense that normal diplomatic relations were impossible.

The situation was so bad, few believed it could get worse. But matters deteriorated even more when the desperately ill Shah requested to come to the United States for cancer treatment. Distinguished Americans, like David Rockefeller, pressured the beleaguered president to grant the request. Well-placed Iranian officials warned Carter that to do so would result in reprisals against Americans. He decided that it would be morally wrong to deny the request to a long-time loyal friend who was dying. On November 4, 1979, an angry Iranian mob stormed the American embassy in Tehran and held the Americans inside captive.

Iran demanded the return of the Shah to stand trial, in exchange for the hostages. Fifty-three Americans remained in captivity for 444 days. Feeling personally responsible, Carter agonized over what he could do. As Carter obsessed over his powerlessness, so did the nation. Newspapers and television reported each day of the captivity, each one a further international humiliation. The television program, *Nightline*, began as a daily report on the continued plight of the hostages.

The crisis intensified the divisions between Vance and Brzezinski. Vance advocated negotiation. Brzezinski pushed for force, maintaining that international respect for the United States was far more important than a few lives. In April 1980, Carter agreed to a desperate hostage rescue attempt. It ended in failure. Eight crewmen lost their lives when their helicopters crashed and burned in the Iranian desert. Vance, who had always opposed the mission, resigned as Secretary of State. This embarrassing defeat, perhaps unfairly, reinforced the image of presidential incompetence.

An agreement to free the hostages could be reached only after the Shah's death in 1980 through the efforts of both the Algerians and Canadians. They were finally released on January 20, 1981, the day Carter left office. The entire episode revealed the real limitations of traditional foreign policy in dealing with terrorism and terrorist governments. This revelation of American impotence also crippled Jimmy Carter's chances for re-election in 1980.

After 444 days the Iranian hostage crisis ended, but it destroyed Carter's chances for re-election.

THE CHANGING FACE OF AMERICA IN THE 70S

The failures in the administrations of Richard Nixon, Gerald Ford, and Jimmy Carter may have been affected by much larger issues confronting the United States. These included economic competition in a new global economy, establishing a place in the post Vietnam world, and coming to terms with significant internal changes. How would Americans adjust to these domestic transformations?

Demographic transitions produced a striking new reality. The 1980 federal census revealed more than half of all Americans now lived in either the South or the West. Population rates in the East and Midwest, in contrast, were stagnant. Northern cities were the greatest losers. The Sunbelt states of California, Florida, and Texas gained the most. Because corporate America re-located in these states,

young professionals and skilled workers were compelled to follow. Thus, in the decade when New York City almost went bankrupt and lost close to a million residents, the hub of the nation's oil industry, Houston, Texas, grew by 26 percent. By 1980, Houston's population reached 1.5 million, making it the fifth largest city in the nation.

Another significant demographic change was that for the first time since 1940, the birth rate began its steady decline. In 1970, there were 18.4 births for every 1,000 people, but by 1975, the rate dipped below 15. (It had been 25.3 at the height of the baby boom in 1957.) While the birth rate decreased, life expectancy increased. Importantly, the poverty rate among the elderly decreased throughout the decade. As Americans lived longer, political priorities changed. Politicians had to pay more attention to this increasingly important interest group and its concerns about Medicare, Medicaid, and, Social Security. Unquestionably, it was a group des-

In the 1950s, child-care responsibilities were mainly the responsibility of mothers who stayed home with their children. Fathers, perhaps, helped on the weekends or after work.

tined to be more visible and even more important on into the twenty-first century.

As it had almost a century earlier, the character of immigration to the United States underwent very important changes in both character and volume. The once European flow of humanity changed to Asian and Latin American. More legal immigrants entered the land in the 1970s, some four million, than had since the era of immigration restriction. This figure says nothing about the many thousands of others who entered illegally. By the decade's end, the annual flow of humanity into the "land of opportunity" was over 700,000. Of these, only 10 percent were European in origin. It should be noted, however, that immigration, once 10 percent of the total population each decade, declined to less than 2 percent in the 1970s.

Life Styles of the 1970s

The traditional American family, the one that most school children of the 1950s read about in the elementary grades, became increasingly hard to find as the 1970s wore on. The family found in *Fun With Dick and Jane* was no longer the sole American norm. Many couples opted not to have children. Widespread use of the reliable and easy-to-use birth con-

trol pill made this choice possible. Although marriage remained the predominant choice, there were other socially accepted options. The fastest growing of these was "living together." By the mid 1980s, unmarried partners living together, and other non-traditional households, constituted 30 percent of all households in the United States. Not all the unwed couples were heterosexual. In urban areas particularly, greater acceptance of gay life-styles led to a substantial increase in homosexual households in the 1970s and 1980s. Even among traditional couples, there were substantial changes. The divorce rate doubled between 1960 and 1980. By the mid-1980s nearly one out of two first marriages ended in divorce. Popular television sitcoms such as *Kate and Allie* replaced *Father Knows Best* in reflecting this new reality.

A 1970s social stereotype, the young urban professional or "yuppie," embraced the new life styles most enthusiastically. Yuppies were the first generation of the baby boom to turn thirty. Many were affluent Americans who, as they became well established professionally, focused on the accumulation of wealth and possessions. Although they did not totally dismiss social issues—feminism and environmentalism, for example—they were primarily concerned with self.

One of their expressions of self concern was the quest for physical fitness. Whether it was skiing, playing tennis, working out at home or in clubs, or jogging, yuppies exercised with great determination. This concern about physical well-being and the environment led to the appeal of health foods, free of chemical additives and pesticide residues. Once they discovered that cigarette smoking was directly related to a host of respiratory problems, heart disease, and cancer, many gave up smoking.

The Yuppie generation also sought to find psychological fulfillment To that end, they became involved in consciousness-raising groups and transcendental meditation. Most often these searches were harmless, but sometimes they became cults like those of the Maharishi Mahesh Yogi or Sun Myung Moon. Sometimes self-improvement turned into selfishness, a type of "therapeutic sensibility." In his thought provoking book, *The Culture of Narcissism: American Life in An Age of Diminishing Expectations*, historian Christopher Lasch maintained, "People [of the 1970s] hunger not for personal salvation, let alone for the restoration of an earlier golden age, but for the feeling, the momentary illusion, of personal well-being, health, and psychic security." Another author simply characterized his contemporaries in the 1970s as the "Me Generation."

Women

Because women in the 1970s had fewer children (less than two by the middle of the decade), they also enjoyed fewer constraints in their life styles. Smaller families, for example, meant that more women were able to enter the job market. In 1950, only 21 percent of wives worked, but by 1980, the figure was over 50 percent. This female labor force included many women with school-age children, some of whom took on part-time, seasonal, or temporary work.

Child care became a big problem for many mothers striving to return to paid employment after the birth of their children. Some women found employment by caring for the children of other working mothers. Safe and licensed child care is still a difficult problem for many working mothers today.

Under Title XI of the 1972 Educational Amendments Act, college sports were required to be funded equally for male and female students. Tremendous growth resulted in women's sports.

Many of the new working women were middle class. The growing service economy required sales, clerical, and office workers. Elementary schools, rapidly expanding to accommodate the baby boom, required more teachers. Others entered the professions, as many more women had been able to obtain college and university education. By 1979, more women were enrolled in college than men. Between 1971 and 1981, the percentage of lawyers and judges who were women grew from 4 percent to 14 percent; the proportion of doctors from 9 percent to 22 percent. In the first half of the 1970s, the proportion of female PhDs awarded just about doubled from 11 to 21 percent. Still, most working women were subjected to economic and job discrimination. At the close of the decade, a working woman made only 60 percent of a working man's wage. Many of these women had to work due to the ever increasing pressures brought on by stagflation and the decline of wages in terms of purchasing power. They tended to view paid labor as a family necessity, rather than fulfilling any personal inclination or individual goal.

Society sent mixed signals to these "new women." In 1972, President Nixon vetoed a bill to provide a nationwide network of day-care centers to assist working mothers. He attacked the "communal approach to child-rearing" and the "family weakening implications" of the legislation. One psychologist in 1972 discussed the "fear of success" demonstrated by 80 percent of the college women in her survey. They had internalized society's continuing view "that competition, success, competence, and intellectual achievement are basically inconsistent with femininity." The resulting "fear of looking aggressive" was a limiting factor in the work world.

With the advent of "sexual liberation" organizations such as Planned Parenthood found an increasing need for their services, such as birth control. By the 1970s, sexual behavior patterns of women became more similar to those of men.

The push for "sexual liberation" and the new emphasis on female sexuality also had diverse consequences. By 1970, surveys among college students showed a substantial rise in premarital sex, especially among women. Magazines, like *Cosmopolitan*, trumpeted the arrival of the independent "Single Girl" who was, above all, "available." Feminists noted that women's role as a "sexual object" seemed to have increased, rather than declined. Sexual competition for marriageable men became a lifelong obsession for many. One article in *Ms* magazine on the sexual revolution commented ruefully, "Women [have] been liberated only from the right to say 'no.'"

By the beginning of the 1970s, the movement for full equality for women had developed a wide-ranging agenda and ideology. Just like the civil rights movement, the women's movement divided into two distinct camps. The moderate faction advocated working to achieve equality through the passage of specific laws. The radical faction wanted to eliminate restrictive gender roles. Both factions, despite their differences, adamantly opposed "sexism." NOW, for example, advocated passage of the Equal Rights Amendment, the establishment of a nation-wide child-care system, enactment of equal oppor-

tunity legislation, and repeal of anti-abortion laws. One historian has noted that the more "revolutionary" radicals "were indeed a vital part of the feminist campaign, if only because they made more moderate demands seem reasonable and legitimate by comparison."

One key issue for the women's movement involved the Equal Rights Amendment. First proposed in 1923, it read, "Equality of rights under the law shall not be denied or abridged by the United States or by any state on account of sex." After years of neglect, NOW resuscitated the amendment. Finally, in 1972, Congress overwhelmingly passed the amendment, and twenty-eight states promptly ratified it. Thereafter, support waned. In 1979, Congress granted its supporters three more years for ratification to take place. The amendment process for the ERA ended in 1982, only three states short of the needed three-fourths. The long and turbulent struggle for passage had pitted women in the professions against those who feared the amendment would endanger protective legislation for non-professional women workers. Other, more conservative women, worried that the amendment would threaten traditional family roles, mandate unisex bathrooms, and require drafting women into the armed forces.

Another broader cause of dissension involved sensitive and private concerns: abortion, marriage, male/female relationships, and homosexuality. "Consciousness-raising" groups sought to make women aware of sexual oppression, including rape and abuse. Some argued that they encouraged "man-hating." "Radicalesbians" argued that "Heterosexual relations locked women into second-class status." But by far the most divisive of all issues emerged following the 7-to-2, 1973 Supreme Court decision of *Roe v. Wade*, protecting a woman's constitutional right to abortion. The majority opinion asserted that "the right to privacy" guaranteed women's freedom of choice, based on the due process clause of the Fourteenth Amendment. Because of the ruling, the number of women having legal abortions greatly increased. Anti-abortion sentiment also increased.

Various religious denominations joined with conservatives and established a "Right to Life" opposition designed to oppose abortion on both legal and moral grounds. The Right to Lifers prevailed on Congress to pass the Hyde Amendment in 1976, forbidding the use of federal Medicaid funds to pay for abortions. This was most damaging to indigent women across the country. Pro-choice factions tried to respond by helping to establish privately funded abortion clinics and agencies to protect all women's right to choose.

Despite setbacks, feminists had made progress. Many joined forces for a massive Strike for Equality on August 26, 1970. Significantly, the Strike marked the fiftieth anniversary of the ratification of the Nineteenth Amendment to the Constitution. Women's groups all across the country established abortion counseling clinics, shelters for battered women, rape crisis centers, and feminist book stores. In 1971, Gloria Steinem and other feminists began to pub-

lish *Ms*, the first national feminist magazine. Feminists succeeded in getting sexist stereotypes eliminated from many textbooks. Such all-male strongholds as the U. S. Military Academy and the great Ivy League institutions opened their doors to women. Colleges offered thousands of women's studies courses. The armed forces integrated women in 1979 (though in non-combat roles), just as they had integrated African Americans in the 1950s.

The Supreme Court issued a number of other important opinions related to sex discrimination. In one, the Court determined that "job-related classifications, based on gender or race, were inherently suspect." In 1976, the Supreme Court decided that, to be constitutional, a policy that engaged in discrimination based on gender had to be "substantially related to an important government objective." Fi-

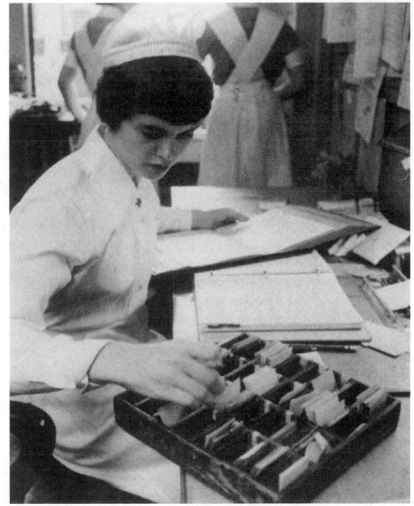

Nursing, teaching and secretarial work traditionally had been jobs for women. Until recently, nurses' salaries did not acknowledge the scientific training necessary for the job. Part of the problem was that work was valued differently according to whether women or men performed the job.

nally, Congress itself took action by passing the Equal Credit Opportunity Act in 1974. Recognizing the significant increase in the number of women in the work force, it allowed women the opportunity to secure bank loans and obtain credit cards on the same terms as men.

Despite these advances, gender discrimination remained, particularly in the workplace. Changing sexual mores led to a substantial increase in single, usually female headed, households. Often these households were African American or Hispanic and, just as often, they were very poor. Although feminists had achieved many successes, they realized that there was much that still needed to be done. By the late 1970s, however, opponents of feminism were uniting under a "pro-family" emblem, and the nation was shifting to a more conservative suspicion of social activism.

African Americans

Lyndon Johnson's vision of a Great Society had included an America in which "every human being had dignity and every worker has a job...education is blind to color and unemployment is unaware of race." Although his programs did not succeed in creating that ideal state, there was a great deal of progress by the end of the 1960s. During the 1960s the median income of black families rose 53 percent, and the proportion of those below the poverty line fell from 55 to 27 percent.

President Nixon denounced many of the Great Society programs as wasteful and eliminated some of them. Despite the position of the president, however, changes stemming from African-American protest as well as major federal programs and efforts of the last several decades could not be entirely undone. Significant social, as well as economic, gains had already been achieved and had become institutionalized within American society. Numerous barriers impeding economic opportunity and advancement were destroyed or seriously weakened. By 1980 there were over 2 million African Americans enrolled in institutions of higher education. Affirmative-action programs and more equitable educational opportunities meant that, by 1976, twice as many African

Americans held white-collar occupations than in 1960.

There were a few different African-American worlds in America by the late 1970s. The upper class of business people and professionals enjoyed their affluence and resented the lack of acceptance they met with from upper-class white society. The middle class, key supporters of civil rights and integration, lived in "gilded ghettos" and struggled to differentiate themselves from the poor in the slums.

The African-American lower classes lived in ghettos from Harlem in New York to Watts in Los Angeles. These neighborhoods included an energetic culture of churches, lodges, lively music, and soul food. But they also were centers of overwhelming problems that America had not yet addressed. By 1986, 45 percent of all African-American children in the United States were born into impoverished female-headed households. Early in 1981, the median income for a lower-class African-American family was $12,674, a little over half of its white counterpart. Even in traditionally structured lower-class families, African-American males increasingly disappeared from the work force of the nation. Profound changes in the economic infrastructure of the United States led to their elimination. The new middle-class and working-class African Americans fled and established new communities or integrated formerly all-white suburbs. A number of the more affluent professionals even returned to the South to the bustling new cities of the Sunbelt.

As great as the advances were for those who departed, the tragedy for those they left behind was equally great. The reasonably steady and well-paid jobs were gone. The best that could be found for those who remained were low paying service occupations, such as a fast-food worker, hospital orderly, or janitor. A once diverse community had become a more uniform community—one populated by "single mothers on welfare, out-of-work men hustling on the streets, drugs, gangs." In one Chicago section, where churches, banks, and stores once flourished "a population of around sixty-six thousand...had exactly one bank, one super market, but...forty-eight state-lottery agents, fifty currency exchanges, and ninety-nine licensed liquor stores and bars."

An insidious problem began to invade the United States in the 1970s in the growing popularity of cocaine. Although it could be found in all places and all levels of society, its use was especially pervasive in the nation's urban ghettos. The passage of strict antidrug laws like the Comprehensive Abuse Drug Act of 1970 did little to ameliorate its deadly consequences in the country's inner cities.

Despite these problems and class divisions, African Americans were still united emotionally by race. The popularity of folk hero Muhammed Ali demonstrates these feelings. Like Jack Johnson, a black boxing champion of an earlier era, Ali flouted the rules of white society. After the Supreme Court reversed his conviction for draft evasion, he regained his title and continued his colorful taunts of his opponents. As an imposing, defiant, triumphant, and charitable black man, Ali represented the aspirations of many African Americans of all classes in the 1970s. As the years went on, he became an icon in the larger society as well.

Native Americans

Perhaps no people in America were more disadvantaged than Native Americans. In 1970, the life expectancy for Native Americans was nearly ten years lower than the national average and the infant mortality rate was twice as great. At least a half million American Indians lived in conditions of abject poverty, comparable to those in the poorest nations of the world. Their homes were often unsanitary, dilapidated, and, all too frequently, abandoned automobiles. Forty percent of all American Indians lived below the poverty level, and their unemployment rate was ten times the nation's average. Disease and alcoholism were rampant on the reservations and among Indians in American cities. Angered by policies of termination and assimilation and inspired by the social activism of other groups in the 1960s, the American Indian began to organize and strike back.

Many tribes began to take legal action against the U. S. government and numerous state governments to regain land, water, hunting, and fishing privileges guaranteed to them by treaty. In one such instance, the Passamaquoddies and the Penobscots of Maine sued in 1972 to recover 12.5 million acres of land they maintained had been seized illegally by the state. In 1980, the Indians settled for 300,000 acres of land and a $27 million tribal trust fund. Earlier, in 1971, various native peoples of Alaska prevailed when they were awarded forty million acres of land and a one billion dollar financial settlement for numerous long-standing claims.

Since they were a relatively small group compared to other minorities, Native Americans could not depend on political clout based on ability to mobilize votes. They had to gain the assistance of repentant whites to achieve any real social or political change. The civil rights movement had sensitized whites to Native American culture. Native Americans were portrayed in more sympathetic ways in films such as *Little Big Man*, on television programs, and even in antipollution commercials that portrayed an Indian's grief at the exploitation of the land. Best selling books such as Dee Brown's *Bury My Hear At Wounded Knee* (1970), criticized historic white mistreatment of Native Americans. *God is Red* (1973) by Vine Deloria, a Sioux, and many other works, celebrated Native American values. Many Native Americans opposed liberal suggestions for job training programs that would have assimilated them into the white economy. They preferred efforts to make reservations more self-sufficient.

The American Indian Movement (AIM), the best known of the Native American protest organizations, staged some of the most dramatic protests. In 1969, they seized Alcatraz Island in San Francisco Bay where they remained until mid-1971. In 1972, they led a demonstration called the "Trail of Broken Treaties," echoing the "Trail of Tears" their ancestors had been forced on over a century earlier. Marching to the nation's capital, the demonstrators captured the offices of the Bureau of Indian Affairs. Their most publicized demonstration occurred in 1973, when two hundred armed Indians took over Wounded Knee, South Dakota. For seventy-one days they occupied the town that had once been the site of the 1890 massacre of the Sioux by the U. S. army cavalry. Shots were fired, and an FBI agent was killed. Some older Native Americans opposed AIM radicalism.

Native Americans stepped up their efforts to re-establish control over their tribal resources and their culture. Richard Nixon demonstrated his sympathy by appointing Indians to important positions in the Bureau of Indian Affairs. He also expanded federal programs in support of Native Americans to encourage greater self-determination. In 1975, the Indian Self-Determination and Cultural Assistance Act took effect. This important legislation gave tribes authority over the various federal programs on their reservations. It also increased their control of reservation schools.

Renewed tribal life, more public awareness of the social and economic status of Native Americans, government willingness to honor treaties, and a new attitude by federal officials were all positive indications of a more promising life and future for the American Indian. These positives did not eliminate the very real problems, such as the high incidence of alcoholism, disease, and high unemployment rates among Native Americans that persisted as the decade ended.

Hispanics

The fastest growing minority group in the 1970s was a mixture of peoples lumped together as Hispanics. Their numbers increased from 9 million in 1970 to 26 million in 1995. This significant increase was due to two factors: immigration and high birth rates. Approximately 45 percent of immigrants to America after 1960 came from the Western Hemisphere. There were also millions of illegal immigrants. This was especially true of Mexicans who, since the middle of the 1960s, crossed over the border hoping to find better lives for themselves and their families. Despite the efforts of the United States to control and curtail this great influx, it continued. Best estimates are that, by the end of the 1970s, the population of Mexican Americans had increased by around 60 percent.

Even though there are many differences in history and customs among Hispanic people, they share some similarities in religion, language, and a fusion of Spanish and Native-American values. These newest of arrivals concentrated in specific places in the country. Thus, in the Southwestern states of Arizona, California, Colorado, New Mexico, and Texas one could travel for hours at a time and see and hear only indications of Mexican-American life and culture. Puerto Ricans and Cubans settled mainly in New York, New Jersey, and Florida.

Just like the other immigrants who had come before them, Hispanics hoped to improve their lot. What they found waiting for them was poverty and discrimination. Many endeavored to retain their native language and traditions, but the language barrier was also an obstacle to educational success. The lack of a good education limited employment to unskilled and semi-skilled occupations, especially in agriculture. Mexican Americans, the largest group, demonstrate this point. Their average educational attainment was under nine years in 1970. As a result, their average income was about 60 percent of that of the rest of the population.

Puerto Ricans, who are American citizens, moved back and forth to mainland America more easily. They tended to settle in urban ghettoes in the Northeast. They entered the cities just as job opportunities were moving to suburban areas. In addition, their inability to speak English, love of large families, and suspicion of bureaucracies hampered their attempts at economic improvement. Almost half had poverty-level incomes, and nearly 40 percent received some form of welfare assistance. By contrast, most of the earlier Cuban refugees from Castro's communist regime were middle class people with a strong entrepreneurial spirit. They tended to be more successful than other Hispanic groups. In 1980, however, the Mariel boatlift brought in 100,000 more Cubans, largely of working class origin. This group encountered more problems than the earlier immigrants.

Whatever its origins, a new social activism energized Hispanic Americans. Younger Mexican Americans adopted a new name for themselves—Chicano. "Chicano" implied a rejection of Anglo society and the more moderate accommodationist Mexican American. One Texas group formed a political party, *La Raza Unida*, in 1970, committed to community control of Mexican-American counties. Some Puerto Ricans turned to militant nationalism, demanding Puerto Rican independence. One group even "oc-

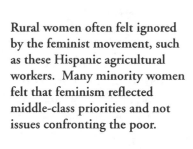

Rural women often felt ignored by the feminist movement, such as these Hispanic agricultural workers. Many minority women felt that feminism reflected middle-class priorities and not issues confronting the poor.

cupied" the Statue of Liberty in 1977 to publicize their demands.

There were also some political gains. In 1981, two major American cities elected Mexican-American mayors: Henry Cisneros in San Antonio and Federico Pena in Denver. Earlier, in 1971, two Mexican Americans were elected state governors: Raul Castro in Arizona and Jerry Apodaca in New Mexico.

Despite these accomplishments, in reality, Hispanics exercised only a small amount of political, economic, or social power. Meanwhile, more Hispanics were entering the United States from Central and South America and the Dominican Republic. Aside from sharing a language and religion, the greatest similarity among these people was poverty. For the nation's second largest minority group, the long struggle to make a place for themselves in the United States was still a formidable task that lay ahead.

Other Americans

Immigration from Asia also increased in the 1970s. Large numbers of people arrived from Korea, the Philippines, and China, as a result of more liberal immigration laws. The Vietnam War and its subsidiary conflicts throughout Indochina led to a wave of refugees, particularly after the fall of South Vietnam

in 1975. In the 1970s most Asian Americans continued to respect traditional values of family loyalty and high achievement. Some Asian Americans, influenced by other militant groups, attempted to create a pan-Asian spirit and a yellow-power movement. The basic cultural differences among the various Asian groups proved too great to surmount and the movement generated little support. Nevertheless, Asian Americans seemed more concerned about equality and less willing to accept conformity than they ever had been before.

In the summer of 1969, New York City police raided a gay Greenwich village bar, the Stonewall Inn. Although such raids had long been commonplace in the United States, this time the bar patrons fought the police. This incident and the civil disobedience that followed led to an era of "gay pride." Gays and lesbians began to "come out of the closet" and join activist organizations demanding an end to discriminatory laws and customs. They achieved some success in decriminalizing sexual acts between consenting adults. Several states repealed anti-sodomy laws. In 1973, the American Psychiatric Association removed homosexuality from its list of mental illnesses. This was only the beginning of a long and continuous struggle.

Traditional white ethnic groups found all this new militancy very unsettling. Continued swings in the business cycle and decline in blue collar jobs increased their unease. Black power movements caused white ethnic expressions of community pride. Bumper stickers began to appear announcing, "Polish power" or "Slovak power," or "Irish power." The enormous popularity of the 1977 television serialization of Alex Haley's *Roots* and the 1978 presentation, *Holocaust*, led many whites as well as African Americans to search for their own origins. Ethnic studies programs spread.

These white ethnics, however, felt threatened when the federal government in the 1970s tried to enforce open housing laws, bus children to integrate schools, and impose racial quotas in business hiring and college admissions. White ethnic groups supported Allan Bakke when he sued the University of California for denying him admission to medical school as a result of reserving places for disadvantaged minorities. In a landmark 1978 decision, the Supreme Court ruled against rigid racial quotas. Demands for "law and order," which African Americans saw as code words for prejudice, appealed to traditional white ethnic groups. As a result of these growing social tensions, many of these white ethnics began to abandon their traditional attachment to the Democratic Party.

TURN TO THE RIGHT

Ethnic groups and yuppies were not the only Americans in the 1970s to attempt a search for a more meaningful existence. Whether it was in the Reverend Sun Myung Moon's Unification Church or the International Society for Krishna Consciousness, the decade was one of religious resurgence. The growth in evangelical Protestant sects like the Southern Baptists and Assemblies of God was particularly impressive. Despite a host of differences between them, these Protestant groups, led by such men as Jerry Falwell and his Moral Majority, shared a core of common beliefs. Among these was a belief that an individual could be "born-again" as a convert to faith; a commitment to a strict moral life ruled by individual piety; and a literal interpretation of the Bible as absolute truth.

Greatly troubled by more liberal attitudes toward divorce, abortion, homosexuality, pornography, the absence of prayer in public schools, and the lack of values in popular culture, they began to engage in political activities. Jerry Falwell, a highly successful radio and television evangelist, sought to use his Moral Majority to create a political base dedicated to "family values" and the American way of life.

But Evangelical Christians were not the only Americans who had moved to the right as the decade came to its end. The old liberal New Deal coalition was in disarray. Taking advantage of society's new mood, the Republicans began cutting into Democratic bulwarks like labor unions, the South, and white ethnic Americans. Furthermore, they had mastered newly developed organizational techniques like political action committees, vehicles for effective fund raising. They also created direct-mail lists and telephone banks. Through these devices, they raised millions of dollars and got voters to turn out for their candidates.

Evangelical Christians politically represented "the human disposition to preserve what we love and to oppose changes which threatened to disrupt accustomed life-patterns." Republican Party conservatives also incorporated "possessive conservatism," which included, in the words of one political scientist, "those who have the most to lose should society undergo rapid social and economic change." Historically, this basic "defense of property rights" has been the essence of what Americans have understood to mean conservative. Added to these in the 1970s was a new respectability for a "philosophical" conservatism that expressed a great reverence for the past.

"Neo-conservative" intellectuals totally disavowed social engineering programs like racial and gender quotas in hiring and school admissions, school busing to achieve racial integration, affirmative action, and the welfare state. They represented a significant defection from New Deal and Great Society activism. They established "think tanks" that reaffirmed their faith in capitalism and individual social mobility and claimed that they believed in equality of opportunity as opposed to government guarantees of equality of outcome. They maintained it was time Americans looked to see what was right rather than wrong about their country. One man more than any capitalized on and popularized the emotional appeal of conservatism. He was the former Governor of California, Ronald Reagan.

The Election of 1980

The problems of the Carter administration intensified as the election of 1980 drew closer. The energy crisis with its staggering increases in costs of oil led to ever rising prices. The continuing Iranian hostage crisis sapped the energies of the president and the nation. The discontent of white ethnics led to their disaffection with the Democrats. Americans, who had begun to turn inward in the decade of the 1970s, as the decade ended, turned increasingly to the right. They turned to tinseltown, to Hollywood, to Ronald Reagan, a candidate who seemed to offer different solutions.

Reagan brought together the various streams of conservative thought. To a nation traumatized by the Vietnam War and the hostage crisis, he promised to restore American "strength and pride." He criticized the supposed excesses of federal government activism and promised major tax cuts in accordance with tax revolts that were spreading across the nation. His personal attributes, magnified by television, included self-confidence, cheerfulness, and, despite his 69 years, the appearance of youthful vigor. He also possessed a unique ability to reduce complex issues to the most simple explanations. In television debates Reagan constantly reminded voters of the "misery index,"—a combination of the unemployment and inflation rate that hovered at 20 percent—and asked, "Are you better off now than you were four years ago?"

The American electorate answered Reagan's question by giving him 51 percent of the vote to Carter's 41 percent. (Seven percent voted for the independent candidacy of a moderate Republican congress man, John Anderson.) The election was hardly a ringing affirmation of support for Reagan. Only 52 percent of those eligible bothered to vote. One eighteen-year-old declared, "I didn't want to be responsible for electing either one." Many merely believed it was "time for a change." Carter left office forlorn and rejected by the American people. He later reestablished his reputation by launching the most notable career of any ex-president as a leader in promoting international peace and in humanitarian activities. In 2002 Carter was awarded the Nobel Peace Prize for his lifetime achievements in these areas. But, in 1981, few regretted his departure. America seemed ready to embrace a new vision of the future.

CONCLUSION

In the decade of the 1970s public faith and confidence in government continued to decline. The revelations in the *Pentagon Papers* about deceptions in the Vietnam War and the corruption and abuses of power shown by the Watergate scandal shook public trust to the core. Although Presidents Ford and Carter demonstrated personal morality, they both lacked the political skills to restore national confidence in government. Internationally, despite a better outlook in the Middle East and restoration of relations with China, the hostage crisis demonstrated to many Americans the decline of American power in the world. Changes in American society based on the ongoing struggle for equal rights continued. The government, however, appeared helpless in coping with major economic problems of lack of growth, unemployment combined with inflation, and a seeming inability to compete in the world economic markets. In the "Me Decade," many Americans also worried that the day of American political and economic power was ending.

Chronology

1968 Richard Nixon elected president

1969 Apollo 11 lands Americans on moon
Nixon begins withdrawal of U. S. troops from
Vietnam; orders secret bombing of Cambodia
"Stonewall Riot" sets in motion gay liberation
movement

1970 Pentagon Pagers published
Nixon implements wage-and-price freeze
"All in the Family" premieres on television,
introducing sharp social commentary

1972 Nixon visits China and the Soviet Union
Congress approves Equal Rights Amendment
Salt I Treaty signed
Break-in discovered at Democratic National
Committee headquarters in Watergate
Eleven Israeli athletes killed in terrorist
attacks at Munich Summer Olympics
Nixon wins landslide re-election
Nixon orders "Christmas bombing" of North
Vietnam

1973 Watergate burglars tried and convicted
Native Americans demonstrate at Wounded Knee
Senate special committee investigates Watergate;
scandal widens
Roe v. Wade decision issued by Supreme Court
Vietnam ceasefire agreement signed;
America withdraws its troops
Yom Kippur War between Arabs and Israel
leads to Arab oil embargo and energy crisis
Vice President Spiro Agnew resigns; Gerald
Ford appointed vice president

1974 House institutes impeachment proceedings
against Nixon
Nixon resigns; Ford becomes president
Ford pardons Nixon for any crimes committed in his
presidency

1975 Government of South Vietnam falls to communists
Khmer Rouge seize power in Cambodia and
begin systematic genocide

1976 Jimmy Carter elected president

1977 Carter pardons Vietnam draft resisters
Panama Canal treaty ratified

1978 Beginning of "stagflation"—high inflation and
interest rates and slow growth
Supreme Court issues Bakke decision against
"reverse" discrimination

1979 Egyptian-Israeli peace settlement, mediated
by Carter, signed at White House
Serious nuclear power accident occurs at
Three Mile Island plant in Pennsylvania
Carter restores full diplomatic relations with
Communist China
Oil prices double
Soviets invade Afghanistan
Iranian militants seize American hostages at
embassy in Teheran

1980 Hostage crisis troubles nation; attempt to
rescue hostages fails
Ronald Reagan elected president

SUGGESTED READINGS

Stephen Ambrose, *Nixon: The Triumph of a Politician, 1962-1972* (1989).

William C. Berman, *America's Right Turn from Nixon to Bush* (1994).

James A. Bill, *The Eagle and the Lion: The Tragedy of American-Iranian Relations* (1988).

Peter G. Bourne, *Jimmy Carter: A Comprehensive Biography* (1997).

Fawn Brodie, *Richard Nixon: The Shaping of His Character* (1981).

Peter N. Carroll, *It Seemed Like Nothing Happened: The Tragedy and Promise of the 1970s* (1990).

William H. Chafe, *Women and Equality: Changing Patterns in American Culture* (1977).

Ronald Dewing, *Wounded Knee: The Meaning and Significance of the Second Incident* (1985).

P.J. Dolan and E. Quinn (eds.), *The Sense of the 70s* (1978).

Martin Duberman, *Stonewall* (1993).

John Dumbrell, *The Carter Presidency: A Reevaluation* (1995).

Marian Faux, *Roe v. Wade* (1988).

L.H. Gann and Peter J.Duignan, *The Hispanics in the United States: A History* (1987).

David Garrow, *Liberty and Sexuality: The Right to Privacy and the Making of Roe v. Wade* (1994).

Paul Gottfried, *The Conservative Movement* (1993).

John R. Greene, *The Limits of Power: The Nixon and Ford Administrations* (1992).

——, *The Presidency of Gerald R. Ford* (1995).

Susan M. Hartmann, *From Margin to Mainstream: Women and Politics Since 1960* (1989).

Joan Hoff, *Nixon Reconsidered* (1994).

Burton I. Kaufmann, *The Presidency of James Earl Carter, Jr.* (1993).

Stanley J. Kutler, *The Wars of Watergate* (1990).

Nicholas Lemann, *The Promised Land: The Great Black Migration and How it Changed America* (1991).

Stanley Lieberson and Mary Water, *From Many Strands: Ethnic and Racial Groups in Contemporary America* (1988).

Matt S. Meier and Feliciano Rivera, eds., *Mexican Americans/American Mexicans* (1993).

Herbert Parmet, *Richard Nixon and His America* (1989).

William B. Quandt, *Camp David* (1987).

David Reimers, *Still the Golden Door: The Third World Comes to America* (1985).

Rosalind Rosenberg, *Divided Lives: American Women in the 20th Century* (1992).

Barry Rubin, *Paved with Good Intentions: The American Experience and Iran* (1983).

Leigh W. Rutledge, *The Gay Decade: From Stonewall to the Present* (1992).

Robert Schulzinger, *Henry Kissinger: Doctor of Diplomacy* (1989).

Ronald Takaki, *Strangers from a Distant Shore: A History of Asian Americans* (1989).

——, *A Different Mirror: A History of Multicultural America* (1993).

Reed Ueda, *Postwar Immigrant America* (1994).

Winifred Wandersee, *On the Move: American Women in the 1970s* (1988).

Theodore H. White, *Breach of Faith* (1975).

Tom Wicker, *One of Us: Richard Nixon and the American Dream* (1991).

Garry Wills, *Nixon Agonistes* (1970).

——, *Under God: Religion and American Politics* (1990).

Bob Woodward and Carl Bernstein, *All the President's Men* (1974).

——, *The Final Days* (1976).

Chapter Twenty-four

IN OUR TIMES:
Reagan to Bush

It was clear and pleasant on that September 11 morning. United Airlines Flight 93, scheduled to depart Newark at 8:01 for San Francisco, took off 40 minutes late. There were only 40 aboard the plane; 15 of them had decided to take that flight at the last minute. There was the usual combination of business and pleasure travelers. One passenger, with a heavy heart, was recovering the remains of a stepson killed in an auto accident on his honeymoon.

At 9:28 four (or three, according to the passengers) Middle Eastern men wearing bandanas hijacked the plane. One claimed to have a bomb strapped to his body. An air-traffic control tape revealed that the pilot yelled, "Get out of here!" This was followed by a breathless terrorist announcing, with bizarre decorum, "Ladies and gentlemen, here, it's the captain. Please sit down. Keep remaining sitting. We have a bomb on board." But the passengers did not passively remain seated. Through more than two dozen in-flight phone calls they learned that three planes had crashed into the World Trade towers and the Pentagon with horrendous consequences. Jeremy Gluck, a former college judo champion, told his wife that there were three other passengers as big as he. Mark Bingham had played on a championship college

rugby team. Tom Burnett, a former high school quarterback, informed his wife that "a group of us" were planning to get control of the plane. Todd Beamer, a baseball and basketball player in college, prayed with a telephone operator he had reached. She heard him say, "Let's roll," at the end of their conversation. A flight attendant told her husband, "They're forcing their way into the cockpit." The passengers seemed to have broken into the cockpit using a food cart as a battering ram. In those final desperate minutes a ferocious struggle took place. At 10:03 the Boeing 757 crashed into thousands of pieces in an old strip mine outside of Shanksville, Pennsylvania. All aboard died, but they had prevented the plane from reaching its destination, the Capitol building or the White House, with further disastrous consequences.

The passengers on Flight 93 were not the only heroes of the 9/11 atrocity. Thousands of fire fighters, police officers, emergency medical technicians, and ordinary people rushed to the twin towers to help. Partially as a result of deadly flaws and failures of communication in their rescue efforts, 343 fire fighters died. One woman, after descending 80 floors, along with dozens of others, found the stairway blocked. A fire fighter broke through an office wall with his ax, locating a way out. "Come this way – move quickly," he shouted, illuminating the path with his flashlight. She and the others made it to the street at 10:24, four minutes before the north tower collapsed. The survivors did not include the firefighter. "He stayed there because there were more people behind us," she recalled.

Mohammed Salman Hamdani, a Muslim Pakistani, was a research technician at Rockefeller University. He had experience as an emergency worker, so he dashed into the towers to assist in the rescue efforts. He was never heard from again. There were insulting rumors about his disappearance and loyalty to America that were dispelled by the recovery of his remains.

The events of 9/11 penetrated the consciousness of Americans who had a sense of invulnerability. Although, "we all know that we are going to die," one observer noted, "Americans see suffering and death as aberrations." The 9/11 catastrophe, "presented us with this massive reminder of death, and how unpredictable, uncontrollable and arbitrary death can be," a social psychologist commented. The public saw the ghastly details on television: the towers collapsing, the people jumping, the billows of smoke, and felt it personally. "Everybody felt that it had happened to them." So the stories of heroism were a balm to wounded souls. The people on Flight 93 quickly acted after they learned about "the unthinkable." The son of one of the passengers said, "I think it is a message to the world that the American spirit is alive and kicking."

THE REAGAN REVOLUTION

Ronald Reagan and the "Moral Majority"

When Ronald Reagan took office in January 1981 he was the oldest man ever to be elected president, turning 70 a few weeks later. Despite this, he always appeared to be vigorous and dynamic. He was a talented public speaker with a carefully crafted image, particularly suited to the demands of television.

In a variety of ways Ronald Reagan's ascent to the White House was a reflection of those elements in American society who had supported him, especially the "Moral Majority." The son of a devout mother, active in the Disciples of Christ church, and an alcoholic father, Reagan spent his formative years in the small town of Dixon, Illinois. He went to Eureka College, near Peoria, Illinois, and from there to Des Moines, Iowa, where he worked as a sportscaster. In 1937, he embarked on his Hollywood career, starring in fifty-four moderately successful films. Perhaps his best known role was in *Knute Rockne, All American* (1940). He played the relatively small role of George Gipp, a Notre Dame football player whose death inspired Rockne in the film to implore his team to "win one for the gipper."

Reagan became far more successful, beginning in 1954, as the television spokesperson for General Electric. This fork in his life coincided with his political shift from a New Deal enthusiast to a right-wing conservative. This move was foreshadowed by his strong anti-Communist actions as head of the Screen Actors' Guild after World War II.

Reagan was finally fully embraced by conservatives after his 1964 speech on behalf of Republican presidential hopeful, Barry Goldwater. Sensing his great political potential, a group of wealthy and well-placed Californians catapulted Reagan into the governor's office in 1966. While the governor of California, an office he held for two terms, Reagan continued to serve as a popular spokesperson for conservative ideas, although his actions as governor were far more pragmatic. Narrowly defeated by Gerald Ford for the party's presidential nomination in 1976, he was their clear choice four years later.

Reagan received the backing of those conservative elements who historically opposed any government regulation of business and finance and also won the favor of the "moral majority." These Christian rightists were attracted by Reagan's "sacramental vision" of America. "God's unique relation to America was the central chord from which all else followed," according to one historian.

Even those who opposed Reagan's ideas and policies often found themselves attracted to his engaging public persona. In March 1981, Reagan was shot departing from a D. C. hotel after delivering a speech. The lone gunman, John Hinckley, was a deranged young man whose attempt failed. Not only did the

Secret service agents rush an assailant who fired six shots at President Reagan as he was leaving the Washington Hilton on March 30. This photo released by the White House shows the door on the presidential limousine being closed (right) after Reagan was pushed in, and Press Secretary James Brady and patrolman Thomas Delahanty on the ground after being hit by gunfire.

president survive, he gained additional public sympathy for showing great bravery under fire. He was able to walk into the hospital on his own and joke to the doctors, "Please tell me you're all Republicans." Later he sent a note from his hospital bed to his wife, Nancy: "Honey, I forgot to duck." James Brady, his press secretary, was more seriously injured, suffering permanent disability. This led Brady and his wife, Sarah, to become gun-control activists.

Reagan not only survived the physical attack, he always seemed to land on his feet even when things went wrong. His ability to evade criticism for the blunders of his administration led some observers to call him the "Teflon president."

Reaganomics

The conservative forces that backed Reagan were bound together by their shared hostility to the federal government's regulatory and taxing power. Thus, after only six days in office, the new president eliminated all allocation and price controls on oil. By

March, federal payrolls had been considerably reduced. The new cabinet appointments were conservatives like the anti-regulatory activist, Secretary of the Interior James Watt. Funds were to be cut from all federal agencies except the Defense Department. He even attempted to abolish the Departments of Energy and Education.

The proposed budget cuts of some $40 billion from domestic programs like Medicare and Medicaid, urban aid, food stamps, school lunches, and welfare assistance for the poor were only part of a larger economic program known as supply-side economics. Essentially grounded in the classical economic doctrine of laissez faire, the theory held that a reduction in taxes would increase supply by fostering production. This would stimulate the necessary investment and savings needed to support business development. Reagan fully embraced the supply-side theory and offered a bold three-year tax rate reduction of 30 percent on corporate and individual taxes.

On August 13, 1981, the Economic Recovery Tax Act became law. The bill slashed corporate and

Nancy Reagan looks at her husband, Ronald Reagan, as he takes the oath of office as 40th President of the U. S.

personal income taxes. The act lowered the maximum tax on all income from about 70 percent to around 50 percent. Taxes paid on all profitable investments, called capital gains, were reduced from 28 percent to 20 percent. The wealthiest Americans received a tremendous boon from the law that eliminated the distinction between unearned versus earned income. Such changes were definitely in line with the thoughts of conservative writers, one of whom had written, "A successful economy depends on the proliferation of the rich."

Deregulation

Another thrust of the Reagan administration's economic plan was to hasten the trend toward deregulation that had begun under President Carter. In fact, not only did the new president accelerate deregulation, he took it into entirely new arenas, including transportation and communications, banking, and the savings-and-loan industry. Reagan's conservative appointees to the Environmental Protection Agency, the Consumer Product Safety Commission, and the Occupational Safety and Health Administration curtailed or eliminated hundreds of regulations designed to protect the American public. This zeal even carried over into cabinet departments like the Department of the Interior. James Watt, Secretary of the Interior, was a leader of the anti-environmental group, the Sagebrush Rebellion. He opened up coastal waters, forest lands, and federal wilderness areas for private development.

Military Buildup and the Strategic Defense Initiative

While campaigning for the presidency in 1980, Ronald Reagan had charged that United States military capability had been greatly weakened. President Carter's seeming inability to resolve the Iranian hostage crisis reinforced that perspective. While there were substantial budget cuts in domestic programs, they would not extend into defense expenditures. The Pentagon budget, under Reagan, ballooned from $171 billion in 1981 to over $300 billion by 1985.

An emphasis on nuclear weaponry was a major thrust in this buildup of America's military strength. The president proposed to close the so-called "window of vulnerability" by greatly enlarging the nation's nuclear strike force. Multiple-warhead MX missiles housed in permanent silos were located in the western states. Pershing II missiles, along with Cruise missiles, were deployed in Western Europe, not far from the borders of the Soviet Union. In addition, the president strongly advocated building a hundred new B-1 bombers.

The development of a mentality that maintained that the country could fight and survive nuclear war accompanied the massive increase in weaponry. Less than a year into his presidency, Reagan approved a secret plan for the United States "to prevail in a protracted nuclear war." A "National Security Decision Document" charted the plan. For the first time, the government of the United States endorsed the idea that, "a global nuclear war [could] be won." The president believed it was "ridiculous" to think that a nuclear conflict meant mutual destruction. Some Reagan advisors asserted that humanity could survive such a conflict because "ants eventually build another hill." As long as there were enough shovels, Americans could dig their own holes in the dirt.

Some fearful people began organizing a political campaign to achieve a verifiable freeze on the manufacture and deployment of nuclear weapons between the world's superpowers. Early in 1982 a number of communities ratified freeze resolutions. A massive demonstration that summer in New York City's Central Park followed. By year's end nine states had adopted freeze resolutions.

Mr. Reagan became a strong believer in the Strategic Defense Initiative, popularly known as "Star Wars." The president claimed that an impregnable shield composed of X-ray lasers could be designed to protect the United States from Soviet launched missiles. Some scientists, like Edward Teller, father of the hydrogen bomb, shared this view. Reagan began to pressure Congress for the necessary moneys beginning in March of 1983. Congress appropriated well over $17 billion for the required research, spanning the next six years. There were critics who questioned the effectiveness of such a system. Many others maintained that the only sure way of achieving international security and preventing a nuclear holocaust was to arrive at an arms control agreement.

Economic and Social Consequences

An attack on inflation complemented Reaganomics and the massive military buildup. The Federal Reserve Board led the way by increasing the discount rate significantly. This bold strategy, along with a major decrease in international oil prices, worked. By 1983 the inflation rate had dropped to around 4 percent where it was to remain.

On the other hand, high interest rates, while they stemmed the tide of inflation, inflicted hardship on the nation's poor and minorities. The old industrial core of the country—the Midwest and the Northeast—was especially hard hit. In large part this was due to a decreased demand for American products abroad. High U. S. interest rates made American goods too expensive to buy. An increase in imports matched the decline in exports. As more people purchased Japanese automobiles and electric equipment, a major U. S. trade deficit resulted. In 1981, the gap between exports and imports stood at $31 billion. By 1984 it had increased to $111 billion. Thus the industrial infrastructure of the United States largely completed at the end of the nineteenth century was not only obsolete but confronted with increasing foreign competition and decreasing exports. During Reagan's presidency, the United States went from being the world's largest creditor nation to being the world's largest debtor nation.

Even the nation's agricultural sector was hurt. The fall in exports adversely effected staple crops like corn and wheat. Farm foreclosures resulted. Many Americans lost homes and land that their families had managed for generations. The phenomena was so common in the 1980s that Hollywood films depicted their plight. In 1984, two films, *Country* and *Places in the Heart*, portrayed the struggle of the American farmer. Popular entertainers, especially musicians like Willie Nelson and John Mellencamp, established Farm Aid in an attempt to raise funds for the rapidly disappearing small farmer.

On the other hand, increases in defense spending, especially in Sun Belt states, stimulated tremendous prosperity. Defense contracts in the Reagan years reflected a major shift in the government's priorities, away from "human" expenditures and into defense expenditures.

By 1983, the "Reagan recession" was over. The inflation rate continued to hold steady at 4 percent and the unemployment rate dropped from an 11 percent high to a 7.5 percent low. The recovery resulted from lower oil prices, coupled with an increase in world trade. Furthermore, the recovery was very selective. The West Coast and Sun Belt regions prospered, but the old industrial heartland continued its decline. The rich grew much richer and the poor much poorer. Hordes of homeless Americans became the grim symbol of an administration that seemed to pamper the rich and punish the poor. The recovery did not create new industrial jobs, stem the decline of the dollar, address the federal deficit that reached a record high of $200 billion by 1986, or correct the imbalance of trade.

Women in High Places

Many women criticized Reagan. If, in fact, only women had voted, Reagan might not have won the election in 1980. Some women objected strongly to his conservative positions in opposition to the Equal Rights Amendment and abortion rights. Although conservatives were not able to reverse *Roe v. Wade*, they made the ERA, which Reagan never supported, a powerful symbolic threat to traditional family values. As a result of well-organized conservative op-

position, despite the congressional time extension to 1982, the Equal Rights Amendment failed to become the law of the land.

By 1983, other variables contributed to the administration's "gender gap." These included budget cuts to education, health, and social welfare programs that struck most heavily at working women and children, including slashing moneys for food stamps and school meals. Occupational segregation persisted. By 1985, 80 percent of all women in the workforce were trapped in low-paying occupations like grade-school teaching, clerking, and waitressing.

Despite this lurch to the right on women's issues, Ronald Reagan appointed more women to high-level government positions than any previous president in American history. Most of them, such as Jeane Kirkpatrick, Reagan's U.S. representative to the United Nations, shared his conservative convictions.

The president's most historic appointment was to the Supreme Court. On July 7, 1981, Reagan announced that he had found "a person for all seasons," Sandra Day O'Connor, the first woman ever appointed to the Supreme Court. Although known for her fundamentally conservative viewpoints, O'Connor did support the Equal Rights Amendment and abortion rights. Though some conservative Republicans did not support her nomination, she was easily confirmed by the Senate.

A native of Arizona and graduate of Stanford University, O'Connor led the life of a rather typical American woman. A happily married mother of three sons, she had faced employment discrimination and the difficulties of juggling family and career. For a time she ran her own law firm when she found it difficult to secure a position in Phoenix. She eventually became active in Republican politics and from there was appointed assistant attorney general for Arizona. From 1979 until her appointment to the Supreme Court, O'Connor served as a judge in the Arizona Court of Appeals.

In her early years on the Court, Sandra Day O'Connor remained close to the conservative faction of that body. Yet, she was not hesitant to chart her own course and in time moved to a more centrist position ideologically. She continued, however, to believe that the rights of states required protection from federal power and that the Court should avoid activism in setting social policy.

RONALD REAGAN CONFRONTS THE WORLD

Part of Ronald Reagan's appeal in the 1980 election was the assertion that the United States needed to re-establish its rightful role in the international arena. He saw the United States as besieged by evil, "whereby the nation's chosenness stood against the powers of darkness." In March 1983, Reagan characterized the Soviet Union as "an evil empire." His first term in office was a decided turn away from the Carter administration's emphasis on human rights and the Nixon and Ford administration's policy of détente. Reagan argued that U. S. military strength had fallen dangerously behind the Soviets. "A window of vulnerability" existed because of nuclear armaments agreements like SALT I.

Although the chairman of the Joint Chiefs of Staff strongly rejected this "window of vulnerability" claim, the government doubled defense expenditures between 1981-84 from $130 billion to $260 billion. Reagan charged that the Soviet Union was actively sponsoring world terrorism. He also tried to prevent sophisticated technical equipment from entering the Soviet Union via NATO nations. In addition, he imposed economic sanctions on Poland after the government crushed the independent labor organization, Solidarity. The right to intervene anywhere in the world to combat communism became known as the "Reagan Doctrine." Thus the United States supported anti-government elements in Afghanistan and Nicaragua, two nations dependent on or directly under the influence of the Soviets.

The Middle East

Except for the Soviet invasion of Afghanistan, the model of the "evil empire" did little to explain the complexities in the Middle East. Here, the Arab-Israeli conflict, terrorism, and nationalism were far more significant than communism.

In the troubled nation of Lebanon, for example, Muslims killed Christians. The Palestine Liberation Organization (PLO) intensified its raids against the state of Israel. Everywhere illusive Islamic terrorist groups attacked Israel and her Western allies. Throughout the region, fanatics bombed public facilities, hijacked ships and planes, and kidnapped innocent victims. Reagan placed blame on the Soviet Union, which had established a strong military relationship with Syria. Syria, in turn, gave major military and economic support to Yasser Arafat and the PLO. The PLO headquartered themselves in Lebanon and from here launched their attacks against Israel. In response, Israel invaded Lebanon in 1982. An international contingent of troops remained after the state of Israel removed her troops. The troops struggled to maintain the uneasy peace.

They were less than successful, especially after terrorists bombed the U.S. embassy in early 1983, killing sixteen Americans. Reagan ordered a naval task force to the Lebanese coast. When the terrorists continued their attacks, the president ordered heavy artillery to fire into the hillsides surrounding the city of Beirut. But the militants won in the end. In October 1983, a suicide terrorist drove a bomb-laden truck into the U.S. marine headquarters causing the death of 241 Americans. Congress threatened to enforce the War Powers Act of 1973 and Reagan, under pressure, withdrew the remaining troops. The best he could do was to redeploy them on naval vessels situated throughout the Mediterranean Sea. In contrast to the way the hostage-taking in Iran destroyed Carter, Reagan's popularity was untouched by this appalling disaster. America's retreat may well have emboldened later terrorists.

Elsewhere trouble brewed in the Persian Gulf where Iran and Iraq had gone to war in 1980. Using third parties, the Reagan administration supplied both sides with money and weapons. The objective was clear—prevent either country from becoming dominant and assure adequate oil supplies for the United States. By 1986, U.S. warships were actually escorting and protecting oil tankers located in the Gulf. U.S. interests in the region increased when the government began to supply the Saudi Arabians with sophisticated military technology.

Libyan ruler, Moamar Qaddafi, was also tied to terrorist activities, specifically the 1986 bombing of a West Berlin disco in which an American soldier was killed and scores of others seriously wounded. Reagan ordered a military reprisal. American planes bombed several Libyan targets, including Qaddafi's quarters. As a result, one of his children was killed. Despite the reprisal, Qaddafi remained in power. Reagan demanded that pressure on him continue in the form of political and economic isolation. These demands increased after the explosion of an airliner over Lockerbie, Scotland in late 1988. This unjustifiable attack, linked to the Libyan government, caused the death of 250 innocent passengers.

Central America

In the Western Hemisphere, closer to home, issues seemed clearer to Reagan. He believed he could prevent the rise of another Castro regime by vigorously implementing the Reagan Doctrine. U.N. ambassador, Jeane Kirkpatrick, announced early in 1981, "Central America is the most important place in the world for the United States today." The Reagan administration hoped to re-establish American dominance in the region.

Consistent with his economic philosophy at home, the president attempted to rebuild relationships and revitalize nations through what he called "the magic of the marketplace." Unfortunately, the Reagan administration had very little understanding of the region's history or contemporary realities. From 1980 to 1983, the United States government pumped more military aid into the region than had been given in the thirty preceding years.

Military action often followed military aid, as in the tiny southern Caribbean island of Grenada. There, the Prime Minister led a "People's Revolutionary Government" with links to Cuba and Eastern bloc Communist nations. The government violated human rights, became very militarized, and refused to schedule elections. Neighboring Carib-

U. S. Marines walk down a street of Greenville, Grenada after landing near the town.

bean governments became alarmed, especially after the government fell to an even more radical group and Cubans began building an airport. They formally requested that the United States intervene. Using the pretext of needing to protect American medical students, Reagan was only too happy to comply. In 1983, just two days after the marine disaster in Lebanon, U. S. soldiers invaded Grenada. They met with little opposition and restored order quickly. With the installation of a pro-American government, Reagan announced that the "brutal gang of thugs were gone" and that the U.S. "Vietnam syndrome" had ended.

The situation in El Salvador was more complicated. The United States supported an "authoritarian" pro-American regime, engaged in a military struggle with leftist rebel insurgents. The U.S. military trained Salvadoran soldiers and massive sums of economic assistance arrived to prevent a social revolution. Unfortunately, tortures and assassinations resulted, including the murder of a Roman Catholic archbishop. Finally, in 1984, a political moderate was elected president. But the bloodshed continued. Thousands of Salvadorans lost their lives, and well over 300,000 entered the United States, many as illegal aliens.

The events in Nicaragua were most troublesome. In 1979, Jimmy Carter had extended financial aid to revolutionaries, called Sandinistas, after they toppled a brutal dictatorship. Reagan charged that the new regime was attempting to transform Nicaragua into a Castro-like state under Soviet control. The CIA financed and organized a resistance guerrilla force called the contras. They based their operations in nearby countries and carried out various acts of sabotage in Nicaragua. Some Americans worried that Nicaragua might become the next Vietnam. Congress responded in 1982 and 1984 by passing laws forbidding the CIA to supply the rebels with either direct or indirect military assistance. Only humanitarian aid was now legal.

The Iran-Contra Scandal

The administration vehemently opposed this act of Congress. Some CIA officials and other administra-

Lt. Col. Oliver North takes the oath before the House Foreign Affairs Committee. North invoked the Fifth Amendment and refused to answer any questions in the Iran arms-contra aid hearing.

tion members thought they had found a way around it by late 1985. Eventually exposed in 1987, the scheme known as the Iran-Contra affair was the most damaging of the many Reagan presidency scandals.

The plot aimed to arm the contras and gain the release of American hostages held in Lebanon. These goals seemed possible to achieve as a result of the war between Iran and Iraq. Iraq was receiving weapons from the Soviet Union, as well as other nations. Iran, on the other hand, was finding foreign weapon procurement more difficult as a result of its hatred of the United States. Shady Israeli arms' dealers convinced Robert McFarlane, head of the National Security Council and his aide, Lieutenant Colonel Oliver North, that if America sold arms to Iranian "moderates," they could facilitate the release of American hostages. The profits from the sales were funneled to the Nicaraguan contras who could purchase weapons to overthrow the Sandinistas.

By November 1986, American newspapers began to report accounts of the plan. Four congressional committees eventually examined the evidence. An Independent Counsel was appointed.

The nation, watching on television, learned that the National Security Council and the Central Intelligence Agency had acted without the approval or knowledge of Congress. Furthermore, they had lied to Congress about the nature of their secret operations. President Reagan called the whole story, "utterly false," and added, "We did not—repeat—did not trade weapons or anything else for hostages." The average American never really seemed to understand the significance of the charges or followed their intricacies.

Robert McFarlane, Oliver North, and five other conspirators were found guilty and given prison sentences. North's conviction was subsequently reversed on a legal technicality, and President George Bush pardoned six others in 1992, as he was leaving office. North, who had become a hero of the right wing, claimed to be vindicated and never admitted any wrong-doing. On the witness stand, in the summer of 1987, he stated, "I saw the idea of using the Ayatollah Khomeini's money to support the Nicaraguan freedom fighters as a good one...I don't think it was wrong. I think it was a neat idea." Later, North established a very profitable publishing and public-speaking career. In 1991, he lost a close election for U.S. Senator from Virginia. In 1994 the independent prosecutor, Lawrence Welsh, issued a final report. He concluded that President Reagan had "knowingly participated or at least acquiesced in

the efforts" of his aides to cover up the affair. By then no one cared. The cover-up had been successful.

THE ELECTION OF 1984

With the election year of 1984 fast approaching, criticisms mounted about the immense foreign-trade gap and an unprecedented budget deficit. The administration's nuclear arms buildup alarmed many Americans. They feared it greatly increased the likelihood of a nuclear confrontation with the Soviet Union. Public opinion polls indicated that an overwhelming majority of Americans wanted a U.S./Soviet nuclear freeze agreement. The president seemed to make no effort to improve relations with the Soviet Union in his first term of office.

Re-election strategists were also well aware that a majority of the nation's minorities and women did not favor the president—that there existed a so-called "gender gap." The active opposition of organized labor was another problem. In fact, the 1980s had been a difficult decade for labor. Reagan had appointed anti-labor people to the National Labor Relations Board. Most dramatically, the president single-handedly destroyed the Professional Air Traf-

Geraldine Ferraro became the first woman nominated for the office of vice president when she was picked as a running mate by the 1984 Democratic presidential candidate Walter Mondale. Here she is seen campaigning with Senator Paul Simon of Illinois.

fic Controllers Organization during their 1981 strike. This action was a major setback to the labor movement, signalling a significant change in government policy towards unions

If the Reagan-Bush ticket seemed to have problems in 1984, the Democratic Party was in even more serious difficulty. As the year progressed, the Gross Domestic Product (GDP) continued to rise and unemployment continued to fall. Inflation remained at 4 percent, a fourteen-year low. Unlike the Reagan and Bush supporters, who remained united behind their candidates, the Democrats were in a state of disarray, fragmented into special interest groups. Few Americans seemed to believe the Democrats represented America as a whole.

Former Vice President Walter Mondale, chosen as the Democratic candidate, proposed to revitalize the social programs dismantled by Reagan in his first term of office. Mondale's most dramatic action was his choice of New York congresswoman, Geraldine Ferraro, as his vice presidential running mate. Ferraro was the first woman ever selected as a candidate for a major-party presidential ticket. This choice was both lauded and condemned.

Although Mondale raised important issues throughout the campaign, such as the armaments race and the mounting federal deficit, he was doomed to failure. Reagan and Bush barely acknowledged their opponents. Instead they relied on the president's popularity and slogans like "America is Back," and "It's Morning in America." The Republicans won a landslide victory. They carried every state but Minnesota and the District of Columbia. The 59 percent who voted for Reagan included many traditional Democrats, especially blue-collar wage-earners. Even the "gender-gap" vanished as 54 percent of the women's vote went to the Republicans. The landslide was largely a personal victory for Reagan, as the Democrats actually gained a Senate seat and retained their control over the House of Representatives.

Many Reagan followers viewed the 1984 election as the triumphant beginning of a conservative era. Few could have predicted the unprecedented changes that would revolutionize the world and America's role within it. The 1984 election was the final one of the cold war era.

FOREIGN POLICY IN THE SECOND TERM

The greatest fear people had about Ronald Reagan in 1981 was that he might precipitate a nuclear confrontation with the Soviet Union. That fear began to lessen when, during the first few weeks of his second term, Reagan abruptly changed his course on arms limitations talks and called for their resumption. The death of the old-fashioned Communist, Leonid Brezhnev, precipitated monumental changes. The president invited Mikhail Gorbachev, who had gained power after a brief interval, for a visit to the United States.

Reagan and Gorbachev ultimately met in Geneva in 1985, where they openly argued with each other. Despite important differences, the two men began to develop a friendship. It may well have begun when the Soviet leader expressed interest in Hollywood and American movies.

Despite his lifelong Communist affiliation and education, Gorbachev was younger and different from previous leaders of his nation. He was an advocate of change who opened up political discussion and encouraged criticisms of Soviet politics and society. Returning from Geneva, Gorbachev announced two new revolutionary programs of reform in economics and politics. These were called *glasnost* (openness) and *perestroika* (restructuring). This new kind of Soviet leader—worldly, charismatic, and clever—appealed to the American public who responded with an outburst of "Gorbymania."

Gorbachev realized that the Soviet economy was in serious difficulty and would benefit from a reduction of armaments spending. At a Washington, D.C. summit held in December of 1987, the two men signed the Intermediate Nuclear Force Agreement (INF). It stipulated a reduction in medium and short range nuclear missiles and their removal from Europe. The treaty also provided for mutual on-site inspections and helped pave the way for Ronald Reagan's historic visit to the "evil empire" in 1988. By this time it was also politically easier for the president to travel to Moscow because the most ideologically conservative members of his administration were gone. In addition, the Soviets withdrew their forces from their ill-fated invasion of Afghanistan, eliminating another important source of contention between the two super powers.

UNSOLVED PROBLEMS

Any meaningful and comprehensive assessment of the Reagan presidency must allow for the passage of some additional time. At present, it seems that Ronald Reagan was not able to muster the full power of his amazing personal popularity to achieve repudiation of the fundamental economic, political, and social programs established by the New Deal. However, because the American people so embraced Reagan, the man, he was able to lift their morale at this crucial juncture in the American experience. Perhaps that was and will remain his most significant contribution. If Americans could feel better about themselves and their country, they could step forward and learn to confront a world filled with enormous opportunities and enormous risks. Often this would mean grappling with challenges to traditional values and lifestyles.

The Culture of Wealth

When Ronald Reagan left office, he described America as, "More prosperous, more secure and happier than it was eight years ago." It was undoubtedly true for those who made the great fortunes celebrated during a decade in which 100,000 new millionaires arose each year.

"Greed is not a bad thing. You shouldn't feel guilty," financier Ivan Boesky announced. As Reagan took office, ABC launched a successful new show, *Dynasty*, dedicated to the same idea. *Dallas*, the prime time soap opera that glamorized the greed of the superrich, was the number one rated show. Madonna's hit proclaimed her to be a "Material Girl."

Baby boomers, known as "yuppies" (young urban professionals), pursued the good life and frenzied consumption. Not since the Gilded Age of the late nineteenth century had conspicuous consumption been so openly exhibited.

The concentration of wealth continued as the income of the richest 20 percent continued to grow and the number of billionaires climbed from 13 to 51. Many of the great fortunes came from Wall Street speculation, "corporate raiders," and "junk" bond dealers. At the same time, however, the post World War II trend of increased economic equality was reversed. The yearly earnings of the bottom 20 percent fell, and poverty increased. By the end of the decade, even some of the beneficiaries of the financial excesses began to suffer its consequences. Ivan Boesky, who had so boldly endorsed greed, was convicted of insider trading, sentenced to prison, and fined $100 million. Serious problems still facing American society remained untouched.

AIDS

Throughout most of the twentieth century Americans struggled with the social problem of sexually transmitted diseases. Moral indignation, matched by public apathy, ill-prepared them for a perplexing, new disease, first discovered in cities like New York, Los Angeles, and San Francisco. First documented in 1981, it was called AIDS (acquired immune deficiency syndrome). Homosexual men in these metropolitan centers began to die from rare varieties of cancer and pneumonia. By 1983, other affected groups included recipients of blood transfusions, hemophiliacs, and intravenous drug users.

Ignored and poorly researched, it was initially labeled the "gay" plague because the preponderance of the early victims in America were homosexual men. Some 21,000 Americans died before the larger society really took notice. Subsequent research revealed definitively that the disease was a threat to all, not just select groups. A deadly HIV virus, transmitted through semen or blood, caused the disease. That full-blown AIDS might not develop for as long as ten years after the initial HIV infection was most ominous. Nonetheless, almost all those initially infected died.

Unfortunately, especially for those sufferers, the discovery of AIDS coincided with countervailing forces of the 1980s. These forces included the election of President Reagan and his conservative agenda,

I AM GAY & I VOTE

GAYS ARE HERE AGAIN

GCDM GAY COALITION DES MOINES

WE EVER

A coalition of gay and lesbian activists gather for a parade in downtown Des Moines June 25, 1983, to kick-off the start of National Gay and Lesbian Pride Week.

coupled with a new wave of Christian fundamentalism. Because it was so closely identified with male homosexuals in the United States, not only was the disease neglected or ignored, it caused a serious setback for the modern Gay Liberation Movement.

The 1969 Stonewall incident had helped promote homosexual unity. The gay community united to educate the larger society about their plight, including job discrimination and police harassment. An expanded base of openly gay citizens provided a stronger political base for addressing various forms of discrimination and oppression. By 1992, there were some 1,580 gay and lesbian organizations across the country. These organizations included student groups, political groups, and activists' groups. This increased visibility, along with AIDS, made them a target of the "new right" and moral majority, both of

whom had played an important role in Reagan's victory.

Responding to this segment of its political base, the Reagan administration equated homosexuality with disease, and they denied any "self-professed homosexual" entry into the country. White House Director of Communications, Patrick Buchanan, stated homosexuals had "declared war on nature, and now nature is extracting an awful retribution." Evangelical minister Jerry Falwell told his faithful to "stop gays DEAD in their perverted tracks."

As the number of AIDS victims mounted, the gay community increased the momentum of its organizational and political activity. The Gay Men's Health Crisis was established in New York City in 1981. Volunteers raised money for research and education. They cared for the sick and dying and lobbied actively for federal funds to find a cure for AIDS.

Gay communities in cities across the United States also took up the cause, even though the White House largely ignored them. Only C. Everett Koop, Surgeon General of the United States, chose to become involved. He advocated education about the disease and comprehensive sex education in the nation's schools, including information about the use of condoms. American communities and school boards bitterly divided over the course of action to be taken on these delicate issues of sexual behavior and sexually transmitted disease.

Nonetheless, the movement went forward. On October 11, 1987, the largest ever gay-rights demonstration in American history took place. On that day, some 250,000 lesbians, homosexual men, and their supporters paraded in the streets of the nation's capital. They mourned those who had died of AIDS. But they also held a huge marriage ceremony to mock laws that forbade same sex marriages. Then, they staged a mass civil disobedience demonstration at the Supreme Court to protest a 1986 decision that had upheld state sodomy laws.

The societal tide began to turn only when Americans started to realize that they, too, could be afflicted with the HIV virus. Revelations that prominent movie stars and athletes were infected added significantly to this realization. The list of famous victims included movie actor Rock Hudson, who had concealed his homosexuality; tennis star Arthur Ashe, infected during heart surgery; and basketball great Ervin (Magic) Johnson, whose disease came from heterosexual contact. Public education and political efforts then intensified.

Eventually modern medical research did develop treatment in the form of new drugs like AZT. Even when more important breakthroughs occurred in the late 1990s like Protease inhibitors, AIDS was still without a cure. In 1994, the Center for Disease Control and Prevention reported that, "Since 1993, AIDS has been the leading cause of death among Americans 25-44 years of age." By the late 1990s, a "cocktail" of many different drugs was showing dramatic results in cutting the death rate among HIV-infected individuals. Unfortunately, this treatment was extremely expensive and very complicated. While the death rate plummeted for educated and affluent homosexuals, it continued to rise in poor, particularly African American, communities and reached epidemic proportions in less developed areas of the world in Africa and elsewhere.

Drugs and Crime

Drug trafficking and drug addiction reached startling new proportions, especially as the 1980s progressed. Significant increases in violent crime coincided with the arrival of crack, a smokable form of cocaine. An extremely potent drug, crack provided its users with an almost instant high, reaching the brain within eight seconds. However, because its effects are extremely short-lived and more intense than powder cocaine, there is a much greater need for repeated use.

Crack first hit the streets of the United States in 1985, causing violent crimes to rise significantly. The enormous demand for drugs, crack in particular, gave birth to a multi-billion dollar industry within the country. Well-organized and financed organizations like the Medellin cartel of Colombia arose to take advantage of the new opportunities. Crack induced violent behavior. Studies conducted during the decade revealed that well over half the males arrested in the country's largest cities, tested positive for cocaine. Increased drug use also helped to spread AIDS. People under the influence of potent drugs were much less likely to engage in safe sex. And intravenous drug addicts, by sharing their dirty needles, also hastened the spread of the epidemic.

The new generation of drug dealers in the nation's inner cities was especially disturbing. Often young minority males were willing to risk incarceration or death to gain tremendous profits in the business. Consequently, for many young Americans crack dealing became "a rational career choice," just like the booze runners of the Prohibition era. They were the victims, according to one observer, of "the devastating consequences for inner-city residents of the Reagan-Bush era's domestic spending policies, and...the collapse of opportunity during the 1980s for those at the bottom of the economic heap—especially poor blacks."

Homeless Americans

Another sad development during the Reagan years occurred in the urban housing market, coupled with failed government housing policies. A rent squeeze affected a majority of urban tenants who paid rents exceeding the federal government's definition of affordable housing—not more than 30 percent of a household's income.

Adding to the problem, by the early 1980s, less than 1 out of 10 families could afford to buy an average-priced new home without spending more than one-quarter of their income. Home foreclosures reached record highs throughout the decade. This development added to the rent squeeze as the marketplace was flooded. This was a contributing factor in the urban crisis of homelessness as well.

These hapless Americans were heavily concentrated in the nation's largest cities. As people walked the streets of great metropolises, they encountered disoriented, dirty, ill-clothed street people. These were the Americans who slept over heating grates, in parks and subways, often in filthy sleeping bags or blankets with sheets of plastic for warmth. They searched out scraps of food from trash barrels, and they panhandled for money.

The ranks of human beings with no place to call home included battered women, female-headed families, alcoholics, drug addicts, and those squeezed out of their dwellings by foreclosures and high rents. About one third were mental patients released during the massive de-institutionalization movement that had occurred in the 1970s. These poor and unfortunate Americans reflected ultimate human desperation in the midst of abundance.

The Immigrant Flood

During the 1980s, approximately eight million immigrants entered the United States, the largest influx since 1900-1910. The change in character of this human flood was equally important, due to the Immigration Reform Act of 1965, which had removed all quotas based on national origins. Two groups, Asians and Hispanics, added to the new cultural diversity.

Asian immigrant groups included the Chinese, the Vietnamese, Koreans, and Filipinos. Collectively they totaled almost 50 percent of all immigrants naturalized during the 1980s, and they achieved U.S. citizenship at the fastest rate. Mexicans, the largest Hispanic group, were much slower to naturalize. Their proximity to Mexico made it easier for them to consider returning home. Other important Hispanic immigrant groups included Salvadorians, Cubans, Puerto Ricans, and Dominicans.

As in the past, these newest arrivals came to the United States for complex reasons. They were both pushed out of their homelands by poverty and political repression and pulled to America by hopes and dreams for a better life. Like their predecessors, cultural differences, language barriers, and discrimination handicapped them. Often this meant they held the most menial, low-income occupations. However, among them was a significant number of educated individuals who possessed highly marketable skills. In particular, this was true of many of the Asian groups. Asians also tended to be rooted in very stable middle-class families. As a consequence, all Asian groups, except the Vietnamese, had achieved significantly higher educational levels than native-born Americans by the mid 1980s.

Even though the 1965 Immigration and Nationality Act had eliminated national origin quotas, it continued to give preferential treatment to better educated aliens seeking enhanced professional opportunities in the United States. Limits of 120,000 immigrants per year from the Western Hemisphere and 170,000 for those outside the Western Hemisphere did not allow adequately for all those who wished to come to the United States. The result was a flood of illegal aliens causing public concern by the middle 1980s.

Although their number is impossible to determine, their dire plight was especially visible. Like an earlier period of the so-called huddled masses, employers, who hoped to exploit them as cheap laborers, welcomed these latest arrivals. Others, who believed they lowered wages or took employment opportunities from "real" Americans, deeply resented them.

Is honesty the best policy? In the 1988 presidential election, Michael Dukakis informed Americans he would raise taxes to cut the deficit. George Bush then delivered his famous "No New Taxes" pledge and won the election. Shortly after assuming office, President Bush recanted his pledge. The tactic hurt his bid for reelection in 1992.

The issue intensified as a political issue, resulting in the passage of the Simpson-Mazzoli Act of 1987. One objective of the legislation was to stem the immense flow of illegal immigrants from Mexico. The act stipulated that employers had to prove the legal status of their employees to authorities. If they were unable to do this, they faced the possibility of fines or criminal penalties. But this concession was tempered by the growing political influence of Hispanics. The 1987 act also offered amnesty to all those undocumented immigrant workers who had entered the United States before 1982. Nevertheless, as the decade ended, it became increasingly clear that the legislation had failed to accomplish its objective—illegals continued to flood into the country at record levels.

THE ELECTION OF 1988

The glow of the Reagan Era, although not that of Reagan himself, began to dim long before the presidential election of 1988. Indications of this came when the Democratic Party recaptured control of the Senate in 1986. They even hoped that one of their own could move back into the White House. Scandals increased in number throughout Reagan's second term. Besides Iran-contra, these included problems involving officials in the Environmental Protection Agency and the Defense Department, the attorney general, and widespread misuse of funds by the Department of Housing and Urban Development. The latter scandal was so severe that it threatened the continued survival of the department. The unfulfilled agendas of women, Hispanics, African Americans, the AIDS epidemic, homelessness, and the greatly accelerated disparity between the rich and the poor remained and even intensified as the decade came to a close. In addition, the stock market, a central element in the economic boom, endured the largest one-day price decline in history in October 1987. Although the market eventually recovered, trust in the business-dominated economy suffered some erosion.

Despite the political opportunity, no truly popular or prominent Democratic candidate came forward. The little known, three-term governor of Massachusetts, Michael Dukakis, became the leading contender based on the so-called "Massachusetts miracle" in which the state had achieved an amazing economic resurgence. Dukakis proved to be a dry and dull campaigner. In this respect he was not much different from his Republican opponent, Vice President George Bush. Yet Democrats had much to be hopeful about because Dukakis was way ahead of Bush in national polls.

Surprisingly, George Bush achieved a remarkable political victory in November. He did so as a result of one of the roughest political campaigns of the century. The Bush campaign used the fears and anger that were latent in the American electorate. While the vice president called for a "kinder, gentler" America, he painted Dukakis as a "card carrying" member of the American Civil Liberties Union and branded him with the hated "L" word—liberal. Bush claimed that Dukakis opposed the Pledge of Allegiance and ran brutal television ads linking him to the African-American convict, Willie Horton. Horton had benefited from a Massachusetts prison furlough program and, while on parole, had raped and murdered a white woman.

These tactics proved to be effective, especially when Bush capped them with the famous statement, "Read my lips, no new taxes." Dukakis hurt his cause by his inability to exhibit any kind of passion, even when a television questioner asked him how he would react if someone raped and murdered his wife! George Bush became the 41st president of the United States by capturing 54 percent of the popular vote to his opponent's 46 percent. Bush won 426 electoral college votes to Dukakis' 111. The newly elected president was not able to carry other Republicans into office on his coat tails as the Democratic Party maintained significant majorities in both houses of Congress.

GEORGE BUSH AS PRESIDENT: DOMESTIC POLICY

Like his political mentor, Richard Nixon, newly elected president George Bush had little interest in domestic policy. He was born into a prosperous and politically active family—his father was a Senator from Connecticut. He was educated at prestigious private schools and Yale University from which he graduated Phi Beta Kappa in 1948. Bush served with distinction in the navy during World War II where he was the youngest active pilot.

He moved to Texas and made his fortune in the oil industry. There, Bush first entered politics and was elected in 1966 to the House of Representatives. Although he failed in later efforts to obtain higher elective office, Richard Nixon appointed him U.S. ambassador to the United Nations in 1971. During the Watergate years he was chairperson of the Republican National Committee and President Gerald Ford named him Director of the Central Intelligence Agency.

Although usually considered a moderate Republican, George Bush was also an ideological chameleon. He had condemned Reagan's supply side economics as "voodoo economics" when he ran for the Republican presidential nomination in 1980, but he reversed himself and later embraced it. Once an advocate of family planning and a woman's right to choose abortion, Bush later courted the right-wing of his party and labeled it murder.

Savings and Loan Crisis

Unfortunately for George Bush it was the wrong time to be disengaged from American domestic policy. This became increasingly apparent as so many of the effects of Reaganomics began to be felt. The first of these was the collapse of the savings-and-loan industry. Reagan tax cuts had allowed capital to pour into the nations S&L's.

Savings-and-loan institutions had responded to the inflation of the 1970s by paying very high interest rates to induce new deposits. Economically, this was unwise since long-term fixed-rate mortgages tied up their assets. In the rush to deregulate American business and industry, the government greatly eased the provisions governing the operation of the savings-and-loan institutions. They continued to make very risky loans. The bottom began to fall out when the economy started to cool down. The impact was especially profound in the Southwest. Between 1988-1990, some 600 savings-and-loan companies collapsed.

Because the United States government insured all savings-and-loan deposits, the Bush administration had to establish a plan to repay the depositors. To pay, real estate had to be dumped on an already depressed market. This included massive office complexes and apartment buildings, forced into foreclosures. In the end, it was the American taxpayer who had to foot the $400 billion bill.

The Economic Crisis

In addition to the savings-and-loan debacle, George Bush had to watch as the economy experienced a nose-dive. The nation's gross domestic product grew at a snail's pace of only 0.7 per cent. Several million Americans were without jobs. Factory workers suffered most as their opportunities continued to decline. Median household income fell by 3.5 per cent. The result was that, by 1992, more and more Americans were living in poverty.

Americans began to worry about the fate of the middle class. The United States had long been thought of as a middle class nation. This perception was greatly strengthened in the three decades following World War II in which home ownership soared and the world envied the living standards of the middle class. Television sitcoms like "the Adventures of Ozzie and Harriet" and "Leave it to Beaver" had reflected this reality.

But, by the early 1990s, the entertainment industry, began to produce programs demonstrating profound economic and social changes. Families like the Cleavers and the Nelsons were gone from the TV screen. They had been replaced by new families like the Simpsons, the Bundys, and the Conners who mirrored the contemporary economic crunch. Unlike June Cleaver who never worked outside the home, Roseanne Conner held six different jobs in eight television seasons. While June Cleaver had worried about the dust accumulating on her kitchen cupboard ketchup bottles, Roseanne Conner worried about making ends meet.

Not only were there more Roseannes who worked year round in 1993—one out of three as compared to one out of five in 1979—their incomes helped prevent middle class families from experiencing economic disaster. Even with the ever increasing number of Roseannes in the workforce, the average middle class family saw its income stagnate. It rose only slightly from $36,556 in 1973 to $37,056 by 1993, a gain of only 1.35 per cent for twenty years! This reality stood in sharp contrast to the gains made to the richest fifth of the nation's households.

An ever mounting federal deficit, caused by the Reagan tax cuts and massive military expenditures, compounded this national dilemma. And the problem continued to worsen, even after 1990 when the Congress and president agreed on a deficit reduction plan. By 1992, the federal deficit had climbed to $290 billion. The total federal debt exceeded $3 trillion. No solution was forthcoming, especially because Bush had campaigned in 1988 on a pledge of no new taxes.

The Bush administration reacted in a passive fashion even when the entire country experienced the consequences of a recession beginning in the late months of 1990. It worsened throughout 1991 and 1992. Frustration, fear, and anger mounted as, increasingly, American citizens worried about their futures and the ever mounting costs of essentials like health care.

The president appeared to have no response to these issues. George Bush seemed to be operating according to his motto—"First, do no harm." This embodied his lifelong predilection of avoiding government involvement in either social or economic problems. Consequently, the president's popularity fell, and there were even those who began to compare him to another Republican president in economic hard times, Herbert Hoover.

The Environment

Whenever possible, George Bush spoke publicly in favor of a conservative social agenda and then adeptly sidestepped action. Another strategy was to unleash the more conservative voices within his administration to ridicule social and domestic reformers like the environmentalists.

But declarations on this issue met head-on with a major environmental disaster in March 1989. The 987-foot oil tanker, the *Exxon Valdez,* ran aground in one of the world's most beautiful places—Alaska's Prince William Sound. A spill of over ten million gallons of crude oil despoiled six hundred coastal acres. Wildlife was destroyed, and the very important Alaskan herring and salmon industries were placed in jeopardy.

More bad environmental news came when, later that year, the Environmental Protection Agency announced that more than one hundred American cities exceeded the standards for air pollution. Furthermore, the EPA claimed that the ozone layer over the United States was being depleted far more rapidly than scientists had predicted.

President Bush responded to these events by attempting to please all factions. He labeled the *Exxon Valdez* accident a major environmental tragedy but, like the good oil man he was, asserted that drilling and oil exploration had to continue. However, the government did take action on the disposal of nuclear waste materials. In 1990, a stricter Federal Clean Air Act passed Congress with the president's assistance.

The Supreme Court

One way that George Bush could pay his debt to conservative elements within the Republican Party was to move the Supreme Court further to the right. There had been no Democratic appointments since the 1960s. By 1989, the Court had experienced a decided shift to the right on a host of important social issues, such as rights of the accused, prayer in the schools and other separation of church/state matters, and abortion. Abortion was the most socially divisive of these issues. The Republican platforms of Reagan and Bush had promised to eliminate abortions and appoint Supreme Court justices to achieve that end.

But the ever popular Reagan failed in his attempt when the Senate refused to approve his nomination of the conservative ideologue, Robert Bork, in 1987. The best President Reagan was able to achieve was the appointment of centrist, Anthony Kennedy. Kennedy showed himself to be extremely cautious when it came to tampering with controversial social and moral issues, abortion in particular.

Despite the failure to appoint Bork, the right to choose was not secure. In the early years of Bush's term, the Court, by a 5 to 4 majority, voted to uphold a Missouri law that restricted abortions by prohibiting public employees from performing the procedure unless the life of the mother was endangered. It also outlawed abortions in public facilities and mandated medical testing to determine if the fetus could survive after twenty weeks.

One more conservative jurist on the nation's highest Court could conceivably tip the balance. In July 1990, President Bush had his first opportunity to accomplish this objective. William Brennan, one of the Supreme Court's most respected liberals, retired. Bush selected David Souter, a New Hampshire Court judge, to replace him. Souter was easily confirmed, although little was known about his views on social issues. As often occurs in Supreme Court appointments, once on the Court, Souter disappointed his conservative backers in his decisions.

The process went less smoothly after Thurgood Marshall, the Court's only African American and a leading liberal supporter of civil rights, announced his resignation. Bush nominated another African American, Clarence Thomas, an Appeals Court judge who was Marshall's ideological opposite. Adamantly conservative, Thomas opposed all affirmative action programs, private or governmental. As head of the Equal Employment Opportunity Commission (EEOC), Thomas had asserted that action by the commission was appropriate only in situations of obvious individual discrimination, rather than class actions. This view, his position favoring prayer in the schools, and his opposition to abortion made Thomas popular among conservatives. However, he received the lowest possible rating, "qualified" rather than "well qualified," by the American Bar Association. The NAACP and the National Organization of Women strongly opposed his appointment.

Bush's selection of a very conservative African American was a politically shrewd move. It was a way to divide the nation and the Democrats. The confirmation of Thomas seemed assured until *Newsday* and National Public Radio reported sexual harassment claims against Thomas by Anita Hill, an African-American law professor at the University of Oklahoma. Hill accused Judge Thomas of unwanted sexual advances during the time she worked under him at the EEOC. Before the all-male Senate Judiciary Committee, she graphically described his discussions with her about pornographic materials and his own sexual prowess. The televised hearings mesmerized and divided the nation. When Thomas's time came to defend himself, he forcefully denied everything, dramatically adding, "I will not provide the rope for my own lynching." This counterattack worked brilliantly, and he was narrowly confirmed 52 to 48. Bush now had his conservative majority on the Supreme Court.

President Bush's victory proved to be less complete than expected. The right of a woman to choose was not lost. In fact, in the Court's 1991-1992 session a majority decision, co-authored by Justice Sandra Day O'Connor, reaffirmed that right. While upholding a Pennsylvania law that placed some restrictions on unfettered abortion, the centrist block on the Court reaffirmed *Roe v. Wade*. Furthermore, the charges leveled against Justice Thomas by Anita Hill evoked a national discussion of the issue of sexual harassment. The discussion revealed its pervasiveness in the workplace, on university and college campuses, and in the nation's schools. A few weeks after the hearing, Congress passed a new Civil Rights Bill that allowed damages to victims of sexual harassment, as well as other discrimination.

The hearing also had important political consequences. Angered by the treatment of Professor Hill by the all-male members of the Senate Judiciary Committee, women all across the country entered the political arena. Women running for office were able to capitalize on the anger, sometimes defeating male opponents of long political standing. They helped to make 1992 the electoral "Year of the Woman."

Anti-abortion extremists, disappointed by the Court and by traditional politics, took to the streets. Groups like Operation Rescue harassed patients and physicians; they attempted to block entry into abortion clinics and tried to close down abortion facilities. Sadly, in a few cases, they went even further. In 1993 and 1994, the most extreme right-to-lifers murdered two Florida physicians known to have performed abortions.

Explosion in Los Angeles

If the issues of abortion and sexual harassment indicated a moral and gender divide in the United States, events in Los Angeles seemed to show that the country itself was ripping apart at the seams. The precipitating incident was routine—a drunken driver speeding away from the police. Rodney King, on parole for armed robbery, decided to elude the Los Angeles patrol car chasing after him with its siren blaring loudly. After a helicopter and ten other police cars entered the chase, King decided to pull over to the side of the road. It was early morning, Sunday, March 3, 1991.

The sirens, the helicopter, and the bright lights attracted residents in a nearby apartment complex. One of them got out his camcorder and began to film the scene below. His film was first shown on a local Los Angeles television and was quickly picked up by the major networks. The film shocked the nation. It showed a man on the ground being beaten by several police officers. The video seemed to confirm what many Angeleno minorities had long claimed—the widespread nature of racism and police brutality.

After the beating, the state of California filed charges against the LAPD officers involved. After a 29-day trial, the jury in a white suburb acquitted the accused officers. It took only 90 minutes after the verdict was announced for an explosion to erupt resulting in the worst riot in the history of Los Angeles. Disorder and violence raged for three long days and nights. Before the National Guard and police were able to re-establish peace, the *Los Angeles Times* reported 58 people were dead, over 2,000 injured, and millions of dollars in property losses. Among those injured was a hapless truck driver, Reginald Denny, dragged and brutally beaten with bottles and bricks by several young black men. Adding to the deadly climate, the Denny incident was broadcast almost as soon as it happened. (Denny was rescued and his life saved by other African Americans in the community.)

A California legislative committee initially compared the events of 1992 to the Watts disorders of 1965. There were some significant differences, however. Not only was the 1992 explosion more destructive and more deadly, it was clearly more complex. Rather than a strictly black-white confrontation, this was a multicultural riot, involving significant numbers of Koreans and Latinos. The deaths and arrests of Latinos matched those of African Americans.

Korean merchants located in South Central Los Angeles, and nearby, were repeatedly looted, attacked, and burned out—over 300 in Koreatown alone. African Americans deeply resented their presence and their success in South Central. There was also lingering anger and frustration over the death of a 15-year-old black girl shot by a Korean storekeeper who received the token sentence of five years on probation.

Close analysis of the disturbance revealed that 60 percent of those arrested for riot-related activities had no previous criminal records. Large numbers of them were poor, non-English speaking immigrants. Those employed tended to be in minimum wage occupations hard hit during the previous two years of economic recession.

Urban Problems

The events in Los Angeles reflected the deteriorating conditions that had occurred for the most disadvantaged Americans during the preceding decade. In South Los Angeles the poverty rate was more than twice the national average, at about 30.3 percent. One quarter of the city's African Americans were on the welfare rolls, and about 40 percent of its black males were unemployed.

Three thousand miles eastward, in New York City in the south Bronx community called Mott Haven, conditions were as bad, if not worse. Mott Haven was the center of one of the nation's poorest congressional districts. In 1991 the *New York Times* reported that the median household income was $7,600. Of the 800 children attending the neighborhood elementary school, only seven did not qualify for free school lunches. Heroin use and crack cocaine addiction were at the very center of these children's lives. AIDS was omnipresent, as well as death in other forms, for "in 1991, 84 people, more than half of whom were 21 or younger, were murdered."

Humid hot summers in Mott Haven brought out roaches, creatures that crawled "on virtually every surface of the houses in which many of the chil-

dren live...." A five-year federally financed study released in early May 1997 revealed why asthma was the most common illness among Mott Haven youngsters. The study concluded that children allergic to cockroaches and exposed to high levels of roach saliva, feces, and other insect proteins have the most severe cases of asthma.

These manifestations of human tragedy tell only one part of changes facing urban Americans. Population and industry were relocating out of the Northeast and Midwest to the Sunbelt. People moved from large cities to smaller cities. By 1980, "for the first time in the twentieth century, more Americans lived in cities with populations of less than half a million people than in larger cities." Within the nation's metropolitan areas fewer people lived inside the once dense central city while more moved to suburbs.

Cities like Buffalo, New York, and Detroit, Michigan lost nearly half of their populations between 1950 and the early 1990s. St. Louis, Missouri lost more than half of its residents. The core of these catastrophic losses occurred in the ghettos of these cities. The "new ghetto" remained predominantly poor, Hispanic, and African American but now underpopulated. Middle income residents, who could afford to flee, did so. Thus tax bases eroded at the same time that social expenses rose.

Newark, New Jersey, home to 439,000 residents in 1950, had less than 270,000 by 1994. Where houses once stood and businesses once flourished, people sold second-hand kitchen appliances and old mattresses from the back of pick-up trucks. Detroit's Book-Cadillac Hotel, the world's tallest hotel when it opened in 1924; the impressive Michigan Central Railroad station; and Hudson's, once the nation's largest department store, were all empty.

Suburban Cities and Shopping Malls

These urban shifts did not mean an across-the-board urban decay. Two-thirds of the country's seventy-six largest cities actually grew significantly between 1950 and 1990. Most, however, were in the Sunbelt. Much of this growth reflected greater metropolitan areas, indicating suburban rather than inner city growth. In fact, the very word "suburb" really became a misnomer as it implies dependency on the city. Increasingly, these outlying areas provided more and more of their residents with employment, entertainment, and shopping.

New market places—shopping centers or malls—had major effects on American community life. In terrible heat waves, people could spend their leisure time in enclosed shopping malls. One observer called them, "placeless, timeless cathedrals of the air conditioned culture." They also privatized public spaces since shopping centers were privately owned, something that was never true of the older metropolitan commercial centers. Privately owned space also meant restrictions on traditional rights of free speech and assembly. This same space became increasingly feminized, enhancing women's claim to suburban America. However, women tended to be empowered more as consumers of goods rather than as producers of goods.

The decades 1950 to 1990 witnessed the completion of these important changes from one type of social order to another. This new landscape, based on postwar mass consumption, established a metropolitan civilization in which Americans no longer came together in a central marketplace, in public buildings, in public parks, or on public streets. Rather, they became segmented into different commercial shopping centers by class, race, and gender. This, in the view of one observer, "has made more precarious the shared public sphere upon which...democracy depends."

Rising Health-Care Costs

Throughout most of the twentieth century, the costs of health care rapidly increased. Between 1950 and 1994, per capita health-care expenditures increased over thirty fold. These figures mean that the United States spends more for health care, in both total dollars and percentage of the gross domestic product, than any other industrialized nation. The American health-care system developed into the most technologically sophisticated and best staffed in the world. Despite this, Americans began to wonder what kind of return they were receiving on their investment as other industrialized nations had longer life expect-

ancy and lower infant mortality while spending far less.

The best explanation for this is that health care in the United States is based on the ability to pay. It was, therefore, a superb system for those of means and woefully deficient for those without means. Wealthy Americans enjoy the best physicians, surgeons, hospital care, and modern medical technology. On the other hand, millions of citizens without health insurance are outside the health-care system altogether.

Despite this very real crisis, President Bush proposed no solutions. Again, he chose inaction, increasing the number of critics who labeled his administration the "status quo presidency."

Americans with Disabilities Act

Surprisingly, the president did move on another important domestic front when he signed the Americans with Disabilities Act of 1990. This legislation prohibited employment discrimination against the mentally retarded, the blind, the deaf, and the physically impaired. Victims of cancer or HIV-positive citizens could not be denied equal employment opportunities. The act was applicable to all companies that employed 25 or more workers. It was believed to cover around 87 percent of all the nation's occupations. In addition the legislation mandated "reasonable accommodations" including such things as wheelchair ramps for the disabled. Many businesses claimed that this unfunded mandate imposed significant financial burdens on them. Unfunded mandates, a form of the government's indirect role on the economy, came under increasing attack by President Bush's own party.

Racial Intolerance

For a time, it appeared that conditions for racial minorities were improving and government policies to end injustice would remain in place.

Yet by the 1970s special actions and programs like busing and affirmative action came under increasing attack by many white Americans. In the 1980s both the Reagan and Bush administrations tended to side with the anti-busing forces. Finally, in 1992, a far more conservative Supreme Court ruled that busing should not be used to integrate school systems segregated by de facto housing patterns.

Affirmative action also came under fire in the late 1970s and on into the 1980s. By this time the United States had become a very different society from the 1960s. Restructuring of the American economy had created new economic dislocations for both whites and African Americans. Increasingly white Americans grew uncomfortable with race-conscious policies in the workplace and school. Politicians adopted race baiting tactics in their efforts to win and remain in office. Racial tensions mounted, causing further debates on the equity of policies based on race.

A number of white power organizations, like the Ku Klux Klan, asserted that the future of white civilization was at stake. At public rallies such groups professed their hatred for gays, feminists, Asians, African Americans, and Hispanics. Between 1980 and 1986 hate crimes increased from less than 100 a year to over 270 a year. One such incident occurred when African-American teens entered the all-white neighborhood of Howard Beach, in Queens, New York City in 1986. The white teenagers attacked and beat the black youths. One black youngster died—hit by a car while fleeing his assailants.

The racial divide in the United States persisted in other ways as well. White Americans believed that their African-American counterparts already enjoyed equality of opportunity, or even an edge with affirmative action, and that they could achieve the American dream. On the other hand, most black Americans believed discrimination persisted. The 1994-5 O.J. Simpson trial vividly revealed the great racial divide in American society. When a largely black jury acquitted the former football star of the murder of his white ex-wife, a CBS poll found that "six in ten whites believed the wrong verdict was reached, while nine in ten blacks said the jury had reached the right conclusion."

Blacks, even those in the middle class, were the objects of special surveillance in department stores. They continued to have a more difficult time getting a taxi. Blacks were still less likely to be served courteously and quickly in a restaurant. Some noted how often they were stopped by police for "DWB—Driving While Black."

THE BUSH FOREIGN POLICY

The presidency of George Bush was especially notable for a number of important and dramatic events in the international arena. The president even claimed credit for "winning" the cold war. The Bush administration dealt carefully and constructively with the collapse of the Soviet Union. It worked to ease tensions in the ever volatile Middle East, moved positively in Latin America, and took decisive action following Iraq's invasion of Kuwait.

The Collapse of Communism

All the world stood by in shocked amazement as the communist governments in Eastern Europe disintegrated. Almost in a flash the world that had existed since the end of the Second World War vanished. In the Soviet Union the disintegration began with the political reforms initiated by Mikhail Gorbachev. In the middle of the 1980s, he advocated a new openness and spirit of democracy by brashly confronting the system that had dominated Soviet society with an iron hand for most of the twentieth century. Gorbachev intended for these reforms to reach into the other Communist nations in Eastern Europe.

In November 1989, the ultimate symbol of the cold war, the Berlin Wall, collapsed. The Soviet Union announced it would withdraw all of its forces from East Germany by 1994.

In rapid succession, the Baltic Republics of Estonia, Latvia, and Lithuania declared themselves independent of the Soviet Union. Other Soviet republics followed suit. By this time Poland had already held its first free elections since the Communists took it over after World War II. The Communist Party of Hungary changed its name and advocated a new multi-party system. Demonstrations began in Romania, Bulgaria, and Czechoslovakia late in 1989. Their Communist leaders were rapidly toppled. Signifying the final death knell to the cold war and nuclear armaments race of almost fifty years' duration, President Bush and Mikhail Gorbachev signed a treaty in August 1991. It reduced their nations' nuclear arsenal by 25 percent.

At home Soviet reformers struggled to establish a capitalist economy amidst economic crisis and political reaction. The conflict brought the President of the Russian Republic, Boris Yeltsin, to power. "Gorbachev knew how to bring us freedom but he did not know how to make sausage," one discontented Muscovite noted. Gorbachev's hopes of reforming the political and economic system, while preserving the Soviet Union, ultimately failed. Yeltsin announced the end of the USSR and proclaimed a new Commonwealth of Independent States. Many issues remained unresolved in the wake of such cataclysmic changes. One of the most crucial involved the arsenal of nuclear weapons in the various newly independent states of the former Soviet Union.

The overall policy of the Bush administration in dealing with the collapse of the Communist world was cautious and wise. The policy had a two-pronged objective; a unified Germany inside NATO along with the liberation of Central and Eastern Europe. These were the preconditions for the establishment of continued good relations between the United States and Russia.

An important indication of improved relations between the U.S.S.R. and America occurred in Nicaragua and Panama. In December 1989, the United States invaded Panama. The objective of the mission was the overthrow of the corrupt regime of Manuel Noriega. Noriega had gone from friend and ally to drug runner and potential threat to U.S. interests in the Canal. The conflict was short-lived as Noriega quickly surrendered. He was later transported to Miami, Florida where he was tried, convicted, and sentenced to a life term in prison. Throughout this ordeal Gorbachev was supportive of the United States. The Bush administration ended the U.S. flow of moneys to the contras in their battle against the Sandinista government of Nicaragua. This change of direction helped pave the way for national elections, which were held in 1990, resulting in an anti-Sandinista victory.

War in the Persian Gulf

With the cold war over, the world could breathe a sigh of relief. The end of superpower rivalry greatly reduced the danger of a nuclear holocaust. President Bush acknowledged these changes with a new sense of hope. He spoke optimistically of a "New World Order, . . . freer from the threat of terror, stronger in the pursuit of justice, and more secure in the quest for peace...." These noble and eloquent expressions, however, did not solve the problems of ethnic and religious conflicts, especially in troubled regions like the Middle East.

While the brutal but inconclusive war between Iran and Iraq raged in the late 1980s, the United States cautiously supported Saddam Hussein with a moderate supply of weapons and other war materials. The United States hoped that Iranian militant Islamic fundamentalism would be crushed by Iraq. Finally, in the late summer of 1988 the war ended. America's willingness to overlook Saddam's brutality to his own people and meetings with the American Ambassador led him to believe that he had a free hand in the area. Hussein turned his attention to the small but oil rich nation of Kuwait, hoping to replenish his war-depleted treasury. He had been involved in a long-running border dispute with his neighbor and advanced historical Iraqi claims to the area. Iraqi troops invaded and quickly occupied Kuwait. Saddam Hussein, an unpredictable tyrant, now had possession of its huge oil reserves and Persian Gulf ports.

Bush immediately denounced Iraq's actions as did the Soviet Union, Egypt, Saudi Arabia, and various countries of Western Europe. All joined under the skillful direction of President Bush, who worked carefully for concerted action through the auspices of the United Nations. On August 6, 1990, the U.N. Security Council established an economic blockade of Iraq and denounced the invasion of Kuwait. By the middle of October there were some 230,000 American forces in the Persian Gulf, and by the middle of January this number had more than doubled.

On November 29, 1990, the United Nations issued an ultimatum to Iraq: leave Kuwait by January

15, 1991, or face the consequences. A joint resolution to use military force against Iraq passed both Houses of Congress in January, despite the argument of some Democrats that economic sanctions should have been given more time to work. When last minute attempts to achieve peaceful resolution failed, the U.N. military operation, called Desert Storm, began on January 16, 1991.

For 42 days Allied and U.S. air forces pounded Iraqi positions, smashing power plants, oil refineries, and transportation facilities, as well as military targets. The ground war began on February 24 and lasted only one hundred hours. Hussein was forced out of Kuwait. U.S. forces lost 146 in action, compared to estimates as high as 100,000 Iraqi deaths.

Most Americans supported the venture. Glued to their televisions, they watched carefully documented, sometimes staged, footage of the conflict, and they celebrated the great accomplishment of U.S. technology. The technology seemed to bring a stunning victory with very little blood and gore. Only later did Americans learn that Iraq's infrastructure had been devastated. Furthermore, the troublesome Saddam Hussein remained in power. He brutally crushed uprisings by Iraqi Kurds and Shiite Muslims as the United States stood by.

Despite lingering questions about Iraq, the Persian Gulf War was the high point of the Bush presidency. George Bush, his commanding General Norman Schwarzkopf, and his chairman of the Joint Chiefs of Staff, Colin Powell, all became new American heroes. Their swift, all but painless, and well-crafted victory reassured Americans about their leaders, U.S. military might, and U.S. role as world leader. "By God, we've kicked the Vietnam syndrome once and for all," President Bush declared happily. Public approval of his presidency reached an astounding 88 percent.

ELECTION OF 1992

On the eve of the presidential election, however, public opinion polls gave George Bush his lowest approval rating, a dismal 40 percent. The president was unable to win long lasting public affection for his victory over Iraq or his skillful diplomacy in directing the course for the end of the cold war. Americans had turned their attention to their nation's economic woes.

By the middle of 1990, the nation was mired in an economic recession that worsened during the Gulf War because of rising fuel prices. At the same time, the national debt continued to mount, reaching four trillion dollars by 1992. The Reagan boom was over, and all of its excesses were becoming apparent. These included corporate raiding, questionable insider financial transactions, and unsound real estate ventures.

The president wanted the recession to end before election time and, to that end, he took a fatal step. He agreed to work with Congress on a tax increase. Breaking his 1988 promise of "no new taxes," Bush and Congress came to terms in October 1990 on a tax bill. It imposed higher rates on upper income Americans and increased excise taxes on gasoline, beer, and cigarettes. The broken promise not only angered the public, it alienated him from his own party. They voted against the legislation, and Bush had the worst of both worlds. Increasingly, he appeared weak, unprincipled, and politically vulnerable. Worse, the recession continued. Concern about their pocket books dominated the American people's view of the 1992 election.

Top Democrats stayed out of the primaries since President Bush appeared politically invincible right after the Gulf War. Instead a field of dark horse candidates entered the fray. The governor of Arkansas, Bill Clinton, was perhaps least known of all. He also had to overcome a number of concerns about his character. There were questions about his opposition to the war in Vietnam, his evasion of the draft, his womanizing, and his history of extra-marital affairs. Equally important for Clinton, the times seemed to be decidedly conservative. The candidate was viewed as a liberal, and he brought along with him an activist liberal, politically astute wife, Hillary Rodham Clinton.

Despite these problems and the grueling primaries, Clinton went on to capture the Democratic Party nomination. In an unusual unbalanced ticket, he chose another Southerner of the baby-boomer generation, Senator Albert Gore, Jr. of Tennessee as his running mate. At the Democratic convention in July, the platform promised the end of politics as usual in Washington, D.C.; to clean up the environment; to increase employment opportunities; to ease the economic crisis for middle-class Americans; and to address the nation's serious health-care crisis. On the extremely volatile issue of abortion, Bill Clinton was firmly pro-choice.

George Bush prevailed over his ultra-conservative challengers also. Easily renominated by their party, the Bush-Quayle ratings in the nation's polls remained low. Right-wing domination of the Republican convention proved to be a problem. Divisive speeches were delivered by conservative activists, summoning the Republican Party to a moral crusade against sexual permissiveness, gay rights, racial feminists, cultural pluralists, and supporters of abortion rights. Their outspokenness hurt Bush's chances for re-election and divided the Republican Party from within. Dan Quayle raised eyebrows when he attacked the television character, Murphy Brown, for being a single mother by choice.

The eccentric billionaire, H. Ross Perot of Texas, was the most colorful candidate, and the most serious third party candidate since Theodore Roosevelt in 1912. As a consummate political outsider, Perot pledged to change politics by ridding Washington of politicians. Politicians would be replaced by businessmen who would engage in sound business practices. If elected, Perot promised to hold electronic "town meetings" where the public would have an opportunity to vote on his proposals. He also put forward a general plan to eliminate the federal deficit and to reorganize the federal government from top to bottom. Perot's candidacy probably hurt the president the most. Perot's constituency was suburban, middle-aged, and white, all expected Bush supporters. He might also, however, have siphoned economic malcontents from the Clinton camp.

Throughout the campaign, Clinton centered on the issues of a stagnant economy and the continued erosion of America's middle class. He demonstrated that he was a persistent as well as shrewd candidate. President Bush and Vice President Quayle ran another negative campaign. Perot, on the other hand, used his money, ambition, and folksy charisma to transform the entire campaign away from the issue of character to issues like the federal deficit and the economy.

In the end this shift benefited Clinton the most. Forty-three percent of the voters elected him president. Bush mustered 38 percent of the vote. Ross Perot captured 19 percent of the popular vote, more than any third-party candidate since Theodore Roosevelt in 1912. George Bush won 168 electoral votes to Bill Clinton's 370. Twelve years of Republican Party rule had ended, although the Democrats had not carried a majority of the popular vote. The new president succeeded in luring back large numbers of "Reagan Democrats," including suburban residents and blue-collar workers. Apparently this campaign aroused the interest of more Americans as 55 percent of all eligible voters went to the polls.

Incumbents tended to fare well in Congress, but they were joined by many more minorities and women. There were 47 women in the new House and six in the new Senate. Illinois elected the nation's first African-American female senator, Carol Moseley Braun. California was the first state to have two women senators, Dianne Feinstein and Barbara Boxer. Other minorities included 17 Hispanic Americans and 38 African Americans in Congress. A congressional district in California elected the first-ever Korean American legislator, and Colorado elected a Native-American senator—Ben Nighthorse Campbell. This was a Congress more representative of all Americans.

THE BABY BOOMERS IN POWER

A new generation of politicians was ushered into national office with the election of Bill Clinton and Al Gore, Jr. They were the first post World War II candidates to occupy the executive branch of government, shaped by Vietnam rather than Pearl Harbor, technology and the environment rather than New Deal politics. Vice President Gore had even established a reputation as a specialist in the environment from his 1992 book *Earth in the Balance: Healing the Global Environment.*

WILLIAM JEFFERSON CLINTON

Both men professed to be "new" Democrats who would move their party to the center of the political spectrum. Clinton spoke of modernizing liberalism by supporting business and being tough on crime. Clinton even favored capital punishment and pledged to put more police on the streets. The new president promised to end welfare as "we know it" and to address the serious health-care crisis confronting the nation. Yet he still left room for more traditional Democratic concerns like increased spending on education, job training, and re-building the nation's crumbling infrastructure.

While Al Gore, Jr. had been groomed to follow in the footsteps of his father, a long-time senator from Tennessee, Bill Clinton came from very different origins. Born in Hope, Arkansas in 1946, his childhood had been turbulent. His father died before he was born, and his mother married an abusive, alcoholic man. Despite this inauspicious beginning, young Clinton was chosen as a "senator" from Arkansas for the American Legion Boy's Nation. This

1963 experience in which he met and shook hands with President Kennedy helped push him into public service, rather than pop music. (He played the saxophone.) The poor boy from Arkansas with an overwhelming need for love and approval, graduated from Georgetown University, became a Rhodes scholar at Oxford University, and gained a degree from Yale Law School. It was there that he met and married Hillary Rodham, an assertive and talented lawyer in her own right.

The Democrats in Control

Although Democrats and liberals had very high expectations for the Clinton presidency, new administration had important political weaknesses. Having won only 43 percent of the popular vote, Clinton had no clear national mandate. The Democrats did control both Houses of Congress, but their majority was not a large one. The Republican leadership was hostile and unified in its opposition.

Clinton tried to make his cabinet positions more reflective of the American population. His appointments included two Hispanics as Secretaries of Transportation and Housing and Urban Development. The Secretary of Agriculture and the Secretary of Commerce, Ron Brown, a close presidential adviser, were African Americans. After appointing Donna Shalala to the traditionally female cabinet post of Health and Human Service, Clinton appointed Janet Reno to the trail blazing position of Attorney General. In 1993, Ruth Bader Ginsberg became the second female justice to serve on the Supreme Court.

"Don't Ask, Don't Tell"

When Clinton attempted to make good on his campaign promise to end discrimination against gays in the military, he encountered a firestorm of opposition from a large portion of the public, the Congress, and the military. These groups believed that allowing openly homosexual Americans into the military would impair the morale and cohesion of military units.

Recognizing the intensity of the opposition, the president chose to compromise. Military officials would no longer question service members about sexual orientation or investigate as long as homosexuals (or bisexuals) would tell no one about their sexual preferences and refrain from "homosexual acts" or marriage. The compromise became known as "Don't Ask, Don't Tell." It left those on both sides of the controversy unhappy. Commanders did not seem well informed about the nature of the new rules. In 1998 the Pentagon released figures showing that the number of homosexuals dismissed from service rose 67 percent since the new policy went into effect. One critical reporter commented that "Don't Ask, Don't Tell" had "created a world of fear and deceit."

Confronting the Economy

Candidate Clinton's campaign had been based on the notion, "It's the Economy, Stupid!" He pledged to bring an end to the recession, stimulate economic growth through a tax reduction for the middle-class, and create new employment opportunities. In February 1993, President Clinton presented his economic package that proposed spending cuts, especially in the military, and tax increases to lower the deficit. The tax proposal aroused considerable Republican opposition. Clinton also proposed substantial expenditures to stimulate economic growth and create new jobs.

As a result of strong Republican opposition, the bill was passed only because the vice president cast the tie breaking vote and without the president's economic stimulus package. Although it fell short of the president's proposals in many ways, the legislation did represent a new direction from the Reagan/Bush years. Increased revenues would be achieved through higher taxes on gasoline, corporations, and more affluent Americans. For example, individuals who earned over $115,000 would pay a 5 percent tax increase, from 31 to 36 percent. At the same time, the legislation increased tax credits to those low-income families who were struggling to lift themselves out of poverty.

The president also signed "Family Leave" legislation that required the nation's employers to allow male and female workers unpaid leaves to handle family emergencies like an illness or the birth of a child. Cuts were made by limiting Medicare allotments, cost-of-living adjustments, and by freezing discretionary spending.

NAFTA and GATT

Two important trade agreements were also central to the administration's economic package. Building on the activities of both the Reagan and Bush administrations to foster free trade and expand markets, the Congress passed the North American Free Trade Agreement (NAFTA) in November 1993. It created the largest free trade zone in the world by eliminating most trade barriers between Mexico, Canada, and the United States.

The General Agreement on Tariffs and Trade (GATT), approved by Congress in 1994, reduced tariffs on thousands of goods worldwide. In addition, it gradually eliminated import quotas established by the industrialized nations of the world, including the United States. Finally, GATT created the World Trade Organization whose task was to mediate the disputes between its 117 member nations.

Both pieces of legislation met with considerable opposition and passed after bitter political battles. The strongest advocates of the agreements were Republicans rather than liberal members of the president's own party. Organized labor feared free trade would mean the loss of jobs for U.S. workers and a greater influx of illegal immigrants into the country. The opposition also predicted that GATT would jeopardize high paying skilled labor, especially in the automobile industry.

It cannot be determined definitively whether these initiatives had a positive or negative impact on the nation's economy. However, by the second quarter of 1993, the U.S. economic situation began to show signs of improvement. Retail sales increased. By the end of 1994 America's steel and auto industries reported increased profits. The country's unemployment rate reached its lowest level in four years. Inflation appeared under control, and by 1998 there was actually a budget surplus.

Senator Dick Durbin (D-IL) talks at the podium on the issue of handgun control. In the wheelchair to his left is Jim Brady, who was hit by gunfire when John Hinkley shot at President Reagan. The Brady Act is a congressional law mandating that state law enforcement agencies conduct criminal background checks prior to allowing an individual to purchase a handgun.

Crime and Gun Control

Crime and violence were important issues that had been debated throughout the presidential campaign, and they re-emerged after the election was over. The Clinton administration took action on a variety of fronts. After heated debate Congress passed the Brady Bill on November 30, 1993. This bill was named for Ronald Reagan's former communications director, James Brady, who had been seriously wounded in the assassination attempt on Reagan. The legislation had failed to pass in previous attempts as a result of opposition from the powerful National Rifle Association, supported by the Republican administrations. Its provisions established a five-day waiting period before a handgun could be legally purchased. The following year, the Clinton admin-

istration secured the passage of legislation that banned the sale of certain types of assault weapons. Finally, the crime bill of 1994 increased funds for drug treatment, prisons, and promised to put additional police officers on the streets.

Whether due to these very initiatives or not, the nation's crime rate began to fall faster from 1995 to the present than any other period in recent history. From 1994 to 1995, for example, the overall drop in violent crime was 12.4 percent. Experts disagreed on what this meant for the future. While some maintained the figures heralded a less violent America, others argued that demographics favored a decrease in crime for the short term, not the long term. This was because the teenage population, statistically the most criminally prone group, was at its lowest level since the beginning of the Baby Boom. Despite this negative assessment, however, violent crime continued to drastically decline, particularly in New York City, which developed new techniques of community policing.

Health-Care Reform

A major theme of the Clinton campaign had been the need for a sweeping reform of the nation's health-care system. In his second year in office, the president put his wife in charge of a task force to design a major overhaul. Mrs. Clinton, a successful lawyer and effective lobbyist, had been an important and divisive issue during the campaign. Those who labeled her a liberal zealot, had their worst fears confirmed with this appointment.

When the task force made its plan public, almost 40 million Americans had no health insurance at all. Many of these people could not afford prohibitive health insurance costs. Others could not find a carrier because of their pre-existing health problems—cancer, chronic heart disease, or perhaps AIDS. In the world of modern medical technology, a long-term illness could wipe people out financially. Millions of other Americans had health-care plans through their place of employment. What would be their fate if they changed jobs or, worse, lost them?

By the 1990s the national burden for health care was tremendous, constituting about one-seventh of the entire domestic economy. If it were to continue its rate of growth, experts projected it would rapidly rise to close to one-fifth of the GDP. Employer costs were equally burdensome. Such costs were obviously passed on to the American consumer.

President Clinton presented the task force plan before a joint session of Congress in September 1993. The massive plan sought to find a middle ground between conservatives and liberals. Essentially, conservatives wanted to "fine tune" the current system by making private coverage available to all Americans. Liberals argued that health care was a basic right to which all citizens were entitled and advocated a federal government program. Some Democrats favored a system like Canada's that was universal in scope and government operated.

The proposed plan was very complex, long, and difficult to understand. Supporters argued the "managed competition" would provide most Americans with medical coverage. The plan mandated that employers pay for 80 percent of their workers' health insurance costs. The start-up expenses of $100 billion would be financed by stiff new taxes on tobacco. Private insurance companies would retain their position at the center of the new system.

The plan was immediately attacked. It was probably doomed to fail because of its complexity. To ensure its demise, pressure groups spent more than $100 million in a fifteen-month period to oppose the legislation. Critics included Chambers of Commerce, Republicans, conservative Democrats, the National Association of Manufacturers, and perhaps most significantly, the Health Insurance Association of America,. The latter launched a brilliant media blitz featuring two "ordinary" citizens, "Harry and Louise," worrying about the impact of government "interference" on their ability to obtain health care.

At the outset of the debate the majority of the American people supported the proposed plan. But support fell off sharply as the political wrangling continued and, by the fall of 1994, it was clear that the legislation was dead. The failure of health-care reform was a significant blow to the Clintons. In particular, Hillary Rodham Clinton had not paid close enough attention to political realities. The already controversial first lady had proposed a plan advocating a total overhaul of America's health-care system when this was not what most Americans wanted. In the end, health-care reform was the real victim, and the nation's health-care problems remained.

Welfare Reform

The president then turned his focus to another campaign issue—welfare. In June 1994, Clinton introduced a reform bill to "end welfare as we know it." It confronted the largest part of the system, Aid to Families with Dependent Children (AFDC), head-on. Many people felt that AFDC created a permanent class of dependent Americans. Between 1989 and 1994 alone there had been a 31 percent increase in the number of women and children on the welfare roles.

The Clinton legislation proposed to end all AFDC payments after two years. Former recipients would have to work, possibly in a public-service occupation. Absent fathers would be compelled to support their children. The legislation had provisions for child care and job training. It included a provision allowing states to deny extra payments to mothers who continued to have children while on the welfare rolls.

After vetoing two Republican measures as too punitive, Clinton signed the Personal Responsibility and Work Opportunity Reconciliation Act in 1996. This law reversed the social policy of a safety net for the poor that had been in place since the 1930s. It replaced AFDC with a system of grants to the states, coupled with limits on the duration of welfare. While it is too soon to evaluate the long term consequences of this dramatic change, welfare rolls have been reduced. In states like Wisconsin, where serious efforts have been made to substitute workfare for welfare, the per-person yearly cost for those on welfare has gone up from $9,000 to $15,000, due to the services provided.

CLINTON FOREIGN POLICY: A NEW PRAGMATISM

Service as a two-term governor from a poor, southern state had provided Bill Clinton no foreign policy experience. The tremendous changes that had occurred in the final years of the Bush presidency did not allow Clinton the luxury of avoiding foreign affairs. With the Soviet Union gone, the United States remained the world's only super power. What role would America assume in a new and uncertain world? Old dangers like the threat of nuclear proliferation and of Arab-Israeli conflict remained. But new crises, such as an Africa stalked by famine and ravaged by AIDS and genocide, emerged. Centuries of old ethnic hatreds took on frightening new dimensions. And they gave birth to horrible new terms like "ethnic cleansing" in the war-torn country that was once Yugoslavia. Clinton and his secretary of state, the

veteran diplomat, Warren Christopher, were very tentative in dealing with this crisis-ridden world. Without the cold war as a guideline, both the Clinton administration and the public labored to determine when American interests justified intervention in foreign countries. Basically, the administration found it difficult to draw up a clear coherent policy to replace containment.

Russia

Russia found the transition from a planned to a free market economy perplexing. There was economic chaos, terrible inflation, and a flourishing violent underworld of black market gangsters. Fear mounted, giving birth to a very anti-western, nationalistic political party that many predicted would win the 1993 elections. Clinton developed a personal relationship with Boris Yeltsin and helped him to persevere through an attempted coup by extreme nationalists and Communists in October 1993. When the presidents of the two countries met in 1994, Clinton pledged to give Russia and the Ukraine economic aid. Significantly, the U.S. and the Ukraine agreed on the elimination of Russian nuclear weapons situated there when the Ukraine had been part of the Soviet Union. Even after Yeltsin stepped down, Russia was mired in corruption and an economy spiraling downward. The health-care system collapsed and the life expectancy of the ordinary Russian dropped precipitously. Slow improvements began with the regimer of Vladimir Putin.

The Balkans

The changing world order caused centuries-old ethnic conflicts to be rekindled. The multiethnic country of Yugoslavia had once been held together by the authoritarian rule of Marshall Tito, the nationalist Communist who defied the Soviet Union. In 1991 civil war first broke out among the various nationalities that had been part of Yugoslavia. Serbians engaged in acts of genocide, that they called "ethnic cleansing." The Serb intent was to eliminate non-Serbian groups in Bosnia, particularly Muslims.

Citizens with Serbian ties protest the bombing of Yugoslavia. On the other side of the street marched those with ties to the ethnic Albanians.

During the 1992 campaign, candidate Clinton had scolded George Bush for ignoring the suffering of Bosnian victims and failing to end the violence. President Clinton found it far more difficult to resolve the situation than he had anticipated. He vacillated on what course of action to take as the carnage continued unabated. Clinton finally authorized limited military air attacks. United States air power enabled NATO forces to bomb Serbian positions. The president also pledged to support United Nations relief and peacekeeping activities. But the violence continued to intensify. Emboldened by signs of U.N. weakness, the Serbs quickly captured the Muslim city of Srebrenica in August 1995. This placed other so-called U.N. "safe zones" like the Bosnian capitol of Sarajevo in danger. The United States responded by mobilizing new airstrikes and pressured to keep the peacekeeping moving forward.

Finally, in November 1995, the leaders of Serbia, Croatia, and Bosnia were brought to Dayton, Ohio where they signed a peace treaty after arduous negotiations. The accords divided Bosnia into separate ethnic republics. Free and fair elections were to be held. A war crimes tribunal was set up to try those responsible for the atrocities committed during the four-year conflict. New conflicts erupted between the Serbs and ethnic Albanians in Kosovo in 1997.

Africa

Clinton also seemed to lack direction in dealing with the problems he inherited in Africa. The East African nation of Somalia was caught in the midst of political chaos, famine, and starvation. President Bush had intervened militarily in 1992 as a humanitarian response to help the victims. Late in 1992 U.S. and U.N. military forces attempted to create the foundation for a political settlement. But this situation changed for the worse when American forces found themselves caught in the middle of firefights among conflicting Somali factions and eighteen Americans were killed. The public was particularly horrified when the body of one serviceman was dragged through the dusty streets before gleeful onlookers. An outcry arose from the public and many members in Congress demanded U.S. withdrawal. By April 1994 Clinton had complied. It was clear that Americans were unwilling to sacrifice the lives of their soldiers when it seemed as though no vital national interests were involved.

When ancient tribal hatred erupted in the small central African country of Rwanda in 1994, the Somali disaster made the administration reluctant to become involved. The genocidal conflict in which at least half-a-million were slaughtered and over a million terrified refugees fled to Zaire made it impossible for the administration to remain completely detached. Clinton sent in 4,000 troops but strictly limited them to humanitarian aid. In 1996 a similarly limited effort was launched to ameliorate suffering in Zaire. Later, President Clinton felt impelled to apologize for the lack of American response to the Rwanda genocide.

The Middle East

The most dramatic success in foreign policy seemed to take place in the oldest area of conflict, the Middle East. The Clinton administration encouraged negotiations that led to a breakthrough. In September 1993, as Clinton presided, Yitzhak Rabin, Prime Minister of Israel, and his old enemy, Yasser Arafat, the chairman of the Palestine Liberation Organization, shook hands in an electrifying ceremony. They agreed to mutual recognition and the beginning of self-rule for the Palestinians in Gaza and the West Bank. The following year, Clinton presided over another momentous occasion as Rabin and King Hussein of Jordan signed a treaty of peace and cooperation.

The progress toward lasting peace in the Middle East suffered a crushing blow, however, when a right-wing Israeli, opposed to the peace efforts, murdered Rabin in 1995. His death, coupled with continued terrorist attacks by militant Palestinians, led to the election of a new right-wing Israeli prime minister, Benjamin Netanyahu, who was far more skeptical of the agreements. By 1998, negotiations appeared to have ground to a halt. In October, however, Clinton got the antagonists to meet at Wye Plantations, Maryland. With the assistance of a desperately ill King Hussein of Jordan, Netanyahu, and Arafat agreed to further limited Israeli withdrawal from the West Bank in return for guarantees of a security crackdown against terrorists. The following year, Israelis elected a war hero, Ehud Barak, who seemed anxious to arrive at a final peace and willing to make substantial concessions. President

Clinton took an increasingly active role in the negotiations.

Ireland

Another significant accomplishment in foreign policy occurred in the centuries-old conflict in Northern Ireland. Clinton ignored the disapproval of his State Department and the anger of the British government to allow Gerry Adams, a leader of Sinn Fein (the political arm of the Irish Republican Army), to come to the United States. The president employed the prestige of his office to encourage the warring factions to negotiate. He appointed George Mitchell, the former majority leader of the Senate, to help facilitate an agreement. The arrangement, which was eventually agreed to by both Protestants and Catholics, represented the first hope for peace in the area in hundreds of years.

CONGRESSIONAL ELECTIONS OF 1994

By the middle of his first term, Bill Clinton appeared to be floundering. Health-care reform lay in ruins, and the president's budget had barely passed. Although Democrats controlled both Houses of Congress, and the presidency, the badly divided party appeared to be incapable of decisive action on any front.

The president seemed incapacitated as the old issue of his character re-emerged. A former employee in Arkansas filed an embarrassing sexual harassment suit. Paula Jones claimed that, while governor, Clinton had crudely propositioned her in a Little Rock hotel room. The president's lawyers countered with the argument that the office of the presidency, with its unique burdens, warranted "temporary immunity" from answering civil lawsuits. The case was appealed to the Supreme Court. At the same time, important questions about the Whitewater real estate development corporation were swirling around. Both the president and his wife had made unsuccessful investments in this questionable corporation a decade earlier. Under great political pressure, Attorney General Reno was forced to ask a three-judge panel to appoint an independent counsel, Kenneth Starr, to investigate.

Many Americans were annoyed with the lingering questions about the president's character. The administration did not seem able to resolve a host of social and cultural concerns including crime, school prayer, abortion, and the demise of American "family values."

Conservative groups believed they had a golden opportunity to persuade the electorate that major political change was in order. Rush Limbaugh, a right wing radio commentator, viciously denounced the Clintons. The National Rifle Association lobbied to elect candidates that would reverse recent gun control legislation. Pat Robertson, leader of the Christian Coalition, organized evangelicals across the country to bring about a political revolution at the polls.

The Republican Party in Congress was led by the aggressive Newt Gingrich of Georgia who had propelled himself from the fringes of his party to its very center. A powerful and effective leader, Gingrich denounced big government and contemporary American counter culture. Equally important, Gingrich was an energetic fund raiser and organizer.

Leading the assault on sixty years of New Deal liberalism, Newt Gingrich accurately interpreted the public mood and translated it into his "Contract with America." The Contract promised a balanced-budget amendment, congressional term limits, tax cuts, and tougher crime laws, all popular reforms the public seemed to favor. Three hundred Republican candidates, most of them Gingrich protégés, signed the Contract in a media-driven ceremony on the steps of the nation's Capitol.

This new order of Republicans succeeded in capturing control of both Houses of Congress in 1994, for the first time in forty years. They also increased their hold of state governments toppling such well-known Democratic governors as Ann Richards in Texas (who lost to George W. Bush, the former president's son) and Mario Cuomo of New York. They captured a total of thirty-one state capitals.

This new cadre of state leaders asserted the states, not Washington, D.C., were the real center of political leadership. States began to show new energy in pushing for change. They pioneered in introducing charter schools and vouchers for private schools. They initiated "three strikes" laws and mandatory sentencing for criminals. They enacted or reversed various bills on gay rights, including unmarried partners' benefits. In the field of health, they contemplated regulations involving assisted suicide, late-term abortions, insurance for AIDs victims, and Health Maintenance Organizations (HMOs). They tested different kinds of job training, compulsory work, and child care in dealing with welfare. Even President Clinton revived the Progressive era designation of states as "laboratories of democracy."

Once in office the new Speaker of the House, Newt Gingrich, and his supporters set about the business of enacting the "Contract with America." They debated a plethora of tax cuts, tax credits, and tax benefits, especially for the wealthy and the middle class. Focusing on what they called the "cultural elite," they slashed the budgets of the National Endowment for the Humanities and the Public Broadcasting Corporation.

Most importantly, they turned their attention to the welfare legislation that was still in limbo. It was at this point that President Clinton signed the revised welfare legislation. Advocates argued this law would end welfare dependency, substitute work for passivity, discourage out-of-wedlock births and teenage parenthood, reduce the size of welfare families, and reduce government costs.

CLINTON'S RE-ELECTION: 1996

Clinton's compromise with the Republicans on welfare reform was a move to the center of the political spectrum. Although still under scrutiny in Whitewater and the sexual harassment charges, he was looking toward the 1996 election.

The Senate majority leader, Robert Dole of Kansas, emerged as the front runner for the Republicans. At 72, Mr. Dole was the oldest candidate to ever seek the presidency. Originally a Nixon protégé, Dole had served in the Senate for thirty years. Despite his long career in politics, many found his political philosophy hard to define. A World War II

Bob Dole, 1996 Republican presidential nominee, served with distinction in the military and the U. S. Senate. But, he had image problems according to his own vice-presidential running mate. "I love Bob Dole," Jack Kemp said. "I just hope that our party doesn't come across ... as a party of grumpy old men."

hero, he offered the American people the opportunity to return to the values of that generation if elected. This appeal did not seem to resonate with the majority of American voters. Dole tried to capture the electorate's imagination by resigning from the Senate to focus full attention on his campaign. Despite his long-standing belief in deficit reduction, Dole also made an ambitious 15 percent across-the-board tax cut a centerpiece of his campaign.

Clinton offered himself as the leader for the future. He proclaimed his administration would build a "bridge to the 21st century." The Democrats, seizing the political center, successfully made traditional Republican issues like crime, welfare, and a balanced budget their own. With the country's economy going strong, the American voter seemed to have very little interest in the ongoing issues about Clinton's character. Ahead in the polls throughout, Clinton captured 49 percent of the popular vote to Dole's 41 percent. Perot, in the contest once again, gained only 8 percent, enough to insure federal financing for his

party in 2000 but little else. The president received 375 electoral college votes and Dole 156. Despite his successful re-election, Clinton was unable to reverse the 1994 Republican capture of Congress. The Republicans retained their control over both the Senate and the House. The public seemed satisfied with divided government.

THE SECOND TERM

Clinton's re-election did not diminish the many daunting challenges that faced him. The specter of various scandals continued to loom. In the spring of 1997, the Supreme Court cleared the way for the politically embarrassing case of sexual harassment to move forward against the president. In a unanimous decision, the Court maintained that Clinton was not immune from a civil trial on Paula Jones' charges while still in office, simply because he was the president. The Court, perhaps shielded from the realities of American political life, said that the trial would not distract the president from his duties in office.

This proved to be wildly inaccurate. Although the civil case was eventually thrown out of court as lacking any merit, the president had been asked in pretrial examination whether he had sexual relations with a White House intern, Monica Lewinsky. The president, relying perhaps on a narrow definition of what constituted sexual relations, denied any such relationship. Lewinsky, however, had been taped by a "friend," discussing a sexual connection with the president. The Independent Counsel, Kenneth Starr, then began an investigation as to whether the president had committed perjury or tried to persuade Monica Lewinsky to perjure herself. (She had also denied a sexual relationship under oath.)

The initial reaction of the American public to this mess was surprising to many observers. They were far angrier at Starr for bringing the matter up than they were at the president. Starr's approval rating fell to 11 percent, while the president's remained over 65 percent. Some people said that Clinton had become like Ronald Reagan, a "teflon president" untouched by any scandal. Others pointed to the economic prosperity that most Americans felt far outweighed any personal peccadilloes. Many Americans expressed annoyance at public airing of private matters. Nevertheless, Starr pushed on and released a report alleging, with graphic details, that the president had committed impeachable acts. The public was alternately fascinated and horrified by the report but eventually tired of the entire issue. In the midterm elections of 1998 the Democrats gained five seats in the House, the first time since 1934 that the president's party had gained seats in a midterm election. This seemed to take the steam out of the push for impeaching the president. Despite this clear demonstration of public opinion, the House of Representatives proceeded to impeach (indict) the president on an almost entirely party-line vote. In the Senate, however, where a two-thirds vote was required to convict, President Clinton was found not guilty. The House impeachment managers failed to get even a majority in the Senate to vote for conviction.

In March 2002 Robert Ray, who had replaced Kenneth Starr as independent counsel, released his 2090-page, five volume final report in which he concluded that he could not charge the Clintons with any crime in the Whitewater matter. The investigation, which had cost $64 million, ended with a "heavy thud." Monica Lewinsky denounced the turn the investigation had taken as a journey "through the banal details of two people's mistakes."

Madeleine Albright and NATO

The most historic cabinet change in the second Clinton administration was the appointment of Madeleine K. Albright. She became the first woman secretary of state in American history. Albright, who had been Ambassador to the United Nations, seemed to signal a more activist foreign policy than her cautious predecessor, Warren Christopher. The issues facing her were daunting and complex. The ancient feuds in the Balkans remained unresolved, and new troubles in Africa had developed. Ms. Albright had to be very mindful that Congress and the president were often at odds with one another as demonstrated in the struggle to ratify the Chemical Weapons Convention, banning chemical warfare. This was finally approved in April 1997.

Now that the Soviet Union was gone and the cold war was over, questions arose about the future of the North Atlantic Treaty Organization (NATO). In 1949, twelve western European nations and the United States had pledged themselves to defend each other in case of armed attack. The clear purpose of the treaty had been to protect against possible Soviet aggression. Should NATO continue to function now that the Soviet Union was gone? Could the Russians and other eastern European nations join NATO? How would the Russians respond if eastern European nations on their border were allowed into NATO?

President Clinton traveled to Europe in the spring of 1997 and invited Poland, Hungary, and the Czech Republic to join NATO. Such an expansion would mean the United States would have to defend these countries against aggression. Recognizing the need to muster support in a Republican-controlled Congress, the president declared that adding new members to NATO "will reduce the likelihood that Americans will have to die in Europe in the 21st century."

In 1999 NATO felt impelled to take action to prevent continued atrocities resulting from renewed efforts by the Serbians to eliminate ethnic Albanians from Kosovo. America and its NATO allies, to force the Serbian government to agree to autonomy for Kosovo and to end "ethnic cleansing," launched air strikes against the Serbians. Despite questions about the effectiveness of these actions, the situation eventually stabilized. The Serbian people turned against the architect of their disasters, Milosovic, and voted for a democratic opposition group.

Extremists and Violence

The history of the United States is filled with examples of violent dissident groups and organizations like the Ku Klux Klan. In the 1990s, right-wing terrorist groups were particularly active. They were responsible for the bombing of more than forty abortion clinics and various government offices. Their targets included the Forest Service office in Carson City, Nevada, the U.S. Bureau of Land Management office in Reno, Nevada, and even the Olympic site in Atlanta. The bombing of the Oklahoma City federal building on April 19, 1995, was the most destructive of all. This appalling act killed 169 innocent people, including 19 children at a day-care center. Another 500 people were injured.

The men responsible for these violent acts represent an expression of deep anger by an American subculture, the radical right. The anger of these radical right groups was greatly exacerbated by some serious government blunders. One such incident occurred in a 1992 Idaho raid by the Bureau of Alcohol, Tobacco, and Firearms (ATF) on the property of white supremacist, Randy Weaver, wanted on a weapons violation charge. An ATF sniper mistakenly killed his wife and son. The 1993 incident involving a religious cult, the Branch Davidians and their leader, David Koresh, was even more outrageous to these militants. In another siege over gun violations, eighty-six members of this religious sect died in a flaming inferno.

Two of these anti-government extremists, Terry Nichols and Timothy McVeigh, sought revenge by planning the Oklahoma City bombing. They chose April 19 for its symbolism. The day was the anniversary of the Branch Davidian raid. It was also the day that white supremacist Richard Wayne Snell was executed in Arkansas for the murder of a Jewish shopkeeper and a black state trooper. "Look over your shoulder; justice is coming," he said before being put to death. Nichols and McVeigh were charged with what was then the most deadly act of terrorism in U.S. history. On June 2, 1997, McVeigh was found guilty on all eleven charges brought against him and was sentenced to death. Nichols was found guilty of the lesser charge of conspiracy and sentenced to life in prison.

Mentally disturbed people have always existed in every society. There seemed to be evidence in 1990s, however, that the policy of emptying mental institutions and failing to provide any support to the hundreds of thousands of schizophrenics now in the larger society could have dire consequences. Schizophrenia can be controlled by medications, and most of its sufferers are not violent. But a handful of sensational incidents demonstrated what happened when violent paranoids went untreated. The

"Unabomber" who believed he was striking a blow against the tyranny of technology by mailing bombs to innocent people was apprehended in his isolated cabin in Montana. Other horrifying incidents included the dragging death of a black man and the torture-murder of a young gay man.

A 1997-9 rash of shootings at schools was also disquieting to Americans. The killers tended to be young white male adolescents in rural communities or small towns. In 2002 sniper shootings in the Washington D.C. area left 10 dead and 3 injured. The nation's capital and its suburbs ground to a standstill until the two gunmen, one a teenager, were apprehended. Some people argued that the proliferation of unsecured guns in those areas was responsible for the shooting sprees. They maintained that more effective gun control laws were needed. Conservatives responded that the violence portrayed in the media had desensitized young people to death. They ascribed the events to a continued moral breakdown in American society. One historian asked why it is that "violence and disorder constitute the primal problem of American history, the dark reverse of its coin of freedom and abundance?"

THE CLINTON LEGACY

In the last few days of the Clinton administration a cartoon appeared in the *Journal News* depicting Bill Clinton attempting to make a diving catch of a large ball labeled "Greatness." The ball lands just beyond his reach. Many observers have commented on a presidency that didn't seem to reach its potential. There seemed little doubt that, by almost any measurable standard, he left the nation stronger than he found it. Crime rates were down and the economy was in the longest economic expansion in decades. He compiled, as the *New York Times* noted, "the best conservation record of any president since Theodore Roosevelt." His achievements in this area included tighter air pollution controls, a strengthened Clean Water Act, new protections for wildernesses and national parks, and negotiation of a global warning treaty (which was not yet ratified). Progressives often criticized Clinton for being willing to accept small increments to help the disadvantaged, rather than working for big programs. These steps included an expanded earned-income tax credit for poor families; a health program for poor children; welfare-to-work aid; doubling of Head Start and school aid for disadvantaged children; and increased college aid for lower-income students. Together, these programs channeled $64 billion to poor families each year. In fact, lowest-income families gained the most from good times for the first time in decades.

Despite these accomplishments, there was a sense of disappointment as his tenure came to a close. Few political leaders came close "to matching his capacity to assimilate information and formulate policy, his skill and zest as a campaigner and his uncanny ability to connect with an audience," in the words of one observer. And yet, even his closest associates spoke of him in tones of regret about squandered opportunities. His sense of indestructibility that led him to call himself the "comeback kid," also led him to disastrous rash behavior and major ethical lapses. His recklessness and character flaws made it impossible to achieve the greatness that had seemed possible. Wasted opportunities, bitter partisanship and inability to deal with national challenges characterized the last two years of his second term

As if to punctuate this point, Clinton spent the last few sleepless nights of his administration granting pardons to people who had access to his associates. These included a fugitive multi-millionaire whose ex-wife was a major contributor to the Clinton library and other well-connected people. To many, it appeared to be an appropriate end to a president who was the first to be impeached since 1868 and who also presided over the greatest era of sustained economic growth.

THE ELECTION OF 2000

As the 2000 election campaign began, the key issue seemed to be whether "Clinton fatigue," the disenchantment caused by the president's ethical lapses would outweigh the achievement of America's longest economic expansion. After rather bitter primary struggles, the two parties picked candidates one ob-

server described as "a matched set of dauphins." The Democrats chose Vice President Al Gore, the son of a senator, who was described as a "policy wonk." The Republicans picked the Governor of Texas, George W. Bush, son of President George Bush and grandson of a senator from Connecticut. Despite his privileged background, Bush presented himself as a "regular guy." A less sympathetic commentator saw him as a "frat boy" who lacked seriousness. The public was faced with choosing between "a man who knew too much and one who knew too little." The media framed the public perception of the two candidates. Missteps by Gore were presented as further evidence of deception, while mistakes by Bush brought up questions about his preparedness. Gore's factually accurate boast that he had played a crucial role in the legislation that brought about the Internet was changed into the preposterous claim that he "invented" the Internet and continually repeated. Since lack of experience can be remedied while dishonesty cannot, two experts on media and public policy argue, "the dominant press frame in the 2000 election hurt Gore more than Bush."

Both candidates tried so hard to present themselves as centrists that much of the electorate found it hard to distinguish between them. It was in the words of columnist Ellen Goodman, "a campaign by two self-described moderates aiming to the center of the center of the undecided center of the country as if they were both trying to straddle a two-lane blacktop." Bush proclaimed himself to be a "compassionate conservative," rather than an extreme right-wing ideologue. Gore declared himself to be a supporter of "fiscal responsibility" and ran on a platform that one writer noted, "sounds as if it was written by the GOP."

A series of three debates highlighted some differences between the two men along traditional Democratic/Republican lines. But many observers felt that the major impact of the debates was to prove that George W. Bush could hold his own and to convey the perception (whether justified or not) that Al Gore was arrogant and untrustworthy. People who watched the debates tended to remain unchanged in their opinions about Gore, but those who didn't came to describe him as less and less honest in the following days, showing the influence of the coverage of the debates rather than the debates themselves. Gore made history in the campaign by choosing Senator Joseph Lieberman of Connecticut as his running mate. Lieberman was the first Jew to run for Vice President in American history. Aside from attracting some interest for his Orthodox observances, this did not turn out to be much of a factor. Bush selected his father's Secretary of Defense, Dick Cheney as his running mate.

The actual election was extraordinary in many ways. It showed a nation so evenly divided that it was virtually at equilibrium. The two parties were very close in the House, with a slight Republican majority. The Senate was a dead heat: 50-50. This was due in part to the election of a dead Democrat from Missouri (his wife was picked to succeed him) and the extraordinary election of First Lady Hillary Rodham Clinton as Senator from New York.

The presidential election was even more of a cliffhanger in which the media played a key role. Early in the evening, based on erroneous poll results, the networks projected that Al Gore won the state of Florida, which would have given him the election. A few hours later they declared that Bush won Florida and declared him the new president. Millions went to bed assuming that Bush had won, but they awakened to a contested election. When Gore challenged the results, the Republicans were able to portray him as a "sore loser" who was trying to divide the country. The news media reinforced this assumption and created an atmosphere that may well have encouraged the Supreme Court to take the election in hand. In the end, the election was so close that it came down to a few hundred votes in Florida and the vagaries of confusing punch card ballots.

The election was still in doubt in December when the case was eventually brought to the Supreme Court. Conservative justices on the court had long championed court "minimalism," criticizing judges who impose "their solutions to national problems on the popularly elected branches of government and on the people." Chief Justice Rehnquist had written, "the states are themselves sovereign entities with their own system of laws and courts, and the supreme court of a state is concededly the final authority in construing the meaning of its own constitution and laws." Despite this, Rehnquist led the conservative majority of the Court to vote 5-4 to overturn the Florida Supreme Court's order to recount the votes. The angry Court minority characterized the decision as "a self-inflicted wound."

Despite the controversy, the result was final and George W. Bush was declared president with 271 electoral votes to 267 for Gore. Gore won the popular vote by more than 500,000 votes. This had last happened in the 1888 presidential election. Despite the closeness of the election, there were clear differences that the election revealed in America. Liberals backed Gore with 80% of their vote, while a similar margin of conservatives voted for Bush. Abortion rights supporters voted overwhelmingly for Gore, as opponents of gun control did for Bush. Poor people, African-Americans, Jews, Hispanics, and women gave large majorities to Gore. Rich people, white Protestants, and men did the same for Bush. There was a rural/urban divide. *Newsweek* commented that American politics seemed to have crashed: "Voters were hopelessly Balkanized, as if two distinct countries voted, Gore controlling the coasts and the shores of the Great Lakes and Bush nearly everything else." It will take many years for scholars to explain why such sharp divisions led to a virtual dead heat.

THE BUSH PRESIDENCY

Bush began his presidency with a cabinet largely composed of people who had served in his father's or Gerald Ford's administration. He did make history by appointing two African-Americans to lead American foreign policy: General Colin Powell as Secretary of State and Condoleeza Rice as National Security Advisor. As he started his new administration, observers wondered if he could overcome the shadow over his victory and work with an evenly divided congress to achieve his goals in education, national security, and tax reduction.

The president's popularity declined as a result of worsening economic news. Some observers wondered if he would suffer the fate of the other four men who had been elected with fewer popular votes

Historians will certainly view the destruction of the World Trade Center in New York City, on September 11, 2001, as a turning point in American foreign, as well as domestic, policy.©Danny C. Sze Photography

than their opponents and failed to win reelection. Bush was determined to avoid the mistakes that had made his father a one-term president.

The Impact of 9/11

The terrible events of September 11, 2001, when terrorists hijacked three planes and crashed them into the World Trade Center towers and the Pentagon, killing more than 3,000 people, completely transformed the political and social landscape. Initially, President Bush did not project an image of great strength. Americans speculated that he was fearful of returning to Washington as Air Force One bounced around the country in the hours after the attack. He was compared unfavorably to New York City's mayor, Rudolph Guiliani who had impressed the nation with his indomitable performance. However, the president had asserted himself by September 20 in a powerful speech to Congress, and his approval rating as commander in chief climbed to an astounding 90 percent.

The nation experienced a fear it had never known. Some commentators called it "a second day of infamy," comparing September 11 to December 7, the attack on Pearl Harbor. In both instances there was an unexpected attack preceded by a massive failure of intelligence. The enemy in the earlier assault, however, was an established nation with identifiable

aims, and the attack took place on a military target (although many civilians also were killed). Now the enemy was a shadowy terrorist organization, Al Qaeda, whose cells could be anywhere and whose aims were unclear. The actions of these 19 Arab men (16 were from our ally, Saudi Arabia), forced Americans to recognize that there were people who detested the United States so intensely that they would commit "suicidal acts of massacre to make this hatred plain." American anxiety was compounded by the discovery of the deadly anthrax in letters sent to media companies and political figures. No evidence was found to connect this possible bioterrorism to Al Qaeda, but the mere possibility left people even more apprehensive.

President Bush immediately declared war on terrorism, proclaiming that Osama bin Laden would be captured, "dead or alive." By October 7 bombers, fighter planes, and missiles pulverized Al Qaeda camps in Afghanistan and destroyed airfields and military strongholds of the Taliban, the extremist group that was protecting bin Laden and his followers. Within a few days the Afghan skies were under control. Shortly thereafter, the Taliban administration collapsed, and the United State was able to install a new friendly government. A more daunting task would be the rebuilding of an Afghanistan battered by years of conflict and the actions of Taliban zealots. Despite intensive efforts to root the terror-

Reactionary Muslim terrorists of the Al Qaeda organization, led by Osama bin Laden, crashed an American Airlines flight into the Pentagon with the resulting destruction seen here.

ists out of their mountain cave hideaways, both Osama bin Laden and Mullah Muhammad Omar, the Taliban leader, thwarted American efforts to capture or kill them. Al Qaeda terrorist cells were responsible for attacks that killed more than 200 people in Indonesia and Kenya. Some Defense Department officials began to argue that America should launch a more sweeping campaign against other state sponsors of terrorism, particularly Iraq. As the attention of the American government turned elsewhere, Taliban, who had fled across the border to Pakistan, began to drift back into a beleaguered Afghanistan.

A shaken public demanded answers about intelligence failures that had allowed Islamic radicals to enter the country, study at American flight schools, and launch an unimaginably successful terrorist suicide attack. Congressional investigation revealed vast collections of unanalyzed material and unheeded warnings. "We didn't know what we knew," a former FBI official lamented. After considerable agitation by the families of 9/11 victims, a reluctant administration agreed to the formation of a commission to examine what had gone wrong. The Commission eventually concluded that there had been a massive failure of intelligence agencies to share and coordinate information that they possessed. After much prodding by the commission's leaders and the fami-

lies of 9/11 victims, the administration agreed to an intelligence overhaul that included the establishment of a new Director of Intelligence above all the agencies involved.

September 11 caused a substantial change in what had been a growing American concern with invasion of privacy. Strong public support developed for such domestic security measures as wiretaps approved by secret courts, delivery people as informants, and government surveillance of churches, mosques and rallies. All these became part of the October 2001 USA Patriot Act which modified the precarious balance between government and privacy. Federal appeals courts endorsed these changes. The public also tolerated closed immigration hearings and prisoners being held without benefit of attorneys. The government conducted sweeps arresting some 1200 Arab and South Asian men who has overstayed visas or entered the country illegally. Many had quietly lived in the United States for years, unmolested by immigration authorities. They were often held in solitary confinement for months and nearly 500 were deported. Although some people worried about profiling of Muslims, concerns about threats to civil liberties were muted. As a public policy expert noted, "One thing 9/11 did was to make Americans a little less reflexively supportive of civil liberty."

Right after 9/11 Democrats suggested the creation of a new cabinet department to combine all agencies involved with America's security. Initially, the administration resisted, but public opinion led it to embrace the concept. After some political infighting, a Department of Homeland Security was created to deter future terrorist attacks. It was designed to include border security, emergency preparedness, the Secret Service, and intelligence handling. It would be the second largest agency in the federal government after the Pentagon.

The American economy was already somewhat wobbly when it was hit by the events of September 11, leading to further uncertainty and a steep decline in the stock market. There had seemed to be a tentative recovery, but on October 16, 2001, the Enron Corporation, listed as the seventh largest in the country with a reported $101 billion in revenue, was forced to disclose $1 billion in losses. This initiated a chain of events that annihilated Enron's stock price and propelled the company into bankruptcy, eliminating thousands of jobs and wiping out billions of dollars in savings.

The company, created in the 1980s in the wave of the deregulation of energy markets by the Reagan administration, had impressed Wall Street commentators as "the most innovative company in the nation." In reality, the ever-expanding profits were only an illusion. Enron had utilized the perplexing intricacy of its financial affairs to cover up its true nature. It was, as one observer noted, "a fundamentally self-destructive institution, a house of cards where human error and a culture of ambition, secrecy and greed made collapse inevitable." Its failure exposed the deficiencies of supposed watchdogs at all levels. These included a board of directors that neglected its oversight role, outside accountants who ignored the rules of their profession, lawyers who sanctioned deceptive deals, and regulators who were bewildered by Enron's complicated finances. Wall Street analysts recommended the stock at the same time that their firms secured gigantic banking fees from the company. The fall of Enron was followed by a series of business scandals enveloping such seemingly solid companies as WorldCom and Tyco International. These events destroyed investor faith and led to a multi-trillion dollar stock market slide. Many people believed that corporate reform was essential to restore public confidence, but the political clout of large corporations limited any steps the government would take in that direction.

President Bush had long favored tax cuts as the measure to solve any and all economic woes. He had succeeded in gaining the passage of tax cuts that were weighted so that more than a third of the money went to 1 percent of the taxpayers. It was assumed that "a rising tide lifts all boats." As the economy continued to falter and 1.4 million jobs were lost, the president suggested further cuts in taxes. These included the repeal of the inheritance tax, a significant source of revenue. It was dubbed the "death tax" by Republicans, even though only the top 2 percent of estates paid any tax at all and half of the tax was paid by estates over $5 million, 0.16 percent of the total. The president also argued for a complicated repeal of the tax on most dividends to rebuild the confidence of investors. Democrats argued that the $360 billion in revenue this would cost would worsen the federal deficit and do little to stimulate the economy. The combination of tax cuts and growing expenses as a result of 9/11 had turned the budget surplus of the Clinton years into a growing deficit that reached $300 billion by 2003.

Domestic Policies

Although George Bush had run as a centrist in his election campaign, he was well aware of the problems his father had faced when he appeared to ignore his conservative core constituency. He attempted to roll back many of the environmental initiatives of the Clinton administration. Shortly after taking office, he rejected the Kyoto Protocol, the global warming treaty negotiated by his predecessor. Believing that mandatory reductions in emissions linked to global warming would harm the economy, the president sent senior officials around the country to collect voluntary written promises from industries to curb such emissions. He also favored legislation to open part of the Arctic National Wildlife Refuge to oil drilling, although the Democrats blocked this effort.

President Bush continued to press for his Faith Based Initiative that would turn some federal welfare funds over to religious charitable organizations. While this had yet to pass Congress, the president was more successful in efforts to modify the historic 1973 *Roe v. Wade* decision that had established a woman's right to end her pregnancy. He attempted to fill the judiciary with individuals hostile to that decision. The status of a fetus or fertilized egg was elevated by the administration to that of a person with rights equivalent to that of women. Federal financing for research on all new embryonic stem-cell lines was prohibited, despite arguments that such research could be valuable in finding treatment for a variety of diseases. He favored the Abortion Non-Discrimination Act that would permit government-supported health-care providers to refuse to perform abortions or even prohibit their doctors from informing their female patients about the option of obtaining an abortion. On his first day in office the president reinstated the global "gag" rule that had been instituted by Ronald Reagan and then lifted by President Clinton. It barred any health providers that received American assistance from in any way counseling or even discussing abortion. As a consequence, millions of dollars were frozen intended for programs to combat AIDS and improve reproductive health, sponsored by the World Health Organization and the United Nations Population Fund. In the summer of 2002 the president revoked support for Senate ratification of a women's rights treaty, barring nations from discriminating against women in such areas as health care and legal rights. American delegations at international conferences opposed endorsement of condom use to prevent AIDS and efforts to help girl war crime rape victims, worrying that his might mean information about abortion.

Conservative Republicans had long fantasized about making Social Security more like a private pension system. In his post 2002 election news conference President Bush reiterated his commitment to that point of view: "I still strongly believe that the best way to achieve security in Social Security for younger workers is to give them the option of managing their own money through a personal savings account." Democrats declared that they would welcome a fight on this issue in the 2004 election, but they didn't offer any plan of their own to solve the issue of the system running out of money when the baby boomers retired.

"The Axis of Evil"

In his 2002 State of the Union address President Bush spoke of an "axis of evil" in the world. He identified the nations in this axis as Iraq, Iran, and North Korea. World leaders worried that the heightening rhetoric was reminiscent of the Cold War campaign against Communism. Vice President Dick Cheney declared that the war was divided into the forces of darkness and light and that "the United States and only the United States can see this effort through to victory."

As the war on terrorism settled into a stalemate, officials in the Defense Department argued that the time was right to go to war with Iraq to oust Saddam Hussein. They contended that Saddam was in the process of accumulating weapons of mass destruction and posed a "grave and growing danger." President Bush declared, "I will not wait on events while dangers gather. I will not stand by as peril draws closer and closer." In the following weeks Bush and his top aides invariably added warnings about the Iraqi threat in their speeches and interviews to bolster their argument for the necessity of "regime change."

Secretary of State Colin Powell and others in the State Department believed that it was important to gain support of a coalition of nations for any action by going to the United Nations and demanding a return of international weapons inspectors to Iraq. On September 12, 2002 the president appeared before the United Nations and challenged its members to act or risk rendering the world body "irrelevant." Powell was able to push through a Security Council resolution demanding that Saddam disarm and cooperate with arms inspectors or face "serious consequences." Although the resolution passed unanimously, its vague phrasing papered over serious division among the member nations. The administration expected Hussein to shuffle his weapons of mass destruction around the country, showing that he was hiding something. But conclusive evidence to convince undecided nations and people proved difficult to uncover. Secretary Powell attempted to break the deadlock by disclosing what he claimed was undeniable evidence of Iraq's weapons of mass destruction and ties to terrorism. Despite the backing of Britain's Tony Blair, the Europeans, particularly the French, Germans and Russians, were not convinced and opposed any new resolution that could lead to war. In the meantime American troop deployment in the Persian Gulf area escalated in early 2003 in preparation for war. Finally, on March 17, Bush addressed the nation. He issued an ultimatum: "Saddam Hussein and his sons must leave Iraq within 48 hours. Their refusal to do so will result in military conflict to commence at a time of our choosing."" Within two days the nation was at war.

At the same time that the Iraqi situation was worsening, North Korea announced that it was pulling out of a 1994 agreement under which it froze its nuclear reactor and renounced any development of nuclear weapons. The North Koreans acknowledged that they had cheated on that accord. It was difficult to understand whether the reclusive "Great Leader," Kim Jong Il, an isolated tyrant, wanted a nuclear arsenal or a new relationship with the West. Administration hard-liners pressed the president to further isolate North Korea to increase pressure on Kim or lead to the collapse of his regime, even though it might intensify the crisis. As thousands of American troops were heading to the Persian Gulf, President Bush did not want to risk a military confrontation with North Korea and South Korea, usually a reliable American ally, opposed any punitive policy. The president declared that the problem could be "solved in a peaceful way" and that America might be willing to negotiate to reward "right behavior" by the North Koreans. Cynics noted that the lesson of the two nations was that it was better to already have nuclear weapons: blackmail was more effective.

The Elections of 2002

Historically, the post-World War II average loss by a president's party in the first midterm after his election was 22 House and two Senate seats. In the 2002

congressional elections the Republicans gained 6 seats in the House and 2 in the Senate. This unprecedented outcome came from careful planning by Karl Rove, the president's "political mastermind." Rove determined by early August to make security the overarching theme of the campaign and to rely on Bush's positive ratings as commander in chief and leader of the war on terror. Iraq would be the central story bolstered by congressional approval obtained before Election Day.

As usual, Republicans tended to be more disciplined and ideologically united than the Democrats, particularly in matters involving use of force. Polls showed that Americans, as Karl Rove informed party leaders, "trust the Republican Party to do a better job of protecting and strengthening America's military might and thereby protecting America."

A crucial moment at the end of September was the failure to reach a compromise with the Democrats on the homeland-security bill. Ironically, the creation of such a department had been a Democratic idea, initially resisted by Bush. But when the Democrats sought to protect their union constituency by opposing limitations on federal employee unions in the bill, Bush had gained an issue. In several "Red" States (states that had voted for Bush), Democrats were charged with being soft on tackling terrorism. Some ads showed their faces alongside Saddam Hussein and Osama bin Laden. The Democrats, the president charged, were more responsive to "special interests" than to the security of America. In Georgia these charges of lack of patriotism succeeded in causing the defeat of Senator Max Cleland who had lost three of his limbs fighting in his nation's armed forces. "The issue resonated, " Rove noted with some glee.

No sooner did the 2002 results come in, than Rove and his colleagues began planning for the presidential election of 2004. While the president's approval ratings remained high, by early 2003 they had fallen below 60 percent for the first time since September 11, 2001. A majority disapproved of his management of the economy, tax cuts, and even foreign policy. The author of several books about President Reagan once remarked, "Reagan invited us to underestimate him. He felt that gave him an advantage." The same often seemed true of President Bush.

THE 2004 ELECTION

The Democrats were heartened by polls that seemed to show declining approval ratings for the president. They chose Senator John Kerry of Massachusetts as their standard-bearer, ignoring warnings about the difficulties of electing long-term senators with substantial numbers of legislative votes that could be attacked. As his running mate, Democrats picked Senator John Edwards of North Carolina who balanced the ticket geographically and was attractive and charismatic. Kerry believed that his background as a decorated Vietnam war veteran would immunize him against any charges of softness in matters of national security. The Republicans were able to counter this by producing a television commercial by Swift Boat Veterans for Truth that disputed Kerry's claims to bravery. Although their charges were never proven, the Kerry campaign was slow to respond to them, and they were successful in confusing the public's understanding of the differences between the Kerry and Bush war record.

Despite the passage of a campaign finance reform law, the election revealed a loophole in allowing so-called "soft-money" contributions. As a result, an astounding $3.9 billion was spent on the campaign. Despite this, Kerry was unsuccessful in turning the campaign into a referendum on the economy or in articulating his vision for America. He was also harmed by the appearance on television on the weekend before the election of a tape by Osama bin Laden that seemed to urge the defeat of George Bush. Others argued that "moral issues" were the key, but later close analysis appears to contradict this view.

Whatever the reason, President Bush was able to accomplish what one Democrat called a "monumental achievement" of winning the election despite polls that showed concern with the direction of the country and unhappiness with his job performance and the public's clear belief that Kerry had won the presidential debates. This time George Bush won the popular vote with 51 percent of the vote, a margin of three and a half million votes. Few of the "red" or "blue" states switched their positions from 2000. (New Mexico and Iowa went for Bush this time, and New Hampshire moved to Kerry.) Bush did better in the states he had won the last time, and Kerry improved the Democratic totals in some showdown states. Despite the fact that this was a much clearer victory, a switch of less than 60,000 votes in Ohio would have changed the results. The nation continued to be closely and bitterly divided.

The results, however, were more clear-cut on the president's psyche. No longer would there hang over his administration the issue of whether he was the legitimate president. He could now feel free to argue that free market principles should prevail in environmental and social policies. It was not clear whether he could convince the country that he had a true conservative mandate on these and on moral issues. His early efforts to change the social security system were met with resistance and skepticism, and his intervention in an end-of-life case provoked public opposition. By the middle of 2005 his approval ratings had fallen well below 50 percent, but he had always shown a capacity to overcome obstacles.

There were substantial changes in the president's cabinet for his second term. The beleaguered and disillusioned Secretary of State Colin Powell resigned. Condoleeza Rice, who became the first African-American woman to reach such a high position in government, replaced him. The controversial Attorney General John Ashcroft also left office. Alberto Gonzalez, who took his place, was the first Hispanic American to hold that job. Donald Rumsfield, however, despite public demands that he too should be removed, remained in his position as Secretary of Defense.

THE NEW MILLENIUM

In the 1990s Bill Clinton had spoken of building a bridge to the twenty-first century. In the early years of the new century many Americans wondered how sturdy a structure that bridge would be as the United States entered its third century as a nation.

The American Economy and Social Classes

The 1990s saw one of the longest and most robust booms in American history, a period of normally incompatible low unemployment and low inflation. Stock prices had risen to unimaginable heights. A combination of an increase in minimum wages and earned-income tax credit had even led to improvements in the bottom 20 percent on the national wage scale.

Even as some experts were arguing that the nation was entering a new economic era, there were cracks in the picture of economic well being. In the 29 years from 1970 to 1999, the average income of middle class families had risen only 10 percent, compared to a 157 percent increase of those in the top 1-percent. In 1970 the 100 top C.E.O.'s earned 39 times the pay of the average worker. By 1999 they made more than 1,000 times the pay of workers. The reconcentration of wealth in America had gotten so great the 13,000 richest families had about as much income as the 20 million poorest. Many observers worried about this growing inequality. Although the United States has the highest per capita income of the world's advanced countries, that is mainly because the rich are so much richer. The poorest Swedes, for example, have incomes 60 percent higher than the poorest Americans do, while their rich are not nearly as affluent. Life expectancy in the United States is well below that in Western Europe, Canada and Japan, and infant mortality and illiteracy rates are much higher. The darkening economic picture after 2001 exacerbated these problems.

The health-care system was also experiencing major difficulties as premiums continued to rise while coverage was shrinking. In 2001 alone, nearly 1.5 million Americans lost their insurance, leaving more than 40 million Americans without any health coverage. By 2004 that number had risen to 45 million. This happened despite the fact that Americans spent nearly twice as much on health care as the average for other industrialized nations. In spite of an effort by the Democrats to address this crucial issue in the 2004 election, it did not have a decisive impact upon the results. As a consequence, there were no efforts mounted to improve the health-care system.

Most Americans, unlike Europeans, express very little class antagonism. They seemed willing to tolerate tremendous inequality in income, disposable wealth, and social privilege. Some say this is because they have bought the "American dream" and expect to join the ranks of the privileged themselves some day. Others have argued that, as the rich get even richer, they can use their money to buy political influence and to shape public perceptions. The result, according to one economist, has been the increasing income gaps, "far from leading to demands to soak the rich, have been accompanied by a growing movement to let them keep more of their earnings and to pass their wealth on to their children." The second Bush administration worked to make the tax cuts that benefited the wealthiest Americans permanent, thus institutionalizing income disparities and increasing the budget deficit.

Would the new millenium bring about the creation of a hereditary elite in America? Kevin Phillips, warned in his book, *Wealth and Democracy,* "Either democracy must be renewed with politics brought back to life, or wealth is likely to cement a new and less democratic regime—plutocracy by some other name."

Demographics and Social Issues:
The Next Half-Century

The Census Bureau projected a demographic transformation of the American population by 2050 that has no precedent in history. In 1965 America was more than 80 percent non-Hispanic white and about 10 percent black. By 2050 the bureau suggested that America will be barely half white, 26 percent Hispanic, 14 percent black, and 8 percent Asian. Hispanic increases, due to high immigration and fertility rates, will coincide with a decline in the non-Hispanic white population. The report stated that, by the year 2028, the number of white Americans who die would exceed the number of those born.

How will Americans react to this dramatic change? As one reporter commented, it will "challenge the existing notions of what it means to be white, redefine the content and character of race relations, and metamorphose the look and feel of American identity."

Many people worry that racism is far from dead in American society. A December 1997 poll, however, revealed rather complex views about affirmative action. Most Americans rejected the idea of making hiring and college admissions decisions based on race, while continuing to endorse the goal of racial diversity in schools and jobs. They favored "special efforts" to help minorities compete and affirmative action programs giving preference to poor people, regardless of race. Although President Bush urged the rejection of a University of Michigan policy to increase diversity in its student body, the majority of Americans expressed disagreement with him on this issue.

Observers were heartened by a report from the National Center for Health Statistics showing that the birth rate for unmarried black women had reached its lowest point in over 40 years. Demographers believed that the trend would continue due to an increase in contraceptive use, sex education, and efforts by community groups to encourage abstention. Large gaps between African Americans and whites in educational accomplishment, infant mortality, income, and poverty rates continued to plague society. However, studies showed substantial improvements in life expectancy, income, murder rates, completion of high school, and other measures of well being by African Americans.

As birth rates continued to decline, immigrants were expected to account for most of the nation's population rise over the next 50 years. Contrary to common perception, a study of the economic and fiscal effects of immigration by the National Academy of Sciences reported that "immigration produces substantial economic benefits for the United States as a whole. . . ." Young immigrant workers will help provide the necessary tax revenues to support the ever-increasing ranks of retirees.

Earlier estimates regarding the graying of America were also reconfirmed. By the middle of the next century the Census Bureau forecast that people 85 years of age would be the fastest growing age cohort in the United States. In 1995, 1.4 percent of the population was over 85. However, by 2050, there would be approximately 18 million Americans over that age, 4.6 percent of the population. By that year, 20 percent of the population will be over 65. This had serious implications for the future viability of the social security system, a political hot-potato that politicians were gingerly attempting to handle. The Bush administration pushed for the introduction of private investment accounts funded by a portion of social security contributions. Democrats argued that such a program would increase the deficit, endanger people's guaranteed social security benefits, and not solve the underlying problem. However, neither Democrats or Republicans seemed willing to discuss such possible solutions as raising the income level taxed by social security, raising the retirement age, or changing the way in which benefits are calculated.

Other social issues faced an anxious nation. At the same time that rural areas of poverty were becoming increasingly dysfunctional, agribusinesses were producing 3,800 calories of food a day for every American, about a thousand calories more than most people need. The result was an effort to convince Americans to eat more by "supersizing." Americans became the fattest people on earth, 6 out of 10 being overweight. One consequence was an epidemic of the dangerous Type 2 diabetes, as well as other health problems.

The "New World Order"

The end of the cold war and the collapse of the Soviet Union created a "new world order" that seemed all the more dangerous in its unpredictability. Countries that were once part of the Soviet state became a vast supermarket for arms dealers. Third world countries could now acquire weapons of terror—missiles, gas, germs—the "poor man's nukes." One observer commented that attempts to control these weapons of mass destruction were "like plugging a gaping leak with chewing gum—again and again." Little has been done to stop the booming arms trade.

There were some victories in avoiding a nuclear disaster. In 1996, leaders of most nuclear powers approved a comprehensive test ban treaty at the United Nations headquarters. President Clinton, employing the same pen that John F. Kennedy had used for the first limited test ban treaty in 1963, declared, "Our children deserve to walk the earth in safety." Anti-nuclear advocates were heartened when South Africa voluntarily gave up its bombs, and Britain, France and Russia signed the pact.

The fragility of attempts to prevent nuclear proliferation quickly became apparent, however. India and Pakistan, two enemies that had not signed the test ban agreement, tested nuclear missiles in 1998. American entreaties and sanctions failed to persuade either nation to abandon nuclear testing. North Korea's overt rejection of nuclear limitations was even more alarming. Outlaw states like Iran and North Korea, unlike the stable and relatively reliable opponents during the cold war, could potentially supply international terrorists with weapons of mass destruction. Despite its overwhelming military power, America's main enemy was not a nation that could be deterred by threat of force, but an indistinct, loosely organized group of zealots who could not be contained and who seized a great religion, Islam, to obtain an endless supply of recruits and loyalists. The destruction of Soviet power did not seem to have made the world a safer place.

Clinton made the achievement of a Mideast peace accord his highest foreign policy priority. Down to his last few days in office, he was working hectically to achieve this elusive peace that seemed tantalizingly close. At the end he had to acknowledge that the agreement he "really wanted with all my heart" had slipped away and "we've got a mess on our hands." As America pursued its war with Iraq, peace between Israel and the Palestinians became more imperative. Instead, Palestinian suicide terrorists mounted more assaults against innocent civilians within Israel, and Sharon retaliated by strengthening settlements inside the West Bank and attacking Palestinian towns. There seemed to be a glimmer of hope after the death of Palestinian leader and obstacle to peace, Yassir Arafat, in November 2004. Mahmoud Abbas, a more moderate advocate of a peaceful solution, succeeded him. In 2005 the Palestinian people ratified this choice in a surprisingly fair and scandal free election. Sharon, meanwhile, despite opposition from the right wing of his own party, announced his intentions to withdraw from the Gaza Strip by the summer of 2005. Hopeful, though cautious, talks began between the two sides over a final compromise on the West Bank.

On March 19, 2003, after failing to get United Nations support, President Bush addressed the nation. "At this hour, American and coalition forces are in the early stages of military operations to disarm Iraq to free its people and to defend the world from grave danger." He assured the country, "I will accept no outcome but victory." As most observers had expected, the war was a swift one. Aided by air strikes and "smart bombs," American forces easily cut the Iraqi military to pieces and destroyed its will to resist. The predicted "death traps" in the streets of Iraqi cities failed to materialize. The Iraqi army "just melted into the population" and the feared showdown with the vaunted Republican Guard turned out to be "an unqualified rout." The official conflict was over in less than four weeks. There was some sporadic resistance from irregulars and suicide bombers, but the total "coalition" (American and British) death toll was under 200. The death toll of Iraq soldiers and civilians was not calculated.

The results, however, were not as clear-cut as televised scenes of exultant crowds cheering the toppling of a giant statue of Saddam in Baghdad and pelting the severed head with shoes, the ultimate Arab insult. Mass burial grounds disclosed the savagery of Saddam's regime. One aspect of "Operation Iraqi Freedom" had ended, but a second far more difficult phase was about to begin. The United States had conquered a fragmented and chaotic nation. The simplest institutions of public order, as well as power and water supplies, had to be restored. Plundering included an orgy of looting and vandalism at the Iraqi National Museum. No American soldiers or marines had been detailed to guard the precious records of the early history of civilization. American authorities had to balance conflicting claims of Sunni Muslims, Kurds and the Shiite Muslim majority. Although the Shiites, who had been severely persecuted under Hussein, welcomed his defeat, they also demonstrated against American occupation. The growing influence of their clergy led to fears that they would attempt to establish a radical Muslim state similar to that of Iran. Extensive searches failed to uncover the tons of weapons of mass destruction that Colin Powell had eloquently described. Despite the capture of Saddam Hussein in December of 2003 from his hiding place in a hole, the suspected ties between his regime and Al Qaeda terrorists could not be verified. Although the American public quickly forgot the original justification for the invasion of Iraq in the euphoria that followed the swift victory, the rest of the world did not. In the face of American occupation, insurgent cells bent on killing American troops and Iraqis who cooperated with them, sprouted up throughout the country. They were particularly effective in the areas of the country where disaffected Sunni Muslims lived. By the middle of 2005 more than 1500 American troops had died in Iraq, the overwhelming majority after victory had been declared. Thousands more were wounded and many more thousands of Iraqis had perished. America's self-image was dealt a crushing blow by the exposure of the torture of Iraqi prisoners by American military police, intelligence agents, and outside contractors at Abu Ghraib prison in Iraq. Although early reports place the blame on relatively low-level operatives, later investigation revealed that the problem was more widespread than originally supposed.

On a more positive note, Iraqis flocked to the polls in January 2005 to choose a government, bravely ignoring threats to their lives if they did so. The democratic election in Palestine, and the success of popular efforts in Lebanon to force a Syrian withdrawal from their country, encouraged the Bush administration, which had changed its justification of the war in Iraq to a struggle to establish democracy. This elation was tempered somewhat by the inability of the various ethnic groups in Iraq to avoid factional divisions and reach some consensus to establish an effective government. In addition to its human cost, the bill for the war in Iraq had reached $300 billion by 2005 with the end not yet in sight, further exacerbating the budget deficit.

September 11 and reactions to the invasion of Iraq made Americans aware of the hatred aroused by the nation's status as the world's sole superpower. Only America now policed the world with five global military commands; maintained armed forces on four continents; drove the engine of global commerce; assembled carrier battle ships in every ocean; and pledged to maintain the survival of nations from South Korea to Israel, as well as the creation of a new democracy in Iraq. This was, as one observer noted, an "empire lite," an empire acquired by a people who considered themselves supporters of democracy and free trade and were dismayed to discover that their good intentions were not appreciated by all the peoples of the world. America had never been clear about whether it valued stability and profits more than its own eloquence about democracy. Events in Iraq tested this ambiguity. A new global order could not be fashioned by America standing alone. Europeans would have to take part in the reconstruction, peacekeeping, and nation building in this new world. Despite this, the Bush administration had appeared to insist that the United States could act on its own. It expressed a distrust of international agreements, organizations, and alliances and an eagerness to displace tyrannical or dangerous governments. At the same time, President Bush attempted to mend fences in Europe, even visiting France and quoting the great existentialist writer Albert Camus that "freedom is a long distance race." The president's ambiguity on the issue of what to do about nations like Iran that posed a nuclear threat in spite of the Iraq war was illustrated in his comment: "The notion that the United States is getting ready to attack Iran is simply ridiculous. Having said that, all options are on the table."

One observer compared the changing international role of the United States to a variation of the film, *The Gladiator.* "We entered the arena reluctantly but once inside vanquished all challengers." Now we are victorious and alone inside the Coliseum, without any idea of what to do with Rome. "What's more, we're not even very sure where the exit signs leading out of the Coliseum are located."

CONCLUSION

The 1990s had ended with many Americans decrying the decline of American morals and grandeur. The media and the public had seemed addicted to a mindless sensationalism. This continued in the new millennium. More observers detected an on-going culture war, epitomized in the divisions between red and blue states. In 2005 these differences were starkly revealed in the media and political frenzy over the end of the life of one American, Terri Schiavo. After she had been declared by her physicians to be in a "persistent vegetative state," her husband had petitioned to have her feeding tube removed. Her parents opposed this, arguing that she was still a sentient human being. When the courts ruled in her husband's favor, Jeb Bush, the Governor of Florida, the Congress of the United States and President Bush, all sought to overturn those decisions. Ultimately, the tubes were removed and Terri Schiavo died, but the bitterness across the cultural divide remained.

The corporate scandals, economic uncertainties, the terrible events of 9/11, the seemingly endless conflict in Iraq, the national divisions over the meaning of life and personal choice, and the problems of a dangerous world left Americans deeply troubled as the nation entered the new millenium. Despite this feeling of despondency, the study of American history reveals a nation of great resilience. Hazards may persist in the new millennium, but this nation of many peoples has endured for more than two centuries with a continuous vision of an even better future.

Chronology

1981   Ronald Reagan takes office as president
Hostages released from Iran
Severe recession begins (to 1983)
Reagan wins major cuts in taxes and domestic spending and increases in military spending
Researchers identify cause of AIDS
Sandra Day O'Connor appointed first female Supreme Court justice

1982   U. S. supports contra war against Sandinista government in Nicaragua
Equal Rights Amendment dies

1983   U. S. invades Grenada
Terrorist attack in Beirut kills American marines/ U. S. pulls out of Lebanon
Reagan proposes Strategic Defense Initiative

1984   Democrats choose Geraldine Ferraro, first woman vice presidential candidate
Reagan defeats Walter Mondale in land-slide for re-election as president

1985   Mikhail Gorbachev becomes leader of Soviet Union
Increase of terrorist acts like airline hijackings

1986   Iran-contra scandal begins to leak out
U. S. bombs Libyan targets
Insider trading scandals rock Wall Street
Challenger space shuttle blows up after takeoff

1987   Congressional hearings held on Iran-contra
Stock market suffers record decline

1988   George Bush elected president

1989   Berlin Wall is torn down; Communism collapses in Eastern Europe
U. S. invades Panama
Chinese government crushes prodemocracy students in Tiananmen Square
Alaska hit by massive oil spill from *Exxon Valdez*

1990   Bush and Congress agree on tax increases to reduce budget deficit
Federal Clean Air Act is passed
Iraq invades Kuwait; United Nations imposes sanctions
Gorbachev wins Nobel Peace Prize as Soviet troops withdraw from Eastern Europe

1991   Soviet Union disintegrates as Soviet republics declare independence
U. S. ousts Iraqi army from Kuwait in Gulf war (Operation Desert Storm)
After controversial hearings, Clarence Thomas confirmed as Supreme Court justice

1992   Bill Clinton elected president
Major race riot in Los Angeles follows "not guilty" verdict in Rodney King case

1993   Janet Reno becomes first female attorney general
Israel and the Palestine Liberation Organization sign Oslo peace accord
U. S. soldiers killed in humanitarian mission in Somalia

Congress approves North American Free Trade
   Agreement (NAFTA)
Gun control, anticrime and Family and
   Medical Leave laws passed
Terrorist bomb explodes in World Trade
   Center in New York City

1994 U. S. troops intervene in Haiti to
   return democratic government to power
Nelson Mandela elected president of
   South Africa
Republicans win control of Congress after
   declaring "Contract with America"

1995 Bomb explodes in Federal Building in
   Oklahoma City, killing 169
Israeli Prime Minister Yitzhak Rabin
   assassinated by opponent of Oslo accords
U. S. arranges Dayton accords to temporarily
   end conflict in former Yugoslavia

1996 Personal Responsibility and Work Opportunity
   Reconciliation Act seeks to end federal welfare
Clinton re-elected president
Comprehensive nuclear test ban treaty
   signed by leaders of nuclear powers

1997 Economy reaches new heights
Madeleine Albright becomes first
   female secretary of state

1998 Monica Lewinsky case embroils Clinton presidency
Democrats gain seats in Congress
Clinton impeached, found not guilty in
   Senate trial.

1999 Nuclear Test Ban treaty rejected in Senate

2000 George W. Bush elected president
   Gore wins popular vote
   Senate divided 50-50

2002 Republicans gain 6 House and 2 Senate seats
   in election

2003 War with Iraq

2004 George W. Bush wins reelection

SUGGESTED READINGS

Richard Bernstein, *Out of the Blue: the Story of September 11* (2002).

Mary Francis Berry, *Why ERA Failed* (1986).

Lou Cannon, *President Reagan: The Role of a Lifetime* (1990).

Richard Clarke, *Against All Enemies: Inside America's War on Terror* (2004).

Theodore Draper, *A Very Thin Line: the Iran-Contra Affair* (1991).

Martin Duberman, *Stonewall* (1993).

Lawrence Freedman and Efraim Karsh, *The Gulf Conflict, 1990-1991* (1993).

John Lewis Gaddis, *Surprise, Security, and the American Experience* (2004).

Andrew Hacker, *Two Nations: Black and White, Separate, Hostile, Unequal* (1992).

Seymour Hersh, *Chain of Command: The Road from 9/11 to Abu Ghraib* (2004).

Christopher Jencks, *The Homeless* (1994).

Haynes Johnson, *Sleepwalking Through History: America in the Reagan Years* (1991).

Michael Katz, *The Undeserving Poor: From the War on Poverty to the War on Welfare* (1989).

John Keegan, *The Iraq War* (2004).

Joe Klein, *The Natural: The Misunderstood Presidency of Bill Clinton* (2002).

Jere Longman, *Among the Heroes: United Flight 93* (2002).

David Mervin, *George Bush and the Guardianship Presidency* (1996).

National Commission on Terrorist Attacks, the *9/11 Commission Report* (2004).

Kevin Phillips, *The Politics of Rich and Poor: Wealth and the American Electorate in the Aftermath of the Reagan Presidency* (1990).

Arthur M. Schlesinger Jr., *The Disuniting of America* (1991)

James B. Stewart, *Den of Thieves* (1991).

Sanford J. Unger, *Fresh Blood: The New American Immigrants* (1995).

Gary Wills, *Reagan's America: Innocents At Home* (1987).

___, *Under God: Religion and American Politics* (1990).

Bob Woodward, *Plan of Attack* (2004).

Declaration of Independence

Congress, July 4, 1776

When, in the course of human events, it becomes necessary for one people to dissolve the political bonds which have connected them with another, and to assume, among the powers of the earth, the separate and equal station to which the laws of nature and of nature's God entitle them, a decent respect to the opinions of mankind requires that they should declare the causes which impel them to the separation.

We hold these truths to be self-evident: That all men are created equal; that they are endowed by their Creator with certain unalienable rights; that among these are life, liberty and the pursuit of happiness; that, to secure these rights, governments are instituted among men, deriving their just powers from the consent of the governed; that whenever any form of government becomes destructive of these ends, it is the right of the people to alter or to abolish it, and to institute new government, laying its foundation on such principles, and organizing its powers in such form, as to them shall seem most likely to effect their safety and happiness. Prudence, indeed, will dictate that governments long established should not be changed for light and transient causes; and accordingly all experience hath shown that mankind are more disposed to suffer, while evils are sufferable, than to right themselves by abolishing the forms to which they are accustomed. But when a long train of abuses and usurpations, pursuing invariably the same object, evinces a design to reduce them under absolute despotism, it is their right, it is their duty, to throw off such government, and to provide new guards for their future security. Such has been the patient sufferance of these colonies; and such is now the necessity which constrains them to alter their former systems of government. The history of the present King of Great Britain is a history of repeated injuries and usurpations, all having in direct object the establishment of an absolute tyranny over these states. To prove this, let facts be submitted to a candid world.

He has refused his assent to laws, the most wholesome and necessary for the public good.

He has forbidden his governors to pass laws of immediate and pressing importance, unless suspended in their operation till his assent should be obtained; and, when so suspended, he has utterly neglected to attend to them.

He has refused to pass other laws for the accommodation of large districts of people, unless those people would relinquish the right of representation in the legislature, a right inestimable to them, and formidable to tyrants only.

He has called together legislative bodies at places unusual, uncomfortable, and distant from the depository of their public records, for the sole purpose of fatiguing them into compliance with his measures.

He has dissolved representative houses repeatedly, for opposing, with many firmness, his invasions on the rights of the people.

He has refused for a long time, after such dissolutions, to cause others to be elected; whereby the legislative powers, incapable of annihilation, have returned to the people at large for their exercise; the state remaining, in the mean time, exposed to all the dangers of invasions from without and convulsions within.

He has endeavored to prevent the population of these states; for that purpose obstructing the laws for naturalization of foreigners; refusing to pass others to encourage their migrations hither, and raising the conditions of new appropriations of lands.

He has obstructed the administration of justice, by refusing his assent to laws establishing judiciary powers.

He has made judges dependent on his will alone, for the tenure of their offices, and the amount and payment of their salaries.

He has erected a multitude of new offices, and sent hither swarms of officers to harass our people and eat out their substance.

He has kept among us, in times of peace, standing armies, without the consent of our legislatures.

He has affected to render the military independent of, and superior to, the civil power.

He has combined with others to subject us to jurisdiction foreign to our constitution, and unacknowledged by our laws, giving his assent to their acts of pretended legislation:

For quartering large bodies of armed troops among us;

For protecting them, by a mock trial, from punishment for any murder which they should commit on the inhabitants of these states;

For cutting off our trade with all parts of the world;

For imposing taxes on us without our consent;

For depriving us, in many cases, of the benefits of trial by jury;

For transporting us beyond seas, to be tried for pretended offenses;

For abolishing the free system of English laws in a neighboring province, establishing therein an arbitrary government, and enlarging its boundaries, so as to render it at once an example and fit instrument for introducing the same absolute rule into these colonies;

For taking away our charters, abolishing our most valuable laws, and altering fundamentally the forms of our governments;

For suspending our own legislatures, and declaring themselves invested with power to legislate for us in all cases whatsoever.

He has abdicated government here, by declaring us out of his protection and waging war against us.

He has plundered our seas, ravaged our coasts, burned our towns, and destroyed the lives of our people.

He is at this time transporting large armies of foreign mercenaries to complete the works of death, desolation and tyranny already begun with circumstances of cruelty and perfidy scarcely paralleled in the most barbarous ages, and totally unworthy the head of a civilized nation.

He has constrained our fellow-citizens, taken captive on the high seas, to bear arms against their country, to become the executioners of their friends and brethren, or to fall themselves by their hands.

He has excited domestic insurrections among us, and has endeavored to bring on the inhabitants of our frontiers the merciless Indian savages, whose known rule of warfare is an undistinguished destruction of all ages, sexes, and conditions.

In every stage of these oppressions we have petitioned for redress in the most humble terms; our repeated petitions have been answered only by repeated injury. A prince, whose character is thus marked by every act which may define a tyrant, is unfit to be the ruler of a free people.

Nor have we been wanting in our attentions to our British brethren. We have warned them, from time to time, of attempts by their legislature to extend an unwarrantable jurisdiction over us. We have reminded them of the circumstances of our emigration and settlement here. We have appealed to their native justice and magnanimity, and we have conjured them, by the ties of our common kindred, to disavow these usurpations, which would inevitably interrupt our connections and correspondence. They, too, have been deaf to the voice of justice and of consanguinity. We must, therefore, acquiesce in the necessity which denounces our separation, and hold them, as we hold the rest of mankind, enemies in war, in peace friends.

We, therefore, the representatives of the United States of America, in General Congress assembled, appealing to the Supreme Judge of the world for the rectitude of our intentions, do, in the name and by authority of the good people of these colonies, solemnly publish and declare, that these United Colonies are, and of right ought to be, FREE AND INDEPENDENT STATES; that they are absolved from all allegiance to the British crown, and that all political connection between them and the state of Great Britain is, and ought to be, totally dissolved; and that, as free and independent states, they have full power to levy war, conclude peace, contract alliances, establish commerce, and do all other acts and things which independent states may of right do. And for the support of this declaration, with a firm reliance on the protection of Divine Providence, we mutually pledge to each other our lives, our fortunes, and our sacred honor.

JOHN HANCOCK

BUTTON GWINNETT
LYMAN HALL
GEO. WALTON
WM. HOOPER
JOSEPH HEWES
JOHN PENN
EDWARD RUTLEDGE
THOS. HEYWARD, JUNR.
THOMAS LYNCH, JUNR.
ARTHUR MIDDLETON
SAMUEL CHASE
WM. PACA
THOS. STONE
CHARLES CARROLL OF CARROLLTON
GEORGE WYTHE
RICHARD HENRY LEE
TH. JEFFERSON
BENJ. HARRISON

THOS. NELSON, JR.
FRANCIS LIGHTFOOT LEE
CARTER BRAXTON
ROBT. MORRIS
BENJAMIN RUSH
BENJA. FRANKLIN
JOHN MORTON
GEO. CLYMER
JAS. SMITH
GEO. TAYLOR
JAMES WILSON
GEO. ROSS
CAESAR RODNEY
GEO READ
THO. M'KEAN
WM. FLOYD
PHIL. LIVINGSTON
FRANS. LEWIS
LEWIS MORRIS

RICHD. STOCKTON
JNO. WITHERSPOON
FRAS. HOPKINSON
JOHN HART
ABRA. CLARK
JOSIAH BARTLETT
WM. WHIPPLE
SAML. ADAMS
JOHN ADAMS
ROBT. TREAT PAINE
ELBRIDGE GERRY
STEP. HOPKINS
WILLIAM ELLERY
ROGER SHERMAN
SAM'EL HUNTINGTON
WM. WILLIAMS
OLIVER WOLCOTT
MATTHEW THORNTON

APPENDIX B

The Constitution of the United States of America

PREAMBLE

We the people of the United States, in order to form a more perfect union, establish justice, insure domestic tranquility, provide for the common defense, promote the general welfare, and secure the blessings of liberty to ourselves and our posterity, do ordain and establish this Constitution for the United States of America.

ARTICLE I.—THE LEGISLATIVE ARTICLE

Section 1. All legislative powers herein granted shall be vested in a Congress of the United States, which shall consist of a Senate and a House of Representatives.

Passages in longer in effect are printed in italic type.

House of Representatives: Composition, Qualification, Apportionment, Impeachment Power

Section 2. The House of Representatives shall be composed of members chosen every second year by the people of the several States, and the electors in each State shall have the qualifications requisite for electors of the most numerous branch of the State Legislature.

No person shall be a Representative who shall not have attained to the age of twenty-five years, and been seven years a citizen of the United States, and who shall not, when elected, be an inhabitant of that State in which he shall be chosen.

Representatives and direct taxes shall be apportioned among the several States which may be included within this Union, according to their respective numbers, *which shall be determined by adding to the whole number of free persons, including those bound to service for a term of years and excluding Indians not taxed, three-fifths of all other persons.* The actual enumeration shall be made within three years after the first meeting of the Congress of the United States, and within every subsequent term of ten years, in such manner as they shall by law direct. The number of Representatives shall not exceed one for every thirty thousand, but each State shall have at least one Representative; *and until each enumeration shall be made, the State of New Hampshire shall be entitled to choose three, Massachusetts eight, Rhode Island and Providence Plantations one, Connecticut five, New York six, New Jersey four, Pennsylvania eight, Delaware one, Maryland six, Virginia ten, North Carolina five, South Carolina five, and Georgia three.*

When vacancies happen in the representation from any State, the Executive authority thereof shall issue writs of election to fill such vacancies.

The House of Representatives shall choose their Speaker and other officers; and shall have the sole power of impeachment.

Senate Composition: Qualifications, Impeachment Trials

Section 3. The Senate of the United States shall be composed of two Senators from each State, *chosen by the legislature thereof,* for six years; and each Senator shall have one vote.

Immediately after they shall be assembled in consequence of the first election, they shall be divided as equally as may be into three classes. The seats of the Senators of the first class shall be vacated at the expiration of the second year, of the second class at the expiration of the fourth year, and of the third class at the expiration of the sixth year, so that one-third may be chosen every second year; and if vacancies happen by resignation or otherwise, during the recess of the legislature of any State, the Executive thereof may make temporary appointments until the next meeting of the legislature, which shall then fill such vacancies.

No person shall be a Senator who shall not have attained to the age of thirty years, and been nine years a citizen of the United States, and who shall not, when elected, be an inhabitant of that State for which he shall be chosen.

The Vice President of the United States shall be President of the Senate, but shall have no vote, unless they be equally divided.

The Senate shall choose their other officers, and also a President *pro tempore,* in the absence of the Vice President, or when he shall exercise the office of President of the United States.

The Senate shall have the sole power to try all impeachments. When sitting for that purpose, they shall be on oath or affirmation. When the President of the United States is tried, the Chief Justice shall preside: and no person shall be convicted without the concurrence of two-thirds of the members present.

Judgment in cases of impeachment shall not extend further than to removal from the office, and disqualification to hold and enjoy any office of honor, trust or profit under the United States; but the party convicted shall nevertheless be liable and subject to indictment, trial, judgment and punishment, according to law.

Congressional Elections: Time, Place, Manner

Section 4. The times, places and manner of holding elections for Senators and Representatives shall be prescribed in each State by the legislature thereof; but the Congress may at any time by law make or alter such regulations, except as to the places of choosing Senators.

The Congress shall assemble at least once in every year, and such meeting *shall be on the first Monday in December, unless they shall by law appoint a different day.*

Powers and Duties of the Houses

Section 5. Each house shall be the judge of the elections, returns and qualifications of its own members, and a majority of each shall constitute a quorum to do business; but a smaller number may adjourn from day to day, and may be authorized to compel the attendance of absent members, in such manner, and under such penalties, as each house may provide.

Each house may determine the rules of its proceedings, punish its members for disorderly behavior, and with the concurrence of two-thirds, expel a member.

Each house shall keep a journal of its proceedings, and from time to time publish the same, excepting such parts as may in their judgment require secrecy; and the yeas and nays of the members of either house on any question shall, at the desire of one-fifth of those present, be entered on the journal.

Neither house, during the session of Congress, shall, without the consent of the other, adjourn for more than three days, nor to any other place than that in which the two houses shall be sitting.

Rights of Members

Section 6. The Senators and Representatives shall receive a compensation for their services, to be ascertained by law and paid out of the treasury of the United States. They shall in all cases except treason, felony and breach of the peace, be privileged from arrest during their attendance at the session of their respective houses, and in going to and returning from the same; and for any speech or debate in either house, they shall not be questioned in any other place.

No Senator or Representative shall, during the time for which he was elected, be appointed to any civil office under the authority of the United States, which shall have been created, or the emoluments whereof shall have been increased, during such time; and no person holding any office under the United States shall be a member of either house during his continuance in office.

Legislative Powers: Bills and Resolutions

Section 7. All bills for raising revenue shall originate in the House of Representatives; but the Senate may propose or concur with amendments as on other bills.

Every bill which shall have passed the House of Representatives and the Senate, shall, before it become a law, be presented to the President of the United States; if he approve he shall sign it, but if not he shall return it with objections to that house in which it originated, who shall enter the objections at large on their journal, and proceed to reconsider it. If after such reconsideration two-thirds of that house shall agree to pass the bill, it shall be sent, together with the objections, to the other house, by which it shall likewise be reconsidered, and if approved by two-thirds of that house, it shall become a law. But in all such cases the votes of both houses shall be determined by yeas and nays, and the names of the persons voting for and against the bill shall be entered on the journal of each house respectively. If any bill shall not be returned by the President within ten days (Sundays excepted) after it shall have been presented to him, the same shall be a law, in like manner as if he had signed it, unless the Congress by their adjournment prevent its return, in which case it shall not be a law.

Every order, resolution, or vote to which the concurrence of the Senate and House of Representatives may be necessary (except on a question of adjournment) shall be presented to the President of the United States; and before the same shall take effect, shall be approved by him, or being disapproved by him, shall be repassed by two-thirds of the Senate and House of Representatives, according to the rules and limitations prescribed in the case of a bill.

Powers of Congress

Section 8. The Congress shall have power
To lay and collect taxes, duties, imposts and excises, to pay the debts and provide for the common defense

and general welfare of the United States; but all duties, imposts and excises shall be uniform throughout the United States;

To borrow money on the credit of the United States;

To regulate commerce with foreign nations, and among the several States, and with the Indian tribes;

To establish an uniform rule of naturalization, and uniform laws on the subject of bankruptcies throughout the United States;

To coin money, regulate the value thereof, and of foreign coin, and fix the standard of weights and measures;

To provide for the punishment of counterfeiting the securities and current coin of the United States;

To establish post offices and post roads;

To promote the progress of science and useful arts by securing for limited times to authors and inventors the exclusive right to their respective writings and discoveries;

To constitute tribunals inferior to the Supreme Court;

To define and punish piracies and felonies committed on the high seas and offenses against the law of nations;

To declare war, grant letters of marque and reprisal, and make rules concerning captures on land and water;

To raise and support armies, but no appropriation of money to that use shall be for a longer term than two years;

To provide and maintain a navy;

To make rules for the government and regulation of the land and naval forces;

To provide for calling forth the militia to execute the laws of the Union, suppress insurrections, and repel invasions;

To provide for organizing, arming, and disciplining the militia, and for governing such part of them as may be employed in the service of the United States, reserving to the States respectively the appointment of the officers, and the authority of training the militia according to the discipline prescribed by Congress;

To exercise exclusive legislation in all cases whatsoever, over such district (not exceeding ten miles square) as may, by cession of particular States, and the acceptance of Congress, become the seat of the government of the United States, and to exercise like authority over all places purchased by the consent of the legislature of the State, in which the same shall be, for erection of forts, magazines, arsenals, dock-yards, and other needful buildings;—and

To make all laws which shall be necessary and proper for carrying into execution the foregoing powers, and all other powers vested by this Constitution in the government of the United States, or in any department or officer thereof.

Powers Denied to Congress

Section 9. *The migration or importation of such persons as any of the States now existing shall think proper to admit shall not be prohibited by the Congress prior to the year 1808; but a tax or duty may be imposed on such importation, not exceeding $10 for each person.*

The privilege of the writ of habeas corpus shall not be suspended, unless when in cases of rebellion or invasion the public safety may require it.

No bill of attainder or ex post facto law shall be passed.

No capitation, or other direct, tax shall be laid, unless in proportion to the census or enumeration herein before directed to be taken.

No tax or duty shall be laid on articles exported from any State.

No preference shall be given by any regulation of commerce or revenue to the ports of one State over those of another; nor shall vessels bound to, or from, one State, be obliged to enter, clear, or pay duties in another.

No money shall be drawn from the treasury, but in consequence of appropriations made by law; and a regular statement and account of the receipts and expenditures of all public money shall be published from time to time.

No title of nobility shall be granted by the United States; and no person holding any office of profit or trust under them, shall, without the consent of the Congress, accept of any present, emolument, office, or title, of any kind whatever, from any king, prince, or foreign state.

Powers Denied to the States

Section 10. No State shall enter into any treaty, alliance, or confederation; grant letters of marque and reprisal; coin money; emit bills of credit; make anything but gold and silver coin a tender in payment of debts; pass any bill of attainder, ex post facto law, or law impairing the obligation of contracts, or grant any title of nobility.

No State shall, without the consent of the Congress, lay any imposts or duties on imports or exports, except what may be absolutely necessary for executing its inspection laws: and the net produce of all duties and imposts, laid by any State on imports or exports, shall be for the use of the treasury of the United States; and all such laws shall be subject to the revision and control of the Congress.

No State shall, without the consent of Congress, lay any duty of tonnage, keep troops or ships of war in time of peace, enter into any agreement or compact with another State, or with a foreign power, or engage in war, unless actually invaded, or in such imminent danger as will not admit of delay.

ARTICLE II.—THE EXECUTIVE ARTICLE

Nature and Scope of Presidential Power

Section 1. The executive power shall be vested in a President of the United States of America. He shall hold his office during the term of four years, and, together with the Vice President, chosen for the same term, be elected, as follows:

Each State shall appoint, in such manner as the legislature thereof may direct, a number of electors, equal to the whole number of Senators and Representatives to which the State may be entitled in the Congress; but no Senator or Representative, or person holding an office of trust or profit under the United States, shall be appointed an elector.

The electors shall meet in their respective States, and vote by ballot for two persons, of whom one at least shall not be an inhabitant of the same State with themselves. And they shall make a list of all the persons voted for, and of the number of votes for each; which list they shall sign and certify, and transmit sealed to the seat of government of the United States, directed to the President of the Senate. The President of the Senate shall, in the presence of the Senate and House of Representatives, open all the certificates, and the votes shall then be counted. The person having the greatest number of votes shall be the President, if such number be a majority of the whole number of electors appointed; and if there be more than one who have such majority, and have an equal number of votes, then the House of Representatives shall immediately choose by ballot one of them for President; and if no person have a majority, then from the five highest on the list said house shall in like manner choose the President. But in choosing the President the votes shall be taken by States, the representation from each State having one vote; a quorum for this purpose shall consist of a member or members from two-thirds of the States, and a majority of all the States shall be necessary to a choice. In every case, after the choice of the President, the person having the greatest number of votes of the electors shall be the Vice President. But if there should remain two or more who have equal votes, the Senate shall choose from them by ballot the Vice President.

The Congress may determine the time of choosing the electors, and the day on which they shall give their votes; which day shall be the same throughout the United States.

No person except a natural-born citizen, *or a citizen of the United States at the time of the adoption of this Constitution*, shall be eligible to the office of President; neither shall any person be eligible to that office who shall not have attained to the age of thirty-five years, and been fourteen years a resident within the United States.

In case of the removal of the President from office or of his death, resignation, or inability to discharge the powers and duties of the said office, the same shall devolve on the Vice President, and the Congress may by law provide for the case of removal, death, resignation, or inability, both of the President and Vice President, declaring what officer shall then act as President, and such officer shall act accordingly, until the disability be removed, or a President shall be elected.

The President shall, at stated times, receive for his services a compensation, which shall neither be increased nor diminished during the period for which he shall have been elected, and he shall not receive within that period any other emolument from the United States, or any of them.

Before he enter on the execution of his office, he shall take the following oath or affirmation: —"I do solemnly swear (or affirm) that I will faithfully execute the office of President of the United States, and will to the best of my ability preserve, protect, and defend the Constitution of the United States."

Powers and Duties of the President

Section 2. The President shall be the commander in chief of the army and navy of the United States, and of the militia of the several States, when called into the actual service of the United States; he may require the opinion, in writing, of the principal officer in each of the executive departments, upon any subject relating to the duties of their respective offices, and he shall have power to grant reprieves and pardons for offenses against the United States, except in cases of impeachment.

He shall have power, by and with the advice and consent of the Senate, to make treaties, provided two-thirds of the Senators present concur; and he shall nominate, and by and with the advice and consent of the Senate, shall appoint ambassadors, other public ministers and consuls, judges of the Supreme Court, and all other officers of the United States, whose appointments are not herein otherwise provided for, and which shall be established by law: but the Congress may by law vest the appointment of such inferior officers, as they think proper, in the President alone, in the courts of law, or in the heads of departments.

The President shall have power to fill up all vacancies that may happen during the recess of the Senate, by granting commissions which shall expire at the end of their next session.

Section 3. He shall from time to time give to the Congress information of the state of the Union, and recommend to their consideration such measures as he shall judge necessary and expedient; he may, on extraordinary occasions, convene both houses, or either of them, and in case of disagreement between them, with respect to the time of adjournment, he may adjourn them to such time as he shall think proper; he shall receive ambassadors and other public ministers; he shall take care that the laws be faithfully executed, and shall commission all the officers of the United States.

Section 4. The President, Vice President and all civil officers of the United States shall be removed from office on impeachment for, and on conviction of, treason, bribery, or other high crimes and misdemeanor.

ARTICLE III.—THE JUDICIAL ARTICLE

Section 1. The judicial power of the United States shall be vested in one Supreme Court, and in such inferior courts as the Congress may from time to time ordain and establish. The judges, both of the Supreme and inferior courts, shall hold their offices during good behavior, and shall, at stated times, receive for their services a compensation which shall not be diminished during their continuance in office.

Jurisdiction

Section 2. The judicial power shall extend to all cases, in law and equity, arising under this Constitution, the laws of the United States, and treaties made, or which shall be made, under their authority;—to all cases affecting ambassadors, other public ministers and consuls;—to all cases of admiralty and maritime jurisdiction;—to controversies to which the United States shall be a party;—to controversies between two or more States;—*between a state and citizens of another state*;—between citizens of different States;—between citizens of the same State claiming lands under grants of different States, and between a State, or the citizens thereof, and foreign states, citizens or subjects.

In all cases affecting ambassadors, other public ministers and consuls, and those in which a State shall be party, the Supreme Court shall have original jurisdiction. In all the other cases before mentioned, the Supreme Court shall have appellate jurisdiction, both as to law and fact, with such exceptions, and under such regulations, as the Congress shall make.

The trial of all crimes, except in cases of impeachment, shall be by jury; and such trial shall be held in the State where said crimes shall have been committed; but when not committed within any State, the trial shall be at such place or places as the Congress may by law have directed.

Treason

Section 3. Treason against the United States shall consist only in levying war against them, or in adhering to their enemies, giving them aid and comfort. No person shall be convicted of treason unless on the testimony of two witnesses to the same overt act, or on confession in open court.

The Congress shall have power to declare the punishment of treason, but no attainder of treason shall work corruption of blood, or forfeiture except during the life of the person attained.

ARTICLE IV.—INTERSTATE RELATIONS

Full Faith and Credit Clause

Section 1. Full Faith and credit shall be given in each State to the public acts, records, and judicial proceedings of every other State. And the Congress may by general laws prescribe the manner in which such acts, records and proceedings shall be proved, and the effect thereof.

Privileges and Immunities; Interstate Extradition

Section 2. The citizens of each State shall be entitled to all privileges and immunities of citizens in the several States.

A person charged in any State with treason, felony or other crime, who shall flee from justice, and be found in another State, shall on demand of the executive authority of the State from which he fled, be delivered up, to be removed to the State having jurisdiction of the crime.

No person held to service or labor in one State, under the laws thereof, escaping into another, shall, in consequence of any law or regulation therein, be discharged from such service or labor, but shall be delivered up on claim of the party to whom such service or labor may be due.

Admission of States

Section 3. New States may be admitted by the Congress into this Union; but no new State shall be formed or erected within the jurisdiction of any other State; nor any State be formed by the junc-
tion of two or more States, or parts of States, without the consent of the legislatures of the States concerned as well as of the Congress.

The Congress shall have power to dispose of and make all needful rules and regulations respecting the territory or other property belonging to the United States; and nothing in this Constitution shall be so construed as to prejudice any claims of the United States, or of any particular State.

Republican Form of Government

Section 4. The United States shall guarantee to every State in this Union a republican form of government, and shall protect each of them against invasion; and on application of the legislature, or of the executive (when the legislature cannot be convened) against domestic violence.

ARTICLE V.—THE AMENDING POWER

The Congress, whenever two-thirds of both houses shall deem it necessary, shall propose amendments to this Constitution, or, on the application of the legislatures of two-thirds of the several States, shall call a convention for proposing amendments, which, in either case, shall be valid to all intents and purposes, as part of this Constitution, when ratified by the legislatures of three-fourths of the several States, or by conventions in three-fourths thereof, as the one or the other mode of ratification may be proposed by the Congress; *provided that no amendment which may be made prior to the year one thousand eight hundred and eight shall in any manner affect the first and fourth clauses in the ninth section of the first article*; and that no State, without its consent, shall be deprived of its equal suffrage in the Senate.

ARTICLE VI.—THE SUPREMACY ACT

All debts contracted and engagements entered into, before the adoption of this Constitution, shall be as valid against the United States under this Constitution, as under the Confederation.

This Constitution, and the laws of the United States which shall be made in pursuance thereof; and all treaties made, or which shall be made, under the authority of the United States, shall be the supreme law of the land; and the judges in every State shall be bound thereby, anything in the Constitution or laws of any State to the contrary notwithstanding.

The Senators and Representatives before mentioned, and the members of the several State legislatures, and all executive and judicial officers, both of the United States and of the several States, shall be bound by oath or affirmation to support this Constitution; but no religious test shall ever be required as a qualification to any office or public trust under the United States.

ARTICLE VII.—RATIFICATION

The ratification of the conventions of nine States shall be sufficient for the establishment of this Constitution between States so ratifying the same.

Done in Convention by the unanimous consent of the States present, the seventeenth day of September in the year of our Lord one thousand seven hundred and eighty-seven and of the Independence of the United States of America the twelfth. In witness whereof we have hereunto subscribed our names.

GEORGE WASHINGTON
President and Deputy from Virginia

New Hampshire
JOHN LANGDON
NICHOLAS GILMAN

Massachusetts
NATHANIEL GORHAM
RUFUS KING

Connecticut
WILLIAM S. JOHNSON
ROGER SHERMAN

Virginia
JOHN BLAIR
JAMES MADISON, JR

South Carolina
J. RUTLEDGE
CHARLES G. PINCKNEY
PIERCE BUTLER

New York
ALEXANDER HAMILTON

New Jersey
WILLIAM LIVINGSTON
DAVID BREARLEY
WILLIAM PATERSON
JONATHAN DAYTON

Pennsylvania
BENJAMIN FRANKLIN
THOMAS MIFFLIN
ROBERT MORRIS
GEORGE CLYMER
THOMAS FITZSIMONS
JARED INGERSOLL
JAMES WILSON
GOUVERNEUR MORRIS

Delaware
GEORGE READ
GUNNING BEDFORD, JR.
JOHN DICKINSON
RICHARD BASSETT
JACOB BROOM

Maryland
JAMES MCHENRY
DANIEL OF ST. THOMAS JENIFER
DANIEL CARROLL

North Carolina
WILLIAM BLOUNT
RICHARD DOBBS SPRAIGHT
HU WILLIAMSON

Georgia
WILLIAM FEW
ABRAHAM BALDWIN

THE BILL OF RIGHTS

The first ten Amendments (the Bill of Rights) were adopted in 1791.

AMENDMENT I.—RELIGION, SPEECH ASSEMBLY, AND PETITION

Congress shall make no law respecting an establishment of religion, or prohibiting the free exercise thereof; or abridging the freedom of speech, or of the press; or the right of the people peaceably to assemble, and to petition the government for a redress of grievances.

AMENDMENT II.—MILITIA AND THE RIGHT TO BEAR ARMS

A well-regulated militia being necessary to the security of a free State, the right of the people to keep and bear arms shall not be infringed.

AMENDMENT III.—QUARTERING OF SOLDIERS

No soldier shall, in time of peace, be quartered in any house without the consent of the owner, nor in time of war, but in a manner to be prescribed by law.

AMENDMENT IV.—SEARCHES AND SEIZURES

The right of the people to be secure in their persons, houses, papers, and effects, against unreasonable searches and seizures, shall not be violated, and no warrants shall issue but upon probable cause, supported by oath or affirmation, and particularly describing the place to be searched, and the persons or things to be seized.

AMENDMENT V.—GRAND JURIES, SELF-INCRIMINATION, DOUBLE JEOPARDY, DUE PROCESS, AND EMINENT DOMAIN

No person shall be held to answer for a capital, or otherwise infamous crime, unless on a presentment or indictment of a grand jury, except in cases arising in the land or naval forces, or in the militia, when in actual service in time of war or public danger; nor shall any person be subject for the same offense to be twice put in jeopardy of life or limb; nor shall be compelled in any criminal case to be a witness against himself, nor be deprived of life, liberty, or property, without due process of law; nor shall private property be taken for public use without just compensation.

AMENDMENT VI.—CRIMINAL COURT PROCEDURES

In all criminal prosecutions, the accused shall enjoy the right to a speedy and public trial, by an impartial jury of the State and district wherein the crime shall have been committed, which district shall have been previously ascertained by law, and to be informed of the nature and cause of the accusation; to be confronted with the witnesses against him; to have compulsory process for obtaining witnesses in his favor, and to have the assistance of counsel for his defense.

AMENDMENT VII.—TRIAL BY JURY IN COMMON LAW CASES

In suits at common law, where the value in controversy shall exceed twenty dollars, the right of trial by jury shall be preserved, and no fact tried by a jury shall be otherwise reexamined in any court of the United States, than according to the rules of the common law.

AMENDMENT VIII.—BAIL, CRUEL AND UNUSUAL PUNISHMENT

Excessive bail shall not be required, nor excessive fines imposed, nor cruel and unusual punishments inflicted.

AMENDMENT IX.—RIGHTS RETAINED BY THE PEOPLE

The enumeration in the Constitution, of certain rights, shall not be construed to deny or disparage others retained by the people.

AMENDMENT X.—RESERVED POWERS OF THE STATES

The powers not delegated to the United States by the Constitution, nor prohibited by it to the States, are reserved to the States respectively, or to the people.

PRE-CIVIL WAR AMENDMENTS

AMENDMENT XI.—SUITS AGAINST THE STATES
[Adopted 1798]

The judicial power of the United States shall not be construed to extend to any suit in law or equity, commenced or prosecuted against one of the United States by citizens of another State, or by citizens or subjects of any foreign state.

AMENDMENT XII.—ELECTION OF THE PRESIDENT
[Adopted 1804]

The electors shall meet in their respective *States*, and vote by ballot for President and Vice President, one of whom, at least, shall not be an inhabitant of the same State with themselves; they shall name in their ballots the person voted for as President, and in distinct ballots the person voted for as Vice President, and they shall make distinct lists of all persons voted for as President, and of all persons voted for as Vice President, and of the number of votes for each, which lists they shall sign and certify, and transmit sealed to the seat of the government of the United States, directed to the President of the Senate;—the President of the Senate shall, in the presence of the Senate and House of Representatives, open all the certificates and the votes shall then be counted;—the person having the greatest number of votes for President shall be the President, if such number be a majority of the whole number of electors appointed; and if no person have such majority, then from the persons having the highest numbers not exceeding three on the list of those voted for as President, the House of Representatives shall choose immediately, by ballot, the President. But in choosing the President, the votes shall be taken by States, the representation from each State having one vote; a quorum for this purpose shall consist of a member or members from two-thirds of the States, and a majority of all the States shall be necessary to a choice. And if the House of Representatives shall not choose a President whenever the right of choice shall devolve upon them, before *the fourth day of March* next following, then the Vice President shall act as President, as in the case of the death or other constitutional disability of the President.

The person having the greatest number of votes as Vice President shall be the Vice President, if such a number be a majority of the whole number of electors appointed; and if no person have a majority, then from the two highest numbers on the list the Senate shall choose the Vice President; a quorum for the purpose shall consist of two-thirds of the whole number of Senators, and a majority of the whole number shall be necessary to a choice. But no person constitutionally ineligible to the office of President shall be eligible to that of Vice President of the United States.

CIVIL WAR AMENDMENTS

AMENDMENT XIII.—PROHIBITION OF SLAVERY
[Adopted 1865]

Section 1. Neither slavery nor involuntary servitude, except as a punishment for crime whereof the party shall have been duly convicted, shall exist within the United States, or any place subject to their jurisdiction.

Section 2. Congress shall have power to enforce this article by appropriate legislation.

AMENDMENT XIV.—CITIZENSHIP, DUE PROCESS, AND EQUAL PROTECTION OF THE LAWS
[Adopted 1868]

Section 1. All persons born or naturalized in the United States, and subject to the jurisdiction thereof, are citizens of the United States and of the State wherein they reside. No State shall make or enforce any law which shall abridge **the privileges or immunities** of citizens of the United States; nor shall any State deprive any person of life, liberty, or property, without **due process of law**; nor deny to any person within its jurisdiction the **equal protection of the laws**.

Section 2. Representatives shall be apportioned among the several States according to their respective numbers, counting the whole number of persons in each State, excluding Indians not taxed. But when the right to vote at any election for the choice of Electors for President and Vice President of the United States, Representatives in Congress, the executive and judicial officers of a State, or the members of the legislature thereof, is denied to any of the male inhabitants of such State, being twenty-one years of age and citizens of the United States, or in any way abridged, except for participation in rebellion, or other crime, the basis of representation therein shall be reduced in the proportion which the number of such male citizens shall bear to the whole number of male citizens twenty-one years of age in such State.

Section 3. No person shall be a Senator or Representative in Congress, or Elector of President and Vice President, or hold any office, civil or military, under the United States, or under any State, who, having previously taken an oath, as a member of Congress, or as an officer of the United States, or as a member of any State legislature, or as an executive or judicial officer of any State, to support the Constitution of the United States, shall have engaged in insurrection or rebellion against the same, or given aid or comfort to the enemies thereof. Congress may, by a vote of two-thirds of each house, remove such disability.

Section 4. The validity of the public debt of the United States, authorized by law, including debts incurred for payment of pensions and bounties for services in suppressing insurrection or rebellion, shall not be questioned. But neither the United States nor any State shall assume or pay any debt or obligation incurred in aid of insurrection or rebellion against the United States, or any claim for the loss or emancipation of any slave; but all such debts, obligations and claims shall be held illegal and void.

Section 5. The Congress shall have power to enforce, by appropriate legislation, the provisions of this article.

AMENDMENT XV.—THE RIGHT TO VOTE
[Adopted 1870]

Section 1. The right of citizens of the United State to vote shall not be denied or abridged by the United States or by any State on account of race, color, or previous condition of servitude.

Section 2. The Congress shall have power to enforce this article by appropriate legislation.

AMENDMENT XVI.—INCOME TAXES
[Adopted 1913]

The Congress shall have power to lay and collect taxes on incomes, from whatever source derived, without apportionment among the several States, and without regard to any census or enumeration.

AMENDMENT XVII.—DIRECT ELECTION OF SENATORS
[Adopted 1913]

Section 1. The Senate of the United States shall be composed of two Senators from each State, elected by the people thereof, for six years; and each Senator shall have one vote. The electors in each State shall have the qualifications requisite for electors of (voters for) the most numerous branch of the State legislatures.

Section 2. When vacancies happen in the representation of any State in the Senate, the executive authority of such State shall issue writs of election to fill such vacancies: Provided, that the Legislature of any State may empower the executive thereof to make temporary appointments until the people fill the vacancies by election as the Legislature may direct.

Section 3. This amendment shall not be so construed as to affect the election or term of any Senator chosen before it becomes valid as part of the Constitution.

AMENDMENT XVIII.—PROHIBITION
[Adopted 1919; Repealed 1933]

Section 1. *After one year from the ratification of this article the manufacture, sale, or transportation of intoxicating liquors within, the importation thereof into, or the exportation thereof from the United State and all territory subject to the jurisdiction thereof, for beverage purposes, is hereby prohibited.*

Section 2. *The Congress and the several States shall have concurrent power to enforce this article by appropriate legislation.*

Section 3. *This article shall be inoperative unless it shall have been ratified as an amendment to the Constitution by the legislatures of the several States, as provided by the Constitution, within seven years from the date of the submission thereof to the States by the Congress.*

AMENDMENT XIX.—FOR WOMEN'S SUFFRAGE
[Adopted 1920]

Section 1. The right of citizens of the United States to vote shall not be denied or abridged by the United States or by any State on account of sex.

Section 2. The Congress shall have power to enforce this article by appropriate legislation.

AMENDMENT XX.—THE LAME DUCK AMENDMENT
[Adopted 1933]

Section 1. The terms of the President and Vice President shall end at noon on the 20th day of January, and the terms of the Senators and Representatives at noon on the 3rd day of January, of the years in which such terms would have ended if this article had not been ratified; and the terms of their successors shall then begin.

Section 2. The Congress shall assemble at least once in every year, and such meeting shall begin at noon on the 3rd day of January, unless they shall by law appoint a different day.

Section 3. If, at the time fixed for the beginning of the term of the President, the President-elect shall have died, the Vice President-elect shall become President. If a President shall not have been chosen before the time fixed for the beginning of his term, or if the President-elect shall have failed to qualify, then the Vice President-elect shall act as President until a President shall have qualified; and the Congress may by law provide for the case wherein neither a President-elect nor a Vice President-elect shall have qualified, declaring who shall then act as President, or the manner in which one who is to act shall be selected, and such persons shall act accordingly until a President or Vice President shall have qualified.

Section 4. The Congress may by law provide for the case of the death of any of the persons from whom the House of Representatives may choose a President whenever the right of choice shall have devolved upon them, and for the case of the death of any of the persons from whom the Senate may choose a Vice President whenever the right of choice shall have devolved upon them.

Section 5. Section 1 and 2 shall take effect on the 15th day of October following the ratification of this article.

Section 6. This article shall be inoperative unless it shall have been ratified as an amendment to the Constitution by the Legislatures of three-fourths of the several States within seven years from the date of its submission.

AMENDMENT XXI.—REPEAL OF PROHIBITION
[Adopted 1933]

Section 1. The eighteenth article of amendment to the Constitution of the United States is hereby repealed.

Section 2. The transportation or importation into any State, Territory, or Possession of the United States for delivery of use therein of intoxicating liquors, in violation of the laws thereof, is hereby prohibited.

Section 3. This article shall be inoperative unless it shall have been ratified as an amendment to the Constitution by conventions in the several States, as provided in the Constitution, within seven years from the date of submission thereof to the States by the Congress.

AMENDMENT XXII.—NUMBER OF PRESIDENTIAL TERMS
[Adopted 1951]

Section 1. No person shall be elected to the office of President more than twice, and no person who has held the office of President, or acted as President, for more than two years of a term to which some other person was elected President shall be elected to the office of President more than once. But this article shall not apply to any person holding the office of President when this article was proposed by the Congress, and shall not prevent any person who may be holding the office of President, or acting as President, during the term within which this article becomes operative from holding the office of President or acting as President during the remainder of such term.

Section 2. This article shall be inoperative unless it shall have been ratified as an amendment to the Constitution by the legislatures of three-fourths of the several States within seven years from the date of its submission to the States by the Congress.

AMENDMENT XXIII.—PRESIDENTIAL ELECTORS FOR THE DISTRICT OF COLUMBIA [Adopted 1961]

Section 1. The District constituting the seat of Government of the United States shall appoint in such manner as the

Congress may direct:

A number of electors of President and Vice President equal to the whole number of Senators and Representatives in Congress to which the District would be entitled if it were a State, but in no event more than the least populous State; they shall be in addition to those appointed by the States, but they shall be considered for the purposes of the election of President and Vice President, to be electors appointed by a State; and they shall meet in the District and perform such duties as provided by the twelfth article of amendment.

Section 2. The Congress shall have power to enforce this article by appropriate legislation.

AMENDMENT XXIV.—THE ANTI-POLL TAX AMENDMENT
[Adopted 1964]

Section 1. The right of citizens of the United States to vote in any primary or other election for President or Vice President, for electors for President or Vice President, or for Senator or Representative in Congress, shall not be denied or abridged by the United States or any State by reason of failure to pay any poll tax or other tax.

Section 2. The Congress shall have power to enforce this article by appropriate legislation.

AMENDMENT XXV.—PRESIDENTIAL DISABILITY, VICE-PRESIDENTIAL VACANCIES
[Adopted 1967]

Section 1. In case of the removal of the President from office or his death or resignation, the Vice President shall become President.

Section 2. Whenever there is a vacancy in the office of the Vice President, the President shall nominate a Vice President who shall take office upon confirmation by a majority vote of both Houses of Congress.

Section 3. Whenever the President transmits to the President pro tempore of the Senate and the Speaker of the House of Representatives his written declaration that he is unable to discharge the powers and duties of his office, and until he transmits to them a written declaration to the contrary, such powers and duties shall be discharged by the Vice President as Acting President.

Section 4. Whenever the Vice President and a majority of either the principal officers of the executive departments or of such other body as Congress may by law provide, transmit to the President pro tempore of the Senate and the Speaker of the House of Representatives their written declaration that the President is unable to discharge the powers and duties of his office, the Vice President shall immediately assume the powers and duties of the office as Acting President.

Thereafter, when the President transmits to the President pro tempore of the Senate and the Speaker of the House of Representatives his written declaration that no inability exists, he shall resume the powers and duties of his office unless the Vice President and a majority of either the principal officers of the executive department{s} or of such other body as Congress may by law provide, transmit within four days to the President pro tempore of the Senate and the Speaker of the House of Representatives their written declaration that the President is unable to discharge the powers and duties of his office. Thereupon Congress shall decide the issue, assembling within forty-eight hours for that purpose if not in session. If the Congress, within twenty-one days after receipt of the latter written declaration, or, if Congress is not in session, within twenty-one days after Congress is required to assemble, determines by two-thirds vote of both Houses that the President is unable to discharge the powers and duties of his office, the Vice President shall continue to discharge the same as Acting President; otherwise, the President shall resume the powers and duties of his office.

AMENDMENT XXVI.—EIGHTEEN-YEAR-OLD VOTE
[Adopted 1971]

Section 1. The right of citizens of the United States, who are eighteen years of age or older, to vote shall not be denied or abridged by the United States or by any State on account of age.

Section 2. The Congress shall have power to enforce this article by appropriate legislation.

AMENDMENT XXVII.—VARYING CONGRESSIONAL COMPENSATION
[Adopted 1992]

No law varying the compensation for the service of the Senators and Representatives shall take effect until an election of Representatives shall have intervened.

APPENDIX C

PRESIDENTIAL ELECTIONS

Year	Name	Party	Popular Vote	Electoral College Vote
1789	George Washington	Federalist	—	69
1792	George Washington	Federalist	—	132
1796	John Adams	Federalist	—	71
	Thomas Jefferson	Democratic-Republican	—	68
1800	Thomas Jefferson	Democratic-Republican	—	73
	John Adams	Federalist	—	65
1804	Thomas Jefferson	Democratic-Republican	—	162
	Charles C. Pinckney	Federalist	—	14
1808	James Madison	Democratic-Republican	—	122
	Charles C. Pinckney	Federalist	—	47
1812	James Madison	Democratic-Republican	—	128
	George Clinton	Federalist	—	89
1816	James Monroe	Democratic-Republican	—	183
	Rufus King	Federalist	—	34
1820	James Monroe	Democratic-Republican	—	231
	John Quincy Adams	Democratic-Republican	—	1
1824	John Quincy Adams	Democratic-Republican	108,740	84
	Andrew Jackson	Democratic-Republican	153,544	99
	William Crawford	Democratic-Republican	46,618	41
	Henry Clay	Democratic-Republican	47,136	37
1828	Andrew Jackson	Democrat	647,286	178
	John Quincy Adams	National Republican	508,064	83
1832	Andrew Jackson	Democrat	687,502	219
	Henry Clay	National Republican	530,189	49
	Electoral votes not cast		2	
1836	Martin Van Buren	Democrat	765,483	170
	William Henry Harrison	Whig	550,816	73
	Hugh White	Whig	146,107	26
	Daniel Webster	Whig	41,201	14
	Total for the 3 Whigs		739,795	113
1840	William Henry Harrison	Whig	1,274,624	234
	Martin Van Buren	Democrat	1,127,781	60
1844	James K. Polk	Democrat	1,338,464	170
	Henry Clay	Whig	1,300,097	105
1848	Zachary Taylor	Whig	1,360,967	163
	Lewis Cass	Democrat	1,222,342	127

Year	Name	Party	Popular Vote	Electoral College Vote
	Martin Van Buren	Free-Soil	291,263	—
1852	Franklin Pierce	Democrat	1,601,117	254
	Winfield Scott	Whig	1,385,453	42
	John P. Hale	Free-Soil	155,825	—
1856	James Buchanan	Democrat	1,832,955	174
	John Frémont	Republican	1,339,932	114
	Millard Fillmore	Whig-American	871,731	8
1860	Abraham Lincoln	Republican	1,865,593	180
	John C. Breckinridge	Democratic	848,356	72
	Stephen Douglas	Democrat	1,382,713	12
	John Bell	Constitutional Union	592,906	39
1864	Abraham Lincoln	Unionist (Republican)	2,206,938	212
	George McClellan	Democrat	1,803,787	21
	Electoral votes not cast		81	
1868	Ulysses S. Grant	Republican	3,013,421	214
	Horatio Seymour	Democrat	2,706,829	80
	Electoral votes not cast		23	
1872	Ulysses S. Grant	Republican	3,596,745	286
	Horace Greeley	Democrat	2,843,446	
	Thomas Hendricks	Democrat	—	42
	Benjamin Brown	Democrat	—	18
	Charles Jenkins	Democrat	—	2
	David Davis	Democrat	—	1
1876	Rutherford B. Hayes	Republican	4,036,572	185
	Samuel Tilden	Democrat	4,284,020	184
	Peter Cooper	Greenback	81,737	—
1880	James A. Garfield	Republican	4,453,295	214
	Winfield S. Hancock	Democrat	4,414,082	155
	James B. Weaver	Greenback-Labor	308,578	—
1884	Grover Cleveland	Democrat	4,879,507	219
	James G. Blaine	Republican	4,850,293	182
	Benjamin Butler	Greenback-Labor	175,370	—
	John St. John	Prohibition	150,369	—
1888	Benjamin Harrison	Republican	5,447,129	233
	Grover Cleveland	Democrat	5,537,857	168
	Clinton Fisk	Prohibition	249,506	—
	Anson Streeter	Union Labor	146,935	—
1892	Grover Cleveland	Democrat	5,555,426	277
	Benjamin Harrison	Republican	5,182,690	145
	James B. Weaver	People's	1,029,846	22
	John Bidwell	Prohibition	264,133	—
1896	William McKinley	Republican	7,102,246	271
	William J. Bryan	Democrat	6,492,559	176
	John Palmer	National Democratic	133,148	—
	Joshua Levering	Prohibition	132,007	—
1900	William McKinley	Republican	7,218,491	292
	William J. Bryan	Democrat	6,356,734	155

Year	Name	Party	Popular Vote	Electoral College Vote
	John C. Wooley	Prohibition	208,914	—
	Eugene V. Debs	Socialist	87,814	—
1904	Theodore Roosevelt	Republican	7,628,461	336
	Alton B. Parker	Democrat	5,084,223	140
	Eugene V. Debs	Socialist	402,283	—
	Silas Swallow	Prohibition	258,536	—
	Thomas Watson	People's	117,183	—
1908	William Howard Taft	Republican	7,675,320	321
	William J. Bryan	Democrat	6,412,294	162
	Eugene V. Debs	Socialist	420,793	—
	Eugene Chafin	Prohibition	253,840	—
1912	Woodrow Wilson	Democrat	6,296,547	435
	William Howard Taft	Republican	3,486,720	8
	Theodore Roosevelt	Progressive	4,118,571	86
	Eugene V. Debs	Socialist	900,672	—
	Eugene Chafin	Prohibition	206,275	—
1916	Woodrow Wilson	Democrat	9,127,695	277
	Charles E. Hughes	Republican	8,533,507	254
	A. L. Benson	Socialist	585,113	—
	J. Frank Hanly	Prohibition	220,506	—
1920	Warren Harding	Republican	16,143,407	404
	James M. Cox	Democrat	9,130,328	127
	Eugene V. Debs	Socialist	919,799	—
	P. P. Christensen	Farmer-Labor	265,411	—
	Aaron Watkins	Prohibition	189,408	—
1924	Calvin Coolidge	Republican	15,718,211	382
	John W. Davis	Democrat	8,385,283	136
	Robert La Follette	Progressive	4,831,289	13
1928	Herbert C. Hoover	Republican	21,391,993	444
	Alfred E. Smith	Democrat	15,016,169	87
	Norman Thomas	Socialist	267,835	—
1932	Franklin D. Roosevelt	Democrat	22,809,638	472
	Herbert C. Hoover	Republican	15,758,901	59
	Norman Thomas	Socialist	881,951	—
	William Foster	Communist	102,785	—
1936	Franklin D. Roosevelt	Democrat	27,752,869	523
	Alfred M. Landon	Republican	16,674,665	8
	William Lemke	Union	882,479	—
	Norman Thomas	Socialist	187,720	—
1940	Franklin D. Roosevelt	Democrat	27,307,819	449
	Wendell Willkie	Republican	22,321,018	82
1944	Franklin D. Roosevelt	Democrat	25,606,585	432
	Thomas E. Dewey	Republican	22,014,745	99
1948	Harry S. Truman	Democrat	24,179,345	303
	Thomas E. Dewey	Republican	21,991,291	189
	Strom Thurmond	Dixiecrat	1,176,125	39
	Henry Wallace	Progressive	1,157,326	—
	Norman Thomas	Socialist	139,572	—
	Claude A. Watson	Prohibition	103,900	—

Year	Name	Party	Popular Vote	Electoral College Vote
1952	Dwight D. Eisenhower	Republican	33,936,234	442
	Adlai Stevenson II	Democrat	27,314,992	89
	Vincent Hallinan	Progressive	140,023	—
1956	Dwight D. Eisenhower	Republican	35,590,472	457
	Adlai Stevenson II	Democrat	26,022,752	73
	T. Coleman Andrews	States' Rights	111,178	—
	Walter B. Jones	Democrat	—	1
1960	John F. Kennedy	Democrat	34,226,731	303
	Richard M. Nixon	Republican	34,108,157	219
	Harry Byrd	Democrat	—	15
1964	Lyndon B. Johnson	Democrat	43,129,566	486
	Barry Goldwater	Republican	27,178,188	52
1968	Richard M. Nixon	Republican	31,785,480	301
	Hubert H. Humphrey	Democrat	31,275,166	191
	George Wallace	American Independent	9,906,473	46
1972	Richard M. Nixon	Republican	47,170,179	520
	George McGovern	Democrat	29,171,791	17
	John Hospers	Libertarian	—	1
1976	Jimmy Carter	Democrat	40,830,763	297
	Gerald R. Ford	Republican	39,147,793	240
	Ronald Reagan	Republican	—	1
1980	Ronald Reagan	Republican	43,904,153	489
	Jimmy Carter	Democrat	35,483,883	49
	John Anderson	Independent candidacy	5,719,437	—
1984	Ronald Reagan	Republican	54,455,074	525
	Walter F. Mondale	Democrat	37,577,137	13
1988	George Bush	Republican	48,881,278	426
	Michael Dukakis	Democrat	41,805,374	111
	Lloyd Bentsen	Democrat	—	1
1992	Bill Clinton	Democrat	43,727,625	370
	George Bush	Republican	38,165,180	168
	Ross Perot	Independent candidacy	19,236,411	0
1996	Bill Clinton	Democrat	45,628,667	379
	Bob Dole	Republican	37,869,435	159
	Ross Perot	Independent candidacy	7,874,283	0
2000	George W. Bush	Republican	49,820,518	271
	Albert Gore Jr.	Democrat	50,158,094	267
2004	George W. Bush	Republican	58,900,000	286
	John Kerry	Democrat	55,400,000	252

APPENDIX D

ADMISSION OF STATES TO THE UNION

State	Date of Admission	State	Date of Admission
Delaware	December 7, 1787	Michigan	January 16, 1837
Pennsylvania	December 12, 1787	Florida	March 3, 1845
New Jersey	December 18, 1787	Texas	December 29, 1845
Georgia	January 2, 1788	Iowa	December 28, 1846
Connecticut	January 9, 1788	Wisconsin	May 29, 1848
Massachusetts	February 6, 1788	California	September 9, 1850
Maryland	April 28, 1788	Minnesota	May 11, 1858
South Carolina	May 23, 1788	Oregon	February 14, 1859
New Hampshire	June 21, 1788	Kansas	January 29, 1861
Virginia	June 25, 1788	West Virginia	June 19, 1863
New York	July 26, 1788	Nevada	October 31, 1864
North Carolina	November 21, 1789	Nebraska	March 1, 1867
Rhode Island	May 29, 1790	Colorado	August 1, 1876
Vermont	March 4, 1791	North Dakota	November 2, 1889
Kentucky	June 1, 1792	South Dakota	November 2, 1889
Tennessee	June 1, 1796	Montana	November 8, 1889
Ohio	March 1, 1803	Washington	November 11, 1889
Louisiana	April 30, 1812	Idaho	July 3, 1890
Indiana	December 11, 1816	Wyoming	July 10, 1890
Mississippi	December 10, 1817	Utah	January 4, 1896
Illinois	December 3, 1818	Oklahoma	November 16, 1907
Alabama	December 14, 1819	New Mexico	January 6, 1912
Maine	March 15, 1820	Arizona	February 14, 1912
Missouri	August 10, 1821	Alaska	January 3, 1959
Arkansas	June 15, 1836	Hawaii	August 21, 1959

APPENDIX E

SUPREME COURT JUSTICES

Name	Service	Appointed by	Name	Service	Appointed by
John Jay*	1789–1795	Washington	David Davis	1862–1877	Lincoln
James Wilson	1789–1798	Washington	Stephen J. Field	1863–1897	Lincoln
John Blair	1789–1796	Washington	**Salmon P. Chase**	1864–1873	Lincoln
John Rutledge	1790–1791	Washington	William Strong	1870–1880	Grant
William Cushing	1790–1810	Washington	Joseph P. Bradley	1870–1892	Grant
James Iredell	1790–1799	Washington	Ward Hunt	1873–1882	Grant
Thomas Johnson	1791–1793	Washington	**Morrison R. Waite**	1874–1888	Grant
William Paterson	1793–1806	Washington	John M. Harlan	1877–1911	Hayes
John Rutledge†	1795	Washington	William B. Woods	1880–1887	Hayes
Samuel Chase	1796–1811	Washington	Stanley Matthews	1881–1889	Garfield
Oliver Ellsworth	1796–1799	Washington	Horace Gray	1882–1902	Arthur
Bushrod Washington	1798–1829	J. Adams	Samuel Blatchford	1882–1893	Arthur
Alfred Moore	1799–1804	J. Adams	Lucious Q. C. Lamar	1888–1893	Cleveland
John Marshall	1801–1835	J. Adams	**Melville W. Fuller**	1888–1910	Cleveland
William Johnson	1804–1834	Jefferson	David J. Brewer	1889–1910	B. Harrison
Henry B. Livingston	1806–1823	Jefferson	Henry B. Brown	1890–1906	B. Harrison
Thomas Todd	1807–1826	Jefferson	George Shiras	1892–1903	B. Harrison
Gabriel Duval	1811–1836	Madison	Howell E. Jackson	1893–1895	B. Harrison
Joseph Story	1811–1845	Madison	Edward D. White	1894–1910	Cleveland
Smith Thompson	1823–1843	Monroe	Rufus W. Peckham	1896–1909	Cleveland
Robert Trimble	1826–1828	J. Q. Adams	Joseph McKenna	1898–1925	McKinley
John McLean	1829–1861	Jackson	Oliver W. Holmes	1902–1932	T. Roosevelt
Henry Baldwin	1830–1844	Jackson	William R. Day	1903–1922	T. Roosevelt
James M. Wayne	1835–1867	Jackson	William H. Moody	1906–1910	T. Roosevelt
Roger B. Taney	1836–1864	Jackson	Horace H. Lurton	1910–1914	Taft
Philip P. Barbour	1836–1841	Jackson	Charles E. Hughes	1910–1916	Taft
John Catron	1837–1865	Van Buren	Willis Van Devanter	1910–1937	Taft
John McKinley	1837–1852	Van Buren	Joseph R. Lamar	1911–1916	Taft
Peter V. Daniel	1841–1860	Van Buren	**Edward D. White**	1910–1921	Taft
Samuel Nelson	1845–1872	Tyler	Mahlon Pitney	1912–1922	Taft
Levi Woodbury	1845–1851	Polk	James C. McReynolds	1914–1941	Wilson
Robert C. Grier	1846–1870	Polk	Louis D. Brandeis	1916–1939	Wilson
Benjamin R. Curtis	1851–1857	Fillmore	John H. Clarke	1916–1922	Wilson
John A. Campbell	1853–1861	Pierce	**William H. Taft**	1921–1930	Harding
Nathan Clifford	1858–1881	Buchanan	George Sutherland	1922–1938	Harding
Noah H. Swayne	1862–1881	Lincoln			
Samuel F. Miller	1862–1890	Lincoln			

***Chief Justices appear in bold type.**
†Acting Chief Justice; Senate refused to confirm appointment.

Name	Service	Appointed by	Name	Service	Appointed by
Pierce Butler	1923–1939	Harding	Potter Stewart	1958–1981	Eisenhower
Edward T. Sanford	1923–1930	Harding	Byron R. White	1962–1993	Kennedy
Harlan F. Stone	1925–1941	Coolidge	Arthur J. Goldberg	1962–1965	Kennedy
Charles E. Hughes	1930–1941	Hoover	Abe Fortas	1965–1969	Johnson
Owen J. Roberts	1930–1945	Hoover	Thurgood Marshall	1967–1991	Johnson
Benjamin N. Cardozo	1932–1938	Hoover	**Warren E. Burger**	1969–1986	Nixon
Hugo L. Black	1937–1971	F. Roosevelt	Harry A. Blackmun	1970–1994	Nixon
Stanley F. Reed	1938–1957	F. Roosevelt	Lewis F. Powell Jr.	1972–1988	Nixon
Felix Frankfurter	1939–1962	F. Roosevelt	William H. Rehnquist	1972–1986	Nixon
William O. Douglas	1939–1975	F. Roosevelt	John Paul Stevens	1975–	Ford
Frank Murphy	1940–1949	F. Roosevelt	Sandra Day O'Connor	1981–	Reagan
Harlan F. Stone	1941–1946	F. Roosevelt	**William H. Rehnquist**	1986–	Reagan
James F. Byrnes	1941–1942	F. Roosevelt	Antonin Scalia	1986–	Reagan
Robert H. Jackson	1941–1954	F. Roosevelt	Anthony M. Kennedy	1988–	Reagan
Wiley B. Rutledge	1943–1949	F. Roosevelt	David H. Souter	1990–	Bush
Harold H. Burton	1945–1958	Truman	Clarence Thomas	1991–	Bush
Frederick M. Vinson	1946–1953	Truman	Ruth Bader Ginsburg	1993–	Clinton
Tom C. Clark	1949–1967	Truman	Stephen Breyer	1994–	Clinton
Sherman Minton	1949–1956	Truman			
Earl Warren	1953–1969	Eisenhower			
John Marshall Harlan	1955–1971	Eisenhower			
William J. Brennan Jr.	1956–1990	Eisenhower			
Charles E. Whittaker	1957–1962	Eisenhower			

APPENDIX F

POPULATION GROWTH, 1630-2000

Year	Population	Percent Increase
1630	4,600	—
1640	26,600	473.3
1650	50,400	89.1
1660	75,100	49.0
1670	111,900	49.1
1680	151,500	35.4
1690	210,400	38.9
1700	250,900	19.3
1710	331,700	32.2
1720	466,200	40.5
1730	629,400	35.0
1740	905,600	43.9
1750	1,170,800	30.0
1760	1,593,600	36.1
1770	2,148,100	34.8
1780	2,780,400	29.4
1790	3,929,214	41.3
1800	5,308,483	35.1
1810	7,239,881	36.4
1820	9,638,453	33.1
1830	12,866,020	33.5
1840	17,069,453	32.7
1850	23,191,876	35.9
1860	31,443,321	35.6
1870	39,818,449	26.6
1880	50,155,783	26.0
1890	62,947,714	25.5
1900	75,994,575	20.7
1910	91,972,266	21.0
1920	105,710,620	14.9
1930	122,775,046	16.1
1940	131,669,275	7.2
1950	150,697,361	14.5
1960	179,323,175	19.0
1970	203,302,031	13.4
1980	226,542,199	11.4
1990	248,718,301	9.8
2000	274,634,000*	11.0

*Projected
Source: *Historical Statistics of the U. S.* (1960), *Historical Statistics of the U.S. from Colonial Times to 1970* (1975), and *Statistical Abstract of the U. S., 1996* 1996).

Index